Building Bones

Bone Formation and Development in Anthropology

Bone is the tissue most frequently recovered archaeologically and is the material most commonly studied by biological anthropologists, who are interested in how skeletons change shape during growth and across evolutionary time. This volume brings together a range of contemporary studies of bone growth and development to highlight how cross-disciplinary research and new methods can enhance our anthropological understanding of skeletal variation. The novel use of imaging techniques from developmental biology, advanced sequencing methods from genetics, and perspectives from evolutionary developmental biology improve our ability to understand the bases of modern human and primate variation. Animal models can also be used to provide a broad biological perspective to the systematic study of humans. This volume is a testament to the drive of anthropologists to understand biological and evolutionary processes that underlie changes in bone morphology and illustrates the continued value of incorporating multiple perspectives within anthropological inquiry.

Christopher J. Percival is a postdoctoral researcher at the University of Calgary. His research focusses on the basis for variation in skull form.

Joan T. Richtsmeier is Distinguished Professor of Anthropology at Pennsylvania State University. Her research looks to understand the complex genetic and developmental basis of variation in head shape in development, disease, and evolution.

Cambridge Studies in Biological and Evolutionary Anthropology

Consulting editors

C. G. Nicholas Mascie-Taylor, *University of Cambridge*

Robert A. Foley, *University of Cambridge*

Series editors

Agustín Fuentes, *University of Notre Dame*

Nina G. Jablonski, *Pennsylvania State University*

Clark Spencer Larsen, *The Ohio State University*

Michael P. Muehlenbein, *The University of Texas, San Antonio*

Dennis H. O'Rourke, *The University of Utah*

Karen B. Strier, *University of Wisconsin*

David P. Watts, *Yale University*

Also available in the series

53. *Technique and Application in Dental Anthropology* Joel D. Irish & Greg C. Nelson (eds.) 978 0 521 87061 0
54. *Western Diseases: An Evolutionary Perspective* Tessa M. Pollard 978 0 521 61737 6
55. *Spider Monkeys: The Biology, Behavior and Ecology of the Genus Ateles* Christina J. Campbell 978 0 521 86750 4
56. *Between Biology and Culture* Holger Schutkowski (ed.) 978 0 521 85936 3
57. *Primate Parasite Ecology: The Dynamics and Study of Host-Parasite Relationships* Michael A. Huffman & Colin A. Chapman (eds.) 978 0 521 87246 1
58. *The Evolutionary Biology of Human Body Fatness: Thrift and Control* Jonathan C. K. Wells 978 0 521 88420 4
59. *Reproduction and Adaptation: Topics in Human Reproductive Ecology* C. G. Nicholas Mascie-Taylor & Lyliane Rosetta (eds.) 978 0 521 50963 3
60. *Monkeys on the Edge: Ecology and Management of Long-Tailed Macaques and their Interface with Humans* Michael D. Gumert, Agustín Fuentes & Lisa Jones-Engel (eds.) 978 0 521 76433 9
61. *The Monkeys of Stormy Mountain: 60 Years of Primatological Research on the Japanese Macaques of Arashiyama* Jean-Baptiste Leca, Michael A. Huffman & Paul L. Vasey (eds.) 978 0 521 76185 7
62. *African Genesis: Perspectives on Hominin Evolution* Sally C. Reynolds & Andrew Gallagher (eds.) 978 1 107 01995 9
63. *Consanguinity in Context* Alan H. Bittles 978 0 521 78186 2
64. *Evolving Human Nutrition: Implications for Public Health* Stanley Ulijaszek, Neil Mann & Sarah Elton (eds.) 978 0 521 86916 4
65. *Evolutionary Biology and Conservation of Titis, Sakis and Uacaris* Liza M. Veiga, Adrian A. Barnett, Stephen F. Ferrari & Marilyn A. Norconk (eds.) 978 0 521 88158 6
66. *Anthropological Perspectives on Tooth Morphology: Genetics, Evolution, Variation* G. Richard Scott & Joel D. Irish (eds.) 978 1 107 01145 8
67. *Bioarchaeological and Forensic Perspectives on Violence: How Violent Death is Interpreted from Skeletal Remains* Debra L. Martin & Cheryl P. Anderson (eds.) 978 1 107 04544 6
68. *The Foragers of Point Hope: The Biology and Archaeology of Humans on the Edge of the Alaskan Arctic* Charles E. Hilton, Benjamin M. Auerbach & Libby W. Cowgill (eds.) 978 1 107 02250 8

Building Bones

Bone Formation and Development in Anthropology

Edited by

CHRISTOPHER J. PERCIVAL
University of Calgary, Canada

and

JOAN T. RICHTSMEIER
Pennsylvania State University, USA

CAMBRIDGE
UNIVERSITY PRESS

University Printing House, Cambridge CB2 8BS, United Kingdom

Cambridge University Press is part of the University of Cambridge.

It furthers the University's mission by disseminating knowledge in the pursuit of
education, learning and research at the highest international levels of excellence.

www.cambridge.org
Information on this title: www.cambridge.org/9781107122789

© Cambridge University Press 2017

First published 2017

Printed in the United Kingdom by TJ International Ltd. Padstow Cornwall

A catalogue record for this publication is available from the British Library

Library of Congress Cataloguing in Publication data
Names: Percival, Christopher J., editor. | Richtsmeier, Joan T., editor.
Title: Building Bones: Bone Formation and Development in Anthropology /
edited by Christopher J. Percival and Joan T. Richtsmeier.
Other titles: Cambridge studies in biological and evolutionary anthropology.
Description: Cambridge; New York : Cambridge University Press, 2016. |
Series: Cambridge studies in biological and evolutionary anthropology |
Includes bibliographical references and index.
Identifiers: LCCN 2016049379 | ISBN 9781107122789 (hardback : alk. paper)
Subjects: | MESH: Bone Development | Anthropology, Physical |
Biological Evolution | Anthropometry
Classification: LCC GN70 | NLM GN 70 | DDC 599.9/47–dc23
LC record available at https://lccn.loc.gov/2016049379

ISBN 978-1-107-12278-9 Hardback

Contents

The color plates are between pages 180 and 181.

Contributors

Timothy G. Bromage
Department of Basic Sciences and Department of Biomaterials and Biomimetics, New York University, College of Dentistry, New York, NY, USA

David B. Burr
Department of Anatomy and Cell Biology, Indiana University, School of Medicine, Indianapolis, IN, USA

Terence D. Capellini
Human Evolutionary Biology, Harvard University & The Broad Institute of MIT and Harvard, Cambridge, MA, USA

John G. Clement
Department of Oral Anatomy, Medicine and Surgery, Melbourne Dental School, University of Melbourne, Melbourne, Victoria, Australia

Paul C. Dechow
Department of Biomedical Sciences, Texas A&M University College of Dentistry, Dallas, TX, USA

Valerie B. DeLeon
Department of Anthropology, University of Florida, Gainesville, FL, USA

Brigitte Demes
Department of Anatomical Sciences, Stony Brook Medicine, Stony Brook, NY, USA

Heather Dingwall
Department of Human Evolutionary Biology, Harvard University, Cambridge, MA, USA

Sarah E. Freidline
Department of Human Evolution, Max Planck Institute for Evolutionary Anthropology, Leipzig, Germany

Haviva M. Goldman
Department of Neurobiology and Anatomy, Drexel University, Philadelphia, PA, USA

James H. Gosman
Department of Anthropology, Ohio State University, Columbus, OH, USA

Philipp Gunz
Department of Human Evolution, Max Planck Institute for Evolutionary Anthropology, Leipzig, Germany

Russell T. Hogg
Department of Rehabilitation Sciences, Florida Gulf Coast University, Ft. Myers, FL, USA

Yuan Huang
Department of Biostatistics, Yale University, New Haven, CT, USA

Jean-Jacques Hublin
Department of Human Evolution, Max Planck Institute for Evolutionary Anthropology, Leipzig, Germany

Stefan Judex
Department of Biomedical Engineering, Stony Brook University, Stony Brook, NY, USA

Julia A. Katris
Department of Basic Sciences and Department of Biomaterials and Biomimetics, New York University, College of Dentistry, New York, NY, USA

Kazuhiko Kawasaki
Department of Anthropology, Pennsylvania State University, University Park, PA, USA

Kelsey M. Kjosness
Department of Anthropology, Pennsylvania State University, University Park, PA, USA

Runze Li
Department of Statistics, Pennsylvania State University, University Park, PA, USA

Cayetana Martinez-Maza
Department of Paleobiology, Museo Nacional de Ciencias Naturales (CSIC), Madrid, Spain

Jason M. Organ
Department of Anatomy and Cell Biology, Indiana University School of Medicine, Indianapolis, IN, USA

Christopher J. Percival
Alberta Children's Hospital Institute for Child and Maternal Health, The McCaig Bone and Joint Institute, Department of Cell Biology and Anatomy, University of Calgary, Calgary, AB, Canada

David A. Raichlen
School of Anthropology, University of Arizona, Tucson, AZ, USA

Philip L. Reno
Department of Anthropology, Pennsylvania State University, University Park, PA, USA

Joan T. Richtsmeier
Department of Anthropology, Pennsylvania State University, University Park, PA, USA

Alfred L. Rosenberger
Department of Anthropology and Archaeology, Brooklyn College, CUNY, NY, USA

Timothy M. Ryan
Department of Anthropology, Pennsylvania State University, University Park, PA, USA

Timothy D. Smith
School of Physical Therapy, Slippery Rock University, Slippery Rock, PA, USA

Ian J. Wallace
Department of Human Evolutionary Biology, Harvard University, Cambridge, MA, USA

Ethylin Wang Jabs
Department of Genetics and Genomic Sciences, Icahn School of Medicine at Mount Sinai Atran Berg Laboratory, New York, NY, USA

Kenneth Weiss
Department of Anthropology, Pennsylvania State University, University Park, PA, USA

Introduction

Christopher J. Percival and Joan T. Richtsmeier

There is little doubt that much of what we know in biological anthropology is based on the experimentation with and excavation, measurement, and analysis of mineralized tissues. From the earliest excavation and recovery of fossil primate specimens, anthropologists have routinely used comparative skeletal materials and particular features on those materials to classify human and nonhuman primate species and to infer evolutionary relationships. Although early studies of skeletal biomechanics were primarily done by anatomists and orthopedists, anthropologists adopted biomechanical principles to infer activity from the shape of bones and to make inferences about life histories and habitual behaviors in the early part of the twentieth century (Washburn, 1951; Ruff, 2008). Our current interpretation of human and nonhuman primate origins and evolutionary history is still based primarily on osseous traits, although genetic and genomic data are being effectively used to resolve phylogenetic relationships that have resisted consensus based solely on skeletal traits (e.g., Perelman et al., 2011; Meyer et al., 2016). Currently, anthropologists explicitly recognize that the development and evolution of mineralized tissues are intertwined, with changes in developmental processes serving as a basis for phenotypic change (e.g., Lovejoy et al., 1999; Chiu and Hamrick, 2002; Hlusko et al., 2004). Consequently, anthropologists have been early adopters of technologies and approaches from other disciplines (e.g., genome-wide association study (GWAS), quantitative trail locus (QTL) analysis, quantitative imaging, breeding experiments), and have contributed to the design of new methods to acquire and measure data pertaining to changing biomechanical properties and to ontogenetic change of mineralized tissues (e.g., Cheverud et al., 1983; Ruff and Hayes, 1983; Richtsmeier et al., 1992; Richtsmeier and Lele, 1993; Smith and Tompkins, 1995; Strait et al., 2005, 2007; Slice, 2007; Raichlen et al., 2015). The adoption of a developmental focus has helped to shift emphasis away from the anatomy and classification of particular skeletal traits towards questions pertaining to developmental processes that underlie the production of those traits and their variation (Hallgrímsson & Lieberman, 2008; Reno et al., 2008; Hallgrímsson et al., 2009; Young et al., 2010; Serrat, 2013; Kjosness et al., 2014; Reno, 2014; Rolian, 2014). In this way, anthropological analyses of skeletal remains have expanded from comparisons based on external features and metrics that are used to build phylogenies to the advance of approaches aimed at uncovering the developmental basis for variation in skeletal morphology and evolution. This book includes research conducted by a broad sample of anthropological researchers who are using their expertise to dissect the ways in which development of both the cranial and postcranial skeleton can be used to further our understanding of the basis of novel variation and the role that changes in developmental processes play in the evolution of skeletal morphology.

Because biological anthropological data sets have historically been principally skeletal in nature, anthropologists have always been favorable toward developing or adopting new technology and novel approaches to the analysis of skeletal tissues. During the twentieth century, investigators began to interrogate bone in new ways. Engineering principals as applied to bony architecture were codified by Wolff's law and anthropologists applied this law in the study of skeletal samples under the paradigm that bone is a living tissue that responds mechanically to stress and/or strain in ways that insure tissue strength and resistance to loads where it is needed. The patterns visualized in bone were interpreted as forming in response to mechanical loading. Wolff's law, and predictions stemming from it, were routinely used to check the relationship between lifestyle and bone architecture in living primate species and to propose the locomotory mode of recovered fossil species. However, further laboratory work showed that bone can have highly variable responses to similarly applied forces and that variations in the skeleton can derive from a complex mix of genetic and epigenetic influences (Pearson and Lieberman, 2004; Ryan and Shaw, 2014). Genetic history, sex, nutrition, diet, hormonal influences, life history, phylogenetic history, maturity, microstructural properties of a particular bone region, and body size comprise some of the additional factors that are found to contribute to the osseous response to applied forces. Mineralized tissues may be those most accessible to anthropologists, but the information they contain relating to life history, function and evolution might be harder to tease from inert and sometimes fossilized samples than once thought. Such realizations provided an impetus for the use of experimental animals by anthropologists where certain of these variables can be experimentally controlled and the influence of the others can be tested.

Bone is a living tissue whose characteristics, even within species, are highly variable in time and space. In the 1970s and 1980s, bioarcheologists began to take advantage of this variation to pose population-level questions of skeletal series. Skeletal remains came to be used as the primary data set of problem-oriented research aimed at the investigation of mortuary practice (e.g., Buikstra, 1981), disease vectors in paleopathology (e.g., Armelagos et al., 2005; Wolfe et al., 2007), population dynamics and paleodemography (e.g., Wood et al., 1992), fracture healing (e.g., Boldsen et al., 2015), and biological (genetic) relationships among populations (e.g., Buikstra et al., 1990). In these applications, skeletal variation became the criterion upon which hypotheses pertaining to the sociocultural context of associated populations represented by the skeletal remains were tested. These approaches are the foundation of modern bioarcheology that recognizes the necessity of large sample sizes for understanding processes at the population level.

In addition to these important research directions that remain valid and currently in use, anthropologists have always shown an interest in the changing shapes of bones during growth and in the differences observed between immature and mature skeletons. Anthropologists have led the way in developing methods that tease more information from the bones than would seem evident at first glance. In the simplest examples, knowledge of the sequence of developmental events and how bone grows (e.g., the order and timing of closure of epiphyses and of cranial sutures, the changing morphology of bones throughout life) have enabled the aging of single skeletons and the analysis of population dynamics and demography when these data are available from samples of known provenience. More complex analyses of growth patterns using varied types of morphological data from varied skeletal tissues and multiple methods of analysis have been used to estimate the age of fossil specimens (e.g., Holly, 1992; Smith and Tompkins, 1995), to compare growth between species (e.g., Ackermann and Grovitz, 2002; Bastir and Rosas, 2004; Berge and Penin, 2004; Bulygina *et al.*, 2006; Bastir *et al.*, 2007; Boughner and Dean, 2008), to determine the influence of particular patterns of growth on known morphologies (e.g., Richtsmeier *et al.*, 1993), and to predict the morphology of "hypothetical forms" by mathematically applying estimated growth trajectories to given morphologies (e.g., Richtsmeier and Lele, 1993; McNulty *et al.*, 2006). These approaches have largely been based on what could be coaxed from measured morphological changes associated with bone growth, namely change in size and shape. More recently, anthropologists have been able to use advanced imaging technologies to study important morphological indicators of growth at much smaller scales, develop novel methodologies for their use in the study of populations, and derive new knowledge from these observations. The field of genetics has also become increasingly relevant to the anthropological study of phenotypes and their growth. Not only does knowledge of the genetics of bone development inform us of how bone is formed (e.g., Long, 2012), but correlations between specific genetic variants and variation in quantitative skeletal traits over developmental time point to the contribution of genetic variation to variation in skeletal phenotypes. For example, Hager and colleagues (2009) conducted a series of quantitative trait loci experiments to identify genomic regions that affect body size growth processes revealing that distinct genomic regions affect early postnatal growth (1–3 weeks) while others affect later growth (4–10 weeks) (Hager *et al.*, 2009).

With the advent of evolutionary developmental biology, additional experimental tools, laboratory methods, and genetic approaches became available to anthropologists interested in determining the developmental basis for evolutionary change within the fossil record and phylogenetic differences between living species. Approaches developed within the emerging field of evolutionary developmental biology (evo–devo) enabled the characterization how change occurring within developmental programs is fundamental to evolutionary processes (Carrol *et al.*, 2001). Evo–devo encompasses research on how variation in development relates to the evolutionary changes that occur between generations. Early traces of the evo–devo perspective can be found in the work of, for example, Bonner (1982), Gould (1977), Waddington (1942), and De Beer (1940), but the molecular revolution that occurred in the last decade of the twentieth century made a new set of tools and resources (e.g., increasingly accessible sequencing technology; increasing computational power; novel immunohistochemistry assays; increased understanding of the complexity of the genome) potentially available to anyone with an interesting question pertaining to the mechanisms that link the genotype with the phenotype and how change measured within a single generation relates to change across many generations.

Although first developed and widely used in other disciplines, resources including specific reagents, transgenic technologies, techniques for gene editing (e.g., CRISPR), genomic sequencing, and genotyping and biological imaging technologies, have become increasingly available at diminishing cost. The traditional training offered in anthropology graduate programs meant that, at their introduction, few anthropologists were appropriately trained to adopt and apply these tools. Thankfully, there were investigators from other disciplines with the appropriate expertise who were eager to work on anthropological problems and to work collaboratively with anthropologists on subjects pertaining to human evolution. These collaborative beginnings, followed by a rapid increase in the number of biological anthropologists seeking training in these techniques, prompted a maturation of the field that is now evident in many aspects of biological anthropology. For example, while the relevance of experimental studies in mice in studies of human evolution was openly questioned only 20 years ago, it is now commonplace for anthropologists to propose and test hypotheses about human and nonhuman primate growth, development and evolution using data from non-primate animal models. The amazing number of genomes now sequenced, along with emerging knowledge of the evolution of genomes, enables an even more direct connection of human biology with fish, mammal and chick biomedical models, illuminating the relevance of distantly related species to understanding the evolution of human developmental processes and the function of human regulatory sequences (see, for example, Lamason *et al.*, 2005; Braasch *et al.*, 2016).

These new research trends in anthropology have not occurred due to a directed reorganization of the discipline, but instead represent an organic expansion of the field of biological anthropology as scientists observe what is happening in the larger world of biological research and imagine how they might apply those technologies and skill sets to anthropologically inspired research questions. Bridges have always existed across the subfields of anthropology (biological, cultural, and archeology traditionally, and more recently with ecological, forensic, and genetic anthropology), but connections between biological anthropology and other disciplines are creating collaborative links that previously would have seemed incongruent. These relationships serve as the foundation for necessary changes in anthropological training programs and independent research projects that welcome the incorporation of methods, knowledge, and perspectives from outside of anthropology. The push towards collaborative, cross-disciplinary research in many universities is evident in the chapters presented in this book, and we hope that this volume helps to create and inspire additional connections within the field and across disciplines by exposing anthropologists to a variety of new perspectives in the study of bone development.

The diverse training becoming progressively available to students of biological anthropology provides new knowledge for those eager to translate observations of lifeless skeletal remains into hypotheses that concern behavioral, molecular and morphological evolution, mechanisms of osseous development, and the relationship between organisms and their environment. These new opportunities enable anthropologists to expand their work from theory-driven analyses of skeletal features to experimental approaches that are aimed at revealing biological mechanisms that underlie phenotypic changes evidenced in skeletal remains. Developmental biology, evolutionary developmental biology, genetics and genomics are probably the fields that have contributed most to the changing world of biological anthropology research, and our chapters reflect that contribution. However, the influence of other disciplines is also apparent in this volume, and it would be premature to predict which fields will provide important discoveries and collaborative inputs in the future. Because anthropologists are trained broadly to consider problems pertaining to human evolution, they often can make connections that might be missed by people working in other fields. The challenge for current and future generations of anthropologists is to maintain this broad perspective *and* obtain adequate training in their chosen area of specialization including becoming proficient in necessary technological, computational and/or laboratory skills while resisting the impulse of becoming overspecialized.

This book presents explicit examples of cross-disciplinary research in biological anthropology with the uniting principle of a focus on early formation and growth of bone, the tissue most often left behind in paleoanthropological and archeological contexts. Although the book is organized according to studies that focus on the appendicular versus axial skeleton, many of the chapters focus on fundamental issues that could apply to either part of the skeleton. Our volume starts with an introductory and historical perspective from **Ken Weiss**. By asking the question "What is a biological trait?" this chapter provides important observations of both theoretical and practical concern by considering the genetic basis for traits like those that have been used by biological anthropologists to assign specimens to a taxon. The development of these traits is complex and this complexity must be acknowledged when attempting to understand the production of these phenotypic traits from genetic information. What besides the genetic information that can be tabulated contributes to the morphology produced? What role do those additional components have? And what, in reality, is a complex trait?

The chapter by **Christopher Percival and Joan Richtsmeier and colleagues** provides a brief review of processes underlying skull formation and development, followed by the description of primary research in a mouse model that helps to illuminate the role that blood vessels play during craniofacial osteogenesis. The results of this work suggest ways in which dysregulation of the relationship between blood vessels and bone might contribute to variation within and between extant primate species, while also illustrating how the quantification of multiple aspects of craniofacial skeletal phenotypes can provide a more complete understanding of how genetic changes modify osteogenesis in the skull. While existing biomedical models can be leveraged to develop a more complete understanding of potential developmental bases for evolutionary change in the skull, anthropologists and evolutionary biologists must take the lead in applying these models to evolutionary questions because researchers interested in disease will not.

Kazuhiko Kawasaki and Joan Richtsmeier present a detailed embryological description of the anatomy of the chondrocranium: that part of the endoskeleton that protects the brain and three principal sense organs but does not include the pharyngeal endoskeleton. After years of studying the genetic basis of bones and teeth (Kawasaki) and the morphology and growth of the mammalian skull (Richtsmeier), these authors provide precise definitions and detail the distinction between the cranial base and the chondrocranium. To provide definitions that are based on the evolution of the endoskeleton and dermal skeleton, these authors combine developmental, evolutionary, and anatomical approaches in the analysis of cranial evolution, and use embryological observations of the laboratory mouse to define the chondrocranium and the dermatocranium and the coordinated development of these structures. Finally, the authors use data relating to the spatiotemporal associations of the chondrocranium and dermatocranium to suggest their dynamic interaction during skull formation and suggest implications for understanding cranial modularity and integration.

Postorbital septation in primates has long been a morphological trait of interest. Valerie DeLeon, Alfred Rosenberger, and Tim Smith describe the unique ontogenetic patterns of postorbital septation in tarsiers and apply their findings to the question of trait homology to show how ontogeny of skeletal elements can provide evidence of phylogenetic relationships. Using a comparative ontogenetic approach, the authors show that early postnatal tarsier orbits show ontogenetic adaptations that delay osseous closure of the orbital fossa to allow eye enlargement, followed by the development of an osseous septum that serves to support the overly large eye. The authors conclude that postorbital septation in tarsiers is secondary to eye hypertrophy. Based on this conclusion, they propose possible scenarios for the evolution of septation in tarsier and anthropoid lineages and emphasize the importance of ontogenetic continuity in evaluating hypotheses about trait homology.

In a chapter about facial shape change during growth, Sarah Freidline, Cayetana Martinez–Maza, Philipp Gunz, and Jean–Jacques Hublin combine data pertaining to patterns of bone modeling (formation and resorption fields on the face and mandible) and morphometric measures of facial shape and form in an attempt to understand the correspondence between large-scale morphological shape changes and bone modeling patterns at a microstructural level. These investigators characterize the size and shape of a cross-sectional ontogenetic sample of human skulls of various ages whose patterns of facial bone formation and resorption fields were previously mapped to investigate whether or not these two types of data can be combined to create informative growth models. Interesting observations pertaining to the correspondence in patterns of variation at both the microscopic and macroscopic levels of analysis are provided.

Paul Dechow uses a unique human and porcine data set to show how cortical bone material properties can be used to reveal changing complex biomechanical properties of individual bones during ontogeny. This valuable and informative data set provides a first glimpse at the potential regularities of the ontogeny of bone material variation within humans and pigs and enables hypothesis-building about these properties across species. The implications of this study provide novel evidence that analyses of bone function and evolution that are limited to a purely structural–mechanical approach can lead to uninformed conclusions about adaptation. Dechow uses the mandible in this study, a skeletal element that is both widely studied and whose loading patterns are adequately known, so these results might be corroborated across additional species in the future. Dechow's observations also lay the ground work for studies of variation in such properties that could represent evolutionary adaptations to unique craniofacial functions or patterns of development.

David Burr and Jason Organ offer a comprehensive review of endochondral growth of long bones and synovial joints with the goal of revealing how changes in patterns of skeletal growth and development drive morphological change evidenced in the evolution of the postcranial skeleton. The authors discuss the influence of postnatal physiologic adaptions on the size and shapes of joints and how these are constrained by evolution. A discussion of the relative contributions of mechanical environment and genetic and epigenetic mechanisms to the evolution of limb bone morphology, especially joint morphology, provides insight into the physiologic adaptations that are primarily mechanical, but also thermoregulatory, hormonal and dietary, and lead to change in bone shape. The authors show how these influences operate within an evolutionary template and how small changes in genetic or epigenetic regulatory mechanisms contribute to change in bone shape during growth and during evolution.

Terence Capellini and Heather Dingwall discuss our current lack of knowledge about the genotypes that underlie phenotypic variation in primate skeletal morphology. Because most genes have pleiotropic effects and complex traits are known to have a polygenic basis rather than being controlled by a single locus, gaining knowledge of the mechanisms that bridge genotype and phenotype presents a formidable challenge. Using appendage skeletal development as their example, Capellini and Dingwall provide a timely and insightful guide to the genetic, molecular, and developmental tools that are available to the anthropologist interested in filling in gaps along the genotype–phenotype continuum in the context of primate skeletal variation and evolution. The authors show that understanding the inherited basis of morphological variation requires the coordinated application of cutting-edge experimental techniques in genetics, functional genomics, and developmental genetics. In this context, the authors provide guidance on how advances in genetics help to identify and connect a genetic locus to variation in skeletal morphology, whereas novel functional genomics tools help to sift through the numerous genetic variants within an associated locus for putative variants responsible for changes in a species-specific phenotype. Finally, the use of novel developmental biology tools provide for a direct assessment of the functional causality of an identified sequence to reveal molecular mechanisms and their impacts on the development of a phenotype. They reveal that the combined use of data sets generated from the most recent advances in each of the above fields allows researchers to identify the causal genetic variants the control variation, and the likely mutations that natural selection has acted upon to sculpt skeletal morphology in primates.

Kelsey Kjosness and Phil Reno provide a complete description of growth plates and how work with knockout murine models has greatly expanded our understanding of growth plate design and function. The authors demonstrate the differences between growth of bones of the hands and feet and growth of long bones of the limbs, the latter being most commonly studied by those interested in skeletal growth. They take advantage of this normal variation in endochondral ossification to identify mechanisms of growth plate development. First, therian mammal metapodials and phalanges form a single growth plate at only one end, while typical long bones form a growth plate at both ends. Second, the mammalian pisiform and calcaneus are unique among the bones of the wrist and ankle in forming a growth plate. The authors take advantage of this situation in the developing mouse, where skeletal development and growth plate biology can be queried experimentally during prenatal growth to analyze patterns of chondrocyte proliferation and explore the expression of specific genes to growth plate formation. Using further comparisons with metatarsal formation in alligators, which still form a growth plate at each end of the bone, the authors provide information pertaining to the association between the expression of the Indian hedgehog receptor, Patched, and patterns of cellular proliferation that distinguish growth plate forming and non-forming sites. In addition, Hox genes are hypothesized to be fundamental to growth plate formation, a view supported by their reduced expression in the developing wrist and ankle which generally lack growth plates. The authors demonstrate the expression of *Hoxd11* adjacent to the growth plate containing pisiform in the wrist as further evidence for the important role of Hox genes in growth plate formation. These authors provide a valuable example of how the identification of these types of patterns in model and non-model organisms can be used to discover and affirm the evolution of growth mechanisms responsible for phenotypic variation.

Ian Wallace, Brigitte Demes, and Stefan Judex provide a useful description of bone responsiveness to mechanical signals, from the molecular to organ level, in order to provide context for a consideration of the non-genetic factors (age and genetic background) that contribute to bone mechanoresponsiveness. There is a huge anthropological literature in which functional loading history of organisms known only by their skeletal remains is inferred from what is known from work with experimental animals (mostly laboratory mouse) and studies of humans. By focusing on what is known of the genetic and ontogenetic influence on bone mechanoresponsiveness in humans, these researchers demonstrate that the primary basis for variation in bone structure is youth physical activity, even in the bones of adults. In addition, the significant influence of genetic background on mechanoresponsiveness means that multiple species or populations may exhibit different degrees of structural evidence for the same activities. These observations indicate additional complications when interpreting loading history from morphological studies of bone, but provide an impetus to broaden our perspective on mechanobiology and scope of inquiry when studying functional skeletal morphology.

Russ Hogg, Tim Bromage, Haviva Goldman, Julia Katris, and John Clement explore the relationship between oscillations in the sympathetic nervous system and growth increments visible in mineralized tissue to try to uncover a circadian mechanism that leads to histologically identified bone growth increments. Specifically, the biorhythm known as Havers–Halberg oscillation (HHO), is expressed as growth increments in mineralized tissues in various forms; e.g., lamellae in bone, and striae of Retzius in dental enamel. The authors review the relationships among bone formation, neuroendocrine physiology, and bone metabolism aimed at relating these subjects to long-period rhythms in bone and teeth, and ultimately to mammalian life history evolution. The authors hypothesize an important role for HHO cycles in the evolution of life history traits among primates and suggest that associated patterns of bone remodeling can be used to estimate life-history characteristics of skeletal and fossil specimens.

Tim Ryan, David Raichlen, and James Gosman emphasize the impact of age and ontogeny on variation in skeletal mechanical responsiveness in a study of changes in the humeral and femoral metaphyses of human juveniles. These authors use computed tomography images to estimate three-dimensional trabecular bone structural features and determine the difference in these features as individuals age. This study shows the difference in trabecular bone architecture of these two bones throughout growth. Femoral measures show patterns that are significantly correlated with age, but measures in the humerus, whose role in bipedality is quite different, do not. Given that the differences between femoral and humeral metaphyseal trabecular bone architecture develop only after the onset of walking in children, the authors suggest that these architectural patterns directly reflect the divergent loading regimes experienced by these two skeletal regions.

Although they are quite diverse, these chapters represent some of the most advanced approaches to the study of bone development by leading anthropologists, and illustrate how these new avenues can inform evolutionary research. In combination, the chapters of this volume provide a snapshot view of the discipline at the time of publication and links work by researchers with different perspectives on bone growth and development, fostering cross-disciplinary dialogue and encouraging collaborative research.

References

Ackermann, R. and Grovitz, G. (2002). Common patterns of facial ontogeny in the hominid lineage. *Anatomical Record*, 269, 142–147.

Armelagos, G., Brown, P. and Turner, B. (2005). Evolutionary, historical and political economic perspectives on health and diseaase. *Social Science and Medicine*, 61, 755–765.

Bastir, M., O'Higgins, P. and Rosas, A. (2007). Facial ontogeny in Neanderthals and modern humans. *Proceedings of the Royal Society B: Biological Sciences*, 274, 1125–1132.

Bastir, M. and Rosas, A. (2004). Comparative ontogeny in humans and chimpanzees: similarities, differences and paradoxes in postnatal growth and development of the skull. *Annals of Anatomy*, 186, 503–509.

Berge, C. and Penin, X. (2004). Ontogenetic allometry, heterochrony, and interspecific differences in the skull of African apes, using tridimensional Procrustes analysis. *American Journal of Physical Anthropology*, 124, 124–138.

Boldsen, J. L., Milner, G. R. and Weise, S. (2015). Cranial vault trauma and selective mortality in medieval to early modern Denmark. *Proceedings of the National Academy of Scencesi USA*, 112, 1721–1726.

Bonner, J. (1982). *Evolution and Development. Report of the Dahlem Workshop on Evolution and Development Berlin 1981, May 10–15*. Berlin: Springer-Verlag.

Boughner, J. and Dean, M. (2008). Mandibular shape, ontogeny and dental development in bonobos (*Pan paniscus*) and chimpanzees (*Pan troglodytes*). *Evolutionary Biology*, 35, 296–308.

Braasch, I., Gehrke, A. R., Smith, J. J., *et al.* (2016). The spotted gar genome illuminates vertebrate evolution and facilitates human–teleost comparisons. *Nature Genetics*, 48, 427–437.

Buikstra, J. (1981). Mortuary practices, paleodemography and paleopathology: a case study from the Koster site (Illinois). *In:* Chapman, R., Kinnes, I. and Randsborg, K. (eds.) *Archaeology of Death*. Cambridge: Cambridge University Press.

Buikstra, J. E., Frankenberg, S. R. and Konigsberg, L. W. (1990). Skeletal biological distance studies in American physical anthropology: recent trends. *American Journal of Physical Anthropology*, 82, 1–7.

Bulygina, E., Mitteroecker, P. and Aiello, L. (2006). Ontogeny of facial dimorphism and patterns of individual development within one human population. *American Journal of Physical Anthropology*, 131, 432–443.

Carrol, S., Grenier, J. and Weatherbee, S. (2001). *From DNA to Diversity: Molecular Genetics and the Evolution of Animal Design*. Oxford: Blackwell Sciences.

Cheverud, J., Lewis, J. L., Bachrach, W. and Lew, W. D. (1983). The measurement of form and variation in form: an application of three-dimensional quantitative morphology by finite-element methods. *American Journal of Physical Anthropology*, 62, 151–165.

Chiu, C. and Hamrick, M. (2002). Evolution and development of the primate limb skeleton. *Evolutionary Anthropology*, 11, 94–107.

De Beer, G. (1940). *Embryos and Ancestors*. Oxford: Clarendon Press.

Gould, S. (1977). *Ontogeny and Phylogeny*. Cambridge, MA: Belknap Press.

Hager, R., Cheverud, J. and Wolf, J. (2009). Relative contribution of additive, dominance, and imprinting effects on phenotypic variation in body size and growth between divergent selection lines of mice. *Evolution*, 63, 1118–1128.

Hallgrímsson, B., Jamniczky, H., Young, N.M., *et al.* (2009). Deciphering the palimpsest: studying the relationship between morphological integration and phenotypic covariation. *Evolutionary Biology*, 36, 355–376.

Hallgrímsson, B. and Lieberman, D.E. (2008). Mouse models and the evolutionary developmental biology of the skull. *Integrative and Comparative Biology*, 48, 373–384.

Hlusko, L. J., Suwa, G., Kono, R. T. and Mahaney, M. C. (2004). Genetics and the evolution of primate enamel thickness: a baboon model. *American Journal of Physical Anthropology*, 124, 223–233.

Holly, B. (1992). The physiological age of KNM-WT 15000. *In:* Walker, A. and Leakey, R. (eds.) *The Homo erectus Skeleton from Nariokotome*. Cambridge, MA: Havard University Press.

Kjosness, K., Hines, J., Lovejoy, C. and Reno, P. (2014). The pisiform growth plate is lost in humans and supports a role for Hox in growth plate formation. *Journal of Anatomy*, 225, 527–538.

Lamason, R. L., Mohideen M. P. K., Mest, J. R., *et al.* (2005). SLC24A5, a putative cation exchanger, affects pigmentation in zebrafish and humans. *Science*, 310(5755), 1782–1786.

Long, F. (2012). Building strong bones: molecular regulation of the osteoblast lineage. *Nature Reviews Molecular Cell Biology*, 13, 27–38.

Lovejoy, C. O., Cohn, M. J. and White, T. D. (1999). Morphological analysis of the mammalian postcranium: a developmental perspective. *Proceedings of the National Academy of Scencesi USA*, 96, 13247–13252.

Mcnulty, K. P., Frost, S. R. and Strait, D. S. (2006). Examining affinities of the Taung child by developmental simulation. *Journal of Human Evolution*, 51, 274–296.

Meyer, M., Arsuaga, J. L., De Filippo, C., *et al.* (2016). Nuclear DNA sequences from the Middle Pleistocene Sima de los Huesos hominins. *Nature*, 531, 504–507.

Pearson, O. M. and Lieberman, D. E. (2004). The aging of Wolff's "law": ontogeny and responses to mechanical loading in cortical bone. *American Journal of Physical Anthropology*, Suppl 39, 63–99.

Perelman, P., Johnson W.E., Roos, C., *et al.* (2011). A molecular phylogeny of living primates. *PLoS Genetics*, 7(3), 1–17.

Raichlen, D. A., Gordon, A. D., Foster, A. D., *et al.* (2015). An ontogenetic framework linking locomotion and trabecular bone architecture with applications for reconstructing hominin life history. *Journal of Human Evolution*, 81, 1–12.

Reno, P. L. (2014). Genetic and developmental basis for parallel evolution and its significance for hominoid evolution. *Evolutionary Anthropology*, 23, 188–200.

Reno, P.L., McCollum, M.A., Cohn, M.J., *et al.* (2008). Patterns of correlation and covariation of anthropoid distal forelimb segments correspond to Hoxd expression territories. *Journal of Experimental Zoology (Mol Dev Evol)*, 310, 240–258.

Richtsmeier, J., Cheverud, J. and Lele, S. (1992). Advances in anthropological morphometrics. *Annual Review of Anthropology*, 21, 283–305.

Richtsmeier, J., Corner, B., Grausz, H., Cheverud, J. and Danahey, S. (1993). The role of postnatal growth pattern in the production of facial morphology. *Systematic Biology*, 42, 307–330.

Richtsmeier, J. T. and Lele, S. (1993). A coordinate-free approach to the analysis of growth patterns: models and theoretical considerations. *Biological Reviews of the Cambridge Philosophical Society*, 68, 381–411.

Rolian, C. (2014). Genes, development, and evolvability in primate evolution. *Evolutionary Anthropology*, 23, 93–104.

Ruff, C. (2008). Biomechanical analyses of archaeological human skeletons. *In:* Katzenberg, M. and Saunders, S. (eds.) *Biological Anthropology of the Human Skeleton*, 2nd ed. New York, NY: John Wiley.

Ruff, C. B. and Hayes, W. C. (1983). Cross-sectional geometry of Pecos Pueblo femora and tibiae – a biomechanical investigation: I. Method and general patterns of variation. *American Journal of Physical Anthropology*, 60, 359–381.

Ryan, T. and Shaw, C. (2014). Gracility of the modern *Homo sapiens* skeleton is the result of decreased biomechanical loading. *Proceedings of the National Academy of Sciences USA*, 112, 372–377.

Serrat, M. A. (2013). Allen's rule revisited: temperature influences bone elongation during a critical period of postnatal development. *The Anatomical Record*, 296, 1534–1545.

Slice, D. (2007). Geometric morphometrics. *Annual Review of Anthropology*, 36, 261–281.

Smith, B. and Tompkins, R. (1995). Toward a life history of the Hominidae. *Annual Review of Anthropology*, 257–279.

Strait, D. S., Wang, Q., Dechow, P. C., *et al.* (2005). Modeling elastic properties in finite-element analysis: how much precision is needed to produce an accurate model? *The Anatomical Record. Part A, Discoveries in Molecular Cellular and Evolutionary Biology*, 283, 275–287.

Strait, D. S., Richmond, B. G., Spencer, M. A., *et al.* (2007). Masticatory biomechanics and its relevance to early hominid phylogeny: an examination of palatal thickness using finite-element analysis. *Journal of Human Evolution*, 52, 585–599.

Waddington, C. (1942). Canalization of development and the inheritance of acquired characters. *Nature*, 3811, 563–565.

Washburn, S. L. (1951). The new physical anthropology. *Transactions of the New York Academy of Sciences*, 13, 298–304.

Wolfe, N. D., Dunavan, C. P. and Diamond, J. (2007). Origins of major human infectious diseases. *Nature*, 447, 279–283.

Wood, J., Milner, G., Harpending, H. and Weiss, K. (1992). The osteological paradox: problems of inferring prehistoric health from skeletal samples. *Current Anthropology*, 33, 343–370.

Young, N. M., Chong, H. J., Hu, D., Hallgrímsson, B. and Marcucio, R. S. (2010). Quantitative analyses link modulation of sonic hedgehog signaling to continuous variation in facial growth and shape. *Development*, 137, 3405–3409.

1 What Is a Biological 'Trait'?

Kenneth Weiss

1.1 Introduction

Assertions are often made that sound precisely technical – and hence "scientific," but on closer examination make less sense. Precise understanding and causal prediction require underlying conditions or processes that we know, or can assume, to be true either exactly or to some specifiable degree of approximation.

In physics, where there seem to be at least some rigorous primal "laws" of nature that apply always and everywhere, a procedural rule of thumb is that one should frame well-posed questions about cause and effect. A well-posed question has a specific answer that is presumably exact and *unique* except for measurement errors and the like. That answer applies universally where similar causal situations might arise – on Earth or anywhere in the known cosmos. And changing the causal conditions in a *continuous* way changes the result in a precisely predictable and continuous way. That means that we can, in principle at least, "predict" the past from knowing the present. Physics at least seems to have these rigorous underpinnings because, as Galileo said, the cosmos is "written in the language of mathematics."

Such foundations have largely been problematic in evolutionary, developmental, and genetic biology. Because these areas are fundamentally connected through shared physical and chemical processes, we should be able to ask well-posed questions about these fields of study that have specific answers. However, with no shortage of care, intelligence, or thoughtful intentions, our understanding is currently too generic and fragmentary to enable us to ask questions that are not also themselves too generic and fragmentary. It is not always obvious what an adequate base foundation might be, if it exists. In particular, unlike much of the physics world, genes, cells, individuals, and species are discrete entities for which the continuous nature of cause and effect is, at best, an approximation. In addition to discontinuity, much of life is, for all practical purposes, probabilistic.

Examples of best-intended but poorly posed questions that sound perfectly sensible are "What makes us 'human'?" and "What is the genetic basis of the skeleton?" One reason these questions are problematic is they hinge on unstated definitions of their own terms. Terms like "genetic" or "skeleton" or "human" or "makes" are semantic constructs about which there can be considerable, even fundamental debate. Does "genetic" refer only to nuclear DNA sequence rather than, say, mitochondrial DNA or epigenetic packaging and usage of DNA? Who or what is to be considered "human"? What specific items comprise the "skeleton"? And what, causally, is meant by "makes"?

The assumption that its basic principles are rigorously mathematical is vital to physics because, as has been often acknowledged, we humans cannot really intuit or visualize abstractions like dimensions greater than three, quantum superposition, or billions of light-years of galaxies. Physics uses the rigorous, unexceptionably rule-bound tools of mathematics to represent, characterize, make predictions, and ask well-posed questions about aspects of the physical world that are too small to see, too fast to understand, or too probabilistic or complex to grasp directly via our senses. Remarkably, we can even use imaginary or negative numbers, which don't actually exist, to address real, empirical questions. Things don't get much more generically powerful than that!

Life as a phenomenon is part of the physical, material world, but in trying to understand it, one needs to be wary of physics envy. Does biology have the luxury of a similarly rigorous basis? Can it? If not, how do we know how to frame what for us would be well-posed questions? One might think that when we refer to billions of humans or nucleotides in DNA sequence, millions of years of evolution, or even of "adaptations," that we are speaking in well-posed terms the way physicists do. However, this may often be more colloquial than practically useful.

A critical fact, perhaps, is that the laws of physics are general, so we know how to apply them to a given situation and they always work the same way. Physical nature is formally replicable, in the sense that when you've seen one star or galaxy, in many ways you've seen them all, and we can (reasonably) safely assume such entities have always behaved in the same way. All electrons are alike! Higher-level entities like stars and galaxies build up in useful ways from these universally replicable entities and principles. However, it is a *central* part of the evolutionary "laws" of biology that things are *not* all alike: the discreteness of organisms and their components means that when you've seen one species or developmental process you have definitively *not* seen them all. The fundamental nature of evolution is that its dynamics are about context-specific *differences* that can't automatically be extrapolated to other situations.

What we usually must do in biological research is to construct an ad-hoc "model" or hypothesis of what we think is going on in a particular situation, collect some data and *fit* those data to the model, usually through sampling-based statistical methods, to draw inferences about the goodness of that fit, and hence, importantly, to feel that we have confirmed a hypothesis with causally generalizable implications for cases not yet studied. However, in most situations the model rather generically makes statistically based *internal* comparisons in some particular situation, like a mouse model of a trait of interest in which we compare "normal" to genetically engineered mice of some specific strain, or between people with some disease and those who are "normal." This is quite different from using *externally* derived theory, like the theory of universal gravitation, to make predictions in some new situation. Similar characteristics apply to our necessarily indirect ways to try to reconstruct causal evolutionary history from fragmentary geological and indirect contemporary comparative genetic data.

These are not faults, but reflect what are at least the current limitations of our knowledge, as well as basic differences between biology and physics at relevant levels of observation. At the same time, the use of modern genetic research technology has been revealing mechanisms underlying specific cases that we can study in focused ways, opening new understanding and new sorts of hopefully well-posed questions we might be able to address. Skeletal traits provide some specific examples from which we can see the issues.

1.2   Skeletal Traits: Human Stature

Human stature has been studied extensively in these respects. Stature is cheap, easy to measure, and highly replicable. Studies to identify ('map') genomic regions whose variation affects variation in normal (non-pathological) stature have found hundreds or even thousands of such regions (Lango Allen et al., 2010; Wood et al., 2014). These include a few functionally interpretable DNA sequence variants in protein-coding "genes" along with the majority of genome locations that presumably affect gene expression or serve currently unknown genetic functions.

The vast majority of these genome regions have individually trivially small average effects on normal stature variation, but even the combined contribution of these many individually minor sites only account for a fraction of the overall genetic contribution to stature variation. Like the grains of sand that comprise a beach, the contributions of the remainder are collectively important to stature, but individually simply cannot be statistically detected by observational studies. In essence, this is again because of the absence of an adequate mechanistic theory of developmental genetics, forcing us to rely on internal comparisons (of subjects' individual stature measures and their genotypes at each such site) to detect effects using statistical rather than deterministically biological decision-making criteria.

At the same time, abnormal or pathogenic stature has been found to be associated with many different individually identifiable genomic sites, many or most of which do *not* appear in the mapping results of stature in the normal range. The reason is that these major sites can't vary in a healthy way, or at least that the effects of their non-pathogenic variation are rare or very small. Their major mutational effects are what modern developmental genetics is proving excellent at finding, but it seems likely that adaptive evolution, one of our central interests, works mainly through adjustments of numerous, individually tiny effects. While the adaptation itself is important, in a phenomenon called "phenogenetic drift," the individual contributing genomic elements are not, because they are essentially exchangeable among individuals and over time and place (Weiss and Fullerton, 2000). It is the result, rather than the specific set of causal contributors, that selection "sees."

Even more problematic is that the effects of individual causal contributions are not absolute but are fundamentally context-dependent. The genome region will only be seen to contribute if its relevant variants happen to be included in any given sample in sufficient numbers for their effect to be detected statistically. Each person has a different combination of such variants, and the genotypic overlap among those with essentially the same stature measure may be minimal. That means that the estimate of a given variant's effect depends on its net genomic contexts in available samples, as well as, of course, the sampled individuals' lifestyle histories. The same will be true in experimental developmental genetic studies in model systems like laboratory mice, where results typically depend on the particular strain being used.

Because sequence variants are numerous but mostly rare, their individual frequencies and hence net effects will vary substantially from sample to sample even within the same population set: the stature data to date are mainly from Europeans, and of course adding other populations will make the picture more complex than it already seems. In addition, stature mapping is generally adjusted for sex and age, despite the likelihood that genetic contributions to stature will change with age, and that age includes more than just maturity or old-age shrinking but is also a surrogate for cohort-specific factors like diet or chronic infectious disease. That is, the mapping finds genome regions contributing to stature variation *after* the known major contributing factors are removed.

Yet ironically, as noted above and as developmental genetic studies effectively show, we can identify the genes whose time- and location-specific expression are fundamental to the development of the bones that determine stature. And we can test this by experimentally inactivating the genes. This suggests that there is currently a gap between our understanding of development and of its adaptive evolution.

Although it is a classical anthropometric trait, it is obvious that stature is not in itself a unitary trait, so that asking "What is the genetic basis of stature?" is *not*, after all, really asking a well-posed question. There is no reason to think that overall stature necessarily evolved per se, given that it is comprised of components that, as seen in Figure 1.1, serve different functions, including posture, locomotion, childbearing, lung capacity, and so on – and given the strong environmental effects such as dietary intake. An obvious reflection of this complexity is that different genome-wide contributions to sitting and total height are different among male and female African- and European-Americans (Chan *et al.*, 2015). Of course, sitting and leg-based height are themselves determined by multiple components. Well-controlled experiments, mostly with laboratory mice, also show clearly that different genes are involved in the development of different parts of the skeleton that contribute to body length.

In addition to their different underlying developmental genetic contributors, there is no reason to assume that these separate parts vary or have evolved in a unitary way nor jointly at the same historical times or places.

So what, then, would be a well-posed question about stature? The answer is not obvious. A major objective is to be able to extend such findings on humans (not to mention mice) to other primates, or to the fossil record, and to make guesses; they are educated guesses, but they go beyond existing data.

The appendicular skeleton presents essentially the same challenges: it is made of different longitudinal (medial–distal) elements, each growing more or less

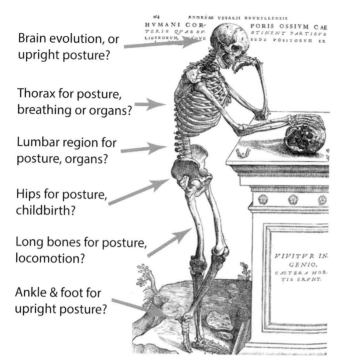

Brain evolution, or upright posture?

Thorax for posture, breathing or organs?

Lumbar region for posture, organs?

Hips for posture, childbirth?

Long bones for posture, locomotion?

Ankle & foot for upright posture?

Figure 1.1 Stature is a composite trait. Background drawing from Vesalius's De humani corporis fabrica, 1543 (image from the Wellcome Library, London).

independently and with specialized functions. Limbs are interesting and great amounts are known about limb development itself, but that is not the same as asking about the genes "for" limb-length variation and its evolution.

These facts do not undermine current mapping and experimental results. Instead, those results show us the terrain we are investigating by revealing mechanisms within each locally studied region or subregion that are relevant to its development. However, this also shows that the overall net stature measure, or perhaps its definition as a biological trait, is in important ways incomplete. This may be because we are not asking well-enough posed questions. So, let us move on up the body, to the head; one component of stature that may seem a more sensibly restricted and unitary structure, one that is present at birth and at least substantially less vulnerable to lifelong environmental and aging effects than is stature.

1.3   Skeletal Traits: Craniofacial Development

"The head" might seem like a sensible structure to study as such. One can take replicable measures of craniofacial dimensions, on model systems, like crosses among laboratory mouse strains, where conditions can be well-controlled, and then use genome-wide sequence variation to search for regions whose variation contributes (statistically) to one or more given dimensions. Unfortunately, genome mapping of

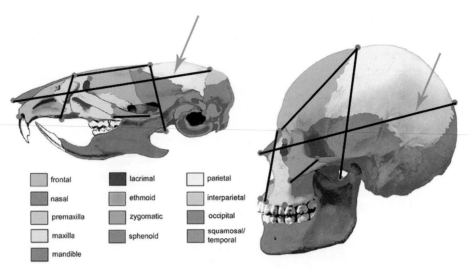

Figure 1.2 Mouse and human skulls with some standard craniometric distances shown. From Weiss *et al.* (2015).

craniofacial distance measures has found complexity that is qualitatively comparable to the findings for stature (Weiss *et al.*, 2015). The reasons are similar as well.

The head has many parts that serve different sensory, postural, vocal, defensive, and mechanical functions, each with its own set of contributing tissues, and each with its own evolutionary history. Even a single part, such as the face, serves many uses. The fossil record shows that these characteristics evolved in their own time and location. Yet the assembled parts develop and work together, and most importantly, they did evolve! That evolution necessarily involved coherent development and its genomic basis. In that a-priori sense, it should be meaningful to consider the head as a biological unit and ask questions about it.

Genomic studies of craniofacial structures or dimensions or structures have been revealing the various signaling and structural (e.g., osteogenic) mechanisms that are involved. There have been surprises, such as that the development of capillary branches may contribute to, not just reflect, developing bone structures (Chapter 2). Correlations of craniofacial metric dimensions reveal genome regions that contribute to one or to many different structures. The challenge is to put these facts together.

A generic evolutionary explanation for the apparent unity within complex causal variety is the simple, powerful Darwinian premise that any individual head that didn't develop in a functionally viable way never made a successful appearance in the world. It was notably hypothesized by C. H. Waddington back in 1942 that complex early developmental processes, once in place, "canalize" or constrain what can viably occur thereafter (Waddington, 1942, 1957). That "thereafter" means a long history of variation that was to be tinkered with mainly around the proverbial edges (Huang, 2012). What works, works, and what's left is left behind. The result today is a hodgepodge, perhaps, something an engineer might design differently, but something that worked well enough in the ad-hoc thread of evolutionary history, with no notion of optimality or causal neatness necessary. This is entirely consistent with the genomic complexity being revealed by mapping. Evolution just said: here's the head; it works!

What we see in our own heads and among those of evolutionarily related species exists *because* of that historical relationship. It is coherent in an adaptive and patterned sense, because evolution is slow and orderly in that it excludes the failed while modifying the workable. Authors investigating different structures like the cranial base or vault, sutures, orbits, mandible and the like find coherence within species and gradually changed differences as well as correlations among them. One way to put this, as anthropological research by Jim Cheverud and colleagues have long been showing, is that there are modular subunits within the overall structure, but that the pleiotropic use of genes – that is, their expression in many different functions – means that these modules are correlated during development at higher levels of overall organization (Cheverud, 1982, 1996, 2004; Cheverud *et al.*, 1991; Mezey *et al.*, 2000; Klingenberg *et al.*, 2004). Rather than individual genes "causing" a trait, it is the dynamic interactions among genes, over embryologic time and space, that lie at the heart of development and its evolution.

Anatomically local questions may be well-posed in that they have a specific genetic answer, but it is less clear how such reductionist studies focused on single structures will yield a picture of the overall process. We have no theory that tells us what the multiple, integrated usage of a web of mechanisms could be in any given case. However, I can at least suggest a general kind of precedent for this by considering another trait that develops within the head, the dentition.

1.4 Nested Segmental Patterning: The Dentition

One of the repeated patterns of evolutionary development is, so to speak, repeated patterns. Repetition in various forms, often with nested branching of subsequent sets of elements, is one of the signal "strategies" of developmental biology and its evolution (Weiss and Buchanan, 2004, 2008, 2009; Buchanan *et al.*, 2009; Kawasaki *et al.*, 2009).

The formation of segmental elements has been at the core of traits like the skeleton and its evolution. Repeated bony elements were observed as important to Bateson even in the late nineteenth century (Bateson, 1894). He suggested some rather mystical mechanisms, but we now have a number of clearly known intercellular signaling mechanisms that generate repetitive patterning, first rigorously suggested as "reaction-diffusion" patterning by Alan Turing (1952), going on. There has been a wealth of recent research showing clearly that a variety of higher-level repetitive patterning processes are indeed at work in many different skeletal (Tabin, 1992; Burke *et al.*, 1995) as well as dental traits (Kondo and Asai, 1995; Jernvall and Jung, 2000; Jernvall and Thesleff, 2000; Salazar-Ciudad and Jernvall, 2002, 2004; Maini *et al.*, 2006; Kondo and Miura, 2010; Sheth *et al.*, 2012; Watanabe and Kondo, 2015). Indeed, most organs and even physiological systems are built of repeated elements, including gene family members.

The basic mechanism is that quantitative concentration differences between various signaling factors are detected by cells along a tissue and can induce local activation of mechanisms producing a structure, like a rib, vertebra, limb component, tooth or cusp, with gaps in between these activation areas. Such patterning often includes nesting, with overall repetition of elements that have local regions of subdifferentiation nested within them. Areas of cells activated by their signaling environment are interspersed with areas of inactivation, yielding a series of spaced elements along a tissue. The patterning mechanisms use slight topographic variation in well-entrenched intercellular signaling mechanisms to alter patterning details in adaptive ways.

An important adaptive phenomenon that provides a good and relevant example of repetitive patterning is the evolution of the number and arrangement of different types of teeth in mammalian dentitions, with their highly regular internal cuspal structure. The tooth row has an evolutionary history, derived ultimately perhaps from exoskeletal scales, that shows an early stage of basic replication of many identical units, to the evolution of local regions of intraregionally similar structures (incisors, canine, premolars, molars). Known signaling molecules induce transcription factors in various combinatorial ways to generate this nested, highly orderly pattern of repetition. The basic genetic mechanisms are used in different tissues (i.e., not just the dentition), and remarkably, traces of genetic dental patterning mechanisms can still be found in birds, who have no teeth (Chen *et al.*, 2000). But while the *process* is conserved and its use adaptable, there are not many genes that are tooth-specific, and even those that are do so only because the local context has been prepared by earlier patterning (Tucker *et al.*, 1998).

Causal complexity and phenogenetic drift also mean that the same genetic elements may come and go while the structures or developmental processes like mineralization retain their basic characteristics (Kawasaki *et al.*, 2005, 2009). The key to understanding such processes is that, rather than enumeration of causal elements, it is their spatiotemporal *combinations* that bear the specifying role. Combinatorial gene expression similarly accounts for vertebral and axial modularity.

To ask how *this* tooth is made is to ask a poorly posed question, once one realizes that it is a quantitative, combinatorial, repeated, and nested *overall* process by which local "decisions" are made. The individual unit, be it a cusp, tooth, tooth type or tooth row, is but one product of a nested process whose basic patterning may be laid out very early in preparing tissues to respond, but played out much later in development when the right tissue-signaling context arises. Critically, there is no gene "for" a premolar or a cusp, but the structures arise by *interactions* among genes and over space that are interpreted by cells in a dynamic process. At some point in development, the process in the upper and lower jaws, rather amazingly, independently produces the dentition's up–down mirror-image symmetries. If mirror-image pre-patterning is made early on, prepared cells spreading linearly in opposite directions from some signaling center, upper and lower jaws can form appropriately aligned proximo-distal dental patterns.

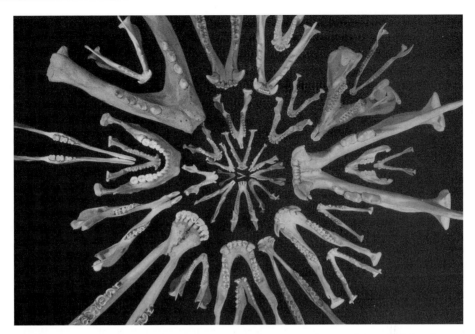

Figure 1.3 Repetitive patterning in mammalian dentitions. To see the cuspal details, see ib.berkeley.edu/node/19. Courtesy Leslea J. Hlusko and Tim D. White.

1.5 Nested Segmental Patterning: A General Developmental Strategy

Repetitive patterning is widespread in living nature and perhaps could be called the fundamental means by which complex organisms are produced. Most organs are structured by repetitive structures arranged linearly, as in intestinal villi, or in branching patterns as in lung alveoli, or in other spatial patterns. Other repetitive patterning is bilateral or radial, and work by other mechanisms, but the strategy for making complexity in conceptually simple ways is similar.

What about the skull itself, within which these dentitions are nested? Much like the evolution of scales and dentitions, vertebrate skulls have evolved from being encased in rather loosely organized sets of covering plates, often of variable number, into the much more tightly and regularly arranged plates in mammals, in which except for a few wormian bones the numbers, shapes, and locations of the cranial plates and other internal bones are highly fixed and regular – to the point that irregularities are damaging and classified as diseases.

There is embryologic evidence not only that bony cranial plates have origins in ossification areas that grow from separately arising sources, and one can speculate (and I think it is likely) that some sort of repetitive patterning process analogous to those in axial skeleton, limbs, and teeth is responsible for these plate origins. Further, collaborative work with Joan Richtsmeier and colleagues using computed tomography (CT) scan data found morphological but not yet genetic evidence that bones themselves may begin as forms of lattices of ossification that can be interpreted as peaks and valleys of spatiotemporal processes generating waves of ossification separated by vacant areas later filled in by ossification, as a way of structuring within the bony plates once they have been initiated (unpublished results). If so, studies of cranial plate initiation, ossification, and so on may integrate higher-level spatiotemporal signaling with more local developmental specificity.

1.6   Anthropological Implications

Anthropologists, indeed most evolutionary and other biologists, have traits they would like to understand, based on what is present today and seems reasonable to define. Stature is a good example. It is obvious if one thinks about it that "stature" is not a self-evidently evolutionary unitary trait. All the individual elements identified in Figure 1.1 combine to make one's stature, but there is no reason to think that that overall measure is what evolved as such. It may have had evolutionary relevance per se, but the individual segments may have, or may still have, their own independent adaptive (or chance) histories.

Even if a component of stature, say neck length, is part of overall stature, selection favoring longer necks could have led to compensating selection favoring shorter femur length if there were some advantage to not being too tall. After the fact, it may be impossible to know what indirect, compensating selection (or chance events) may be responsible for aspects of what we otherwise think is a meaningful "trait."

Similarly elusive is the fact that a trait that anthropologists may be interested in because of its obvious functional nature may have been achieved by any manner of individual component changes that had no particular selective advantage or disadvantage – that is, if the net result, like stature, was being screened by selection, different ways may have been taken to achieve it. So, for example, people in different human populations may have similar stature but different contributing body proportions. We may be able to infer, or guess at, the reasons for having a given large or small stature (say, East African peoples vs. the shorter people in the African rainforest), but not the reasons – if there were any – for the different relative proportions. The same would be true of different people with similar stature but different proportions.

Decomposing a trait by taking a developmental (experimental) approach can perhaps identify contributing genetic mechanisms, as can be done using the mouse models described here. This may provide clues as to what genes to study in humans or other primates, to see if particular variants may be informative about the subjects' different trait measures (such as stature or craniofacial components).

We can learn about how traits are assembled developmentally, or how their variation within and between individuals, or populations, or species (e.g., primates, or different hominins based on fossil data), but how or even whether we can identify histories of chance or natural selection is not clear. What is clear is that we should frame our questions properly to answer questions in ways that are most interpretable without straying too far in purely speculative directions.

Anthropologists and others with evolutionary or ecological interests may not really care about the mechanistic details of development, but both comparative and experimental genetic studies can provide information, of unique kinds, that will be helpful for addressing more holistic questions.

1.7   Conclusion

Research focused on specific skeletal traits defined in traditional ways but using modern genomic approaches is rapidly providing potentially transformative evidence for the involvement of genes, and of the nature of the evolution, of those traits (see Chapters 8 and 9 for review and illustration of the value of modern genetic and developmental biology methods in understanding skeletal variation). This work takes us beyond traditional morphological evolutionary concepts upon which anthropology has traditionally had to rely, by identifying underlying mechanisms, which must ultimately be genomic.

Tissue-specific projects may not directly address higher-level issues, but they provide what one might call tangential evidence that can help triangulate an approach to those higher-level developmental processes. They identify the actions among specific genes whose more general involvement is likely to be relevant. Time will tell. The point is that one way to ask a well-posed question is to notice processes, rather than things, that might in a unifying way account for complex patterns.

Research on various classically and anthropologically relevant traits like the shape or spacing of orbits, the length or proportions of limb bones, correlations among measures, or the activity of various genes in tissues in the developing head seem more narrowly focused than the overall question of organization. But could even that sense of focus itself also somewhat illusory?

For example, once we have found evidence of modules that interact at higher levels, as noted above, should we not immediately think, as well, that they might be relevant at *lower* levels of organization as well? And is this a nested set of levels, like Russian dolls, or are we somehow discretizing phenomena by thinking in terms of modules and their interactions, rather than a more continuous flow of causal genetic information? After all, modules themselves are identified as distinct units by statistical cutoff criteria (e.g., significance tests), which are basically subjective ways to define categories, even if underlying processes are more continuous and pleiotropic, meaning that many of the same genes are involved.

Is there something seriously missing in our attempt to define well-posed questions or define traits appropriately in the contexts I have discussed? Each piece of the puzzle is important and informative. It may be that we do not yet have an adequately precise or agreed-on idea of what the most well-posed types of question for the "traits" we care to understand should be.

We are in early stages in the genetics of the evolution of development and its resulting complex traits. Evolution generates messy, statistically noisy results that must only satisfy the "theorem" that what is, is what has survived best – even if that may not yield "clean" or simple answers to questions we have been asking. There may not be neat, unitary underlying genomic causation. The questions we ask may not be the same ones "asked" by evolution itself, and we should probably try to ask them too.

Still, there is every reason to think that careful thought about questions that are currently being investigated can lead to better-posed questions with clearer, or one may say more satisfyingly rigorous and less statistical answers. Many are pursuing such ends with the various technologies and methods that are now available. Their questions are varied and typically focused, because we know how to turn such questions into practicable research projects. As with evolution itself, there is no predicting what these studies will lead to, except that it surely will be interesting.

References

Bateson, W. (1894). *Materials for the Study of Variation, Treated with Special Regard to Discontinuity in the Origin of Species.* London: Macmillan.

Buchanan, A. V., Sholtis, S., Richtsmeier, J. and Weiss, K. M. (2009). What are genes "for" or where are traits "from"? What is the question? *BioEssays*, 31, 198–208.

Burke, A. C., Nelson, C. E., Morgan, B. A. and Tabin, C. (1995). Hox genes and the evolution of vertebrate axial morphology. *Development*, 121, 333–346.

Chan, Y., Salem, R. M., Hsu, Y. H., *et al.* (2015). Genome-wide analysis of body proportion classifies height-associated variants by mechanism of action and implicates genes important for skeletal development. *American Journal of Human Genetics*, 96, 695–708.

Chen, Y., Zhang, Y., Jiang, T. X., *et al.* (2000). Conservation of early odontogenic signaling pathways in Aves. *Proceedings of the National Academy of Sciences USA*, 97, 10044–10049.

Cheverud, J. (1982). Phenotypic, genetic, and environmental morphological integration in the cranium. *Evolution*, 36, 1737–1747.

Cheverud, J. (1996). Developmental integration and the evolution of pleiotropy. *American Zoologist*, 36, 44–50.

Cheverud, J. (2004). Modular pleiotropic effects of quantitative trait loci on morphological traits. *In:* Schlosser, G. & Wagner, G. (eds.) *Modularity in Development and Evolution.* Chicago, IL: University of Chicago.

Cheverud, J. M., Hartman, S. E., Richtsmeier, J. T. and Atchley, W. R. (1991). A quantitative genetic analysis of localized morphology in mandibles of inbred mice using finite element scaling analysis. *Journal of Craniofacial Genetics and Developmental Biology*, 11, 122–137.

Huang, S. (2012). The molecular and mathematical basis of Waddington's epigenetic landscape: a framework for post-Darwinian biology? *Bioessays*, 34, 149–157.

Jernvall, J. and Jung, H. S. (2000). Genotype, phenotype, and developmental biology of molar tooth characters. *American Journal of Physical Anthropology*, Suppl 31, 171–190.

Jernvall, J. and Thesleff, I. (2000). Reiterative signaling and patterning during mammalian tooth morphogenesis. *Mechanisms of Development*, 92, 19–29.

Kawasaki, K., Suzuki, T. and Weiss, K. M. (2005). Phenogenetic drift in evolution: the changing genetic basis of vertebrate teeth. *Proceedings of the National Academy of Sciences USA*, 102, 18063–18068.

Kawasaki, K., Buchanan, A. V. and Weiss, K. M. (2009). Biomineralization in humans: making the hard choices in life. *Annual Review of Genetics*, 43, 119–142.

Klingenberg, C. P., Leamy, L. J. and Cheverud, J. (2004). Integration and modularity of quantitative trait locus effects on geometric shape in the mouse mandible. *Genetics*, 166, 1909–1921.

Kondo, S. and Asai, R. (1995). A reaction-diffusion wave on the skin of the marine angelfish *Pomacanthus*. *Nature*, 376, 765–768.

Kondo, S. and Miura, T. (2010). Reaction-diffusion model as a framework for understanding biological pattern formation. *Science*, 329, 1616–1620.

Lango Allen, H., Estrada, K., Lettre, G., *et al.* (2010). Hundreds of variants clustered in genomic loci and biological pathways affect human height. *Nature*, 467, 832–838.

Maini, P. K., Baker, R. E. and Chuong, C. M. (2006). Developmental biology. The Turing model comes of molecular age. *Science*, 314, 1397–1398.

Mezey, J. G., Cheverud, J. M. and Wagner, G. P. (2000). Is the genotype–phenotype map modular? A statistical approach using mouse quantitative trait loci data. *Genetics*, 156, 305–311.

Salazar-Ciudad, I. and Jernvall, J. (2002). A gene network model accounting for development and evolution of mammalian teeth. *Proceedings of the National Academy of Science USA*, 99, 8116–8120.

Salazar-Ciudad, I. and Jernvall, J. (2004). How different types of pattern formation mechanisms affect the evolution of form and development. *Evolution and Development*, 6, 6–16.

Sheth, R., Marcon, L., Bastida, M. F., *et al.* (2012). Hox genes regulate digit patterning by controlling the wavelength of a Turing-type mechanism. *Science*, 338, 1476–1480.

Tabin, C. (1992). Why we have (only) five fingers per hand: Hox genes and the evolution of paired limbs. *Development*, 116, 289–296.

Tucker, A., Matthews, K. and Sharpe, P. (1998). Transformation of tooth type induced by inhibition of BMP signaling. *Science*, 282, 1136–1138.

Turing, A. (1952). The chemical basis of morphogenesis. *Philosophical Transactions of the Royal Society of London, Series B*, 237, 37–72.

Waddington, C. H. (1942). Canalization of development and genetic assimilation of acquired characters. *Nature*, 183, 1654–1655.

Waddington, C. H. (1957). *The Strategy of the Genes: A Discussion of Some Aspects of Theoretical Biology*. London: George Allen & Unwin.

Watanabe, M. and Kondo, S. (2015). Is pigment patterning in fish skin determined by the Turing mechanism? *Trends in Genetics*, 31, 88–96.

Weiss, K., Buchanan, A. and Richtsmeier, J. (2015). How are we made? Even well-controlled experiments show the complexity of our traits. *Evolutionary Anthropology*, 24, 130–136.

Weiss, K. M. and Buchanan, A. V. (2004). *Genetics and the Logic of Evolution*. New York, NY: Wiley-Liss.

Weiss, K. M. and Buchanan, A. V. (2008). The cooperative genome: organisms as social contracts. *International Journal of Developmental Biology*, 53, 753–763.

Weiss, K. M. and Buchanan, A. V. (2009). *The Mermaid's Tale: Four Billion Years of Cooperation in the Making of Living Things*. Cambridge, MA: Harvard University Press.

Weiss, K. M. and Fullerton, S. M. (2000). Phenogenetic drift and the evolution of genotype–phenotype relationships. *Theoretical Population Biology*, 57, 187–195.

Wood, A. R., Esco, T., Yang, J., *et al.* (2014). Defining the role of common variation in the genomic and biological architecture of adult human height. *Nature Genetics*, 46, 1173–1186.

2 The Contribution of Angiogenesis to Variation in Bone Development and Evolution

Christopher J. Percival, Kazuhiko Kawasaki, Yuan Huang, Kenneth Weiss, Ethylin Wang Jabs, Runze Li and Joan T. Richtsmeier

2.1 Background

The craniofacial skeleton reflects many important evolutionary trends of primates, including derived orbit morphology (Ross, 1995; Ravosa et al., 2000), cranial base shape (Lieberman et al., 2000), and increased relative cranial vault size (Isler et al., 2008). Similar to findings in many other clades that are not reviewed here, differences in primate dentition (Lambert et al., 2004) and the morphology of the semicircular canal system (Spoor et al., 2007) provide evidence of diet and locomotion, respectively, while the degree of sexual dimorphism provides hints about social behavior (Plavcan, 2001). Morphology of the cranial vault, including cranial volume and relative neurocranial height, are important characteristics that help to distinguish different primate clades (Fleagle et al., 2010). In particular, the human skull is highly derived and cranial elements are useful for determining phylogenetic relationships among hominins (Lahr, 1996; Schwartz and Tattersall, 2003), with vault morphology being an important diagnostic feature in operational definitions of Pleistocene hominin species and descriptions of new fossils (Athreya, 2009). The skull houses structures that enable many important functions associated with the human condition, including cognition (Holloway, 1969; Falk, 1992; Sherwood et al., 2008), vocalization (Kay et al., 1998; MacLarnon and Hewitt, 1999), and thermoregulation (Beals et al., 1984; Weaver, 2009), and as such, human craniofacial evolution raises particularly intriguing questions about our species' origins (Lieberman et al., 2008).

Ontogenetic analysis of fossil and extant primates allows anthropologists to explore the developmental bases of morphological variation, the contribution of mechanical stresses to derived morphology, and ontogenetic shifts that are associated with phylogeny (Lieberman et al., 2002; Lovejoy et al., 2003; Zollikofer and Ponce de León, 2010). Since Stephen J. Gould's discussion of the relationship between ontogeny and phylogeny (Gould, 1977), ontogenetic shifts, including changes in life-history characteristics, have been used to explain the origin of morphological differences between modern humans and other hominid species including chimpanzees (Leigh, 2004; Robson and Wood, 2008), *Ardipithecus ramidus* (Suwa *et al.*, 2009), *Homo erectus* (Dean *et al.*, 2001; Smith, 2004), and Neanderthals (Tillier, 1995; Ponce de León and Zollikofer, 2001), typically using postnatal morphological data.

While studies of postnatal craniofacial development are important, studies of prenatal developmental mechanisms are necessary to complete our understanding of the ontogenetic bases of many important craniofacial features. It is likely that variation in prenatal processes contributes significantly to diagnostic differences in craniofacial morphology that already exist during the earliest postnatal years (Richtsmeier *et al.*, 1993), including those between hominins (Richtsmeier and Walker, 1993; Krovitz, 2000; Ponce de León and Zollikofer, 2001; Cobb and O'Higgins, 2004; Lieberman *et al.*, 2008). Additionally, it has been shown that diagnostic human craniofacial features, including cranial base angle, are known to develop prenatally (Jeffery and Spoor, 2002; Lieberman *et al.*, 2008) and fetal growth patterns of macaques and humans are significantly different (Zumpano and Richtsmeier, 2003). The prenatal appearance of diagnostic morphology should not be surprising given that phenotypic novelties often result from changes in gene regulation during early embryonic stages of development (Raff, 1996; Hall, 1999, 2003; Carroll *et al.*, 2001). Although studies of prenatal specimens are necessary to identify the developmental mechanisms underlying evolutionary change in craniofacial morphology, primate fetal specimens are rare and often not available for study (although see Chapters 4 and 6). Studies using non-primate animal models provide excellent alternatives for anthropologists (Reno *et al.*, 2008; Serrat *et al.*, 2008; Menegaz *et al.*, 2010; Carmody *et al.*, 2011; Young and Devlin, 2012), because of the high degree of conservation of developmental processes across mammalian taxa (Reeves *et al.*, 2001) and because adequate samples of any prenatal stage can be analyzed.

Work with animal models has provided significant insight on the role that gene signaling and tissue interactions play in determining skull form. Among the best understood interactions that underlie integration between tissues of the head are the epithelial–mesenchymal regulatory gene interactions that regulate the formation and fusion of facial prominences, portions of which will ossify into the facial bones, including bones of the upper jaw and palate (e.g., Abzhanov *et al.*, 2007; Marcucio *et al.*, 2011). Once skull bone formation (osteogenesis) is initiated within a condensation of mesenchymal cells, a host of other regulatory genes are necessary for its normal development, whether it ossifies endochondrally from an intermediate cartilage model (Karaplis, 2008; Mackie *et al.*, 2008) or intramembranously ossifies directly from the mesenchymal condensation (Abzhanov *et al.*, 2007; Franz-Odendaal, 2011). More detailed reviews of the cellular origin, genetic regulation, and osteogenesis of skull bones are available elsewhere (e.g., Chapter 3; Karaplis, 2008; Franz-Odendaal, 2011; Percival and Richtsmeier, 2013).

Physical interactions between developing skull bones and adjacent tissues also contribute to craniofacial form. For instance, bones surrounding the orbit may not develop normally without the growing eye (Kish *et al.*, 2011; Dufton *et al.*, 2012; Smith *et al.*, 2014; Dufton and Franz-Odendaal, 2015) and the growth of the brain is necessary for normal cranial vault shape (Moss and Young, 1960; Richtsmeier *et al.*, 2006; Richtsmeier and Flaherty, 2013). On the other hand, the combination of a normally growing brain combined with a failure in the genetic regulation of vault bone growth can lead to craniofacial dysmorphology. Just as long bone growth is dependent on the maintenance of an unfused growth plate, normal skull growth is dependent on the maintenance of cartilaginous synchondroses between endochondral bones of the cranial base and the unossified fibrous tissue in cranial sutures of the facial skeleton and cranial vault. Early vault suture fusion can contribute to significant changes in overall skull morphology as other portions of the skull must compensate for the continued increases in brain volume (Opperman, 2000; Herring, 2008; Heuzé *et al.*, 2014; Twigg and Wilkie, 2015).

2.1.1   Angiogenesis and Skull Development

Another interaction necessary for normal skull development is between blood vessels and osteogenic cells. Although loose populations of craniofacial mesenchyme are associated with blood vessels, the mesenchymal condensations that differentiate into cartilage precursors of bone during endochondral osteogenesis are avascular at the time of their formation (Drushel *et al.*, 1985; Eames *et al.*, 2003; Eshkar-Oren *et al.*, 2009). Vascular invasion of the subsequent avascular cartilage anlage is necessary for the initial ossification of long bones (Zelzer *et al.*, 2002; Colnot *et al.*, 2004; Takimoto *et al.*, 2009), while continued vascular sprouting and growth (angiogenesis) from the diaphysis towards growth plates is necessary for normal metaphyseal bone growth (Bloom and Fawcett, 1994; Kronenberg, 2003; Mackie *et al.*, 2008; Amizuka *et al.*, 2012). Similarly, there is evidence that the mesenchymal condensation precursors of intramembranous bones are avascular for chick sclera (Jourdeuil and Franz-Odendaal, 2012; Jabalee and Franz-Odendaal, 2015), chick frontal (Thompson *et al.*, 1989), chick mandible (Eames and Helms, 2004), and rat mandible prior to ossification (Zernik *et al.*, 1990). As with endochondral bones, the expression of vascular endothelial growth factor, known to be important in driving angiogenesis, is associated with the ossification of chick sclera (Jabalee and Franz-Odendaal, 2015) and rat mandibles (Yang *et al.*, 2012). Furthermore, angiogenesis into the avascular mesenchymal condensation of the chick frontal bone occurs at the same time that intramembranous osteogenesis is initiated (Thompson *et al.*, 1989). These observations combined with the fact that access to oxygen, calcium, and circulating factors within the vasculature is critical to bone formation of any kind suggests that angiogenesis plays an important role during the ossification of both intramembranous and endochondral bones of the skull (reviewed in Percival and Richtsmeier, 2013).

We have proposed that changes in the regulation of angiogenesis can have significant impacts on the timing, speed, and nature of intramembranous osteogenesis within the skull. Such changes in skull growth and development could produce novel variation that is associated with evolutionary change (Percival and Richts-meier, 2013). Within this chapter, we present the results of an investigation into how modifications to angiogenesis perturb the development of craniofacial bone size, shape, and relative density. By focusing on how experimental perturbations of gene expression in the endothelial cells that line blood vessels are associated with variation in the skull, we hoped to elucidate fundamental relationships between bone and vasculature during development.

In this study, we focus on a mouse model where fibroblast growth factor receptor 2 (FGFR2) expression is modified. Fibroblast growth factors (FGF) and receptors (FGFR) are highly pleiotropic, playing critical roles during normal morphogenesis, development, and tissue maintenance. The tissue-specific expression of FGFR iso-forms and FGF ligands, combined with FGF ligand binding specificity of the recep-tor isoforms, gives rise to a complex system of intercellular signaling that is critical for normal development. Although known to be important in the development of many organs, including the brain (Saarimäki-Vire et al., 2007), kidney (Bates, 2007), and lungs (Warburton et al., 2000), we became interested in FGFR2 because muta-tions of this receptor have been associated with changes in skull development, leading to chondroplasia and craniosynostosis (Ornitz and Marie, 2015).

FGFR2 regulates mesenchymal cell activity during osteogenesis (Iseki et al., 1999; Eswarakumar et al., 2002; Ornitz and Marie, 2002) and some FGFR2 mutations are associated with craniosynostosis syndromes (Cohen Jr and Maclean, 2000; Heuzé et al., 2014; Twigg and Wilkie, 2015). FGFR2 is part of a family of receptors whose members are also associated with the regulation of endothelial cells (Suhardja and Hoffman, 2003), cells that make up the walls of capillaries and the inner layers of larger blood vessels. In addition, some of the ligands with which FGFR2 interacts are known to regulate blood vessel sprouting, or angiogenesis (Javerzat et al., 2002). Furthermore, FGFR2 mutations may influence endothelial cell activity, because this gene is expressed in endothelial cells, including a cell line derived from murine brain capillaries (Kanda et al., 1996). Inhibition of FGFR2 in rat glioma cells reduces the vascularity and associated growth of resulting tumors (Auguste et al., 2001), suggesting that FGFR2 signaling plays an important role in promoting angiogenesis in some contexts. Specifically, FGFR2 has been shown to regulate cell migration but not proliferation of brain capillary endothelial cells within cell cultures (Nakamura et al., 2001). In addition, it has been reported that the relatively brittle calvar-ial bones of some patients with Crouzon syndrome, a craniosynostosis syndrome associated with FGFR2 and FGFR3 mutations, display poorly formed vessels of increased diameter (Tholpady et al., 2004). It is not clear from this study whether the vascular and skeletal phenotypes in these patients are independent results of FGFR mutations or whether one is secondary to the other.

Previous studies have indicated that mice carrying a specific missense mutation of Fgfr2 (Fgfr2$^{+/P253R}$ mice), a mutation associated with Apert craniosynostosis syn-drome, display significant craniofacial dysmorphology including midfacial hypo-plasia, premature fusion of some craniofacial sutures, and abnormal cranial vault shape (Wang et al., 2010; Martínez-Abadías et al., 2010), as well as decreased bone volume and density of some bones during early ossification (Percival *et al.*, 2014). Given that FGFR2 likely plays a role in regulating angiogenesis, which is critical for normal bone ossification and development, we hypothesize that some of the craniofacial skeletal dysmorphology previously noted in these $Fgfr2^{+/P253R}$ mice is secondary to the dysregulation of angiogenesis by aberrant FGF/FGFR signaling. To test this hypothesis, we measured the effect of conditional expression of the *Fgfr2* P253R mutation within endothelial cells on skull bone phenotypes during the first week of postnatal development. This conditional expression should remove the direct effect of the mutation on bone cell activity, suggesting that any changes in osteogenesis or in bone shape are the result of modified FGFR2 expression within the vasculature. We hypothesized that these mice would display bone dysmorphology when compared to non-mutant littermates, although this dysmorphology will not be as severe as noted in the $Fgfr2^{+/P253R}$ mice, in whom the mutation is expressed globally.

By quantifying early postnatal variation across multiple aspects of gross skull phenotype, we captured a more complete picture of the skeletal phenotypic effect of the conditional expression of this gene knockout in vascular endothelial cells than would have been possible with analysis limited to craniofacial landmarks. While this study does not definitively show that changes in bone morphology are secondary to dysregulation of angiogenesis, it provides a solid foundation for further study of the interaction between angiogenesis and osteogenesis in the skull. The combination of the research presented here along with similar studies of the influence of various tissues and processes on skull development will allow researchers to make more precise and testable hypotheses about the basis of novel variation that serves as the foundation for evolutionary change.

2.2   Methods

2.2.1   Sample and Imaging

Mice heterozygous for the *Fgfr2* P253R mutation with a neo cassette (+/P253Rneo) (Wang *et al.*, 2010) were bred with *Tek*-cre hemizygote (+/−) mice (Kisanuki *et al.*, 2001) to exclusively remove the cassette within endothelial cells, allowing for conditional expression of the mutation. This cross leads to litters containing four genotypes with similar frequency. $Tek^{+/-}; Fgfr2^{+/P253R}$ mice are heterozygous for the P253R mutation and hemizygous for *Tek*-cre so should express the P253R mutation in endothelial cells only. The other three genotypes ($Tek^{-/-}; Fgfr2^{+/P253R}$, $Tek^{-/-}; Fgfr2^{+/+}$, $Tek^{+/-}; Fgfr2^{+/+}$) represent controls that should not express the *Fgfr2* mutation at all and were independently compared to the affected sample. Because the results of these comparisons were similar (Percival, 2013), we present the results of a comparison between $Tek^{+/-}; Fgfr2^{+/P253R}$ and $Tek^{-/-}; Fgfr2^{+/P253Rneo}$, the latter representing the control genotype with the highest sample size. For the rest of the chapter, $Tek^{+/-};$ $Fgfr2^{+/P253R}$ will be referred to as affected mice and $Tek^{-/-}; Fgfr2^{+/P253Rneo}$ will be referred to as control mice.

Table 2.1 Sample sizes for genotype groups used during landmark-based analyses (LandM) and volume/density analyses (Vol/Den) for P0 and P8, including the voxel size and slice thickness of associated µCT images.

Genotype	P0		P8	
	LandM	Vol/Den	LandM	Vol/Den
$Tek^{-/-}; Fgfr2^{+/P253Rneo}$	24	22	7	7
$Tek^{+/-}; Fgfr2^{+/P253R}$	14	9	4	4
Voxel size (µm)	13.8		19.8	
Slice thickness (µm)	15.4		21.8	

Litters were sacrificed at postnatal days zero (P0) and eight (P8) and fixed in 4% paraformaldehyde (sample sizes in Table 2.1). Care and use of mice were approved by Penn State University Institutional Animal Care and Use Committee. Micro-computed tomography (µCT) images (130 kVp/0.15 mA) of mouse heads (Table 2.1) were acquired in air at the Center for Quantitative X-Ray Imaging at Pennsylvania State University (www.cqi.psu.edu). Solid hydroxyapatite phantoms (QRM GmbH, Möehrendorf, Germany) scanned with each set of skulls allowed for relative X-ray attenuation values to be associated with bone mineral density estimates.

We verified that Tek-cre removes neo cassettes extensively and exclusively in vascular endothelial cells by breeding Tek-cre hemizygotes (+/–) with R26 Rosa reporter homozygotes (+/+) (Soriano, 1999). After LacZ staining and clearing embryonic day 17.5 (E17.5) specimens in glycerol, whole mounts of $Tek^{+/-}; Rosa^{+/+}$ embryos revealed staining of apparently complete vasculature, while littermates without Tek-cre display no staining (Percival, 2013), suggesting that Tek-cre expression leads to heterozygous expression of the P253R $Fgfr2$ mutation in endothelial cells of $Tek^{+/-}; Fgfr2^{+/P253R}$ mice.

2.2.2   Landmark Identification and Analysis

3D coordinates of anatomical landmarks (Figure 2.1, Table 2.2), were manually recorded on µCT-derived bone surfaces produced with a minimum threshold of 62 mg/cm³ partial density of hydroxyapatite. The locations of 25 landmarks were recorded on the skull surfaces of P0 mice while 29 cranial landmarks were recorded for the P8 mice. Differences in skull form were assessed using the Euclidian Distance Matrix Analysis (EDMA) Form method (Lele and Richtsmeier, 1991) to estimate the form of each specimen as a matrix of all unique linear distances between all landmarks. A given linear distance differs between two genotypes if a bootstrap algorithm (1000 iterations) that determines the linear distance ratio between the genotype averages is significantly different than one ($\alpha = 0.10$). This allows morphometric differences between genotypes to be localized to specific linear distances and their associated landmarks. Specimens with damaged skulls or those with

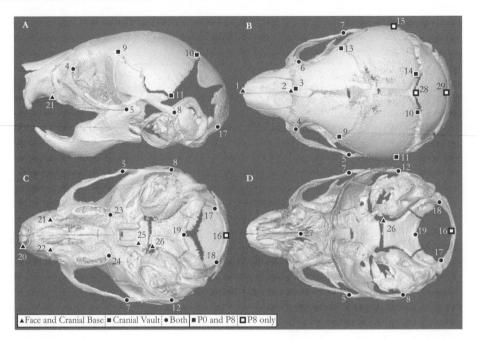

Figure 2.1 The locations of landmarks used for EDMA Form analyses of the face–cranial base (triangles), the vault (squares), or both (circles) on surface reconstructions of a μCT image of a P8 mouse head from the following views: (A) left lateral, (B) superior, (C) inferior with mandible removed, and (D) superior with the calotte removed. Dark outlines on a landmark symbol indicates it was included in the analysis of P8 mice but not P0 mice. All landmarks were used for MorphoJ analyses. Landmark numbers correspond to those listed in Table 2.2.

unique outlier morphology (i.e., a specimen with only one eye and another with fused upper incisors) were not included in this analysis. Two subsets of landmarks representing the facial skeleton/cranial base and the cranial vault were analyzed separately (Table 2.2, Figure 2.1) at both P0 and P8. We analyzed the vault separately from the facial skeleton and cranial base to test whether any changes in the affected mice, who express a mutation associated with premature fusion of cranial vault sutures in their endothelial cells, occur just in the vault or in other parts of the skull as well.

To test whether skull size differs between affected and controls at each age, pairwise two-sample Wilcoxon (Mann–Whitney) tests of centroid size were completed in R (R Developmental Core Team, 2008). To test for differences in static allometry between genotypes at each age, we performed a multivariate regression in MorphoJ (Klingenberg, 2011) of all Procrustes landmark coordinates against centroid size. This regression produced a plot of the regression summary score, a summary of skull shape variation (Drake and Klingenberg, 2008), against centroid size of each specimen at P0 and P8.

Table 2.2 Definitions for all landmarks used in EDMA Form analysis assigned to the face or cranial base (F-B) and landmarks assigned to the cranial vault (Vault) for P0 and P8 specimens. MorphoJ-based analyses included all landmarks. Landmark numbers correspond to those found in Figure 2.1.

	P0		P8			
Number	F-B	Vault	F-B	Vault	Name	Definition
1	y		y		rnsla	Most antero-medial point of the right nasal bone
2	y		y		rnslp	Most postero-medial point of the right nasal bone
3		y		y	ramf	Most medio-anterior point of right frontal bone
4	y	y	y	y	lflac	Intersection of frontal process of maxilla with frontal and lacrimal bones, left side
5	y	y	y	y	lzyt	Intersection of zygoma with zygomatic process of temporal, taken on zygoma, left side
6	y	y	y	y	rflac	Intersection of frontal process of maxilla with frontal and lacrimal bones, right side
7	y	y	y	y	rzyt	Intersection of zygoma with zygomatic process of temporal, taken on zygoma, right side
8	y	y	y	y	lpsq	Most posterior point on the posterior extension of the left squamous temporal
9		y		y	lpfl	Most lateral intersection of the frontal and parietal bones, taken on the left parietal
10		y		y	lpto	Most postero-medial point on the left parietal
11		y		y	lpip	Most postero-inferior point on the left parietal
12	y	y	y	y	rpsq	Most posterior point on the posterior extension of the right squamous temporal
13		y		y	rpfl	Most lateral intersection of the frontal and parietal bones, taken on the right parietal
14		y		y	rpto	Most postero-medial point on the right parietal
15				y	rpip	Most postero-inferior point on the right parietal
16				y	opi	Mid-point on the anterior margin of the foramen magnum, taken on basioccipital
17	y	y	y	y	loci	The superior posterior point on the ectocranial surface of the left lateral occipital
18	y	y	y	y	roci	The superior posterior point on the ectocranial surface of the right lateral occipital
19	y	y	y	y	bas	Mid-point on the posterior margin of the foramen magnum, taken on squamosal occipital
20	y		y		rpmsp	Anterior superior edge of the right premaxilla at the nasal aperture
21	y		y		lpmx	Most infero-lateral point of the premaxillary–maxillary suture, taken on the left premaxilla
22	y		y		rpmx	Most infero-lateral point of the premaxillary–maxillary suture, taken on the right premaxilla
23	y	y	y	y	lmma	Posterior lateral point on the maxillary portion of the left medial alveolus
24	y	y	y	y	rmma	Posterior lateral point on the maxillary portion of the right medial alveolus

(*continued*)

Table 2.2 (*cont.*)

	PO		P8			
Number	F-B	Vault	F-B	Vault	Name	Definition
25	y		y		rptyp	Most posterior tip of the medial right pterygoid process
26	y		y		rsyn	Most antero-lateral point on corner of the right basioccipital
27	y	y	y	y	ethmp	Most posterior point on the body of the vomer
28				y	pari	The anterior midline point on the interparietal bone
29				y	paro	The midline superior point of the squamous occipital bone

2.2.3   Bone Volume and Density Measurement

Semiautomatic segmentation (Percival *et al.*, 2012, 2014) was performed within Avizo 3D analysis software (Visualization Sciences Group, Burlington, MA) to identify the individual craniofacial bones of each specimen, based on a minimum bone threshold of 74 mg/cm^3 partial density of hydroxyapatite. Single manually segmented P0 and P8 reference specimens served as the basis for the semiautomatic segmentation of other specimens of the same age. A subset of 16 relatively large midline and left-side craniofacial bones with low segmentation error were included in our analysis (Figure 2.2). Specimens with relatively high bone identification error during semiautomatic segmentation were excluded from our volume/density analysis.

Bone density histograms, bone volumes, and standardized bone density histograms were estimated for all bones in our analysis, as previously described (Percival *et al.*, 2014). Bone volume, based on the number of voxels over the minimum threshold, serves as a proxy for bone size, while differences in volume between ages represent bone growth. Single bone volume standardized by total volume of all measured bones represents the relative development of that bone at a given age. In order to identify differences in volume between genotypes, pairwise comparisons of mean individual bone volumes were completed between genotypes at both ages with two-sample Wilcoxon (Mann–Whitney) tests in R, including Bonferroni correction for multiple testing.

Cubic spline curves approximating standardized bone density histograms (ranging between 74 and 372 mg/cm^3 partial density of hydroxyapatite), called relative density curves, provide the basis for the quantitative evaluation of bone maturation. Mean relative density curves representing typical bone maturation of control specimens were plotted for P0 and P8 time points to investigate whether bones cluster by patterns of bone maturation across

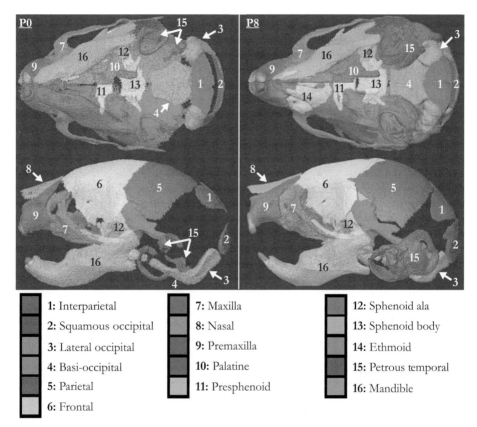

Figure 2.2 The subset of bones analyzed, as identified from the surface reconstructions of P0 and P8 specimens from the inferior view (top) and the left lateral view (bottom). Bones included in our analysis are opaque, while the rest of the skull is translucent. As identified in this figure, the maxilla includes the lacrimal bone and the petrous temporal includes the ectotympanic. A black and white version of this figure will appear in some formats. For the color version, please refer to the plate section.

the early postnatal period. With the $Tek^{-/-}$; $Fgfr2^{+/P253Rneo}$ mice controls as a baseline, functional data analysis was completed, using the fda package in R (Ramsay *et al.*, 2009), to determine the influence of endothelial expression of the *P253R* mutation on bone maturation across the early postnatal period. Because image saturation would have a strong artificial influence on functions estimated from histograms, the five highest bone density values were discarded during functional analysis. A functional multivariate regression was computed for each bone with a genotype dummy variable representing the affected specimens and age as a binary variable.

$$E(y(d)) = \beta_0(d) + \beta_1(d)I + \beta_2(d)Age$$

In this regression model, *d* refers to bone density values, *I* is the genotype identity for affected mice and *Age* represents the postnatal age of the specimen. Because the ethmoid does not exist as an ossified bone at P0, a regression analysis was not completed for this bone. Ninety-five percent confidence intervals of the resulting coefficient curves were computed to determine whether the associated covariates had a significant effect on relative bone density curves.

2.3   Results

2.3.1   Typical Growth and Maturation

The volumes of individual bones at postnatal day 0 (P0) (Table 2.3), relative to overall ossified volume, are similar to those previously reported for P0 mice on the same C57BL/6 inbred background (Percival *et al.*, 2014). Between P0 and P8, we note a major shift in the relative volume of the bones that are relatively large in the adult. The mandible, which accounts for the majority of ossified material between E15.5 and P0 (Percival *et al.*, 2014), is rivaled in size by the petrous temporal at P8. The ethmoid, which displayed no ossified volume at P0, displays the third highest relative volume at P8, followed by the maxilla and frontal bones.

Table 2.3 Comparison of patterns of bone growth between genotypes. In the first numeric row are mean total volumes of the 16 bones under study by age measured as mm³, with standard deviation in parentheses. The rest of the numeric rows include the mean relative volume of each bone by age and genotype, calculated as the percentage of mean total bone volume at the associated age, with standard deviation in parentheses.

	Controls		Affected	
	Mean total bone volume in mm³ by age (standard deviation)			
	P0	P8	P0	P8
	8.02 (1.57)	37.68 (1.85)	7.55 (1.78)	33.98 (4.03)
	Mean % of total volume at each age (standard deviation)			
	P0	P8	P0	P8
Mandible	26.00 (1.95)	14.81 (0.72)	27.29 (1.01)	14.80 (0.95)
Frontal	12.00 (0.61)	8.55 (0.26)	12.24 (0.33)	8.57 (0.44)
Maxilla	10.52 (0.51)	8.97 (0.16)	10.49 (0.60)	8.97 (0.43)
Basi-occipital	8.54 (0.83)	4.60 (0.11)	8.73 (1.17)	4.90 (0.27)
Premaxilla	6.31 (0.39)	5.81 (0.18)	6.02 (0.48)	5.88 (0.09)
Parietal	6.18 (0.53)	5.61 (0.52)	5.91 (0.71)	6.16 (0.65)
Sphenoid body	5.58 (0.52)	4.07 (0.19)	5.58 (0.53)	4.22 (0.16)
Lateral occipital	5.49 (0.78)	3.07 (0.17)	5.64 (0.59)	3.11 (0.26)
Sphenoid ala	3.57 (0.12)	2.46 (0.13)	3.60 (0.17)	2.33 (0.11)
Palatine	3.41 (0.25)	2.14 (0.10)	3.58 (0.36)	2.08 (0.03)
Squamous occipital	3.39 (0.77)	5.36 (0.47)	2.96 (0.96)	5.30 (0.61)
Interparietal	3.30 (0.70)	5.05 (0.53)	3.10 (0.76)	5.11 (0.57)
Presphenoid	2.52 (0.54)	1.83 (0.15)	2.27 (0.40)	1.76 (0.08)
Petrous temporal	1.77 (0.81)	15.17 (0.36)	1.22 (0.39)	14.59 (0.27)
Nasal	1.43 (0.35)	2.65 (0.12)	1.37 (0.32)	2.66 (0.11)
Ethmoid	0.00 (–)	9.85 (0.35)	0.00 (–)	9.54 (0.74)

The mean standardized bone density curves of control mice indicate that all bones typically approach a similar level of bone maturation by P8. Most bones display an increase in relative density as a reduction in the slope of their relative density curves between P0 and P8. Variation in this common pattern is shown by the density curves of the palatine (Figure 2.3A), frontal (Figure 2.3B), and mandible (Figure 2.3C), with the maxilla, parietal, premaxilla, presphenoid, and sphenoid ala also maturing in this pattern. Basi-occipital (Figure 2.3D), lateral occipital, and

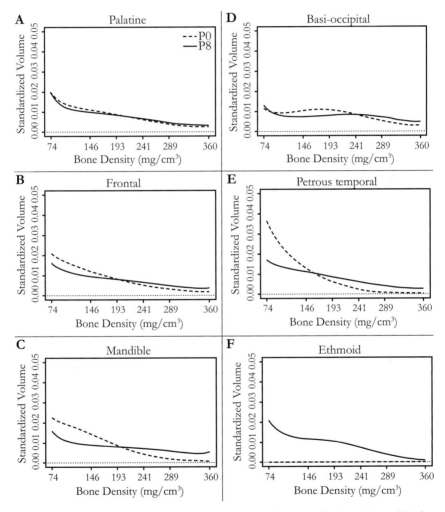

Figure 2.3 The mean standardized density curves for the control mice at P0 and P8 for a representative subset of bones. (A) Palatine, (B) frontal, and (C) mandible bone maturation represent most bones between P0 and P8; relative density increases as the relative density curves become more horizontal, leading to similar relative density curves at P8. (D) Basi-occipital represents a few endochondral bones, increasing in relative density through the movement of a peak frequency towards higher densities. (E) Petrous temporal represents bones that have low relative densities at P0; (F) ethmoid is completely unossified at P0, but both reach a similar relative density to most bones by P8.

sphenoid body start with high relative densities at P0, but further increase in density via the movement of the peak in their curves towards higher density values. The petrous temporal (Figure 2.3E), interparietal, nasal, and squamous occipital bones have relatively low relative density at P0, while the ethmoid (Figure 2.3F) has no ossified material at this stage. However, these five bones still mature into relatively dense bones by P8, although not quite as dense as the others.

Our functional multivariate regression indicates that age is significantly correlated with variation in relative bone density, as measured from standardized bone density curves. With P0 serving as the baseline, an increase in age to P8 is generally associated with a reduction in the proportion of lower density bone and an increase in the proportion of higher density bone. For bones that started at a higher relative density at P0, the age coefficient curve resembles a sine curve (Figure 2.4A). Bones

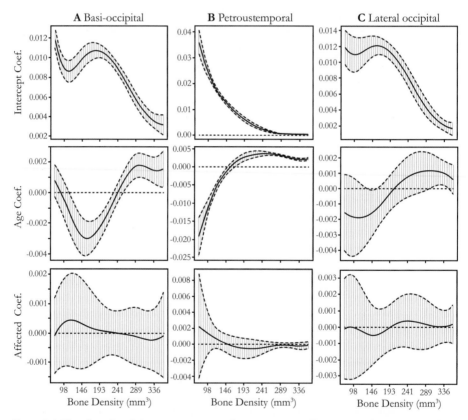

Figure 2.4 The functional intercept, age, and genotype coefficients, with 95% confidence intervals from the multivariate regressions of standardized bone density curves for three bones. The baseline for the regressions are P0 control mice, with an identity coefficient for the affected genotype. (A) Basi-occipital and (B) petrous temporal both display a significant age effect, as most bones do. (C) Lateral occipital does not display a significant age effect between P0 and P8. None of the bones display a significant effect of genotype for this set of multivariate regressions.

that started with a lower relative density at birth display a single convex curve (Figure 2.4B). The lateral occipital is the only bone for which age is not significantly correlated with relative bone density (Figure 2.4C), while the palatine bone displays a significant age coefficient across a limited range of density values.

2.3.2   Effect of Endothelial Cell Expression of $Fgfr2^{+/P253R}$

EDMA Form analysis of control and affected mice, which serve as numerator and denominator of associated linear distance ratios, respectively, indicates most distance ratios are greater than one at both P0 and P8 for both landmark subsets (skull vault, cranial base: Figure 2.5A,B), indicating that the affected mice have generally shorter skull dimensions. Based on the 90% confidence intervals for these comparisons, length is shorter for 71% and 40% of face/cranial base linear distances at P0 and P8, respectively, and 65% and 39% of cranial vault linear distances at P0 and P8, respectively. A similar proportion of skull lengths, widths, and heights are significantly different in the mutant pups, suggesting that the overall linearly measured scale of affected mice is reduced compared to control littermates and that all studied regions of the skull are affected.

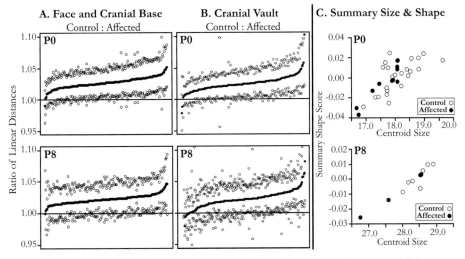

Figure 2.5 Ratios of linear distances of the (A) face–cranial base landmarks and (B) cranial vault landmarks, sorted by estimated ratio (filled circle) with 90% confidence intervals (open circles). Separate EDMA Form tests comparing controls and affected samples were completed for both ages. P0 and P8 ratios tend to be above one, suggesting that linear distances of affected mice (the denominator) tend to be smaller than the control genotypes, often significantly so. (C) Plots of centroid size and a regression summary score representing the landmark-based skull shape accounted for by centroid size for all specimens of both genotypes at shape. The linear relationship between these summary scores is similar for both genotypes, but affected specimens tend to be found towards the left side of both plots. This suggests that the relationship between size and shape is similar for all genotypes, but that the affected skulls are more likely to have smaller size than control skulls.

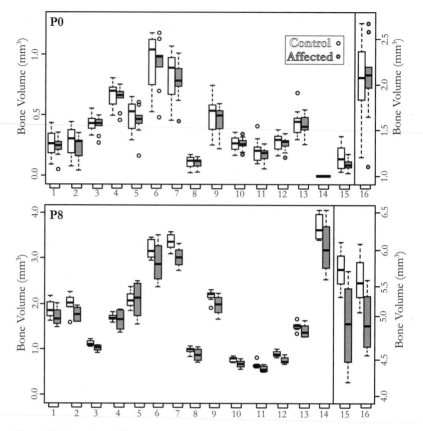

Figure 2.6 Boxplots of bone volumes by age, for control (white) and affected genotypes (gray). Dots represent outlier values that are more than 1.5 times the interquartile range from the box. The values for mandible (16) and petrous temporal (15) may be at a different scale than the other bones within an age. Numbers refer to individual bones, as identified in Figure 2.2: 1, interparietal; 2, squamous occipital; 3, lateral occipital; 4, basi-occipital; 5, parietal; 6, frontal; 7, maxilla; 8, nasal; 9, premaxilla; 10, palatine; 11, presphenoid; 12, sphenoid ala; 13, sphenoid body; 14, ethmoid; 15, petrous temporal; 16, mandible.

Based on similarities in the linear distribution of the multivariate shape summary score against centroid size, a measure of scale, it appears that the relationship between cranial shape and size is similar for both genotypes at P0 and P8 (Figure 2.5C). While the distribution of affected group centroid sizes represents the lower half of the control distribution (Figure 2.5C), no differences in mean centroid size are significant (α = 0.05) at P0 or P8. However, the fact that affected mice appear to be smaller complements the EDMA results that suggest affected mice are reduced in overall scale.

The mean overall ossified volume of affected mice does not differ significantly from control genotypes at either age (Table 2.3). The mean individual volumes of each bone are also similar across genotypes at P0, while trending lower for many bones of affected mice at P8 (Figure 2.6). Without correction for multiple testing, the P8 lateral occipital bone volume would be significantly lower in affected mice. However, no other bone volumes are significantly different across pair-wise genotype comparisons, even though genotype differences for other bones, including petrous temporal and squamous occipital, visually appear more extreme at P8. Functional multivariate regressions do not indicate that genotype significantly influences relative bone density. In summary, there are no significant differences in individual bone volume or relative bone density between genotypes, although some affected bone volumes might have been significantly lower than controls at P8 in marginally larger samples.

2.4   Discussion

Development serves as the mechanistic bridge linking genetic variation and resulting phenotypic variation, including variation acted on by evolution. The palimpsest concept, first conceived by Gregory (1947), and now being championed by Hallgrímsson and colleagues (2009), provides a conceptual framework for studies of the developmental determinants of variation in complex traits. In highly complex structures like the skull, developmental processes underlying variation are probably so complex that it is not possible to divide the structure into definitive morphological modules based on developmental processes (Roseman *et al.*, 2009). Instead, the palimpsest model suggests that we focus on how the combination of semi-independent developmental processes acting at different times and on different anatomical regions leads to patterns of variation and covariation in the adult structure (Hallgrímsson *et al.*, 2009). One possible way to accomplish this is to focus on the spatial associations and developmental interactions between cell populations or tissues that are traditionally studied independently. Another strategy is to modify gene expression and/or a developmental process associated with a specific tissue type (or cell population) in order to see what secondary phenotypic effects occur across the head. Both strategies are designed to measure how modifications in particular developmental pathways or processes, such as blood vessel growth, brain growth, cell condensation, or ossification, produce phenotypic variation in the skull.

The results of our current study help to clarify how modulation of an important regulatory gene within vascular cells influences gross skull morphology and how these changes manifest phenotypically across early bone development. Specifically, our results provide evidence that changes in the regulation of angiogenesis can lead to significant secondary changes in craniofacial phenotypes (i.e., skull form), suggesting another avenue by which the development of skull bones can be influenced by other tissues.

2.4.1   Typical Bone Growth and Maturation

While the typical pace of bone maturation may differ between specific bones prenatally, bones reach similar stages of bone maturation by P8. The mean typical standardized bone density curves of P0 control mice on the C57BL/6 background are similar in this (Figure 2.3) and our previous study (Percival et al., 2014), although bone maturation may progress slightly faster for the mice described here, because they appear to have mildly higher relative density and volume at P0. We previously identified three groups of skull bones with differing patterns of bone maturation in C57BL/6-based control mice, as approximated by changes in relative density, between embryonic day 15.5 (approximately one day after the start of craniofacial osteogenesis) and P0 (Percival et al., 2014). While strong differences in relative bone density exist between bones at P0, these differences are reduced by P8; even for bones that display low density (e.g., nasal) or no bone volume (ethmoid) at birth (Figure 2.3). We anticipate that similarities in relative density between specific bones persist throughout postnatal development and into adulthood, although additional imaging and histological studies are required to verify this.

2.4.2   Genotype Effect

Landmark-based morphometric analysis, as well as volume and relative density analyses were completed on μCT images of mouse heads to quantify any differences in skull bone morphology between the genotypes. Landmark-based comparisons suggest that affected mouse skulls are reduced in scale at P0 and P8, as measured by linear distances. However, the $Tek^{+/-}$; $Fgfr2^{+/P253Rneo}$ mice lack the midfacial hypoplasia, coronal craniosynostosis, and rounded vault form of mice that express the same $Fgfr2$ mutation across all tissues. This indicates that the major craniofacial dysmorphologies associated with Apert syndrome are primarily based on expression of the $Fgfr2$ mutation by cells other than endothelial cells, probably including osteoblast lineage cells and/or surrounding mesenchyme. However, the reduced linear scale of our $Tek^{+/-}$; $Fgfr2^{+/P253Rneo}$ mice indicate that the expression of this mutation by endothelial cells likely contributes to decreased overall skull size. Given the fact that linearly measured cranial dimensions are shorter in affected mice by P0, it is surprising that measures of bone volume are so similar between affected and control mice at birth. It appears that the effect of endothelial specific expression of P253R mutation leads to smaller skulls with a similar volume of ossified material at P0. However, by P8, bone volumes trend lower for affected mice, although not significantly so. In addition, functional multivariate regressions did not indicate any significant differences in relative bone density between the genotypes at P0 or P8.

Given that affected mice lack the gross dysmorphology typical of mice that universally express the P253R mutation, the smaller size of affected mouse skulls might provide evidence for developmental delay of affected mice along the same developmental growth trajectory as the control genotypes. However, only the landmark-defined linear distance measures of size are shorter at P0, while bones contain similar amounts of similarly dense ossified material. This suggests that the endothelial expression of the P253R mutation modifies the ossified form of a bone by P0 without changes to the volume or quality of deposited bone. Based on these observations, we expect to see the same number of osteoblasts with similar activity levels in affected and control mice at P0, but with differences in the spatial distribution of those osteoblasts. With a larger sample size, it is possible that significantly lower bone volume might have been identified in affected mice at P8, indicating a difference in the amount of bone material produced alongside a reduction in the expansion of bone outward. This situation would have suggested that the spatial distribution and the number of osteoblasts are both modified by P8. Incorporation of histological methods (some of which are discussed in Chapters 8 and 9; also see Chapter 5 for analysis of cell activity from bone surface features) is required to test these hypotheses of cellular distribution and activity, but our results indicate that the conditional expression of the P253R *Fgfr2* mutation within endothelial cells influences the growth and development of the craniofacial skeleton.

2.4.3 Osteogenesis Regulated by Angiogenesis

While the critical importance of angiogenesis to the process of osteogenesis has been well documented in the postcranial skeleton and is assumed to operate during cranial bone ossification (Percival and Richtsmeier, 2013), the regulatory mechanisms through which angiogenesis directly influences bone growth and development are not well studied. Endothelial cell-specific loss of *PlexinD1* expression in mice has previously been shown to cause axial skeletal deformations (Zhang *et al.*, 2009), illustrating that endothelial cell-specific changes in gene expression can directly lead to changes in skeletal development. We rely on more indirect lines of evidence to hypothesize a mechanism by which endothelial specific expression of the P253R mutation of *Fgfr2* might lead to the smaller skull noted in our study. A study of the IBE endothelial cell line, derived from murine brain capillaries, suggests that FGFR2 expression in endothelial cells regulates endothelial cell motility, an important aspect of angiogenesis. However, other angiogenic responses including endothelial cell proliferation and capillary tube formation do not appear to be influenced by FGFR2 signaling (Nakamura *et al.*, 2001). While it is possible that the results of this cell-culture study are not generalizable to the process of angiogenesis across developing tissues *in vivo* (Javerzat *et al.*, 2002), endothelial FGFR2 expression may play a similar role during angiogenesis associated with cranial bone osteogenesis.

If FGFR2 expression in endothelial cells only influences angiogenesis via dysregulation of endothelial cell motility, an *Fgfr2* mutation, like the P253R mutation, might only serve to modulate the speed of new capillary outgrowth from existing vasculature during angiogenesis. Given that bones grow outward from initial ossification centers within initially avascular condensations of mesenchyme that have been invaded by blood vessels (reviewed in Percival and Richtsmeier, 2013), and the importance of the proximity of capillaries to osteoblasts during osteogenesis (Percival and Richtsmeier, 2013), we hypothesize that a reduction in the motility of the endothelial cells within $Tek^{+/-}$; $Fgfr2^{+/P253R}$ mice leads to a reduction in the spatial extent of active osteoblasts within developing bones and secondarily, to skull bones of reduced linear scale. It is not clear whether a reduction in motility based on the P253R mutation might lead to a capillary network with shorter capillary segments between branch points, fewer capillary branches, or some other modified network structure. In any case, a reduction in the spatial extent of sprouting capillaries would likely limit the linear range over which osteoblasts could successfully differentiate and produce bone. Logically, this could lead to a situation where the quality and speed of bone-forming activity is unchanged, except for being limited to a smaller spatial extent. If this hypothesis is correct, we expect the capillary network associated with developing bones in our affected mice to be reduced in spatial extent starting during the earliest phases of prenatal cranial ossification, followed by a similar reduction in spatial extent of osteoblast activity and mineralized tissue.

Because signaling between tissues may play a major role in regulating cranial bone development, it is possible that the conditional expression of the *P253R* mutation in endothelial cells directly influences bone cells or their precursors, rather than secondarily influencing them via the dysregulation of angiogenesis. It is also possible that the endothelial expression of this mutation might influence the growth of the cranial bones via abnormal development of vasculature across the developing specimen, including a reduction in blood flow caused by reduced blood vessel diameter. Reduction in blood flow during early development has been previously linked to shorter limb bones in mice (Serrat *et al.*, 2008). Future studies on the covariation between capillary network properties and bone mineralization will be required to determine the regulatory basis of the subtle changes in cranial bone growth and development noted in our *Tek$^{+/-}$; Fgfr2$^{+/P253R}$* mice. We are continuing to pursue methods to quantify the 3D association of embryonic vasculature and bone in developing skulls.

2.4.4   Anthropological Implications

The work presented here adds to our understanding of the types of genetic or developmental changes that might underlie evolutionary morphological variation. Methodologically, we have illustrated how quantifying multiple aspects of craniofacial bone phenotypes can help formulate more specific testable hypotheses about the changes in cellular behavior that might underlie this variation. The appreciation that changes in the regulation of blood vessel growth can secondarily influence craniofacial morphology might have direct implications for current studies of living primates and fossil hominids. We comment on three of these implications below.

(1) Although not directly answering traditional anthropological questions, studies of the basic processes of craniofacial osteogenesis and the role that other tissues can play in modulating bone phenotypes are fundamental to developing hypotheses about the genetic and developmental origins of phenotypic variation. The results of our study on mice that express an *Fgfr2* mutation exclusively in endothelial cells provide further evidence of the developmental complexity of skeletal phenotypes and the pleiotropic nature of important

regulatory genes. Understanding these basic developmental processes is critical as anthropologists move beyond more descriptive quantification of ontogenetic trajectories towards questions of developmental mechanisms underlying differences in ontogeny and adult morphology (e.g., Reno *et al.*, 2008; Serrat *et al.*, 2008; Menegaz *et al.*, 2010; Carmody *et al.*, 2011; Young and Devlin, 2012). Additionally, given the relative lack of basic information about the processes and interactions underlying craniofacial osteogenesis, there is the opportunity for anthropologists to drive basic bone research in new directions that reveal the potential bases of skull variation in primates, mammals, and perhaps other vertebrates.

(2) By combining common methods of morphometrics with complementary measures of bone volume and relative density across the late prenatal period, we previously illustrated differences in typical early bone maturation between three groups of skull bones, and showed that midfacial hypoplasia of a mouse model of a craniosynostosis syndrome displayed shorter facial bones with similar volume at birth (Percival *et al.*, 2014). If landmark- or linear distance-based morphometrics had been applied alone, the reduction in linear size of the facial bones might have been hypothetically associated with a simple reduction in bone cell activity. However, by quantifying other aspects of skeletal phenotypes from the same μCT images, this hypothesis could be discounted and more specific hypotheses about the developmental basis for gross morphological change could be proposed. Similarly, we see that a reduction in the linear scale of the skull in our affected mice is not associated with reduced bone volume or density at birth. This is evidence that the reduced scale is not simply a mild developmental delay, but may be based on a more complex interaction between reduced endothelial cell motility and bone cell differentiation. Landmark-based morphometric studies of bone remain invaluable for anthropologists, but can often be made stronger by incorporating complementary measures of skeletal phenotype. Anyone using CT images standardized with a bone density calibration to study fresh bone can quantify bone volume and relative density of individual bones or regions of the skull from existing images. Given their potential value, we recommend adding these complementary methods to the landmark- or surface-based morphometric methods that are more commonly used to measure skull phenotypes (also see Chapters 6 and 12 for ontogenetic studies of bone material properties).

As a next step, the incorporation of histological approaches is necessary to test the specific hypotheses generated by our work. Collaborations between anthropologists who quantify gross skeletal phenotypes in 3D and developmental biologists who quantify gene expression and cellular activity patterns using histological methods are necessary in our search for the developmental bases of evolutionary change. While there is a wide selection of molecular methods that can link gene expression patterns and local cellular activity, there are also now attempts to directly link gene expression and cellular activity to the type of gross morphological variation that has traditionally interested paleontologists, ecologists, and many anthropologists (Chapters 1, 8, and 9).

(3) Given that our results indicate that dysregulation of angiogenesis can influence the speed of outward bone growth, it is possible that changes in patterns or speed of angiogenesis might contribute to some of the variation we see among extant and extinct primate species. For instance, in species with extreme morphology, such as the wide orbits of the tarsier or the long snouts of baboons, changes in the direction and timing of angiogenesis to match (or perhaps precede) patterns of osteogenesis will be necessary for healthy bone development. More subtly, it is possible that relative differences in the speed of angiogenesis during early postnatal expansion of bones toward each other contributes to differences between species in the relative size of adjacent bones and the position of associated sutures.

Furthermore, it is possible that a delay in angiogenesis might lead to an evolutionarily adaptive phenotype. Although several other mechanisms may explain why the zygomatic and frontal bones of the tarsier do not touch at birth in tarsiers (Smith *et al.*, 2013), it is possible that delay of angiogenesis associated with zygomatic bone growth may maintain a flexible articulation to accommodate significant postnatal growth of the eye. As a second example, our work with mice that express the P253R *Fgfr2* mutation supports the idea that dysmorphology associated with Apert syndrome arises from the direct pleiotropic influence of the P253R mutation on multiple tissue types within the head (Aldridge *et al.*, 2010; Percival and Richtsmeier, 2011; Martínez-Abadías *et al.*, 2013). The midfacial hypoplasia associated with Apert syndrome is grossly similar to the midfacial reduction noted during human evolution. If only angiogenesis (rather than osteogenesis) were dysregulated in the midface, this might contribute to the short midface of humans, although we would expect to see thicker midfacial bones with similar bone volumes and relative bone densities during the earliest stages of this evolutionary change.

Understanding the developmental mechanisms underlying craniofacial variation is critical for determining the basis for the emergence of phenotypic novelties during evolutionary history. While this includes leveraging the work of developmental biologists, anthropologists have increasing opportunities to drive this work forward themselves by making use of existing animal models, thus directing the study of bone development towards answers to anthropologically relevant questions.

Acknowledgments

Many thanks to Talia Pankratz and Tiffany Kim for assistance with mouse breeding and data collection; to Tim Ryan, Patrick Drew, and two anonymous reviewers for their comments on earlier versions of this manuscript; and for the technical expertise and care by Tim Ryan and Tim Stecko at PSU CQI in producing the µCT images used in this study. Our research was supported in part by grants from the National Science Foundation to CJP (BCS-1061554) and JTR/KW (BCS-0725227), from the National Institute of Dental and Craniofacial Research and the American Recovery and Reinvestment Act to JTR/EWJ (R01DE018500; 3R01DE018500-02S1; R01DE022988); and from the National Institute of Child Health and Development to JTR/EWJ (P01HD078233). Additional support to CJP also provided by the CIHR Training Program in Genetics, Child Development and Health through the Alberta Children's Hospital Research Institute for Child and Maternal Health.

References

Abzhanov, A., Rodda, S. J., McMahon, A. P. and Tabin, C. J. (2007). Regulation of skeletogenic differentiation in cranial dermal bone. *Development*, 134, 3133–3144.

Aldridge, K., Hill, C. A., Austin, J. R., et al. (2010). Brain phenotypes in two FGFR2 mouse models for Apert syndrome. *Developmental Dynamics*, 239, 987–997.

Amizuka, N., Hasegawa, T., Oda, K., et al. (2012). Histology of epiphyseal cartilage calcification and endochondral ossification. *Frontiers in Bioscience*, 4, 2085–2100.

Athreya, S. (2009). A comparative study of frontal bone morphology among Pleistocene hominin fossil groups. *Journal of Human Evolution*, 57, 786–804.

Auguste, P., Gürsel, D. B., Lemière, S., et al. (2001). Inhibition of fibroblast growth factor/ fibroblast growth factor receptor activity in glioma cells impedes tumor growth by both angiogenesis-dependent and -independent mechanisms. *Cancer Research*, 61, 1717–1726.

Bates, C. M. (2007). Role of fibroblast growth factor receptor signaling in kidney development. *Pediatric Nephrology*, 22, 343–349.

Beals, K. L., Smith, C. L. and Dodd, S. M. (1984). Brain size, cranial morphology, climate, and time machines. *Current Anthropology*, 25, 301–330.

Bloom, W. and Fawcett, D. W. (1994). *A Textbook of Histology*. New York, NY: Chapman & Hall.

Carmody, R. N., Weintraub, G. S. and Wrangham, R. W. (2011). Energetic consequences of thermal and nonthermal food processing. *Proceedings of the National Academy of Sciences*, 108, 19199–19203.

Carroll, S. B., Grenier, J. K. and Weatherbee, S. D. (2001). *From DNA to Diversity*. London: Blackwell Science.

Cobb, S. N. and O'Higgins, P. (2004). Hominins do not share a common postnatal facial ontogenetic shape trajectory. *Journal of Experimental Zoology Part B: Molecular and Developmental Evolution*, 302, 302–321.

Cohen Jr, M. M. and Maclean, R. E. (2000). *Craniosynostosis: Diagnosis, Evaluation and Management*, 2nd ed. New York, NY: Oxford University Press.

Colnot, C., Lu, C., Hu, D. and Helms, J. A. (2004). Distinguishing the contributions of the perichondrium, cartilage, and vascular endothelium to skeletal development. *Developmental Biology*, 269, 55–69.

Dean, C., Leakey, M. G., Reid, D., et al. (2001). Growth processes in teeth distinguish modern humans from *Homo erectus* and earlier hominins. *Nature*, 414, 628–631.

Drake, A. G. and Klingenberg, C. P. (2008). The pace of morphological change: historical transformation of skull shape in St Bernard dogs. *Proceedings of the Royal Society B: Biological Sciences*, 275, 71–76.

Drushel, R. F., Pechak, D. G. and Caplan, A. I. (1985). The anatomy, ultrastructure and fluid dynamics of the developing vasculature of the embryonic chick wing bud. *Cell Differentiation*, 16, 13–28.

Dufton, M. and Franz-Odendaal, T. A. (2015). Morphological diversity in the orbital bones of two teleosts with experimental and natural variation in eye size. *Developmental Dynamics*, 244, 1109–1120.

Dufton, M., Hall, B. K. and Franz-Odendaal, T. A. (2012). Early lens ablation causes dramatic long-term effects on the shape of bones in the craniofacial skeleton of *Astyanax mexicanus*. *PLoS ONE*, 7, e50308.

Eames, B. F. and Helms, J. A. (2004). Conserved molecular program regulating cranial and appendicular skeletogenesis. *Developmental Dynamics*, 231, 4–13.

Eames, B. F., De La Fuente, L. and Helms, J. A. (2003). Molecular ontogeny of the skeleton. *Birth Defects Research Part A: Clinical and Molecular Teratology*, 69, 93–101.

Eshkar-Oren, I., Viukov, S. V., Salameh, S., *et al.* (2009). The forming limb skeleton serves as a signaling center for limb vasculature patterning via regulation of Vegf. *Development*, 136, 1263–1272.

Eswarakumar, V. P., Monsonego-Ornan, E., Pines, M., *et al.* (2002). The IIIc alternative of Fgfr2 is a positive regulator of bone formation. *Development*, 129, 3783–3793.

Falk, D. (1992). *Evolution of the Brain and Cognition in Hominids*. New York, NY: American Museum of Natural History.

Fleagle, J. G., Babbitt, C. C. and Baden, A. L. (2010). Primate cranial diversity. *American Journal of Physical Anthropology*, 142, 565–578.

Franz-Odendaal, T. A. (2011). Induction and patterning of intramembranous bone. *Frontiers in Bioscience*, 16, 2734–2746.

Gould, S. J. (1977). *Ontogeny and Phylogeny*. Cambridge, MA: Belknap Press.

Gregory, W. K. (1947). The monotremes and the palimpsest theory. *Bulletin of the American Museum of Natural History*, 88, 1–52.

Hall, B. K. (1999). *Evolutionary Developmental Biology*. Dodrecht, The Netherlands: Kluwer Academic Publishers.

Hall, B. K. (2003). Evo–Devo: evolutionary developmental mechanisms. *International Journal of Developmental Biology*, 47, 491–496.

Hallgrímsson, B., Jamniczky, H., Young, N. M., *et al.* (2009). Deciphering the palimpsest: studying the relationship between morphological integration and phenotypic covariation. *Evolutionary Biology*, 36, 355–376.

Herring, S. (2008). Mechanical influences on suture development and patency. *Frontiers of Oral Biology*, 12, 41–56.

Heuzé, Y., Holmes, G., Peter, I., Richtsmeier, J. T. and Jabs, E. W. (2014). Closing the gap: genetic and genomic continuum from syndromic to nonsyndromic craniosynostoses. *Current Genetic Medicine Reports* 2, 135–145.

Holloway, J. R. L. (1969). Culture: a human domain. *Current Anthropology*, 10, 395–412.

Iseki, S., Wilkie, A. O. and Morriss-Kay, G. M. (1999). Fgfr1 and Fgfr2 have distinct differentiation- and proliferation-related roles in the developing mouse skull vault. *Development*, 126, 5611–5620.

Isler, K., Christopher Kirk, E., Miller, J., *et al.* (2008). Endocranial volumes of primate species: scaling analyses using a comprehensive and reliable data set. *Journal of Human Evolution*, 55, 967–978.

Jabalee, J. and Franz-Odendaal, T. A. (2015). Vascular endothelial growth factor signaling affects both angiogenesis and osteogenesis during the development of scleral ossicles. *Developmental Biology*, 406, 52–62.

Javerzat, S., Auguste, P. and Bikfalvi, A. (2002). The role of fibroblast growth factors in vascular development. *Trends in Molecular Medicine*, 8, 483–489.

Jeffery, N. and Spoor, F. (2002). Brain size and the human cranial base: a prenatal perspective. *American Journal of Physical Anthropology*, 118, 324–340.

Jourdeuil, K. and Franz-Odendaal, T. A. (2012). Vasculogenesis and the induction of skeletogenic condensations in the avian eye. *The Anatomical Record: Advances in Integrative Anatomy and Evolutionary Biology*, 295, 691–698.

Kanda, S., Landgren, E., Ljungström, M. and Claesson-Welsh, L. (1996). Fibroblast growth factor receptor 1-induced differentiation of endothelial cell line established from tsA58 large T transgenic mice. *Cell Growth & Differentiation*, 7, 383–395.

Karaplis, A. C. (2008). Embryonic development of bone and regulation of intramembranous and endochondral bone formation. In: Bilezikian, J. P., Raisz, L. G. and Martin, T. J. (eds.) *Principles of Bone Biology*. 3rd ed. New York, NY: Academic Press, pp. 53–84.

Kay, R. F., Cartmill, M. and Balow, M. (1998). The hypoglossal canal and the origin of human vocal behavior. *Proceedings of the National Academy of Sciences*, 95, 5417–5419.

Kisanuki, Y. Y., Hammer, R. E., Miyazaki, J., *et al.* (2001). Tie2-Cre transgenic mice: a new model for endothelial cell-lineage analysis *in vivo. Developmental Biology*, 230, 230–242.

Kish, P. E., Bohnsack, B. L., Gallina, D., Kasprick, D. S. and Kahana, A. (2011). The eye as an organizer of craniofacial development. *Genesis*, 49, 222–230.

Klingenberg, C. P. (2011). MorphoJ: an integrated software package for geometric morphometrics. *Molecular Ecology Resources*, 11, 353–357.

Kronenberg, H. M. (2003). Developmental regulation of the growth plate. *Nature*, 423: 332–336.

Krovitz, G. (2000). Three-dimensional comparisons of craniofacial morphology and growth patterns in Neanderthals and modern humans. PhD Dissertation, Johns Hopkins University.

Lahr, M. M. (1996). *The Evolution of Modern Human Diversity: A Study of Cranial Variation.* Cambridge: Cambridge University Press.

Lambert, J. E., Chapman, C. A., Wrangham, R. W. and Conklin-Brittain, N. L. (2004). Hardness of cercopithecine foods: implications for the critical function of enamel thickness in exploiting fallback foods. *American Journal of Physical Anthropology*, 125, 363–368.

Leigh, S. R. (2004). Brain growth, life history, and cognition in primate and human evolution. *American Journal of Primatology*, 62, 139–164.

Lele, S. and Richtsmeier, J. T. (1991). Euclidean distance matrix analysis: a coordinate-free approach for comparing biological shapes using landmark data. *American Journal of Physical Anthropology*, 86, 415–427.

Lieberman, D. E., Ross, C. F. and Ravosa, M. J. (2000). The primate cranial base: ontogeny, function, and integration. *American Journal of Physical Anthropology*, 113, 117–169.

Lieberman, D. E., McBratney, B. M. and Krovitz, G. (2002). The evolution and development of cranial form in *Homosapiens. Proceedings of the National Academy of Science*, 99, 1134–1139.

Lieberman, D. E., Hallgrímsson, B., Liu, W., Parsons, T. E. and Jamniczky, H. A. (2008). Spatial packing, cranial base angulation, and craniofacial shape variation in the mammalian skull: testing a new model using mice. *Journal of Anatomy*, 212, 720–735.

Lovejoy, C. O., McCollum, M. A., Reno, P. L. and Rosenman, B. A. (2003). Developmental biology and human evolution. *Annual Review of Anthropology*, 32, 85–109.

Mackie, E. J., Ahmed, Y. A., Tatarczuch, L., Chen, K. S. and Mirams, M. (2008). Endochondral ossification: how cartilage is converted into bone in the developing skeleton. *The International Journal of Biochemistry & Cell Biology*, 40, 46–62.

MacLarnon, A. M. and Hewitt, G. P. (1999). The evolution of human speech: the role of enhanced breathing control. *American Journal of Physical Anthropology*, 109, 341–363.

Marcucio, R. S., Young, N. M., Hu, D. and Hallgrimsson, B. (2011). Mechanisms that underlie covariation of the brain and face. *Genesis*, 49, 177–189.

Martínez-Abadías, N., Percival, C., Aldridge, K., *et al.* (2010). Beyond the closed suture in Apert mouse models: evidence of primary effects of FGFR2 signaling on facial shape at P0. *Developmental Dynamics*, 239, 3058–3071.

Martínez-Abadías, N., Motch, S. M., Pankratz, T. L., *et al.* (2013). Tissue-specific responses to aberrant FGF signaling in complex head phenotypes. *Developmental Dynamics*, 242, 80–94.

Menegaz, R. A., Sublett, S. V., Figueroa, S. D., *et al.* (2010). Evidence for the influence of diet on cranial form and robusticity. *The Anatomical Record*, 293, 630–641.

Moss, M. L. and Young, R. W. (1960). A functional approach to craniology. *American Journal of Physical Anthropology*, 18, 281–292.

Nakamura, T., Mochizuki, Y., Kanetake, H. and Kanda, S. (2001). Signals via FGF receptor 2 regulate migration of endothelial cells. *Biochemical and Biophysical Research Communications*, 289, 801–806.

Opperman, L. A. (2000). Cranial sutures as intramembranous bone growth sites. *Developmental Dynamics*, 219, 472–485.

Ornitz, D. M. and Marie, P. J. (2002). FGF signaling pathways in endochondral and intramembranous bone development and human genetic disease. *Genes & Development*, 16, 1446–1465.

Ornitz, D. M. and Marie, P. J. (2015). Fibroblast growth factor signlaing in skeletal development and disease. *Genes & Development*, 29, 1463–1486.

Percival, C. J. (2013). The influence of angiogenesis on craniofacial development and evolution. Dissertation, The Pennsylvania State University. Available at: https://etda.libraries.psu.edu/paper/16838/ [Accessed: 9 July 2013].

Percival, C. and Richtsmeier, J. T. (2011). The epigenetics of dysmorphology: craniosynostosis as an example. *In:* Hallgrímsson, B. and Hall, B. K. (eds.) *Epigenetics: Linking Genotype and Phenotype in Development and Evolution.* San Fransisco, CA: University of California Press.

Percival, C. J. and Richtsmeier, J. T. (2013). Angiogenesis and intramembranous osteogenesis. *Developmental Dynamics,* 242, 909–922.

Percival, C. J., Wang, Y., Zhou, X., Jabs, E. W. and Richtsmeier, J. T. (2012). The effect of a Beare–Stevenson syndrome Fgfr2 *Y394C* mutation on early craniofacial bone volume and relative bone mineral density in mice. *Journal of Anatomy,* 221, 434–442.

Percival, C. J., Huang, Y., Jabs, E. W., Li, R. and Richtsmeier, J. T. (2014). Embryonic craniofacial bone volume and bone mineral density in Fgfr2+/P253R and nonmutant mice. *Developmental Dynamics,* 243, 541–551.

Plavcan, J. M. (2001). Sexual dimorphism in primate evolution. *American Journal of Physical Anthropology,* 116, 25–53.

Ponce de León, M. S. P. and Zollikofer, C. P. E. (2001). Neanderthal cranial ontogeny and its implications for late hominid diversity. *Nature,* 412, 534–538.

Raff, R. A. (1996). *The Shape of Life: Genes, Development, and the Evolution of Animal Form.* Chicago, IL: University of Chicago Press.

Ramsay, J. O., Hooker, G. and Graves, S. (2009). *Functional Data Analysis with R and MATLAB.* New York, NY: Springer.

Ravosa, M. J., Noble, V. E., Hylander, W. L., Johnson, K. R. and Kowalski, E. M. (2000). Masticatory stress, orbital orientation and the evolution of the primate postorbital bar. *Journal of Human Evolution,* 38, 667–693.

R Developmental Core Team (2008). *R: A Language and Environment for Statistical Computing.* Vienna: R Foundation for Statistical Computing. Available at: http://www.R-project.org.

Reeves, R. H., Baxter, L. L. and Richtsmeier, J. T. (2001). Too much of a good thing: mechanisms of gene action in Down syndrome. *Trends in Genetics,* 17, 83–88.

Reno, P. L., McCollum, M. A., Cohn, M. J., *et al.* (2008). Patterns of correlation and covariation of anthropoid distal forelimb segments correspond to Hoxd expression territories. *Journal of Experimental Zoology (Mol Dev Evol),* 310, 240–258.

Richtsmeier, J. T. and Flaherty, K. (2013). Hand in glove: brain and skull in development and dysmorphogenesis. *Acta Neuropathologica,* 125, 469–489.

Richtsmeier, J. T. and Walker, A. (1993). A morphometric study of facial growth. *In:* Walker, A. and Leakey, R. (eds.) *The Nariokotome Homo erectus Skeleton.* Cambridge, MA: Harvard University Press, pp. 391–410.

Richtsmeier, J. T., Corner, B. D., Grausz, H. M., Cheverud, J. M. and Danahey, S. E. (1993). The role of postnatal growth pattern in the production of facial morphology. *Systematic Biology,* 42, 307–330.

Richtsmeier, J. T., Aldridge, K., DeLeon, V. B., *et al.* (2006). Phenotypic integration of neurocranium and brain. *Journal of Experimental Zoology. Part B, Molecular and Developmental Evolution,* 306, 360–378.

Robson, S. L. and Wood, B. (2008). Hominin life history: reconstruction and evolution. *Journal of Anatomy,* 212, 394–425.

Roseman, C. C., Kenny-Hunt, J. P. and Cheverud, J. M. (2009). Phenotypic integration without modularity: testing hypotheses about the distribution of pleiotropic quantitative trait loci in a continuous space. *Evolutionary Biology,* 36, 282–291.

Ross, C. F. (1995). Allometric and functional influences on primate orbit orientation and the origins of the Anthropoidea. *Journal of Human Evolution,* 29, 201–227.

Saarimäki-Vire, J., Peltopuro, P., Lahti, L., *et al.* (2007). Fibroblast growth factor receptors cooperate to regulate neural progenitor properties in the developing midbrain and hindbrain. *The Journal of Neuroscience,* 27, 8581–8592.

Schwartz, J. H. and Tattersall, I. (2003). *The Human Fossil Record: Craniodental Morphology of Genus Homo (Africa and Asia).* Hoboken, NJ: John Wiley and Sons.

Serrat, M. A., King, D. and Lovejoy, C. O. (2008). Temperature regulates limb length in homeotherms by directly modulating cartilage growth. *Proceedings of the National Academy of Sciences,* 105, 19348–19353.

Sherwood, C. C., Subiaul, F. and Zawidzki, T. W. (2008). A natural history of the human mind: tracing evolutionary changes in brain and cognition. *Journal of Anatomy*, 212, 426–454.

Smith, S. L. (2004). Skeletal age, dental age, and the maturation of KNM-WT 15000. *American Journal of Physical Anthropology*, 125, 105–120.

Smith, T. D., DeLeon, V. B. and Rosenberger, A. L. (2013). At birth, tarsiers lack a postorbital bar or septum. *The Anatomical Record*, 296, 365–377.

Smith, T. D., Kentzel, E. S., Cunningham, J. M., *et al.* (2014). Mapping bone cell distributions to assess ontogenetic origin of primate midfacial form. *American Journal of Physical Anthropology*, 154, 424–435.

Soriano, P. (1999). Generalized lacZ expression with the ROSA26 Cre reporter strain. *Nature Genetics*, 21, 70–71.

Spoor, F., Garland, T., Krovitz, G., *et al.* (2007). The primate semicircular canal system and locomotion. *Proceedings of the National Academy of Sciences*, 104, 10808–10812.

Suhardja, A. and Hoffman, H. (2003). Role of growth factors and their receptors in proliferation of microvascular endothelial cells. *Microscopy Research and Technique*, 60, 70–75.

Suwa, G., Kono, R. T., Simpson, S. W., *et al.* (2009). Paleobiological implications of the *Ardipithecus ramidus* dentition. *Science*, 326, 69.

Takimoto, A., Nishizaki, Y., Hiraki, Y. and Shukunami, C. (2009). Differential actions of VEGF-A isoforms on perichondrial angiogenesis during endochondral bone formation. *Developmental Biology*, 332, 196–211.

Tholpady, S. S., Abdelaal, M. M., Dufresne, C. R., *et al.* (2004). Aberrant bony vasculature associated with activating fibroblast growth factor receptor mutations accompanying Crouzon syndrome. *Journal of Craniofacial Surgery*, 15, 431–435.

Thompson, T. J., Owens, P. D. and Wilson, D. J. (1989). Intramembranous osteogenesis and angiogenesis in the chick embryo. *Journal of Anatomy*, 166, 55–65.

Tillier, A. M. (1995). Neanderthal ontogeny: a new source for critical analysis. *Anthropologie*, 33, 63–68.

Twigg, S. R. and Wilkie, A. O. (2015). A genetic–pathophysiological framework for craniosynostosis. *The American Journal of Human Genetics*, 97, 359–377.

Wang, Y., Sun, M., Uhlhorn, V. L., *et al.* (2010). Activation of p38 MAPK pathway in the skull abnormalities of Apert syndrome Fgfr2+/P253R mice. *BMC Developmental Biology*, 10, 22.

Warburton, D., Schwarz, M., Tefft, D., *et al.* (2000). The molecular basis of lung morphogenesis. *Mechanisms of Development*, 92, 55–82.

Weaver, T. D. (2009). The meaning of Neanderthal skeletal morphology. *Proceedings of the National Academy of Sciences*, 106, 16028–16033.

Yang, Y. Q., Tan, Y. Y., Wong, R., *et al.* (2012). The role of vascular endothelial growth factor in ossification. *International Journal of Oral Science*, 4, 64–68.

Young, N. M. and Devlin, M. J. (2012). Finding our inner animal: understanding human evolutionary variation via experimental model systems. Curated Podium Session at the American Association of Physical Anthropologists Annual Meeting, Portland, OR.

Zelzer, E., McLean, W., Ng, Y. S., *et al.* (2002). Skeletal defects in VEGF120/120 mice reveal multiple roles for VEGF in skeletogenesis. *Development*, 129, 1893–1904.

Zernik, J., Twarog, K. and Upholt, W. B. (1990). Regulation of alkaline phosphatase and alpha2 (I) procollagen synthesis during early intramembranous bone formation in the rat mandible. *Differentiation*, 44, 207–215.

Zhang, Y., Singh, M. K., Degenhardt, K. R., *et al.* (2009). Tie2Cre-mediated inactivation of plexinD1 results in congenital heart, vascular and skeletal defects. *Developmental Biology*, 325, 82–93.

Zollikofer, C. P. E. and Ponce de León, M. S. (2010). The evolution of hominin ontogenies. *Seminars in Cell & Developmental Biology*, 21, 441–452.

Zumpano, M. P. and Richtsmeier, J. T. (2003). Growth-related shape changes in the fetal craniofacial complex of humans (*Homo sapiens*) and pigtailed macaques (*Macaca nemestrina*): a 3D-CT comparative analysis. *American Journal of Physical Anthropology*, 120, 339–351.

3 Association of the Chondrocranium and Dermatocranium in Early Skull Formation

Kazuhiko Kawasaki and Joan T. Richtsmeier

Terminology for the branchial/visceral/pharyngeal arches, and for the skull in general, grew out of a number of distinct anatomic and paleontologic traditions and suffers from a lack of cohesion.

Depew *et al.* (2002)

3.1 Introduction

Studies of the skull have long played a fundamental role in anthropological research and many studies support the idea that major changes in the cranial base have played crucial roles in the evolution of early primates, in the origin of anthropoids, and in the origin of *Homo sapiens* (Scott, 1958; Lieberman *et al.*, 2000). The cranial base angle, measured on the sagittal plane according to various designs (McCarthy, 2001), is a measure of the relationship between the anterior (prechordal) and the posterior (parachordal) cranial base and is thought to be key to elucidating developmental and evolutionary events as evidenced in the association of cranial base morphology and skull form (Lieberman *et al.*, 2008). Studies of the influence of brain size and shape on cranial base morphology has a long history in anthropological theory (Lieberman *et al.*, 2000), prompting ideas like the spatial packing hypothesis (Biegert, 1963), which states that basicranial flexion in haplorhines maximizes braincase volume relative to basicranial length, and has motivated recent studies designed to test the hypothesis that a relatively larger brain is accommodated by a more flexed cranial base in anthropoids (Ross and Ravosa, 1993; Ross and Henneberg, 1995; Spoor, 1997; McCarthy, 2001). Additional hypotheses proposed to account for variation in the cranial base angle in primates (and specifically for the increased flexion in *Homo sapiens*) include: that basicranial flexion is an adaptation to repositioning of the foramen magnum to place the center of mass of the head over the axial skeleton (the postural hypothesis) and reduce stresses on the rostral portion of the cranial base; that flexion accommodates a more globular brain that minimizes the distances between neurons thereby facilitating cognitive function; and that flexion accommodates hyolaryngeal descent permitting quantal speech (see McCarthy, 2001 for a detailed list of references to research that has tested these hypotheses).

The cranial base angle has served as a surrogate metric for complex cranial base morphology that can now be measured without difficulty using 3D imaging methods or digitizers. Although the skull is considered an integrated structure, meaning that different cranial traits covary in a coordinated manner, anthropologists have traditionally divided the skull into the cranial base, the cranial vault, and the facial skeleton, each of which comprises a cohesive anatomical unit conceived of as a module and thought to be partially independent. Modules are morphological units whose patterns of interactions (usually measured as correlation or covariation) reveal phenotypes with strong within-module and weak between-module integration (Olson and Miller, 1958; Mezey *et al.*, 2000; Klingenberg, 2014). These patterns are thought to provide information about codependence and interactions within and between units that are the result of a variety of biological processes. Such interactions arise due to communication between local developmental factors and the gene expression profiles of proximate cells, producing coordinated changes in their behaviors (i.e., migration, proliferation, differentiation, apoptosis) that lead to the production of functioning tissue complexes in the adult population. How changes in genetic regulatory networks and developmental pathways initiate or constrain changes in pattern and/or magnitude of modularity leading to changes in complex cranial morphologies is a question central to understanding the evolution of complex traits.

Most anthropological descriptions acknowledge that the cranial base arises embryologically from a complex series of cartilages. Because the majority of cranial base elements in the adult ossify endochondrally from these cartilage precursors, the cranial base is sometimes referred to as the chondrocranium, and the chondrocranium is often loosely defined as the composite of cartilaginous precursors of the anthropologically defined cranial base (Lieberman *et al.*, 2000). However, this definition is inadequate at best, and can be misleading when attempting to understand the embryological development of the skull as well as its evolutionary history.

Our current misunderstanding of exactly what the chondrocranium is may stem from the lack of an easily comprehensible description of chondrocranial development and anatomy. Excellent historical treatments exist (see especially Gaupp (1906) and de Beer (1937)), but they were executed without the advantage of modern biological protocols and imaging techniques. These works are meticulous and the descriptions within them are precise, but the archaic nature of the writing makes these descriptions less accessible and has therefore diminished their impact on contemporary research. The most accurate modern study focuses on embryological development of the cartilaginous skull that will develop into the ossified cranial base in the mouse (McBratney-Owen *et al.*, 2008), but this work does not provide an explicit definition that distinguishes the developing chondrocranium from the cranial base.

Here we provide a clear anatomical exposition of the developing chondrocranium, emphasizing the importance of the chondrocranium in evolutionary developmental research, and we demonstrate how a precise definition can be used to further our understanding of cranial development and evolution. Our chapter has two objectives. First, we provide a precise definition of the chondrocranium with explicit anatomic descriptions of the elements that comprise the chondrocranium

using data from laboratory mice. An extensive Appendix summarizing our laboratory observations is also available for the interested reader (Appendix to Chapter 3).
Second, we use our observations of mouse development to propose a model for the
function of the chondrocranium in development of the dermal bones of the cranial
vault and facial skeleton (the dermatocranium) and in the formation of cranial vault
sutures, acknowledging the potential importance of our observations for the study
of cranial evolution.

3.2   Organization of the head

The skull constitutes an intricate skeletal system that protects the brain and three
principal sense organs (olfactory, optic, and auditory) and contributes to vision,
olfaction, hearing, ingestion, and respiration. There is no single, up-to-date, author-
itative source for the evolutionary developmental study of the skull. Varied and
sometimes conflicting definitions of the skull and jaws, and their elements, come
from studies of anatomy, phylogeny, osteology, and developmental biology. Consequently, many terminological conflicts, inconsistencies, or ambiguities exist in
the vast historical and contemporary literature, and this terminological confusion
is inherent to the study of the skull. A typical example is the basic definition of
the skull. While Romer and Parsons (1977) consider the skull of jawed vertebrates
(gnathostomes) to include the braincase, upper jaw, and dermal roof, but not the
lower jaw, White and colleagues (2012) define the human skull as the entire bony
framework of the head including the lower jaw. Although there are fine books considered the gold standard in human osteology, embryology, evolution, comparative
anatomy, and forensic sciences, the definitions provided are not always consistent
across disciplines.

   Adding to this confusion are the two dominant classification systems that divide
the "skull" into units. The first divides the skull into the neurocranium and splanchnocranium, while the second divides the skull into the chondrocranium, dermatocranium, and splanchnocranium (the splanchnocranium is also referred to as the
pharyngeal skeleton, oropharyngeal skeleton, visceral skeleton, or viscerocranium).
The former classification is usually used in textbooks of anthropology and human
anatomy, while the latter is commonly used in comparative anatomy and paleontology. A corollary of the second system when adopted by anthropologists is the
division of the adult skull into cranial base, cranial vault, and facial skeleton. Both
classification systems have the splanchnocranium as a component, but each system
uses this label to refer to slightly different sets of skeletal units. This fundamental
incongruity, undetected or internalized by many, is responsible for inconsistencies
across these fields of inquiry as researchers adopt a classification system with little
regard for the precise meaning underlying the classification of the osseous members
of these assemblages.

   In the first classification system, the neurocranium and the splanchnocranium
are defined primarily on the basis of their anatomical location and association with

soft tissue anatomy, and are often synonymized with the braincase and the facial skeleton (including the upper and lower jaws). Using this system, it is difficult to classify certain bones. For example, the frontal bone is simultaneously part of the braincase and the facial skeleton and is classified as part of the neurocranium in some textbooks and as part of the splanchnocranium in others. Additionally, bones can simultaneously contribute to the neurocranium and splanchnocranium. For example, the body of the sphenoid bone underlies the brain and holds the pituitary gland and so is part of the neurocranium. However, the greater wings contribute to the middle cranial fossae and cranial vault (neurocranium) as well as the orbit (splanchnocranium), and the medial pterygoid plates contribute to the skeleton of the posterior nasal passages (choanae) and the hard palate of the splanchnocranium.

The second classification system (chondrocranium, dermatocranium, splanchnocranium) embraces the phylogenetic distinction between the *endoskeleton* (composed of chondrocranium and splanchnocranium) and the *dermal skeleton* (dermatocranium) (see Section 3.4), but also imparts differences in material composition. The endoskeleton is based in cartilage that may be replaced by bone, whereas the dermal skeleton consists primarily of dentin and bone (Hall, 2014). Although bone is a tissue of both skeletal systems, endoskeletal bone and exoskeletal bone are distinct ontogenetically and/or phylogenetically. We adopt the second classification system as it combines information from evolution and development of the skull. We adopt the terms chondrocranium and dermatocranium, but substitute the term pharyngeal skeleton in place of splanchnocranium to acknowledge the evolutionary history of the pharyngeal component.

3.3   Skeletal Tissues of the head

3.3.1   Cartilage and Bone

Cartilage and bone are two principal skeletal tissues, comprising different components (Kawasaki *et al.*, 2009). Cartilage is primarily composed of water, fibrillar collagens, and proteoglycans, whereas bone is largely composed of mineral reinforced with fibrillar collagens. Fibrillar collagens are the primary component of the organic matrix in both tissues, but their composition is different. Cartilage is rich in type-II collagen, whereas bone is rich in type-I collagen. Type-I and type-II collagens are coded by different genes and show different biochemical characteristics (Kawasaki *et al.*, 2009).

Cartilage forms in the organic matrix secreted by chondrocytes and grows in two modes, interstitial and appositional. Interstitial growth involves proliferation of chondrocytes within cartilage and their subsequent secretion of cartilage matrix (e.g., proliferative zone of the growth plate). Interstitial growth of cartilage is unique among skeletal tissues and enables a rapid increase in size. Appositional growth occurs in the perichondrium (the outer surface of cartilages) through the recruitment of newly differentiated chondrocytes, which peripherally secrete new cartilage matrix.

Bone forms in the matrix secreted by osteoblasts through two different processes, intramembranous ossification and endochondral ossification. Intramembranous ossification represents direct secretion of bone matrix by osteoblasts and its mineralization, both taking place in perichondral, periosteal (the outer surface of bones), and endosteal (the inner or medullary surface of bone) regions. Endochondral ossification embodies bone formation by replacement of an already-formed morphogenic cartilage model and progresses through three consecutive steps: mineralization of the cartilage model, partial resorption of the cartilage by chondroclasts, and secretion of bone matrix onto the resorbed cartilage surface by osteoblasts that invade the cartilage.

3.3.2   Types of Bone

Bone formed either intramembranously or endochondrally is classified into three types: cartilage bone (also called cartilage-replacement bone or chondral bone), dermal bone, and membrane bone (Patterson, 1977). *Cartilage bone* is bone that is formed by ossification of preformed cartilage initially in the perichondrial region. Later in development, the cartilage bone may or may not ossify endochondrally (within the preformed cartilage), periosteally, and endosteally. Consequently, perichondral bone that does not undergo endochondral ossification is considered as cartilage bone. Finally, cartilage bone may develop membrane bone outgrowths. Figure 3.1 illustrates the formation of cartilage bone and membrane bone in the alisphenoid (see the legend for details).

Dermal bone is not preformed in cartilage, but forms directly through intramembranous ossification. Dermal bone is part of the dermal skeleton that forms in contact with the ectoderm either during evolution or development (Hall, 2015). The dermal skeleton arose in jawless vertebrates (agnathans) as the dermal armor and descended to gnathostomes (Giles *et al.*, 2013). The ancient dermal skeleton is a composite structure, the surface being comprised of dermal denticles that consist of dentin (enamel or functionally equivalent tissue, enameloid, may also be included). Although dermal denticles may have been secondarily lost during evolution, homologs of ancient dermal bones remain as dermal skeletal elements in modern vertebrates (Patterson, 1977).

Membrane bone ossifies by intramembranous ossification, but does not form in contact with the ectoderm. Any cartilage bone can evolve into membrane bone, if the initial cartilaginous stage is secondarily lost (Bellairs and Gans, 1983). Evolutionary history is therefore necessary to precisely classify membrane bone. In addition, neoformations, such as an outgrowth from the perichondrium (Figure 3.1), heterotopic, and pathological bones are membrane bones (Patterson, 1977). Although "membrane bone" is often used interchangeably with "dermal bone," these types of bones are distinct (Patterson, 1977) due to the dissimilarity between the endoskeleton and the dermal skeleton (Hirasawa and Kuratani, 2015). Both the frontal and the parietal are dermal bones and are part of the dermal skeleton, whereas membrane bone and cartilage bone are part of the endoskeleton. The evolutionary significance

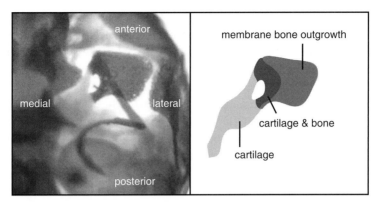

Figure 3.1 Cartilage bone and membrane bone formation illustrated by the alisphenoid at embryonic day 16.5 (E16.5; ventral view). In the left box, cartilage is stained in blue, while bone is stained in red. The ala temporalis is depicted in the right box. At E14.5, the lateral ascending edge of the ala temporalis (Figure 3.2B) undergoes perichondral ossification and extends a membrane bone outgrowth laterally from the ossified surface. Inside the perichondral bone, the cartilage becomes hypertrophic and initiates mineralization at E15.5. The mineralized cartilage is subsequently replaced by bone by endochondral ossification. At E16.5, the ala temporalis is being ossified into the alisphenoid primarily by endochondral ossification and membranous outgrowth. Later during bone remodeling, the endochondrally ossified portion is resorbed and replaced by intramembranously formed new endosteal bone. A black and white version of this figure will appear in some formats. For the color version, please refer to the plate section.

of the dermal skeleton and the endoskeleton lies in the evolution of skeletal tissues, as we describe next.

3.4   Skull Systematics: Endoskeleton Versus Dermal (Exo)Skeleton

3.4.1   The Evolution of Skeletal Tissues in Vertebrates

The *endoskeleton* is composed of cartilage, cartilage bone, and/or membrane bone, whereas the *dermal skeleton* comprises dermal bone, dentin, and/or enamel/enameloid. Thus, the origin and distinction of these skeletal systems are based on the phylogenetic history and distribution of these tissues. In bony vertebrates (osteichthyans), formation of bone, dentin, enameloid, and enamel involves various secretory calcium-binding phosphoprotein (*SCPP*) genes, which arose from a common ancestral gene by duplication (Kawasaki and Weiss, 2003). The tissue distribution of *SCPP* gene expression suggests that these four mineralized tissues arose by modification of an ancient bone-like tissue that originated early in vertebrates (Kawasaki, 2011). In contrast with these mineralized skeletal tissues, cartilage or cartilage-like tissues originated earlier in evolution as they are found broadly in metazoans, including cephalopods and arthropods (Cole and Hall, 2004). Among deuterostomes, amphioxus and acorn worms develop a pharyngeal skeleton (but not a cranial skeleton) that consists of collagenous cartilage-like tissues (Meulemans and Bronner-Fraser, 2007), although these tissues are acellular and structurally different from cellular cartilage that is commonly found in vertebrates (Rychel *et al.*, 2006).

Within the vertebrates, modern agnathans (hagfish and lampreys) have no bony skeleton but develop cartilaginous endoskeletons in the cranial, pharyngeal, and postcranial regions (de Beer, 1937; Oisi *et al.*, 2013). Although their cranial skeleton is distinct from that of gnathostomes in architectural design and organization, hagfish and lampreys have a cartilaginous cranial skeleton (chondrocranium) that protects the brain and sense organs (Oisi *et al.*, 2013). In hagfish and lamprey, the type-II collagen gene and its presumed regulatory genes are expressed during cartilage formation (Zhang and Cohn, 2006; Zhang *et al.*, 2006; Wada, 2010), suggesting that type-II collagen-based cartilage is a synapomorphy of vertebrates (Zhang *et al.*, 2009). Importantly, cartilage of the cranial and pharyngeal skeletons of hagfish and lampreys is cellular, similar to that in gnathostomes (Cattell *et al.*, 2011). To date, the evolutionary relationship of the pharyngeal skeleton in non-vertebrates (amphioxus and acorn worms) and vertebrates is not well understood (Zhang *et al.*, 2009; Hall and Gillis, 2013). However, if we accept that acellular cartilage is the evolutionary precursor of cellular cartilage, then the most ancient cartilaginous endoskeleton that developed in the lineage leading to vertebrates would be the pharyngeal skeleton, and the chondrocranium arose subsequently. Because the cartilaginous endoskeleton does not mineralize in hagfish and lampreys, and because they are phylogenetically basal to the armored agnathans (Donoghue and Keating, 2014), the earliest vertebrate skeleton presumably consisted entirely of the non-mineralized cartilaginous endoskeleton. The dermal skeleton (also called exoskeleton to distinguish it from the endoskeleton) originated subsequent to the endoskeleton initially as the dermal armor in extinct agnathans (Janvier, 1996; Donoghue *et al.*, 2006).

The endoskeletal cartilage, including the chondrocranium (braincase) and pharyngeal skeleton (jaws), can be partly mineralized in cartilaginous fish (chondrichthyans, the phylogenetically basal clade among modern gnathostomes) (Janvier, 1996), but their mineralized cartilage is not replaced by bone. Furthermore, cartilaginous fish develop teeth, scales, and spines that are composed of dentin and enameloid, but these dermal skeletal elements do not contain bone (Eames *et al.*, 2007). Given the early evolution of dermal bone in extinct agnathans, the lack of dermal bone in chondrichthyans is thought to represent a secondary loss in this lineage (Giles *et al.*, 2013).

In contrast to chondrichthyans, many endoskeletal cartilages in osteichthyans are ontogenetically replaced by cartilage bones through perichondral/endochondral ossification. Furthermore, dermal denticles were secondarily lost in most modern osteichthyans. In some lineages, membrane bones may have replaced some cartilage bones, and/or membrane bones may have newly evolved.

The archetypal endoskeleton and dermal skeleton in osteichthyans may have changed during evolution by cartilage secondarily forming in the dermal skeleton or dermal bone forming in the endoskeleton. However, the only known example of cartilage forming in the dermal skeleton, or dermal bone in the endoskeleton, is *secondary cartilage*, which forms adjacent to a developing dermal bone relatively late in ontogeny, and hence independently from endoskeletal cartilages (Patterson, 1977). Secondary cartilage has been found only in mammals and birds. In mammals, secondary cartilage develops in various locations including the condylar and coronoid processes, the cranial sutures, and during the reparative process of dermal bones (de Beer, 1937; Hall, 1970; Moore, 1981). With the exception of this single derived character, the endoskeleton and dermal skeleton are distinct in terms of their composition, development, and/or phylogenetic distribution.

3.4.2 Chondrocranium, Pharyngeal Skeleton, and Dermatocranium

The distinction between endoskeleton and dermal skeleton forms the basis of the division of the skull into chondrocranium, pharyngeal skeleton, and dermatocranium. The chondrocranium and the pharyngeal skeleton compose the endoskeleton in the skull and the lower jaw. It is initially (ontogenetically or phylogenetically) formed as cartilage and, when ossified, consists of cartilage bone and/or membrane bone. This is in contrast with the dermatocranium that ossifies as dermal bone. The chondrocranium functions similarly in both agnathans and gnathostomes, protecting the brain and principle paired sense organs. The pharyngeal skeleton arose as simple gill supports, which became progressively functionally specialized into more complex structures (e.g., upper and lower jaws, jaw supports, ear ossicles). In all vertebrates that develop the dermatocranium, the chondrocranium and the pharyngeal skeleton are more or less covered with the dermatocranium.

3.5 Development of the Chondrocranium and Topological Association with the Dermatocranium

3.5.1 Analysis of Mouse Chondrocranium – Materials and Methods

In this section, we provide a detailed treatise of chondrocranial development and anatomy based primarily on the mouse. Our goal is to clarify the functional properties of the chondrocranium, its distinction from the cranial base, and its relationship to the dermatocranium. Development of the chondrocranium was described in detail for various vertebrate species, including humans and various primates, in the late nineteenth and early twentieth centuries by several investigators (e.g., Gaupp, 1906; Goodrich, 1930; de Beer, 1937). However, they did not study the laboratory mouse, which is currently the most extensively used experimental model for studying human development and disease. The basic structure of the rodent chondrocranium has been documented for *Microtus amphibius* (Fawcett, 1917), *Xerus* (Fawcett, 1923), and *Otomys tropicalis* (Eloff, 1948), and specific topics relevant to chondrocranial development have been presented for different rodents (e.g., Youssef, 1966, 1969; Kadam, 1976). Depew's recent comprehensive analysis (Depew *et al.*, 2002) and McBratney-Owen's intensive investigation of the developing cranial base focus on mice (McBratney-Owen *et al.*, 2008), but development of the chondrocranium has never been systematically described for this species. Here we combine our own observations of C57BL/6J mouse development with data presented by other authors to provide a detailed description of the development and ossification of the chondrocranium, and its spatiotemporal associations with dermatocranial elements. In our work, cartilage and bone were stained using Alcian blue and Alizarin red, respectively, and other tissues were optically cleared using glycerol (McLeod, 1980). The developmental descriptions are based on timed matings and expressed in terms of embryonic days postconception (e.g., 17 days postconception is E17) and postnatal days (e.g., P2 is the second postnatal day). Because many structures are transient, they are described according to their appearance during developmental time that is approximate due to variation among littermates (Flaherty *et al.*, 2015).

3.5.2   Chondrocranium – Overall Structure

The chondrocranium is that part of the endoskeleton that protects the brain and three principal sense organs but does not include the pharyngeal endoskeleton that consists of Meckel's cartilage, Reichert's cartilage, the malleus, incus, stapes, ala temporalis, and others. The chondrocranium is organized into regions that are named for their anatomical contribution to protecting the brain and sense organs: braincase, nasal capsule, and otic capsule (Moore, 1981). The *braincase* consists of the *floor*, *roof*, and *lateral wall*, which protect the brain, and parts of the braincase also support the eyes. The *nasal capsule* protects the olfactory organs and olfactory bulbs, whereas the *otic capsule*, composed of the pars cochlearis (PCO) and pars canalicularis (PCA), accommodates the hearing and balancing organs (PCO protecting the saccule and cochlear duct, and PCA protecting the semicircular canals and utricle). These and all other anatomical abbreviations in this chapter are defined in a list found within Section 3.5.3.

3.5.3   Braincase floor

The floor of the braincase arises as composite cartilages: the trabecular (T), hypophyseal (H), acrochordal (AR), and parachordal (P) from anterior to posterior (Figure 3.3). These cartilages subsequently fuse and develop into the bony floor, consisting of the mesethmoid (see Section 3.5.6), presphenoid (PS), basisphenoid (BS), and basioccipital bones (BO in Figure 3.2E).

   The braincase floor forms by E12.5 with the appearance of parachordal cartilage (Figure 3.3). At this stage, the trabecular cartilage arises as the septum nasi (SN), an anterior extension of the braincase floor. The hypophyseal and acrochordal cartilages subsequently form and join with the parachordal by E13.5. As the trabecular cartilage extends posteriorly, these four composite cartilages form a continuous plate at E14.5.

   Perichondral/endochondral ossification of the floor begins with the basioccipital between E14.5 and E15.5. The basioccipital grows anteriorly from the boundary with the foramen magnum (fmg) by replacing the parachordal cartilage (P, Figs. 3.2A & 3.2E). The basisphenoid arises at E15.5 by ossification of the hypophyseal cartilage on both sides of the hypophyseal fenestra (fhy), while the presphenoid appears at E17.5 by ossification of the trabecular cartilage medial to the pila metoptica (PMO).

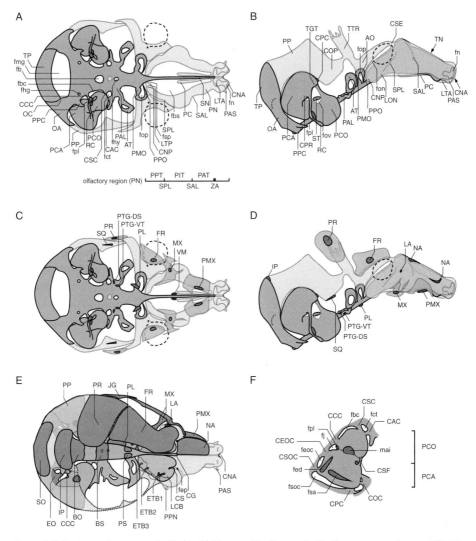

Figure 3.2 Embryonic mouse skull. (A, B) The cartilaginous skull of a mouse embryo at E15.5, (A) inferior view and (B) lateral view, with nose to the right and occiput to the left. Cartilages that are partly or entirely replaced by bone via endochondral ossification are shown in darker blue, while those that are resorbed and substituted by dermal bones are depicted in light blue. The globes of the eyes are shown by a dashed outline. (A) The scale at the bottom corresponds with coronal cuts that define the three parts of the paries nasi (PPT, PIT, and PAT) separated by the two sulci (SPL and SAL, shown in dotted line in Figure 3.2B) and the zona annularis (ZA). (C, D) Dermatocranial bones associated with the chondrocranial elements, (C) inferior view, and (D) lateral view, with nose to the right and occiput to the left. Dermatocranial elements formed at E15.5 are shown in pale red with the initial location of their formation shown in dark red. Although the nasal and lacrimal bones are not yet formed at E15.5, they are illustrated in the region where they will form later in development. (E) Spatial association of cartilages (blue/pale blue) and bones at E17.5, superior view. Both dermal and cartilage bones are shown in red. On the right half of the skull (lower half), part of the cranial vault and the lateral wall (dotted line) are removed. (F) An enlarged superior view of the pars cochlearis and the pars canalicularis at E17.5, anterior to the right, posterior to the left. Note that the inferior part of the pars canalicularis in this figure extends dorsally (see Figure 3.2B). A black and white version of this figure will appear in some formats. For the color version, please refer to the plate section.

List of Abbreviations used throughout Chapter 3 and Appendix

AO, ala orbitalis; AR, acrochordal cartilage; AT, ala temporalis; avpm, alveolar process of maxilla; avppm, alveolar process of premaxilla; BO, basioccipital; BS, basisphenoid; CAC, alicochlear commissure; CCC, chordo-cochlear commissure; CEOC, exoccipitocapsular commissure; CG, crista galli; CNA, cupula nasi anterior; CNP, cupula nasi posterior; COC, orbitocapsular commissure; cola, orbital crest of lacrimal; COP, orbitoparietal commissure; CPC, parietocapsular commissure; CPR, crista parotica; cps, caudal process of squamosal; CPTG, pterygoid cartilage; CS, crista semicircularis; CSC, sphenocochlear commissure; CSE, sphenethmoid commissure; CSF, suprafacial commissure; CSOC, supraoccipitocapsular commissure; EO, exoccipital; ETB1, ethmoturbinal I; ETB2, ethmoturbinal II; ETB3, ethmoturbinal III; fb, basicranial fenestra; fbc, basicapsular fissure; fbs, fenestra basalis; fct, foramen caroticum; fed, foramen endolymphaticum; feoc, exoccipitocapsular fissure; fep, foramen epiphinale; fhg, foramen hypoglossum; fhy, hypophyseal fenestra; fj, foramen jugulare; fmg, foramen magnum; fn, fenestra nasi; fon, orbitonasal fissure; fop, foramen opticum; fov, fenestra ovalis; fpdal, dorsal ascending lamina of frontal process; fpl, foramen perilymphaticum; fpla, facial process of lacrimal; fplap, lateral ascending portion of frontal process; fpmap, medial ascending portion of frontal process; FR, frontal; fsa, subarcuate fossa; fsoc, supraoccipitocapsular fissure; fsp, septo-paraseptal fissure; H, hypophyseal cartilage; hppl, horizontal plate of palatine; iof, infraorbital foramen; IP, interparietal; JG, jugal; LA, lacrimal; LCB, lamina cribrosa; LON, lamina orbitonasalis; LTA, lamina transversalis anterior; LTP, lamina transversalis posterior; mai, internal acoustic meatus; MC, Meckel's cartilage; MX, maxilla; NA, nasal; O, orbital cartilage; OA, occipital arch; OC, occipital condyle; opla, orbital process of lacrimal; P, parachordal cartilage; PAL, processus alaris; PAT, pars anterior; PAS, processus alaris superior; PC, paraseptal cartilage; PCA, pars canalicularis; PCO, pars cochlearis; pdppm, posterodorsal process of premaxilla; PIT, pars intermedia; PL, palatine; PMO, pila metoptica; PMX, premaxilla; PN, paries nasi; PP, parietal plate; PPC, paracondylar process; ppm, palatine process of maxilla; PPN, paranasal process; PPO, pila preoptica; pppm, palatine process of premaxilla; PPT, pars posterior; PR, parietal; PS, presphenoid; PTG-DS, pterygoid dorsal element; PTG-VT, pterygoid ventral element; RC, Reichert's cartilage; rtps, retrotympanic process of squamosal; SAL, sulcus anterior lateralis; sbp, squamous basal plate; SDN, sulcus dorsalis nasi; SN, septum nasi; SO, supraoccipital; SPL, sulcus posterior lateralis; SQ, squamosal; ST, stapes; T, trabecular cartilage; TGT, tegmen tympani; TN, tectum nasi; TP, tectum posterius; TTR, tectum transversum; VM, vomer; vppl, vertical plate of palatine; Y, hypochiasmatic cartilage; ZA, zona annularis; zpm, zygomatic process of maxilla; zps, zygomatic process of squamosal.

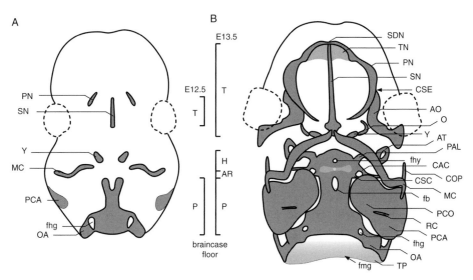

Figure 3.3 Anteroventral view of cartilages in the head and lower jaw at E12.5 (A) and E13.5 (B), rostrum at top, occiput at bottom. The vertical bars provided for each stage identify the segments of the braincase floor, formed along the midline: trabecular (T), hypophyseal (H), acrochordal (AR), and parachordal (P). Globes of the eyes are shown with a dashed outline.

Dermatocranium Associations – Vomer, Palatine, and Pterygoid. Between E14.5 and E15.5, cartilages of the braincase floor associate with three pairs of forming dermatocranial bones: the vomers (VM), palatines (PL), and pterygoids (PTG-VT and PTG-DS in Figure 3.2C,D; Table 3.1), which comprise part of the palatal series defined in early vertebrates (Goodrich, 1930). The palatine bones arise first by E15.5 ventral to the pila metoptica (Figure 3.2A,C) and grow anteromedially and posterolaterally with the lateral edge inclined ventrally. At E16.5, each palatine bone forms a vertical plate (vppl), from which a horizontal plate (hppl) buds and extends (Figure 3.4B). At E17.5, the vertical plate approaches the cupula nasi posterior (CNP) anteriorly and posteriorly overlies the anterior end of the ventral element of the pterygoid, while the horizontal plate forms a suture posteriorly with the anterior end of the ventral element of the pterygoid (Figure 3.4B). This suture is located ventral to the intersphenoid synchondrosis at P7.

Around E15.5, the vomer (VM) arises as a pair of nearly vertical plates medial to the posterior end of the paraseptal cartilages (PC in Figure 3.2A) and lateral to the ventral edge of the septum nasi (Figure 3.2C). As the vomer extends anteriorly at E16.5, the plates grow dorsolaterally and medioventrally; the two plates ventrally contact each other or open slightly (Figure 3.4), separating the ventral edge of the septum nasi from the medial border of the paraseptal cartilage on each side. Posterior to the paraseptal cartilage, distantly positioned ventral edges underlie the septum nasi. At E17.5, the ventral edge of each vomer anteriorly forms a suture with the dorsal edge of the palatine process of the premaxilla (pppm). By P0, the

Table 3.1 Select association between chondrocranium and dermatocranium described in the text and Appendix.

Chondrocranium	Dermatocranium
Braincase floor	
Presphenoid	Palatine
Hypophyseal	Pterygoid, ventral element
Alicochlear commissure	Pterygoid, dorsal element
Lateral wall	
Pila metoptica	Palatine
Parietal plate	Interparietal
Ala temporalis	Pterygoid dorsal/ventral elements
Tectum posterius	Interparietal
Ala orbitalis	Frontal
Sphenethmoid commissure	Frontal
Tectum transversum	Parietal
Orbitoparietal commissure	Parietal
Parietal plate	Parietal
Orbitoparietal commissure	Squamosal
Nasal capsule	
Cupula nasi posterior	Palatine
Paraseptal	Vomer
Septum nasi	Vomer
Lamina transversalis posterior	Vomer
Pars anterior	Premaxilla
Paraseptal	Premaxilla
Pars intermedia	Maxilla
Septum nasi	Maxilla
Paraseptal	Maxilla
Pars intermedia	Lacrimal
Paranasal process	Lacrimal
Tectum nasi	Nasal
Pars anterior	Nasal
Lamina cribrosa	Nasal
Otic capsule	
Tegmen tympani	Squamosal

posterior end of the vomer becomes a narrow process extending toward the cupula nasi posterior (Figure 3.2A) between the septum nasi and the lamina transversalis posterior (LTP). More anteriorly, the ventral edge of the vomer widens and curls laterally, and the curled posterior edge apparently contacts the anterior edge of the lamina transversalis posterior.

Each of the paired pterygoid bones appear around E15.5 from two separate ossification centers that form the ventral (PTG-VT) and dorsal elements (PTG-DS in

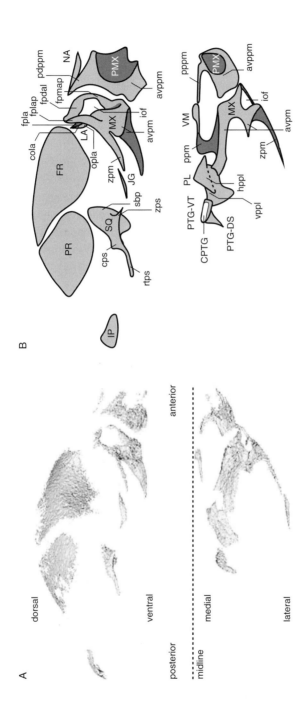

Figure 3.4 Lateral (top) and inferior (bottom) view of the dermatocranium at E16.5, obtained by micro–CT (A) and optical microscope after alizarin red staining (B). Note that the development of the samples and the detection sensitivity are different in these two methods. The vomer, palatine, and pterygoid overlap partly or entirely with other bones and are not shown in the lateral view.

Figure 3.2C,D). The ventral elements are the first to develop ventral to the hypophyseal cartilage and medial to the ventral ridge that formed at the base of the ala temporalis (AT; Figs. 3.2A & 3.2C). The dorsal elements form next, near the posterior end of the ventral element, and extend posterolaterally along the ventral surface of the alicochlear commissure (CAC) (de Beer and Woodger, 1930). Soon after their formation, the posterior end of the ventral element connects with the medial end of the dorsal element (Figure 3.4). At E16.5, the ventral element extends posteriorly beneath the medial end of the dorsal element, while the dorsal surface of the dorsal element connects with the base of the alisphenoid (perichondrally ossified ala temporalis; Figure 3.1). Both elements originate as members of the palatal series of the dermatocranium, but a portion of the ventral pterygoid element consists of cartilage (CPTG in Figure 3.4B). This cartilage is considered as secondary cartilage (de Beer, 1937; Presley and Steel, 1978; Moore, 1981), as it arises after deposition of the bone matrix in the rat (Presley and Steel, 1978). However, in our observation, both the pterygoid cartilage and the bony ventral element arise nearly simultaneously. The pterygoid cartilage undergoes endochondral ossification and persists postnatally at least to P14.

3.5.4   Lateral Wall and Roof of the Occipital Region

The part of the chondrocranium composing the lateral wall and roof of the occipital region arises as the paired occipital arches (OA in Figure 3.2B) at E12.5 and the tectum posterius (TP) at E13.5. The occipital arch dorsally continues to the tectum posterius that appears as a thin cartilage mesh and covers the posterior aspect of the brain. The tectum posterius blend with the parietal plate (PP) anteriorly dorsal to the pars canicularis.

By E15.5, perichondral/endochondral ossification begins at a middle region of the occipital arch to form the exoccipital bone and extends dorsoventrally. By P0, the exoccipital ventrally grows beyond the boundary between the occipital arch and the parachordal cartilage (i.e., foramen hypoglossum, fhg). During this process, the paracondylar process (PPC) grows anterolaterally from the anterior edge of the occipital arch at E15.5 (Figure 3.2A). By E16.5, the base of the paracondylar process undergoes ossification, but its apex remains cartilaginous even at P14. The posterior edge of the exoccipital bounding the foramen magnum is partly covered with cartilage at E16.5, forming the occipital condyle (OC), while the reminder of the occipital arch largely ossifies.

The supraoccipital bone (SO) appears at E17.5 as a pair of cartilage bones by ossification of the tectum posterius on both sides of the posterior edge near the midline. These two bony plates spread superiorly and join along the midline (Figure 3.2E), while the inferomedial edge remains cartilaginous until around P2.

Dermatocranium Association – Interparietal. At E15.5, the interparietal (IP) bone arises as a pair of thin dermatocranial plates, which soon join at the midline to form a crescent-shaped bone (Figure 3.2D). The medial region of the interparietal coincides with the anterior edge of the tectum posterius (Table 3.1). The lateral extremities of the interparietal barely overlie the parietal plate initially, but by E17.5 the interparietal overlies the posterodorsal edge of the parietal plates (Figure 3.2E and Table 3.1). Those portions of the parietal plate and tectum posterius that are completely covered by the interparietal are poorly chondrified, appearing only as a coarse meshwork from this stage onward.

By P7, the tectum posterius is reduced to a narrow channel as the interparietal and supraoccipital bones grow. By P14, the tectum between the interparietal and supraoccipital is completely resorbed, and only a small, poorly chondrified cartilage remains within the supraoccipital bone near the boundary with the parietal bone (PR in Figure 3.2E; lateral to the interparietal). In our observations, although the bone and the cartilage continue to grow, chondrification is relatively poor in all regions of the chondrocranium that are covered by a dermal bone. We propose this as evidence of a growth mechanism, by which localized expansion of dermal bone and resorption of cartilage are coordinated and coupled. Similar patterns are observed also in the preoccipital region, as we describe below.

3.5.5   Lateral Wall and Roof of the Preoccipital Region

The lateral wall of the preoccipital region bridges the nasal capsule and the occipital cartilages and is composed, from anterior to posterior, of the sphenethmoid commissure (CSE), ala orbitalis (AO), orbitoparietal commissure (COP), and parietal plate (PP) (Figure 3.2B). The pila preoptica (PPO) and pila metoptica (PMO), which connect with the braincase floor, also contribute to the lateral wall (Goodrich, 1930; Moore, 1981). While dermatocranial frontal, parietal, and squamosal bones develop superficial to these cartilages (Figure 3.2C,D), some cartilages are progressively resorbed and eventually substituted by these bones.

Between E12.5 and E13.5, the ala orbitalis (AO) arises medial to the eye and joins anteriorly with the dorsal ridge of the nasal capsule via the sphenethmoid commissure (Figure 3.2B), while the orbitoparietal commissure grows anteriorly from the parietal plate and reaches the ala orbitalis at the base and the posterior edge of the tectum transversum (TTR) (de Beer, 1937). Medial to the ala orbitalis, the orbital cartilage (O) and the hypochiasmatic cartilage (Y) arise by E13.5 (Figure 3.3) (McBratney-Owen et al., 2008). These two cartilages join with a narrow process extending medially from the orbital cartilage (Figure 3.3B). At E14.5, the orbital cartilage also extends a U-shaped rod laterally, anteriorly, and then medially with the medial (distal) end reaching the trabecular cartilage. As this rod laterally joins with the ala orbitalis, the orbital and hypochiasmatic cartilages are integrated into the ala orbitalis (Figure 3.2B) (Eloff, 1948). The hypochiasmatic cartilage medially fuses with the trabecular cartilage at E15.5; thereafter, the trabecular cartilage connects with the lateral wall (ala orbitalis) by the pila preoptica and the pila metoptica that bound the foramen opticum (fop) (Goodrich, 1930). The pila preoptica initiates perichondral/endochondral ossification at E17.5, and the area surrounding the foramen ossifies into the orbitosphenoid by P7.

Dermatocranium Associations – Frontal, Parietal, and Squamosal. The frontal bones (FR) appear by E14.5 as a pair of dermatocranial elements (Figure 3.2C,D). Before mineralization, the frontal is discernible as a lattice-like matrix dorsal to the ala orbitalis, spreading from the sphenethmoid commissure to the base of the tectum transversum. Mineralization initiates within this matrix, but the exact location varies among samples. From E15.5 to E16.5, the frontal extends anteriorly to the sphenethmoid commissure (Table 3.1). The posterior edge of the frontal only slightly overlaps with the ala orbitalis but not with the tectum transversum (Figure 3.2D and Table 3.1). As the frontal expands apically and posteriorly at E17.5, the underlying cartilages are resorbed rapidly, thereby limiting the superimposition of frontal ossification with surrounding cartilages.

Appearing later than the frontal bones, the parietals are discernible at E14.5 before mineralization as a lattice-like matrix that slightly overlies the dorsal edge of the tectum transversum and spreads dorsally. Anteriorly, the parietal matrix extends towards the dorsal extension of the anterior edge of the tectum transversum. Mineralization initiates between E14.5 and E15.5 along (or slightly above) the dorsal edge of the tectum transversum (Figure 3.2D and Table 3.1). Between E15.5 and E16.5, the parietal bone overlies the tectum transversum considerably and extends anteriorly up to the dorsal extension of its anterior edge. Posteroventrally, the parietal grows toward the dorsal edge of the orbitoparietal commissure (Table 3.1). By E17.5, the parietal bone slightly overlies the anterior edge of the parietal plate (Table 3.1). Any portion of any cartilage that is superimposed by the parietal bone undergoes a rapid resorption and appears mesh-like because of poor chondrification. At E17.5, the majority of the tectum transversum is considerably resorbed, but its anterior edge remains slightly and is aligned with the anterior edge of the parietal bone. Thus, as the frontal bone extends posteriorly, its approaching edge contributes to a suture forming with the parietal along a line initially defined and maintained by the anterior edge of the tectum transversum (Figure 3.2B,D). This growth pattern suggests that the location of the future frontal–parietal (coronal) suture is predetermined by the anterior edge of the tectum transversum that arose by E13.5, long before mineralization of these bones.

The squamosal (SQ) appears between E14.5 and E15.5 as a bilateral pair of dermatocranial bones (Figure 3.2C,D). Each bone initially forms as a squamous basal plate (sbp) and an outer ridge (Figure 3.4), appearing lateral to the ventral edge of the orbitoparietal commissure (Table 3.1) (de Beer and Woodger, 1930). The ridge develops into the zygomatic process (zps) anteriorly and the retrotympanic process (rtps) posteriorly (Figure 3.4). Between E15.5 and E17.5, the squamous plate slightly overlies the ventral edge of the orbitoparietal commissure, while it grows medioventrally toward the posterodorsal edge of the alisphenoid (part of the membrane bone outgrowth in Figure 3.1). The caudal process (cps in Figure 3.4) completely superimposes the lateral wall where the underlying cartilage is rapidly resorbed.

After E16.5, as the frontal, parietal, and squamosal bones gradually expand, the cartilages beneath these dermal bones are progressively resorbed. As a result, the tectum transversum and its ventral connection with the ala orbitalis and the orbitoparietal commissure degenerate into a narrow tract along the gap formed by the frontal, parietal, and squamosal bones with little overlap between the tract and these bones at E17.5. The remnant of the cartilage is completely resorbed by P0, confirming what we found in the occipital region: thick, growing dermatocranial bone does not overlie thick chondrocranial cartilage.

3.5.6   Olfactory Region

Among the components of the nasal capsule, the lateral walls (parietes nasi, PN) arise first at E12.5, followed by the roof (tectum nasi, TN) at E13.5 (Figure 3.3A,B) (Zeller, 1987). The tectum nasi forms a furrow called the sulcus dorsalis nasi (SDN) along the dorsal midline, and the sulcus connects with the septum nasi that separates the left and right nasal passages (Figure 3.3B). The tectum nasi laterally joins with the paries nasi, also forming a furrow along the joint. At E13.5 and later, the paries nasi is separated into the anterior (PAT), intermediate (PIT), and posterior (PPT) regions by the sulcus anterior lateralis (SAL) and sulcus posterior lateralis (SPL; see the scale in Figure 3.2A). Around E14.5, the lamina orbitonasalis (LON) connects with the trabecular cartilage anterior to the pila preoptica (Figure 3.2B).

At E14.5, the fenestra nasi (fn) is bounded anteriorly by the cupula nasi anterior (CNA) and posteroventrally by the laminae transversalis anterior (LTA in Figure 3.2A,B). The processus alaris superior (PAS) anterolaterally extends posteroinferior to the fenestra nasi (Zeller, 1987). By E15.5, the lamina transversalis anterior connects with the septum nasi medially and the paries nasi dorsally, so that this region is surrounded by a ring of cartilage: the zona annularis (ZA).

At E14.5, the paired paraseptal cartilages arise inferolateral to the inferior edge of the septum nasi to accommodate the vomeronasal organ. Between E15.5 and E16.5, the inferior edge of the pars posterior medially forms the lamina transversalis posterior (Fawcett, 1917; Eloff, 1948). The posterior end of the capsule is referred to as the cupula nasi posterior. At this stage, the floor of the nasal capsule (solum nasi) is formed by the lamina transversalis anterior, paraseptal cartilage, and lamina transversalis posterior (Figure 3.2A).

Various paired nasal turbinals grow inside the nasal capsule (Fawcett, 1917; Starck, 1979; Maier and Ruf, 2014). The ethmoturbinal I (ETB1) extends inward from the sulcus posterior lateralis at E13.5, and the ethmoturbinals II (ETB2) and III (ETB3) grow posteroventral to the ethmoturbinal I at E14.5 and E16.5, respectively (Figure 3.2E). The nasoturbinal develops antero-posteriorly inside the pars anterior at E14.5, and the maxilloturbinal forms along the ventral edge of pars anterior at E15.5. In addition to nasal turbinals, the cristae semicircularis (CS) extend inward from the sulci anterior lateralis at E14.5. The laminae cribrosa (LCB) arise as the posterior roof of the nasal capsule to support the olfactory bulbs at E15.5. Each lamina cribrosa is separated medially by the septum nasi, the dorsal corner of which forms the crista galli (CG in Figure 3.2E).

Perichondral/endochondral ossification of the olfactory region initiates at a mediodorsal region of the laminae cribrosa, ethmoturbinals, nasoturbinals, and maxilloturbinals around P4, while the tectum nasi, paries nasi, and paraseptal cartilage are progressively resorbed. A central portion of the posterior edge of the septum nasi begins to ossify into the mesethmoid at P4, but anteriorly and dorsally it remains cartilaginous at P14.

Dermatocranium Associations – Premaxilla, Maxilla, Lacrimal, and Nasal. The paired premaxillae (PMX) arise between E14.5 and E15.5, with the appearance of the alveolar process (avppm) beneath the pars anterior (Figures 3.2C,D, 3.4, and Table 3.1). The alveolar process subsequently grows superiorly to form the ascending portion of the premaxilla. At E16.5, the growing ascending portion forms the posterodorsal process (pdppm) along the surface of the pars anterior. Within the alveolar process, a large pit forms to accommodate the developing incisor. The alveolar process grows medially and continues to the palatine process (Figure 3.4) that elongates posteriorly along the ventral surface of the paraseptal cartilage (Table 3.1). The posteriorly growing palatine process extends superiorly along the medial surface of the paraseptal cartilage (medial ascending process) at E17.5 and along the lateral surface of the paraseptal cartilage (lateral ascending process) at P0 (Eloff, 1948). By P7, the palatine, medial ascending, and lateral ascending processes unite at the end of the paraseptal cartilage. The paraseptal cartilage begins to be resorbed by P1 and almost completely disappears by P7, leaving the premaxillae to provide postnatal protection for the vomeronasal organ (Eloff, 1948).

The paired maxillae (MX) arise subsequent to the premaxillae between E14.5 and E15.5 (Figure 3.2C,D), the alveolar process (avpm) appearing beneath the pars intermedia (Table 3.1). From the lateral portion of this process, the zygomatic process (zpm) extends posterolaterally, while the lateral ascending portion of the frontal process (fplap) elongates superomedially (Figure 3.4) (Eloff, 1948). The lateral ascending portion terminates anterior to the lateral apex of the pars intermedia and abruptly turns anteriorly 90 degrees to form the lateral bar. The medial ascending portion of the frontal process (fpmap) grows along the sulcus anterior lateralis and joins with the anterior end of the alveolar process inferiorly (Figure 3.4) (Eloff, 1948). At E16.5, as the posterior edge of the premaxilla approaches the anterior edge of the maxilla (Figure 3.4), the premaxilla–maxillary suture forms in line with the sulcus anterior lateralis (Figure 3.2B). At this stage, the lateral bar connects with the two ascending portions of the frontal process, forming the infraorbital foramen (iof). The lateral bar also forms a dorsal ascending lamina of the frontal process (fpdal) alongside the pars intermedia. At E16.5, the alveolar process extends medially and continues to the palatine process (ppm), which elongates anteriorly inferolateral to the septum nasi (inferior to the vomer; Figure 3.4). At P2, the anterior end of the palatine process of the maxilla underlies the posterior end of the palatine process of the premaxilla, forming a suture inferior to the posterior end of the paraseptal cartilage (Table 3.1). Furthermore, the posterior end of the palatine process of the maxilla forms a suture with the anterior end of the palatine bone.

The paired lacrimal (LA) bones appear between E15.5 and E16.5 as tiny nodules and grow into thin plates lateral to the pars intermedia (Figure 3.2D and Table 3.1).

The orbital crest (cola) forms apparently parallel to the ridge of the pars intermedia and splits the plate into the facial (fpla) and orbital (opla) processes (Figure 3.4) (Wible, 2011). The facial process is inserted between the pars intermedia and the lateral ascending portion of the maxilla. The orbital crest articulates with the posterior edge of the lateral ascending portion anteriorly around P2 and with the anterior end of the supraorbital crest of the frontal posterodorsally at P4 (Wible, 2011). The orbital process reaches the paranasal process (PPN; Table 3.1), a cartilaginous hamulus holding the nasolacrimal duct (Figure 3.2E), inferiorly at P2 (Macklin, 1921).

The nasal (NA) bones form as a pair of dermal bony plates that cover the tectum nasi and a dorsal portion of the pars anterior (Figure 3.2D and Table 3.1). Each nasal plate begins ossification at E16.5 from two sites: one on the anterolateral corner and the other on the posteromedial corner (Figure 3.2D,E). The medial region of each plate ossifies subsequently by E17.5. Anteriorly, the nasal bones reach the level of the posterior edge of the lamina transversalis anterior, coincident with the anterior edge of the premaxilla (Figure 3.4). The lateral edge of the nasal forms a suture with the dorsal edge of the premaxilla (Wible, 2011), and the posterior edge of the nasal aligns with the posterior edge of the posterodorsal process of the premaxilla along the sulcus anterior lateralis (Figures 3.2E and 3.4). The posterior edge of the nasal reaches the dorsal edge of the lamina cribrosa (Table 3.1) and the anterior edge of the frontal at P0.

3.5.7   Otic Region

Each auditory capsule consists of two parts, the dorsolateral pars canalicularis (PCA) and the ventromedial pars cochlearis (PCO) (Figure 3.2F). The auditory capsule begins chondrification from the lateral side of the pars canalicularis by E12.5 (Figure 3.3) (de Beer and Woodger, 1930), and the semicircular canals and the endolymphatic duct form internally by E13.5 (Kaufman and Bard, 1999). By contrast, the pars cochlearis appears to chondrify only superficially, especially the dorsal half poorly chondrified even at E14.5 (Figure 3.2B). The crista parotica (CPR in Figure 3.2B) is a shallow ridge, formed by the lateral surface of the pars canalicularis that overhangs the pars cochlearis (de Beer and Woodger, 1930). The tegmen tympani (TGT) appears anterior to the crista parotica, and dorsally roofs the epitympanic recess at E15.5 (Fawcett, 1917). A forming cochlear duct is first detected as an internal ridge at this stage. The suprafacial commissure (CSF) bridges the anterior surfaces of the pars cochlearis and the pars canalicularis (Figure 3.2F).

The auditory capsule is linked with surrounding cartilages by seven commissures (Figure 3.2F) (Starck, 1979). At E13.5, the pars cochlearis connects with the hypophyseal cartilage via the alicochlear commissure (i) and with the acrochordal cartilage via the sphenocochlear commissure (ii, CSC; Figure 3.3B). At E15.5, the pars cochlearis connects with the parachordal via the chordo-cochlear commissure (iii, CCC), whereas the pars canalicularis joins with the parietal plate via the parietocapsular commissure (iv, CPC). At E16.5, the pars canalicularis connects with the orbitoparietal commissure via the orbitocapsular commissure (v, COC) (Fawcett,

1917; Zeller, 1987), and the pars canalicularis connects with the tectum posterius via the supraoccipitocapsular commissure (vi, CSOC). Finally, the pars canalicularis connects with the exoccipital bone at the base of the cartilaginous paracondylar process through the exoccipitocapsular commissure by E17.5 (vii, CEOC).

Perichondral/endochondral ossification of the auditory capsule initiates at P1 to form the petromastoid portion of the temporal bone at two locations: one around the tegmen tympani and the other around the foramen perilymphaticum (Figure 3.2B). Ossification progresses in the pars cochlearis at P2 and extends to an inferior region of the pars canalicularis. At P7, the lateral surface of the pars canalicularis is still largely cartilaginous but mostly ossified by P14.

Dermatocranium Association – Squamosal. The tegmen tympani anteriorly continues to the orbitocapsular commissure, and both are located medial to the retrotympanic process of the squamosal at E16.5 (Table 3.1).

3.5.8   The Role of the Chondrocranium

As we have described, large portions of the initially cartilaginous chondrocranium are either replaced by cartilage bone or resorbed and substituted by dermal bone during embryonic or early postnatal development in osteichthyans. Nevertheless, the chondrocranium appears to be essential to vertebrates, as suggested by the simple fact that no modern vertebrates have lost this skeleton during evolution. This is in contrast with the dermatocranium that is thought to have been lost secondarily in modern cartilaginous fish (Giles *et al.*, 2013). The significance of the chondrocranium and its fundamental role has been attributed to the interstitial growth of cartilage, which enables rapid production of complex structures and their continued growth necessary for embryonic development of the head in vertebrates (de Beer, 1937; Romer, 1963). While bone is superior to cartilage as a protective or supporting material, construction of an architecturally complicated bony skull without the aid of cartilage precursors seems unlikely (Romer, 1963). The formative brain and other sensory organs need support from an early developmental stage. Cartilage is a tissue that provides a reasonably strong foundation while facilitating rapid growth of intricate cranial soft tissues. Our analysis provides hints that the chondrocranium might also serve as a scaffold for the later development of dermatocranial elements.

We have shown that the development of the dermatocranium is tightly linked with the chondrocranium spatially and temporally, and that this link often persists for long periods over developmental time. For example, the location of the coronal suture corresponds exactly with, and we propose is predetermined by, the anterior edge of the tectum transversum established as early as E13.5, much earlier than mineralization of the frontal and parietal bones. However, the link between the two skeletal systems appears to have the ability to vary and thus can evolve, with the link being rewired in different species. Indeed, most primates have a large gap between the ala orbitalis and parietal plate, hence no orbitoparietal commissure or tectum transversum (de Beer, 1937). Without the tectum transversum, the location of the coronal suture cannot be determined by this structure, but may be determined by an alternate chondrocranial element. Remarkably, most dermatocranial elements show a developmental association with the chondrocranium. In our experience, the jugal (JG in Figure 3.4) is the only dermatocranial bone whose appearance, development, and/or growth does not show any direct association with the chondrocranium.

Of note, we demonstrated that many portions of the chondrocranium are resorbed when superimposed by the growing dermatocranium, and we suggest that these observations signal the existence of a mechanism for the coordinated, localized expansion (dermal bones) and resorption (cartilage) of two developmentally and evolutionarily separate tissues. Mice that lack the type-II collagen gene cannot deposit well-formed cartilage matrix, but the dermatocranium shows apparently normal mineralization (Li *et al.*, 1995). This result suggests that growing bone induces cartilage resorption, not that cartilage or its resorption induces bone formation. The slight but consistent spatial and temporal overlap between resorbing cartilage and growing bone appears to facilitate structural integrity during development. Early skull formation depends on a dynamic interplay between the chondrocranium and the dermatocranium.

3.6   Anthropological Implications

The skeleton of the head in the Craniata is made up of various elements of diverse origin which become more or less closely combined to form what we loosely call the 'skull' and visceral arches. Many of these constituent elements are more clearly distinguishable in lower than in higher forms, in earlier than in later stages of development.

Goodrich, 1930

Morphological structures are thought to be modular if they can be subdivided into relatively autonomous, internally highly connected units that covary in a hierarchical manner where interactions among traits within units are relatively high (modular) and interactions among units relatively low. The statistical evidence for modularity of morphological structures (covariance and correlation patterns) is thought to signal molecular, developmental, and/or evolutionary mechanisms (Cheverud *et al.*, 2004; Wagner *et al.*, 2007). Anthropologists have traditionally divided the skull into units that are thought to be partially independent and are conceived of as modules. How cranial modules arise, and how changes in genetic regulatory networks and developmental pathways instigate changes in pattern or magnitude of modularity leading to changes in complex cranial morphologies, are questions of significant interest to anthropologists.

Morphological integration refers to the cohesion among traits in an organism that could bias the direction and rate of morphological change, so that estimation of patterns and magnitudes of morphological integration and modularity and their consequences on development are central to understanding how complex traits evolve (Wagner *et al.*, 2007; Klingenberg, 2008; Porto *et al.*, 2009; Koyabu *et al.*, 2014).

Often the cranial base is identified as fundamental to the heterogeneity found in crania, and so it figures prominently in studies of skull integration. Reasons for assigning an especially important role to the cranial base include: relatively early formation, endochondral ossification and the presence of synchondroses that serve as important growth sites; early completion of growth relative to the face and vault; anatomical positioning between the cranial vault and facial skeleton; and increased evolutionary age relative to the facial skeleton and cranial vault.

A few clarifications are pertinent here. First, when defining cranial modules, many researchers use the labels cranial base, facial skeleton, and cranial vault interchangeably with chondrocranium, splanchnocranium, and dermatocranium, respectively. Although correspondences do exist across the two sets of labels, they are not equivalent. Specifically, although there is some overlap among structures of the chondrocranium and the cranial base, the chondrocranium and the cranial base are distinct. Nor is the chondrocranium the appropriate term to describe the embryological precursors of the postnatal bony cranial base. The chondrocranium is that part of the endoskeleton that protects the brain and three principal sense organs but does not include the pharyngeal skeleton. By contrast, the cranial base represents that part of the neurocranium that underlies the brain. In adult humans, the cranial base consists of both endoskeletal and dermal skeletal elements and, although defined variably by researchers, it usually includes parts of the ethmoid, sphenoid, occipital, temporal, frontal, and parietal bones. Importantly, the components of the cranial base change during evolution. For example, the greater wing of the sphenoid (alisphenoid) constitutes a significant part of the cranial base in humans (Lieberman *et al.*, 2000). However, this position is derived evolutionarily from part of the endoskeletal upper jaw (Hopson and Rougier, 1993), which grows outside the neurocranium and does not contribute to the cranial base. Furthermore, the frontal and parietal bones do not contribute to the cranial base in most non-primate animals, including the mouse. It is only the braincase floor that contributes to the cranial base consistently in vertebrates, although its individual cartilage or cartilage-bone elements may change during evolution. This is in contrast with the evolutionarily stable dichotomy between the endoskeleton and the dermal skeleton (see Section 3.4.1). Evolutionarily stable skeletal systematics has led to a classification system that partitions the skull into chondrocranium, pharyngeal skeleton, and dermatocranium. We consider this system appropriate for studies that combine developmental, evolutionary, and anatomic information in the analysis of cranial evolution.

Second, with very few exceptions, studies of modularity and integration of the skull are conducted using postnatal (often adult) data, where the morphology of skeletal units is relatively static and established. It is likely that the composition of modules is dynamic, changing throughout ontogeny so that analysis of data from adult skulls may be inadequate for the study of certain developmental questions. Third, modularity and integration are currently operationalized in most anthropological studies using patterns of covariation or correlation and the processes responsible for these patterns (molecular, developmental, evolutionary) are inferred, usually *post hoc*. Alternative strategies will have to be employed to identify and verify the mechanism(s) responsible for modular development in order to more fully understand its role in evolution. Finally, and probably obvious to most anthropologists, modules may likely be composed of both skeletal and non-skeletal components so that osseous data may provide an incomplete assessment of skull or head modularity.

We have demonstrated the usefulness of a classification system that clearly demarcates between the endoskeleton and the dermal skeleton, two components of the skull that evolved separately. We have provided a detailed definition of the embryonic mouse chondrocranium using data from historical texts and our own laboratory observations. Visualizing the appearance (and disappearance in some cases) of chondrocranial elements, their ossification, and/or their association with formation and mineralization of dermatocranial elements enabled the formulation of a novel hypothesis regarding the function of the chondrocranium in establishing the initial formation and spatial distribution of the dermatocranium. When validated, our observations of chondrocranial development may identify the cell and molecular processes that underlie the integrative properties of the chondrocranium in development and evolution.

Acknowledgments

We are grateful to Dr. Chris Percival and an anonymous reviewer for providing helpful comments that improved the quality and clarity of the manuscript. This study was funded in part by the National Institute of Child Health and Human Development, the National Institute of Craniofacial and Dental Research, the American Recovery and Reinvestment Act (grant numbers R01-DE018500, R01-DE018500-S1, R01-DE022988, P01HD078233-01A1) and the National Science Foundation (BCS-0725227).

References

Bellairs, A. D. and Gans, C. (1983). A reinterpretation of the amphisbaenian orbitosphenoid. *Nature*, 302, 243–244.

Biegert, J. (1963). The evaluation of chracteristcs of the skull, hands and feet for primate taxonomy. *In:* Washburn, S. L. (ed.) *Classification and Human Evolution*. Chicago, IL: Aldine Publishing.

Cattell, M., Lai, S., Cerny, R. and Medeiros, D. M. (2011). A new mechanistic scenario for the origin and evolution of vertebrate cartilage. *PLoS ONE*, 6, e22474.

Cheverud, J. M., Ehrich, T. H., Vaughn, T. T., *et al.* (2004). Pleiotropic effects on mandibular morphology II: differential epistasis and genetic variation in morphological integration. *Journal of Experimental Zoology Part B, Molecular and Developmental Evolution*, 302, 424–435.

Cole, A. G. and Hall, B. K. (2004). The nature and significance of invertebrate cartilages revisited: distribution and histology of cartilage and cartilage-like tissues within the Metazoa. *Zoology*, 107, 261–273.

de Beer, G. R. and Woodger, J. H. (1930). The early development of the skull of the rabbit. *Philosophical Transactions of the Royal Society B*, 230, 373–414.

de Beer, G. R. (1937). *The Development of the Vertebrate Skull*. New York, NY: Oxford.

Depew, M. J., Tucker, A. S. and Sharpe, P. T. (2002). Cranifacial development. *In:* Rossant, J. and Tam, P. P. L. (eds.) *Mouse Development*. San Diego, CA: Academic Press.

Donoghue, P. C., Sansom, I. J. and Downs, J. P. (2006). Early evolution of vertebrate skeletal tissues and cellular interactions, and the canalization of skeletal development. *Journal of Experimental Zoology Part B, Molecular and Developmental Evolution*, 306, 278–294.

Donoghue, P. C. J. and Keating, J. N. (2014). Early vertebrate evolution. *Palaeontology*, 57, 879–893.

Eames, B. F., Allen, N., Young, J., *et al.* (2007). Skeletogenesis in the swell shark *Cephaloscyllium ventriosum*. *Journal of Anatomy*, 210, 542–554.

Eloff, F. C. (1948). The early development of the skull of *Otomys tropicalis*. *Annals of the Transvaal Museum*, 21, 103–152.

Fawcett, E. (1917). The primordial cranium of *Microtus amphibius* (water-rat), as determined by sections and a model of the 25-mm stage. *Journal of Anatomy*, 51, 309–359.

Fawcett, E. (1923). The primordial cranium of *Xerus* (spiny squirrel) at the 17 and 19 millimeters stages. *Journal of Anatomy*, 57(Pt 3), 221–237.

Flaherty, K. V., Musy, M., Sharpe, J. and Richtsmeier, J. T. (2015). Patterns of asynchrony between developmental age and chronological age *in utero*. *American Journal of Physical Anthropology*, Suppl 60, 134.

Gaupp, E. (1906). Die Entwickelung des Kopfskelettes. *In:* Hertwig, O. (ed.) *Entwickelungslehre der Wirbeltiere*. Jena: Gustav Fischer.

Giles, S., Rucklin, M. and Donoghue, P. C. (2013). Histology of "placoderm" dermal skeletons: implications for the nature of the ancestral gnathostome. *Journal of Morphology*, 274, 627–644.

Goodrich, E. S. (1930). *Studies of the Structure and Development of Vertebrates*. London: Macmillan.

Hall, B. K. (1970). Cellular differentiation in skeletal tissues. *Biological Reviews*, 45, 455–484.

Hall, B. K. (2014). Endoskeleton/exo (dermal) skeleton – mesoderm/ neural crest: two pair of problems and a shifting paradigm. *Journal of Applied Ichthyology*, 30, 608–615.

Hall, B. K. (2015). *Bones and Cartilage*. San Diego, CA: Elsevier.

Hall, B. K. and Gillis, J. A. (2013). Incremental evolution of the neural crest, neural crest cells and neural crest-derived skeletal tissues. *Journal of Anatomy*, 222, 19–31.

Hirasawa, T. and Kuratani, S. (2015). Evolution of the vertebrate skeleton: morphology, embryology, and development. *Zoological Letters*, 1, 2.

Hopson, J. A. and Rougier, G. W. (1993). Braincase structure in the oldest known skull of a therian mammal: implications for mammallian systematics and cranial evolution. *American Journal of Science*, 293, 268–299.

Janvier, P. (1996). *Early Vertebrates*. New York, NY: Oxford University Press.

Kadam, K. M. (1976). The development of the chondrocranium in the golden hamster, *Mesocricetus auratus* (waterhouse). *Gegenbaurs Morphologisches Jahrbuch*, 122, 796–814.

Kaufman, M. H. and Bard, J. B. L. (1999). *The Anatomical Basis of Mouse Development*. San Diego, CA: Academic Press.

Kawasaki, K. and Weiss, K. M. (2003). Mineralized tissue and vertebrate evolution: the secretory calcium-binding phosphoprotein gene cluster. *Proceedings of the National Academy of Sciences USA*, 100, 4060–4065.

Kawasaki, K., Buchanan, A. V. and Weiss, K. M. (2009). Biomineralization in humans: making the hard choices in life. *Annual Review of Genetics*, 43, 119–142.

Kawasaki, K. (2011). The *SCPP* gene family and the complexity of hard tissues in vertebrates. *Cells Tissues Organs*, 194, 108–112.

Klingenberg, C. P. (2008). Morphological integration and developmental modularity. *Annual Review of Ecology Evolution and Systematics*, 39, 115–132.

Klingenberg, C. P. (2014). Studying morphological integration and modularity at multiple levels: concepts and analysis. *Philosophical Transactions of the Royal Society of London B*, 369, 20130249.

Koyabu, D., Werneburg, I., Morimoto, N., *et al.* (2014). Mammalian skull heterochrony reveals modular evolution and a link between cranial development and brain size. *Nature Communications*, 5, 3625.

Li, S. W., Prockop, D. J., Helminen, H., *et al.* (1995). Transgenic mice with targeted inactivation of the *Col2a1* gene for collagen II develop a skeleton with membranous and periosteal bone but no endochondral bone. *Genes & Development*, 9, 2821–2830.

Lieberman, D. E., Ross, C. F. and Ravosa, M. J. (2000). The primate cranial base: ontogeny, function, and integration. *American Journal of Physical Anthropology*, 43, 117–169.

Lieberman, D. E., Hallgrimsson, B., Liu, W., Parsons, T. E. and Jamniczky, H. A. (2008). Spatial packing, cranial base angulation, and craniofacial shape variation in the mammalian skull: testing a new model using mice. *Journal of Anatomy*, 212, 720–735.

Macklin, C. C. (1921). The skull of a human fetus of 43 millimeters greatest length. *Contributions to Embryology*, 10, 57–103.

Maier, W. and Ruf, I. (2014). Morphology of the nasal capsule of primates – with special reference to *Daubentonia* and *Homo*. *Anatomical Record*, 297, 1985–2006.

McBratney-Owen, B., Iseki, S., Bamforth, S. D., Olsen, B. R. and Morriss-Kay, G. M. (2008). Development and tissue origins of the mammalian cranial base. *Developmental Biology*, 322, 121–132.

McCarthy, R. C. (2001). Anthropoid cranial base architecture and scaling relationships. *Journal of Human Evolution*, 40, 41–66.

McLeod, M. J. (1980). Differential staining of cartilage and bone in whole mouse fetuses by Alcian blue and Alizarin red S. *Teratology*, 22, 299–301.

Meulemans, D. and Bronner-Fraser, M. (2007). Insights from amphioxus into the evolution of vertebrate cartilage. *PLoS ONE*, 2, e787.

Mezey, J. G., Cheverud, J. M. and Wagner, G. P. (2000). Is the genotype–phenotype map modular? A statistical approach using mouse quantitative trait loci data. *Genetics*, 156, 305–311.

Moore, W. J. (1981). *The Mammalian Skull*. New York, NY: Cambridge University Press.

Oisi, Y., Ota, K. G., Fujimoto, S. and Kuratani, S. (2013). Development of the chondrocranium in hagfishes, with special reference to the early evolution of vertebrates. *Zoological Science*, 30, 944–961.

Olson, E. C. and Miller, R. L. (1958). *Morphological Integration*. Chicago, IL: University of Chicago.

Patterson, C. (1977). Cartilage bones, dermal bones and membrane bones, or the exoskeleton versus endoskeleton. *In:* Andrews, S. M., Miles R. S. and Walker, A. D. (eds.) *Problems in Vertebrate Evolution*. New York, NY: Academic Press.

Porto, A., de Oliveira, F. B., Shirai, L. T., De Conto, V. and Marroig, G. (2009). The evolution of modularity in the mammalian skull I: morphological integration patterns and magnitudes. *Evolutionary Biology*, 36, 118–135.

Presley, R. and Steel, F. L. (1978). The pterygoid and ectopterygoid in mammals. *Anatomy and Embryology*, 154, 95–110.

Romer, A. S. (1963). The "ancient history" of bone. *Annals of the New York Academy of Sciences*, 109, 168–176.

Romer, A. S. and Parsons, T. S. (1977). *The Vertebrate Body*. Philadelphia, PA: Saunders.

Ross, C. and Henneberg, M. (1995). Basicranial flexion, relative brain size, and facial kyphosis in *Homo sapiens* and some fossil hominids. *American Journal of Physical Anthropology*, 98, 575–593.

Ross, C. F. and Ravosa, M. J. (1993). Basicranial flexion, relative brain size, and facial kyphosis in nonhuman primates. *American Journal of Physical Anthropology*, 91, 305–324.

Rychel, A. L., Smith, S. E., Shimamoto, H. T. and Swalla, B. J. (2006). Evolution and development of the chordates: collagen and pharyngeal cartilage. *Molecular Biology and Evolution*, 23, 541–549.

Scott, J. H. (1958). The cranial base. *American Journal of Physical Anthropology*, 16, 319–348.

Spoor, F. (1997). Basicranial architecture and relative brain size of Sts 5 (*Australopithecus africanus*) and other Plio-Pleistocene hominids. *South African Journal of Science*, 93, 182–186.

Starck, D. (1979). *Vergleichende Anatomi der Wirbeltiere auf evolutionsbiologischer Grundlage.* New York, NY: Springer.

Wada, H. (2010). Origin and genetic evolution of the vertebrate skeleton. *Zoological Science, 27,* 119–123.

Wagner, G. P., Pavlicev, M. and Cheverud, J. M. (2007). The road to modularity. *Nature Review Genetics, 8,* 921–931.

White, T. D., Black, M. T. and Folkens, P. A. (2012). *Human Osteology.* San Diego, CA: Academic Press.

Wible, J. R. (2011). On the treeshrew skull (Mammalia, Placentalia, Scandentia). *Annals of the Carnegie Museum, 79,* 149–230.

Youssef, E. H. (1966). The chondrocranium of the albino rat. *Acta Anatomica, 64,* 586–617.

Youssef, E. H. (1969). Development of the membrane bones and ossification of the chondrocranium in the albino rat. *Acta Anatomica, 72,* 603–623.

Zeller, U. (1987). Morphologenesis of the mamalian skull with special reference to *Tupaia. In:* Kuhn, H.-J. (ed.) *Morphogenesis of the Mamalian Skull.* Hamburg: Paul Parey.

Zhang, G. and Cohn, M. J. (2006). Hagfish and lancelet fibrillar collagens reveal that type II collagen-based cartilage evolved in stem vertebrates. *Proceedings of the National Academy of Sciences USA, 103,* 16829–16833.

Zhang, G., Miyamoto, M. M. and Cohn, M. J. (2006). Lamprey type II collagen and Sox9 reveal an ancient origin of the vertebrate collagenous skeleton. *Proceedings of the National Academy of Sciences USA, 103,* 3180–3185.

Zhang, G., Eames, B. and Cohn, M. (2009). Evolution of vertebrate cartilage development. *Current Topics in Developmental Biology, 86,* 15–42.

4 Unique Ontogenetic Patterns of Postorbital Septation in Tarsiers and the Issue of Trait Homology

Valerie B. DeLeon, Alfred L. Rosenberger and Timothy D. Smith

4.1 Introduction

Homology of postorbital closure is a critical issue in primate phylogenetics, because it is variably expressed within the Order Primates and has been used to infer phylogenetic relationships among extant and fossil taxa. *Homology* is a term used to describe a suite of biological phenomena in the scientific literature (reviewed briefly below and more extensively in, e.g., Hall, 1994; Kleisner, 2007; Wagner, 2014). Here we explicitly use the term *homology* to refer to traits shared by descent from a common ancestor in which the trait is also expressed. However, this simple definition masks the operational difficulties involved in establishing homology, because trait homology cannot be observed – it can only be inferred. On a practical level, this holds true even when two taxa are confidently linked as an ancestor and descendant because we generally have limited knowledge of the underlying biological properties of structures and structural similarity – from genes to form itself – that were potentially inherited from one generation to the next. This problem is theoretically compounded when the taxa being compared are living, and the trait is shared by descent with modification from an extinct (and often unknown) fossil ancestor. Our purpose in this chapter is to illustrate one approach that has the power to resolve some of these issues. We describe developmental evidence regarding postorbital closure in the tarsier and discuss the implications for defining expectations for postorbital traits in fossil primates.

Extant primates are commonly grouped into six clades: lemurs, lorises and galagos, tarsiers, New World monkeys, Old World monkeys, and apes (including humans). In recent decades, a general consensus has been reached on the phylogenetic structure of these groups, confirming proposals made earlier in the twentieth century (e.g., Szalay & Delson, 1979; Martin, 1990; Fleagle, 2013). The clade including lemurs, lorises, and galagos is referred to the Suborder Strepsirrhini. The sister Suborder Haplorhini includes tarsiers and anthropoids, which comprises all monkey, apes, and humans. The genus *Tarsius* commands a unique position within Primates as a result of the very early divergence of the group from other living primate lineages. Tarsiers retain many primitive characters, but have also accumulated a suite of highly derived traits. The product is an unusual, complex

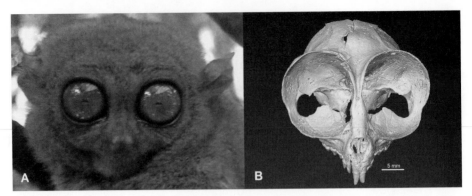

Figure 4.1 (A) All tarsiers are characterized by extremely large eyes. *Tarsius syrichta* is shown in its habitual resting position associated with vertical clinging and leaping (photo modified and licensed through CCA-SA 3.0 by JT Lim Majuro~enwiki at http://wikipedia.com). (B) Reconstruction of an adult *Tarsius syrichta* cranium in comparable orientation illustrates the profound influence of eye hypertrophy on the shape of the cranium and bony orbit. A black and white version of this figure will appear in some formats. For the color version, please refer to the plate section.

primitive-and-derived mosaic. Among the most remarkable features of tarsiers are their extraordinarily large eyes (Figure 4.1). These, in conjunction with their insectivorous teeth and highly modified postcranial adaptations for vertical clinging and leaping, make it difficult to identify phylogenetic relationships based on skeletal anatomy alone. This had led to a debate over tarsier systematics that continued for well over a century. Historically, tarsiers were aligned with strepsirrhines in a group called Prosimii (Illiger, 1811). Many still use the term informally (i.e., prosimian) in referring to any non-anthropoid. More recently, the addition of molecular evidence (e.g., Hartig *et al.*, 2013) to the accumulated database of soft-tissue traits (e.g., foveate eyes, hemochorial placentation, oronasal complex) has overwhelmingly persuaded researchers that tarsiers are more closely related to Anthropoidea than to Strepsirrhini, supporting their inclusion in the Suborder Haplorhini (Pocock, 1918).

The relationship of tarsiers to known *fossil* primates is more hotly debated. The earliest specimens attributed by some to the Order Primates are the paraphyletic Plesiadapiformes from the Paleocene of North America and Europe (e.g., *Purgatorius coracis*; Fox and Scott, 2011; reviewed in Silcox *et al.*, 2015). In this model, the crown group Euprimates, including all living primates and their closest fossil relatives, are believed to derive from one of these taxa, or more likely, from an as-yet-unknown plesiadapiform ancestor. During the Eocene, two apparently distinct groups appear in the fossil record: the Adapiformes and the Omomyiformes (reviewed in Godinot, 2015). Although there is some disagreement about the relationship of these fossils to modern primates, many researchers believe that strepsirrhines are derived from an adapiform ancestor, and haplorrhines are derived from one or more omomyiform ancestors (Szalay *et al.*, 1987; Ross, 2000). However, molecular evidence suggests a divergence date of the modern tarsier lineage from that of living anthropoids between 61 and 70 Ma, following closely after the divergence of Haplorhini and Strepsirrhini (reviewed in Raaum, 2015). These dates suggest long ghost lineages for the major clades of living primates (strepsirrhines, tarsiers, and anthropoids) through the Paleocene, as ancestral strepsirrhines and haplorhines would have temporally coexisted with a diverse assemblage of plesi-adapiforms.

Many researchers look to Eocene fossils attributed to the Omomyiformes for clues about the haplorhine ancestor that gave rise to both tarsier and anthropoid lineages. Homologous traits shared by tarsiers and anthropoids are expected also to be shared with these earliest haplorhines and provide evidence for morphological traits of the earliest anthropoids. As a result, assumptions about homology constrain the interpretation of the fossil record. This sometimes creates a circularity in reasoning: we use phylogenetic relationships to define homologous characters, and then we use those homologous characters to test hypotheses about phylogenetic relationships. This limits our ability to recognize possible candidates for the earliest haplorhines in the fossil record, especially in cases where data are limited and the comparative morphology proves difficult. In this chapter, we summarize aspects of homology and discuss them in the context of postorbital septation in primates. We present our own observations of growth of this region in primates, and use this as an example of how growth can provide important information that influences assumptions and interpretations about homology.

4.2   Homology

One of these things is not like the others. One of these things just doesn't belong.
                                                                        –Sesame Street

In any comparison of organisms (plants or animals), it is easy to see that some aspects of structure are shared across groups and distinct among other groups. The sorting of objects into groups that are similar and groups that are different is a key part of how we as humans process information about the world around us. Classification and naming are fundamental processes of human cognition. Our conceptions of similarity and difference are based on observations that we make, but are themselves artificial labels that we impose on the world. These labels do not change the inherent nature of the objects being observed (but consider Schroedinger's cat for an alternative view). In some cases, the labels that we apply may align with the true evolutionary history of the animals involved, but this alignment cannot be assumed. Instead, our assumptions of similarity and differences should be framed as valid hypotheses, subjecting those assumptions to testing and the potential for falsification. Only then can we have confidence that our labels reflect biological reality.

The recognition of similarity in structure across different taxa has been a fundamental part of biological study since the Classical period (e.g., Aristotle, cited in

Hall, 1994). In his studies of comparative anatomy, Cuvier described the similarity of particular anatomical structures which could be discerned by their common connections within the bodies of different animals.

> the number, direction, and shape of the bones that compose each part of an animal's body are always in a necessary relation to all the other parts, in such a way that – up to a point – one can infer the whole from any one of them and vice versa. (Cuvier, 1798)

However, Cuvier was adamant in his belief in the fixity of species, and did not allow for any *natural* mechanism through which one structure might be modified from another.

By the early nineteenth century, in the rich, expanding scientific community of European naturalists and comparative anatomists, Geoffrey Saint-Hilaire had proposed his *Philosophie Anatomique* (1818–1822), which included as a key tenet the "unity of plan" in which all organisms reflect modifications from a common archetype. He used the term "analogie" to describe structures shared across multiple taxa and derived from the same archetypal structure. This theory was shared by Lamarck, although they differed on the primary causal factor influencing modification from the archetype. Owen (1848) was the first to apply the term "homologue" to the biological context in which it is used today: "the same organ in different animals under every variety of form and function." He contrasted this meaning with his definition of "analogue" as "a part or organ in one animal which has the same function as another part or organ in a different animal." Owen's definitions were powerful for (1) indicating that different taxa could share the *same* character that might differ in structure and in function, and (2) allowing also that similarities could arise in two distinct structures by commonality in function, but that these similarities do not create a shared identity in those structures.

Darwin's *Origin of Species* and the theory of evolution by descent that he advanced along with Alfred Russell Wallace provided an evolutionary framework for understanding the origin of shared traits. For some structures, similarities among related taxa were understood to reflect descent with modification from a common ancestor. This led to a shift from a gradistic concept of homology applied to the classification of similarity in structure to a phylogenetic concept of homology, in which "similarity" carried assumptions about the shared inheritance of that trait from a common ancestor. The phylogenetic concept of homology assumes that hierarchies of homology reflect phylogenetic relationships.

Similarities in structure thus provide persuasive evidence of inheritance from a common ancestor, and therefore phylogenetic affinity. However, similarities may also arise through separate paths of adaptation to comparable environmental factors or to serve the same or similar function. These derived similarities, then, are considered to be *homoplasies*, a result of parallel or convergent evolution, rather than homologies. The generalized anatomy of adaptations for flight in birds and bats are a commonly cited example of convergent evolution. Each has accumulated a set of morphological and physiological adaptations that allow that group to exploit the functional niche of flight, although they evolved in different lineages.

The Modern Synthesis in the middle of the twentieth century incorporated population genetics and developmental biology into the explanatory model of homology and evolutionary relationships. Statements about homology carried with them assumptions about genetic affinity. Consequently, once the structure and function of DNA were deciphered, Van Valen (1982, p. 305) would describe homology as "correspondence caused by a continuity of information." The understanding of how genetic modification could accumulate over time to produce speciation events also led to a widely accepted cladistic reconceptualization of phylogenetic systematics. The founding father of this approach, Hennig (1950), relied on the identification of homologous characters to distinguish shared derived traits ("synapomorphies") from shared ancestral traits ("symplesiomorphies"). The cladistic contribution to taxonomic principles stresses the idea that monophyletic clades are biologically meaningful, but that paraphyletic taxonomic groups are an artificial construct. The biological "reality" of a monophyletic grouping is assumed, because all organisms in the group descend from a common ancestor, and all descendants of that ancestor are included in the group. Patterson (1982) thus further defined homology as traits shared within a monophyletic group.

Wagner (2014) and others have pointed out that there often seems to be a different concept of homology for every research program. Absent known ancestor–descendant relationships, we still often identify traits as phylogenetically homologous between two taxa. When we do this, we are inferring that the last common ancestor must have shared a similar trait. Homologous traits are also used to formulate *a priori* expectations for the traits that will be present in a fossil specimen or species that potentially represents the ancestral state. In the case of fossil taxa, we use homologous traits in extant organisms to identify specific characters that are expected to be present in the last common ancestor. These conclusions are heavily influential in identifying fossil specimens and attributing them to particular taxonomic groups. At the same time, we are inferring that the genetic code and epigenetic effects producing that trait are also shared with the last common ancestor and inherited by the descendants that share the trait. This link between the trait and the underlying genetic code in the taxa under consideration is a fundamental assumption when we make claims about phylogenetic homology.

4.3 Postorbital Septation

Postorbital septation has been among the most important skeletal traits linking tarsiers and anthropoids, thereby uniting living Haplorhini (Pocock, 1918). Euprimates (the clade excluding plesiadapiforms) are characterized by a *bony* posterolateral support framing the orbital fossa. The zygomatic process of the frontal articulates with the ascending process of the zygomatic to form a continuous bony bridge posterolateral to the eyeball. In strepsirrhines, often considered to preserve the ancestral Euprimate form, this simple *postorbital bar* is the full extent of posterolateral bony closure. The orbital fossa and its contents are confluent with the temporal fossa posteriorly. Haplorhine primates, on the other hand, invariably display a thin sheet of bone extending posteromedially from the lateral orbital rim to the neurocranium to fully or partially enclose the orbit on its lateral and/or posterior aspect. This *postorbital septum* effectively separates the orbital and temporal fossae. In other words, strepsirrhines display a postorbital bar, and living haplorhines display both postorbital bar and postorbital septum as a composite structure. In tarsiers, the postorbital septum includes contributions from the frontal bone, the alisphenoid (the portion of the sphenoid bone contributing to the greater wings), and the zygomatic. The relative contribution of each bone is debated (see below), but regardless, they each contribute substantially to a septum that *partially* separates the orbit from the temporal fossa. Therefore, in tarsiers, the structure is usually called a *partial postorbital septum.* In contrast, the postorbital septum of anthropoids is disproportionately composed of a posterior lamina from the zygomatic bone that essentially separates the orbital and temporal fossae. The frontal and alisphenoid make only minimal contributions to this separation of the orbital and temporal fossae. The apparent similarity among the haplorhine primates is a trait that has been used to unite this clade, and the homology of postorbital septation in these taxa has been debated for decades (e.g., Simons and Russell, 1960; Cartmill, 1980, 1994a; Simons and Rasmussen, 1989). A consequence of the uncertainty has important implications for interpreting the primate fossil record. At issue is whether fossils with *no* evidence of postorbital septation could be included within the clade represented by tarsiers and anthropoids, i.e., whether tarsiers are actually more closely related to anthropoids or to fossils resembling tarsiers in many ways but not in postorbital septation.

The postorbital bar is a trait that has evolved in parallel in multiple groups of living mammals and is shared by some ungulates (e.g., sheep), tree shrews, hyraxes, some bats and diverse fossil taxa. Many mammals also display processes of the frontal and zygomatic that partially frame the orbit posterolaterally, and this is often regarded as a precondition for the evolution of the postorbital bar. A postorbital bar is also present in the horse; however, in these animals the inferior portion of the bar ascends from the squamosal, rather than the zygomatic (Hillman, 1975). The independent appearance of a complete postorbital bar across this diverse range of animals indicates convergent evolution and demonstrates the plasticity of this anatomical region. It suggests the possibility that this trait develops in response to similar ontogenetic mechanisms and may serve a similar function in many of these taxa.

The bony postorbital enclosure observed in humans and other haplorhines is often conceptualized to comprise two distinct parts: a postorbital bar anteriorly (uniting frontal and zygomatic bones to form the lateral orbital margin), and the postorbital septum posteriorly (uniting frontal, zygomatic, and alisphenoid bones to partition the orbital fossa from behind). The temporal line, which indicates the superior extent of the proximal temporalis muscle insertion and the transition of temporalis fascia to periosteum, is a visible osteological feature that divides these two parts. In most cases, the postorbital bar is triangular in cross-section (Cartmill, 1980), and the postorbital septum is a thin layer of bone that conforms in shape to the contents of the orbit.

As noted, characteristics of postorbital anatomy across primates have always played a key role in evidence of phylogenetic relationships. In what is probably the most influential work on the topic, Cartmill (1980) addressed the question of homology of the postorbital septum in haplorhines. He considered anatomic structure of the septum in adult extant haplorhines and evaluated competing hypotheses about its function, in order to infer the evolutionary history of the septum. Cartmill provided an excellent comparative analysis of the septum in tarsiers, platyrrhines, and catarrhines, and laid out an argument that strepsirrhines, tarsiers, and anthropoids demonstrate a transformational series in postorbital septation (see also Hershkovitz, 1977). Strepsirrhines possess a postorbital bar, representing the ancestral state. Tarsiers display an intermediate conformation described as a partial postorbital septum, including a small articulation between zygomatic and alisphenoid bones. Finally, anthropoids represent the final stage with complete postorbital septation. Cartmill (1980, p. 245) illustrated a "pseudophylogenetic" series demonstrating the specific anatomical changes or potential trajectories in growth patterns that would be required to transform a strepsirrhine (*Galago*, bushbaby) postorbital bar to a tarsier partial postorbital septum, and from that configuration to an anthropoid (*Saimiri*, a squirrel monkey) complete postorbital septum (Figure 4.2). Specifically,

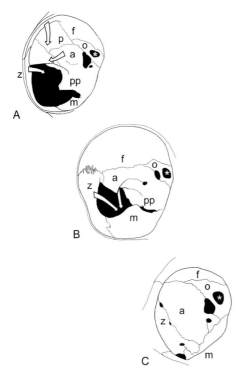

Figure 4.2 Schematic demonstration of Cartmill's (1980) hypothesized changes in postorbital anatomy. Anterior views of the right orbit are shown for (A) *Galago*, (B) *Tarsius*, and (C) *Saimiri*. Arrows illustrate transformations intended to represent an ordered set of character states. Used with permission from Cartmill (1980), figure 2, with modification based on personal observation. Key: f, frontal; z, zygomatic; m, maxilla; p, parietal; a, alisphenoid; o, orbitosphenoid; pp, pterygoid plates; *, optic canal.

he described small posterior processes from the frontal and zygomatic, and another from the alisphenoid between the superior orbital fissure and foramen rotundum that he observed in *Galago*, which (if expanded) would approximate the contributions of these bones in the tarsier orbit. Further, the continued inferior expansion of the alisphenoid and zygomatic processes would produce the elongated zygomatic–alisphenoid suture observed in anthropoids, along with complete postorbital septation and the complete separation of the orbital and temporal fossae.

In the transformational scenario that he proposed, Cartmill (1980) considered fascial planes and sites for potential bone growth that incorporated the surrounding soft tissues. These fascial planes included: the periorbita that surrounds and encloses the contents of the orbit, and the deep fascia of the anterior temporalis muscle. He described the triangular cross-section of the *Galago* postorbital bar, noting that the three surfaces of the postorbital bar are associated with three distinct soft tissue layers: medially, the periorbita; laterally, the subcutaneous tissue; and posteriorly, the deep fascia of the temporalis muscle. He further noted that growth of bone from the postorbital bar in *Galago* was most likely to occur at the posteromedial apex at the interface between periorbita and temporalis fascia.

Cartmill (1980) dismissed the possibility that formation of the postorbital septum was a side effect or by-product of snout reduction as had been previously proposed by Jones (1916). Instead, he adopted a functionalist approach to explain the appearance of postorbital septation in haplorhine primates. He reviewed many of the functions that had been proposed for this bony enclosure, including: support of the eyeball, protection of the eyeball, increased area for proximal insertion of temporalis muscle, and transmission of masticatory stresses. He continued by focusing on a fifth proposed function of postorbital septation, specifically that it acts to isolate the eye from displacement produced by the temporalis muscle. Haplorhine primates share the derived trait of retinal foveae, which are regions of the retina with a high density of photoreceptor cells, devoid of retinal capillaries, and contribute to visual acuity. Cartmill (1980) noted that retinal foveae occur in conjunction with at least some degree of postorbital septation in all living haplorhines. This combination, unique among mammals, suggested to him that the characteristics of muscle, eye, and bony orbit are linked. Based on this association, he hypothesized that postorbital septation is a functional adaptation that isolates the eyeball from masticatory muscles (his "insulation hypothesis"), therefore protecting an ability to discern fine visual detail during feeding. Retinal foveae are also observed in other non-mammalian animals (e.g., some birds), but Cartmill noted that the eye and temporalis muscle are not adjacent in these animals, obviating any adaptive need for formation of a postorbital septum. Nevertheless, multiple lines of evidence supported the notion that early anthropoids were increasingly reliant on visual acuity, and Cartmill's hypothesis that postorbital septation and mechanical isolation of the eye provided a selective advantage related to vision in early haplorhine primates was well reasoned and widely accepted.

Based on the assumption of homology and a single, unified function in the origin of the septum, Cartmill (1980) laid out a hypothesized evolutionary history.

First, homology of the septum suggests that it must be shared exclusively by the last common ancestor (LCA) of the tarsier/anthropoid clade. This hypothesis eliminates many of the Eocene omomyiform omomyids *sensu lato* (e.g., *Tetonius*, *Necrolemur*), which have only a postorbital bar, from being closely related to tarsiers, monophyletically. He argued that this conclusion was further supported by basicranial evidence (Cartmill and Kay, 1978). To offer a scenario explaining the origin of the tarsier/anthropoid LCA, Cartmill, like others, invoked the omomyids as a model ancestral stock. Omomyids were likely small nocturnal animals, many with fairly large eyes, eating insects and fruits (like galagos). Some omomyid relatives, it was proposed, shifted to a more *Saimiri*-like fruit-eating diurnal lifestyle. This context led to selective pressure favoring visual acuity, resulting in loss of the tapetum lucidum, which advantages night vision, and formation of an optic fovea and postorbital septation in the LCA of tarsiers and anthropoids. Afterwards, the tarsier lineage split off and reverted to an exclusively predatory nocturnal niche. In order to compensate for the earlier loss of a tapetum lucidum, the tarsiers developed very large eyes to increase the amount of light collected by the retina.

The essential element underlying this hypothesis is that postorbital septation represents a transformational series in primates, and this is premised on the assumption that the postorbital septum of tarsiers and anthropoids are homologous characters. However, a number of researchers have noted the differences in the shape and relative contribution of zygomatic, frontal, and alisphenoid to the postorbital septum, and determined that the differences are significant enough to deny the homology of septation in tarsiers and anthropoids. Simons and Russell (1960) described the structural anatomic differences in postorbital septation between tarsiers and anthropoids, stating that the septum in tarsiers is composed primarily of frontal and alisphenoid, whereas that in anthropoids is derived almost entirely from the zygomatic. This difference led them to conclude that that the postorbital septum had evolved independently in tarsiers and anthropoids. In response, Cartmill (1980) attributed their conclusion to an inaccurate portrayal of the frontal contribution to the septum and, instead, argued that the septum of *Tarsius* is formed primarily by the zygomatic, as in anthropoids. Further, he made the point that the presence of *any* alisphenoid contribution to the septum of tarsiers argues in favor of its homology with that of anthropoids.

Simons and Rasmussen (1989) addressed Cartmill's comments in a subsequent paper evaluating the tarsier–anthropoid clade in light of the Oligocene primate *Aegyptopithecus*. This taxon is confidently placed in Anthropoidea, and is well represented in the fossil record. Simons and Rasmussen discussed three characters that had been described as synapomorphies of an exclusive tarsier–anthropoid clade: (1) an apical interorbital septum; (2) the postorbital septum; and (3) a perbullar pathway for the internal carotid artery. They noted that *Aegyptopithecus* has a periorbital process of the zygomatic that articulates with the frontal and alisphenoid near the braincase. They also noted that the zygomatic of *Aegyptopithecus* makes a significantly greater contribution to the septum than that observed in tarsiers.

Simons and Rasmussen (1989) further considered fetal and young tarsiers and noted that they do not exhibit any posterior expansion of the frontal process of the zygomatic as seen in anthropoids. Instead, they described it as a narrow band of bone that was much more similar to the postorbital bar of strepsirrhines. They argued that the orbits of juvenile tarsiers resembled those of adult *Necrolemur*, as described in an earlier paper (Simons and Russell, 1960). Based on these observations, Simons and Rasmussen (1989) concluded that "the evolution of partial postorbital closure in tarsiers has resulted primarily from the expansion of periorbital flanges of the frontal and alisphenoid out to the postorbital bar" (p. 9).

Simons and Rasmussen (1989) also criticized Cartmill's conclusions regarding function of the postorbital septum, and identified multiple aspects of tarsier postorbital septation that are inconsistent with his insulation hypothesis. Specifically, they noted the maxillary flange on the inferior aspect of the orbit, and the circumorbital flanges of the frontal bone, both of which act to support the eyeball. They argued that, because they are not directly related to the temporalis or other masticatory muscles, these bony features have no apparent role in insulating the eyeball. Given that the structure and function of the septum in tarsiers appears to be distinct from that in anthropoids, Simons and Rasmussen (1989) concluded that evolution of the postorbital septum occurred independently in these two lineages. This, in combination with their observations on the variable appearance of the apical interorbital septum and the perbullar internal carotid artery, led them to conclude that there is no evidence to support an exclusive tarsier–anthropoid clade to the exclusion of Eocene fossil groups. Although they supported an adapid origin for Anthropoidea, they noted that their conclusions were also relevant for a phylogeny that includes an omomyid origin for anthropoids. In either case, they concluded that modern tarsiers are descended from large-eyed Eocene tarsiiforms as stated in their earlier work (Simons and Rasmussen, 1989, citing Simons and Russell, 1960).

Cartmill responded to Simons and Rasmussen (1989), acknowledging the lack of agreement in the scientific community on cladistic and gradistic issues regarding anthropoid origins (Cartmill, 1994a). He attributed these conflicts to underlying defects in the traditions of comparative morphological study, specifically the *a priori* determination of non-homology, which can be inappropriately used to skew the results of any phylogenetic analysis. He also called into question the common practice of redescribing anatomy that had already been well described in the literature. As an example, he criticized Simons and Rasmussen (1989) for redefining the anatomy to discount the cranial similarities shared by tarsiers and anthropoids, including specifically the way that they were defining the postorbital septum. Simons and Rasmussen (1989) appear to have included the entire postorbital bony enclosure in their scope, focusing on differences in the relative contribution of frontal, zygomatic, and alisphenoid. In contrast, Cartmill (1994a) argued that the postorbital septum should be considered as a whole, rather than emphasizing relative contributions of individual bone elements. However, he subsequently emphasized a more precise definition of the septum to include only that part of the postorbital bone enclosure bounded by the temporal line. In other words, he explicitly distinguished the postorbital bar and the postorbital septum in tarsiers (and other haplorhines). The temporal line marks the superior insertion of the temporalis fascia. It runs along the lateral wall of the neurocranium and extends rostrally onto the frontal bone. In strepsirrhines, this corresponds to the posterolateral edge of the postorbital bar. In haplorhines, this corresponds to a posterolateral ridge that merges inferiorly with the superior edge of the zygomatic arch.

We are left with two issues stemming from this debate. First, does the developmental evidence about tarsiers noted by Simons and Rasmussen (1989) affect our determination of homology of postorbital septation? The arguments they put forth on the basis of their observations of juvenile tarsiers suffered by lack of visual evidence of the character state in tarsiers that preceded eye growth. Our current work seeks to rectify that problem. Second, even if developmental evidence is suggestive of non-homology, should this evidence influence our choices *a priori* for phylogenetic analysis? Clearly, our anatomic descriptions are influenced by preconceived notions about development, function, homology, and phylogenetic relationships. Because of this inherent flaw in our character definitions, Cartmill (1994a,b) argued that a proper approach would be to collect discrete, objective observations (e.g., genetic data) en masse for phylogenetic analysis, and then determine homology post hoc from the phylogeny determined by the preponderance of evidence. However, only in limited circumstances are genetic data a feasible option to resolve the phylogenetic position of fossil forms. Conclusions from that analysis would be limited to inferences about fossil forms based primarily on living animals. Such an analysis would not be able to resolve the position of fossil omomyiform primates relative to the LCA of tarsiers and anthropoids. However, as Cartmill (1980, p. 256) stated, "If it could be shown that the septa of the various haplorhine groups are not homologous, it would be easier to develop a coherent set of hypotheses about their evolutionary histories."

More recent experimental and anatomical studies of the postorbital region in primates and other mammals have provided additional insight into the role of postorbital processes, postorbital bars, and postorbital septa. Comparative analyses of orbit orientation angles led Ross (1995a,b) to conclude that orbital convergence and frontation in anthropoids is the primary factor driving formation of the postorbital septum. In analyses of a broad sample of living and fossil primates, he found an allometric effect on orbit orientation and an inverse relationship of convergence and relative orbit size (Ross, 1995a). He also used dissection to study muscular attachments and infer transmission of muscular forces in a similarly broad sample of living primates (Ross, 1995b). Based on his findings in these studies, he concluded that the insulation function of postorbital septation may be independent of a need for pronounced visual acuity and may have arisen in the evolutionary history of primates *prior to* the occurrence of a retinal fovea (Ross, 1995a,b). Additional analyses of orbit orientation across a broader range of taxa have extended those results and provided support for this hypothesis (Noble *et al.*, 2000; Ravosa *et al.*, 2000), also addressing allometry as a factor (Ravosa & Savakova, 2004). In an extensive study of comparative postorbital anatomy across 16 mammalian orders, Heesy (2005) used landmark-based morphometric analyses and found that a decreased orbitotemporal angle was associated with more developed postorbital processes. Further, he determined that orbitotemporal angle was influenced primarily by reorientation of the orbit, in particular frontation (Heesy, 2005).

Other studies have used *in vivo* bone strain data and experimental models to study the role of postorbital anatomy. Ross and Hylander (1996) combined *in vivo* bone strain data with an *in vitro* experimental model in which the postorbital septa of an anthropoid primate had been cut. Their combined results proved equivocal regarding the contribution of the postorbital septum toward structural integrity during mastication and determined that expansion of the postorbital bar into a postorbital septum was unlikely to be driven by the need to dissipate forces related to feeding (Ross and Hylander, 1996). In another study using bone strain data, Ravosa and colleagues (2000) showed low (but not inconsequential) loading on the postorbital bar in galagos, inadequate to explain its observed strength, and concluded that other factors must play a role in driving expression of the postorbital bar. This study and related work by this research group are reviewed in detail by Ravosa *et al.* (2007). Menegaz and Kirk (2009) combined metric and anatomic data collected from owls and found support for the insulation hypothesis and an association with nocturnal predation. Additional experimental studies have considered the effect of masticatory loading on the postorbital ligament in animals with incomplete postorbital bars (pigs, Herring *et al.*, 2011; rabbits, Jašarević *et al.*, 2010). Finally, finite element analysis has been used to model the transmission of masticatory forces through the postorbital region (e.g., Nakashige *et al.*, 2011). However, despite continued focus on the functional role of postorbital anatomy, few have addressed function of the postorbital septum during growth and development of the skull (but see Ravosa, 1991; Smith *et al.*, 2013)

4.4   Ontogeny of Postorbital Septation in Tarsiers

Using a developmental series of *T. syrichta* specimens (four perinatal specimens from late fetal to six days postnatal, and one adult specimen), we have studied growth of the orbit. Infant specimens of strepsirrhines (e.g., *Eulemur*) and anthropoids (e.g., *Cebuella*) provided comparative data and were chosen as representative of their taxonomic groups. We also studied infant specimens of *Galago* sp. and *Saimiri* sp. to correspond to the specimens illustrated in Cartmill (1980). Most specimens were obtained from Duke Lemur Center. Computed tomography (CT) images allow us to visualize three-dimensional (3D) spatial anatomic relationships, and histological sections provide microstructural detail. A subset of the specimens have been previously damaged by necropsy or prior study, and some 3D reconstructions include virtual correction via transformation of volumetric or surface data using AMIRA software (FEI Vizualization, Inc.; see example reported in Lindsay *et al.*, 2015). Some of these findings have been reported elsewhere (Smith *et al.*, 2013; DeLeon et al., 2015, in press).

We have documented previously the surprising degree of eye hypertrophy that is delayed until the postnatal period in tarsiers (Cummings *et al.*, 2012). Prior to birth, although the relative size of the orbit is similar to that of generalized anthropoids, the relation of the orbit to braincase and dental arcade is quite different (DeLeon *et al.*, 2015). On the other hand, the size of the tarsier's orbits *and* their position relative to braincase and dental arcade appear very similar to the generalized strepsirrhine conformation at the same stage (Figure 4.3). Two notable structures

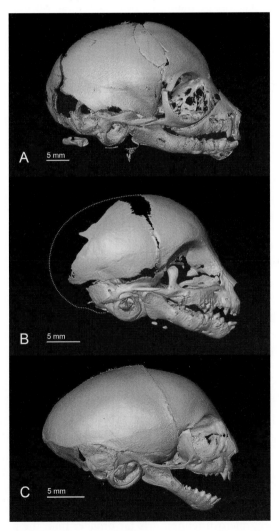

Figure 4.3 Neonatal specimens of (A) *Eulemur* (strepsirrhine), (B) *Tarsius*, and (C) *Cebuella* (anthropoid) skulls in right lateral view. The posterior contour of the skull is estimated by the dotted line in *Tarsius*, which was damaged postmortem. Note the similarity of relative orbit size among all specimens, and the similarity in relative position of orbit, neurocranium, and dentition between *Tarsius* and *Eulemur*, despite the closer phylogenetic relationship between *Tarsius* and *Cebuella*.

distinguish the tarsier orbit from strepsirrhines: first, the apparent loss of a frontal spur; and second, the appearance of a broad ligament in the path of the postorbital bar (Smith *et al.*, 2013). The perinatal tarsier orbit is also distinct from the anthropoid condition, and three of these features are highlighted here: lack of expansion of the zygomatic in the postorbital region, extension of an alisphenoid process toward the zygomatic, and minimal contribution of the alisphenoid and frontal to the interface between endocranial and orbital fossae. In fact, ontogeny of the orbit in tarsiers is unique among the mammals we have studied.

Comparison to Strepsirrhines. All perinatal strepsirrhines that we have studied display a zygomatic process of the frontal in the form of a *frontal spur* (Smith *et al.*, 2013). An analogous process is commonly found among other mammals, such as dogs and cats, even when they lack a postorbital bar. In strepsirrhines, this bony projection appears as a thin, narrow band originating along the superolateral quadrant of the orbital rim, lengthened to reach the ascending process of the zygomatic, and contoured to the shape of the lateral eyeball. It contains no diploe. The frontal spur is continuous with the transient postorbital ligament in fetal strepsirrhines. The frontal spur and the ascending process of the zygomatic maintain a constant anteroposterior width along their length, suggesting the complete postorbital bar may be produced by ossification of these two elements within the postorbital ligament. The strepsirrhine frontal spur is also notable in that it extends as a process inferiorly along the lateral margin of the orbit substantially below the orbital roof and the rest of the frontal bone. In contrast, this process appears to be significantly reduced in tarsiers and anthropoids (Figure 4.4). In both tarsiers and anthropoids, the remnant of the zygomatic process of the frontal bone is quite short and robust, with a diploe core and minimal extension of cortical bone. In some anthropoid infants (e.g., *Alouatta*), this process extends somewhat further, but not substantially more inferior than the rest of the frontal bone (DeLeon, personal observation).

The connection between the frontal and zygomatic bones in infant tarsiers is maintained by the *postorbital membrane* (POM). This fan-shaped ligament is composed of parallel bundles of collagen and contains both fibroblast and chondrocyte-like cells (Smith *et al.*, 2013). The POM extends from its inferior distal attachment on the ascending process of the zygomatic to its proximal attachment on the zygomatic process of the frontal bone, and reaches posteriorly to the anterolateral fontanelle at pterion. In older infant specimens, the proximal insertion of the POM extends posteriorly to the alisphenoid (DeLeon *et al.*, in press). We have suggested that the POM itself functions like a fontanelle, allowing rapid growth of the bony orbit in association with rapid expansion of the eyeball (Smith *et al.*, 2013). The POM is unique to tarsiers. Although it takes the form of a fan-shaped ligament (see Smith *et al.*, 2013, regarding microstructure), it is far broader than the postorbital ligament that precedes the formation of the postorbital bar in strepsirrhines. It also differs from the fully formed suture that characterizes hard tissue frontozygomatic articulation in infant anthropoids.

Comparison to Anthropoids. All perinatal anthropoids that we have studied display an expansive *posterior lamina of the zygomatic* enclosing the posterolateral wall of

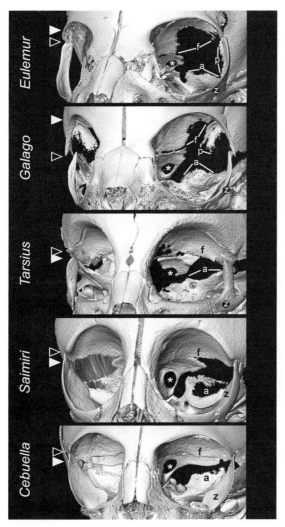

Figure 4.4 CT reconstructions of the orbital region in *Eulemur*, *Galago*, *Tarsius*, *Saimiri*, and *Cebuella*. In strepsirrhines (*Eulemur* and *Galago*), the zygomatic process of the frontal (black arrows) extends inferiorly beyond the neurocranial margin of the frontal (level indicated by white arrow). The opposite relationship is observed in tarsiers and anthropoids (*Saimiri* and *Cebuella*). Posterior cranial structures are intentionally erased from the left orbit to clarify orbital bone margins. Key: f, frontal; z, zygomatic; a, alisphenoid; p, parietal; *, optic canal.

the orbit. The robust, paddle-like zygomatic of the infant tarsier lacks this feature, and is instead much more similar to that of strepsirrhines (Figure 4.5). The ascending process of the zygomatic in anthropoids articulates with the frontal bone in the upper quadrant of the orbit. The anterior portion of this process along the lateral orbital rim is thickened, as if to withstand bending forces, comparable to a postorbital bar. Posteriorly, a thin sheet of bone (the posterior lamina) follows the contour of the orbital contents all the way to the neurocranium to articulate in an elongated

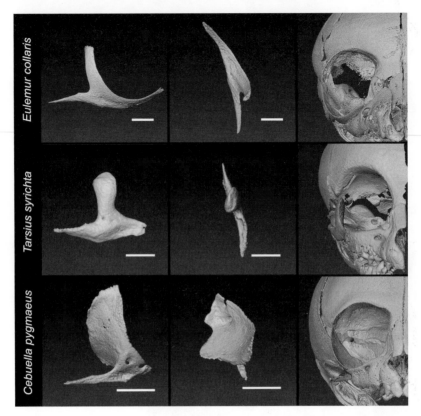

Figure 4.5 Zygomatic bone in infant *Eulemur*, *Tarsius*, and *Cebuella*. Right lateral (left column) and superior (middle column) views of the isolated zygomatic highlights distinct features of the ascending process in these taxa. The right column illustrates the position of the zygomatic (green in color plate) relative to the skull. Scale bars: *Eulemur* = 3 mm; *Tarsius* = 2 mm; *Cebuella* = 2 mm. A black and white version of this figure will appear in some formats. For the color version, please refer to the plate section.

suture with the alisphenoid. The frontozygomatic and zygomaticosphenoid sutures are continuous, and this posterior lamina separates the orbital and temporal fossae (Figures 4.4 and 4.5). In contrast, the zygomatic in tarsiers is much more limited, with no posterior lamina apparent through the oldest infant specimen that we studied (6 days old). The zygomatic is separated from the alisphenoid and the neurocranium by the length of the POM. Instead, the ascending process of the zygomatic (APZ) in the infant tarsier is paddle-shaped with a rounded superior edge at the connection to the POM. The medial (deep) face of the process is smooth and appears to be closely adjacent to the eyeball. The lateral (superficial) surface of the process is rounded. Prior to birth, when the eyeball is still of a relative size comparable to other primates, the APZ is oriented in a parasagittal plane. As the eyeball undergoes rapid growth in the postnatal period, the APZ appears to undergo modeling under the influence of pressure from the eyeball, rotating externally into a more coronal plane. By 6 days of age, the eye has grown substantially. There is no extension of the APZ as a posterior lamina, but a thin sheet of bone extends anterolaterally from the alisphenoid at the apparent proximal attachment of the POM. We have referred to this as the *alisphenoid slip* (DeLeon *et al.*, in press).

The *structure of the alisphenoid* in infant tarsiers is distinct from that in anthropoids in other respects, as well (see Figure 4.4). In all primates, the endocranial surface of the alisphenoid (greater wing of the sphenoid) is associated with the middle cranial fossa and the inferior and lateral contours of the temporal lobe of the brain. The lateral alisphenoid extends superiorly, separating the endocranial fossa internally from the temporal fossa externally. The anterior portion of the alisphenoid contributes to the orbital plate, which separates the endocranial fossa from the orbit. The orbital plate in anthropoids is substantial, reflecting an extensive shared interface between endocranial and orbital fossae. In contrast, the orbital plate of the alisphenoid in tarsiers is minimal. In a frontal view of the orbit in an infant tarsier, the alisphenoid is visible only as the axially oriented floor of the middle cranial fossa on the level of the foramen rotundum (consistent with descriptions in Cartmill, 1980; Schwartz *et al.*, 1978). The alisphenoid slip is actually an anterior extension of the calvarial surface of the alisphenoid in the temporal fossa.

The growth trajectory between our oldest perinatal specimen (6 days postnatal) and adult anatomy will require additional specimens to evaluate in detail. However, with the available specimens, we can make the following conclusions. First, volumetric expansion of the eyeball is associated with modeling of the cranial skeleton. Evidence of this modeling is apparent in the comparative anatomy of the 0-day-old, 6-day-old, and adult specimens. The transversely oriented orbital roof is transformed to an oblique orientation, effectively pushing the frontal lobes of the brain dorsally and posteriorly. The APZ is rotated from a parasagittal to a coronal plane. Our preliminary metric analyses also suggest that the dental arcade and the cranial base maintain a consistent spatial relationship, and that modeling occurs primarily in the frontal and zygomatic skeletal elements (DeLeon *et al.*, 2015).

Second, expansion of bony postorbital processes occurs in the fascial planes that are attached to them, as described by Cartmill (1980). The region for growth of the postorbital septum is constrained to fascial planes that connect the postorbital bar to other structures, including other bones. These fascial planes establish a framework within which ossification may occur. In this way, preexisting bony and soft tissue spatial relationships contain the range of potential morphological variation in the skeleton, particularly for structures formed by intramembranous ossification (Enlow and Hans, 1996). However, the specific identity of the membranes to which the postorbital bar connects (and could presumably expand) is not clear. Cartmill (1980) notes connections between the periorbital membrane and the postorbital bar. However, this has not been thoroughly studied in primates in our view, certainly not at the histological level.

Finally, ossification of the postorbital septum in the tarsier appears to result from forces transmitted by the postorbital membrane to its insertions on the frontal and alisphenoid bones (for mechanical induction of osteogenesis, see Herring & Teng, 2000; Henderson *et al.*, 2004). Ossification does not appear to be initiated at the zygomatic bone at these early stages. This suggests that the bony processes that complete the postorbital septum in tarsiers would not appear without the prior influence of eye hypertrophy. We propose that, absent the mechanical influence of eye hypertrophy, the bony connection of frontal and zygomatic would have eventually been established, but that the all-important contact of zygomatic and alisphenoid bones would never have formed.

4.5   Can Ontogeny Inform Our Understanding of Homology?

Homologues are identified based on similarities in location, form, function, and development (reviewed in Wagner, 2014). Many developmental processes are shared across living mammals, including cellular processes establishing the tetrapod bauplan and tissue interactions that produce the homologous elements of the skeleton (reviewed in, e.g., Hall, 1994 (multiple chapters)). Bones of the skull are derived from mesenchymal condensations, formation of cartilage precursors, and a combination of intramembranous and cartilaginous ossification (Enlow and Hans, 1996), and these bone elements and their precursors are conserved across related taxa (de Beer, 1937; also see Chapter 3 for detailed review of skull bone origins, development, and evolution). Early researchers recognized the logical expectation that homologous characters may diverge as distinct endpoints of similar developmental processes (e.g., Geoffroy Saint-Hilaire, 1818). In most cases, the "sameness" of a character in two organisms is inversely correlated with the time that has elapsed since the LCA of those taxa. More time allows the potential for more divergence in character states. Following the same logic, similarity in underlying developmental processes is also inversely correlated with the time since divergence from the LCA. Organisms sharing a recent LCA are expected to share more similar developmental mechanisms than more distantly related animals. As a result, the developmental processes themselves may be considered homologous.

The intersection of developmental and functional evidence arguably offers insight into how selection drives development (and not simply the resultant morphology). The utility of developmental data for recognizing homology is especially clear in cases where the adult morphology is difficult to compare between species due to their iterative nature or when structures are the result of multiple precursor elements combined. Two such examples are serial and composite structures.

Serial elements can be vexing to comparative morphologists because organisms may possess a different number of structures that develop in a sequence (e.g., vertebrae). In cases where differing numbers of segments are present (e.g., related primate taxa with 12 vs. 13 thoracic vertebrae), how can individual elements be said to be homologous? In part, the question is irrelevant to our current discussion because of the very nature of development of vertebrae. "Serial" homologues are similar at adjacent levels because of a similar regulatory control of development (Favier and Dollé, 1997), which leads to similar patterning of morphogenesis, and similar phenotype. Vertebrae and teeth have been thoroughly discussed elsewhere in this regard (Favier and Dollé, 1997; Maas and Bei, 1997; Jernvall and Thesleff, 2000, 2012). In recent years, the iterative nature of development of nasal turbinals has been described (Maier, 1993; Smith and Rossie, 2008; Maier and Ruf, 2014), presenting what may be another example in which determining homology of serial structures between species is rendered difficult. In all of these cases it is difficult (but not impossible, see Macrini, 2014) to determine how sequential structures within the series compare between species, especially where different numbers of elements eliminate the possibility of a one-to-one correspondence.

"Composite" osseous structures are those that form by the coalescence of multiple precursor elements, and present another example of developmental complexity that may make determination of homology difficult. One of the best-understood examples is the vertebrate lower jaw (reviewed in Maier and Ruf, 2015). The lower jaw of reptiles comprises multiple dermal bones; only the dentary bears teeth. In mammals this arrangement is fundamentally altered, such that only the dentary (plus some secondary cartilage) forms the lower jaw (other elements are derived as middle ear ossicles). Our understanding of vertebrate jaws based on location, form, and function is not fundamentally altered: the tooth-bearing portion of the lower jaw is the same in reptiles and mammals, but the elements of the composite lower jaw are not identical. The postorbital septum is another example of a composite structure. In all such cases, developmental data provide the narrative of how these complex structures emerge.

However, if there are *differences* in developmental pathways that yield a particular structure or trait, can we infer that the LCA did *not* share that structure? Some unquestionably homologous structures appear to be built using different developmental processes, even using differing precursor tissues (Hall, 1995). Common examples include the regeneration of the tail in anoles, and digit formation in urodeles and other tetrapods. As a result, there has been considerable skepticism over the use of developmental evidence in the determination of *non*-homology. In a discussion of literature on "biological homology," Hall (1999, p. 349) noted: "Although common developmental processes may aid in the identification of homologous structures, *lack of common development* neither speaks for or against homology" (emphasis added). These convincing examples lead some researchers to dismiss out of hand any developmental evidence from consideration of homology (e.g., Richmond and Strait, 2001). However, this ignores the potentially informative evidence to be gained from understanding the ontogenetic origin of morphological traits.

Homology requires continuity of information not only from individual to individual through phylogenies, but also continuity of information through ontogeny within an individual (Van Valen, 1982). Morphological characters are not made out of whole cloth, but must modify existing developmental mechanisms and growth trajectories to produce the features that characterize a given organism. Hypotheses regarding the homology of two traits in different organisms must acknowledge the practical necessity of getting from Point A to Point B. How can we resolve the dilemma presented by the requirement for ontogenetic continuity on the one hand, and the numerous examples of homologous structures formed by different developmental mechanisms on the other? If we are presented with similar traits in two related taxa that are shown to involve different developmental processes, do we have to ignore the developmental evidence? Or can we hypothesize a chain of ontogenetic and phylogenetic continuity consistent with the homology of that trait (i.e., shared with the LCA). If we find that chain of continuity to be unlikely, then we have to allow for the possibility of homoplasy (i.e., parallel evolution) and the conclusion that the trait is not shared with the LCA. The challenge of distinguishing homology and homoplasy in primate evolution was addressed by Hall (2007) in a special issue of the *Journal of Human Evolution* that includes many papers on this topic.

If the tarsier partial postorbital septum and the anthropoid postorbital septum are truly homologous, then there must be both phylogenetic *and* ontogenetic continuity in postorbital anatomy among modern tarsiers, anthropoids, and the tarsier–anthropoid LCA. Developmental evidence allows us to assess the plausibility of this hypothesis. It offers a literal framework for developing realistic scenarios of how this composite morphological structure may have changed through evolutionary time. The ontogenetic data described above illustrate that the postorbital bony enclosure of primates forms in a preexisting framework of periorbita, temporalis fascia, and in some cases, postorbital ligament or membrane. In tarsiers and anthropoids, osteogenic fronts at frontal, zygomatic, and alisphenoid contribute to ossification of this complex structure. In the case of the neonate tarsier, the separation of the zygomatic from the neurocranium, the lack of a posterior lamina that could contribute to postorbital septation, and the presence of a fontanelle-like arrangement of soft tissue – rather than bone – closing the compartment posteriorly provide evidence that the osseous postorbital septum might not form in the absence of (postnatal) eye hypertrophy (Figure 4.6). Given this information, we propose the following three scenarios regarding the evolution of tarsier and anthropoid orbits. Note that all three of these scenarios are predicated on the assumption that the mechanisms of ossification, specifically intramembranous ossification, are conserved in the postorbital region, and only the external forces that initiate and maintain bone growth and modeling differ.

Scenario 1 – Homology (Eye Hypertrophy). If eye hypertrophy is prerequisite for postorbital septation in the tarsier lineage, one could hypothesize that the LCA shared with anthropoids also had large eyes. Adaptations relating to this morphology would establish the functional basis for postorbital septation. Both are maintained in the tarsier lineage. In the anthropoid lineage, eye hypertrophy is lost, but the postorbital septum is maintained, with or without the same functional significance.

Scenario 2 – Homology (Mechanical Loading). Postorbital septation in the last common ancestor of extant haplorhines occurred independent of eye hypertrophy. Septation occurs by the confluence of bony laminae from the zygomatic and/or alisphenoid. This feature forms prenatally, likely in response to mechanical loads transmitted via fascial planes and possibly as a result of spatial relationships of eye and temporalis muscle. Other functional requirements may also contribute to the adaptive potential of this feature (e.g., isolation of the foveate eye). In the tarsier lineage, eye hypertrophy influences delayed ossification of the postorbital septum. In this scenario, the last common ancestor of haplorhines would have a partial or complete postorbital septum.

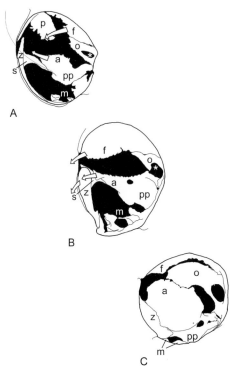

Figure 4.6 Schematic illustration of perinatal postorbital anatomy. Anterior views of the right orbit are shown for perinatal specimens of (A) *Galago*, (B) *Tarsius*, and (C) *Saimiri*. In panel (A), arrows indicate the lateral expansion of frontal and alisphenoid bone in the galago that would be required to produce a tarsier-like orbit. The zygomatic does not undergo significant expansion, although it does become paddle-shaped in the tarsier. In panel (B), arrows indicate the trajectory of growth observed in the tarsier as a result of eye hypertrophy. The zygomatic does not show the expansion expected by Cartmill's (1980) model until *after* the onset of eye hypertrophy. Panel (C) shows the "complete" status of the postorbital septum attained in an anthropoid by a comparable developmental stage in the absence of eye hypertrophy. Key: f, frontal; z, zygomatic; m, maxilla (or exposed molar cusps); p, parietal; a, alisphenoid; o, orbitosphenoid; pp, pterygoid plates; s, squamosal; *, optic canal.

Scenario 3 – Parallel Evolution. The LCA of extant haplorhines does *not* have postorbital septation. This septation evolves in the tarsier lineage as a postnatal response to eye hypertrophy. In the anthropoid lineage, septation evolves as a feature that forms prenatally, arguably in response to mechanical loads transmitted via fascial planes and possibly as a result of orbit orientation and spatial relationships of eye and temporalis muscle that are unique to anthropoids. In this scenario, a fossil representing the LCA of haplorhines would show evidence of a postorbital bar, or possibly an incomplete postorbital bar.

The case of postorbital anatomy in primates highlights the potential role for ontogenetic evidence in evaluating lack of homology. Similarity in developmental processes is one possible mechanism for parallel evolution in primate crania; specifically, a mechanistic explanation for homoplasy. *Differences* in development are relevant to the extent that they are consistent or conflict with scenarios for ontogenetic continuity in a given clade. As a result, ontogeny provides necessary information for developing hypotheses about homology (or *lack* of homology) that are subject to further testing.

4.6   Anthropological Implications

Ever since Darwin, by studying living forms and the fossil record, anthropologists have sought to understand the deep-time origins of humans within the Order Primates as a means to comprehend how human anatomy and behavior were assembled over time. Identifying the branch of the primate phylogenetic tree that first initiated the novelties distinguishing our most remote ancestors – anthropoids – from primates that represent an alternative span of the tree, and may share more in common with non-primate mammals, has been a powerful theme. The living tarsiers, a small group of species whose anatomy is nothing short of bizarre when compared with hominins, apes, and the more familiar monkeys, has long been held to be a key that can unlock this puzzle. Serendipitously, the morphology of the cranium, one of evolution's richest sources of information, is the region that has been central to this question from more than a century.

For anthropoids, our results neither contradict nor confirm the functional interpretation of the postorbital septum as providing insulation of the orbital contents proposed by Cartmill (1980) and further developed by others (e.g., Ross, 1995a,b; Heesy, 2005). Instead, they challenge the relevance of this explanation for tarsiers. Our results demonstrate that orbital morphology in the tarsier is more similar to that of strepsirrhines at early developmental stages, prior to eye hypertrophy. From this, one could infer that postorbital ossification might be limited to a strepsirrhine-like postorbital bar in a tarsier ancestor that did not display such massive eye growth. This has important phylogenetic implications. The debate between Cartmill and Simons and colleagues described above (i.e., Simons and Russell, 1960; Cartmill, 1980, 1994a; Simons and Rasmussen, 1989) is framed in the context of anthropoid origins and the definition of cranial characters used to determine the relative position of fossil taxa in the clade Haplorhini. If the postorbital septum is a synapomorphy of the tarsier-anthropoid clade, then the Eocene tarsiiform omomyids that have only a postorbital bar are excluded from this group. On the other hand, if the postorbital septum of tarsiers and anthropoids developed independently, and possibly to serve different functions, then modern tarsiers may be derived from one of those Eocene omomyiforms, challenging anthropoid origins scenarios based on the tarsier–anthropoid hypothesis. This also would leave expectations for the postorbital anatomy of the earliest anthropoids unresolved.

If developmental evidence casts doubt on a proposed scenario for the ontogenetic continuity of characters, then it becomes relevant for a hypothesis of *lack of* homology and therefore cannot be dismissed in comparative studies. In a broader sense, therefore, the debate over postorbital septation illuminates the more philosophical discussion of how useful information about ontogenetic trajectories actually is for determining homology, and whether deeply probing such information should be considered a necessary step in phylogenetic analyses, especially when other indicators suggest the presence of widespread homoplasy in the group under study.

4.7   Acknowledgments

We thank Chris Percival and Joan Richtsmeier for inviting us to contribute to this volume and participate in the excellent symposium on which it was based. Their suggestions to improve the manuscript, along with the insightful comments of two reviewers, were greatly appreciated. We are grateful to Mary Silcox and Callum Ross for conversations that helped to clarify our position regarding how ontogeny can inform homology. We thank Chris Vinyard and Jesse Young for providing CT scans of the specimens studied. This research was made possible by National Science Foundation grants BCS-1231717, BCS-1231350, and BCS-0959438.

References

Cartmill, M. (1980). Morphology, function, and evolution of the anthropoid postorbital septum. *In:* Ciochon, R. L. and Chiarelli, A. (eds.)*Evolutionary Biology of the New World Monkeys and Continental Drift*. New York, NY: Plenum Press, pp. 243–274.

Cartmill, M. (1994a). Anatomy, antinomies, and the problem of anthropoid origins. *In:* Fleagle, J. G. and Kay, R. F. (eds.) *Anthropoid Origins*. New York, NY: Plenum, pp. 549–566.

Cartmill, M. (1994b). A critique of homology as a morphological concept. *American Journal of Physical Anthropology*, 94(1), 115–123.

Cartmill, M. and Kay, R. (1978). Cranio-dental morphology, tarsier affinities, and primate suborders. *In:* Chivers, D. and Joysey, J. (eds.) *Recent Advances in Primatology*, 3rd ed. London: Academic Press, pp. 205–214.

Cummings, J. R., Muchlinski, M. N., Kirk, E. C., *et al.* (2012). Eye size at birth in prosimian primates: life history correlates and growth patterns. *PloS ONE*, 7(5), e36097.

Cuvier, J. L. (1798). *Tableau élémentaire de l'histoire naturelle des animaux*. Baudouin Freres.

De Beer, G. R. (1937). *The Development of the Vertebrate Skull*. Chicago, IL: University of Chicago Press (reprinted 1971).

DeLeon, V. B., Smith, T. D. and Rosenberger, A. L. (2015). Changing perspectives: ontogeny of facial orientation and eye hypertrophy in tarsiers [Abstract]. *American Journal of Physical Anthropology*, 156, 118–118.

DeLeon, V. B., Smith, T. D. and Rosenberger, A. L. (in press). Ontogeny of the postorbital region in tarsiers and other primates. *The Anatomical Record*.

Enlow, D. H. and Hans, M. G. (1996). *Essentials of Facial Growth*. Philadelphia, PA: WB Saunders Company.

Favier, B. and Dolle, P. (1997). Developmental functions of mammalian Hox genes. *Molecular Human Reproduction*, 3(2), 115–131.

Fleagle, J. G. (2013). *Primate Adaptation and Evolution*, 3rd ed. New York, NY: Academic Press.

Fox, R. C. and Scott, C. S. (2011). A new, early Puercan (earliest Paleocene) species of *Purgatorius* (Plesiadapiformes, Primates) from Saskatchewan, Canada. *Journal of Paleontology*, 85(3), 537–548.

Geoffroy Saint-Hilaire, E. (1818). *Philosophie Anatomique*. Paris: J.B. Baillière.

Godinot, M. (2015). Fossil record of the Primates from the Paleocene to the Oligocene. In: Henke, W. and Tattersall, I. (eds.) *Handbook of Paleoanthropology*, 2d ed. Berlin: Springer, pp. 1137–1259.

Hall, B. K. (1994). *Homology: The Hierarchial Basis of Comparative Biology.* San Diego, CA: Academic Press.

Hall, B. K. (1995). Homology and embryonic development. *Evolutionary Biology,* 28, 1–37.

Hall, B. K. (1999). *Evolutionary Developmental Biology,* 2d ed. Dordrecht: Kluwer Academic Publishers.

Hall, B. K. (2007). Homoplasy and homology: dichotomy or continuum? *Journal of Human Evolution,* 52(5), 473–479.

Hartig, G., Churakov, G., Warren, W. C., *et al.* (2013). Retrophylogenomics place tarsiers on the evolutionary branch of anthropoids. *Scientific Reports,* 3, 1756.

Heesy, C. P. (2005). Function of the mammalian postorbital bar. *Journal of Morphology,* 264(3), 363–380.

Henderson, J. H., Longaker, M. T. and Carter, D. R. (2004). Sutural bone deposition rate and strain magnitude during cranial development. *Bone,* 34(2), 271–280.

Hennig, W. (1950). *Grundzuge einer Theorie der phylogenetischen Systematik.* Berlin: Deutscher Zentralverlag.

Herring, S. W. and Teng, S. (2000). Strain in the braincase and its sutures during function. *American Journal of Physical Anthropology,* 112(4), 575–593.

Herring, S. W., Rafferty, K. L., Liu, Z. J. and Lemme, M. (2011). Mastication and the postorbital ligament: dynamic strain in soft tissues. *Integrative and Comparative Biology,* p.icr023.

Hershkovitz, P. (1977). *Living New World Monkeys (Platyrrhini).* Chicago, IL: University of Chicago Press.

Hillman, D. (1975). Equine osteology: skull. *In:* Getty, R. (ed.) *Sisson and Grossman's Anatomy of the Domestic Animals,* 5th ed. Philadelphia, PA: WB Saunders, pp. 318–348.

Illiger, C. (1811). *Prodromus systematis mammalium et avium additis terminis zoographicis utriudque classis.* Berlin: C. Salfeld.

Jašarević, E., Ning, J., Daniel, A. N., *et al.* (2010). Masticatory loading, function, and plasticity: a microanatomical analysis of mammalian circumorbital soft-tissue structures, *The Anatomical Record,* 293(4), 642–650.

Jernvall, J. and Thesleff, I. (2000). Reiterative signaling and patterning during mammalian tooth morphogenesis. *Mechanisms of Development,* 92(1), 19–29.

Jernvall, J. and Thesleff, I. (2012). Tooth shape formation and tooth renewal: evolving with the same signals. *Development,* 139(19), 3487–3497.

Jones, F. W. (1916). *Arboreal Man.* London: E. Arnold.

Kleisner, K. (2007). The formation of the theory of homology in biological sciences. *Acta Biotheoretica,* 55(4), 317–340.

Lindsay, K. E., Rühli, F. J. and DeLeon, V. B. (2015). Revealing the face of an ancient Egyptian: synthesis of current and traditional approaches to evidence-based facial approximation. *The Anatomical Record,* 298(6), 1144–1161.

Maas, R. and Bei, M. (1997). The genetic control of early tooth development. *Critical Reviews in Oral Biology and Medicine,* 8(1), 4–39.

Macrini, T. E. (2014). Development of the ethmoid in *Caluromys philander* (Didelphidae, Marsupialia) with a discussion on the homology of the turbinal elements in marsupials. *The Anatomical Record,* 297(11), 2007–2017.

Maier, W. (1993). Cranial morphology of the therian common ancestor, as suggested by the adaptations of neonate marsupials. *In:* Szalay, F. S., Novacek, M. J. and McKenna, M. C. (eds.) *Mammal Phylogeny: Mesozoic Differentiation, Multituberculates, Monotremes, Early Therians, and Marsupials.* New York, NY: Springer-Verlag, pp. 165–181.

Maier, W. and Ruf, I. (2014). Morphology of the nasal capsule of primates – with special reference to *Daubentonia* and *Homo. The Anatomical Record,* 297(11), 1985–2006.

Maier, W. and Ruf, I. (2015). Evolution of the mammalian middle ear: a historical review. *Journal of Anatomy,* 228(2), 270–283.

Martin, R. D. (1990). *Primate Origins and Evolution: A Phylogenetic Reconstruction.* London: Chapman and Hall.

Menegaz, R. A. and Kirk, E. C. (2009). Septa and processes: convergent evolution of the orbit in haplorhine primates and strigiform birds. *Journal of Human Evolution,* 57(6), 672–687.

Nakashige, M., Smith, A. L. and Strait, D. S. (2011). Biomechanics of the macaque postorbital septum investigated using finite element analysis: implications for anthropoid evolution. *Journal of Anatomy*, 218(1), 142–150.

Noble, V. E., Kowalski, E. M. and Ravosa, M. J. (2000). Orbit orientation and the function of the mammalian postorbital bar. *Journal of Zoology*, 250(3), 405–418.

Owen, R. (1848). *On the Archetype and Homologies of the Vertebrate Skeleton*. London: J. Van Voorst.

Patterson, C. (1982). Morphological characters and homology. *Problems of Phylogenetic Reconstruction*, 21, 21–74.

Pocock, R. (1918). On the external characters of the lemurs and of *Tarsius*. *Proceedings of the Zoological Society of London*, 88(1), 19–53.

Raaum, R. L. (2015). Molecular evidence on primate origins and primate evolution. *In:* Henke, W. and Tattersall, I. (eds.)*Handbook of Paleoanthropology*, 2d ed., Berlin: Springer, pp. 1083–1135.

Ravosa, M. J. (1991). Ontogenetic perspective on mechanical and nonmechanical models of primate circumorbital morphology. *American Journal of Physical Anthropology*, 85(1), 95–112.

Ravosa, M. J. and Savakova, D. G. (2004). Euprimate origins: the eyes have it. *Journal of Human Evolution*, 46(3), 355–362.

Ravosa, M. J., Noble, V. E., Hylander, W. L., Johnson, K. R. and Kowalski, E. M. (2000). Masticatory stress, orbital orientation and the evolution of the primate postorbital bar. *Journal of Human Evolution*, 38(5), 667–693.

Ravosa, M. J., Savakova, D. G., Johnson, K. R. and Hylander, W. L. (2007). Primate origins and the function of the circumorbital region: what's load got to do with it? *In: Primate Origins: Adaptations and Evolution*. New York, NY: Springer, pp. 285–328.

Richmond, B. G. and Strait, D. S. (2001). Reply: Did our ancestors knuckle-walk? *Nature*, 410(6826), 326–326.

Ross, C. F. (1995a). Allometric and functional influences on primate orbit orientation and the origins of the Anthropoidea. *Journal of Human Evolution*, 29(3), 201–227.

Ross, C. F. (1995b). Muscular and osseous anatomy of the primate anterior temporal fossa and the functions of the postorbital septum. *American Journal of Physical Anthropology*, 98(3), 275–306.

Ross, C. F. (2000). Into the light: the origin of Anthropoidea. *Annual Review of Anthropology*, 29, 147–194.

Ross, C. F. and Hylander, W. L. (1996). *In vivo* and *in vitro* bone strain in the owl monkey circumorbital region and the function of the postorbital septum. *American Journal of Physical Anthropology*, 101(2), 183–215.

Schwartz, J. H., Tattersall, I. and Eldredge, N. (1978). Phylogeny and classification of the primates revisited. *Yearbook of Physical Anthropology*, 21(1978), 95–133.

Silcox, M. T., Sargis, E. J., Bloch, J. I. and Boyer, D. M. (2015). Primate origins and supraordinal relationships: morphological evidence. *In:* Henke , W. and Tattersall, I. (eds.) *Handbook of Paleoanthropology*, 2d ed. Berlin: Springer, pp. 1053–1081.

Simons, E. L. and Rasmussen, D. T. (1989). Cranial morphology of *Aegyptopithecus* and *Tarsius* and the question of the tarsier–anthropoidean clade. *American Journal of Physical Anthropology*, 79(1), 1–23.

Simons, E. L. and Russell, D. (1960). Notes on the cranial anatomy of *Necrolemur*. *Breviora*, 127, 1–14.

Smith, T. D. and Rossie, J. B. (2008). Nasal fossa of mouse and dwarf lemurs (Primates, Cheirogaleidae). *The Anatomical Record*, 291(8), 895–915.

Smith, T. D., DeLeon, V. B. and Rosenberger, A. L. (2013). At birth, tarsiers lack a postorbital bar or septum. *The Anatomical Record*, 296(3), 365–377.

Szalay, F. S. and Delson, E. (1979). *Evolutionary History of the Primates*. New York, NY: Academic Press.

Szalay, F. S., Rosenberger, A. L. and Dagosto, M. (1987). Diagnosis and differentiation of the order Primates. *American Journal of Physical Anthropology*, 30(S8), 75–105.

Van Valen, L. M. (1982). Homology and causes. *Journal of Morphology*, 173(3), 305–312.

Wagner, G. P. (2014). *Homology, Genes, and Evolutionary Innovation*. Princeton, NJ: Princeton University Press.

5 Exploring Modern Human Facial Growth at the Micro- and Macroscopic Levels

Sarah E. Freidline, Cayetana Martinez-Maza, Philipp Gunz and Jean-Jacques Hublin

5.1 Introduction

A main goal in biological anthropology is to understand how adult morphology is attained through development. During craniofacial growth, complex interactions occur between different skeletal components largely resulting in bone displacement (e.g., relocation, primary and secondary displacements, and rotations). Facial bones are tightly associated with functional spaces, such as the oral and nasal complex and brain. Therefore, the movement (i.e., change in relative location due to growth) of the skeletal elements occur in response to the growth of these organs as well as to neighboring bones in order to maintain proper bone alignment (Moss and Young, 1960). Along these lines, it has been shown that there is a temporal sequence of craniofacial maturation largely related to the differential development of neural and somatic growth (Moss and Young, 1960; Humphrey, 1998; Bastir and Rosas, 2004; Bastir *et al.*, 2006; Bastir, 2008; Enlow and Hans, 2008). The cranial skeletal structures to mature first are those associated with brain, spinal and orbital growth, followed by the mid-facial region and parts of the cranial base, and lastly those associated with the masticatory apparatus (Humphrey, 1998).

Bone modeling takes place throughout life and in particular during development (Figure 5.1). Bone modeling consists of the activity of two cellular groups: osteoblasts (bone formation cells), and osteoclasts (bone resorption cells). Both cellular activities can be identified on the bone surface either as collagen fiber bundles (bone formation) or concavities called Howship's lacunae (resorption). Using microscopy, one can observe the distribution of these fields to obtain individual bone modeling patterns or maps (Bromage, 1989; Enlow and Hans, 2008; Martinez-Maza *et al.*, 2010).

The pioneering work of Enlow (1962, 1963, 1966a, 1966b) showed that structural differences in human and macaque craniofacial skeletons are reflected in specific patterns of bone growth modeling fields. While Enlow's innovative studies on the growth and modeling of the human face were significant contributions to the fields of anthropology, human anatomy, and orthodontics, his samples were restricted because he used cross-sectional histology, an invasive technique. Boyde

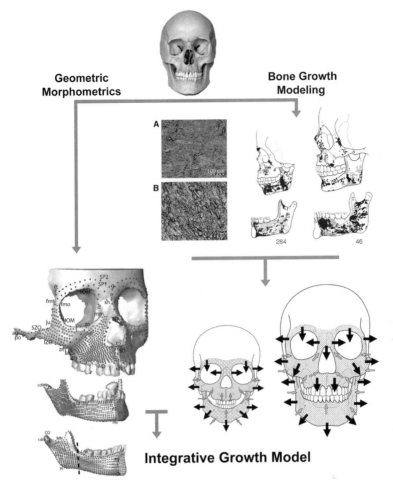

Figure 5.1 Integrative growth model combining geometric morphometric and bone modeling methods. Geometric morphometric analysis: landmarks and curve and surface semilandmarks on the face and mandible used in the geometric morphometric analysis. Red: homologous landmarks; blue: curve semilandmarks; and green: surface semilandmarks. Homologous landmarks (lowercase) and curves (capitalized) are abbreviated and labeled in the figure. The full names of the landmarks, and curves, and surface semilandmarks, and their definitions are listed in Table 5.1. The dashed line on the mandible represents the mandibular corpus and ramus division used in mandibular subset analyses (see text for more details). Bone growth modeling: left: (A) bone formation surface characterized by collagen fiber bundles; (B) bone resorption surfaces characterized by Howship's lacunae (scale bar: 100 μm); right: bone modeling map of external surface of cranial bones made for individual specimens. Bone formation surfaces are shown in black and bone resorption surfaces are shown in gray, while the white areas indicate damaged bone surfaces with no histological data. Generalized bone modeling maps (stippled areas represent bone deposition and gray areas represent bone resorption) are derived from individual patterns and are shown on immature and mature skulls (bottom) and are used to predict growth trajectories (arrows). A black and white version of this figure will appear in some formats. For the color version, please refer to the plate section.

and coworkers soon demonstrated that scanning electron microscopy (SEM) could be used to view surface modeling (Boyde and Hobdell, 1969; Boyde, 1972) and later Bromage (1984, 1985, 1987) implemented high-resolution replicas of the original bone surfaces to study the surface features that result from the process of cranio-facial growth in hominin fossils. Since then, non-destructive studies of craniofacial bone growth modeling have been executed on extant monkeys, chimpanzees and extant and fossil humans (Bromage, 1989; O'Higgins *et al.*, 1991; Walters and O'Higgins, 1992; McCollum and Ward, 1997; O'Higgins and Jones, 1998; McCollum, 1999, 2008; Rosas and Martinez-Maza, 2010; Martinez-Maza *et al.*, 2011, 2013, 2015; Lacruz *et al.*, 2013). Together, these studies suggest that variation in craniofacial bone growth modeling patterns occurs at the species level.

Surface bone modeling studies and associated growth directions are usually interpreted in the framework originally described by Enlow (1962, 1963, 1966a, 1966b). Here the term "growth by bone modeling" is defined as cellular processes responsible for the building up of new bone tissue. Given some bone geometries, the combination of bone formation on one surface and resorption on the surface of the opposite side causes growth movement in the direction of bone-forming surfaces called cortical drift, resulting in repositioning of bone through ontogeny. Consequently, the distribution and direction of surface modeling fields can be indicative of the direction of bone displacement. Therefore, it is generally assumed that bone modeling patterns at a microstructural level correspond to large-scale morphological changes (e.g., Enlow and Hans, 2008).

In a recent publication, one of us (CMM) carried out the first comprehensive bone modeling analysis on the mandible and facial skeleton in a sample of human specimens of various ages (Martinez-Maza *et al.*, 2013). The results revealed differences in growth dynamics between subadults and adults, from a primarily downward displacement before adulthood to a more forward displacement into adulthood. In addition, Martinez-Maza and colleagues (2013) found that the bone modeling patterns were more variable in the nasomaxillary region of the facial skeleton and the mandibular ramus across subadult and adult specimens compared to the zygomatic, the upper face (superciliary arches and glabella), and the mandibular corpus.

As of now, surface bone modeling studies have been descriptive and qualitative, reflecting the last activities of the osteoblasts and osteoclasts in a specific temporal window during the development of the organism. Integrating geometric morphometric (GM) techniques into the interpretation of bone modeling studies offers an additional piece of information to the dynamic component by enabling one to examine bone growth through displacement (O'Higgins and Jones, 1998). At the same time, GM studies can benefit from the direct evidence of bone growth activity provided in bone modeling studies. First, however, the correspondence between these two methods, bone modeling at the microstructural level and large-scale shape changes, must be evaluated.

Advances in GM approaches (O'Higgins, 2000; Adams *et al.*, 2004, 2013; Slice, 2005) have provided novel tools for the investigation of research problems of interest to biological anthropologists. For example, by applying surface semilandmarks one can visualize subtle morphological differences between individuals (Freidline *et al.*, 2012a, 2013). Moreover, GM methods allow one to separate changes in size and shape from changes in shape alone thereby providing another powerful perspective on studies of ontogeny (Mitteroecker *et al.*, 2004; Mitteroecker and Gunz, 2009). As is common in GM studies, we define growth as changes in size and shape (i.e., form), and development as changes in shape during ontogeny (Mitteroecker *et al.*, 2013). Using this methodology one can explore how size and shape, not solely age, covary with bone modeling patterns.

Here we use semilandmark GM methods to capture bone growth and displacement in the same sample of skulls analyzed by Martinez-Maza and colleagues (2013). First, we explore whether variation in bone modeling is also reflected in GM data by evaluating three of the main results found by Martinez-Maza *et al.* (2013): (1) growth is more variable in the nasomaxillary region compared to the zygomatic and upper face; (2): growth is more variable in the mandibular ramus compared to the corpus; and (3) there is more variation in subadults than in adults. Additionally, we explore correspondences between bone modeling patterns during ontogeny and facial shape, form (shape and size), and ontogenetic age.

5.2   Materials and Methods

5.2.1   Sample

The sample (Table 5.1) consists of the same skulls of subadult and adult human specimens from the Department of Life Sciences of the University of Coimbra analyzed by Martinez-Maza *et al.* (2013). Sex and calendar ages for all specimens in this collection are known. Individual ages range from 7 to 38 years and an equal number of males and females were analyzed. Because of the small sample sizes in the original study by Martinez-Maza *et al.* (2013), we chose to pool male and females in all analyses, recognizing that males and females may age and grow differently.

5.2.2   Histological Data

Bone surface replicas were made of the entire facial and mandibular skeleton using non-destructive silicone material. From these negative replicas a positive cast was made and observed under a reflected light microscope. Fields of bone modeling, formation, and resorption were identified on each specimen following the criteria provided by Martinez-Maza and colleagues (2010), among others (Boyde, 1972; Bromage, 1989). All specimens presented regions of slightly damaged bone surface where bone modeling patterns could not be clearly identified. Bone modeling maps illustrating the distribution of bone formation and resorption were drawn for each individual (Figure 5.1, upper right) and generalized modeling patterns for the subadult and adult groups were then established by eye according to intraspecific similarities in the bone modeling field distribution for

Table 5.1 Individuals used in the geometric morphometric and bone modeling analyses adapted from Martinez-Maza *et al.* (2013).

Specimen	Age (years)	Age group	Age group[1]	Sex
101	12	Subadult	2	Female
218	10	Subadult	1	Female
284	17	Subadult	2	Female
100	7	Subadult	1	Male
100A	11	Subadult	1	Male
126	8	Subadult	1	Male
52	38	Adult	3	Female
144	29	Adult	3	Female
342	28	Adult	3	Female
46	38	Adult	3	Male
92	27	Adult	3	Male
98	24	Adult	3	Male

[1] Age groups are defined according to dental eruption. Age group 1 is defined as individuals that have a first permanent molar erupted; Age group 2, second permanent molar erupted; and Age Group 3, third permanent molar erupted (i.e., adults).

each anatomical region (Figure 5.1, lower right). A detailed account of the methods can be found in Martinez-Maza *et al.* (2013).

A caveat to surface bone modeling studies is that while the bone modeling pattern reflects the last bone growth activities at the age of death we cannot say at what age exactly a bone modeling field stopped its activity. Boyde (1972) and Bromage (1989) indicate that it is possible to distinguish between active and inactive modeling activities; however, the identification of this in osteological collections is difficult as they usually show altered bone surfaces resulting from taphonomic processes and/or manipulation during laboratory analyses. Along these lines, the "adult" bone modeling pattern in our histological study could actually represent the moment at which the individual became skeletally mature, near the termination of growth (i.e., late adolescence or early adulthood), or the patterns could represent facial displacements in adulthood as most facial sutures remain patent until late adulthood (e.g., the frontomaxillary, nasomaxillary, and zygomaticomaxillary) and do not start to fuse until the seventh or eighth decade of life (Rice, 2008). For the sake of simplicity, we refer to changes in size and shape (i.e., form) in the adult facial and mandibular structures as "growth," realizing that observed changes may not represent growth dynamics in the sense of what is observed in the subadult specimens.

5.2.3   Semilandmark Geometric Morphometrics and Exploratory Analyses

NextEngine surface scans were acquired from each specimen following the protocol described in Freidline *et al.* (2012a, 2012b, 2013). Landmarks and curve semilandmarks were digitized on three-dimensional reconstructions of the surface scans using the software Landmark Editor (Wiley *et al.*, 2005). A template mesh of surface semilandmarks covering the entire face and mandible was digitized on one individual and a thin-plate-spline (TPS) interpolation was used to warp this template mesh of semilandmarks to the surface of every other specimen according to their landmark and curve data. All semilandmarks were allowed to slide along tangents to the curves and tangent planes to the surface so as to minimize the bending energy of the TPS interpolation between each specimen and the Procrustes consensus configuration. This removes the influence of the arbitrary spacing of the semilandmarks and establishes a geometric correspondence of the semilandmark coordinates within the sample. For a detailed technical account of this method see Gunz (2005) and Gunz *et al.* (2005, 2009).

First, to make the GM data comparable to the bone modeling results of Martinez-Maza *et al.* (2013), we divided the face into three anatomical regions: nasomaxillary, zygomatic, and upper face (superciliary and glabella), consisting of 733, 300, and 72 landmarks and semilandmarks, respectively, and the mandibular landmark data set into corpus (548 landmarks and semilandmarks) and ramus (684 landmarks and semilandmarks) (Figure 5.1 and Table 5.2). Growth variables

Table 5.2 Homologous landmarks, curves and surface semilandmarks used in the analysis; NM: nasomaxillary subset; Z: zygomatic; UF: upper face; C: mandibular corpus; R: mandibular ramus.[1,2,3]

Facial landmarks and semilandmarks

Landmarks	Label	Subset	Definition
Alveolare	ids	NM	
Auriculare[3]	au	Z	
Dacryon[3]	d	NM	
Frontomalare orbitale[3]	fo	Z, UF	
Frontomalare temporale[3]	fmt	Z, UF	
Frontotemporale[3]	ft	UF	
Glabella	g	UF	
Jugale[3]	ju	Z	
Medial orbital margin[3]	mm	NM	
Nasion	n	NM, UF	
Nasospinale	ns	NM	
Porion[3]	po	Z	
Rhinion	rhi	NM	
Sphenopalatine suture[2,3]	ss	NM	
Staphylion[2]	sta	NM	
Superolateral nasion[3]	sn	NM	Superior lateral point where the frontonasal and nasomaxillary sutures cross; the superior lateral corner of the nasal bone
Zygomatic process root superior[3]	zrs	NM	
Zygomaxillare[3]	zm	NM, Z	
Zygoorbitale[3]	zyo	NM, Z	

(continued)

Table 5.2 *(cont.)*

Facial landmarks and semilandmarks

Landmarks	Label	Subset	Definition
Curve semilandmarks			
Alveolar outline[3]	AO	NM	Sphenopalatine suture to alveolare
Inferior orbital margin[3]	IOM	Z	Zygoorbitale to frontomalare orbitale
Inferior zygomatic outline[3]	IZO	Z	Zygomaxillare to porion
Maxillary contour[3]	MC	NM	Zygomatic process root inferior to zygomaxillare
Midsagittal palate[2]	MP	NM	Staphylion to alveolare
Subnasal outline	SO	NM	Alveolare to anterior nasal spine
Superior orbital margin[3]	SOM	UF	Frontomalare orbitale to dacryon
Supraorbital profile 1[3]	SP1	UF	Anterior projection of superciliary arch from frontomalare temporale to nasion
Supraorbital profile 2[3]	SP2	UF	Superior outline of superciliary arch from frontomalare temporale to glabella
Superior zygomatic outline[3]	SZO	Z	Jugale to auriculare
Surface semilandmarks			
Maxillary patch[2,3]		NM	Covering the anterior surface of the maxillary bone
Zygomatic patch[2,3]		Z	Covering the anterior surface of the zygomatic bone

Mandibular landmarks and semilandmarks

Landmarks	Label	Subset	Definition
Coronoid[3]	cr	R	
Infradentale	id	C	
Lateral condyle[3]	cdl	R	
Lingual	l	C	Infradentale on lingual side
Mandibular symphysis	ms	C	Base of mandibular symphysis at center
Medial condyle[3]	cdm	R	
Curve semilandmarks			
Anterior symphysis	AS	C	Infradentale to mandibular symphysis
Buccal alveolar ramal outline[3,4]	BAR	C, R	Infradentale to coronoid
Condyle outline[3]	CO	R	Lateral to medial condyle
Lingual alveolar ramal outline[3,4]	LAR	C, R	Lingual to coronoid
Mandibular notch[3]	MN	R	Coronoid to lateral condyle

Table 5.2 (*cont.*)

Mandibular landmarks and semilandmarks

Landmarks	Label	Subset	Definition
Posteroinferior outline[3,4]	PI	C,R	Medial condyle to mandibular symphysis
Posterior symphysis	PS	C	Mandibular symphysis to lingual
Surface semilandmarks			
Buccal patch[3,4]		C, R	Covering the entire outer surface of the mandible, including body and ramus
Lingual patch[3,4]		C, R	Covering the entire inner surface of the mandible, including body and ramus

[1] See Freidline *et al.* (2012a, 2013) for facial landmark definitions, and White *et al.* (2012) for mandibular landmark definition. Definitions are provided in table for less common landmarks.
[2] Landmarks or curve semilandmarks are not labeled in the figure.
[3] Paired right and left landmarks.
[4] Mandibular curve and surface semilandmarks were arbitrarily divided into corpus and ramus subsets.

(i.e., size–shape variables) were achieved by standardizing the raw landmark configurations for position and orientation using a generalized Procrustes analysis (GPA), but not standardizing for centroid size (Dryden and Mardia, 1998), the square root of the sum of squared distances of a set of landmarks from their centroid. This was done independently for each landmark subset of the face and mandible. The GPA follows a least-squares oriented approach iteratively rotating all configurations until the summed squared distances between landmarks and their corresponding sample average is minimized (Mitteroecker *et al.*, 2013). Consequently, the subsequent growth interpretations are based on this alignment and bound to this reference space, that is, the centroid of the superimposition, which may not correspond exactly to where bone growth occurs.

We used Procrustes variance to quantify the subsequent growth (i.e., form) variables. Procrustes variance is the sum of the diagonal elements of the group covariance matrix (Zelditch *et al.*, 2012). In order to evaluate whether growth is more variable in the nasomaxilla and mandibular ramus, Procrustes variance was estimated separately for each of the landmark subsets (i.e., nasomaxilla, zygomatic, and upper face and mandibular corpus and ramus). To compare Procrustes variance between landmark subsets, we divided the diagonal elements of the covariance block by the number of landmarks of that corresponding block (i.e., number of landmark in each anatomical subset). To evaluate the third hypothesis (subadults are more variable than adults) we further divided the specimens into subadult and adult groups following Martinez-Maza *et al.* (2013) and calculated the Procrustes variance for each landmark subset.

Variation in facial and mandibular growth was explored by means of a principal component analysis (PCA) in form space, including the geometric size (as the natural logarithm of centroid size) of each specimen. A PCA in form space was performed on each of the facial landmark subsets independently (e.g., nasomaxillary, zygomatic, upper face) and the whole mandible. For the mandible, this required aligning all of the mandibular landmark coordinates and standardizing for position and orientation, but not centroid size. Growth was visualized along the first two principal components (PCs) by warping the sample mean shape along the positive and negative ends of PC 1 and 2 plus/minus three standard deviations (± 3 SD), that is, corresponding to a form increase or decrease of three standard deviations from the sample mean.

Centroid size values were calculated for each individual using each facial landmark subset and the whole mandible. In doing so, we are able to investigate possible size differences in anatomical regions for each specimen. Additionally, allometry was calculated for each facial landmark subset and the whole mandible using multivariate regression analysis, regressing all Procrustes form variables on the natural logarithm of centroid size. This was also done to evaluate ontogenetic allometry, using only subadults, and static allometry in adults.

Temporal patterns of development (i.e., shape) and growth (i.e., form) maturation for each anatomical region were also explored and compared to the bone modeling data. Form maturation was estimated by plotting the first PC in form space against the age for each specimen. To explore shape maturation, we first performed separate GPAs for each anatomical region standardizing for position, orientation, and centroid size. Next, a PCA was performed on the resulting shape coordinate and the first PC in shape space was plotted against the age for each specimen. Development (i.e., shape) was visualized along the first PC by warping the sample mean shape along the positive and negative ends of PC 1 plus/minus three standard deviations (± 3 SD). All data processing and statistical analyses were performed in R (R Development Core Team, 2010).

5.3   Results

5.3.1   Centroid Size

Individual centroid size values for each anatomical region are plotted in Figure 5.2. There are clear size differences in males and females in the upper face, nasomaxilla, and zygomatic from at least seven years of age into adulthood. Although male–female size differences are present in the mandible during this time period, they are less extreme in the youngest subadults (e.g., 126 and 100A) compared to the face. Size relationships between anatomical regions are more or less consistent within and between individuals, although there are several outliers. For example, the adult female 52 falls within the range of subadult centroid sizes in the upper face, but in all other anatomical regions it is similar in size to other adult females. The subadult male 101 also has a relatively small upper face compared to other

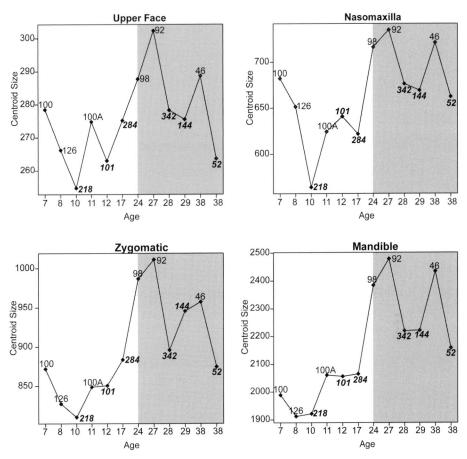

Figure 5.2 Individual centroid size values according to landmark subset. Numbers along the x-axis denote individual age, the y-axis represents centroid size, specimen numbers are given, females are bolded italic, and gray boxes divide subadults and adults.

anatomical regions and individuals of similar age, the adult female 144, has a large zygomatic, and the youngest individuals, 100 and 126, have a much larger nasomaxillary region relative to mandible. In fact, in all facial subsets 100 overlaps in size with adult females.

5.3.2 Growth Variation Across Anatomical Regions

Procrustes variance of the facial and mandibular subsets is listed in Table 5.3. In the face, the nasomaxilla (NM; 4.85) is the most variable region during growth (i.e., in subadults), followed by the zygomatic (Z; 4.2), and the upper face (UF; 2.34). For the subadult mandible, the ramus (R; 1.38) is slightly more variable than the corpus (C; 1.33). In all anatomical regions except the nasomaxilla, adults are more variable than subadults.

Table 5.3 Variance in facial (UF, upper face; NM, nasomaxillary; Z, zygomatic) and mandibular (Mand; R, ramus, C, corpus) subsets using Procrustes form variables.

	Face: UF	*Face: Z*	*Face: NM*	*Mand: R*	*Mand: C*
Subadult	2.34	4.2	4.85	1.38	1.33
Adult	3.9	10.94	3.3	4.56	3.56

5.3.3 Facial and Mandibular Growth and Displacement

For each anatomical region, PCAs in form space were performed in order to explore facial and mandibular growth (Figure 5.3). Principal component 1 documents growth; in general, younger individuals plot along the negative end of PC 1 and adult, male individuals along the positive end. Allometry, calculated for each facial landmark subset and the whole mandible using multivariate regression analysis, is greatest in the mandible, explaining 82.3% of form variation, followed by the zygomatic (80.9%), upper face (57.2%), and nasomaxilla (47.1%). This pattern is maintained in analyses of ontogenetic and static allometry (Table 5.4).

Upper Face

PC1 accounts for 61.3% of total form variance and PC2 accounts for 10.4% and is not correlated with size ($r \approx 0.02$). Although younger individuals tend to plot along the negative end of PC1, there are several exceptions. Specimen 52, an adult female, plots closer to subadults along PC1, and specimen 100, a subadult male, plots closer to adult females. Form changes associated with growth along PC1 are primarily associated with an overall more anteriorly projecting brow ridge, in particular medially at glabella and at the lateral corners, and a superior movement of nasion. Form changes along PC2 are similar to PC1 and also include a more angular superior orbital margin and a pinching of the supero-lateral superciliary arch at the positive end of PC2.

   Individual bone modeling maps of the upper face (Figure 5.3) indicate that in subadults and adults the upper region of the facial skeleton is mainly characterized by bone formation. Resorption fields occur only in small regions around the superciliary arch–glabella contact in subadults 101 and 218 and adults 92, 98, 144, and 342, and the inferior superciliary arch of subadult 100A.

Zygomatic

PC1 accounts for 82.7% of total form variance and PC2 accounts for 4.5%; PC2 is not correlated with size ($r \approx 0.002$). Several adult females (342 and 52) have small zygomatic bones and plot closer to subadults along PC1. Form changes along PC1 associated with growth include greater robusticity in the frontal process, a larger zygomatic body, and a coronal rotation and superior–inferior elongation of the zygomatic body. This latter form change is most evident in the curvature of the

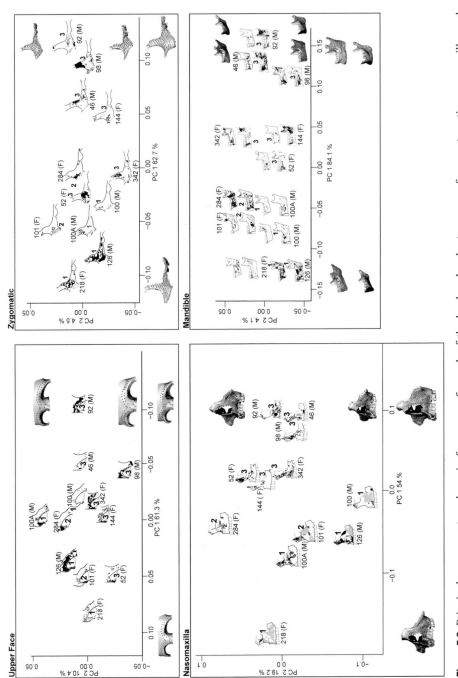

Figure 5.3 Principal component analyses in form space for each of the landmark subsets – upper face, zygomatic, nasomaxilla, and mandible. Individuals are represented by their bone modeling maps (adapted from Martínez-Maza *et al.*, 2013) and are labeled according to specimen number, age group (see Table 5.1 for definition), and sex. Bone formation surfaces are shown in black, bone resorption surfaces are shown in gray, while the white areas indicate damaged bone surfaces with no histological data. The surface visualizations represent the mean shapes warped along the positive and negative ends of PC1 and 2 plus/minus 3 standard deviations (± 3 SD) from the sample mean.

Table 5.4 Percentage of ontogenetic, static, and total allometry in facial (UF, upper face; NM, nasomaxilla; Z, zygomatic) and mandibular growth calculating using multivariate regression analysis.

	Face: UF	Face: Z	Face: NM	Mandible
Total	57.2	80.9	47.1	82.3
Ontogenetic	62.3	80.7	55.4	82.8
Static	68.5	84.8	64	85.6

bone at the zygomaticomaxillary suture, being more pronounced along the positive end of PC1. Form changes along PC2 are primarily associated with the shape of the posterior margin of the frontal process, the length and orientation of the body and the shape of the inferior margin, such that individuals plotting at the positive end of PC2 express a smaller zygomatic body in the sagittal plane, a shorter and less-curved frontal process, and a less-curved inferior margin.

In subadult individuals the zygomatic bone mainly shows signs of bone formation, with small, isolated regions of resorption occurring along the orbital margin and the zygomaticomaxillary suture in several specimens (100 and 100A, respectively). The bone modeling patterns in adults primarily reveals bone formation in specimens 46, 98, 52, and 342, with areas of bone resorption being more variable in size, location and extension than in the subadults and occur along the zygomatico-maxillary suture, inferior zygomatic margin, temporal suture, and isolated patches on the body.

Nasomaxilla

PC1 accounts for 54% of total form variance and PC2 accounts for 19.2% and is less correlated with size ($r \approx 0.24$) than PC1. Subadults plot along the negative end of PC1 and PC2, while adults of both sexes cluster together at the positive ends of PC1 and 2. Form changes associated with nasomaxillary growth along PC1 include a superior–inferior increase in facial height, increase in nasal aperture height and superior projection, alveolar prognathism, and a posterior deepening of the infraorbital plate. Form changes associated with PC2 are primarily related to facial height and infraorbital morphology. Individuals plotting at the positive end of PC2 express a much taller facial height and nasal aperture, and depressed infraorbital surface morphology; whereas those plotting at the negative end of PC2 (mainly subadults associated to age group 1) have a much smaller face and inflated infraorbital surface topography.

The nasomaxillary region shows high variation in the distribution of modeling fields in both subadults and adults. Compared to adults, subadults show more bone resorptive surfaces on the maxilla. This is particularly true for specimens 218, 101, and 300, whereas specimens 101A and 126 show more bone deposition on the max-illa. Unlike the subadults, the adults show a more similar distribution of bone formation fields on the maxilla, with bone resorption fields generally extending from the infraorbital foramen to the canine alveolus. In both subadults and adults, areas of resorption occur around the infero-lateral orbital margin, nasal process of the maxilla, from the infraorbital foramen to the canine alveolus, inferior zygomaticomaxillary suture and along the inferior margin of the zygomatic to the temporal zygomatic suture. The nasal bones are primarily characterized by bone formation surfaces.

Mandible

PC1 accounts for 84.1% of total form variance and PC2 accounts for 4.1% and is not correlated with size ($r \approx 0.04$). Along PC1 there are four clusters: the two smallest individuals 218 and 126 plotting at the extreme negative end; the older subadult (AG 2) females plotting with the subadult (AG 1) males; and among the adults the females and males form two isolated groups, suggesting clear size dimorphism in the adult mandible. Form changes associated with growth along PC1 include the development of the chin, downward displacement of the mandibular corpus and rami, superior lengthening of the rami, deepening of the mandibular notch, and posterior movement of the inferior rami (in the gonial region). Form changes along PC2 are in the angle of the symphysis and development of the chin and a downward and posterior displacement of the inferior rami, such that specimens plotting at the negative end of PC2 express a more vertical mandibular symphysis and antero-posteriorly wider and downwardly displaced rami.

The best preserved subadult mandibular surfaces (126 and 284) display predominately bone formation fields in the symphyseal region, and bone resorption fields are present on the alveolar process on the buccal side for all subadult specimens. The lingual symphysis in these specimens is also primarily characterized by bone formation. The subadult mandibular corpus shows signs of bone formation surfaces on the buccal side and resorbing surfaces on the lingual side. The buccal side of the mandibular ramus in subadults is predominately bone formation with bone resorption fields along the condyle and coronoid process extending inferiorly. The lingual surface of the mandibular ramus is predominately resorptive. Like subadults, the buccal surface of the mandibular symphysis and corpus is primarily bone formation in adults, whereas the buccal ramus is primarily resorptive.

5.3.4   Temporal Patterns in Development and Growth

We explored the relationship between growth (change in form), development (change in shape), and chronological age for each of the anatomical regions analyzed in this study (Figure 5.4). The x-axis represents age and the y-axis either development or growth, estimated using the first PC in shape and form space, respectively. In shape space, PC1 shows the greatest correlation with log centroid size in the mandibular data set ($r \approx 0.9$), followed by the zygomatic ($r \approx 0.71$), upper face ($r \approx 0.51$), and the nasomaxilla ($r \approx 0.42$).

In all plots, apart from the development of the upper face, there is a clear separation between subadults and adults indicating ontogenetic changes in both shape

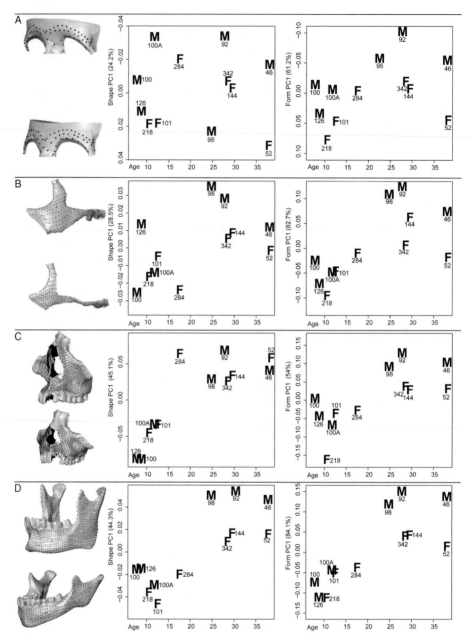

Figure 5.4 Temporal patterns in development and growth. The *x*-axis represents age and the *y*-axis either development or growth, estimated using the first PC in shape and form space, respectively; (A) upper face, (B) zygomatic, (C) nasomaxilla, and (D) mandible. For each individual, specimen number and sex (M, male; F, female) is given. The surface visualizations represent development changes in Procrustes shape space. Mean shapes were warped along the positive and negative ends of PC and 2 plus/minus 3 standard deviations (± 3 SD) from the sample mean. Refer to Figure 5.3 for growth changes (i.e., form space) along PC1.

(development) and form (growth). Male–female shape differences during development are less consistent between anatomical regions during ontogeny. In both the upper face and nasomaxilla there are no differences in male and female shapes in subadults or adults. The zygomatic shows sexually dimorphic shape differences in adults, but not in subadults. Lastly, mandibular shape differences between males and females are present in both subadults and adults, suggesting an early development of sexual dimorphism. Shape changes associated with development (i.e., along PC1 in shape space) are similar to those described for growth (along PC1 in form space) in the previous section.

5.4   Discussion

The aim of this study was to explore patterns of facial and mandibular growth on the micro- and macroscopic scale using surface bone modeling data and semilandmark GM methods, respectively. Using GM data, we evaluated three results derived from the bone modeling study by Martinez-Maza *et al.* (2013): (1) growth is more variable in the nasomaxillary region compared to the zygomatic and upper face; (2) growth is more variable in the mandibular ramus compared to the corpus; and (3) variation in subadults is higher than in adults. Our GM results indicate that the most variable region of the face during ontogeny is the nasomaxillary region (4.85), followed by the zygomatic (4.2), and the upper face (2.34); the mandibular ramus (1.38) is slightly more variable than the corpus (1.33). These results support the first two conclusions by Martinez-Maza and colleagues (2013). The results of their third finding – subadults express more variation than adults – is only upheld in the nasomaxillary region. However, we must emphasize that this is a preliminary investigation of the correspondence between bone modeling and bone displacement; both larger sample sizes and a more thorough evaluation of the effects of sexual dimorphism, in particular in bone modeling patterns, are essential in order to confirm these results.

Both the histological and GM results suggest clear ontogenetic differences in the nasomaxilla between subadults and adults; these changes are more pronounced compared to other regions of the facial skeleton and are correlated less with size. Unlike the other anatomical regions of the face, the nasomaxilla shows a less consistent bone modeling pattern during ontogeny and into adulthood; in subadults it is primarily resorptive, whereas in adults it is characterized by more bone formation. In our GM analysis, the subadult nasomaxillary form (shape + size) is more variable than the upper face and zygomatic and the percentage of allometric variation, both ontogenetic and static, is less.

Our GM study reveals that compared to adults, subadults show a more inflated maxilla, in particular in the inferior maxilla above the canine and premolars. In contrast, the adult infraorbital plate is depressed. Adults also show greater prognathism in the anterior–inferior maxilla above the incisors and canines. The inflated subadult maxilla is surely caused by the development of the permanent dentition under the bone surface in this region. The predominant bone resorption pattern on the subadult maxilla is also most likely related to dental development and movement, combined with bone displacement in other regions of the skull. As it has been described previously (Enlow and Hans, 2008), the subadult maxilla shows bone resorption indicating a backward growth while bone growth is actually occurring in the posterior maxilla and at the craniofacial sutures (e.g., temporozygomatic, frontozygomatic, frontomaxillary, frontonasal). The posterior bone growth and the forward displacement of the facial skeleton result in an upward maxillary rotation during ontogeny (Enlow and Bang, 1965; Björk and Skieller, 1976; Bromage, 1989; McCollum and Ward, 1997; Enlow and Hans, 2008). Consequently, to compensate for this rotation, as well as the predominately forward displacement of the upper face and dental drift, resorption occurs on the external surfaces of the anterior maxilla (Björk and Skieller, 1976). In adulthood, the posterior growth of the facial skeleton has ceased due to the fusion of the craniofacial sutures in this region and therefore the combination of bone modeling and horizontal growth by deposition results in a more protrusive nose and an antero-posteriorly deeper face in the adult morphology (Martinez-Maza et al., 2013). Bone formation in the adult superior maxillary body (inferior orbital margin) and subnasal region combined with resorption in the inferior maxilla result in an anteriorly projecting inferior orbital margin, a depressed infraorbital plate, and a prognathic alveolar region, explaining the adult infraorbital morphology highlighted in the GM analyses.

In both subadults and adults, the bone modeling patterns in the upper face and zygomatic are primarily indicative of bone formation on the external surfaces of these bones during ontogeny. As the zygomatic grows by means of bone formation it increases in size, in particular the zygomatic body and in supero-inferior length, and the frontal process becomes more robust. The brow ridge becomes more anteriorly projecting, in particular at glabella and at the lateral corners by means of bone formation. Both the bone modeling and GM methods show that the upper face and zygomatic regions are less variable in subadults compared to the nasomaxillary region. In this framework, our results could suggest a correspondence between constant patterns of bone formation and a decreased variation in form, indicating a direct relationship between bone modeling and form. However, this should be considered as a working hypothesis that needs to be tested in future work.

The greater form variation in the adult upper face and zygomatic compared to the nasomaxilla is not surprising given these regions often reflect sexual dimorphism in humans and although male–female differences in facial morphology occur during development, they are most pronounced in adulthood (Bulygina et al., 2006). The GM results show clear size differences in males and females in the upper face, nasomaxillary, and zygomatic regions from at least seven years of age into adulthood, consistent with Bulygina et al. (2006), who showed that before puberty males possess a larger facial size than females of a similar age.

Our results also indicate that there are shape differences between subadults and adults in zygomatic morphology that are not obvious from a review of the bone modeling data. In addition to an overall increase in size, growth and developmental shape changes of the zygomatic entail an antero-posterior rotation. In the subadult condition the frontal process is more anteriorly projecting with the zygomatic body appearing more posterior. Conversely, in the adult condition the frontal process is angled posteriorly and the zygomatic body anteriorly. Evidence for this rotation during ontogeny is not obvious in the bone modeling data; however, the bone resorption present in both the subadult and adult zygomaticomaxillary sutures, and around the subadult orbital margin, could be related to this growth rotation, with the resorption fields possibly acting as a compensatory mechanism to the rotation. The zygomatic shape changes described above may also be explained by bone displacements from adjoining regions of the skull, like the frontal bone or maxilla, and/or differential rates of bone formation in different regions of the zygomatic.

The growth trajectories in the mandible are not as clear as in the facial complex emphasizing the importance of understanding both bone modeling and displacement in order to interpret craniofacial growth. Previous work has shown that the bone modeling pattern of the mandible indicates a posterior superior direction as it is simultaneously being displaced, like the nasomaxillary region, in an anteroinferior direction (Enlow and Hans, 2008). The subadult mandibular bone modeling pattern is characterized mainly by bone formation fields in the symphysis and anterior corpus and resorption fields in the anterior alveolar region, consistent with the forward growth of the mandible and development of the chin during ontogeny. These shape changes are visible in the GM analyses in this study and are consistent with other morphometric studies (e.g. Coquerelle *et al.*, 2011).

The modeling pattern in the posterior region of the mandibular corpus and ramus is more complex. The GM data clearly indicate a downward displacement of the ramus during development corroborated by bone formation fields on the buccal surface of the ramus. The bone modeling patterns also suggest a lateral growth of the subadult ramus, an upward movement of the condyle, and a medial and posterior movement of the coronoid. In the GM analysis, the movements associated with the condyle and coronoid are consistent with the bone modeling data; however, form changes in the lateral direction of the ramus are minimal. Given the age of the subadults in our study, growth of the middle cranial fossa is mostly complete (Scheuer and Black, 2000), and consequently the mandible (and nasomaxillary region) grows more vertically than horizontally. To achieve this, condylar and rami growth is more vertical, corroborated by areas of bone formation on its inferior-posterior border. To explain the discrepancy between the bone modeling and GM results we hypothesize that the bone formation rates on the mandibular ramus may be very low or in a resting state.

Our results suggest that chronological age may be a better predictor of an individuals' bone modeling pattern, rather than size or sex. While it is common practice in morphometric studies to use size and sex as substitutes for developmental stage, developmental age, or chronological age, to our knowledge the relationship between facial size and sex, and an individual's bone modeling pattern, has never been explicitly addressed. When plotting chronological age against growth and development, there is a clear separation between subadults and adults in all anatomical regions, except in the development of the upper face, suggesting that age may be a good predictor of bone modeling patterns. This is particularly relevant for the nasomaxilla, which, unlike the upper face, shows obvious changes in both bone modeling and morphology during ontogeny into adulthood. Along these lines, the nasomaxilla of specimen 284, a late adolescent female, plots closer to adults in form space and also exhibits more extensive bone formation, similar to the adult pattern; however, its nasomaxillary size is more similar to specimens that exhibit a more subadult morphology and bone modeling pattern. Whether this result is simply individual variation cannot be determined in this study. Future work, with larger sample sizes, would help to distinguish between ontogenetic trends in the data and interindividual differences in bone modeling patterns.

This study has explored ways of integrating two methodologies that are often employed independently to assess morphological changes in the development and evolution of primates (also see Chapter 2 for combination of bone volume and density with morphometric methods). In addition to the limited sample size, there are several drawbacks inherent in both of the methods applied in this study. To begin with, they both make predictions based on models, which may not precisely reflect reality. In the GM analysis the landmark data are subject to a Procrustes superimposition, and subsequent growth interpretations are based on this alignment, which may not correspond exactly to where bone growth occurs.

Similarly, the generalized bone modeling pattern is derived from intraspecific similarities in bone modeling field distributions. However, in osteological collections perfectly preserved surfaces are rare, and consequently data may be lacking in the generalized bone modeling map. Additionally, the individual bone modeling patterns reflect the last bone growth activities at the age of death, but we cannot say at what age exactly a bone modeling field stopped its activity, and more work needs to be done to better distinguish between active and inactive bone modeling (although see Boyde, 1972, and Bromage, 1989), as well as modeling and remodeling activities. In spite of these limitations, our preliminary results show that GM and histological methods are complementary, and a combination of both methodological approaches could improve our understanding of the complex processes that occur during craniofacial growth.

5.5   Anthropological Implications

Two main aspects of growth are bone modeling and displacement. It is generally assumed that bone modeling patterns at a microstructural level correspond to large-scale morphological shape changes. In this study we explored the relationship between bone modeling patterns during ontogeny and facial shape, form (shape and size), and ontogenetic age using semilandmark GM methods. Throughout this study, we demonstrate how bone modeling and GM data can be combined to further improve our understanding of human facial growth. GM analyses add a quantitative component that pertains to changes in the geometry of the bone, and to bone modeling studies. Bone modeling provides concrete evidence of bone growth activity. Furthermore, in this study, we show that by applying surface semilandmarks,

GM analyses can be used to identify subtle morphological features that may not be obvious in our bone modeling study, such as ontogenetic changes in zygomatic and mandibular rami morphology. Additionally, when using GM techniques, one can explore how size and shape, not solely age, covary with bone modeling patterns. As far as we know, to date, no study has explored the the relationship between facial size and sex, and an individual's bone modeling pattern. Our preliminary results suggest that chronological age may be a better predictor of an individuals' bone modeling pattern, rather than size or sex.

To date, only a few studies have combined bone modeling and GM data (O'Higgins and Jones, 1998; Aporta et al., 2014; Freidline et al., 2014; Martinez-Maza et al., 2015). Recently, we (SEF and CMM) applied both methods in order to explore growth dynamics in gorillas and chimpanzees (Martinez-Maza et al. 2015). As in the present study, the upper face, zygomatic, and mandibular corpus in gorillas and chimpanzees represent more constant areas of bone growth. Ontogenetic changes primarily affect the bone modeling fields on the mandibular ramus and nasomaxilla, and these latter regions are most variable within and between taxa. This pattern is also upheld in the present study. While our results suggest a correspondence between variable patterns of bone formation and an increased variation in form during ontogeny, future research, with a larger sample size, is needed to test this correspondence. Constant patterns in the upper face and mandibular corpus across species and ages may reflect the existence of phylogenetically preserved constraints, likely associated with developmental processes that determine the growth dynamics of these regions (Martinez-Maza et al., 2015). Along these lines, postnatal facial growth differences between two morphologically distinct human groups, the Khoisan (South Africa) and Inuit (Alaska), were recently shown to be concentrated in the nasomaxillary region (Freidline et al., 2015). Taken together, these findings may suggest that anatomical regions that are more variable within and across human and primate populations, like the nasomaxilla, may be less developmentally constrained and subject to greater evolvability.

In humans, regional or geographic difference in facial features develop early in ontogeny and some modern human populations show a distinct pattern of postnatal facial ontogeny that further enhances facial differences (Strand Viðarsdóttir et al., 2002; Freidline et al., 2015). How differences in bone modeling patterns translate to morphological differences in postnatal facial growth has yet to be explored, and could provide valuable insight to modern and fossil human growth variability. A clearer understanding of the biological underpinnings that result in the modern human phenotype will provide us with a more comprehensive framework from which to interpret the variability in our fossil ancestors. Additionally, future studies focusing on how strains, such as pressure, tension, and muscle–activity patterns affect osteogenesis and bone modeling patterns are also needed in order to better understand how behavioral patterns, such as dietary mechanics, help shape the developing skeleton.

As of now, surface bone modeling studies on extant primates are limited. This is most likely because the data are time-consuming to analyze and bone surface preservation is often poor. Consequently, our understanding of the extent of variability in facial and mandibular modeling patterns within and between species is still at its infancy. As a result, differentiating between inter-individual variability and ontogenetic and species patterns is challenging. Future studies on diverse primates, with larger ontogenetic samples, are essential in order to develop more precise and detailed growth models. Additionally, using animal models and controlling for factors, such as sex and diet, could help disentangle patterns attributed to growth from those resulting from function or behavior.

This study raises many new questions for future studies. For example, can the ontogenetic shape changes revealed in the GM analysis that are not evident in the bone modeling data be explained by bone movements from adjoining regions of the skull or mandible, differential rates of bone formation, and/or active versus inactive modeling fields? Cranial integration studies using larger sample sizes and combining GM and histological methods would be a good starting point to address such questions. Furthermore, a better understanding of bone formation rates and improving ways to distinguish active from inactive bone modeling is essential.

Another interesting preliminary finding in this study is that male–female size differences highlighted in our GM analyses do not translate to sex differences in bone modeling patterns. We hypothesize that sex differences in bone formation rate and/or activity (resting versus active modeling fields) during ontogeny may explain some aspects of male–female shape and form differences. For example, a study by Bulygina *et al.* (2006) found that males show faster rates of facial growth and development (i.e., hypermorphosis) relative to females during ontogeny. Heterochronic patterns, defined as the dissociation of size, shape, and age (Gould, 1977; Alberch *et al.*, 1979), associated with facial size dimorphism may also occur at the cellular level. In this context, shape and form changes revealed in semilandmark GM analyses that are not apparent in bone modeling patterns may provide clues to differential rates of bone formation and whether bone is in a resting or active state.

Ultimately, a better understanding of the underlying developmental mechanisms that produce the variation seen in adult primate morphology will aid us in reconstructing the behavior and the evolutionary relationships between our fossil ancestors. With a more comprehensive understanding of the development and displacement of skeletal features during ontogeny we may be able to better differentiate morphological features that develop homologously between taxa from those that look similar, but result from different growth dynamics (see Chapter 4 for detailed discussion of developmental homology). Further research combining bone modeling and GM could also provide greater insight to character state polarity (i.e., ancestral versus derived) and homology to assist in reconstructing phylogenetic relationships between hominin taxa.

5.6   Acknowledgments

We would like to thank Drs. Chris Percival and Joan Richtsmeier for inviting us to participate, and organizing the symposium and subsequent volume. We would also like to thank Eugenia Cunha and Ana Luisa Santos from the Department of Life Sciences at the University of Coimbra for access to the collection and the anonymous reviewers. This work was supported by the Max Planck Society and by the JAE-Doc program (co-funded by CSIC and European Social Fund).

References

Adams, D. C., Rohlf, F. J. and Slice, D. E. (2004). Geometric morphometrics: ten years of progress following the 'revolution'. *Italian Journal of Zoology*, 71, 5–16.

Adams, D. C., Rohlf, F. J. and Slice, D. E. (2013). A field comes of age: geometric morphometrics in the 21st century. *Hystrix – Italian Journal of Mammalogy*, 24, 7–14.

Alberch, P., Gould, S. J., Oster, G. F. and Wake, D. B. (1979). Size and shape in ontogeny and phylogeny. *Paleobiology*, 5, 296–317.

Aporta, N. B., Martinez-Maza, C., Gonzalez, P. N. and Bernal, V. (2014). Bone modeling patterns and morphometric craniofacial variation in individuals from two prehistoric human populations from Argentina. *Anatomical Record – Advances in Integrative Anatomy and Evolutionary Biology*, 297, 1829–1838.

Bastir, M. (2008). A systems-model for the morphological analysis of integration and modularity in human craniofacial evolution. *Journal of Anthropological Science*, 86, 37–58.

Bastir, M. and Rosas, A. (2004). Facial heights: evolutionary relevance of postnatal ontogeny for facial orientation and skull morphology in humans and chimpanzees. *Journal of Human Evolution*, 47, 359–381.

Bastir, M., Rosas, A. and O'Higgins, P. (2006). Craniofacial levels and the morphological maturation of the human skull. *Journal of Anatomy*, 209, 637–654.

Björk, A. and Skieller, V. (1976). Postnatal growth and developmemt of the maxillary complex. *In:* McNamara, F. A. (ed.) *Factors Affecting the Growth of the Midface. Craniofacial Growth Series*. Ann Arbor, MI: University of Michigan Press, pp. 61–69.

Boyde, A. (1972). *Scanning Electron Microscope Studies of Bone*. New York, NY: Academic Press.

Boyde, A. and Hobdell, M. H. (1969). Scanning electron microscopy of primary membrane bone. *Zeitschrift fur Zellforschung und Mikroskopische Anatomie*, 99, 98–108.

Bromage, T. G. (1984). Interpretation of scanning electron microscopic images of abraded forming bone surfaces. *American Journal of Physical Anthropology*, 64, 161–178.

Bromage, T. G. (1985). Systematic inquiry in tests of negative/postive replica combinations for SEM. *Journal of Microscopy*, 137, 209–216.

Bromage, T. G. (1987). The scanning electron microscopy/replica technique and recent applications to the study of fossil bone. *Scanning Microscopy*, 1, 607–613.

Bromage, T. G. (1989). Ontogeny of the early hominid face. *Journal of Human Evolution*, 18, 751–773.

Bulygina, E., Mitteroecker, P. and Aiello, L. (2006). Ontogeny of facial dimorphism and patterns of individual development within one human population. *American Journal of Physical Anthropology*, 131, 432–443.

Coquerelle, M., Bookstein, F. L., Braga, J., *et al.* (2011). Sexual dimorphism of the human mandible and its association with dental development. *American Journal of Physical Anthropology*, 145, 192–202.

Dryden, I. L. and Mardia, K. V. (1998). *Statistical Shape Analysis*. Chichester: John Wiley & Sons.

Enlow, D. H. (1962). A study of the post-natal growth and remodeling of bone. *American Journal of Anatomy*, 110, 79–101.

Enlow, D. H. (1963). *Principles of Bone Remodeling*. Springfield, IL: Charles C. Thomas Publisher.

Enlow, D. H. (1966a). A comparative study of facial growth in *Homo* and *Macaca*. *American Journal of Physical Anthropology*, 24, 293–308.

Enlow, D. H. (1966b). A morphogenetic analysis of facial growth. *American Journal of Orthodontics*, 52, 283–299.

Enlow, D. H. and Bang, S. (1965). Growth and remodeling of the human maxilla. *American Journal of Orthodontics*, 51, 446–464.

Enlow, D. H. and Hans, M. G. (2008). *Essentials of Facial Growth*. Ann Arbor, MI: Needham Press.

Freidline, S. E., Gunz, P., Harvati, K. and Hublin, J.-J. (2012a). Middle Pleistocene human facial morphology in an evolutionary and developmental context. *Journal of Human Evolution*, 63, 723–740.

Freidline, S. E., Gunz, P., Janković, I., Harvati, K. and Hublin, J. J. (2012b). A comprehensive morphometric analysis of the frontal and zygomatic bone of the Zuttiyeh fossil from Israel. *Journal of Human Evolution* 62, 225–241.

Freidline, S. E., Gunz, P., Harvati, K. and Hublin, J.-J. (2013). Evaluating developmental shape changes in *Homo antecessor* subadult facial morphology. *Journal of Human Evolution* 65, 404–423.

Freidline, S. E., Martinez-Maza, C. and Hublin, J. J. (2014). An integrative approach to studying craniofacial development in great apes and humans. *American Journal of Physical Anthropology*, S58, 121.

Freidline, S. E., Gunz, P. and Hublin, J. J. (2015). Ontogenetic and static allometry in the human face: contrasting Khoisan and Inuit. *American Journal of Physical Anthropology*, 158, 116–131.

Gould, S. J. (1977). *Ontogeny and Phylogeny*. Cambridge, MA: Harvard University Press.

Gunz, P. (2005). Statistical and geometric reconstruction of hominid crania: reconstructing Australopithecine ontogeny. PhD Thesis, University of Vienna.

Gunz, P., Mitteroecker, P. and Bookstein, F. (2005). Semilandmarks in three dimensions. *In:* Slice, D. E. (ed.) *Modern Morphometrics in Physical Anthropology*. New York, NY: Plenum Publishers, pp. 73–98.

Gunz, P., Mitteroecker, P., Neubauer, S., Weber, G. W. and Bookstein, F. L. (2009). Principles for the virtual reconstruction of hominin crania. *Journal of Human Evolution*, 57, 48–62.

Humphrey, L. T. (1998). Growth patterns in the modern human skeleton. *American Journal of Physical Anthropology*, 105, 57–72.

Lacruz, R. S., de Castro, J. M., Martinon-Torres, M., *et al.* (2013). Facial morphogenesis of the earliest Europeans. *PLoS ONE*, 8, e65199.

Martinez-Maza, C., Rosas, A. and Nieto-Diaz, M. (2010). Brief communication: Identification of bone formation and resorption surfaces by reflected light microscopy. *American Journal of Physical Anthropology*, 143, 313–320.

Martinez-Maza, C., Rosas, A., García-Vargas, S., Estalrrich, A. and de la Rasilla, M. (2011). Bone remodelling in Neanderthal mandibles from the El Sidrón site (Asturias, Spain). *Biology Letters*, 7, 593–596.

Martinez-Maza, C., Rosas, A. and Nieto-Díaz, M. (2013). Postnatal changes in the growth dynamics of the human face revealed from bone modelling patterns. *Journal of Anatomy*, 223, 228–241.

Martinez-Maza, C., Freidline, S. E., Strauss, A. and Nieto-Diaz, M. (2015). Bone growth dynamicsof the facial skeleton and mandible in *Gorilla gorilla* and *Pan troglodytes*. *Evolutionary Biology*, 43, 1–21.

McCollum, M. A. (1999). The robust australopithecine face: a morphogenetic perspective. *Science*, 284, 301–305.

McCollum, M. A. (2008). Nasomaxillary remodeling and facial form in robust *Australopithecus*: a reassessment. *Journal of Human Evolution*, 54, 2–14.

McCollum, M. A. and Ward, S. C. (1997). Subnasoalveolar anatomy and hominoid phylogeny: evidence from comparative ontogeny. *American Journal of Physical Anthropology*, 102, 377–405.

Mitteroecker, P. and Gunz, P. (2009). Advances in geometric morphometrics. *Evolutionary Biology*, 36, 235–247.

Mitteroecker, P., Gunz, P., Bernhard, M., Schaefer, K. and Bookstein, F. L. (2004). Comparison of cranial ontogenetic trajectories among great apes and humans. *Journal of Human Evolution*, 46, 679–697.

Mitteroecker, P., Gunz, P., Windhager, S. and Schaefer, K. (2013). A brief review of shape, form, and allometry in geometric morphometrics, with applications to human facial morphology. *Hystrix – Italian Journal of Mammalogy*, 24, 59–66.

Moss, M. L. and Young, R. W. (1960). A functional approach to craniology. *American Journal of Physical Anthropology*, 18, 281–292.

O'Higgins, P. (2000). The study of morphological variation in the hominid fossil record: biology, landmarks and geometry. *Journal of Anatomy*, 197, 103–120.

O'Higgins, P. and Jones, N. (1998). Facial growth in *Cercocebus torquatus*: an application of three-dimensional geometric morphometric techniques to the study of morphological variation. *Journal of Anatomy*, 193, 251–272.

O'Higgins, P., Bromage, T. G., Johnson, D. R., Moore, W. J. and McPhie, P. (1991). A study of facial growth in the sooty mangabey *Cercocebus atys. Folia Primatologica (Basel)*, 56, 86–94.

R Development Core Team (2010). *R: A Language and Environment for Statistical Computing.* Vienna: R Foundation for Statistical Computing.

Rice, D. P. (2008). Clinical features of syndromic craniosynostosis. *In:* Rice, D. P. (ed.) *Craniofacial Sutures: Development, Disease, and Treatment. Frontiers in Oral Biology.* Basel: Karger, pp. 91–106.

Rosas, A. and Martinez-Maza, C. (2010). Bone remodeling of the *Homo heidelbergensis* mandible; the Atapuerca-SH sample. *Journal of Human Evolution*, 58, 127–137.

Scheuer, L. and Black, S. M. (2000). *Developmental Juvenile Osteology.* San Diego, CA: Elsevier Academic Press.

Slice, D. E. (2005). Modern morphometrics. *In:* Slice, D. E. (ed.) *Modern Morphometrics in Physical Anthropology.* New York, NY: Kluwer Academic, pp. 1–46.

Strand Viðarsdóttir, U., O'Higgins, P. and Stringer, C. (2002). A geometric morphometric study of regional differences in the ontogeny of the modern human facial skeleton. *Journal of Anatomy*, 201, 211–229.

Walters, M. and O'Higgins, P. (1992). Factors influencing craniofacial growth: a scanning electron microscope study of high resolution facial replicas. *Proceedings of the Australian Society for Human Biology*, 5, 391–402.

White, T. D., Black, M. T. and Folkens, P. A. (2012). *Human Osteology.* Burlington, MA: Academic Press.

Wiley, D. F., Amenta, N., Alcantara, D. A., *et al.* (2005). Evolutionary morphing. *Proceedings of IEEE Visualizations.*

Zelditch, M. L., Swiderski, D. L. and Sheets, H. D. (2012). *Geometric Morphometrics for Biologists.* New York, NY: Academic Press.

6 Changes in Mandibular Cortical Bone Density and Elastic Properties during Growth

Paul C. Dechow

6.1 Introduction

Cortical bone material properties including density and elastic properties (elastic modulus, shear modulus, and Poisson's ratio) are essential for understanding the complex biomechanical responses of individual bones to muscle forces and extrinsic loadings (Dechow and Hylander, 2000; Strait *et al.*, 2005). In particular, variations in cortical bone anisotropies are significant in determining the relationship between stress and strain in bone. In primate and human evolution, research on the craniofacial skeleton, including the mandible, suggests that variations in such properties may represent evolutionary adaptations to unique craniofacial functions or patterns of development (Wang *et al.*, 2006).

While there is a growing body of literature on intraspecific and interspecific adult variation in cortical bone material properties in primate craniofacial skeletons (Ashman et al., 1984; Dechow *et al.*, 1992, 1993, 2008, 2010; Peterson and Dechow, 2002, 2003; Schwartz-Dabney and Dechow, 2002a,b, 2003; Lettry *et al.*, 2003; Nomura *et al.*, 2003; Peterson *et al.*, 2006; Wang and Dechow, 2006; Rapoff *et al.*, 2008; Q. Wang *et al.*, 2010; Chung and Dechow, 2011; Daegling *et al.*, 2011a,b, 2014; Davis *et al.*, 2012; J. Wang *et al.*, 2014), little is known about changes in these properties during growth (Ashman *et al.*, 1984; Hara *et al.*, 1998; Wang *et al.*, 2010; Davis *et al.*, 2012; Daegling *et al.*, 2014). While it is understood that bone increases in mineralization during growth, there is little understanding of whether the regional variations in material properties seen in adults can also be found in juveniles and neonates, or whether these variations develop during growth in response to intrinsic and extrinsic biomechanical factors. Because of the overall unavailability of appropriate cadaver material, regionally comparative studies in primates have been limited to a single study in baboons (Wang *et al.*, 2010) that contrasted juveniles and adults to explore questions of age changes in bone material properties.

This chapter will examine these questions through the use of two unique data sets: (1) material properties of a sample of five neonatal human mandibles are contrasted with data from a sample of 17 adult humans; and (2) material properties of the mandibles of domestic pigs are contrasted across different mandibular regions at different ages. The mandible was chosen as a model skeletal organ for study because of our knowledge of adult variation in material properties of mandibles of selected primates (Schwartz-Dabney and Dechow, 2003; Rapoff *et al.*, 2008; Wang *et al.*, 2010; Daegling *et al.*, 2011a,b), and because of the inherent functional and material variation found throughout the mandible. Pigs were used because of the availability of specimens and because they are frequently used as a model animal in craniofacial studies. Little is currently known about the mechanical properties of pig mandibular bone (Brosh *et al.*, 2014).

Two questions are addressed: (1) how do material properties change in the mandible during postnatal growth, and (2) do patterns of these material properties relative to region and orientation vary with age? Lower bone densities as found in younger animals result in lower elastic moduli in bone, which in turn affects how loads induce bone strain. Lower elastic moduli indicate greater elasticity and thus greater deformation for a given load. Thus, material property changes during growth can have an important impact on how we interpret changes in bone strain, as measured in functional experiments and as estimated in finite element modeling in comparative primate studies (Dechow and Hylander, 2000). The second question is also of importance because regional variation in the changes in material properties during growth can modify regional patterns of bone strain. These patterns, documented as relative differences in bone strain, affect our interpretation of overall strain patterns and our understanding of the relationship between bone function and structure within and between specific regions of the skeleton. Thus the interpretation of skeletal form requires that we also know something about variations in skeletal material properties as these play a large role in how bone is deformed and responds to load.

6.2   Methods and Materials

6.2.1   Human Sample

Cortical bone samples of human adults and stillborn infants were taken from unembalmed human crania from individuals of known age and sex, which were maintained in a frozen state in the Gross Anatomy Laboratory at Texas A&M University College of Dentistry. All crania were frozen shortly after death and were thus maintained in a fresh (unembalmed) condition. The adult cadavers were primarily those of older individuals (> 50 years of age). The adult specimens are dentulous and have not been diagnosed with or died from any primary bone diseases. The sample size consisted of 17 adult and 5 stillborn infant mandibles.

Bone samples were cut with a 5-mm Nobelpharma trephine burr from a site along the lower border of the mandible. In adults, this site was on the buccal surface inferior to the mandibular second molar. In stillborn infants, this site was on the buccal surface of the corpus of the mandible anterior to the insertion of the masseter muscle (Figure 6.1). Because of the small size of the infant mandibles, only a single sample could be taken reliably from the buccal corpus.

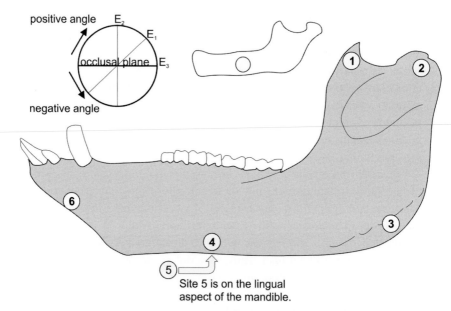

Figure 6.1 Locations of sampled sites on the pig mandible (larger figure) and on the human infant mandible (smaller figure). The circle shows the meaning of the angles for E_3 (maximum stiffness in the cortical plane) presented in Table 6.7 and Figure 6.4. Positive angles are clockwise from the occlusal plane and negative angles are counterclockwise on the buccal surface of the left hemimandible. These directions would be the reverse on the lingual side of the left hemimandible. The orientation of E_2 (minimum stiffness in the cortical plane) is always 90° to E_3 within the cortical plane. The orientation of E_1 is 90° to both E_2 and E_3 and is in the orientation of cortical thickness.

6.2.2   Porcine Sample

Cortical bone samples of porcine infants (newborns), juveniles (70 lbs), and young adult common domestic pigs (*Sus scrofa domesticus*) were taken from unembalmed mandibles within several days of death. All material was obtained from a slaughter house in the Dallas–Fort Worth metroplex. Mandibles were subsequently frozen in case additional bone samples would be needed. The sample size consisted of 10 young adults, 10 juveniles, and 5 infants.

Bone samples were cut in a similar way as in the human samples but were taken from six locations (Figure 6.1) including (1) the coronoid process, (2) the buccal condylar neck, (3) the buccal mandibular angle, (4) a buccal site along the lower border of the mandibular corpus inferior to the first molar, (5) a lingual site along the lower border of the mandibular corpus inferior to the first molar, and (6) the buccal surface of the symphysis.

6.2.3   Preparation and Testing of Bone Samples

The cortical bone samples were stored in a solution of 95% ethanol and isotonic saline in equal proportions. This media has been shown to maintain the elastic properties of bone over time (Ashman *et al.*, 1984). Bone was prepared using a slow-speed dental handpiece, a Unimat miniature lathe, and grinding wheels. All bone preparation procedures were carried out under a hood with the investigator wearing mask, gloves, and gown. All specimens were marked with a posterior-anterior graphite arrow to indicate orientation, thereby allowing the position of the bone to be reconstructed.

Measured properties include cortical thickness, apparent density, and ultrasonic wave velocities (Ashman *et al.*, 1984). Cortical thickness, the linear distance from the periosteal surface to the cortical–trabecular interface (Schwartz-Dabney and Dechow, 2003), was measured using digital calipers (Fowler & NSK Max – Cal Digital Caliper Metric 6"). The apparent density was measured by means of Archimedes' principle of buoyancy (Ashman *et al.*, 1984). A density kit and an Excellence XS105 balance (Mettler Toledo) were used to measure density. Readings were repeated to verify reliability.

Ultrasonic testing was carried out using a pulse transmission technique (Ashman *et al.*, 1984; Dechow *et al.*, 1993; Schwartz-Dabney and Dechow, 2002a; Chung and Dechow, 2011). With this technique, both longitudinal and transverse ultrasonic waves are passed through the specimens in each of the three mutually perpendicular directions. The resulting time delay corresponds to the propagation of the wave through the thickness of the specimen, and it is measured by making a phase comparison of the signal before and after the transmission. Ultrasonic velocities are then calculated knowing the time delay and the thickness of the specimen in the direction of wave transmission. This technique has been demonstrated to be as accurate as the values measured with traditional mechanical testing, and alleviates significant problems associated with fixing the bone specimens to the loading device (Ashman *et al.*, 1984).

Relationships between the various velocities through the specimen and its elastic properties are then derived from the principles of linear elastic wave theory (Ashman *et al.*, 1984). This theory, which is based on Hooke's Law, allows computer generation of a 6×6 algebraic matrix of elastic coefficients, or "C" matrix. This matrix is then used to calculate several elastic moduli as follows: (1) elastic modulus (E), a measure of the ability of a structure to resist deformation in a given direction, (2) shear modulus (G), a measure of the ability of a structure to resist shear stresses, and (3) Poisson's ratio (v), a measure of the ability of a structure to resist deformation perpendicular to that of the applied load.

The method used here requires an assumption of orthotropy and numbers are assigned to each of the three mutually perpendicular orientations determined for each bone specimen. The "1" direction is radial to the cortical plane and is coincident with the cortical thickness. The "2" direction is the axis of minimum stiffness in the cortical plane, and the "3" direction is the axis of maximum stiffness in the cortical plane (Figure 6.1). As an example of how these numbers are used, elastic moduli, such as E_1, signify the value in the "1" direction. Shear moduli, such as G_{23}, signify the value in the plane formed by the "2" and "3" directions. Poisson's ratios, such as v_{23}, signify a ratio of the strain in the "2" direction divided by that in the "3" direction when the load is applied in the "3" direction.

To determine the "2" and "3" directions, longitudinal ultrasonic velocities were measured through the cortical plane at multiple angles around the perimeter of each cylindrical specimen (Schwartz-Dabney and Dechow, 2002a, 2003). The direction of maximal stiffness in the cortical plane corresponds to the direction of peak ultrasonic velocity in the cortical plane. The direction of minimal ultrasonic velocity in the cortical plane was always found at 90° to that of peak velocity, indicating the direction of minimal stiffness in that plane and confirming the assumption of orthotropic symmetry.

6.2.4   Statistical Analysis

Descriptive statistics, including means, standard deviations, and standard errors, were calculated for all measurements using Minitab 17 Statistical Software. Analysis of variance determined whether significant differences for density, cortical thickness, and the elastic coefficients existed among human bone specimens with respect to age and among porcine specimens with respect to age and region. Post-hoc Tukey tests determined significant differences between individual cells. Differences in the orientations of orthotropic axes of stiffness were analyzed with circular statistics (Oriana 4.02, Kovach Computing Services, Anglesey, Wales, UK). Because of the small sample sizes, especially for the human and porcine infant samples, post-hoc power analyses were conducted to determine effect size and power using G*Power 3.1 (Faul et al., 2007). Power analyses were conducted for each comparison involving a t-test for the human samples. For the porcine samples, power analyses were conducted comparing regional differences among sites within each age group for each variable. Analyses were not conducted for age differences as they tended to be much larger than the differences among sites, and the site analyses revealed a large effect size and sufficient power for most comparisons.

6.3   Results

6.3.1   Human Samples

Density, elastic moduli, and shear moduli all showed highly significant differences between infant and adult mandibular cortical bone (Table 6.1). With the exception of v_{23} ($P = 0.034$), Poisson's ratios and anisotropy ratios did not differ between infants and adults. Effect sizes and power were large for most comparisons, except for Poisson's ratios and anisotropy ratios. Given the magnitude of the variance compared to the intergroup differences, much larger sample sizes would be needed to show significant differences, if they exist.

6.3.2   Porcine Samples

6.3.2.1   Cortical Thickness

Cortical thickness showed significant variation among sites ($P < 0.001$) and ages ($P < 0.001$) (Table 6.2 and Figure 6.2) between specimens. Cortical bone was thinner

Table 6.1 Material properties of infant ($N = 5$) and adult ($N = 17$) human mandibular specimens. The P value is the result of a two-sample t-test comparing infant and adult values. Density is given in mg/cm³; elastic (E) and shear (G) moduli are given in GPa; Poisson's ratios (v) and anisotropy ratios are unitless.

Property	Infant		Adult		P	Post-hoc power analysis	
	Mean	SD	Mean	SD		Effect size d	Power
Density	1337	118	1768	116	< 0.001	3.68	1.00
E_1	3.4	0.9	11.3	2.4	< 0.001	4.36	1.00
E_2	4.4	2.0	13.8	2.8	< 0.001	3.86	1.00
E_3	6.4	2.6	19.4	4.0	< 0.001	3.85	1.00
G_{23}	2.4	0.7	6.2	0.7	< 0.001	5.43	1.00
G_{31}	2.0	1.0	5.2	1.0	0.001	3.20	1.00
G_{12}	1.3	0.3	4.5	1.0	< 0.001	4.33	1.00
v_{12}	0.35	0.19	0.30	0.16	NS	0.28	0.08
v_{23}	0.21	0.15	0.32	0.16	NS	0.71	0.26
v_{31}	0.16	0.11	0.32	0.06	.034	1.81	0.92
E_2/E_3	0.70	0.14	0.75	0.26	NS	0.24	0.07
E_1/E_3	0.57	0.12	0.59	1.10	NS	0.17	0.06
E_1/E_2	0.84	0.20	0.84	0.19	NS	0.00	0.05

among infants and thicker among juveniles and adults. No difference was found between juveniles and adults in the following regions: coronoid, condyle, buccal corpus, or symphysis. Cortices were thicker in adults at the angle of the mandible and in the lingual corpus. The angle of the mandible in juveniles did not differ from that in infants. Post-hoc power analyses showed large effect sizes and power.

6.3.2.2 Density

Density of cortical bone showed significant variation among sites ($P < 0.001$) and ages ($P < 0.001$) (Table 6.2 and Figure 6.2). In adults, cortical bone was most dense on the buccal and lingual corpus and least dense at the symphysis. Juvenile bone was less dense than that of adults at all sites and denser than infant bone at all sites, except at the condyle. Post-hoc power analyses showed large effect sizes and power.

6.3.2.3 Elastic Moduli

The elastic moduli for the three principal axes showed a distinct pattern. E_3 is by definition larger than E_2, although the relative differences varied by region (see section on anisotropy below) and both E_3 and E_2 were larger than E_1 at all sites. This pattern of elastic moduli indicated orthotropy. All three elastic moduli showed significant variation among sites ($P < 0.001$) and ages ($P < 0.001$) (Table 6.3 and Figure 6.3). Patterns of stiffness by site varied among elastic moduli and among ages

Table 6.2 Cortical thickness and density.

Region	Age	N	Thickness (mm)		Density (mg/cm³)	
			Mean	SD	Mean	SD
Coronoid	Infant	5	1.86	0.27	1495	83
	Juvenile	10	2.62	0.47	1683	81
	Adult	10	2.85	0.88	1779	106
Condyle	Infant	5	2.27	0.35	1399	104
	Juvenile	10	3.97	1.26	1421	116
	Adult	10	3.68	1.01	1774	108
Angle	Infant	5	1.98	0.39	1386	73
	Juvenile	10	2.27	0.35	1580	121
	Adult	10	3.24	0.81	1799	126
Buccal	Infant	5	2.05	0.48	1497	71
Corpus	Juvenile	10	3.39	0.80	1739	100
	Adult	10	3.91	0.87	1902	56
Lingual	Infant	5	1.37	0.19	1612	208
Corpus	Juvenile	10	2.66	0.61	1835	43
	Adult	10	3.60	0.68	1928	65
Symphysis	Infant	5	2.36	0.15	1463	139
	Juvenile	10	4.07	1.49	1588	110
	Adult	10	4.00	1.17	1724	96
ANOVA			F	P	F	P
Age			31.7	<0.001	117.9	<0.001
Site			6.0	<0.001	19.3	<0.001
Age × Site			1.3	NS	2.84	0.003
Post-hoc power analysis			Effect size, f	Power	Effect size, f	Power
Infant			1.05	0.99	0.66	0.96
Juvenile			0.83	0.96	1.38	0.97
Adult			0.44	0.96	0.78	0.97

for each elastic modulus. Overall, the lingual corpus site had the greatest stiffness while the symphysis and condyle had the least stiffness. Post-hoc power analyses showed large effect sizes and power.

6.3.2.4 Shear Moduli

All three shear moduli showed significant variation among sites ($P < 0.001$) and ages ($P < 0.001$) (Table 6.4 and Figure 6.3). Overall, G_{23} had the largest shear moduli, followed by G_{31} and G_{12}. The lingual symphysis became stiffer at a younger age, showing little difference among juveniles and adults in all three planes. Otherwise, adult cortical bone was stiffer than that of juveniles which was stiffer than that of infants. Post-hoc power analyses showed medium to large effect sizes and power.

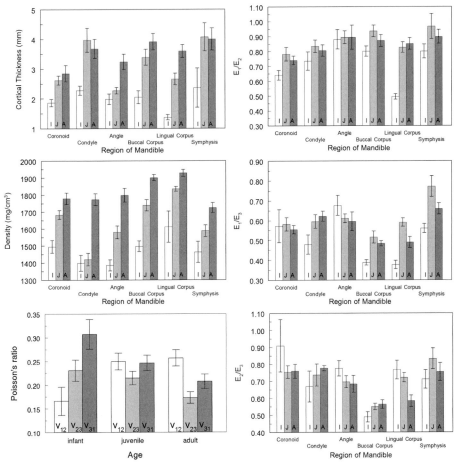

Figure 6.2 Variations in cortical thickness (top left; cortical density, middle left; Poisson's ratio, lower left; and cortical anisotropy, right figures) in the pig mandible. Bars are standard errors. I, infants; J, juveniles; A, adults. For cortical thickness, density, E_1/E_2 cortical anisotropy, and E_1/E_3 cortical anisotropy, ANOVA indicated significant differences between ages ($P < 0.001$) and sites ($P < 0.001$). For E_2/E_3 cortical anisotropy, ANOVA indicated significant differences between sites ($P < 0.001$), but not between ages. For Poisson's ratios, there were no significant differences by region, so overall comparisons are shown by age only ($P < 0.001$).

6.3.2.5 Poisson's Ratios

Poisson's ratios showed significant variation among ages (v_{12}, $P = 0.009$; v_{23}, $P = 0.021$; v_{31}, $P = 0.004$), but not among sites (Table 6.5, Figure 6.2). Overall, v_{31} and v_{23} declined with age while v_{12} increased with age. Post-hoc power analyses showed medium to large effect sizes and power.

6.3.2.6 Anisotropy

Anisotropy showed significant variation among sites ($P < 0.001$) and ages ($P < 0.001$), except for E_2/E_3, which showed no age related differences (Table 6.6 and Figure 6.2).

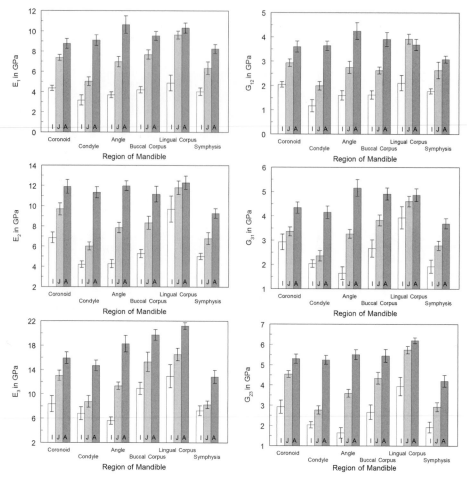

Figure 6.3 Variations in cortical elastic moduli (left figures) and shear moduli (right figures) in the pig mandible. Bars are standard errors. ANOVA indicated significant differences between ages ($P < 0.001$) and sites ($P < 0.001$) for all elastic and shear moduli.

For E_2/E_3, the greatest anisotropy was found in the buccal corpus of all ages and in the lingual corpus of adults, while other sites were similar and less anisotropic. For E_1/E_3, little difference was found between juveniles and adults and the greatest anisotropy was found in the buccal and lingual cortices. In infants, greater anisotropy was also found at these sites and anisotropy was greater than that found in juveniles and adults. For E_1/E_2, anisotropy was greater overall in infants than in juveniles and adults. The lingual corpus in infants had remarkably greater anisotropy than all other sites and ages. Post-hoc power analyses showed large effect sizes and power.

6.3.2.7 Directions of the Axes of Maximum Stiffness

Variation in the axes of maximum stiffness varied among sites and among ages at some sites, specifically at the angle of the mandible and at the lingual corpus

Table 6.3 Elastic moduli.

Region	Age	N	E_1 (GPa)		E_2 (GPa)		E_3 (GPa)	
			Mean	SD	Mean	SD	Mean	SD
Coronoid	Infant	5	4.4	0.6	6.9	0.5	8.4	3.0
	Juvenile	10	7.4	0.9	9.7	1.9	13.0	2.7
	Adult	10	8.8	1.6	11.9	2.1	15.9	3.1
Condyle	Infant	5	3.2	1.1	4.2	0.3	6.8	2.3
	Juvenile	10	5.0	1.4	6.0	1.3	8.6	3.0
	Adult	10	9.1	1.7	11.3	1.7	14.7	2.8
Angle	Infant	5	3.7	0.6	4.3	0.4	5.6	1.4
	Juvenile	10	7.0	1.6	7.8	1.6	11.3	1.9
	Adult	10	10.6	2.7	12.0	1.5	18.2	4.3
Buccal	Infant	5	4.2	0.7	5.3	0.4	10.9	2.2
Corpus	Juvenile	10	7.7	1.4	8.3	1.9	15.3	3.8
	Adult	10	9.5	1.4	11.2	2.4	19.7	2.8
Lingual	Infant	5	4.9	1.7	9.7	1.3	12.9	4.3
Corpus	Juvenile	10	9.6	1.3	11.8	2.1	16.5	3.3
	Adult	10	10.3	1.6	12.3	2.1	21.2	1.8
Symphysis	Infant	5	4.0	0.8	5.0	0.3	7.3	1.8
	Juvenile	10	6.3	1.9	6.8	1.9	8.3	1.9
	Adult	10	8.2	1.4	9.3	1.5	12.3	3.4
ANOVA			F	P	F	P	F	P
Age			123.6	< 0.001	98.3	< 0.001	92.4	< 0.001
Site			7.2	< 0.001	17.8	< 0.001	22.3	< 0.001
Age × Site			2.3	0.015	3.0	0.002	1.4	NS
Post-hoc power analysis			Effect size, f	Power	Effect size, f	Power	Effect size, f	Power
Infant			0.58	0.99	3.60	1.00	1.00	0.98
Juvenile			0.98	0.98	1.07	0.96	1.12	0.97
Adult			0.48	0.96	0.53	0.95	1.00	0.98

(Table 6.7 and Figure 6.4). Symphyseal cortical bone samples did not show consistent orientation of maximum stiffness among specimens except in infants. Post-hoc power analyses showed large effect sizes and power.

6.4   Discussion

Two questions are addressed by this study: (1) how do material properties change in the mandible during growth, and (2) do patterns of these material properties relative to region and orientation vary with age? The results confirm that the material properties do change during growth. However, different regions of the mandible change at different rates, and further, the changes in orientation and in anisotropy suggest that these changes involve differential changes in

Table 6.4 Shear moduli.

Region	Age	N	G_{12} (GPa)		G_{31} (GPa)		G_{23} (GPa)	
			Mean	SD	Mean	SD	Mean	SD
Coronoid	Infant	5	2.0	0.3	2.1	0.3	2.9	0.7
	Juvenile	10	2.9	0.5	3.4	0.6	4.5	0.5
	Adult	10	3.6	0.7	4.3	0.7	5.3	0.7
Condyle	Infant	5	1.2	0.6	1.4	0.2	2.0	0.3
	Juvenile	10	2.0	0.5	2.4	0.7	2.8	0.7
	Adult	10	3.6	0.6	4.1	0.8	5.2	0.7
Angle	Infant	5	1.6	0.4	2.1	0.7	1.6	0.6
	Juvenile	10	2.7	0.8	3.3	0.6	3.6	0.6
	Adult	10	4.2	1.1	5.1	1.1	5.5	0.8
Buccal	Infant	5	1.6	0.4	2.6	0.6	2.7	0.8
Corpus	Juvenile	10	2.6	0.4	3.8	0.7	4.3	0.9
	Adult	10	3.9	0.9	4.9	0.8	5.4	1.0
Lingual	Infant	5	2.1	0.7	2.5	0.8	3.9	1.0
Corpus	Juvenile	10	3.9	0.6	4.6	0.7	5.7	0.6
	Adult	10	3.7	0.7	4.9	0.8	6.2	0.5
Symphysis	Infant	5	1.8	0.2	2.2	0.6	1.9	0.6
	Juvenile	10	2.6	1.1	2.8	0.6	2.9	0.7
	Adult	10	3.1	0.4	3.7	0.7	4.2	0.9
ANOVA			F	P	F	P	F	P
Age			82.2	P<0.001	118.3	P<0.001	155.8	P<0.001
Site			5.2	P<0.001	12.0	P<0.001	28.6	P<0.001
Age × Site			3.1	P=0.002	2.5	P=0.008	3.4	P=0.001
Post-hoc power analysis			Effect size, f	Power	Effect size, f	Power	Effect size, f	Power
Infant			0.69	0.74	0.73	0.80	1.15	1.00
Juvenile			0.36	0.95	1.08	0.96	1.50	0.99
Adult			0.46	0.95	0.61	0.96	0.76	0.96

microstructure and not simply increases in density (also see Chapter 2 for more simplistic estimates of perinatal bone density changes across mouse craniofacial bones).

The standard model of cortical bone growth attributes changes in material properties to increases in mineralization and hence density. Increased density results in mature bone that is stiffer, stronger in bending, but less tough (Currey, 2001). These changes in density may be accompanied by alterations in micro-structure, including bone remodeling, and associated changes in collagen ori-entation. It is unclear whether these growth changes are adaptive or are merely correlates of the growth process itself. Here, findings from the pig mandible are compared with what is known from the study of primate mandibles, including the human results presented in this paper and the results from an earlier study of

Table 6.5 Poisson's ratios.

Region	Age	N	ν_{12}		ν_{23}		ν_{31}	
			Mean	SD	Mean	SD	Mean	SD
Coronoid	Infant	5	0.05	0.05	0.26	0.15	0.34	0.19
	Juvenile	10	0.22	0.12	0.21	0.06	0.25	0.09
	Adult	10	0.18	0.11	0.18	0.09	0.24	0.12
Condyle	Infant	5	0.30	0.20	0.23	0.15	0.33	0.21
	Juvenile	10	0.24	0.13	0.24	0.11	0.29	0.15
	Adult	10	0.21	0.13	0.21	0.10	0.26	0.12
Angle	Infant	5	0.16	0.16	0.31	0.07	0.35	0.08
	Juvenile	10	0.27	0.12	0.19	0.06	0.22	0.10
	Adult	10	0.24	0.09	0.15	0.11	0.17	0.15
Buccal	Infant	5	0.26	0.18	0.17	0.13	0.23	0.19
Corpus	Juvenile	10	0.30	0.14	0.18	0.16	0.21	0.15
	Adult	10	0.23	0.16	0.20	0.07	0.22	0.08
Lingual	Infant	5	0.10	0.04	0.18	0.12	0.32	0.21
Corpus	Juvenile	10	0.21	0.12	0.19	0.12	0.22	0.13
	Adult	10	0.35	0.11	0.09	0.06	0.11	0.07
Symphysis	Infant	5	0.12	0.19	0.23	0.12	0.28	0.15
	Juvenile	10	0.26	0.19	0.28	0.11	0.29	0.14
	Adult	10	0.32	0.14	0.20	0.07	0.23	0.10
ANOVA			F	P	F	P	F	P
Age			4.9	0.009	4.0	0.021	5.7	0.004
Site			1.8	0.116	2.1	0.067	1.3	NS
Age × Site			1.9	0.050	1.2	NS	0.7	NS
Post-hoc power analysis			Effect size, f	Power	Effect size, f	Power	Effect size, f	Power
Infant			0.63	0.65	0.39	0.27	0.24	0.12
Juvenile			0.22	0.95	0.35	0.95	0.25	0.95
Adult			0.50	0.96	0.51	0.96	0.46	0.96

the baboon mandible (Wang *et al.*, 2010). These comparisons are made regionally and accompanied by speculation on whether any differences represent unique adaptations.

6.4.1 Mandibular Corpus

The body of the mandible was investigated in our pig model by taking samples from the buccal and lingual cortices inferior to the second molar. Comparisons show that the buccal corpus compared to the lingual corpus tends to be thicker and less dense in infants and juveniles but not in adults. Similar differences are found for the elastic modulus in the radial direction (1) and in the direction of minimum stiffness in the cortical plane (2), but not for the direction of maximum

Table 6.6 Anisotropy.

Region	Age	N	E_2/E_3		E_1/E_3		E_1/E_2	
			Mean	SD	Mean	SD	Mean	SD
Coronoid	Infant	5	0.91	0.35	0.57	0.19	0.64	0.07
	Juvenile	10	0.75	0.12	0.58	0.11	0.78	0.15
	Adult	10	0.76	0.13	0.56	0.07	0.74	0.09
Condyle	Infant	5	0.67	0.20	0.48	0.11	0.74	0.14
	Juvenile	10	0.74	0.21	0.60	0.11	0.83	0.13
	Adult	10	0.78	0.05	0.62	0.08	0.81	0.12
Angle	Infant	5	0.77	0.10	0.68	0.11	0.88	0.14
	Juvenile	10	0.70	0.11	0.61	0.07	0.89	0.14
	Adult	10	0.68	0.16	0.60	0.15	0.89	0.26
Buccal	Infant	5	0.49	0.07	0.39	0.03	0.80	0.08
Corpus	Juvenile	10	0.55	0.06	0.52	0.09	0.94	0.12
	Adult	10	0.56	0.08	0.48	0.04	0.87	0.13
Lingual	Infant	5	0.76	0.12	0.38	0.05	0.50	0.04
Corpus	Juvenile	10	0.72	0.09	0.59	0.07	0.83	0.11
	Adult	10	0.58	0.11	0.49	0.09	0.85	0.12
Symphysis	Infant	5	0.71	0.12	0.56	0.05	0.80	0.10
	Juvenile	10	0.83	0.20	0.77	0.17	0.97	0.27
	Adult	10	0.75	0.17	0.66	0.09	0.90	0.15
ANOVA			F	P	F	P	F	P
Age			0.8	NS	10.4	<0.001	10.1	<0.001
Site			9.5	<0.001	13.4	<0.001	6.4	<0.001
Age × Site			1.7	0.081	2.6	0.007	1.3	NS
Post-hoc power analysis			Effect size, f	Power	Effect size, f	Power	Effect size, f	Power
Infant			1.176	1.00	1.25	1.00	3.68	1.00
Juvenile			0.65	0.95	0.76	0.96	0.44	0.95
Adult			0.73	0.97	0.73	0.97	0.36	0.95

stiffness in the cortical plane (3). Similar differences in shear moduli suggest that the lingual cortex matures more rapidly than the buccal cortex. However, variations in anisotropies are more pronounced throughout growth in the lingual cortex. Cortical specimens from the mandibular body in humans show similar changes as in the pig with increases in density, elastic moduli, and shear moduli throughout growth. However, the anisotropy in humans is not significantly different in infants and adults, suggesting that pigs undergo different structural changes in cortical bone during growth than humans. Likewise, baboons show increases in cortical density and stiffness during growth but, as in humans, do not have pronounced changes in anisotropy. In absolute terms, the bone in adult baboons has a similar density to that of adult pigs, although the pig bone is greater than 1/3 thicker.

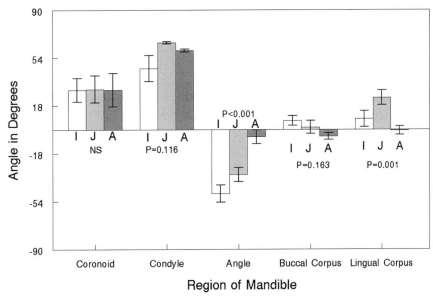

Figure 6.4 Mean orientations of the direction of maximum stiffness in cortical bone samples from pig mandibles. The zero orientation is parallel to the occlusal plane. The orientation of positive and negative angles is shown in Figure 6.1. I, infants; J, juveniles; A, adults.

6.4.2 Mandibular Symphysis

In pigs, cortical bone at the mandibular symphysis tends to be the thickest, least dense, and least stiff of all bone in the mandible in all age groups. Density and stiffness do increase consistently throughout growth but there are few differences in age groups in anisotropies and those that are apparent (E_1/E_3), do not have a consistent pattern of change from infants to adults. This general pattern is similar to that found in baboons between juveniles and adults.

6.4.3 Mandibular Ramus

In pigs, cortical bone was examined separately in different parts of the ramus, namely at the angle, coronoid process, and condylar neck, whereas in baboons (Wang *et al.*, 2010) data from sites throughout the ramus were lumped for analysis. This makes some direct comparisons difficult as the pigs showed interesting differences between these regions. Overall, differences in pigs were not great between these regions in adults. However, there were marked growth differences, with the coronoid process showing more rapid maturation than the angle or the condylar process. For instance, cortical thickness reached that of adults by the juvenile stage at the coronoid process and condylar neck, but lagged behind at the mandibular angle. Conversely, density lagged behind at the condylar neck compared to cortical bone at the coronoid process and angle. There were no marked differences in anisotropy in any of the regions of the ramus during growth. From the available data,

Table 6.7 Mean direction of maximum stiffness (D_3) by site in degrees.

Site	Age	N	Orientation in degrees			Watson–Williams F-test among ages
			Mean	SD	Rayleigh test (P)	
Coronoid	Infant	5	29.8	14.0	0.011	NS
	Juvenile	10	30.5	10.2	0.026	
	Adult	10	29.7	33.2	0.070	
Condyle	Infant	5	46.0	15.5	0.015	F=2.2
	Juvenile	10	65.3	26.1	0.009	P=0.116
	Adult	10	59.4	19.3	<0.001	
Angle	Infant	5	-48.2	10.1	0.005	F=13.6
	Juvenile	10	-33.9	14.3	<0.001	P<0.001
	Adult	10	-5.5	14.0	<0.001	
Buccal	Infant	5	6.7	5.8	0.002	F=1.9
Corpus	Juvenile	10	1.7	12.9	<0.001	P<0.163
	Adult	10	-5.1	6.7	<0.001	
Lingual	Infant	5	7.9	9.3	0.004	F=7.5
Corpus	Juvenile	10	23.9	15.3	<0.001	P=0.001
	Adult	10	-0.7	8.4	<0.001	
	Infant	5	-76.6	15.7	0.015	
Symphysis	Juvenile	10	69.6	44.8	NS	
	Adult	10	17.8	41.2	NS	

Watson–Williams F-tests by age among sites
Infant $F = 29.6, P < 0.001$
Juvenile $F = 37.7, P < 0.001$
Adult $F = 23.5, P < 0.001$

Post-hoc power analysis
Infant: effect size f = 3.68, power = 1.00
Juvenile: effect size f = 1.73, power = 1.00
Adult: effect size f = 1.13, power = 0.97

it appears that maturation of the ramus is similar in baboons and pigs. As in pigs, thickness of the cortical bone of the ramus is similar between juveniles and adults, but density and stiffness are not and they increase with maturation.

6.4.4   Significance and Comparisons with Other Skeletal Regions

The differences in mandibular cortical material properties among pigs, baboons, and humans at various ages suggest different patterns of maturation in both mineralization and microstructure. Unfortunately, similar data from multiple ages do not exist for the mandibles of other vertebrates. There are some interesting growth studies of different bony organs in various species, although none of these examine three-dimensional material properties and are thus not comparable to the data in the current study. For example, Carrier and Leon (1990) show that elastic moduli of various limb bones mature at variable rates in California gulls, but little is known about orientations and anisotropies in these bones. Similar growth changes in the femurs of polar bears are compared with deer and humans by Brear and Currey (1990). They show increases in strength and elastic moduli that correspond with changes in bone density in all three species; however, variations in timing and degree of mineralization exist among species. The methodology did not allow investigation of orientations of axes of stiffness and anisotropies. See also Chapter 12 for a review of differences in the development of trabecular bone properties between appendicular bones.

6.4.5   Anthropological Implications

Measurement of *in vivo* bone strain in the craniofacial skeletons of primates has been used to determine how these skeletons deform during function; this information is then used to make inferences about the relationship between function and skeletal form. The addition of material properties to the analysis of bone strain patterns can have important effects on the interpretation of those patterns. Work by Dechow and Hylander (2000) examined these effects in great detail by applying material property information to the results of *in vivo* strain gage studies in the mandibles of adult macaques. A comparison was made between magnitudes and orientations of measured strains and magnitudes and orientations of stresses calculated from measured strains and material properties. This comparison is equivalent to examining the differences between stresses in an isotropic material (strains without material property data incorporated) and stresses in an orthotropic material. In other words, they show the effects of the material properties on the functional interpretations of mandibular loading. Despite studies showing theoretical divergences in stress orientations of up to 45° when orthotropic materials are modeled as isotropic (Cowin and Hart, 1990), actual differences were much smaller, with empirical differences found up to 12°. Ratios between maximum and minimum stresses had greater maximum differences of nearly 2.5 times. Dechow and Hylander (2000) examined the implications of these differences for interpretations of the function of the mandible. It was found to make little difference in interpretations of balancing side function, but showed greater effects, especially in maximum and minimum stress ratios, on the working side. Dechow and Hylander concluded (p. 573): "The significance of differences (resulting from the inclusion of material properties) between the orientations and relative magnitudes of stress and strains must be addressed on a case by case basis."

The problem of requiring material property information to adequately interpret skeletal strain patterns is magnified in finite element studies. A number of these investigations have looked at the impact of using isometric material properties compared to orthotropic material properties. Studies of the human femur have received the greatest attention (Peng *et al.*, 2006; Baca *et al.*, 2008; Yang et al., 2010; Geraldes and Phillips, 2014). Overall, these studies have noted that overall patterns of strain tend to be similar in the femur regardless of the use of either isometric or orthotropic material properties. The greatest differences tend to be found when local patterns of deformation are considered or when working with small pieces of bone. However, the results of these studies may be strongly influenced by the loading patterns in the finite-element simulations because longitudinal compression of a long bone tends to align the direction of the load with the orientation of maximum stiffness, which is also longitudinal. When loading orientation and maximum stiffness orientation are aligned, deviations between the orientations and relative magnitudes of stress and strain are minimized (Dechow and Hylander, 2000).

Several studies in the anthropology literature have addressed the issue of including material properties in the interpretation of finite-element models of jaws and crania (Strait *et al.*, 2005; Cox *et al.*, 2011; Wood *et al.*, 2011; Berthaume *et al.*, 2012; Groning *et al.*, 2012). These sensitivity studies have looked at the impact of a number of factors, including material properties, on the results of finite element models. Overall, the addition of orthotropic material properties to the models improves the models, yielding results more similar to *in vivo* testing. However, these studies take more global views and note that overall patterns of stress and strain are similar when considering whole skeletal structures. Larger deviations tend to be found locally, suggesting that the impact of including material properties needs to be analyzed on a case-by-case, or region-by-region, basis. In other words, the impact of material properties on the interpretation of strain patterns depends on local-bone geometry and loading. Future bone strain and finite-element studies need to consider the use of material properties in their analyses and conduct sensitivity studies to see if the inclusion of this information makes a difference in the outcome.

In this study, differences in the material properties of the pig mandible at different stages revealed a complex pattern of growth and maturation, much of which can be attributed to increasing bone density with age, especially regarding elastic and shear moduli. Other variables such as anisotropy and orientation of maximum stiffness, which do not correlate with density, also show some changes with age indicating changes in internal microstructure with growth (Dechow *et al.*, 2008). Detailed examination of the results suggests different patterns in different regions. For instance, along the buccal corpus, the angle of maximum stiffness is similar at different ages, although E_2/E_3 anisotropy decreases slightly with maturation. In contrast, the angle of the mandible shows a 42.7° shift from infant to adult while E_2/E_3 anisotropy increases. Interpretation of the impact of these differences between regions on the relationship between stress and strain patterns would require an understanding of the different loading and boundary conditions at each region. For this reason, it is doubtful whether one can generalize from region to region and across ages on the impact of including material properties in a functional analysis. The comparison of the human infant to the adult on the buccal portion of the mandible reveals no difference in anisotropy. This finding is different from that in the pigs and calls into question how much we can generalize about material property changes during growth across species. More data from multiple species are needed to resolve this issue.

A few recent studies in rats and mice (for example, Alippi *et al.*, 2005; Main *et al.*, 2010; Checa *et al.*, 2015) have considered the interplay between skeletal structure and intrinsic material properties during growth, and their adaptive significance. These studies strengthen the notion that changes in material properties during growth coincide with structural changes to produce anatomical structures that are well adapted to that particular phase of life history. Exploring this concept in different skeletal organs in primate growth and development shows promise for understanding the dynamics of bone growth in primate evolution.

6.5   Acknowledgments

This research was supported by the National Science Foundation Physical Anthropology HOMINID program, grant number NSF BCS 0725141. I thank Chris Percival and Joan Richtsmeier for inviting me to participate in this volume and I thank the late Dr. Edward Shinedling for help with data collection in this research.

References

Alippi, R. M., Olivera, M. I., Bozzini, C., Huygens, P. A. and Bozzini, C. E. (2005). Changes in material and architectural properties of rat femoral diaphysis during ontogeny in hypophysectomized rats. *Comparative Clinical Pathology*, 14, 76–80.

Ashman, R. B., Cowin, S. C., Van Buskirk, W. C; and Rice, J. C. (1984). A continuous wave technique for the measurement of the elastic properties of cortical bone. *Journal of Biomechanics*, 17, 349–361.

Baca, V., Horak, Z., Mikulenka, P. and Dzupa, V. (2008). Comparison of an inhomogeneous orthotropic and isotropic material models used for FE analysis. *Medical Engineering & Physics*, 30, 924–930.

Berthaume, M. A., Dechow, P. C., Iriarte-Diaz, J., *et al.* (2012). Probabilistic finite element analysis of a craniofacial finite element model. *Journal of Theoretical Biology*, 300, 242–253.

Brear, K. and Currey, J. D. (1990). Ontogenetic changes in the mechanical properties of the femur of the polar bear *Ursus maritimus*. *Journal of Zoology*, 222, 49–58.

Brosh, T., Rozitsky, D., Geron, S. and Pilo, R. (2014). Tensile mechanical properties of swine cortical mandibular bone. *PLoS ONE*, 91(2), e113229.

Carrier, D. and Leon, L. R. (1990). Skeletal growth and function in the California gull (*Larus californicus*). *Journal of Zoology*, 222, 375–389.

Checa, S., Hesse, B., Roschger, P., *et al.* (2015). Skeletal maturation substantially affects elastic tissue properties in the endosteal and periosteal regions of loaded mice tibiae. *Acta Biomaterialia*, 21, 154–164.

Chung, D. H. and Dechow, P. C. (2011). Elastic anisotropy and off-axis ultrasonic velocity distribution in human cortical bone. *Journal of Anatomy*, 218, 26–39.

Cowin, S. C. and Hart, R.T. (1990). Errors in the orientation of the principal stress axes if bone tissue is modeled as isotropic. *Journal of Biomechanics*, 23, 349–352.

Cox, P. G., Fagan, M. J., Rayfield, E. J. and Jeffery, N. (2011). Finite element modelling of squirrel, guinea pig and rat skulls: using geometric morphometrics to assess sensitivity. *Journal of Anatomy*, 219, 696–709.

Currey, J. D. (2001). Ontogenetic changes in compact bone material properties. *In:* Cowin, S. C. (ed.) *Bone Mechanics Handbook, Second Edition*. Boca Raton, FL: CRC Press, pp. 19.1–19.16.

Daegling, D. J., Granatosky, M. C., McGraw, W. S. and Rapoff, A. J. (2011a). Reduced stiffness of alveolar bone in the colobine mandible. *American Journal of Physical Anthropology*, 144, 421–431.

Daegling, D. J., Granatosky, M. C., McGraw, W. S. and Rapoff, A. J. (2011b). Spatial patterning of bone stiffness variation in the colobine alveolar process. *Archives of Oral Biology*, 56, 220–230.

Daegling, D. J., Granatosky, M. C. and McGraw, W. S. (2014). Ontogeny of material stiffness heterogeneity in the macaque mandibular corpus. *American Journal of Physical Anthropology*, 153, 297–304.

Davis, M. T., Loyd, A. M., Shen, H. H., *et al.* (2012). The mechanical and morphological properties of 6 year-old cranial bone. *Journal of Biomechanics*, 45, 2493–2498.

Dechow, P. C. and Hylander, W. L. (2000). Elastic properties and masticatory bone stress in the macaque mandible. *American Journal of Physical Anthropology*, 112, 553–574.

Dechow, P. C., Schwartz-Dabney, C. L. and Ashman, R. (1992). Elastic properties of the human mandibular corpus. In: Goldstein, S. A. and Carlson, D. S (eds.) *Bone Biodynamics in Orthodontic and Orthopedic Treatment, Volume 27*. Craniofacial Growth Series. Ann Arbor, MI: Center for Human Growth and Development, The University of Michigan, pp. 299–314.

Dechow, P. C., Nail, G. A., Schwartz-Dabney, C. L. and Ashman, R. B. (1993). Elastic properties of human supraorbital and mandibular bone. *American Journal of Physical Anthropology*, 90, 291–306.

Dechow, P. C., Chung, D. H. and Bolouri, M. (2008). Relationship between three dimensional microstructure and elastic properties of cortical bone in the human mandible and femur. *In:* Vinyard, C. J., Ravosa, M. J. and Wall, C. E. (eds.) *Primate Craniofacial Function and Biology*. New York, NY: Springer, pp. 265–292.

Dechow, P. C., Wang, Q. and Peterson, J. (2010). Edentulation alters material properties of cortical bone in the human craniofacial skeleton: functional implications for craniofacial structure in primate evolution. *Anatomical Record*, 293, 618–629.

Faul, F., Erdfelder, E., Lang, A.-G. and Buchner, A. (2007). G*Power 3: a flexible statistical power analysis program for the social, behavioral, and biomedical sciences. *Behavior Research Methods*, 39, 175–191.

Geraldes, D. M. and Phillips, A. T. M. (2014). A comparative study of orthotropic and isotropic bone adaptation in the femur. *International Journal of Numerical Methods in Biomedical Engineering*, 30, 873–889.

Groning, F., Fagan, M. and O'Higgins, P. (2012). Modeling the human mandible under masticatory loads: which input variables are important? *The Anatomical Record*, 295, 853–863.

Hara, T., Takizawa, M., Sato, T. and Ide, Y. (1998). Mechanical properties of buccal compact bone of the mandibular ramus in human adults and children: relationship of the elastic modulus to the direction of the osteon and the porosity ratio. *Bulletin of the Tokyo Dental College*, 39, 47–55.

Lettry, S., Seedhom, B. B., Berry, E. and Cuppone, M. (2003). Quality assessment of the cortical bone of the human mandible. *Bone*, 32, 35–44.

Main, R. P., Lynch, M. E. and van der Meulen, C. H. (2010). *In vivo* tibial stiffness is maintained by whole bone morphology and cross-sectional geometry in growing female mice. *Journal of Biomechanics*, 43, 2689–2694.

Nomura, T., Gold, E., Powers, M. P., Shingaki, S. and Katz, J. L. (2003). Micromechanics/structure relationships in the human mandible. *Dental Materials*, 19, 167–173.

Peng, L., Bai, J., Zeng, X. and Zhou, Y. (2006). Comparison of isotropic and orthotropic material property assignments on femoral finite element models under two loading conditions. *Medical Engineering & Physics*, 28, 277–233.

Peterson, J. and Dechow, P. C. (2002). Material properties of the inner and outer cortical tables of the human parietal bone. *Anatomical Record*, 268, 7–15.

Peterson, J. and Dechow, P. C. (2003). Material properties of the human cranial vault and zygoma. *Anatomical Record*, 274, 785–797.

Peterson, J., Wang, Q. and Dechow, P. C. (2006). Material properties of the dentate maxilla. *Anatomical Record*, 288, 962–972.

Rapoff, A. J., Rinaldi, R. G., Hotzman, J. L. and Daegling, D. J. (2008). Elastic modulus variation in mandibular bone: a microindentation study of Macaca fascicularis. *American Journal of Physical Anthropology*, 135, 100–109.

Schwartz-Dabney, C. L. and Dechow, P. C. (2002a). Accuracy of elastic property measurement in mandibular cortical bone is improved by using cylindrical specimens. *Journal of Biomechanical Engineering*, 124, 714–723.

Schwartz-Dabney, C. L. and Dechow, P. C. (2002b). Edentulation alters material properties of cortical bone in the human mandible. *Journal of Dental Research*, 81, 613–617.

Schwartz-Dabney, C. L. and Dechow, P. C. (2003). Variations in cortical material properties throughout the human dentate mandible. *American Journal of Physical Anthropology*, 120, 252–277.

Strait, D. S., Wang, Q., Dechow, P. C., *et al.* (2005). Modeling elastic properties in finite-element analysis: how much precision is needed to produce an accurate model? *Anatomical Record*, 283, 275–287.

Wang, J., Zou, D., Li, Z., *et al.* (2014). Mechanical properties of cranial bones and sutures in 1–2-year-old infants. *Medical Science Monitor*, 20, 1808–1813.

Wang, Q. and Dechow, P. C. (2006). Elastic properties of external cortical bone in the craniofacial skeleton of the rhesus monkey. *American Journal of Physical Anthropology*, 131, 402–415.

Wang, Q., Strait, D. S. and Dechow, P. C. (2006). A comparison of cortical elastic properties in the craniofacial skeletons of three primate species and its relevance to the study of human evolution. *Journal of Human Evolution*, 51, 375–382.

Wang, Q., Ashley, D. W. and Dechow, P. C. (2010). Regional, ontogenetic, and sex-related variations in elastic properties of cortical bone in baboon mandibles. *American Journal of Physical Anthropology*, 141, 526–549.

Wood, S. A., Strait, D. S., Dumont, E. R., Ross, C. F. and Grosse, I. R. (2011). The effects of modeling simplifications on craniofacial finite element models: the alveoli (tooth sockets) and periodontal ligaments. *Journal of Biomechanics*, 44, 1831–1838.

Yang, H., Ma, X. and Guo, T. (2010). Some factors that affect the comparison between isotropic and orthotropic inhomogeneous finite element material models of femur. *Medical Engineering & Physics*, 32, 553–560.

7 Postcranial Skeletal Development and Its Evolutionary Implications

David B. Burr and Jason M. Organ

7.1 Introduction

Changes in patterns of skeletal growth and development have taken a back seat to attempts to understand morphology strictly as the result of adaptive changes in the adult form. However, small changes in genetically determined developmental patterns can have large and significant effects on adult structure (Towers and Tickle, 2009; Rolian, 2014) that may have less to do with fully adult behaviors and adaptations, and have everything to do with ensuring survival of the developing child until he or she can reach the minimum age to reproduce. Epigenetic interactions between morphological adaptations to environment and the genetic changes that are permissive to those adaptations to an unpredictable environment are complex and interrelated. Development carries out the genetic blueprint, while it also influences the variability of phenotypic expression (Rolian, 2014). Genetic alterations provide the palette of potential adaptive responses, giving the organism the flexibility to respond to its own particular environment (for the developmentalist argument, see Roseman and Weaver, 2007). Thus, growth and skeletal development do not proceed along a completely predetermined path, but can follow a variety of different paths depending on specific morphogens or other environmental factors (ten Broek et al., 2012). These environmental factors can in fact be passed along to the next generation through adaptive events that change the expression of DNA sequences that regulate development (Grossniklaus et al., 2013). Evolution involves a constant interplay between slow and seemingly random genetic changes and more rapid, predictable adaptations of body form.

The goal of this chapter is to describe the mechanisms for normal human growth and development of long bones and synovial joints as a basis for understanding growth and development in an evolutionary framework. In that context, normal human growth and development can help to explain variations in body size and proportion, allometric relationships, the evolutionary limitations on somatic adaptation (see Bateson, 1963), and the diversity of primate and early human form and function.

7.2   Postcranial Skeletal Development

Development of the postcranial skeleton occurs through two separate processes of ossification. Bone lengthens through a program of endochondral ossification in which a cartilage "model" (or *anlage*) of the bone shape is produced first, and subsequently replaced by mineralized tissue. Bone width increases in part through a process of intramembranous ossification, in which the fibrocellular perichondrium (the perichondrial ring) encircling the cartilage *anlage* expands and mineralizes.

7.2.1   Longitudinal Growth through Endochondral Ossification

Longitudinal growth occurs by endochondral ossification, in which a cartilage anlage is formed and is eventually replaced by bone. A pre-cartilage model of the eventual bone is formed between the fifth and the twelfth weeks of intrauterine development from lateral plate somatic mesoderm. The pre-cartilage model initially is composed of loose, undifferentiated mesenchyme that is continuous with general mesenchyme in the mesodermal layer. By the sixth embryonic week, the hyaline cartilage model begins to form as the mesenchyme for bone formation begins to differentiate from muscle mesenchyme. At this time, a mesenchymal condensation forms the perichondrium at the periphery of the model to surround the *anlage*. At about the eighth week of development, vascular invasion of the anlage occurs, bringing mesenchymal cells that can differentiate into osteoblasts to form bone, but which will also allow development of the synovial joint and capsule. Between the seventh and twenty-eighth weeks of development, primary centers of ossification are established across the width of the developing shaft of the model, extending in both directions usually to form two ossification fronts (Figure 7.1).

7.2.2   Appositional Growth through Intramembranous Ossification

The periosteum is a condensation of general mesenchyme that forms a fibrous sheath around the cartilage model during growth. It ends by attaching to the margin of the developing joint, where it forms a fibrous condensation of tissue called the perichondrial ring. This ring has its own blood supply, initially separate from those of the epiphysis or the capillary buds that supply the primary spongiosa (Figure 7.2). As the bone grows in width, progenitor cells lying in the deep layers of the fibrous membrane next to the cartilage anlage will differentiate into bone-forming osteoblasts and contribute to the formation of a mineralized ring around the anlage. This appositional process continues throughout life, even after longitudinal growth has stopped. During longitudinal growth, both the cellular and the fibrous layer of the periosteal sheath will migrate to cover the new bone as it grows longitudinally (Ochareon and Herring, 2007). It has been suggested that the insertion of the periosteum into the mineralized bone regulates longitudinal growth by constraining it, and that periosteal release can permit and accelerate growth (Wilde and Baker, 1987; Hernandez *et al.*, 1995; Forriol and

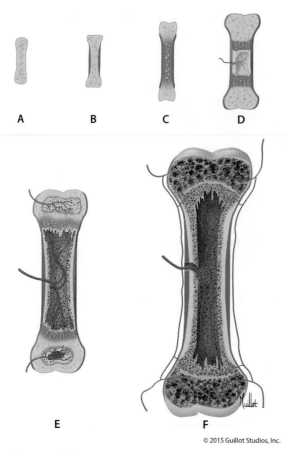

© 2015 Guillot Studios, Inc.

Figure 7.1 (A) A cartilage model of the developing bone is formed from general mesenchyme. (B) A periosteal collar is formed around the circumference of the cartilage model. This collar contributes to appositional growth of the bone, as the cartilage in the primary center begins to calcify (C). Subsequent vascular growth into the calcified cartilage core (D) allows the cartilage to be remodeled into bone. (E) Postnatally, secondary centers of ossification (epiphyses) develop at the ends of the long bones, separated from the primary center by the epiphyseal, or growth, plate. Note that at this time the blood supplies to the primary and secondary centers are independent, and if the supply to the secondary center is disrupted for any reason, it can die. (F) When growth ceases, the epiphysis fuses to the diaphysis, and the cartilaginous growth plate disappears, although an ossified ghost of it may still be visible by x-ray. At this time, there is collateral circulation between the diaphysis and the epiphyseal region.

Shapiro, 2005). This was thought to be a physical constraint because the periosteal sheath is highly pre-stressed and physically retracts and shortens when cut (McBride *et al.*, 2011), but the tensile stresses generated by the fibrous periosteum are not large enough to provide such physical constraint (Foolen *et al.*, 2009). The mechanism for this constraint is more likely through mechanically regulated cellular pathways that allow intracellular sensing of tensile stress (Foolen *et al.*, 2011), which results in the release of soluble inhibitory factors by the periosteal

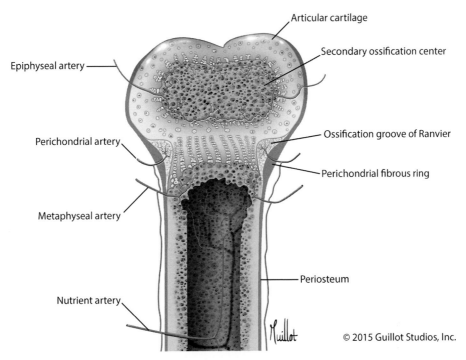

Articular cartilage

Secondary ossification center

Epiphyseal artery

Ossification groove of Ranvier

Perichondrial artery

Perichondrial fibrous ring

Metaphyseal artery

Periosteum

Nutrient artery

© 2015 Guillot Studios, Inc.

Figure 7.2 A more detailed drawing of the growth plate, showing the various regions of the growth plate and their vascular supply.

osteoblasts (Bertram *et al.*, 1998; Di Nino *et al.*, 2001). When the periosteum is incised, bone morphogenetic proteins (e.g., BMP-2 and BMP-4) are released, accelerating additional longitudinal growth.

7.2.3   The Development of Synovial Joints

At about the time when the cartilage model begins to form from the undifferentiated mesenchyme (the sixth week of human development), the mesenchyme between the ends of two adjacent cartilage models condenses to form dense laminae that surround the articulating surface of each cartilage anlage. Between them is an intermediate zone or lamina composed of general mesenchyme between the two dense condensations (Figure 7.3). This *trilaminar disk* serves to allow the longitudinal growth of the anlage from the ends, but will also develop into the synovial joint cavity. The dense laminae are continuous with the perichondrium surrounding the anlage, and are chondrogenic. The loose cells of the intermediate lamina are avascular but continuous with the general mesenchyme along the margins of the joint that will develop into the fibrous capsule and periosteal membrane.

The general mesenchyme at the margins of the joint condenses and becomes continuous with the perichondrium, investing the joint surfaces like a sleeve, and becoming embedded in the cartilage model to eventually form Sharpey's fibers. The

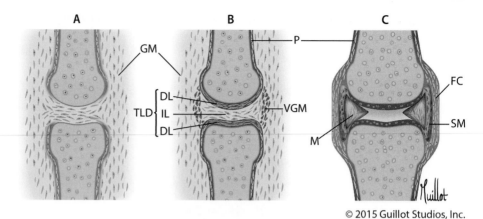

© 2015 Guillot Studios, Inc.

Figure 7.3 The synovial joint develops from general mesenchyme (GM), which is avascular in the region that will become the joint cavity, but is vascular peripherally where the synovial membrane will develop. Eventually, the mesenchyme of the joint will differentiate into two dense laminae (DL), and an intermediate zone (IL); the three regions are collectively called the trilaminar disk (TLD). The intermediate zone degenerates to form a cavity, whereas the dense laminae are chondrogenic and form the articular cartilage. The peripheral vascular mesenchyme (VGM) forms the fibrous capsule (FC), the synovial lining of the capsule (SM), and intra-articular structures such as menisci (M) and intra-articular ligaments (not shown). Note that the perichondrium (P) becomes continuous with the fibrous capsule.

mesenchyme subsequently differentiates into an outer fibrous layer, the fibrous portion of the joint capsule that is continuous with perichondrium (and eventually with the periosteum), and an inner vascular membrane, which becomes the synovial membrane. The synovial membrane develops from a portion of the vascular mesenchyme that becomes separated from the general mesenchyme as the fibrous capsule forms. This synovial mesenchyme forms all the intra-articular structures (ligaments and intra-articular disks), and envelops all the intra-articular structures except the menisci, intra-articular disks, and articular cartilage. This process also allows the formation of the articular labra (glenoid and acetabular labra). The intra-articular structures form *in situ* prior to joint space cavitation. The vascular synovial membrane contains cells that regulate joint metabolism and produce synovial fluid (mostly hyaluronic acid) to lubricate and nourish the articular cartilage and intra-articular joint structures. It also functions to prevent joint degeneration by phagocytosis of foreign debris from the joint, and by cellular inhibition of lysosomal enzymatic activity that can cause cartilage destruction.

At about 10–12 weeks of embryonic development, the avascular loose interzone mesenchyme condenses into a parallel arrangement, and the cells in this layer begin to secrete hyaluronic acid, which is believed to liquefy the intercellular mesenchyme, starting the process of cavitation. Prior to this, differential replacement of extracellular matrix in the articular interzone weakens the intra-articular connections (Archer *et al.*, 1994). Small fluid-filled spaces appear peripherally, coalesce, and move internally in the joint, causing cavitation and forming the joint space and fluid-filled bursae that surround and protect the joints. Cell death may precede the initiation of cavitation, which corresponds in time to the disappearance of the dense chondrogenic layers of the trilaminar disk and their conversion into articular cartilage. This is coincident with the initiation of ossification of the long bones. The result of this activity is a free cavity, filled with joint fluid, surrounded by a synovial membrane and a fibrous capsule.

By the end of the human embryonic period (12 weeks postconception), all component parts of the joints have developed. Synovial villi are apparent, and the neurovascular supply to the joint is present. For a healthy, morphologically normal synovial joint to form, movement must take place at the joint. Neuromuscular failures that prevent movement can cause joint ankyloses or other forms of joint dysplasias, as well as a poorly shaped diaphysis. This is because muscle contraction leads to high tensile stress in the interzone regions and results in cleavage and eventual cavitation (Drachman, 1969). Cavitation reduces the friction between articulating surfaces, and allows articulating surfaces to develop in tandem. This process explains the initial formation of synovial joint articular surfaces (Carter and Beaupre, 2001).

7.3   Postnatal Growth of the Skeleton

7.3.1   Longitudinal Growth

Because the postcranial skeleton needs to grow in size, but also remain sensitive to changing mechanical forces as it does so, longitudinal growth occurs in a region of cartilage near the end of the bone. In most cases postnatally the secondary centers of ossification (epiphyses) develop where the adjacent bones articulate. This region of growth is called the growth (epiphyseal) plate, or physis. It separates the bony epiphysis from the metaphysis and, following cartilage hypertrophy, matrix calcification, and erosion by vascular elements penetrating from the perichondrium, it mineralizes and fuses when growth stops (Figure 7.1). Usually, there is a secondary center at each end of the bone, although in some bones like the metacarpals and phalanges there is only one (see Chapter 9). During development, the epiphysis is supplied by its own epiphyseal artery, without collateral circulation (Figures 7.1 and 7.2). If this blood supply is disrupted for any reason, the secondary center will fail to develop and the cells in it will die.

Most often, one growth plate contributes more to longitudinal growth than the other. In the femur, this is the distal growth plate; in the tibia, it is the proximal plate (Kuhn et al., 1996; Wilsman et al., 1996b). It has been reported that rates of growth may vary by two to three times in different growth plates from the same bone, and up to sevenfold in different growth plates from different bones (Wilsman et al., 1996b). Most likely, this differential growth occurs through a synergistic interaction of cell division in the resting and proliferative zones (Breur et al., 1991; Liu et al. 2011), matrix synthesis in the proliferative zone (Wilsman et al., 1996b), and hypertrophic cell enlargement (Hunziker et al., 1987; Breur et al., 1991;

Kuhn *et al.*, 1996). The differential cellular swelling of the hypertrophic chondro-cytes may occur under the influence of IGF-1 (Cooper *et al.* 2013), which in turn elevates vascular endothelial growth factor (VEGF) expression (Garcia-Ramirez *et al.*, 2000), although many growth factors, proteins, and enzymes are known to be present and regulated in the growth plate (Breur *et al.*, 1991). VEGF is produced by hypertrophic chondrocytes, and regulates vascular permeability of the bone matrix in addition to providing paracrine regulation at the mineralization front of the growth plate (see Farnum *et al.*, 2006, for a discussion of this). This feedback loop between VEGF and hypertrophic chondrocytes may be functionally driven, as suggested by Cooper and colleagues (2013), and may fuel the differential growth of the lower limb segments in some animals (see Chapter 9 for review of additional genetic factors acting at the epiphyseal growth plate).

In the newborn, the physis is typically a flat, basically circular plate, which increases in diameter through cellular division at its circumference in a region called the zone of Ranvier. Over time, the physis loses its flat shape and becomes curved, often with a complex set of ridges that stabilize the joint and connect the developing cartilage to the underlying mineralized bone. This interlocking between the cartilage and bone protects against failure in response to shear stresses at the bone–cartilage junction.

New cartilage is formed continually throughout growth by cartilage cells, or chon-drocytes, primarily within the proliferative zone of the growth plate. The growth plate is divided into zones, each representing a stage in the life cycle of its chondro-cytes (Figure 7.4). The *reserve zone* (sometimes called the quiescent or resting zone) is furthest from the calcification front. In this zone, the cartilage matrix is composed of randomly oriented collagen fibers and a few irregularly arranged chondrocytes. The relative matrix volume of this zone is more than twice as large as the proliferative and hypertrophic zones combined (Farnum and Wilsman, 1998; Sergerie *et al.*, 2009). Adjacent to this is a *proliferative zone* in which, as the name implies, disc-shaped chondrocytes rapidly divide, and arrange themselves in columns oriented parallel to the longitudinally oriented collagen fibers. It is estimated that each cell produces about twice its own volume in new matrix during its lifetime (Hunziker *et al.*, 1987). As the chondrocytes age they begin to enlarge their volume and surface area by 4–10 times (i.e., they become hypertrophic) (Hunziker *et al.*, 1987; Horton, 1993), they accu-mulate intracellular glycogen, and they die through apoptosis. Chondrocyte hyper-trophy may represent the greatest contribution to longitudinal growth of any zone of the growth plate (Wilsman *et al.*, 1996), and is closely related not only to the amount of longitudinal growth but to the rate of longitudinal growth as well. Breur and col-leagues (1991) reported correlations between hypertrophic cell volume and longitu-dinal growth rate as high as 0.83–0.98 in experimental animals. In this *hypertrophic zone*, the chondrocytes continue to produce matrix, especially in the upper hyper-trophic zone, as actively as in the proliferative zone, but catabolism becomes pre-dominant in the lower hypertrophic zone. The cells stop multiplying and the cartilage between the columns of hypertrophic cells begins to degrade. This leaves columns of cartilage with dying cells that begin to calcify between the remaining cells. This *zone of*

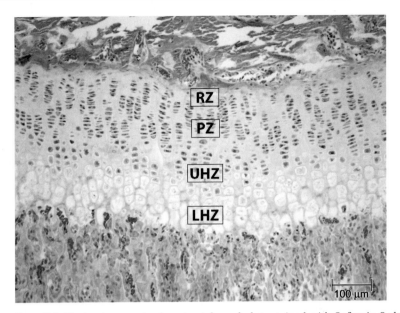

Figure 7.4 Photomicrograph of a rat epiphyseal plate stained with Safranin O show-ing the different cellular regions that contribute to longitudinal growth. The very narrow zone at the top of the cartilage is the *resting zone* (RZ), which here appears to have few cells. Cells in the *proliferative zone* (PZ), where mitosis and cell matrix production primarily occur, organize themselves in columns. These cells are some-what flattened or disc-shaped. These cells eventually begin to enlarge (become hyperotrophic) and are rounder, but in the *upper hypertrophic zone* (UHZ) still pro-duce significant amounts of matrix. These cells become apoptotic, enlarging further with nuclear disintegration, indicated by the loss of staining. Many lacunae in this *lower hypertrophic zone* (LHZ) are empty. The columns between the hypertrophic chondrocytes calcify. As the hypertrophic cells are lost, spaces form that are filled by blood vessels, which will provide cells responsible for remodeling the calcified cartilage columns into bone, or primary spongiosa. A black and white version of this figure will appear in some formats. For the color version, please refer to the plate section.

provisional calcification is the junction between the growth plate and the metaphysis. The process of mineralization is likely a permissive process brought on by an increase in alkaline phosphatase and a reduction in the proteoglycan aggrecan. In this region, the walls between the cell columns continue to disappear, but others will survive to form the primary spongiosa (Farnum and Wilsman, 1989). Frost (1994b) suggested that the mineralization of the cartilage in this zone, which increases its stiffness, creates a region of virtual disuse (i.e., lower strains) that could provide the signal for the resorption of matrix between the columns of hypertrophic cells. Subsequently, capillary invasion brings in cells that differentiate into osteoblasts that deposit bone on the calcified septa that remain. These septa remain attached to the growth plate, but form a zone of weakness where the epiphysis can separate from the rest of the bone (e.g., in a slipped capital femoral epiphysis). The septa continue to remodel to bone, but failure to further remodel can leave primary spongiosa with a calcified cartilage core. If there is any disruption to the base of the growth plate (i.e., near the zone of calcification), the cells cannot form bone and will die. In this case, the physis may develop a fibrous tissue connection with the primary center of ossification.

The groove of Ranvier is a region surrounding the margins of the epiphyseal plate during growth. It is an area of active cell division and appositional growth found at the junction of the growth plate and the metaphysis; it is highly vascular (Farnum et al., 2006). Peripheral to this groove and surrounding it is a ring of collagen-rich fibrous tissue, the perichondrial ring of LaCroix, which is continuous with the periosteum. These structures at the margin of the growth plate can be considered analogous to the fibrous and cellular periosteum surrounding the diaphysis. This ring may provide stability at the junction of the growth plate and metaphysis, preventing lateral forces from dislodging the growth plate from the underlying bone.

The anabolic and catabolic processes that occur at the growth plate are coupled so that, under usual conditions, the width of the growth plate is controlled within limits, while the metaphyseal and diaphyseal parts of the bone are lengthened. New cartilage is produced at the junction closest to the epiphysis, while cartilage at the base of the growth plate adjacent to the metaphysis becomes mineralized, and eventually replaced by bone through remodeling processes (resorption and subsequent replacement with mineralized bone). Usually, a thicker growth plate is associated with rapid growth, and a narrower one with slower growth, so growth rate can be estimated based on plate thickness (Wilsman et al., 1996a). However, under conditions of overloading, growth plate height can expand because matrix proliferation continues (albeit at a reduced rate) but mineralization at the base of the growth plate is suppressed. Therefore, growth plate height is not always the best surrogate for growth rate. However, there are other approaches for assessing growth rate from the epiphyseal plate. Kember (1985) suggested that bone growth could be estimated by the number of proliferative cells and the terminal size of the hypertrophic chondrocytes because these features vary more widely than the more highly regulated rate of cell division. The hypertrophic zone appears to be most influential, because hypertrophic cells elongate mostly in the direction of growth (Cooper et al., 2013), by about fourfold (Hunziker et al., 1987), so that chondrocyte enlargement and matrix synthesis in this zone account for 58–87% of the variability in growth rate (Wilsman et al., 1996a). Another estimate of strictly longitudinal growth rate (R_G, µm/day) can be made (Stokes et al., 2005; Villemure and Stokes, 2009) by considering the product of the number of proliferating cells (N) and their daily rate of division (r_d, cells/day), together with the average height of hypertrophic chondrocytes (h_{mean}, µm/cell):

$$R_G = (N)\,(r_d)(h_{mean})$$

Several assumptions must be made in using this estimate, however, including the estimate that all cells in the proliferative zone will eventually become hypertrophic (rather than dying by necrosis) and that matrix production occurs primarily in the radial direction (and not in the direction of longitudinal growth).

As a child matures, the physes "close" by ossification, connecting the epiphysis to the metaphysis with bone. The blood circulatory systems of the epiphysis and metaphysis, formerly independent, also unite. This region of bone remodels over many years, but the physeal "scar" or "ghost" may persist into old age. Closure of the physes of different bones, and even the proximal and distal ends of the same bone, occurs at different ages and in a specific sequence. This allows one to determine radiographically the skeletal age of an individual by observing which physes have closed. The hands and wrist are most useful because of the number of bones they contain, and the fact that the eight wrist bones are derived only from a primary center of ossification, without epiphyses (see Chapter 9). The primary centers appear radiographically at different ages and grow at different rates. In girls, physes close several years earlier than in boys; this contributes to the shorter average stature of women compared to men, and probably also to their lower overall bone density. About half of an individual's bone mass is accrued during the adolescent growth spurt prior to epiphyseal closure (Rico *et al.*, 1993; Parfitt 1994). Although this rapid increase occurs in both axial and appendicular compartments, there is a greater acceleration in growth in the axial skeleton than in the legs and arms, possibly because of the greater sensitivity of the spine to estrogen and testosterone (Tupman, 1962). Even so, the rapid longitudinal growth in the limbs causes significant cortical porosity to develop during the rapid growth phase, a result of the normal delay between the rapid resorption of bone and the more prolonged replacement of bone. This porosity causes a transient weakening of bone that can result in avulsion type fractures at musculo-tendinous junctions with bone, and can also increase the risk of catastrophic and complete fractures of bone (Alffram and Bauer, 1962; Parfitt, 1986). Following epiphyseal closure, the porosity consolidates, which partly accounts for the postclosure increase in bone mineral density.

7.3.2   Vascular Supply to the Developing Joint

During growth, the epiphysis (secondary center) and metaphysis (primary center) of the bone receive vascular supply from three different sources that do not provide good collateral pathways for circulation. One supply provides for the epiphysis, another for the metaphysis, and a third is found in the groove of Ranvier, primarily supplying the perichondrium/periosteum around the joint (Farnum *et al.*, 2006). The epiphyseal vessels supply the entire secondary center of ossification, and when blood from this source is interrupted, it leads to the death of the bony center. The metaphyseal vessels terminate in a complex of venous sinusoids (Brookes, 1971), and are intimately involved in mineralization at the osteochondral junction at the base of the growth plate. These vessels will penetrate the growth plate once the hypertrophic chondrocytes have died and disappeared, and are central to mineralization of the cartilage prior to its remodeling to bone. When the metaphyseal vessels are disrupted, there is a failure to replace cartilage with bone (Trueta, 1968). Besides maintaining the health of developing bone, these vessels also provide nutrients to the growth plate. Low-molecular-weight molecules, such as some sugars, can enter the growth plate from either the epiphyseal or metaphyseal sides (Farnum et al., 2006), although larger molecules may be required to enter via metaphyseal pathways.

7.3.3   The Cessation of Growth and Growth Plate Senescence

The conventional wisdom suggests that epiphyseal closure stops longitudinal growth, but evidence now suggests that growth stops first, precipitating closure of the physis (Parfitt, 2002). Growth cessation (unlike the separate process of epiphyseal closure) is independent of hormonal changes (Liu et al., 2011) and is regulated by growth itself. Evidence for this comes from experimental animals in which transplantation of growth plates between animals of different ages results in a growth rate of the transplanted tissue that is more similar to the donor animal than to the recipient (Stevens et al., 1999). It is now thought that deceleration of growth is caused by a combination of reduced chondrocyte proliferation that may drive other molecular and catabolic structural changes in the cartilage matrix, a process known as "growth plate senescence" (Nilsson et al., 2005; Liu et al., 2011). Growth plate senescence appears to occur not as a function of chronological age, but is rather determined by the number of cell divisions that chondrocytes in the resting zone, in particular, are capable of undergoing. The capacity of resting zone chondrocytes to proliferate declines with number of replications, and this reduction in proliferative capability ultimately results in the depletion of chondrocyte numbers. The mechanisms for this regulation of cell division are not entirely understood, but one hypothesis is that DNA methylation declines with each subsequent cell division (Nilsson et al., 2005), and that this serves as a "cell-cycle counter." Interestingly, the decline in cell division does not seem to be similarly regulated in the proliferative or hypertrophic zones of the growth plate, even though methylation does not differ between chondrocytes of the resting zone and those in these other regions of the growth plate. This may be explained by the observation that chondrocytes in the proliferative zone do not replicate like those in the resting zone, but rather proceed through various phases to terminal differentiation as hypertrophic chondrocytes (Liu et al., 2011). This may suggest that the process initiates with the declines in the resting zone chondrocyte population, which subsequently has a downstream effect as these chondrocytes move through the proliferative and hypertrophic zones/phases of their existence. Because the number of cell divisions that can occur in vitro is not dependent on the age of the animals from which they came (i.e., the prior number of in vivo replications), it is likely that the processes limiting growth at the epiphyseal plate are also cell–cell, or cell–matrix, dependent. These interactions also may be mediated by alterations in the regulation of a multitude of genes, including igf2, which is downregulated by three orders of magnitude during growth plate senescence (Parker et al., 2007), or by a multitude of other genes and proteins that are expressed in the growth plate (Lazarus *et al.*, 2007; Liu *et al.*, 2010).

7.3.4   Hormonal Effects on Epiphyseal Closure

Once growth has stopped, or slowed sufficiently, epiphyseal closure can proceed to occur as a function of the increase in sex steroids during maturation (Parfitt, 2002). The cessation of growth and the closure of the growth plate are probably under different regulatory controls. This view has merit, as it is well-known that estrogen suppresses long bone growth (Silberberg, 1971). Exogenous administration of estrogens can cause premature closure of the growth plate, whereas a loss of ovarian function or ovariectomy results in decreased mineralization of the hypertrophic zone and delayed epiphyseal closure (Ianotti, 1990). Evidence from a female who could not synthesize estrogen because of an aromatase defect, and a male with an estrogen receptor defect that conferred estrogen resistance, both suggest that it is estrogen in both sexes and not androgens in males that is responsible for epiphyseal closure (Frank, 1995). In both cases, the growth plates did not close, and growth continued.

Humans are considered already to be adults at the time the growth plate closes. For the tibia and femur, the ratio of age at growth plate closure to age at sexual maturity is higher than in many other animals, including nonhuman primates (Kilborn *et al.*, 2002). This means that hormonal changes associated with maturity are already well under way by the time the secondary centers of the femur and tibia begin to close, which also supports the idea that hormonal changes associated with maturation, not the cessation of growth, are the primary cause for epiphyseal closure. This may reflect a change in the regulation of epiphyseal closure that was required by human adaptation to a bipedal mode of locomotion, requires a longer period for growth and longer hindlimbs in order to be most energetically efficient (Steudel-Numbers and Tilkens, 2004), especially at moderate-to-fast walking speeds (Pontzer, 2005). The comparatively late closure of the growth plate also reflects the fact that both humans and nonhuman primates are growing for a greater proportion of their total lifespan than many other mammalian species and is an ideal developmental adaptation for a slow-growing, long-living species.

7.3.5   Mechanical Influences on the Growth Plate

Like the articular cartilage, the growth plate is primarily adapted to high compressive stresses, and is weaker in tension and shear, although this can vary by region of the growth plate (Villemure and Stokes, 2009). Like bone, the growth plate is transversely isotropic, with greater compliance in the axial direction than transversely (Villemure and Stokes, 2009). The reserve zone has the greatest rigidity, and has been suggested to provide mechanical support particularly in larger species that grow more slowly and for longer (Kember and Sissons, 1976). The hypertrophic region, on the other hand, is particularly compliant because of its high cell-to-matrix ratio. Large shear stresses at the junction between the epiphysis and the diaphysis commonly lead to physeal injuries in children. A complex set of ridges in the physis provides an interlocking geometry, which confers some protection against slippage of the epiphysis on the shaft of the bone, and tends to convert tensile stresses to more compressive stresses. High tensile stresses can cause damage in the upper proliferative zone, whereas shear stresses cause damage more often in the hypertrophic zone where cell volume is high in relation to matrix volume. Compressive stresses more often do not damage the growth plate at all, but are absorbed by metaphyseal trabeculae (see Chapter 12 for further discussion of the relationship between activity and trabecular bone structure).

The growth plate can both adapt to externally applied forces, but also may generate its own internal forces during growth that can direct and alter the growth process itself. Recent evidence suggests that the growth plate can generate forces up to 200% of body weight (Bylski-Austrow et al., 2001). It is possible that these forces in the developing joint are bi-directional (Rot et al., 2014), essentially attempting to force the primary and secondary centers apart. These forces may drive the ossification process, affecting the eventual orientation of the articular surfaces.

The adaptation of the growth plate to externally applied forces ultimately shapes the joints' surfaces and the orientation of limb components. The developmental physiologic adaptation that arises during growth occurs on a species-specific evolutionary template, and is maintained within limits by the genetic constraints imposed by the evolutionary process (Parfitt, 1994). However, we know very little about how that occurs. The qualitative Heuter–Volkmann "Law," another piece of conventional wisdom, suggests that large compressive stresses suppress or even inhibit growth, whereas tensile stresses stimulate it. It is unclear whether either Heuter or Volkmann ever stated this (they never collaborated, and we have yet to find an original citation to this Law). This concept is consistent with observations that high compressive loads retard growth (Hert, 1969), whereas distraction osteogenesis will accelerate growth (Apte and Kenwright, 1994; Stokes et al., 2002). Whether these static forces have the same effect as the dynamic loads that occur during movement is not entirely clear.

The relationship between growth and stress is dependent on the magnitude of the load (and perhaps its rate of application; Ménard et al., 2014), in combination with the polarity of the load (i.e., compression or tension). Large compressive loads suppress growth (Hert, 1969; Li et al., 1991; Vico et al., 1999; Robling et al., 2001; Ohashi et al., 2002; Stokes et al., 2005, 2006, 2007; Cancel et al., 2009; Ménard et al., 2014), although other types or magnitudes of load may stimulate growth (Swissa-Sivan et al., 1989; Nyska et al., 1995). Moderate or transversal loads may increase growth rate; for example, tennis players not only have wider bones, but the ulnae on their playing-side arm are about 3% longer than the non-dominant arm (Krahl et al., 1994). Some studies show that moderate exercise increases growth plate thickness and cell volume, but not cell proliferation (Congdon et al., 2012), whereas others suggest that moderate loading of the mammalian limb also stimulates cell proliferation (Hammond *et al.*, 2010). Data from animal models suggest that very high loads may stimulate the conversion of proliferative cells to hypertrophic ones (Robling *et al.*, 2001), while at the same time suppressing mineralization of the hypertrophic zone and reducing vascularity (Ohashi *et al.*, 2002).

Frost's (1979, 1990, 1999) chondral modeling hypothesis attempted to refine the relationship between longitudinal bone growth and loading in terms of load type and load magnitude, based on his observations of skeletal deformities in growing children. That hypothesis, and its accompanying chondral growth force response (CGFR) curve (Figure 7.5), proposes that although large compressive loads will retard longitudinal growth, small compressive loads will accelerate growth. Conversely, Frost proposed that tensile forces will have an alternate effect: large tensile forces will accelerate growth, but smaller tensile forces will have no influence on growth. Unlike the Heuter–Volmann "Law," Frost also proposes that there is a window on the compression side of the curve at the transition from accelerated growth to retarded growth within which simple maintenance of cartilage occurs. This is consistent with the observation that although disuse or muscle weakness (Frost, 1994b), and very high compressive stresses (Hert, 1969), retard growth, longitudinal growth is not accelerated but maintained within the normal range of loading. Niehoff *et al.* (2004) found no effect on femoral length in rats subjected to three different levels of exercise, consistent with the observation of growth in children, which indicates that large differences in activity levels have very little effect on growth rate.

Static forces and dynamic forces applied to the growth plate can have very different effects (Villemure and Stokes, 2009; Congdon *et al.*, 2012), although some experimental studies have shown that growth is equally retarded by static and

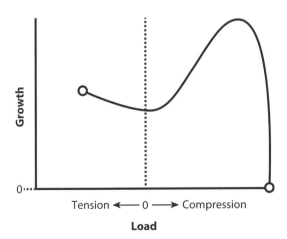

Figure 7.5 The response of cartilage is captured by the chondral modeling curve, proposed by Frost (1979). The hypothesis is that high compressive strains will inhibit cartilage growth, whereas lower compressive strains and tensile strains permit normal growth. Intermediate amounts of compression, within a very narrow window, can stimulate growth.

dynamic loads of the same magnitude (Robling *et al.*, 2001; Valteau *et al.*, 2011). There is also disagreement about whether the suppression of growth is determined by load magnitude (Robling *et al.*, 2001) or by the time-averaged compressive stress (Ménard *et al.*, 2014). Static tensile stresses on the growth plate, as in distraction osteogenesis, result in increased growth plate height as predicted by the CGFR curve, but tensile loads applied in a dynamic fashion may not have the same result.

Current views of loading on growth at the epiphyseal plate are much too simplistic because loading of growth plate cartilage by locomotor functions is not entirely compressive, but involves a complex set of time-varying stresses that change during cycles of movement. Because of the morphology of the cartilage and underlying bone, because of the shape of the joints themselves, and because many joints have "sliding" or "rocking" motions that place different parts of the joint under stress during different phases of movement, the stresses on the growth plate will be highly complex and undoubtedly involve tensile and shear forces throughout the matrix, particularly at the edges of the line of force. During growth, these forces and stresses can alter joint size, shape, and alignment, and perhaps even the material properties of the growth and articular cartilages. Adaptation in these structural and material features serves to reduce stresses on cartilage and to regulate stress gradients. Lateral expansion in the size of a joint has an exponential effect on the bearing surface, so that even small changes in size (and shape) during growth can have significant effects on cartilage and joint stresses. To some extent, the perichondrial ring growth controls this lateral joint expansion. Although shape and orientation of joints can change in adults, size does not and so adults have a limited capacity to adjust to varying loading conditions.

The effects of mechanical adaptation during growth can be seen by comparing the distal femoral growth plate with the proximal tibial plate. Both are similarly thick at birth, but by the time of growth plate closure, the femoral growth plate is twice as wide as the tibial one (Frost, 1994a). Frost suggests this is because the tibial plateau has greater "time-averaged" loading than the femoral condyle, which slides and rolls over the tibial articular cartilage, exposing more of its surface to loading over shorter periods of time. However, these "rules" do not take into account the significant effects of genetics, hormonal status, or solute transport, which may have very real effects on growth rate (see Chapter 10 for a study on the interaction of genotype with loading environment in generating bone phenotypes).

7.4   Anthropological Implications

The first goal of this chapter was to review the processes of postcranial skeletal development and of postnatal skeletal growth. The basic patterns detailed above describe these processes in all mammals. However, differences in adult articular surface morphology and limb length among species (both extant and extinct) can be related back to differences in specific details of skeletal development and postnatal ontogeny. The remainder of this chapter will focus on some of the ways that these processes have been examined to understand two specific questions in hominin paleontology: how do (1) articular surface size and shape, and (2) limb length relate to locomotor behavior and habitat/environment?

7.4.1   Articular Surface Size and Shape

Because the growth plate, like bone, is exquisitely sensitive to its mechanical environment, changes in locomotion or patterns of movement can have significant non-genomic effects on morphology of the postcranial skeleton. These can be used to reconstruct behavioral patterns, or changes in behavior, over an evolutionary timeframe.

As body mass increases during postnatal growth, peak transarticular loading increases exponentially. This has potentially devastating effects for the articular cartilage within the synovial joint because it is avascular and cannot easily repair itself after damage. Thus, from the perspective of evolution, it is advantageous to adapt joint surface morphology to protect the articular cartilage. To do this, the surfaces of synovial joints undergo postnatal growth that reduces stress within the cartilage, in part by increasing articular surface area ontogenetically, thereby attenuating transarticular loads across a larger surface, and reducing the absolute stress at any given location.

In bipedal locomotion, the lower limb bears the most significant mechanical loading, while the upper limb is subjected to no loading as a result of locomotion. To solve the problem of increased transarticular loading in the human lower limb, Ruff and Runestad (1992) demonstrated that humans have larger lower-limb joint surfaces relative to body mass compared to nonhuman primates of similar body mass, but that the size of these joint surfaces within humans scales with body mass at a similar rate as in other primates and mammals. In other words, lower-limb joint surface size increases proportionally to body mass across all mammals (i.e., similar slopes in a bivariate regression of joint size on body size), but humans have consistently larger articular surface sizes compared to other primates and mammals across the whole range of human body size (i.e., different slope elevation). Larger articular surfaces in the human lower limb effectively reduce articular cartilage stress by distributing loads across a larger area. If this hypothesis is correct, then human upper limb articular surfaces should scale differently than those of the lower limb; this test of the hypothesis has not been performed. Such a test of the hypothesis is important, however, in that it will elucidate whether human adaptation to increased loading during bipedal locomotion is a function of loading experienced during life (i.e., the product of ontogenetic mechanical adaptation), or is the product of natural selection, which has acted to increase the relative size of lower limb joints developmentally, either pre- or postnatally (i.e., the product of evolutionary adaptation). This is an excellent example of the dichotomy, expressed above by Parfitt (1994), between physiologic adaptation and evolutionary constraints.

Adaptation to increased loading with changes in body size within or across taxa (measured as intra- or interspecific allometry), as described above, is different than adaptation that occurs during life (measured as ontogenetic allometry). Across taxa, articular surface size can change in response to selection, representing evolutionary adaptation. However, at the individual level, mechanical adaptations to counteract stress are seen as changes in surface topography largely independent of size. For example, the femoral condyles of humans are geometrically structured to reduce stress in cartilage at or near full extension (Kettelkamp and Jacobs, 1972; Maquet et al., 1975; Lovejoy, 1984; Hirokawa, 1993). The ellipitical profile of the lateral femoral condyle in humans is argued to be a clear adaptation to increased cartilage contact during extension (Heiple and Lovejoy, 1971; Lovejoy, 1984). The shape also allows the femoral condyles to "roll and slide" during knee flexion and extension, bringing different parts of the articular surface into contact and further reducing time-averaged loads.

Hamrick's (1999) refinement of Frost's chondral modeling hypothesis (Frost, 1979, 1990) explains how joint surface morphology develops postnatally as a function of mechanical loading. Hamrick (1999) explains that high levels of hydrostatic pressure in the proliferative zone of cartilage under the center of the joint contact area will inhibit chondrocyte mitosis, while adjacent regions will respond through growth because the hydrostatic pressure they experience is lower. Hamrick's hypothesis predicts that central regions of an articular surface experience levels of hydrostatic pressure too high to stimulate chondrocyte division, and therefore grow at a slower rate than adjacent regions experiencing lower hydrostatic pressure. This would suggest that cartilage thickness should be greatest peripherally in the joint, unless mitosis and matrix production are uncoupled, but observations of joints with relatively flat surfaces (such as the tibial plateau or distal radius) clearly show that cartilage thickness is greatest in the central area of primary loadbearing.

Recently, Plochocki et al. (2009) developed a computational model of the growing human knee joint using nonlinear 2D finite element analysis that along with numeric shape optimization procedures was used to test the chondral modeling hypothesis. In this model, stress-regulated morphological changes were simulated ontogenetically until skeletal maturity and the results demonstrated increased joint congruence between the tibia and femur, broader stress distributions in the articular cartilage of the tibiofemoral joint, and a decrease in joint diameter relative to joint size (i.e., joint flattening in response to increased articular loading). These results correspond well with experimental studies evaluating joint surface development postnatally (Hammond et al., 2010; Congdon et al., 2012).

Postnatal chondral modeling responses could be investigated across a wider taxonomic distribution by examining joint surface mechanical adaptation in an ontogenetic series of skeletons (neonates, juveniles, subadults, and adults) for any number of taxa. While adaptation of the articular surface may occur during development, it has not been systematically evaluated across a large taxonomic distribution. Instead, researchers have focused studies on *adult* quadrupedal mammals, demonstrating that most taxa exhibit an isometric or slightly positively inter- or intraspecific allometric relationship between body mass and articular size (Jungers, 1988; Ruff, 1988; Godfrey et al., 1991; Ruff and Runestad, 1992). Adult mammals of differing body sizes, then, employ various degrees of limb excursion during locomotion (Biewener, 1989; Polk *et al.*, 2009; Day and Jayne, 2007). For example, limb postures in mice are dramatically different than those of elephants. In mice, the knee is nearly always loaded in various degrees of flexion, resulting in a crouched posture, whereas in elephants the knee is loaded almost always at or near full extension. For the elephant, this would align its limbs more closely with the ground reaction force experienced during locomotion, reducing the muscle force required to counteract the knee joint moment (and by extension the forces that its bones must resist) (Biewener, 1989). Similar relationships have been demonstrated for felids (Day and Jayne 2007), and more recently for primates (Polk *et al.*, 2009). More vertically oriented limb postures in large mammals presumably place articular cartilage under primarily compressive stress, which cartilage is quite adept at resisting, and reduces the tension and shear experienced by the articular cartilage, which it is poorly constructed to withstand. However, whereas changes in joint surface contours, specifically the flattening of joint surfaces in order to reduce articular cartilage stresses, appear to be driven by changes in body mass and articular loading, studies examining this across taxa or even within taxa across a range of body sizes, do not appear to support this hypothesis. This discrepancy between hypothesis and observation is central to the debate about the nature and evolution of bipedal locomotion among the various fossil hominin species.

Some of the most heated debates about australopith morphology have occurred with reference to the knee joint, in part because of the relative completeness of many specimens, and in part because the human knee joint reflects a number of adaptations to bipedal locomotion (see review in Ward, 2002). As an example, the lateral tibial condyle of fossil hominins has been suggested to vary, with some fossils being described as antero-posteriorly convex (i.e., smaller specimens) like that of African apes, and others described as flat (i.e., larger specimens), as in humans. This morphological variation among taxa (and even within taxa at a single site, like the multiple specimens from Hadar, Ethiopia) has been attributed to differences in locomotor function, with smaller (more convex) lateral tibial condyles reflecting a higher degree of adaptation to arboreal locomotion (Senut and Tardieu, 1985). An alternative hypothesis, proposed to explain morphological variation in radius of curvature of the talar trochlea by Latimer and colleagues (Latimer *et al.*, 1987; Latimer and Lovejoy, 1989), and tested on the lateral tibial condyle by Organ and Ward (2006), predicts that joint convexity scales with negative allometry relative to body mass. This prediction derives, broadly speaking, from the chondral modeling hypothesis. However, the data do not support it; the lateral tibial condyle of Great Apes and humans does not become flatter with increased body mass within a species. However, the scaling analysis of lateral tibial condylar curvature in hominoids does illustrate that there is significant overlap in antero-posterior joint convexity at the lower end of the body mass range for humans and Great Apes. Therefore, while the hominin fossils as a group do appear more ape-like than human-like in their morphology, there is no difference in degree of antero-posterior convexity among the various fossil taxa, and small-bodied australopiths do not differ from large-bodied australoptiths, refuting hypotheses of multiple species at Hadar (Organ and Ward, 2006). Therefore, from this study it is unclear whether antero-posterior joint convexity of the lateral tibial condyle at the lower end of the body size range for Great Apes and humans reflects body size or locomotor mode on transarticular loading.

7.4.2   Limb Length: Locomotor Consequences and Ecogeographic Variation

Reconstructions of body mass (Jungers, 1985), locomotor repertoire and efficiency (Hunt, 1996; Connour et al., 2000; Higgins and Ruff, 2011), and behavioral and feeding ecology often hinge on limb length measures, which are directly influenced by growth plate behavior. This is in part related to the known differences in limb length among various fossil hominins: *Australopithecus* is characterized by substantially shorter lower limbs than *Homo erectus/ergaster* and more recent *Homo* species (Jungers, 1982; Jungers and Stern, 1983), while Neanderthals are known to have had shorter distal lower limb elements than contemporaneous anatomically modern *H. sapiens* (Trinkaus, 1986; Holliday, 1999). Differences in lower limb length have been argued to have consequences for locomotor energetic economy. Some authors have argued based on models of mechanical work during locomotion that shorter limbs would impart an energetic advantage because shorter limbs have lower limb moments of inertia, and therefore a lower energetic cost (Kramer, 1999; Kramer and Eck, 2000; Myers and Steudel, 1997), but the stronger arguments rooted in experimental work suggest that shorter lower limbs are energetically more costly, which has implications for various fossil hominin taxa (Steudel-Numbers and Tilkens, 2004). Steudel-Numbers and Tilkens (2004) estimated that Neanderthals would have had locomotor costs that were 30% larger than contemporaneous anatomically modern humans, and the increase in body size and presumably locomotor cost from early African *Homo* species to later ones would have been mitigated by concomitant increases in lower limb length. These observations on skeletal proportions have profound implications for interpreting the migratory patterns of hominin species leaving Africa and spreading through Europe, Asia, and the New World. However, paleontological studies also have considered the impact of environmental factors such as climate on skeletal proportions, especially in the context of human evolution (Ruff, 1994, 2002; Holliday, 1997; Auerbach, 2007; Temple et al., 2008; Betti et al., 2012; Roseman and Auerbach, 2015).

Variation in long bone morphology, especially length and robustness, has long been associated with two thermoregulatory principles developed from the work of Bergmann (1847) and Allen (1877), and later codified as "ecogeographical" patterns ("rules") by Mayr (1956). In brief, Bergmann's rule states that geographically dispersed polytypic species tend to be larger in body size at higher latitudes. The mechanism proposed to explain this phenomenon is physiological. Larger body sizes have lower surface area to volume ratios, which reduces the gradient for heat loss. Allen's rule compliments Bergmann's by focusing on the reduction in size of the extremities (ears, snouts, limbs, tails) in colder climates, again the emphasis being on the reduction of surface area relative to volume.

Together, these "rules" predict that surface area relative to volume is the determining factor in heat dissipation, and therefore individuals with longer limbs relative to their torsos are able to thermoregulate better than individuals with shorter limbs relative to body size. Therefore, it stands to reason that individuals living in warmer climates would benefit from having longer limbs relative to body size than individuals living in colder climates. Empirical support for this prediction can be found in the clinal distribution of intralimb proportions among humans in Europe (Trinkaus, 1981; Holliday, 1997), although the pattern is not as clear in the Americas, where the history of migration into the region is much more recent (Auerbach, 2007; Auerbach and Ruff, 2010). Perhaps what is most interesting about these patterns, however, is how they develop as a function of growth plate chondrocyte proliferation (Cooper *et al.*, 2013).

Traditionally, the ecogeographic patterns of intralimb proportions, and of body shape at large, have been viewed through the lens of natural selection (Roberts, 1978), with these patterns reflecting adaptations for thermoregulation. Recently, it has been shown that these proportions can been influenced experimentally by altering the ambient temperature during postnatal development (Serrat *et al.*, 2008; Serrat, 2013), suggesting that variations in limb length are at least partially reflective of phenotypic plasticity during development. Serrat (2013) argues, then, that such growth plasticity, irrespective of its potential thermal advantage, may reflect a physiological response to environment, and not an explicit genotypic adaptation for thermoregulation. In fact, there is now evidence that temperature influences vascular access to the growth plate, such that higher physiologic temperatures cause acute vasodilation and increase blood flow velocity in the subperichondrial vascular plexus (Serrat *et al.*, 2014).

Studies employing population genetic variance approaches, however, have cautioned against a strict thermoregulatory cause of ecogeographic variation in limb proportions, arguing instead that population structure and the evolutionary forces of natural selection, gene flow, and genetic drift play an equally important role in the development of human postcranial variation (Betti *et al.*, 2012; Roseman and Auerbach, 2015). Ultimately, whatever mechanisms are responsible for the global distribution of limb length (and other body proportions), the dynamics of the growth plate are central to the discussion.

7.5   Future Directions

It should be clear from this discussion that there remain numerous gaps in our knowledge about the biology and genetic potential of developing joints, as well as how and why patterns of growth have changed through our evolutionary history. There are many questions about the mechanisms of growth plate senescence, the exact conditions under which it occurs, and the molecular processes that contribute to it. Similarly, mechanisms for the regulation of epiphyseal closure, and how they relate to chondrocyte senescence, are a relatively untapped area of investigation. It has been shown that when one artificially delays senescence, epiphyseal closure is also delayed (Liu *et al.*, 2011). If growth plate senescence and epiphyseal closure are so closely linked, it raises the question of how differential alterations in limb length can occur evolutionarily, unless simply through single mutations that can epigenetically alter the regulation of both processes. The coordinated processes of chondrocyte senescence and epiphyseal closure are undoubtedly regulated by complex interactions between the hormonal and metabolic environments, acting on a predetermined genetic template. However, the specific gene products involved, how they are regulated, and whether these products act locally on different parts of the growth plate are unknown.

There is still much debate about how the growth plate cartilage adapts to local stresses, what the loading thresholds and windows are, and whether cartilage responds differently to the polarity of stress (i.e., tension, compression, and shear). This is particularly critical to understanding the adult morphology of the synovial joints of the postcranium. However, this information also could be used to better interpret loading patterns in hominins and how these have changed over evolutionary time. Well-designed *in vivo* studies in experimental animals (expanding on the excellent work of the Stokes laboratory) could prove significant in our interpretations of form and function as it relates to our own evolutionary history. It could also shed light on patterns of differential limb growth and how altered loading patterns may contribute to the process of differential limb growth (see Cooper *et al.*, 2013).

This chapter has concentrated only on postcranial development, and only on the long bones (see Chapter 9 for a study of endochondral growth in metapodial sites without a epiphyseal growth plate). Growth and development of the limb girdles offers another area of investigation that is critically important to our own locomotory evolution. This is likely to be an even more complex project than understanding growth and development of joints in the long bones because it involves processes of both intramembranous and endochondral ossification and both synovial and non-synovial joints. It is further complicated by the convoluted geometry of the limb girdles, which provides special challenges even to our understanding of variations in adult form. However, there can be no question about its relevance and importance to our evolutionary history.

7.6   Conclusion

Although we tend to think of adaptation as an individual adjustment to an alteration in the environment, it is important to consider genetically driven developmental processes that can affect adult form, and which underlie a longer-term process of evolutionary adaptation. These processes are affected by a host of different factors – mechanical, nutritional, hormonal, and metabolic – that modulate the genetic template. There is insufficient space to discuss all of these influences here, but relatively minor alterations in both genetic and epigenetic regulatory mechanisms affecting postcranial development can lead to rapid changes in size and shape of the limb bones, alter differential patterns of limb growth, and affect functional, and therefore behavioral, outcomes that have evolutionary consequences. Developmental changes in the context of evolution have not received as much attention in the anthropological world as they probably should. It is our hope that highlighting them will stimulate further investigative emphasis on the interplay between somatic and evolutionary adaptation, and provide a somewhat different perspective on the evolutionary process.

References

Alffram, P.-A. and Bauer, G.C.H. (1962). Epidemiology of fractures of the forearm: a biomechanical investigation of bone strength. *Journal of Bone and Joint Surgery AM*, 44, 105–114.

Allen, J. A. (1877). The influence of physical conditions in the genesis of species. *Radical Review*, 1, 108–140.

Apte, S. S. and Kenwright, J. (1994). Physeal distraction and cell proliferation in the growth plate. *Journal of Bone and Joint Surgery British Volume*, 76, 837–843.

Archer, C. W., Morrison, H. and Pitsillides, A. A. (1994). Cellular aspects of the development of diarthrodial joints and articular cartilage. *Journal of Anatomy*, 184, 447–456.

Auerbach, B. M. (2007). Human skeletal variation in the New World during the Holocone: effects of climate and subsistence across geography and time. PhD dissertation, Johns Hopkins University, Baltimore, MD.

Auerbach, B. M. and Ruff, C. B. (2010). Stature estimation formulae for indigenous North American populations. *American Journal of Physical Anthropology*, 141, 190–207.

Bateson, G. (1963). The role of somatic change in evolution. *Evolution*, 17, 529–539.

Bergmann, C. (1847). Ueber die Verhältnisse der wärmeökonomie der Thiere zu ihrer Grösse. *Göttinger Studien*, 3, 595–708.

Bertram, J. E., Polevoy, Y. and Cullinane, D. M. (1998). Mechanics of avian fibrous periosteum: tensile and adhesion properties. *Bone*, 22, 669–675.

Betti, L., von Cramon-Taubadel, N. and Lycett, S. J. (2012). Human pelvis and long bones reveal differential preservation of ancient population history and migration out of Africa. *Human Biology*, 84, 139–152.

Biewener, A. A. (1989). Scaling body support in mammals: limb posture and muscle mechanics. *Science*, 245, 45–48.

Breur, G. J., VanEnkevort, B. A., Farnum, C. E. and Wilsman, N. J. (1991). Linear relationship between the volume of hypertrophic chondrocytes and the rate of longtiduinal bone growth in growth plates. *Journal of Orthopaedic Research*, 9, 348–359.

Brookes, M. (1971). *Growth Cartilages. The Blood Supply of Bone: An Approach to Bone Biology*. London: Butterworth, pp. 133–161.

Bylski-Austrow, D. I., Wall, E. J., Rupert, M. P., Roy, D. R. and Crawford, A. H. (2001). Growth plate forces in the adolescent human knee: a radiographic and mechanical study of epiphyseal staples. *Journal of Pediatric Orthopaedics*, 21, 817–823.

Cancel, M., Grimard, G., Thuillard-Crisinel, D., Moldovan, F., and Villemure, I. (2009). Effects of in vivo static compressive loading on aggrecan and type II and X collagens in the rat growth plate extracellular matrix. *Bone*, 44, 306–315.

Carter, D. R. and Beaupre, G. S. (2001). *Skeletal Function and Form: Mechanobiology of Skeletal Development, Aging, and Regeneration*. Cambridge: Cambridge University Press.

Congdon, K. A., Hammond, A. S. and Ravosa, M. J. (2012). Differential limb loading in miniature pigs (*Sus scrofa domesticus*): a test of chondral modeling theory. *Journal of Experimental Biology*, 215, 1472–1483.

Connour, J. R., Glander, K. and Vincent, F. (2000). Postcranial adaptations for leaping in primates. *Journal of Zoology*, 251, 79–103.

Cooper, K. L., Oh, S., Sung, Y., *et al.* (2013). Multiple phases of chondrocyte enlargement underlie differences in skeletal proportions. *Nature*, 495, 375–379.

Day, L. M. and Jayne, B. C. (2007). Interspecific scaling of the morphology and posture of the limbs during the locomotion of cats (Felidae). *Journal of Experimental Biology*, 210, 642–654.

Di Nino, D. L., Long, F. and Linsenmayer, T. F. (2001). Regulation of endochondral cartilage growth in the developing avian limb: cooperative involvement of perichondrium and periosteum. *Developmental Biology*, 240, 433–442.

Drachman, D. (1969). Normal development and congenital malformation of joints. *Bulletin of Rheumatic Diseases*, 19, 536–540.

Farnum, C. E. and Wilsman, N. J. (1989). Cellular turnover at the chondro-osseous junction of growth plate cartilage: analysis by serial sections at the light microscopical level. *Journal of Orthopaedic Research*, 7, 654–666.

Farnum, C. E. and Wilsman, N.J. (1998). Effects of distraction and compression on growth plate function. *In:* Buckwalter, J. A., Ehrlich, M. G., Sandell, L. J. and Trippel, S. B. (eds.) *Skeletal Growth and Development*. Rosemont, IL: American Academy of Orthopaedic Surgeons, pp. 517–530.

Farnum, C. E., Lenox, M., Zipfel, W., Horton, W. and Williams, R. (2006). *In vivo* delivery of fluoresceinated dextrans to the murine growth plate: imaging of three vascular routes by multiphoton microscopy. *The Anatomical Record*, 288A, 91–103.

Foolen, J., van Dopnkelaar, C. C., Murphy, P., Huiskes, R. and Ito, K. (2009). Residual periosteum tension is insufficient to directly modulate bone growth. *Journal of Biomechanics*, 42, 152–157.

Foolen, J., van Donkelaar, C. C. and Ito, K. (2011). Intracellular tension in periosteum/perichondrium cells regulates long bone growth. *Journal of Orthopaedic Research*, 29, 84–91.

Forriol, F. and Shapiro, F. (2005). Bone development. *Clinical Orthopaedics and Related Research*, 432, 14–33.

Frank, G. R. (1995). The role of estrogen in pubertal skeletal physiology: epiphyseal maturation and mineralization of the skeleton. *Acta Paediatrica*, 84, 627–630.

Frost, H. M. (1979). A chondral modeling theory. *Calcified Tissue International*, 28, 181–200.

Frost, H. M. (1990). Structural adaptations to mechanical usage (SATMU): the hyaline cartilage modeling problem. *The Anatomical Record*, 226, 423–432.

Frost, H. M. (1994a). Perspectives: a vital biomechanical model of synovial joint design. *The Anatomical Record*, 240, 1–18.

Frost, H. M. (1994b). Perspectives: a vital biomechanical model of the endochondral ossification mechanism. *The Anatomical Record*, 240, 435–446.

Frost, H. M. (1999). Joint anatomy, design, and arthroses: insights of the Utah paradigm. *The Anatomical Record*, 255, 162–174.

Garcia-Ramirez, M., Toran, N., Andaluz, P., Carrascosa, A. and Audi, L. (2000). Vascular endothelial growth factor is expressed in human fetal growth cartilage. *Journal of Bone and Mineral Research*, 15, 534–540.

Godfrey, L., Sutherland, M., Boy, D. and Gomberg, N. (1991). Scaling of limb joint surface areas in anthropoid primates and other mammals. *Journal of Zoology*, 223, 603–625.

Grossniklaus, U., Kelly, B., Ferguson-Smith, A. C., Pembrey, M. and Lindquist, S. (2013). Transgenerational epigenetic inheritance: how important is it? *Nature Reviews of Genetics*, 14, 228–235.

Hammond, A. S., Ning, J., Ward, C. V. and Ravosa, M. J. (2010). Mammalian limb loading and chondral modeling during ontogeny. *The Anatomical Record*, 293, 658–670.

Hamrick, M. W. (1999). A chondral modeling theory revisiting. *Journal of Theoretical Biology*, 201, 201–208.

Heiple, K. G. and Lovejoy, C. O. (1971). The distal femoral anatomy of *Australopithecus*. *American Journal of Physical Anthropology*, 35, 75–84.

Hernandez, J. A., Serrano, S., Mariñoso, M. L., *et al.* (1995). Bone growth and modeling changes induced by periosteal stripping in the rat. *Clinical Orthopaedics and Related Research*, 320, 211–219.

Hert, J. (1969). Acceleration of the growth after decrease of load on epiphyseal plates by means of spring distractors. *Folia Morphologia (Praha)*, 17, 194–203.

Higgins, R. W. and Ruff, C. B. (2011). The effects of distal limb segment shortening on locomotor efficiency in sloped terrain: implications for Neandertal locomotor behavior. *American Journal of Physical Anthropology*, 146, 336–345.

Hirokawa, S. (1993). Biomechanics of the knee joint: a critical review. *Critical Reviews in Biomedical Engineering*, 21, 79–135.

Holliday, T. W. (1997). Postcranial evidence of cold adaptation in European Neandertals. *American Journal of Physical Anthropology*, 104, 245–258.

Holliday, T. W. (1999). Brachial and crural indices of European Late Upper Paleolithic and Mesolithic humans. *Journal of Human Evolution*, 36, 549–566.

Horton, W. A. (1993). Morphology of connective tissue: cartilage. *In:* Royce, P. M. and Steinman, B. (eds.) *Connective Tissue and its Heritable Disorders*. New York, NY: Wiley-Liss.

Hunziker, E. B., Schenk, R. K. and Cruz-Orive, L.-M. (1987). Quantitation of chondrocyte performance in growth-plate cartilage during longitudinal bone growth. *Journal of Bone and Joint Surgery, American Volume*, 69, 162–173.

Hunt, K. D. (1996). The postural feeding hypothesis: an ecological model for the evolution of bipedalism. *South African Journal of Science*, 92, 77–90.

Ianotti, J. P. (1990). Growth plate physiology and pathology. *The Orthopaedic Clinics of North America*, 21, 1–17.

Jungers, W. L. (1982). Lucy's limbs: skeletal allometry and locomotion in *Australopithecus afarensis*. *Nature*, 297, 676–678.

Jungers, W. L. (1985). *Size and Scaling in Primate Biology*. New York, NY: Plenum Press.

Jungers, W. L. (1988). Relative joint size and hominoid locomotor adaptations with implications for the evolution of hominid bipedalism. *Journal of Human Evolution*, 17, 247–265.

Jungers, W. L. and Stern, J. T. (1983). Body proportions, skeletal allometry and locomotion in the Hadar hominids: a reply to Wolpoff. *Journal of Human Evolution*, 12, 673–684.

Kember, N. F. (1985). Comparative patterns of cell division in epiphyseal cartilage plates in the rabbit. *Journal of Anatomy*, 142, 185–190.

Kember, N. F. and Sisson, H. A. (1976). Quantitative histology of the human growth plate. *Journal of Bone and Joint Surgery, British Volume*, 58, 426–435.

Kettelkamp, D. B. and Jacobs, A. W. (1972). Tibiofemoral contact area: determination and implications. *Journal of Bone and Joint Surgery, American Volume*, 54, 347–358.

Kilborn, S. H., Trudel, G. and Uhthoff, H. (2002). Review of growth plate closure compared with age at sexual maturity and lifespan in laboratory animals. *Contemporary Topics*, 41, 21–26.

Krahl, H., Michaelis, U., Pieper, H. G., Quack, G. and Montag, M. (1994). Stimulation of bone growth through sports. A radiologic investigation of the upper extremities in professional tennis players. *American Journal of Sports Medicine*, 22, 751–757.

Kramer, P. (1999). Modelling the locomotor energetics of extinct hominids. *Journal of Experimental Biology*, 202, 2807–2818.

Kramer, P., and Eck, G. G. (2000). Locomotor energetics and lower limb length in hominid bipedality. *Journal of Human Evolution*, 38, 651–666.

Kuhn, J. L., DeLacey, J. H. and Leenellett, E. E. (1996). Relationship between bone growth rate and hypertrophic chondrocyte volume in New Zealand White rabbits of varying ages. *Journal of Orthopaedic Research*, 14, 706–711.

Latimer, B. M. and Lovejoy, C. O. (1989). The calcaneus of *Australopithecus afarensis* and its implications for the evolution of bipedality. *American Journal of Physical Anthropology*, 33, 369–386.

Latimer, B., Ohman, S. C. and Lovejoy, C. O. (1987). Talocrural joint in African hominoids: implications for *Australopithecus afarensis*. *American Journal of Physical Anthropology*, 74, 155–175.

Lazarus, J. E., Hegde, A., Andrade, A. C., Nilsson, O. and Baron, J. (2007). Fibroblast growth factor expression in the postnatal growth plate. *Bone*, 40, 577–586.

Li, K. C., Zernicke, R. F., Barnard, R. J. and Li, A. F. (1991). The influences of exercise intensity on bone development in growing rats. *Japanese Journal of Physical Education*, 36, 39–51.

Liu, J. C., Andrade, A. C., Forcinito, P., *et al.* (2010). Spatial and temporal regulation of gene expression in the mammalian growth plate. *Bone*, 46, 1380–1390.

Liu, J. C., Nilsson, O. and Baron, J. (2011). Growth plate senescence and catch-up growth. *Endocrine Reviews*, 21, 23–29.

Lovejoy, C. O. (1984). Review of possible animal models for kinematic/utility testing of the Pfizer Anterior Cruciate Ligament Prosthesis (PALCP). Monograph presented to the Howmedica Division of Pfizer Pharmaceutical Company.

Maquet, P. G., Van de Berg, A. J. and Simonet, J. C. (1975). Femorotibial weight-bearing areas. *Journal of Bone and Joint Surgery, American Volume*, 57, 766–771.

Mayr, E. (1956). Geographical character gradients and climactic adaptation. *Evolution*, 10, 105–108.

McBride, S. H., Evans, S. F. and Knothe Tate, M. L. (2011). Anisotropic mechanical properties of ovine femoral periosteum and the effects of cryopreservation. *Journal of Biomechanics*, 44, 1954–1959.

Ménard, A-L., Grimard, G., Valteau, B., *et al.* (2014). *In vivo* dynamic loading reduces bone growth without histomorphometric changes of the growth plate. *Journal of Orthopaedic Research*, 32, 1129–1136.

Myers, M. J. and Steudel, K. (1997). Morphological conservation of limb natural pendular period in the domestic dog (*Canis familiaris*): implications for locomotor energetics. *Journal of Morphology*, 234, 183–196.

Niehoff, A., Kersting, U. G., Zaucke, F., Morlock, M. M. and Bruggemann, G. P. (2004). Adaptation of mechanical, morphological, and biochemical properties of the rat growth plate to dose-dependent voluntary exercise. *Bone*, 35, 899–908.

Nilsson, O., Mitchum, R. D. Jr., Schrier, L., *et al.* (2005). Growth plate senescence is associated with loss of DNA methylation. *Journal of Endocrinology*, 186, 241–249.

Nyska, M., Nyska, A., Swissa-Sivan, A. and Samueloff, S. (1995). Histomorphometry of long bone growth plate in swimming rats. *International Journal of Experimental Pathology*, 76, 241–245.

Ochareon, P. and Herring, S.W. (2007). Growing the mandible: role of the periosteum and its cells. *The Anatomical Record*, 290, 1366–1376.

Ohashi, N., Robling, A. G., Burr, D. B. and Turner, C. H. (2002). The effects of dynamic axial loading on the rat growth plate. *Journal of Bone and Mineral Research*, 17, 284–292.

Organ, J. M. and Ward, C. V. (2006). Contours of the hominoid lateral tibial condyle with implications for *Australopithecus*. *Journal of Human Evolution*, 51, 113–127.

Parfitt, A. M. (1986). Cortical porosity in postmenopausal and adolescent wrist fractures. *In:* Uhthoff, H. and Jaworski, Z. F. G. (eds.) *Current Concepts of Bone Fragility*. Berlin: Springer, pp. 167–172.

Parfitt, A. M. (1994). The two faces of growth: benefits and risks to bone integrity. *Osteoporosis International*, 4, 382–398.

Parfitt, A. M. (2002). Misconceptions (1): epiphyseal fusion causes cessation of growth. *Bone*, 30, 337–339.

Parker, E. A., Hegde, A., Buckley, M., *et al.* (2007). Spatial and temporal regulation of GH-IGF-related gene expression in growth plate cartilage. *Journal of Endocrinology*, 194, 31–40.

Plochocki, J. H., Ward, C. V. and Smith, D. E. (2009). Evaluation of the chondral modeling theory using FE-simulation and numeric shape optimization. *Journal of Anatomy*, 214, 768–777.

Polk, J. D., Williams, S. A. and Peterson, J. V. (2009). Body size and joint posture in primates. *American Journal of Physical Anthropology*, 140, 359–367.

Pontzer, H. (2005). A new model predicting locomotor cost from limb length via force production. *Journal of Experimental Biology*, 208, 1513–1524.

Rico, H., Revilla, M., Villa, L. F., *et al.* (1993). Body composition in children and Tanner's stages: a study in dual-energy x-ray absorptiometry. *Metabolism*, 42, 967–970.

Roberts, D. F. (1978). *Climate and Human Variability*, 2nd ed. Menlo Park, CA: Cummings Publishing Company.

Robling, A. G., Duuvelaar, K. M., Geevers, J. V., Ohashi, N. and Turner, C. H. (2001). Modulation of appositional and longitudinal bone growth in the rat ulna by applied static and dynamic force. *Bone*, 29, 105–113.

Rolian, C. (2014). Genes, development, and evolvability in primate evolution. *Evolutionary Anthropology*, 23, 93–104.

Roseman, C. C. and Auerbach, B. M. (2015). Ecogeography, genetics, and the evolution of human body form. *Journal of Human Evolution*, 78, 80–90.

Roseman, C. C., and Weaver, T. D. (2007). Molecules versus morphology? Not for the human cranium. *BioEssays*, 29, 1185–1188.

Rot, C., Stern, T., Blecher, R., Friesem B. and Zelzer, E. (2014). A mechanical jack-like mechanism drives spontaneous fracture healing in neonatal mice. *Developmental Cell*, 31, 159–170.

Ruff, C. (1988). Hindlimb articular surface allometry in Hominoidea and *Macaca*, with comparisons to diaphyseal scaling. *Journal of Human Evolution*, 17, 687–714.

Ruff, C. B. (1994). Morphological adaptation to climate in modern and fossil hominids. *Yearbook of Physical Anthropology*, 37, 65–107.

Ruff, C. B. (2002). Variation in human body size and shape. *Annual Review of Anthropology*, 31, 211–232.

Ruff, C. B. and Runestad, J. A. (1992). Primate limb bone structural adaptations. *Annual Review of Anthropology*, 21, 407–433.

Senut, B. and Tardieu, C. (1985). Functional aspects of Plio-Pleistocene Hominid limb bones: implications for taxonomy and phylogeny. *In:* Delson, E. (ed.) *Ancestors: The Hard Evidence*. New York, NY: Alan R. Liss, pp. 193–201.

Sergerie, K., Lacoursierem, M. O., Levesqaue, M. and Villemure I. (2009). Mechanical properties of the porcine growth plate and its three zones from unconfined compression tests. *Journal of Biomechanics*, 42, 510–516.

Serrat, M. A. (2013). Allen's rule revisited: temperature influences bone elongation during a critical period of postnatal development. *Anatomical Record*, 296, 1534–1545.

Serrat, M. A., King, D. and Lovejoy, C. O. (2008). Temperature regulates limb length in homeotherms by directly modulating cartilage growth. *Proceedings of the National Academy of Sciences*, 105, 19347–19352.

Serrat, M. A., Efaw, M. L. and Williams, R. M. (2014). Hindlimb heating increases vascular access of large molecules to murine tibial growth plates measured by *in vivo* multiphoton imaging. *Journal of Applied Physiology*, 116, 425–438.

Silberberg, R. (1971). Skeletal growth and ageing. *Acta Rheumatologica*, 26, 1–56.

Steudel-Numbers, K. L. and Tilkens, M. J. (2004). The effect of lower limb length on the energetic cost of locomotion: implications for fossil hominins. *Journal of Human Evolution*, 47, 95–109.

Stevens, D. G., Doyer, M. I. and Bowen, C. V. (1999). Transplantation of epiphyseal plate allografts between animals of different ages. *Journal of Pediatric Orthopedics*, 19, 398–403.

Stokes, I. A. F., Mente, P. L., Iatridis, J. C., Farnum, C. E. and Aronsson, D. D. (2002). Enlargement of growth plate chondrocytes modulated by sustained mechanical loading. *Journal of Bone and Joint Surgery, American Volume*, 84, 1842–1848.

Stokes, I. A. F., Gwadera, J., Dimock, A., Farnum, C. E. and Aronsson, D. D. (2005). Modulation of vertebral and tibial growth by compression loading: diurnal versus full-time loading. *Journal of Orthopaedic Research*, 2, 188–195.

Stokes, I. A., Aronsson, D. D., Dimock, A. N., Cortright, V. and Beck, S. (2006). Endochondral growth in growth plates of three species of two anatomical locations modulated by mechanical compression and tension. *Journal of Orthopaedic Research*, 24, 1327–1334.

Stokes, I. A., Clark, K. C., Farnum, C. E. and Aronsson, D. D. (2007). Alterations in the growth plate associated with growth modulation by sustained compression or distraction. *Bone*, 41, 197–205.

Swissa-Siva, A., Simking, A., Leichter, I., *et al.* (1989). Effect of swimming on bone growth and development in young rats. *Bone and Mineral*, 7, 91–105.

Temple, D. H., Auerbach, B. M., Nakatsukasas, M., Sciulli, P. W. and Larsen, C. S. (2008). Variation in limb proportions between Jomon foragers and Yayoi agriculturalists. *American Journal of Physical Anthropology*, 137, 164–174.

ten Broek, C. M., Bakker, A. J., Varela-Lasheras, V., *et al.* (2012). Evo–Devo of the human vertebral column: on homeotic transformations, pathologies and prenatal selection. *Evolutionary Biology*, 39, 456–471.

Towers, M. and Tickle, C. (2009). Growing models of vertebrate limb development. *Development*, 136, 179–190.

Trinkaus, E. (1981). Neandertal limb proportions and cold adaptation. *In:* Stringer, C. B. (ed.) *Aspects of Human Evolution*. London: Taylor and Francis, pp. 187–224.

Trinkaus, E. (1986). The Neandertals and modern human origins. *Annual Review of Anthropology*, 15, 193–218.

Trueta, J. (1968). *The Effect of Ischaemia on the Epiphyseal Cartilage. Studies of the Development and Decay of the Human Frame*. London: William Heinemann Medical Books, pp. 108–117.

Tupman, G. S. (1962). A study of bone growth in normal children and its relationship to skeletal maturation. *Journal of Bone and Joint Surgery, British Volume*, 44, 42–67.

Valteau, B., Grimard, G., Londono, I., Modovan, F. and Villemure, I. (2011). *In vivo* dynamic bone growth modulation is less detrimental but as effective as static growth modulation. *Bone*, 49, 996–1004.

Vico, L., Barou, O., Larouche, N., Alexandre, C. and Lafage-Proust, M. H. (1999). Effects of centrifuging at 2 *g* on rat long bone metaphyses. *European Journal of Applied Physiology*, 80, 360–366.

Villemure, I. and Stokes I. A. F. (2009). Growth plate mechanics and mechanobiology. A survey of present understanding. *Journal of Biomechanics*, 42, 1793–1803.

Ward, C. V. (2002). Interpreting the posture and locomotion of *Australopithecus afarensis*: where do we stand? *Yearbook of Physical Anthropology*, 45, 185–215.

Wilde, G. P. and Baker, G. C. (1987). Circumferential periosteal release in the treatment of children with leg-length inequality. *Journal of Bone and Joint Surgery, British Volume*, 69, 817–821.

Wilsman, N. J., Farnum, C. E., Green, E. M., Lieferman, E. M. and Clayton, M. K. (1996a). Cell cycle analysis of proliferative zone chondrocytes in growth plates elongating at different rates. *Journal of Orthopaedic Research*, 14, 562–572.

Wilsman, N. J., Farnum, C. E., Leiferman, E. M., Fry, M. and Barreto, C. (1996b). Differential growth by growth plates as a function of multiple parameters of chondrocytic kinetics. *Journal of Orthopaedic Research*, 14, 927–936.

8 Combining Genetic and Developmental Methods to Study Musculoskeletal Evolution in Primates

Terence D. Capellini and Heather Dingwall

8.1 Introduction

Among mammals, primates exhibit remarkable diversity in skeletal morphology. Much of this diversity is readily apparent in the appendages, body parts that interact with substrates during locomotion and positional behavior. Differences in the lengths, shapes, and proportions of the major long bones of the forelimb (scapula, humerus, radius, ulna) and hindlimb (pelvis, femur, tibia, fibula) reflect the myriad skeletal adaptations primates have evolved to occupy diverse ecological niches. This diversity is not only observable at the level of the entire appendage or individual limb segment, but at specific functional zones, such as growth plates, joints, and muscle-attachment sites. From an evolutionary perspective, this striking morphological diversity reflects the actions of natural selection on variation in pre- and postnatal developmental processes (Carroll, 2008). Historically, this diversity has inspired biologists to search for the developmental and genetic underpinnings of skeletal shape. Yet despite many decades of research, relatively little is known about the molecular mechanisms that control the specific shapes of bones, let alone how modifications to pre- and postnatal developmental programs influence the morphological variation within and between species. A deeper exploration of these mechanisms is necessary to establish precise connections between genotype and phenotype (Hartl and Ruvolo, 2011), and in doing so to understand the nature of species adaptation and evolution.

A modern synthetic approach, one which integrates experimental findings from developmental biology, genetics, genomics, and bioinformatics, has the potential to provide increased power and resolution in connecting genotype to phenotype and revealing the causative mutations that underlie adaptive morphological evolution. Given the noticeable and marked variation in animal appendages, the identification of the molecular and cellular mechanisms that control limb skeletal development and diversity has been one of the main areas of research within developmental biology for well over 50 years. This is in part a consequence of the findings that experimental disruptions to limbs or natural mutations that impact limb morphology do not necessarily influence embryonic survival, making limbs a tractable system to study developmental principles (Gilbert, 2013). Thus, studies treating the limb as a developmental system have consistently been at the forefront of revealing the basic molecular and cellular mechanisms underlying developmental processes. Not surprisingly, this area of research has also consistently introduced cutting-edge experimental techniques that have aided in the identification of genes, their expression patterns, and their functions within living organisms. Importantly, such achievements have also been matched by advances in genetics, specifically in the development and improvement of methods that serve to map genetic regions to trait variation. For example, the development of genome-wide association studies (GWAS) and refinements in quantitative trait loci (QTL) mapping has achieved a heightened ability to elucidate regions in the genome that explain variation in limb and skeletal morphology. Most recently, functional genomics techniques, which have taken advantage of next-generation sequencing (NGS) technologies, have permitted the genome-wide identification of gene transcripts and regulatory sequences involved in skeletal development. These newest approaches, when used in the context of bioinformatics and comparative genomics, are beginning to help to refine genomic signals within genetically mapped intervals to causative loci. When all of these approaches are considered collectively, scientists now have a powerful, versatile toolkit to understand limb and skeletal development and to elucidate how nucleotide diversity underlies appendage morphological variation within and between animals.

As alluded to earlier, a major finding that has been experimentally corroborated through achievements in each of the above fields is that as DNA sequences are the units of heredity, modifications to the DNA molecule directly impact molecular processes. These modifications in turn influence the development of a phenotype and phenotypic variation within a species. Under a selective regime, slight perturbations to a developing system, which results in heritable variation, eventually can lead to species-specific adaptations. Indeed, variation in adult skeletal phenotypes often has its roots in changes to early developmental programs *in utero* and/or processes of growth and maturation that occur during postnatal life (e.g., Young *et al.*, 2006; Chan *et al.*, 2010). Within primates, for example, skeletal morphology and proportions of the major long bones are often established *in utero* and/or early in postnatal growth (Young *et al.*, 2006), a likely consequence of natural selection operating on the genes that control the patterning of skeletal elements (e.g., determining the number of cell populations that form the femur versus the tibia), and/or those that control skeletal growth (e.g., regulating proliferation of chondrocytes in the growth plate).

In the context of development, another major finding is that developmentally encoded traits, such as skeletal shape, are often controlled at the level of gene regulation rather than through modifications to the protein-coding portion of the gene (Carroll, 2008). Perhaps because of their visibility in the genome and their relative predictive effects on protein function, for many years mutations in the protein coding portions of genes were argued to play major roles in adaptive phenotypes. While there are examples of this in the literature, it is now understood that the large majority of genes in the genome have many different roles during development and postnatal growth and that alterations to their function via coding mutations can result in an extensive pleiotropism with deleterious consequences to the organism and its fitness. On a comparative genomics level, one signature of this impact has been the finding that coding portions of genes display high sequence conservation across a large number of vertebrate species, indicating a conserved function for the protein during life (Yue *et al.*, 2014). On the other hand, more recent studies, such as those examining the regulatory control of single genes (e.g., Mortlock *et al.*, 2003) or those focusing of the regulatory architecture of different cell types (ENCODE Consortium, 2012), reveal that the majority of genes have complex regulatory sequences (i.e., on/off switches) that function to drive gene expression in highly specific spatial and temporal domains. By controlling gene expression in a modular fashion, these regulatory switches have the ability to mediate specific anatomical outcomes. This specificity in the control of gene expression helps organisms avoid the extensive pleiotropic effects of coding muta-tions and provides a mechanism for natural selection to target specific components of functional anatomy. In light of these findings, it is not surprising that recent comparisons of the regulatory architecture of the genomes of different species has revealed considerable divergence in the regulatory control of genes in similar tis-sues and cell types (Yue *et al.*, 2014).

One additional insight that has emerged into the developmental genetic control of trait variation is that many morphological traits have a polygenic underpinning rather than being controlled by only a single locus. Indeed, it has been known for some time that specific anatomy, even down to a musculotendonous insertion site on bone, may be controlled by tens to hundreds of loci, many of which of are likely regulatory (Carroll, 2008). However, it is also understood, via findings from com-parative genetic mapping experiments, that the extent to which each locus explains heritable variation in a trait is dependent on each species' evolutionary history. For example, in mice, the *Growth Differentiation Factor Five* (*Gdf5*) gene, a bone morphogenetic protein that is expressed in growth plates, controls approximately 10–15% of the growth of normal long bones, whereas in humans, *GDF5* contributes to less than 1% of growth, even in cases when the gene's function is entirely miss-ing (Capellini *et al.*, unpublished). When considering specific evolutionary histories, it is not surprising that there are cases where only a few loci may have been under intense selection and end up explaining large percentages of variation in the trait. For example, mutations within a tissue-specific regulatory element for the *Pitx1* gene explain approximately 65% of variation in pelvic fin presence/absence in some freshwater populations of stickleback fish (Shapiro *et al.*, 2004; Chan *et al.*, 2010). On the other hand, given the nature of selection on highly complex pheno-types, some traits have potentially thousands of underlying loci, none of which control more than a small percentage of variation. For example, human height is likely controlled by thousands of loci; the most potent locus controls only about 1–2% of normal variation in this phenotype (Wood *et al.*, 2014). In lieu of the above, revealing the causative adaptive mutations that control variation in skeletal shape within and/or between species is a daunting task and one that will require insight from multiple scientific angles (see Chapter 1 for further discussion on parsing the genetic basis of complex traits like height).

Given the complicated relationship between genotypes and phenotypes, how then do scientists identify functionally important loci and gauge how much variation they control? How do they sift through the numerous genetic variants within an identified locus to find the variants directly responsible for changes in a species-specific phenotype? Finally, how do they functionally test these sequences to reveal molecular mechanism and their impacts on development? This chapter addresses these questions and issues in the context of appendage skeletal development and evolution. The goal is to inform the evolutionary developmental anthropologist as to the genetic, molecular, and developmental tools that are available for them to explore aspects of the genotype–phenotype puzzle in the context of primate skeletal variation and evolution.

8.2   Connecting Genotype to Phenotype

To connect genotype to phenotype using a developmental genetics perspective, it is imperative that the DNA base-pair sequences that control limb development, growth, and maturation be identified, and this can be accomplished using multiple approaches. For example, geneticists have historically used mapping approaches to reveal loci that underlie variation in skeletal morphology (see Pardo-Diaz *et al.*, 2015, for review), while more recently, functional geneticists and genomicists have used NGS methods to identify and then hone in on the types of genetic muta-tions that affect developmental pathways and underlie variation in morphology and disease risk (Gibson and Muse, 2009; Barrett and Hoekstra, 2011). To estab-lish direct functional links between loci and traits and thus identify precisely how genes and their protein products contribute to morphological development, devel-opmental biologists have used techniques such as gene mis-expression in the chick (e.g., Logan and Tabin, 1999) and targeted gene deletion/replacement in the mouse model systems (e.g., Menke, 2013). When used in concert to address evolutionary questions, these approaches can be quite powerful in revealing the sequences that control adaptive trait variation. These topics are addressed in detail below.

8.2.1   Genetic Methods: Finding the Loci that Control Trait Variation

Studies that focus on identifying loci that control trait variation typically fall into one of two main categories: "forward approaches" or "reverse approaches." When a phenotype is known to vary and researchers are seeking to identify the loci that control its variation, these studies are often classified as either "forward genetics" or "forward genomics." Investigative genetic studies involving twins or family ped-igrees with known phenotypes fall under the "forward genetics" category, as do genetic association studies such as QTL mapping and GWAS. Most recently, "for-ward genomics" has emerged and involves using comparisons of known traits across many taxa (i.e., between group variation) in concert with full genome sequences from those taxa to find recurrent genomic regions that control convergent or divergent biological traits (e.g., Hiller *et al.*, 2012). On the other hand, the "reverse genetics" or "reverse genomics" approach employs a *de novo* scan across a locus or the genome to find sequences that show characteristics of functional and evolutionary change (e.g., evidence of natural selection or drift). Both "reverse approaches" result in the identification of novel sequences, albeit these sequences still need to be linked to biological phenotypes using some of the functional techniques outlined below. This approach is especially powerful in revealing regions of the genome that display evidence of potentially adaptive evolution in different primates and humans (Prabhaker *et al.*, 2006, 2008; McLean *et al.*, 2011; Vitti *et al.*, 2013).

To make sense of any biological outcome, both approaches often rely on previous knowledge of the genomic region under investigation and downstream analyses often focus on known genes with established biological effects in chicks, mice, or humans. This "candidate" gene perspective has been particularly useful in twin and family studies to uncover causative mutations involved in limb skeletal variation (Farooq *et al.*, 2013). For example, novel mutations in a functional domain of the *GDF5* gene were identified in members of a large Pakistani family exhibiting brachydactyly by sequencing the gene's coding region in affected and unaffected individuals (Farooq *et al.*, 2013). These mutations disrupted digit joint development, resulting in the absence of the intermediate phalanx and revealed key functions for *GDF5* in distal joint development. However, many family studies are inherently limited by the availability of families/cohorts with relevant phenotypes and by the fact that the individual genetic influences on a trait are difficult to identify because they can be hidden by the segregation of other genes and/or noise produced by environmental or experimental variation. Often candidate gene studies are conducted in patients and yield no significant results that are then not reported; this is likely due to the fact that many genes and regulatory regions control the trait in question. Moreover, the candidate gene approach is still limited mainly to coding regions, yet mutations in nearby or faraway non-coding regulatory sequences may be the true culprits responsible for the phenotype of interest.

Recent genomics approaches, such as whole exome sequencing (WES) in which untranslated and coding regions of genes are sequenced genome-wide, allow for a more rapid identification of causative mutations (Tetreault *et al.*, 2015). This is an especially powerful approach when affected and non-affected siblings are both sequenced. For example, using WES, Parry and colleagues (2013) identified mutations in the *Goosecoid* gene that cause short stature, auditory canal atresia, mandibular hypoplasia, and skeletal abnormalities. This technique is even more powerful when it is performed on multiple individuals with and without a given phenotype from different families. Nilsson and colleagues (2014) have identified several different causative mutations in the *Aggrecan* gene, which encodes a proteoglycan in the extracellular matrix of growth plate cartilage, underlying idiopathic short stature syndrome in three different families. While WES and related techniques have been important in mapping relatively simple, monogenic Mendelian-inherited traits and diseases, they are only now being used to identify the mutations that underlie complex, polygenic traits and diseases with some (limited) success (e.g., autism via Codina-Solà et al., 2015; neural tube defects via Lemay et al., 2015).

The "forward genetic" approaches of linkage and association mapping (such as GWAS) have more often been used to identify loci that underlie complex, polygenic traits that display patterns of normally distributed variation. Evolutionary biologists routinely use linkage mapping to identify loci that influence quantitative variation in a particular trait, or QTL (Hartl and Ruvolo, 2011). In QTL mapping, often a broad locus can be uncovered if it is linked genetically via some marker in the genome (e.g., microsatellite repeat, or single nucleotide polymorphism (SNP)) to observable variation in a trait. Such markers, when dispersed across the genome, can be tracked for how they co-segregate with variation in the trait in question, especially after analyses are conducted on offspring cohorts across several generations (e.g., F_1 and F_2 generations). Typically, QTL mapping is performed in organisms that have marked genetic and phenotypic diversity. In evolutionary biology contexts (i.e., with model and non-model organisms) researchers take advantage of this extensive trait heterogeneity, and improvements in genome-wide genotyping, and experimentally cross individuals in order to track alleles that influence phenotypic variation in the F_1 and F_2 hybrid generations. Statistical analysis then allows markers to be associated with trait variation and can reveal significant, but often very wide (e.g., megabase) QTL intervals that often harbor many putative functional loci (genes and regulatory sequences). Experimental studies with offspring cohorts possessing many individuals (e.g., thousands) have generally uncovered more loci, including those of slightly smaller effects, as well as loci that are a bit narrower due to the greater number of recombination events that partition meaningful genetic and phenotypic variation into smaller co-segregating blocks. One striking example was by Shapiro and colleagues, who used QTL analyses on stickleback pelvic fin phenotypes to identify a genomic interval that contained numerous genes including *Pitx1*, a key gene involved in pelvic development (Shapiro et al., 2004; Colosimo et al., 2005). Other examples within mice include the identification of the *cadherin 11* locus in the control of femoral microarchitecture (Farber et al., 2011); a locus on chromosome 6 that controls tibial length in LG/J and SM/J inbred lines (Nikolskiy et al., 2015); the *PAPP-A2* locus that controls bone shape and size (Christians et al., 2013), and numerous other loci that have been mapped by Cheverud and colleagues and shown to underlie limb and craniofacial skeletal traits (e.g., see Kenney-Hunt et al., 2006). Within non-human primates, fewer examples exist, but include the identification of QTLs governing craniofacial shape in hamadryas baboons (Sherwood et al., 2008); and the identification of a QTL in baboons governing variation in forearm bone mineral density (Havill et al., 2005).

GWAS, as well as other association mapping experiments, have taken advantage of a highly prevalent class of markers called SNPs, and improvements in genotyping technologies, to map population variation in traits to loci in the human genome (reviewed in Hartl and Ruvolo, 2011). GWAS involve genotyping and phenotyping a large number of individuals (tens to hundreds of thousands) from cases and controls that are age- and sex-matched and are often from similar geographic

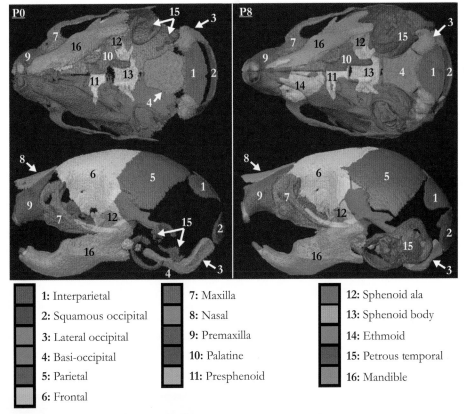

Figure 2.2 The subset of bones analyzed, as identified from the surface reconstructions of P0 and P8 specimens from the inferior view (top) and the left lateral view (bottom). Bones included in our analysis are brightly colored, while the rest of the skull is transparent gray. As identified in this figure, the maxilla includes the lacrimal bone and the petrous temporal includes the ectotympanic.

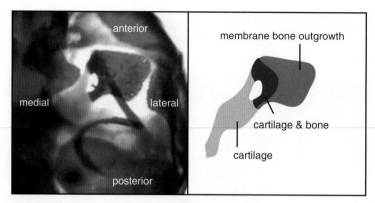

Figure 3.1 Cartilage bone and membrane bone formation illustrated by the alisphenoid at embryonic day 16.5 (E16.5; ventral view). In the left box, cartilage is stained in blue, while bone is stained in red. The ala temporalis is depicted in the right box. At E14.5, the lateral ascending edge of the ala temporalis (Figure 3.2B) undergoes perichondral ossification and extends a membrane bone outgrowth laterally from the ossified surface. Inside the perichondral bone, the cartilage becomes hypertrophic and initiates mineralization at E15.5. The mineralized cartilage is subsequently replaced by bone by endochondral ossification. At E16.5, the ala temporalis is being ossified into the alisphenoid primarily by endochondral ossification and membranous outgrowth. Later during bone remodeling, the endochondrally ossified portion is resorbed and replaced by intramembranously formed new endosteal bone.

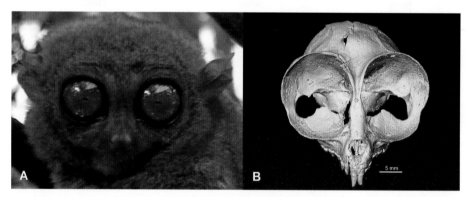

Figure 4.1 (A) All tarsiers are characterized by extremely large eyes. Tarsius syrichta is shown in its habitual resting position associated with vertical clinging and leaping (photo modified and licensed through CCA-SA 3.0 by JT Lim Majuro~enwiki at http://wikipedia.com). (B) Reconstruction of an adult Tarsius syrichta cranium in comparable orientation illustrates the profound influence of eye hypertrophy on the shape of the cranium and bony orbit.

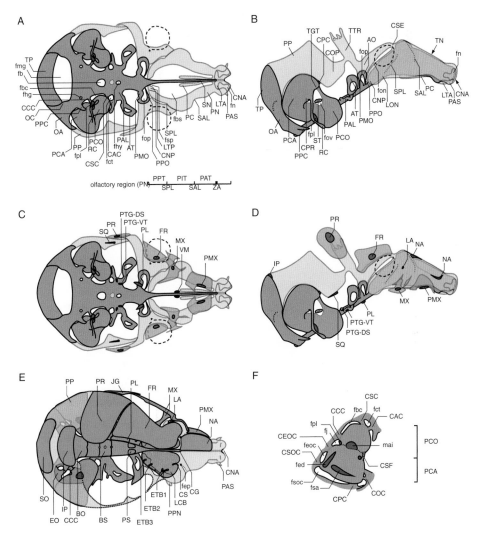

Figure 3.2 Embryonic mouse skull. (A, B) The cartilaginous skull of a mouse embryo at E15.5, (A) inferior view and (B) lateral view, with nose to the right and occiput to the left. Cartilages that are partly or entirely replaced by bone via endochondral ossification are shown in darker blue, while those that are resorbed and substituted by dermal bones are depicted in light blue. The globes of the eyes are shown by a dashed outline. (A) The scale at the bottom corresponds with coronal cuts that define the three parts of the paries nasi (PPT, PIT, and PAT) separated by the two sulci (SPL and SAL, shown in dotted line in Figure 3.2B) and the zona annularis (ZA). (C, D) Dermatocranial bones associated with the chondrocranial elements, (C) inferior view, and (D) lateral view, with nose to the right and occiput to the left. Dermatocranial elements formed at E15.5 are shown in pale red with the initial location of their formation shown in dark red. Although the nasal and lacrimal bones are not yet formed at E15.5, they are illustrated in the region where they will form later in development. (E) Spatial association of cartilages (blue/pale blue) and bones at E17.5, superior view. Both dermal and cartilage bones are shown in red. On the right half of the skull (lower half), part of the cranial vault and the lateral wall (dotted line) are removed. (F) An enlarged superior view of the pars cochlearis and the pars canalicularis at E17.5, anterior to the right, posterior to the left. Note that the inferior part of the pars canalicularis in this figure extends dorsally (see Figure 3.2B).

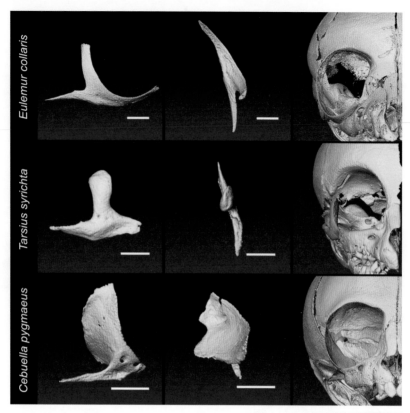

Figure 4.5 Zygomatic bone in infant Eulemur, Tarsius, and Cebuella. Right lateral (left column) and superior (middle column) views of the isolated zygomatic highlights distinct features of the ascending process in these taxa. The right column illustrates the position of the zygomatic (green) relative to the skull. Scale bars: Eulemur = 3 mm; Tarsius = 2 mm; Cebuella = 2 mm.

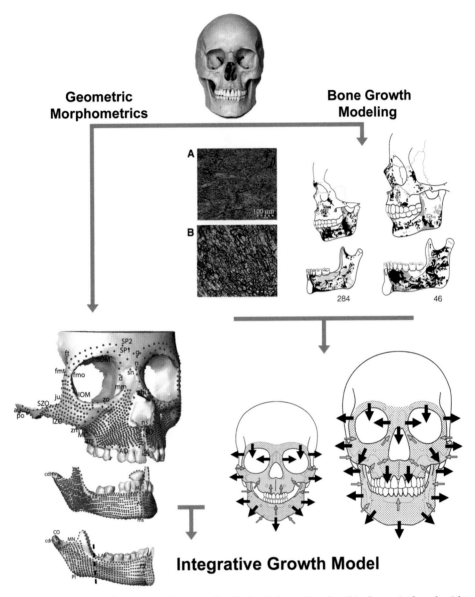

Figure 5.1 To allow for increased image detail, the full caption for this figure is found with Figure 5.1 in the main body of this volume.

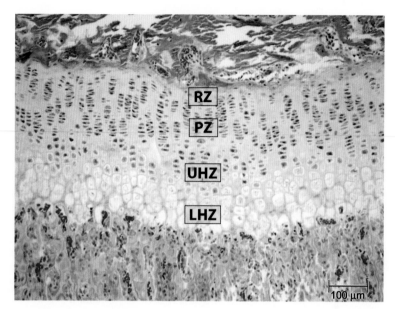

Figure 7.4 Photomicrograph of a rat epiphyseal plate stained with Safranin O showing the different cellular regions that contribute to longitudinal growth. The very narrow zone at the top of the cartilage is the resting zone (RZ), which here appears to have few cells. Cells in the proliferative zone (PZ), where mitosis and cell matrix production primarily occur, organize themselves in columns. These cells are somewhat flattened or disc-shaped. These cells eventually begin to enlarge (become hyperotrophic) and are rounder, but in the upper hypertrophic zone (UHZ) still produce significant amounts of matrix. These cells become apoptotic, enlarging further with nuclear disintegration, indicated by the loss of staining. Many lacunae in this lower hypertrophic zone (LHZ) are empty. The columns between the hypertrophic chondrocytes calcify. As the hypertrophic cells are lost, spaces form that are filled by blood vessels, which will provide cells responsible for remodeling the calcified cartilage columns into bone, or primary spongiosa.

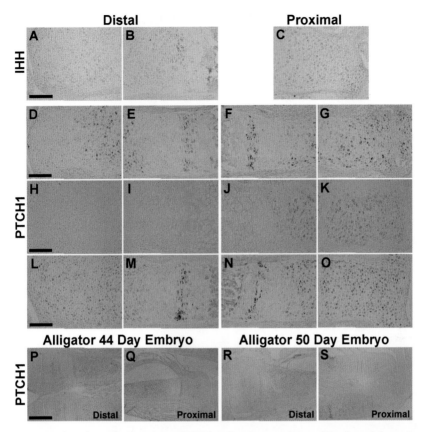

Figure 9.3 (A–C) Similar patterns of IHH localization are detected in the epiphyseal, columnar, and prehypertrophic chondrocytes at each end of P2 MTs. PTCH1 detection is variable in the distal end (D, E, H, I, L, M). Commonly, a gradient of expression is observed in the epiphysis (D), with strong expression detected in prehypertrophic chondrocytes (E, M). However, some specimens show no staining in distal epiphysis (H) or the growth plate (I), and in others staining is uniform across the epiphysis (L). In contrast, proximal staining is highly consistent in prehypertrophic chondroctyes (F, J, N) and uniformly across the epiphysis (G, K, O). (P–S) In the embryonic alligators PTCH1 is detected in epiphyseal chondrocytes adjacent to the columnar zone and prehypertrophic cells at each end, consistent with these bones forming two growth plates in this species.

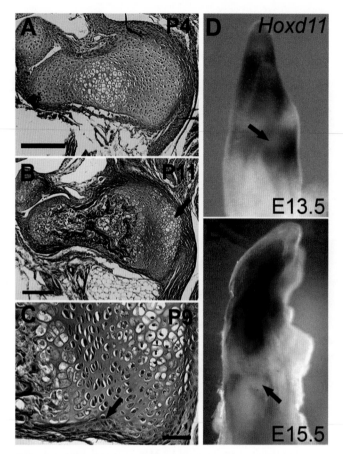

Figure 9.5 (A) Safranin O (red) staining reveals the development of the growth plate in the mouse pisiform. Chondrocyte hypertrophy and calcification is initiating in the central part of the P4 cartilage model. (B) By P11 the pisiform is largely ossified except for the remaining growth plate on the palmar end (right); note the formation of the secondary center (arrow). (C) The pisiform preserves all of the hallmarks of a growth plate with columnar and hyper-trophic cells and an encircling bone collar and perichondrial ring (arrow). Scale bars are 100 μm. In situ hybridization in (D) E13.5 and (E) E15.5 mouse forelimbs reveal late-stage Hoxd11 expression surrounding the developing pisiform (arrows).

localities. Genotyping involves the use of a SNP-chip that often contains over one million SNP markers spread across the genome. The use of more markers as well as knowledge of the non-random association of alleles at different loci, or linkage disequilibrium (LD), recently acquired from the 1000 Genomes and the HapMap projects (Weir *et al.*, 2005), has improved GWAS studies and helped to narrow down genomic intervals of association. Most recently, rare variant imputation (reviewed in Porcu *et al.*, 2013), along with fine-mapping and refined haplotype analyses in diverse human populations (reviewed in Li and Keating, 2014) has lead to even narrower association windows (tens of thousands of kilobases). Given that most GWAS studies are conducted on complex traits that are extremely variable and highly polygenic, often thousands to hundreds of thousands of individuals will need to be analyzed to identify associated loci; for example, the most recent GWAS of skeletal height variation in human populations was conducted on over 250,000 individuals and revealed almost 700 loci that explain at least 20% of heritable variation in height (Wood *et al.*, 2014). Importantly, in all GWAS studies to date, the causative base pairs that control variation remain largely unknown due to the fact that many SNPs are often in strong LD within the association interval (Wood *et al.*, 2014).

8.2.2   Functional Genomics Methods: Defining Functional Sequences

Recently, functional genomics approaches have been implemented by large-scale projects such as The Encode Project (ENCODE Project Consortium, 2012), The Roadmap Epigenomics Project (Roadmap Epigenomics Consortium, 2015), and The Fantom Project (Lizio *et al.*, 2015), providing rich data sets upon which to screen putative associated variants from GWAS or other association studies. These projects have taken advantage of NGS to reveal genome-wide transcript production (transcriptome) and usage, as well as the locations of regulatory sequences and their interactions with target genes in a variety of cell and tissue types in humans and mice.

8.2.2.1 Genome-wide Transcript Detection

Detection of expressed transcripts has been carried out on genomic levels by surveying the transcriptome of a specific tissue or cell type (Gibson and Muse, 2009; Dong and Chen, 2013; Roux *et al.*, 2015). Initially, this was accomplished by way of tissue dissections followed by the generation of complementary DNA (cDNA) libraries, in which double-stranded DNA is synthesized from messenger RNA extracted from a tissue of interest. When cDNA is sequenced and mapped to an assembled genome, these libraries produce a list of the expressed transcripts in that tissue (Gibson and Muse, 2009). Early cDNA libraries did yield the locations of transcripts in the genome and interesting differences in transcript abundance and variation between specific tissues in the body and between different individuals or species (e.g., see Canavez *et al.*, 2001). However, the advent of the DNA microarray (reviewed in Gibson and Muse, 2009), a microchip that contains DNA probes for nearly every known protein coding gene in the genome, made faster, more refined studies of transcript expression and variation possible. In these experiments, cDNA generated from a particular tissue is applied to the chip allowing the sequences to hybridize to gene probes. The hybridized transcripts are then detected using fluorescence or chemiluminescence. This method allows for a relative quantification of which transcripts are either up- or down-represented in the sample, especially when compared to appropriate control genes and tissues. In an effort to characterize the gene expression profile of developing limbs, microarray analyses have been performed on different limb bud zones (Rock *et al.*, 2007; Schreiner *et al.*, 2009), limb types (Shou *et al.*, 2005), limb structures (Pazin *et al.*, 2012), tissue types (Zhang *et al.*, 2008; Chau *et al.*, 2014), and even between different growth zones of developing bones (Wang *et al.*, 2004; Horvat-Gordon *et al.*, 2010; James *et al.*, 2010; Lui *et al.*, 2010).

More recent advancements, such as RNA-sequencing (RNA-seq; reviewed in Ozsolak and Milos, 2011), in which NGS is performed on RNA extracted from whole tissues, cultured cells, and even single cells (see below), provide genome-wide maps of transcriptional output including non-coding RNA transcripts. This technique can be carried out on tissues from different species, although the mapping of reads from NGS can be impacted by the quality of the parent genome. To date, RNA-seq has been performed in a number of different contexts, including on a variety of skeletal tissues and cell types, such as on chondrocyte cell lines and osteoblasts (ENCODE Project Consortium, 2012; Bowen *et al.*, 2014; Mori *et al.*, 2014; Oh *et al.*, 2014; Lizio *et al.*, 2015; Roadmap Epigenomics Consortium, 2015). While these experiments have revealed novel loci that likely reflect cartilage and bone-specific biology, it is important to note that they have been conducted mostly on *in vitro* derived cell lines and therefore transcriptomic profiles may be quite dissimilar to profiles acquired from *in vivo* collected tissues, such as chondrocytes of the growth plate.

Historically, these transcriptomic techniques were more often than not performed on heterogeneous cell populations extracted from a single organ or tissue. However, techniques such as fluorescence-activated cell sorting (FACs) (reviewed in Tung *et al.*, 2007) and laser capture microdissection (reviewed in Datta *et al.*, 2015) now allow for the isolation of specific cell types for use with these functional genomics methods. These approaches enable the identification of all transcripts produced by that cell or tissue type at a given time point. Most recently, microfluidic techniques that permit the isolation of single cells and subsequent "barcoding" of their RNA, permit rapid, single-cell resolution transcriptomics (Macosko *et al.*, 2015).

Using these types of refined data sets, scientists will be able to address a number of issues. For example, they will be able to determine whether GWAS SNPs for height are enriched near genes expressed uniquely within a specific growth plate zone (e.g., in the proliferative zone versus the hypertrophic zone) and this could reveal specific mechanisms that evolution has targeted to drive skeletal variation in human populations. Comparative RNA-seq analyses performed on specific tissues, such as growth plates, or on specific growth plate zones, from several different species with different limb phenotypes will likely shed light on the molecular and evolutionary mechanisms that generate interspecies variation in limb length, segment length, and limb proportions. For example, Cooper and colleagues (2013) have demonstrated that hypertrophic chondrocyte zones from the elongated distal metapodial growth plate of the jerboa, a hopping rodent, are enlarged by over 50% compared to the laboratory mouse. This suggests that genes and regulatory sequences controlling hypertrophic zone formation, differentiation, and maintenance may have been the target of selection during jerboa evolution; if so, it may be interesting to identify whether similar genetic changes are seen in other hopping or jumping rodents with similar distal metapodial elongations. Hypertrophic cells from species with convergent phenotypes may have very similar transcriptome profiles and be quite dissimilar to more closely related (non-elongated) sister species. On the other hand, hypertrophic chondrocyte zones in each hopping rodent species may exhibit significant transcript expression divergence due to the evolution of distinct hierarchical factors regulating growth plate transcriptional programs. In this case, knowledge of underlying genetic variation within and between species will be paramount for identifying mutations linked to expression differences in these rodents.

Transcriptome experiments, such as those described above, can help bridge the genotype–phenotype gap, especially when they are coupled with direct measurements of genome sequence variation in the same individuals. Accordingly, expression quantitative trait loci or eQTLs (reviewed in Gilad *et al.*, 2008; Majewski and Pastinen, 2011) are loci that show expression variation in relation to underlying genomic variation. SNPs have historically been the primary type of genomic variation examined, but more recently insertion/deletion mutations have been analyzed (Huang *et al.*, 2015). For example, RNA-sequencing and SNP genotyping performed on HapMap and/or 1000 Genomes Project lymphoblastoid cell lines have revealed SNPs that are associated with transcript variation for nearby genes (e.g., Lappalainen *et al.*, 2013). These eQTLs will help to narrow down causative mutations among the many associated variants uncovered via GWAS and are useful for honing in on variants within QTL intervals.

8.2.2.2 Genome-wide Regulatory Element Detection

One insight gained from The Encode Project (ENCODE Project Consortium, 2012), The Roadmap Epigenomics Project (Roadmap Epigenomics Consortium, 2015), and The Fantom Project (Lizio *et al.*, 2015) is that most genomic variation (including eQTLs) resides in close proximity to, or directly overlaps with, a sequence with known biochemical function, the majority of which is regulatory in nature. This finding suggests that regulatory portions of the genome are important drivers of developmental variation and evolutionary change. Recent advancements in the genome-wide identification of regulatory sequences are improving our understanding of this domain, specifically with respect to the spatiotemporal control of gene regulation in a cell-type specific manner.

Techniques that reveal regulatory sequences (e.g., enhancers, repressors, promoters) across the genome have been based on several fundamental observations. First, it has been known for some time, via the development of chromatin immunoprecipitation (ChIP) (reviewed in Orlando, 2000), that regulatory sequences are physically bound by transcription factors (TF), which facilitate the expression of target genes (reviewed in Krebs et al., 2014). Some TFs have been shown to act in a general manner; that is, they bind to the same regulatory sequence in many different cell types. Other TFs have been shown to be functional only in a particular cell type, bound to many targets, and/or responsible for hierarchically controlling its transcriptional profile (e.g., Aziz et al., 2010). A typical hypothesis that emerges from these findings is that if a TF is shown to interact biochemically with a regulatory sequence, then a DNA modification (e.g., SNP) at the specific location of binding may reduce or enhance TF binding, producing a functional impact on gene transcription and phenotype. Importantly, recently ChIP has been combined with NGS (i.e., ChIP-seq) to identify all locations in the genome bound by a specific factor (reviewed in Furey, 2012). Projects such as The ENCODE Project (ENCODE Project Consortium, 2012) have performed ChIP-seq on over 125 different human cell types for a number of transcription factors, some of which universally mark enhancers and others that mark enhancers for specific cell types.

ChIP-seq studies have only recently been performed on tissues related to limb and skeletal development. Menke and colleagues performed ChIP-seq on early mouse limb buds for the TF Pitx1 (Infante et al., 2013). As Pitx1 is a hindlimb-specific regulator (Lanctôt et al., 1999), their work has revealed many targets genome-wide that likely regulate hindlimb development in mammals; such targets can be screened for mutations that potentially underlie variation in hindlimb morphology across mammals and primates. ChIP-seq has also been performed on skeletogenic tissues for Sox9 (Oh et al., 2014), a hierarchical regulator of mesenchymal condensation and early chondrocyte development in long bones (Bi et al., 1999; Ohba et al., 2015). This data set of regulatory sequences can be used to identify whether any GWAS variants for height reside within and thus potentially disrupt chondrocyte enhancer function. Likewise, comparative genomic sequence analyses on such an enhancer data set can be used to reveal suites of enhancers that have experienced evolutionary changes between species that have different long bone skeletal phenotypes.

Second, it has also been discovered that chromatin that is wound around histones in the form of nucleosomes is actively unwound before transcription (reviewed in Krebs et al., 2014). Importantly, where chromatin is unwound or "open," it can then be experimentally digested using nucleases, enzymes that cut DNA (Wu et al., 1979a,b; Gross and Garrard, 1988). Numerous assays have been developed that use NGS to sequence "open" digested nucleosome sequences (reviewed in Meyer and Liu, 2014) with the goal of identifying the locations of these potential regulatory sequences across the genome. These techniques include: DNase-seq (Crawford et al., 2004; Sabo et al., 2004), FAIRE-seq (Giresi et al., 2007), and ATAC-seq (Buenrostro et al., 2013). DNase-seq involves the digestion of "open" chromatin by the enzyme DNase I followed by sequencing (Crawford et al., 2004; Sabo et al., 2004). DNase-seq protocols performed on hundreds of cell and tissue types have revealed millions of active regulatory regions across the genome (reviewed in Madrigal and

Krajewski, 2012) and about one-third of these DNase sites are specific to individual cell types, reflecting the cell-type-specific control of gene regulation (ENCODE Project Consortium, 2012). To date, DNase-seq has been performed on mouse fore- and hindlimb buds at gestational day (E) 11.5 revealing a number of loci that regulate early limb bone patterning; on mouse limb buds at E14.5 identifying loci involved in limb chondrogenesis (ENCODE Project Consortium, 2012), and on *in vitro*-derived osteoblasts to study bone development (Inoue and Imai, 2014; Tai *et al.*, 2014).

Of these approaches, ATAC-seq or assay for transposase-accessible chromatin Sequencing (Buenrostro *et al.*, 2013) is quite promising. This approach uses a specific transposase that preferentially cuts open chromatin regions and simultaneously integrates built-in adaptor tags to the ends of the cut sequence that coincide with the regions adjacent to nucleosomes. Using primers that recognize these tagged sites, polymerase chain reaction (PCR) is then performed to amplify the library, which then undergoes NGS and mapping of reads to the parent genome to reveal regulatory sequences. This approach is quite promising because it is relatively simple, that is, it can be accomplished in less than a day, and requires very little starting cellular material. This latter property of ATAC-seq allows scientists to identify regulatory regions on rare tissue samples (for example, human embryonic limb buds) or even highly specific anatomies or cell types. While ATAC-seq has not yet been used on skeletal tissues, one elegant study by Shubin and colleagues (Gehrke *et al.*, 2015) has compared genome-wide ATAC-seq signatures derived from mammalian limb-bud and fish fin-bud tissues to understand the evolution of gene regulation during appendage development over deep evolutionary time.

Third, chromatin wound around nucleosomes experiences chemical modifications that lead to its relaxation and thus potential for active transcription (reviewed in Krebs *et al.*, 2014). At the nucleosome, core histone proteins possess exposed amino acid residues or tails that can be chemically modified or "marked" by a number of processes including acetylation and methylation (reviewed in Rivera and Ren, 2013). Specific histone tail residues, when acetylated, can lead to the loosening of a chromatin–histone complex, which exposes DNA for future occupancy by transcription factors. On the other hand, methylation at specific histone tail residues can lead to repression and a highly wound DNA–histone complex. Thus, based on the type of mark, it has been possible to identify using ChIP-seq active and repressed regulatory sequences on a genome-wide and cell-type specific level. Some of the most studied histone marks include: H3K27ac, a mark of active enhancers (Heintzman *et al.*, 2009; Creyghton *et al.*, 2010; Rada-Iglesias *et al.*, 2011); H3K4me3, a mark of active promoters (Bernstein *et al.*, 2005; Pokholok *et al.*, 2005); and H3K27me3, a mark of a repressed region (Bernstein *et al.*, 2006). The ENCODE Project (ENCODE Project Consortium, 2012) has studied a series of these marks in human cell lines and tissues related to limb development, while the Roadmap Epigenomics Project (Roadmap Epigenomics Consortium, 2015) has focused on a variety of human fetal and adult tissues. With respect to skeletal development, each consortium has performed a number of experiments for different histone marks on chondrocytes and osteoblasts derived from adult long bone marrow cavities. These data sets have not yet been extensively examined.

All three of the approaches discussed above yield regulatory sequences which can be screened and/or filtered for mutations that either have been associated with trait variation, or are different between two species or individuals under study. In addition, these techniques provide an understanding of the localized control of gene expression via the identification of regulatory sequences within a candidate locus. Thus, they can be used to substantially narrow down the number of putative regulatory mutations that need to be considered between affected and unaffected individuals in candidate gene studies or in association intervals. Because these data sets are new, there have not been many examples of their use in the above applications. However, one recent study has revealed that specific enhancers for *SOX9* are physically removed from its coding region due to chromosomal inversions in patients with limb defects such as campomelic dysplasia (Gordon *et al.*, 2009b; Fukami *et al.*, 2012). It is through the identification of the enhancers and their physical displacement that the causative mutations underlying this phenotype were discovered.

8.2.2.3 Intrachromosomal Interactions Between Regulatory Elements and Genes

In order to connect regulatory elements to their specific target genes, and thus be able to understand how mutations within them impact gene expression and phenotypes, assays that gauge biophysical connections, known as chromosomal conformation capture assays, have been developed (reviewed in Rivera and Ren, 2013). These techniques can be performed in a localized manner to reveal intralocus interactions (i.e., chromosomal conformation capture (3C) (Dekker *et al.*, 2002) or chromosomal conformation capture carbon copy (5C) (Dostie *et al.*, 2006)), or on a broader genome-wide level (i.e., circular chromosome conformation capture (4C) (Zhao *et al.*, 2006), chromatin interaction analysis using paired-end tag sequencing (ChIA-PET) (Fullwood *et al.*, 2010), or Hi-C (Lieberman-Aiden *et al.*, 2009)). One common finding of all of these capture techniques is that regulatory sequences can target more than one gene during development, making understanding the regulatory impacts of sequence variants quite complicated. To date, few studies have been conducted using capture assays for limb and skeletal development, although some notable examples exist. Amano and colleagues (2009) used 3C to identify intralocus interactions in the *Sonic hedgehog* (*SHH*) locus, revealing important expression kinematics of the SHH protein in the limb bud. Mutations in *SHH* have been shown to alter digit morphology and likely explain some variation in digit number in different animals (see below). 3C was also used on the *SHOX* locus and revealed that disruptions in enhancer interactions may underlie some cases of idiopathic short stature (Benito-Sanz *et al.*, 2012). Finally, Lupiáñez and colleagues (2015) used 4C assays on patients with brachydactyly and polydactyly and revealed that genomic disruptions (via deletions, inversions, or duplications) to intrachromosomal interactions between enhancers and promoters for the *WNT6;IHH;EPHA4;PAX3* locus are likely the causative mutations underlying these skeletal phenotypes. In time, these methods will be used in a comparative framework to reveal how intrachromosomal interactions vary between species displaying considerable variation in skeletal morphology.

8.2.3 Developmental Biology Methods: Testing Putative Functional Variants and Understanding their Developmental Context and Phenotypic Impacts

While genetic mapping experiments are ideal for identifying loci associated with phenotypic traits, and functional genomic studies can help narrow down association and QTL intervals to a smaller number of putative functional mutations, both lack the ability at this time to directly test mutations for functional impacts on phenotypes. To acquire this level of understanding for a given variant (or region of the genome that markedly differs between individuals or species), developmental biology and molecular biology methods must be utilized, and thus far they have been important for understanding: (1) the identification of the spatiotemporal patterns of expression for transcripts and proteins in specific tissues and cells; (2) the nature of signaling interactions between and within tissues and cells; (3) the tracking of cellular contributions to developing and mature tissues; (4) the identification of specific regulatory sequences for genes used during development and growth; and (5) the functions of gene and regulatory elements in the embryo at specific times and places. Below, each of these contributions is discussed in the context of skeletal development and in the ways they have been helpful in linking genotypes to phenotypes.

8.2.3.1 Detecting Gene Expression and Protein Localization

For a coding or regulatory variant to impact morphological variation, the mutation will likely alter the expression and/or function of the gene in a specific cell type of interest. Therefore, methods have been developed that allow for the precise identification of the spatiotemporal expression pattern of the gene and its protein product. The earliest expression detection methods involved the qualitative detection of just one individual gene or protein product either on a histological section or in a whole embryo using *in situ* hybridization (reviewed in Hauptmann, 2015) or immunohistochemistry (reviewed in Buchwalow and Böcker, 2014). In these cases, the endogenously expressed transcript or protein of interest is first targeted using either a labeled-mRNA probe or antibody, and once the probe is hybridized to the transcript, or the antibody is bound to the protein, they are then detected via a colorimetric or fluorescence reaction. Assays such as these, when simultaneously performed for cell-type specific marker genes or proteins, and/or in conjunction with histological staining techniques (e.g., hematoxylin and eosin staining), allow the researcher to define specific expression zones at the level of cells and tissues (see Chapter 9 for an example). These methods provide important information about where and when a gene is expressed and, if used in the context of gene loss-of-function or mis-expression experiments (see below), they can serve to reveal how the expression of downstream genes and specific molecular pathways are disrupted (e.g., see Capellini *et al.*, 2006, 2010). They can also be used to determine whether species-specific mutations in regulatory elements lead to transcript down- or upregulation at a localized subdomain of an entire gene's expression pattern (e.g., see Shapiro *et al.*, 2004).

8.2.3.2 Identifying How Signaling Interactions Sculpt Phenotypes

Because phenotypic variation arises during development, it is important to understand how genetic mutations alter, ever so finely, signaling interactions within and between tissues. A key component of this approach is characterizing these interactions in model systems, so that the functional ramifications of mutations can be contextualized, especially as they lead to the production of variation. Indeed, some of the earliest studies in developmental biology used model systems such as the chick and the axolotl to examine tissue interactions during development and how they control the formation of distinct tissues (e.g., see Gilbert, 2013). These experiments involved either placing foil barriers between tissues of interest or removing tissues to alter signaling and observe the phenotypic consequences on the development of appendage skeletal elements (e.g., see Summerbell, 1979; Stephens and McNulty, 1981). For example, placement of a foil barrier between the lateral plate mesoderm and somitic dermomyotome at the level of the chick forelimb bud lead to the downregulation of bone morphogenetic protein expression and severe scapula blade phenotypes. Likewise, removal of the somites at the forelimb and hindlimb levels has revealed that signaling interactions between the somites and lateral plate mesoderm are important for the formation of the scapula but not necessarily the pelvis (Huang *et al.*, 2006). These experiments also reveal that one potential source of variation in scapula blade morphology is from the actions of genes in adjacent non-scapula tissues.

Another early experimental approach involved grafting tissues from one part of the body onto another to observe the phenotypic effects of disrupted signaling. For example, early studies in chick limb development revealed that when a specific subpopulation of posterior limb bud cells was grafted onto the anterior portion of a similarly staged limb bud, an ectopic mirror image digit duplication occurred (MacCabe *et al.*, 1973). Furthermore, the grafting of the homologous mouse tissues onto the anterior chick limb bud resulted in similar patterns (Tickle *et al.*, 1976), revealing a conservation of digit patterning mechanisms. These early experiments identified an important signaling center called the zone of polarizing activity (ZPA) that is now known to express *Shh*, which encodes for a protein that signals across the limb bud to drive posterior digit formation (Riddle *et al.*, 1993). Researchers have also used beads soaked in specific proteins or chemical antagonists to explore how signaling occurs within and between tissues. For example, the application of SHH protein-soaked beads to the anterior portion of the chick limb bud yielded mirror image duplications, thus reproducing the result of ectopic application of ZPA tissues (Yang *et al.*, 1997). In addition, distal limb truncations and digit loss occurred in response to the application of SHH antagonists to the ZPA region, revealing the important role of this pathway in digit patterning and outgrowth (Scherz *et al.*, 2007). Beads soaked in bone morphogenetic proteins, such as GDF5 or its antagonist, have helped to reveal their role in the formation of synovial joints (Francis-West *et al.*, 1996; Merino *et al.*, 1999), whereas the application of chemical inhibitors to developing growth plates has demonstrated the important effects of signaling interactions in endochondral ossification (e.g., Nagai and Aoki, 2002; Wu and De Luca, 2006).

8.2.3.3 Fate-mapping

Many protocols have been designed to track or fate-map cellular contributions to distinct tissues during development, thereby providing a context for understanding how functional mutations in specific cells can influence morphological development and variation. For example, studies in chick embryos using DiI labeling have fated cell populations in the early limb bud to different signaling centers as well as to proximal and distal skeletal elements (e.g., Vargesson *et al.*, 1997; Dudley *et al.*, 2002). They have also shed light on the cellular progenitors of both synovial joints (Koyama *et al.*, 2008) and muscles of the limb (e.g., Pacifici *et al.*, 2006). Interspecies (quail–chick) cell labeling experiments, which take advantage of the use of species-specific antibodies for detection, have also revealed the migratory pathways of muscle cells in the limb (e.g., Valasek *et al.*, 2005), as well as the tissues that give rise to both girdles (reviewed in Huang *et al.*, 2006).

The laboratory mouse has been an exceptionally important model system for tracing cell lineages during development (reviewed in Kraus *et al.*, 2014). Using gene-targeting procedures, researchers have created mouse strains harboring specific regulatory sequences placed upstream of the *Cre* gene to drive its expression. The protein product of this gene is the Cre-recombinase enzyme, which can excise artificial sequence tags called loxP sites. For the purpose of fate-mapping, loxP sites have been engineered to flank "stop" sequences upstream of regulatory elements capable of constitutively activating a reporter gene, such as one that produces lacZ or green fluorescent protein (GFP) (e.g., Soriano, 1999). Mouse lines harboring this reporter sequence can be crossed to a line with a tissue-specific regulatory sequence driving the expression of Cre-recombinase. The enzyme will then excise the stop sequence via recombination at the loxP sites, thus activating *lacZ* or *GFP* gene expression in only that cell type. Using detection methods, scientists can then track lacZ- or GFP-labeled cells as they proliferate and migrate to the tissues they help form. For example, this procedure has been used to fate cells that have expressed *Shh* to posterior digits (Harfe *et al.*, 2004), expressed *Gdf5* to developing and mature joints (Koyama *et al.*, 2008), and expressed *Sox9* to chondrogenic populations in the growth plates (Akiyama *et al.*, 2005).

8.2.3.4 Regulatory Element Identification

The discovery that phenotypic variation within and between species is due to regulatory mutations (King and Wilson, 1975), which has been recently documented by genome-wide studies in humans (Grossman *et al.*, 2013) and stickleback fish (Jones *et al.*, 2012), has lead scientists to interrogate conserved non-coding sequences for regulatory function using *in vitro* or *in vivo* assays (reviewed in Davidson, 2001). In these assays, candidate non-coding sequences are cloned upstream of reporter genes (*lacZ* or *GFP*) to see if they can activate reporter expression when transfected in cells or injected into living embryos. While cell assays have been useful in determining that a sequence has regulatory potential, *in vivo* approaches, such as enhancer transgenesis, reveal a sequence's precise spatial–temporal control of gene regulation in the three-dimensional embryo (Mortlock *et al.*, 2003). For example, based on its high sequence conservation in mammals, a specific regulatory enhancer for *Shh* was discovered that drives this gene specifically in the ZPA (Lettice *et al.*, 2003) in mouse embryos. Interestingly, single point mutations in this enhancer in mice, cats, and humans each result in an extra digit in the forepaw and hindpaw (Gurnett *et al.*, 2007; Furniss *et al.*, 2008; Lettice *et al.*, 2008; Sun *et al.*, 2008), demonstrating the role of regulatory mutations underlying phenotypic diversity. Recently, specific long bone and joint regulatory sequences for the *Gdf5* (Capellini, unpublished) and *Gdf6* (Mortlock *et al.*, 2003) genes, along with several other musculoskeletal and limb genes such as *Bmp5* (Guenther *et al.*, 2008), *Fgf8* (Marinić *et al.*, 2013), and *Myf5* (Summerbell *et al.*, 2000) have been discovered also based on strong vertebrate conservation profiles. Importantly, these sequences control variation, as for example, mutations in a long-bone growth plate specific *GDF5* regulatory element underlies limb length variation in humans (Capellini *et al.*, unpublished).

8.2.3.5   Identification of Gene and Regulatory Element Function

A major step in connecting genotype to phenotype is determining the biological function of the RNA transcript, regulatory region, and/or specific DNA base-pair mutation under study. Numerous protocols have been developed that allow for the targeted interference or alteration of a DNA or RNA molecule *in vivo* (reviewed in Behringer *et al.*, 2014). Some of these assays, initially performed in chicks and mice, focused on using small hairpin RNA molecules (shRNAs) and the RNA interference pathway to knock down transcript level in order to reveal a gene's developmental role (reviewed in Campeau and Gobeil, 2011). Other techniques involved gene mis-expression by injecting replication-competent retroviral vectors (RCAS) possessing complementary DNAs for target genes (reviewed in Gordon *et al.*, 2009a). For example, targeted RCAS mis-expression for the genes *TBX4*, *TBX5*, and *PITX1* helped identify their roles in the determination of chick limb identity and early outgrowth (Logan and Tabin, 1999; Rodriguez-Esteban *et al.*, 1999; Takeuchi *et al.*, 1999), whereas similar assays for *Ihh*, *PTHrP*, *Wnt*, *Bmp*, and *Notch* revealed their actions during growth plate chondrocyte biology (Vortkamp *et al.*, 1996; Zou *et al.*, 1997; Hartmann and Tabin, 2000; Church *et al.*, 2002; Provot *et al.*, 2006).

Gene targeting directly in mice has long been the gold standard for identifying how a specific DNA mutation influences biological function (reviewed in Menke, 2013).

The earliest techniques allowed for the removal of a target sequence (known as a "knockout"), or a replacement of an endogenous mouse sequence with a foreign sequence (known as a "knockin"). These early techniques revolved around the process of homologous recombination, which allowed scientists to use the cell's own repair machinery in concert with foreign sequence constructs to replace a targeted sequence with a new sequence or none at all. Some of the earliest "knockout" and "knockin" alleles were performed on loci involved in limb skeletal development. For example, knockout of the *Shh* gene or its long-range regulatory element lead to a severe digit reduction and truncation, which roughly phenocopied early tissue removal and bead experiments in chicks (Chiang *et al.*, 1996; Sagai *et al.*, 2005). Many genes involved in growth plate regulation and joint formation have been experimentally excised using this approach (see Decker *et al.*, 2014; Kozhemyakina *et al.*, 2015). When data generated using gene targeting are coupled with tissue expression and other functional studies, not only has the understanding of the molecular circuitry of limb development, growth plate function, and joint formation been greatly expanded, but now scientists have the ability to contextualize how sequence mutations associated with phenotypes (and apparent within/between species) impact phenotypic variation.

Recently, techniques in genome editing using zinc finger nucleases (Urnov *et al.*, 2010), transcription activator-like effector nucleases (TALENs) (Christian *et al.*, 2010), and clustered regularly interspaced short palindromic repeats (CRISPR) with the CRISPR-associated system (CRISPR-Cas9) (Jinek *et al.*, 2012) have afforded scientists more rapid, cost-effective, and artifact-free ways of making targeted mutations at a locus (reviewed in Gupta and Musunuru, 2014). Of these three techniques, CRISPR-Cas9 editing has proven to be the most popular due to its higher efficiency, greater ease, and lower cost. This technique works when short guide RNA (sgRNA) molecules, which are complementary to the targeted DNA region of interest, are artificially expressed together with a Cas9 nuclease in a cell (reviewed in Zhang *et al.*, 2014). The guides lead Cas9 to the specific DNA site of interest, so that it can cut and induce a double-strand break. CRISPR-Cas9 has been used to create frameshift mutations resulting in premature stop codons and loss-of-function of key developmental genes (e.g., Fossat *et al.*, 2015), as well as to excise enhancers (e.g., Zhou *et al.*, 2014). CRISPR-Cas9 has also been used to "knockin" human sequence (see Zhang *et al.*, 2014), which has revolutionized the study of the functional basis of normal and rare variation underlying animal phenotypes (e.g., Gennequin *et al.*, 2013). Techniques have improved so rapidly that CRISPR-Cas9 can now be used to generate mutations at multiple loci simultaneously (Wang *et al.*, 2013) and it has been adapted to study large-scale structural changes in chromosomes (Kraft *et al.*, 2015) and to recreate human structural rearrangements in the mouse model (Lupiáñez *et al.*, 2015). More recently, CRISPR-Cas9 has been used to manipulate the genomes of other organisms, including humans (Liang *et al.*, 2015), non-human primates (Niu *et al.*, 2014; Chen *et al.*, 2015; Wan *et al.*, 2015), and rats (Shao *et al.*, 2014). CRISPR-Cas9 is also being used extensively *in vitro*, such as in human, primate, and mouse cell lines, to characterize the effects that coding and regulatory mutations have on cellular phenotypes (see Zhang *et al.*, 2014).

8.3   Anthropological Perspectives

The last 10 years have witnessed remarkable progress in the development of a number of important genetic, genomic, and developmental biology tools that help to identify and test the specific base-pairs that control phenotypic variation. Given the specialized nature of these techniques, there has not been a single study to date that has combined all approaches to link a genotype to a skeletal phenotype. However, one landmark project involved the discovery of a recurrent adaptive genotype in different freshwater stickleback populations (Shapiro *et al.*, 2004; Chan *et al.*, 2010). In this study, the causative allele, an approximate 500-bp enhancer deletion near the *Pitx1* gene, was identified due to the use of extensive genetic mapping, population genetic approaches, and functional tests *in vivo*. These approaches helped identify the *Pitx1* locus as a driver of variation in pelvic morphology in sticklebacks, discover freshwater stickleback populations with *Pitx1* haplotypes harboring recurrent enhancer deletions, reveal that these haplotypes were under selection, and focus stickleback transgenic and knockin studies to pinpoint the functional adaptive base-pair deletion controlling pelvic fin loss. This discovery was borne out of the development of several genetic, molecular biology, and developmental biology tools by David Kingsley's laboratory over the last 15 years that has made the stickleback a model system to study the evolutionary mechanisms controlling phenotypic variation.

For practical, ethical, and monetary reasons, Evolutionary Developmental Anthropologists are unlikely going to acquire many of these tools and samples for their primates of interest. For example, given the endangered status of many primates, there will likely always be a dearth of embryonic, infant, and juvenile tissues for functional genomic and developmental biology studies. Even if these samples were made available to a few experts (as in Chapters 4 and 6), they may not be high enough in number to meet the requirements for biological replication. In fact, the most cutting-edge functional genomics studies to date were performed on heterogeneous tissues from only a few individuals of each primate species, each of which differed dramatically in sex, age, health status, and post-mortem processing (e.g., see Khaitovich *et al.*, 2005; Perry *et al.*, 2012). Another example includes the difficulties in acquiring enough wild (and/or captive) individuals in large numbers and of diverse genetic makeup to perform association mapping experiments.

There may be some improvements on some of these fronts in the next several years, although they will only improve a portion of the tool types discussed above. For example, regarding sample size, one possible remedy is the establishment of a unified international system that fosters the opportunistic acquisition of tissues from animals that have died due to injury, illness, or during pregnancy. In the proper organizational setting, low cell number RNA-seq (Ozsolak and Milos, 2011) and ATAC-seq (Buenrostro *et al.*, 2013) protocols can produce important functional genomic data sets from a host of different tissues and cell types from a single animal. Another improvement will be the continued generation, expansion, and use of lymphoblastoid cell lines (LCLs) and induced pluripotent stem cells (IPS) from multiple individuals of a single species (e.g., see Khan *et al.*, 2013; Gallego Romero *et al.*, 2015). These lines will allow for functional genomic studies, although their use will be of limited value to directly understanding three-dimensional skeletal morphology. To strengthen genetic mapping experiments in primates, large-scale efforts are currently underway through a number of projects, such as the International Vervet Research Project (IVRP) (Jasinska *et al.*, 2012); the Southwest National Primate Research Center (SNPRC) (https://www.txbiomed.org/primate-research-center); the UC Davis California National Primate Research Center (UCDCNPRC) (http://www.cnprc.ucdavis.edu/); the Cayo Santiago Rhesus Macaque Study (CSRMS) (e.g., Widdig *et al.*, 2016); and the German Primate Center (GPC) (http://www.dpz.eu/en/home.html). These projects all hold great promise for increasing colony size, expanding knowledge of genetic diversity, improving animal pedigrees, and enhancing the potential for mapping of genotype to phenotype in captive and wild settings.

While these endeavors will improve some tools, Evolutionary Developmental Anthropologists will still be forced to use model systems to understand the developmental and genetic basis of variation and this poses some important issues. For example, recent comparisons of The ENCODE Project (ENCODE Project Consortium, 2012), the Mouse ENCODE Project (Yue *et al.*, 2014), and smaller-scale (e.g., Cotney *et al.*, 2013) data sets have revealed considerable divergence in the regulatory genomes between humans and mice, suggesting that the use of the mouse as a model system may lead to erroneous claims on how a locus controls variation. Yet, for a portion of the regulatory genome, that is, orthologous regulatory sequences that remain syntenic to their putative target genes, there appears to be significant functional conservation (Yue *et al.*, 2014). Additionally, Yue and colleagues (2014) and other researchers (Cheng *et al.*, 2014; Stergachis *et al.*, 2014) have discovered that human and mouse transcription factor binding at target loci, and the associated genetic networks they control, are substantially more conserved than previously believed, indicating that important molecular cascades remain intact from mouse to human. Both findings support the continued use of the mouse to gauge the functional impacts of mutations that alter conserved sequences have on phenotypic variation; although they indicate that the use of the mouse as a model system for functional genomics studies should be carefully undertaken and in a comparative framework. For this reason, recent studies cataloging transcript and regulatory element usage in the mouse have also performed assays on precious human and macaque embryonic tissues (Cotney *et al.*, 2013; Reilly *et al.*, 2015). While this level of experimentation is preferable, it is not very feasible or likely because the acquisition of samples is unpredictable and difficult. In the absence of the appropriate primate tissue data sets, detailed comparisons of novel mouse data sets with those compiled across many tissues from The ENCODE Project (ENCODE Project Consortium, 2012) and The Roadmap Epigenomics Project

(Roadmap Epigenomics Consortium, 2015) should be helpful in revealing the context of important mutations in primates.

Regardless of these suggested difficulties, the laboratory mouse has already had tremendous utility, especially in the context of testing the functional consequences of mutations that differ between human populations and/or primate species. For example, Kamberov and colleagues (2013) generated a coding mutation in the human *Ectodysplasin Receptor* (*EDAR*) gene in mice to recreate a human mutation that is high in frequency in Chinese populations and displays strong evidence of past selection. This mutation resulted in several human-like phenotypes in mice, including morphological changes in hair thickness, mammary biology, and eccrine gland density. Mice will also continue to provide a unique *in vivo* three-dimensional mammalian context for interpreting and/or characterizing morphological differences that result from specific regulatory mutations. For example, by comparing the transcriptome of human and mouse progenitor cell populations in the cortex, Florio and colleagues (2015) identified over 50 genes that were preferentially expressed in humans. One specific human gene, *ARHGAP11B*, when knocked into the orthologous mouse locus, increased basal progenitor generation and self-renewal and increased cortical plate area and gyrification, likely underlying some of the major developmental changes in human brain evolution. Indeed, as more and more gene transcripts and regulatory enhancers are discovered that are found to be expressed in and/or control highly specific anatomy, the mouse will be the only system available to assess how mutations in regulatory elements influence anatomy.

Another major issue that Evolutionary Developmental Anthropologists are up against concerns the acquisition of *adequate* phenotypic data within and between species. While thousands of papers have been published on morphological variation in primates offering tremendous insight into primate biology, most have not acquired genotypic information and many have measured the same trait differently, which makes combining phenotypic data sets for future association mapping studies difficult, misleading, and highly problematic. In addition, measured phenotypes do not necessarily reflect important developmental information, and their use in genetic mapping experiments or comparative genomic studies may lead to many false positives. Fortunately, there have been some recent attempts to remedy these issues. Centers like the IVRP, SNPRC, UCDCNPRC, CSRM, and GPC, along with large-scale phenotype data acquisition and cataloging by Morphobank (www.morphobank.org), are starting to collect the relevant information and standardize measurements.

Finally, for studies to be informative on an evolutionary level, improvements must also be made in addressing how functional mutations reflect and have affected the fitness landscape (Barrett and Hoekstra, 2011; Vitti *et al.*, 2013). While there is agreement that this last aspect is critically important, being able to identify the adaptive value of a specific phenotype encoded by a genetic mutation is extremely difficult. There are a few experimental techniques that help reveal how natural selection directly impacts variation at any functional, putatively adaptive variant and some experiments have laid the foundations for how these studies may be conducted (reviewed in Pardo-Diaz *et al.* 2015). Other than these insights, many scientists have reverted to a "reverse genomics" approach that relies on genome-wide scans to identify loci that display characteristic signatures of natural selection. One comprehensive measure developed by Pardis Sabeti and colleagues, called the composite of multiple signals (CMS) score (Grossman *et al.*, 2013), involves the integration of genome-wide data sets from five different selection methods into one score. CMS has been performed on human genomes spanning different continents and populations and has produced lists of candidate regions in the modern human genome, each of which can be functionally interrogated using all of the methods described above (e.g., see Kamberov *et al.*, 2013). However, these tests do not reveal loci that have experienced selection between species (e.g., between humans and chimpanzees from a last common ancestor), and further improvements in methods that can detect such signatures are highly needed.

As powerful as it is, the CMS test statistic (or any approach that aims to reveal selected regions of primate genomes) relies on sequence and SNP data sets generated on many individuals (e.g., the 1000 Genomes Project). In human genomics, data sets like these are the tip of the iceberg, and they will be greatly expanded upon to include tens of thousands to millions of genomes in the next 5–10 years. Unfortunately, such expansive data sets have not been generated for primates, although there are a few projects that have augmented the number of sequenced genomes. For example, the Great Ape Genome Diversity Project has sequenced genomes from approximately 100 hominoids, and this has improved our understanding of hominoid phylogenetic history, allele sharing, genome-wide methylation patterns, chromosome evolution, and species divergence at the sequence level (Hernando-Herraez *et al.*, 2013; Prado-Martinez *et al.*, 2013; Sudmant *et al.*, 2013; Nam *et al.*, 2015). However, for each sequenced individual, phenotype data are missing. Additionally, the sample size for each hominoid species is still not large enough to perform CMS testing or tests to identify fixed, selected regions of the genome. Given that for African apes we have genetic resources (e.g., linkage maps (e.g., Auton *et al.*, 2012)), reference genomes (Chimpanzee Sequencing and Analysis Consortium, 2005; Prüfer *et al.*, 2012; Scally *et al.*, 2012; Xue *et al.*, 2015), samplings of genomic or exomic diversity (e.g., Prado-Martinez *et al.*, 2013; Bataillon *et al.*, 2015), biological reagents (e.g., iPS and LCLs cells (Khan *et al.*, 2013; Gallego Romero et al., 2015)), molecular tools such as microarrays (e.g., Khaitovich *et al.*, 2004), transcriptomic data sets (e.g., Khaitovich *et al.*, 2005; Perry *et al.*, 2012) and phenotypic data sets (e.g., 100+ years of field observation and sample collection at multiple sites and museums), we should be focusing on large-scale genomic projects that capture nucleotide variation, haplotype diversity, and phenotypic data in thousands of remaining apes from around the world. These data sets may permit novel "reverse genomics" scans for selection, the possibility of revealing broadly mapped loci, and they will help partially transform these wild primates into "model-like" systems so that we can explore adaptation and the genotype–phenotype relationship in animals very pertinent to understanding the evolution of the human condition.

References

Akiyama, H., Kim, J. E., Nakashima, K., *et al.* (2005). Osteo-chondroprogenitor cells are derived from *Sox9* expressing precursors. *Proceedings of the National Academy of Sciences of the USA*, 102(41), 14665–14670.

Amano, T., Sagai, H., Tanabe, Y., *et al.* (2009). Chromosomal dynamics at the *Shh* locus: limb bud-specific differential regulation of competence and active transcription. *Developmental Cell*, 16(1), 47–57.

Auton, A. and McVean G. (2012). Estimating recombination rates from genetic variation in humans. *Methods in Molecular Biology*, 856, 217–237.

Aziz, A., Liu, Q. C. and Dilworth, F. J. (2010). Regulating a master regulator: establishing tissue-specific gene expression in skeletal muscle. *Epigenetics*, 5(8), 691–695.

Barrett, R. D. and Hoekstra, H. E. (2011). Molecular spandrels: tests of adaptation at the genetic level. *Nature Reviews Genetics*, 12(11), 767–780.

Bataillon, T., Duan, J., Hvilsom, C., *et al.* (2015). Inference of purifying and positive selection in three subspecies of chimpanzees (*Pan troglodytes*) from exome sequencing. *Genome Biology and Evolution*, 7(4), 1122–1132.

Behringer R, Vintersten Nagy, G. M. and Nagy, K. (2014). *Manipulating the Mouse Embryo: A Laboratory Manual, Fourth Edition*. New York, NY: Cold Spring Harbor Press.

Benito-Sanz, S., Aza-Carmona, M., Rodriguez-Estevez, A., *et al.* (2012). Identification of the first *PAR1* deletion encompassing upstream *SHOX* enhancers in a family with idiopathic short stature. *European Journal of Human Genetics*, 20(1), 125–127.

Bernstein, B. E., Kamal, M., Lindblad-Toh, K., *et al.* (2005). Genomic maps and comparative analysis of histone modifications in human and mouse. *Cell*, 120(2), 169–181.

Bernstein, B. E., Mikkelsen, T. S., Xie, X., *et al.* (2006). A bivalent chromatin structure marks key developmental genes in embryonic stem cells. *Cell*, 125(2), 315–326.

Bi, W., Deng, J. M., Zhang, Z., Behringer, R. R. and de Crombrugghe, B. (1999). Sox9 is required for cartilage formation. *Nature Genetics*, 22(1), 85–89.

Bowen, M. E., Ayturk, U. M., Kurek, K. C., Yang, W. and Warman, M. L. (2014). SHP2 regulates chondrocyte terminal differentiation, growth plate architecture and skeletal cell fates. *PLoS Genetics*, 10(5), e1004364.

Buchwalow, I. B. and Böcker, W. (2014). *Immunohistochemistry: Basics and Methods*. New York, NY: Springer.

Buenrostro, J. D., Giresi, P. G., Zaba, L. C., Chang, H. Y. and Greenleaf, W. J. (2013). Transposition of native chromatin for fast and sensitive epigenomic profiling of open chromatin, DNA-binding proteins and nucleosome position. *Nature Methods*, 10(12), 1213–1218.

Campeau, E. and Gobeil, S. (2011). RNA interference in mammals: behind the screen. *Briefings in Functional Genomics*, 10(4), 215–226.

Canavez, F., Young, N. T., Guethlein, L. A., *et al.* (2001). Comparison of chimpanzee and human leukocyte Ig-like receptor genes reveals framework and rapidly evolving genes. *Journal of Immunology*, 167(10), 5786–5794.

Capellini, T. D., Di Giacomo, G., Salsi, V., *et al.* (2006). *Pbx1/Pbx2* requirement for distal limb patterning is mediated by the hierarchical control of *Hox* gene spatial distribution and *Shh* expression. *Development*, 133(11), 2263–2273.

Capellini, T. D., Vaccari, G., Ferretti, E., *et al.* (2010). Scapula development is governed by genetic interactions of *Pbx1* with its family members and with *Emx2* via their cooperative control of *Alx1*. *Development*, 137(15), 2559–2569.

Carroll, S. B. (2008). Evo–devo and an expanding evolutionary synthesis: a genetic theory of morphological evolution. *Cell*, 134(1), 25–36.

Chan, Y. F., Marks, M. E., Jones, F. C., *et al.* (2010). Adaptive evolution of pelvic reduction in sticklebacks by recurrent deletion of a *Pitx1* enhancer. *Science*, 327(5963), 302–305.

Chau, M., Lui, J. C., Landman, E. B., *et al.* (2014). Gene expression profiling reveals similarities between the spatial architectures of postnatal articular and growth plate cartilage. *PLoS ONE*, 9(7), e103061.

Chen, Y., Zheng, Y., Kang, Y., *et al.* (2015). Functional disruption of the *dystrophin* gene in rhesus monkey using CRISPR/Cas9. *Human Molecular Genetics*, 24(13), 3764–3774.

Cheng, Y., Ma, Z., Kim, B. H., *et al.* (2014). Principles of regulatory information conservation between mouse and human. *Nature*, 515(7527), 371–375.

Chiang, C., Litingtung, Y., Lee, E., *et al.* (1996). Cyclopia and defective axial patterning in mice lacking *Sonic hedgehog* gene function. *Nature*, 383(6599), 407–413.

Chimpanzee Consortium Analysis. (2005). Initial sequence of the chimpanzee genome and comparison with the human genome. *Nature*, 437(7055), 69–87.

Christian, M., Cermak, T., Doyle, E. L., *et al.* (2010). Targeting DNA double-strand breaks with TAL effector nucleases. *Genetics*, 186(2), 757–761.

Christians, J. K., de Zwaan, D. R. and Fung, S. H. (2013). Pregnancy associated plasma protein A2 (PAPP-A2) affects bone size and shape and contributes to natural variation in postnatal growth in mice. *PLoS ONE*, 8(2), e56260.

Church, V., Nohno, T., Linker, C., Marcelle, C. and Francis-West, P. (2002). Wnt regulation of chondrocyte differentiation. *Journal of Cell Science*, 115(Pt 24), 4809–4818.

Codina-Sola, M., Rodriguez-Santiago, B., Homs, A., *et al.* (2015). Integrated analysis of whole-exome sequencing and transcriptome profiling in males with autism spectrum disorders. *Molecular Autism*, 6, 21.

Colosimo, P. F., Hosemann, K. E., Balabhadra, S. G., *et al.* (2005). Widespread parallel evolution in sticklebacks by repeated fixation of *Ectodysplasin* alleles. *Science*, 307(5717), 1928–1933.

Cooper, K. L., Oh, S., Sung, Y., *et al.* (2013). Multiple phases of chondrocyte enlargement underlie differences in skeletal proportions. *Nature*, 495(7441), 375–378.

Cotney, J., Leng, J., Yin, J., *et al.* (2013). The evolution of lineage-specific regulatory activities in the human embryonic limb. *Cell*, 154(1), 185–196.

Crawford, G. E., Holt, I. E., Mullikin, J. C., *et al.* (2004). Identifying gene regulatory elements by genome-wide recovery of DNase hypersensitive sites. *Proceedings of the National Academy of Sciences of the USA*, 101(4), 992–997.

Creyghton, M. P., Cheng, A. W., Welstead, G. G., *et al.* (2010). Histone H3K27ac separates active from poised enhancers and predicts developmental state. *Proceedings of the National Academy of Sciences of the USA*, 107(50), 21931–21936.

Datta, S., Malhotra, L., Dickerson, R., *et al.* (2015). Laser capture microdissection: big data from small samples. *Histology and Histopathology*, 30(11), 1255–1269.

Davidson, E. (2001). *Genomic Regulatory Systems: Development and Evolution*. San Diego, CA: Academic Press.

Decker, R. S., Koyama, E., Enomoto-Iwamoto, M., *et al.* (2014). Mouse limb skeletal growth and synovial joint development are coordinately enhanced by Kartogenin. *Developmental Biology*, 395(2), 255–267.

Dekker, J., Rippe, K., Dekker, M. and Kleckner, N. (2002). Capturing chromosome conformation. *Science*, 295(5558), 1306–1311.

Dong, Z. and Chen, Y. (2013). Transcriptomics: advances and approaches. *Science in China Series C Life Sciences*, 56(10), 960–967.

Dostie, J., Richmond, T. A., Arnaout, R. A., *et al.* (2006). Chromosome Conformation Capture Carbon Copy (5C): a massively parallel solution for mapping interactions between genomic elements. *Genome Research*, 16(10), 1299–1309.

Dudley, A. T., Ros, M. A. and Tabin, C. J. (2002). A re-examination of proximodistal patterning during vertebrate limb development. *Nature*, 418(6897), 539–544.

ENCODE Project Consortium. (2012). An integrated encyclopedia of DNA elements in the human genome. *Nature*, 489(7414), 57–74.

Farber, C. R., Kelly, S. A., Baruch, E., *et al.* (2011). Identification of quantitative trait loci influencing skeletal architecture in mice: emergence of *Cdh11* as a primary candidate gene regulating femoral morphology. *Journal of Bone and Mineral Research*, 26(9), 2174–2183.

Farooq, M., Nakai, H., Fujimoto, A., *et al.* (2013). Characterization of a novel missense mutation in the prodomain of *GDF5*, which underlies brachydactyly type C and mild Grebe type chondrodysplasia in a large Pakistani family. *Human Genetics*, 132(11), 1253–1264.

Florio, M., Albert, M., Taverna, E., *et al.* (2015). Human-specific gene *ARHGAP11B* promotes basal progenitor amplification and neocortex expansion. *Science*, 347(6229), 1465–1470.

Fossat, N., Ip, C. K., Jones, V. J., *et al.* (2015). Context-specific function of the LIM homeobox 1 transcription factor in head formation of the mouse embryo. *Development*, 142(11), 2069–2079.

Francis-West, P. H., Richardson, M. K., Bell, E., *et al.* (1996). The effect of overexpression of BMPs and GDF-5 on the development of chick limb skeletal elements. *Annals if the New York Academy of Science*, 785, 254–255.

Fukami, M., Tsuchiya, T., Takada, S., *et al.* (2012). Complex genomic rearrangement in the *SOX9* 5' region in a patient with Pierre Robin sequence and hypoplastic left scapula. *American Journal of Medical Genetics A*, 158A(7), 1529–1534.

Fullwood, M. J., Han, Y., Wei, C. L., Ruan, X. and Ruan, Y. (2010). Chromatin interaction analysis using paired-end tag sequencing. *Current Protocol in Molecular Biology*, Chapter 21: Unit 21.15–21.25.

Furey, T. S. (2012). ChIP-seq and beyond: new and improved methodologies to detect and characterize protein–DNA interactions. *Nature Reviews Genetics*, 13(12), 840–852.

Furniss, D., Lettice, L. A., Taylor, I. B., *et al.* (2008). A variant in the *Sonic hedgehog* regulatory sequence (ZRS) is associated with triphalangeal thumb and deregulates expression in the developing limb. *Human Molecular Genetics*, 17(16), 2417–2423.

Gallego Romero, I., Pavlovic, B. J., Hernando-Herraez, I., *et al.* (2015). A panel of induced pluripotent stem cells from chimpanzees: a resource for comparative functional genomics. *Elife* 4.

Gehrke, A. R., Schneider, I., de la Calle-Mustienes, E., *et al.* (2015). Deep conservation of wrist and digit enhancers in fish. *Proceedings of the National Academy of Sciences of the USA*, 112(3), 803–808.

Gennequin, B., Otte, D. M. and Zimmer, A. (2013). CRISPR/Cas-induced double-strand breaks boost the frequency of gene replacements for humanizing the mouse *Cnr2* gene. *Biochemical and Biophysical Research Commununications*, 441(4): 815–819.

Gibson, S. V. and Muse, G. (2009). *A Primer in Genome Sciences*. New York, NY: Sinauer Associates.

Gilad, Y., Rifkin, S. A. and Pritchard, J. K. (2008). Revealing the architecture of gene regulation: the promise of eQTL studies. *Trends in Genetics*, 24(8), 408–415.

Gilbert, S. (2013). *Developmental Biology*. New York, NY: Sinauer Associates.

Giresi, P. G., Kim, J., McDaniell, R. M., Iyer, V. R. and Lieb, J. D. (2007). FAIRE (formaldehyde-assisted isolation of regulatory elements) isolates active regulatory elements from human chromatin. *Genome Research*, 17(6), 877–885.

Gordon, C. T., Rodda, F. A. and Farlie, P. G. (2009a). The RCAS retroviral expression system in the study of skeletal development. *Developmental Dynamics*, 238(4), 797–811.

Gordon, C. T., Tan, T. Y., Benko, S., *et al.* (2009b). Long-range regulation at the *SOX9* locus in development and disease. *Journal of Medical Genetics*, 46(10), 649–656.

Gross, D. S. and Garrard, W. T. (1988). Nuclease hypersensitive sites in chromatin. *Annual Review of Biochemistry*, 57, 159–197.

Grossman, S. R., Andersen, K. G., Shlyakhter, I., *et al.* (2013). Identifying recent adaptations in large-scale genomic data. *Cell*, 152(4), 703–713.

Guenther, C., Pantalena-Filho, L. and Kingsley, D. M. (2008). Shaping skeletal growth by modular regulatory elements in the *Bmp5* gene. *PLoS Genetics*, 4(12), e1000308.

Gupta, R. M. and Musunuru, K. (2014). Expanding the genetic editing tool kit: ZFNs, TALENs, and CRISPR-Cas9. *Journal of Clinical Investigations*, 124(10), 4154–4161.

Gurnett, C. A., Bowcock, A. M., Dietz, F. R., *et al.* (2007). Two novel point mutations in the long-range *SHH* enhancer in three families with triphalangeal thumb and preaxial polydactyly. *American Journal of Medical Genetics A*, 143A(1) , 27–32.

Harfe, B. D., Scherz, P. J., Nissim, S., *et al.* (2004). Evidence for an expansion-based temporal Shh gradient in specifying vertebrate digit identities. *Cell*, 118(4), 517–528.

Hartl, D. and Ruvolo, M. (2011). *Genetics: Analysis of Genes and Genomes*. New York, NY: Jones & Bartlett Learning.

Hartmann, C. and Tabin, C. J. (2000). Dual roles of Wnt signaling during chondrogenesis in the chicken limb. *Development*, 127(14), 3141–3159.

Hauptmann, G. (2015). *In Situ Hybridization Methods (Neuromethods)*. New York, NY: Humana Press.

Havill, L. M., Mahaney, M. C., Cox, L. A., *et al.* (2005). A quantitative trait locus for normal variation in forearm bone mineral density in pedigreed baboons maps to the ortholog of human chromosome 11q. *Journal of Clinical Endocrinology and Metabolism*, 90(6), 3638–3645.

Heintzman, N. D., Hon, G. C., Hawkins, R. D., *et al.* (2009). Histone modifications at human enhancers reflect global cell-type-specific gene expression. *Nature*, 459(7243), 108–112.

Hernando-Herraez, I., Prado-Martinez, J., Garg, P., *et al.* (2013). Dynamics of DNA methylation in recent human and great ape evolution. *PLoS Genetics*, 9(9), e1003763.

Hiller, M., Schaar, B. T., Indjeian, V. B., *et al.* (2012). A forward genomics approach links genotype to phenotype using independent phenotypic losses among related species. *Cell Reports*, 2(4), 817–823.

Horvat-Gordon, M., Praul, C. A., Ramachandran, R., Bartell, P. A. and Leach, R. M. Jr. (2010). Use of microarray analysis to study gene expression in the avian epiphyseal growth plate. *Comparative Biochemistry and Physiology Part D Genomics and Proteomics*, 5(1), 12–23.

Huang, J., Chen, J., Esparza, J., *et al.* (2015). eQTL mapping identifies insertion- and deletion-specific eQTLs in multiple tissues. *Nature Communications*, 6, 6821.

Huang, R., Christ, B. and Patel, K. (2006). Regulation of scapula development. *Anatomy and Embryology*, 211(Suppl 1), 65–71.

Infante, C. R., Park, S., Mihala, A. G., Kingsley, D. M. and Menke, D. B. (2013). Pitx1 broadly associates with limb enhancers and is enriched on hindlimb *cis*-regulatory elements. *Developmental Biology*, 374(1), 234–244.

Inoue, K. and Imai, Y. (2014). Identification of novel transcription factors in osteoclast differentiation using genome-wide analysis of open chromatin determined by DNase-seq. *Journal of Bone and Mineral Research*, 29(8), 1823–1832.

James, C. G., Stanton, L. A., Agoston, H., *et al.* (2010). Genome-wide analyses of gene expression during mouse endochondral ossification. *PLoS ONE*, 5(1), e8693.

Jasinska, A. J., Lin, M. K., Service, S., *et al.* (2012). A non-human primate system for large-scale genetic studies of complex traits. *Human Molecular Genetics*, 21(15), 3307–3316.

Jinek, M., Chylinski, K., Fonfara, I., *et al.* (2012). A programmable dual-RNA-guided DNA endonuclease in adaptive bacterial immunity. *Science*, 337(6096), 816–821.

Jones, F. C., Grabherr, M. G., Chan, Y. F., *et al.* (2012). The genomic basis of adaptive evolution in threespine sticklebacks. *Nature*, 484(7392), 55–61.

Kamberov, Y. G., Wang, S., Tan, J., *et al.* (2013). Modeling recent human evolution in mice by expression of a selected *EDAR* variant. *Cell*, 152(4), 691–702.

Kenney-Hunt, J. P., Vaughn, T. T., Pletscher, L. S., *et al.* (2006). Quantitative trait loci for body size components in mice. *Mammalian Genome*, 17(6), 526–537.

Khaitovich, P., Hellmann, I., Enard, W., *et al.* (2005). Parallel patterns of evolution in the genomes and transcriptomes of humans and chimpanzees. *Science*, 309(5742), 1850–1854.

Khaitovich, P., Muetzel, B., She, X., *et al.* (2004). Regional patterns of gene expression in human and chimpanzee brains. *Genome Research*, 14(8), 1462–1473.

Khan, Z., Ford, M. J., Cusanovich, D. A., *et al.* (2013). Primate transcript and protein expression levels evolve under compensatory selection pressures. *Science*, 342(6162), 1100–1104.

King, M. C. and Wilson, A. C. (1975). Evolution at two levels in humans and chimpanzees. *Science*, 188(4184), 107–116.

Koyama, E., Shibukawa, Y., Nagayama, M., *et al.* (2008). A distinct cohort of progenitor cells participates in synovial joint and articular cartilage formation during mouse limb skeletogenesis. *Developmental Biology*, 316(1), 62–73.

Kozhemyakina, E., Lassar, A. B. and Zelzer, E. (2015). A pathway to bone: signaling molecules and transcription factors involved in chondrocyte development and maturation. *Development*, 142(5), 817–831.

Kraft, K., Geuer, S., Will, A. J., *et al.* (2015). Deletions, inversions, duplications: engineering of structural variants using CRISPR/Cas in mice. *Cell Reports*.

Kraus P., Xing S. V. and Lufkin, T. (2014). Generating mouse lines for lineage tracing and knock-out studies. *In*: Singh, S. R. and Coppola, V. (eds.) *Mouse Genetics: Methods and Protocols, Methods in Molecular Biology*. New York, NY: Springer Science+Business Media.

Krebs, J. E., Gi, E. and Kilpatrick, S. T. (2014). *Lewin's Genes XI*. Burlington, MA: Jones & Bartlett Learning.

Lanctôt, C., Moreau, A., Chamberland, M., Tremblay, M. L. and Drouin, J. (1999). Hindlimb patterning and mandible development require the *Ptx1* gene. *Development*, 126(9), 1805–1810.

Lappalainen, T., Sammeth, M., Friedlander, M. R., *et al.* (2013). Transcriptome and genome sequencing uncovers functional variation in humans. *Nature*, 501(7468), 506–511.

Lemay, P., Guyot, M. C., Tremblay, E., *et al.* (2015). Loss-of-function *de novo* mutations play an important role in severe human neural tube defects. *Journal of Medical Genetics*, 52(7), 493–497.

Lettice, L. A., Heaney, S. J., Purdie, L. A., *et al.* (2003). A long-range *Shh* enhancer regulates expression in the developing limb and fin and is associated with preaxial polydactyly. *Human Molecular Genetics*, 12(14), 1725–1735.

Lettice, L. A., Hill, A. E., Devenney, P. S. and Hill, R. E. (2008). Point mutations in a distant *sonic hedgehog cis*-regulator generate a variable regulatory output responsible for preaxial polydactyly. *Human Molecular Genetics*, 17(7), 978–985.

Li, Y. R. and Keating, B. J. (2014). Trans-ethnic genome-wide association studies: advantages and challenges of mapping in diverse populations. *Genome Medicine*, 6(10), 91.

Liang, P., Xu, Y., Zhang, X., *et al.* (2015). CRISPR/Cas9-mediated gene editing in human tripronuclear zygotes. *Protein and Cell*, 6(5), 363–372.

Lieberman-Aiden, E., van Berkum, N. L., Williams, L., *et al.* (2009). Comprehensive mapping of long-range interactions reveals folding principles of the human genome. *Science*, 326(5950), 289–293.

Lizio, M., Harshbarger, J., Shimoji, H., *et al.* (2015). Gateways to the FANTOM5 promoter level mammalian expression atlas. *Genome Biology*, 16, 22.

Logan, M. and Tabin, C. J. (1999). Role of Pitx1 upstream of *Tbx4* in specification of hindlimb identity. *Science*, 283(5408), 1736–1739.

Lui, J. C., Andrade, A. C., Forcinito, P., *et al.* (2010). Spatial and temporal regulation of gene expression in the mammalian growth plate. *Bone*, 46(5), 1380–1390.

Lupiáñez, D. G., Kraft, K., Heinrich, V., *et al.* (2015). Disruptions of topological chromatin domains cause pathogenic rewiring of gene-enhancer interactions. *Cell*, 161(5), 1012–1025.

MacCabe, A. B., Gasseling, M. T. and Saunders Jr. J. W. (1973). Spatiotemporal distribution of mechanisms that control outgrowth and anteroposterior polarization of the limb bud in the chick embryo. *Mechanisms of Ageing and Development*, 2(1), 1–12.

Macosko, E. Z., Basu, A., Satija, R., *et al.* (2015). Highly parallel genome-wide expression profiling of individual cells using nanoliter droplets. *Cell*, 161(5), 1202–1214.

Madrigal, P. and Krajewski, P. (2012). Current bioinformatic approaches to identify DNase I hypersensitive sites and genomic footprints from DNase-seq data. *Frontiers in Genetics*, 3, 230.

Majewski, J. and Pastinen, T. (2011). The study of eQTL variations by RNA-seq: from SNPs to phenotypes. *Trends in Genetics*, 27(2), 72–79.

Marinić, M., Aktas, T., Ruf, S. and Spitz, F. (2013). An integrated holo-enhancer unit defines tissue and gene specificity of the *Fgf8* regulatory landscape. *Developmental Cell*, 24(5), 530–542.

McLean, C. Y., Reno, P. L., Pollen, A. A., *et al.* (2011). Human-specific loss of regulatory DNA and the evolution of human-specific traits. *Nature*, 471(7337), 216–219.

Menke, D. B. (2013). Engineering subtle targeted mutations into the mouse genome. *Genesis*, 51(9), 605–618.

Merino, R., Macias, D., Ganan, Y., *et al.* (1999). Expression and function of Gdf-5 during digit skeletogenesis in the embryonic chick leg bud. *Developmental Biology*, 206(1), 33–45.

Meyer, C. A. and Liu, X. S. (2014). Identifying and mitigating bias in next-generation sequencing methods for chromatin biology. *Nature Reviews Genetics*, 15(11), 709–721.

Mori, Y., Chung, U. I., Tanaka, S. and Saito, T. (2014). Determination of differential gene expression profiles in superficial and deeper zones of mature rat articular cartilage using RNA sequencing of laser microdissected tissue specimens. *Biomedical Research*, 35(4), 263–270.

Mortlock, D. P., Guenther, C. and Kingsley, D. M. (2003). A general approach for identifying distant regulatory elements applied to the *Gdf6* gene. *Genome Research*, 13(9), 2069–2081.

Nagai, H. and Aoki, M. (2002). Inhibition of growth plate angiogenesis and endochondral ossification with diminished expression of MMP-13 in hypertrophic chondrocytes in FGF-2-treated rats. *Journal of Bone and Mineral Metabolism*, 20(3), 142–147.

Nam, K., Munch, K., Hobolth, A., *et al.* (2015). Extreme selective sweeps independently targeted the X chromosomes of the great apes. *Proceedings of the National Academy of Sciences of the USA*, 112(20), 6413–6418.

Nikolskiy, I., Conrad, D. F., Chun, S., *et al.* (2015). Using whole-genome sequences of the LG/J and SM/J inbred mouse strains to prioritize quantitative trait genes and nucleotides. *BMC Genomics*, 16, 415.

Nilsson, O., Guo, M. H., Dunbar, N., *et al.* (2014). Short stature, accelerated bone maturation, and early growth cessation due to heterozygous *aggrecan* mutations. *Journal of Clinical Endocrinology and Metabolism*, 99(8), E1510–1518.

Niu, Y., Shen, B., Cui, Y., *et al.* (2014). Generation of gene-modified cynomolgus monkey via Cas9/RNA-mediated gene targeting in one-cell embryos. *Cell*, 156(4), 836–843.

Oh, C. D., Lu, Y., Liang, S., *et al.* (2014). SOX9 regulates multiple genes in chondrocytes, including genes encoding ECM proteins, ECM modification enzymes, receptors, and transporters. *PLoS ONE*, 9(9), e107577.

Ohba, S., He, X., Hojo, H. and McMahon, A. P. (2015). Distinct transcriptional programs underlie Sox9 regulation of the mammalian chondrocyte. *Cell Report*, 12(2), 229–243.

1000 Genomes Project Consortium. (2012). An integrated map of genetic variation from 1,092 human genomes. *Nature*, 491(7422), 56–65.

Orlando, V. (2000). Mapping chromosomal proteins in vivo by formaldehyde-crosslinked-chromatin immunoprecipitation. *Trends in Biochemical Science*, 25(3), 99–104.

Ozsolak, F. and Milos, P. M. (2011). RNA sequencing: advances, challenges and opportunities. *Nature Reviews Genetics*, 12(2), 87–98.

Pacifici, M., Koyama, E., Shibukawa, Y., *et al.* (2006). Cellular and molecular mechanisms of synovial joint and articular cartilage formation. *Annals of the New York Academy of Science*, 1068, 74–86.

Pardo-Diaz, C., Salazar, C. and Jiggins, C. D. (2015). Towards the identification of the loci of adaptive evolution. *Methods in Ecology and Evolution*, 6(4), 445–464.

Parry, D. A., Logan, C. V., Stegmann, A. P., *et al.* (2013). SAMS, a syndrome of short stature, auditory-canal atresia, mandibular hypoplasia, and skeletal abnormalities is a unique neurocristopathy caused by mutations in *Goosecoid*. *American Journal of Human Genetics*, 93(6), 1135–1142.

Pazin, D. E., Gamer, L. W., Cox, K. A. and Rosen, V. (2012). Molecular profiling of synovial joints: use of microarray analysis to identify factors that direct the development of the knee and elbow. *Developmental Dynamics*, 241(11), 1816–1826.

Perry, G. H., Melsted, P., Marioni, J. C., *et al.* (2012). Comparative RNA sequencing reveals substantial genetic variation in endangered primates. *Genome Research*, 22(4), 602–610.

Pokholok, D. K., Harbison, C. T., Levine, S., *et al.* (2005). Genome-wide map of nucleosome acetylation and methylation in yeast. *Cell*, 122(4), 517–527.

Porcu, E., Sanna, S., Fuchsberger, C. and Fritsche, L. G. (2013). Genotype imputation in genome-wide association studies. *Current Protocol in Human Genetics*, Chapter 1: Unit 1.25.

Prabhakar, S., Noonan, J.P., Paabo, S. and Rubin, E.M. (2006). Accelerated evolution of conserved noncoding sequences in humans. *Science*, 314(5800), 786.

Prabhakar, S., Visel, A., Akiyama, J.A., *et al.* (2008). Human-specific gain of function in a developmental enhancer. *Science*, 321(5894), 1346–1350.

Prado-Martinez, J., Sudmant, P. H., Kidd, J. M., *et al.* (2013). Great ape genetic diversity and population history. *Nature*, 499(7459), 471–475.

Provot, S., Kempf, H., Murtaugh, L. C., *et al.* (2006). Nkx3.2/Bapx1 acts as a negative regulator of chondrocyte maturation. *Development*, 133(4), 651–662.

Prüfer, K., Munch, K., Hellmann, I., *et al.* (2012). The bonobo genome compared with the chimpanzee and human genomes. *Nature*, 486(7404), 527–531.

Rada-Iglesias, A., Bajpai, R., Swigut, T., *et al.* (2011). A unique chromatin signature uncovers early developmental enhancers in humans. *Nature*, 470(7333), 279–283.

Reilly, S. K., Yin, J., Ayoub, A. E., *et al.* (2015). Evolutionary genomics. Evolutionary changes in promoter and enhancer activity during human corticogenesis. *Science*, 347(6226), 1155–1159.

Riddle, R. D., Johnson, R. L., Laufer, E. and Tabin, C. (1993). Sonic hedgehog mediates the polarizing activity of the ZPA. *Cell*, 75(7), 1401–1416.

Rivera, C. M. and Ren, B. (2013). Mapping human epigenomes. *Cell*, 155(1), 39–55.

Roadmap Epigenomics Project Consortium. (2015). Integrative analysis of 111 reference human epigenomes. *Nature*, 518(7539), 317–330.

Rock, J. R., Lopez, M. C., Baker, H. V. and Harfe, B. D. (2007). Identification of genes expressed in the mouse limb using a novel ZPA microarray approach. *Gene Expression Patterns*, 8(1), 19–26.

Rodriguez-Esteban, C., Tsukui, T., Yonei, S., *et al.* (1999). The T-box genes *Tbx4* and *Tbx5* regulate limb outgrowth and identity. *Nature*, 398(6730), 814–818.

Roux, J., Rosikiewicz, M. and Robinson-Rechavi, M. (2015). What to compare and how: comparative transcriptomics for Evo–Devo. *Journal of Experimental Zoology Series B Molecular Development and Evolution*, 324(4), 372–382.

Sabo, P. J., Humbert, R., Hawrylycz, M., *et al.* (2004). Genome-wide identification of DNaseI hypersensitive sites using active chromatin sequence libraries. *Proceedings of the National Academy of Science of the USA*, 101(13), 4537–4542.

Sagai, T., Hosoya, M., Mizushina, Y., Tamura, M. and Shiroishi, T. (2005). Elimination of a long-range *cis*-regulatory module causes complete loss of limb-specific *Shh* expression and truncation of the mouse limb. *Development*, 132(4), 797–803.

Scally, A., Dutheil, J. Y., Hillier, L. W., *et al.* (2012). Insights into hominid evolution from the gorilla genome sequence. *Nature*, 483(7388), 169–175.

Scherz, P. J., McGlinn, E., Nissim, S. and Tabin, C. J. (2007). Extended exposure to Sonic hedgehog is required for patterning the posterior digits of the vertebrate limb. *Developmental Biology*, 308(2), 343–354.

Schreiner, C. M., Bell, S. M. and Scott Jr., W. J. (2009). Microarray analysis of murine limb bud ectoderm and mesoderm after exposure to cadmium or acetazolamide. *Birth Defects Research Series A Clinical and Molecular Teratology*, 85(7), 588–598.

Shao, Y., Guan, Y., Wang, L., *et al.* (2014). CRISPR/Cas-mediated genome editing in the rat via direct injection of one-cell embryos. *Nature Protocols*, 9(10), 2493–2512.

Shapiro, M. D., Marks, M. E., Peichel, C. L., *et al.* (2004). Genetic and developmental basis of evolutionary pelvic reduction in threespine sticklebacks. *Nature*, 428(6984), 717–723.

Sherwood, R. J., Duren, D. L., Havill, L. M., *et al.* (2008). A genomewide linkage scan for quantitative trait loci influencing the craniofacial complex in baboons (*Papio hamadryas* spp.). *Genetics*, 180(1), 619–628.

Shou, S., Scott, V., Reed, C., Hitzemann, R. and Stadler, H. S. (2005). Transcriptome analysis of the murine forelimb and hindlimb autopod. *Developmental Dynamics*, 234(1), 74–89.

Soriano, P. (1999). Generalized lacZ expression with the ROSA26 Cre reporter strain. *Nature Genetics*, 21(1), 70–71.

Stephens, T. D. and McNulty, T. R. (1981). Evidence for a metameric pattern in the development of the chick humerus. *Journal of Embryology and Experimental Morphology*, 61, 191–205.

Stergachis, A. B., Neph, S., Sandstrom, R., *et al.* (2014). Conservation of *trans*-acting circuitry during mammalian regulatory evolution. *Nature*, 515(7527), 365–370.

Sudmant, P. H., Huddleston, J., Catacchio, C. R., *et al.* (2013). Evolution and diversity of copy number variation in the great ape lineage. *Genome Research*, 23(9), 1373–1382.

Summerbell, D. (1979). The zone of polarizing activity: evidence for a role in normal chick limb morphogenesis. *Journal of Embryology and Experimental Morphology*, 50, 217–233.

Summerbell, D., Ashby, P. R., Coutelle, O., *et al.* (2000). The expression of *Myf5* in the developing mouse embryo is controlled by discrete and dispersed enhancers specific for particular populations of skeletal muscle precursors. *Development*, 127(17), 3745–3757.

Sun, M., Ma, F., Zeng, X., *et al.* (2008). Triphalangeal thumb-polysyndactyly syndrome and syndactyly type IV are caused by genomic duplications involving the long range, limb-specific *SHH* enhancer. *Journal of Medical Genetics*, 45(9), 589–595.

Tai, P. W., Wu, H., Gordon, J. A., *et al.* (2014). Epigenetic landscape during osteoblastogenesis defines a differentiation-dependent *Runx2* promoter region. *Gene*, 550(1), 1–9.

Takeuchi, J. K., Koshiba-Takeuchi, K., Matsumoto, K., *et al.* (1999). *Tbx5* and *Tbx4* genes determine the wing/leg identity of limb buds. *Nature*, 398(6730), 810–814.

Tetreault, M., Bareke, E., Nadaf, J., Alirezaie, N. and Majewski, J. (2015). Whole-exome sequencing as a diagnostic tool: current challenges and future opportunities. *Expert Review of Molecular Diagnostics*, 15(6), 749–760.

Tickle, C., Shellswell, G., Crawley, A. and Wolpert, L. (1976). Positional signalling by mouse limb polarising region in the chick wing bud. *Nature*, 259(5542), 396–397.

Tung, J. W., Heydari, K., Tirouvanziam, R., *et al.* (2007). Modern flow cytometry: a practical approach. *Clinical Laboratory Medicine*, 27(3), 453–468, v.

Urnov, F. D., Rebar, E. J., Holmes, M. C., Zhang, H. S. and Gregory, P. D. (2010). Genome editing with engineered zinc finger nucleases. *Nature Reviews Genetics*, 11(9), 636–646.

Valasek, P., Evans, D. J., Maina, F., Grim, M. and Patel, K. (2005). A dual fate of the hindlimb muscle mass: cloacal/perineal musculature develops from leg muscle cells. *Development*, 132(3), 447–458.

Vargesson, N., Clarke, J. D., Vincent, K., *et al.* (1997). Cell fate in the chick limb bud and relationship to gene expression. *Development*, 124(10), 1909–1918.

Vitti, J. J., Grossman, S. R. and Sabeti, P. C. (2013). Detecting natural selection in genomic data. *Annual Review of Genetics*, 47, 97–120.

Vortkamp, A., Lee, K., Lanske, B., *et al.* (1996). Regulation of rate of cartilage differentiation by Indian hedgehog and PTH-related protein. *Science*, 273(5275), 613–622.

Wan, H., Feng, C., Teng, F., *et al.* (2015). One-step generation of *p53* gene biallelic mutant *Cynomolgus* monkey via the CRISPR/Cas system. *Cell Research*, 25(2), 258–261.

Wang, Y., Middleton, F., Horton, J. A., *et al.* (2004). Microarray analysis of proliferative and hypertrophic growth plate zones identifies differentiation markers and signal pathways. *Bone*, 35(6), 1273–1293.

Wang, H., Yang, H., Shivalila, C. S., *et al.* (2013). One-step generation of mice carrying mutations in multiple genes by CRISPR/Cas-mediated genome engineering. *Cell*, 153(4), 910–918.

Weir, B. S., Cardon, L. R., Anderson, A. D., Nielsen, D. M. and Hill, W. G. (2005). Measures of human population structure show heterogeneity among genomic regions. *Genome Research*, 15(11), 1468–1476.

Widdig, A., Kessler, M. J., Bercovitch, F. B., *et al.* (2016). Genetic studies on the Cayo *Santiago rhesus* macaques: a review of 40 years of research. *American Journal of Primatology*, 78(1), 44–62.

Wood, A. R., Esko, T., Yang, J., *et al.* (2014). Defining the role of common variation in the genomic and biological architecture of adult human height. *Nature Genetics*, 46(11), 1173–1186.

Wu, C., Bingham, P. M., Livak, K. J., Holmgren, R. and Elgin, S. C. (1979a). The chromatin structure of specific genes: I. Evidence for higher order domains of defined DNA sequence. *Cell*, 16(4), 797–806.

Wu, C., Wong, Y. C. and Elgin, S. C. (1979b). The chromatin structure of specific genes: II. Disruption of chromatin structure during gene activity. *Cell*, 16(4), 807–814.

Wu, S. and De Luca, F. (2006). Inhibition of the proteasomal function in chondrocytes downregulates growth plate chondrogenesis and longitudinal bone growth. *Endocrinology*, 147(8), 3761–3768.

Xue, Y., Prado-Martinez, J., Sudmant, P. H., *et al.* (2015). Mountain gorilla genomes reveal the impact of long-term population decline and inbreeding. *Science*, 348(6231), 242–245.

Yang, Y., Drossopoulou, G., Chuang, P. T., *et al.* (1997). Relationship between dose, distance and time in Sonic Hedgehog-mediated regulation of anteroposterior polarity in the chick limb. *Development*, 124(21), 4393–4404.

Young, N. M. (2006). Function, ontogeny and canalization of shape variance in the primate scapula. *Journal of Anatomy*, 209(5), 623–636.

Yue, F., Cheng, Y., Breschi, A., *et al.* (2014). A comparative encyclopedia of DNA elements in the mouse genome. *Nature*, 515(7527), 355–364.

Zhang, F., Wen, Y. and Guo, X. (2014). CRISPR/Cas9 for genome editing: progress, implications and challenges. *Human Molecular Genetics*, 23(R1), R40–46.

Zhang, M., Pritchard, M. R., Middleton, F. A., Horton, J. A. and Damron, T. A. (2008). Microarray analysis of perichondral and reserve growth plate zones identifies differential gene expressions and signal pathways. *Bone*, 43(3), 511–520.

Zhao, Z., Tavoosidana, G., Sjolinder, M., *et al.* (2006). Circular chromosome conformation capture (4C) uncovers extensive networks of epigenetically regulated intra- and interchromosomal interactions. *Nature Genetics*, 38(11), 1341–1347.

Zhou, H. Y., Katsman, Y., Dhaliwal, N. K., *et al.* (2014). A *Sox2* distal enhancer cluster regulates embryonic stem cell differentiation potential. *Genes and Development*, 28(24), 2699–2711.

Zou, H., Wieser, R., Massague, J. and Niswander, L. (1997). Distinct roles of type I bone morphogenetic protein receptors in the formation and differentiation of cartilage. *Genes and Development*, 11(17), 2191–2203.

9 Using Comparisons between Species and Anatomical Locations to Discover Mechanisms of Growth Plate Patterning and Differential Growth

Kelsey M. Kjosness and Philip L. Reno

9.1 Introduction

Despite our shared ancestry, humans and other primates show great diversity in skeletal form. The functional significance of this variation has been well-studied, and our understanding of it continues to be refined. While obviously important for determining the selective pressures that have shaped the skeleton throughout evolutionary history, functional explanations alone do not tell the complete evolutionary story. Each individual is the result of a developmental process that interprets its particular genotype into a functional phenotype. Therefore, to fully appreciate the evolutionary process we must also uncover the genomic and developmental mechanisms that generate the phenotypic variation upon which selection can act (Hendrikse *et al.*, 2007; Rolian, 2008; Reno, 2014, 2016).

The vertebrate postcranial skeleton initially forms as cartilage models during early embryological patterning that are subsequently replaced by bone, a process called endochondral ossification (Long and Ornitz, 2013; also see Chapter 7 for additional review of endochondral ossification). During ontogeny, growth plates preserve regions of cartilage that permit rapid longitudinal growth. The differential growth performance of the individual growth plates gives the skeleton its eventual shape (Wolpert, 1981). This process is commonly studied as two distinct stages. First, skeletal patterning is understood to be guided by developmental control genes that establish body axes, define developmental fields, assign positional information, and direct the aggregation, proliferation, and differentiation of mesenchymal cells (Johnson and Tabin, 1997). Second, differential growth is viewed as the result of cellular organization behaviors and intercellular signaling networks within the growth plate and the surrounding perichondrium (Maes and Kronenberg, 2012). Recent efforts have begun to identify how key developmental patterning genes, including *Hox*, can specify growth behaviors in the long and short bones of the limbs (Villavicencio-Lorini *et al.*, 2010; Kuss *et al.*, 2014). This knowledge is an important step toward understanding processes by which species-specific morphologies, including limb and digit lengths, have evolved.

Three types of biological variation have been used to discover the links between early skeletal patterning and differential growth. First, dramatic changes can be produced through genetic manipulation and gene targeting (Capecchi, 1994). This is the most utilized of the three sources, and the strength of such models is that particular phenotypes and their developmental basis can be ascribed to the action of individual genes. Second, the discovery of the deep conservation of developmental control genes and gene regulatory networks has reinvigorated comparative developmental analyses (Carroll, 2008). Independently evolved phenotypic variants, even between distantly related species, often result from modifications in homologous genes and regulatory networks. Third is the dramatic developmental variation within an individual skeleton that is crucial for understanding mechanisms of differential skeletal growth (Bisgard and Bisgard, 1935; Lacroix, 1951; Ogden *et al.*, 1987; Hunziker, 1994). Such interspecific and intra-individual variation have the benefit of comparing viable phenotypes that are more likely to be evolutionary relevant.

Here we review the recent advances made from studying these three types of skeletal variation to understand the linkage between early skeletal patterning and differential growth. These approaches are beginning to identify how *Hox* genes act to specify the behaviors of individual growth plates. We focus on anatomical and evolutionary differences in growth plate location within mammalian metapodials (metacarpals and metatarsals) and the pisiform of humans and other mammals, information that is contributing to our understanding of how bones are built.

9.2   *Hox* Genes and Skeletal Patterning

One of the most profound and surprising discoveries of evolutionary developmental biology is the surprising degree of conservation of genomic and developmental processes across animals (Mayr, 1963; Carroll, 2008). The quintessential example is the *Hox* family that consists of clusters of related genes that are instrumental in patterning animal form (Krumlauf, 1994; Capecchi, 1997). From flies to vertebrates, these genes have maintained similar chromosomal synteny, biochemical interactions between their protein products and genetic enhancers, and roles in defining the major body axes (Duboule, 2007) (Figure 9.1). *Hox* genes have subtle differences in their binding properties to DNA and associated protein cofactors (Mann *et al.*, 2009). Therefore, their array of expression patterns during embryological development serves to define regional modules of shared gene expression and regulation. In both flies and vertebrates, *Hox* genes are expressed in a temporal and spatial collinear sequence matching their 3' to 5' position in the genome (Duboule, 2007). Those located closest to the 3' position are expressed earlier in the more anterior segments of the fly or vertebrate embryo, progressing toward the 5' end of the cluster with expression of each subsequent gene occurring later and positioned in a more posterior expression

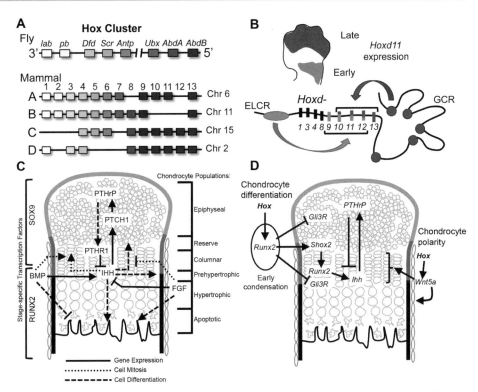

Figure 9.1 (A) Illustration of the fly and mammalian Hox clusters. The shading indicates homologous genes between the clusters. (B) Mammalian *Hox* gene expression in the limb is divided into an early and late phase by extensive regulatory domains flanking the cluster. The early limb control region (ELCR) guides expression in the stylopod and zeugopod, while the global control region (GCR) drives expression in the autopod. (C) During development the end of the bone is divided into the indicated chondrocyte zones. The "reserve" zone is equivalent to "resting" chondrocytes; however, the former term better encapsulates the fact that this progenitor population can be mitotically active. For the same reason, "columnar" is a better descriptor than "proliferative." The extent of the stage-specific transcription factors SOX9 and RUNX2 are indicated. In the growth plate, a feedback loop between PTHrP and IHH serves to maintain a proliferative pool of chondrocytes. In addition, IHH acts to promote differentiation of reserve chondrocytes, proliferation in the columnar zone, and ossification in the bone collar and primary center of ossification. BMPs and FGFs have been shown to interact with IHH to enhance or inhibit these steps, respectively. (D) *Hox* genes appear to regulate skeleton elongation at multiple steps. *Hox* acts upstream of the first wave of *Runx2* expression in the initial mesenchymal condensations (round oval) and *Shox2* during endochondral ossification to promote differentiation from round reserve cells into columnar chondrocytes. *Shox2* is upstream of the second wave of *Runx2* expression in prehypertrophic chondrocytes which results in *Ihh* expression and the stimulation of the IHH/PTHrP feedback loop. In addition, early expression of *Runx2* appears to inhibit the repressive actions of *GLI3R* which would otherwise repress cellular differentiation into columnar and hypertrophic chondrocytes. *Hox* also stimulates the directional growth of the skeleton by establishing the fibrous perichondrium and acts upstream of *Wnt5a* to activate the WNT/Planar Cell Polarity pathway in the perichondrial and columnar chondrocytes.

domain (Dolle *et al.*, 1989; Izpisua-Belmonte *et al.*, 1991). This collinear expression of *Hox* genes serves to pattern the body plan, be it segments in the fly or vertebral identity in humans.

The vertebrate *Hox* cluster has become further organized and undergone multiple rounds of duplication that have enabled the evolution of increased regulatory complexity (Duboule, 2007). There are 39 *Hox* genes in tetrapods arrayed among four clusters labeled A–D. Within each cluster, genes are numbered 1–13 from their 3' to 5' positions (Krumlauf, 1992) (Figure 9.1A). This formation of cohesive clusters and their associated expansive *cis*-regulatory domains enables the redeployment of the *Hox* genes across multiple anatomical systems during development (Capecchi, 1997). *Hox9–13* genes from the A and D clusters are crucial in limb development and skeletal patterning (Nelson *et al.*, 1996; Zakany and Duboule, 2007; Woltering and Duboule, 2010). In tetrapods, these genes are expressed in two phases (Spitz *et al.*, 2003; Deschamps, 2004; Andrey *et al.*, 2013) (Figure 9.1B). In the first phase, *Hox9–11* genes are sequentially activated in the proximal segments of the limbs to pattern the stylopod (humerus and femur), zeugopod (radius/ulna and tibia/fibula), and proximal carpals and tarsals (Reno *et al.*, 2016). For the *Hoxd* genes, first phase expression is controlled by a large regulatory domain named the "early limb control region" (ELCR), located at the 3' side of the cluster (Zakany *et al.*, 2004; Tarchini and Duboule, 2006). In the autopod (hands and feet), *Hox10–13* genes are expressed in reverse numerical order with *Hoxd13* being expressed more anteriorly (including digits I–V) and *Hoxd12* and *Hoxd11* expression restricted to the posterior digits II–V. This second phase is controlled by an expansive regulatory archipelago called the "global control region" (GCR) lying at the 5' end of the *Hox* cluster (Spitz *et al.*, 2003). The *Hoxa* genes reveal comparable expression patterns apparently controlled by a similar regulatory regime (Woltering *et al.*, 2014; Gehrke *et al.*, 2015).

Modification of *Hox* gene expression often results in malformed skeletal elements that are indicative of their role in early skeletal patterning and subsequent longitudinal growth (Dolle *et al.*, 1993; Small and Potter, 1993; Davis *et al.*, 1995; Favier *et al.*, 1995, 1996; Davis and Capecchi, 1996; Fromental-Remain *et al.*, 1996). Additionally, the biphasic regulation has long been observed to result in reduced *Hoxd* expression in the wrist, which is generally thought to lack growth plates (Woltering and Duboule, 2010). This is particularly evident for *Hoxd11*, which is expressed in both phases of limb development, but produces two separate domains of expression: one corresponding to the distal zeugopod and the other to the posterior digits (II–V) (Figure 9.1B) (Yokouchi *et al.*, 1991; Nelson *et al.*, 1996; Spitz *et al.*, 2005). Mice with reduced *Hoxa11*/*Hoxd11* expression experience dramatic shortening of the radius and ulna to the point that they resemble the short bones of the wrist and ankle that typically lack growth plates (Davis *et al.*, 1995; Boulet and Capecchi, 2004; Gross *et al.*, 2012). Experimentally increasing the HOXD11 dosage in the distal forelimb results in longer metacarpals and phalanges (Boulet and Capecchi, 2002). Individual *Hox* genes appear to promote distinct growth behaviors as misactivation of *Hox13* genes in the zeugopod causes growth reduction (Yokouchi *et al.*,

1995; Goff and Tabin, 1997; Zhao and Potter, 2001) and thus appear to work in combination to sculpt the limb skeleton (Davis and Capecchi, 1996).

9.3   Formation of the Endochondral Skeleton

To determine how *Hox* and other developmental control genes pattern skeletal form, it is necessary to review the specific cellular mechanisms that are used to build and grow bones. Four distinct types of growth regions operate during mammalian endochondral skeletal development (Lacroix, 1951). In the embryonic stages, initial cartilaginous condensations undergo isotropic interstitial enlargement. Once mineralization and replacement of cartilage by osseous tissue has begun, growth is restricted to the perichondrial/periosteal sheath responsible for circumferential growth, the articular cartilage that shapes joint surfaces, and the growth plate whose behavior drives skeletal elongation. The morphogenesis of these processes is well understood. Mesenchymal cells of the initial skeletal condensations differentiate into chondrocytes, while a thin layer of surrounding cells forms the fibrous perichondrium. Starting from the center of the cartilage model, chondrocytes undergo sequential differentiation through proliferative, hypertrophic, and apoptotic phases in a front that advances towards each end of the bone (Figure 9.1C). The perichondrium matures into periosteum and begins to form a bone collar encircling the hypertrophic chondrocytes. The periosteum provides the source of invading osteoclasts and osteoblasts to form the primary center of ossification and replace the cartilage with bone (Maes and Kronenberg, 2012). In a typical long bone, the advancing front of chondrocyte differentiation stabilizes and matures into a growth plate at the end of the bone. Between the growth plate and joint, the epiphyseal cartilage is replaced by secondary centers of ossification (Haines, 1942, 1969).

Growth plates preserve these steps of chondrocyte differentiation and consist of four distinct zones: reserve, columnar, prehypertrophic, and hypertrophic (Ballock and O'Keefe, 2003) (Figure 9.1C). Preservation of the distinct zones in the growth plate requires the precise control of chondrocyte differentiation and proliferation through interactions between chondrocyte populations, adjacent tissues (perichondrium and periosteum) and their vascular supply. These interactions have been largely characterized through the use of targeted gene knockouts. These steps in cellular differentiation are associated with changes in stage-specific transcription factors (Figure 9.1C). Initially, *Runx2* (runt-related transcription factor 2; formerly *Cbfa1*) and *Sox9* (sex-determining region on the Y box 9) are expressed in the mesenchymal condensations to promote initial cartilage differentiation (Ducy, 2000; Lefebvre *et al.*, 2001; Akiyama *et al.*, 2002). *Sox9* continues to be expressed in reserve and columnar chondrocytes, while *Runx2* is reactivated in prehypertrophic chondrocytes (de Crombrugghe *et al.*, 2001). A complex regulatory feedback loop acts to maintain and control the timing of chondrocyte maturation (Lanske *et al.*, 1996; Vortkamp *et al.*, 1996) (Figure 9.1C). As cells leave the proliferative zone and begin to undergo hypertrophy they express *Indian hedgehog* (*Ihh*), which signals to cells expressing the surface receptor patched homolog 1 (PTCH1). Upregulation of

Ihh has also been shown to increase parathyroid hormone-related peptide (*PTHrP*) expression in epiphyseal chondrocytes adjacent to the articular surface and to a lesser degree near the columnar chondrocytes (Lee *et al.*, 1995). PTHrP receptors (PTHR1) are found in columnar zone chondrocytes. PTHrP from the epiphyses acts to maintain these cells in their proliferative state and limit the numbers that begin to hypertrophy. Thus, IHH and PTHrP constitute a negative feedback loop that limits the rate of cell maturation and maintains a proliferative pool of chondrocytes in the growth plate throughout ontogeny (Lanske *et al.*, 1996; Vortkamp *et al.*, 1996).

Besides its role in the IHH/PTHrP feedback loop, IHH has a number of PTHrP-independent effects on the growth plate (Long and Ornitz, 2013). Proliferation and organization of columnar chondrocytes are IHH-dependent, and IHH signaling to the epiphyses prompts reserve zone chondrocytes to enter the columnar phase (Figure 9.1C). One mechanism of IHH action is through antagonism of the repressive form of the transcription factor GLI3 in the reserve chondrocytes (Hilton *et al.*, 2005; Koziel *et al.*, 2005).

Hox genes have been shown to regulate the expression of IHH/PTHrP feedback loop constituents (Figure 9.1D). The short radius and ulna of double *Hoxa11;Hoxd11* knockout mice result from perturbed expression of *Ihh*, *PTHrP*, and *Pthr1* (Boulet and Capecchi, 2004). In addition, ablation of *Pbx1* (a Hox binding co-factor) results in reduced growth rate and accelerated endochondral ossification in the growth plates of the humerus (Selleri *et al.*, 2001).

Other signals interact with the IHH/PTHrP feedback loop or act in parallel to regulate growth plate chondrocytes. These include members of the bone morphogenetic protein (BMP) and fibroblast growth factor (FGF) family members that interact with IHH in a dose-dependent manner to provide coordinated modulation of growth rate (Minina *et al.*, 2001, 2002) (Figure 9.1C). In addition, WNT5A and the related WNT5B have been shown to regulate chondrocyte differentiation and proliferation in parallel to the IHH/PTHrP feedback loop (Yang *et al.*, 2003). WNT5A is a key regulator of spatial organization and transitions in cell morphology in multiple mesenchymal tissues (Romereim and Dudley, 2011). Given the expression of *Wnt5a* in the perichondrial and prehypertrophic chondrocytes, it may act in an autocrine or paracrine role to initiate the change to flattened, elongated cellular morphology in the perichondrial and columnar chondrocytes (Yang *et al.*, 2003). Such changes in cell polarity are regulated by a WNT/Planar Cell Polarity pathway that can be activated by WNT5A (Gao *et al.*, 2011; Romereim and Dudley, 2011). Thus, the multiple signaling networks integrate the different tissues of the growth plate such that chondrocytes differentiate and proliferate in a coordinated manner. This ensures that growth plates remain functional throughout the many years it may take for a skeleton to mature.

9.4   Regulation of Differential Growth Rates

Growth plates are maintained by the same gene networks responsible for initial interstitial cartilaginous growth, but less is known about the mechanisms that regulate location-specific growth rate. Differential growth rates can be observed between the same growth plate locations across a population or species (Reno *et al.*, 2000, 2005; Rolian, 2008; Cooper *et al.*, 2013), but also between growth plates within an individual skeleton (Payton, 1932; Bisgard and Bisgard, 1935; Wilsman *et al.*, 1996a,1996b). A variety of study designs have been employed to better understand the phenomena of differential growth rates in growth plates. While exceptionally informative, phenotypes generated by artificial developmental perturbations may not adequately resemble the natural variation in growth plate performance upon which natural selection can act. As such, the diversity of patterns of endochondral ossification that occur within a single skeleton can be an important resource to discern the mechanisms underlying the diversity of skeletal growth behaviors that have been generated through evolution. Even within the same bone, growth plates grow at very different rates (Reno *et al.*, 2005). Comparisons between different locations or ages have improved our understanding of the physiological mechanisms specifying growth rate. For example, faster-growing growth plates characteristic of the proximal tibia and distal radius have greater cell turnover and increased hypertrophy compared to their slower-growing counterparts (Wilsman *et al.*, 1996a). Rolian (2008) observed that the slower growth characteristic of metapodials (MP) resulted from reductions in the pool of proliferating chondrocytes and the ultimate size of hypertrophic chondrocytes. Similar variation in hypertrophy and proliferation has been observed between the growth plates of the bat fore- and hind limbs, in which the faster-growing growth plates of the forelimb bones has disproportionate changes in cell expansion within the hypertrophic zone despite similar rates of cellular turnover (Farnum *et al.*, 2008a).

Cooper and colleagues (2013) recently refined the mechanisms of variation in cell enlargement by observing that hypertrophy occurs in three phases in fast-growing growth plates such as the tibia. Initially, cells enlarge through a proportionate increase in dry mass production and fluid intake. In the second phase, cellular uptake of fluid outpaces dry mass production resulting in a diminishing density within the cell. In the final phase, cells return to a proportionate increase in dry mass production and fluid intake. The slower-growing metatarsals (MT) and proximal radial growth plates truncate phase 2 and eliminate phase 3 resulting in decreased overall cell size.

In a comparison of growth plates across the mouse skeleton, Serrat *et al.* (2007) observed that faster-growing growth plates had higher expression of insulin-like growth factor-1 receptor (IGF-1R), an important component of the growth hormone and IGF-1 regulatory axis in bone growth. Interestingly, IGF-1-deficient mice also have reduced growth by eliminating the third phase of cellular hypertrophy (Cooper *et al.*, 2013).

Comparisons between species reveal that similar changes to cellular behaviors underlie evolutionary differences in growth. Compared to mice, the limbs of Mongolian gerbils, which reach twice the body size of the mouse, and the elongate wings of bats exhibit increased proliferative rates (Farnum *et al.*, 2008b; Rolian, 2008). Furthermore, faster-growing wings of bats (Chiroptera) and long hind limbs in the jerboa (*Jaculus jaculus*) show significant differences in cellular hypertrophy relative to the mouse. Specifically, jerboas extend the third phase of cellular hypertrophy in their MT growth plates (Cooper *et al.*, 2013). Like the differences in growth plate behavior between skeletal sites, it appears that multiple cellular processes can be targeted by selection to produce evolutionary changes in the skeleton. Unfortunately, few examples of gene expression changes have been identified that are associated with interspecific growth patterns. Sears and colleagues (2007) found that bat distal metacarpals (MC) had increased BMP2/4 and phosphorylated SMAD effector protein expression compared to bat MTs and mouse MCs. Such a result fits with the earlier finding that BMP signaling interacts with the IHH pathway to regulate growth plate differentiation, proliferation and hypertrophy in a coordinated manner (Minina *et al.*, 2001, 2002). In total, these studies reveal that differences in growth plate performance rely on both the modification of chondrocyte proliferation and hypertrophy. However, the relative contributions of each can vary between species and skeletal loci, indicating that multiple signaling pathways and regulatory networks can be used to specify particular rates of skeletal growth.

9.5   Comparative Metatarsal Model for Growth Plate Patterning

While long bones garner special attention, the formation of a classic growth plate is not the only outcome of endochondral ossification. The epiphyses, most carpals and tarsals, and one end of each MP and phalanx undergo endochondral ossification without forming true growth plates. Yet, during endochondral ossification, chondrocytes at these sites still proceed through the same basic differentiation steps observed in growth plates (but to a lesser degree) of proliferation, columnar organization and hypertrophy. Growth regions are maintained underlying articular surfaces, and they not only enable short bones to grow in size, but provide an opportunity for articular surfaces to remodel in response to typical loading regimes despite lacking longitudinal growth (Hamrick, 1999). Understanding how these different types of growth behaviors are specified is also fundamental for understanding the variation in skeletal shape both within and between species. Comparisons between sites lacking growth plates to those possessing more typical growth plates can reveal the early patterning mechanisms involved in specifying the locations where growth plates do and do not form.

One striking example is the difference in ossification of the ends of MPs and phalanges of the mammalian autopod (Reno *et al.*, 2006). While their early development is similar to that of long bones, a growth plate forms at only one end. The columnar and hypertrophic zones at the opposite ends progressively disorganize and are obliterated as the primary center of ossification directly invades the epiphysis, a process we have called "direct ossification" (Reno *et al.*, 2006). This model has been used to confirm a distinctive band of proliferation in round chondrocytes sitting atop the columnar zone in the growth plate-forming end that was not observed in the opposite end that does not form a growth plate (Smits *et al.*, 2004;

Reno *et al.*, 2006). This cell population may correspond to the future reserve zone chondrocytes that have an important role in subsequent growth plate organization (Abad *et al.*, 2002).

We also identified that this asymmetrical pattern of MP development is a therian synapomorphy as alligators and lizards still form growth plates at both ends (Reno *et al.*, 2007, 2013). This fact has enabled alligators to serve as a special test case to confirm that signals and behaviors that differ between the two ends of the mouse MP reflect growth plate-specific functions and not simply differences in orientation. Accordingly, alligators exhibit a similar peak of proliferation in round chondrocytes above the columnar zone at both ends of early stage MP ossification (Reno *et al.*, 2007).

9.6   Growth Plate Loss Is Not Dependent on Environment or Systemic Factors

So how does such a pattern manifest during development? One question is whether growth plate loss in the MP is purely a product of developmental patterning or is it influenced by the biomechanical environment resulting from changes in locomotion specific to therians (Reno *et al.*, 2013). To test this hypothesis, we raised embryonic and postnatal mouse MTs in culture. Such systems have long been used to study development in the absence of cues resulting from systemic factors, adjacent tissues, and external loading. These studies include *in vivo* transplantation and *in vitro* culture systems (Felts, 1959; Klement and Spooner, 1992). One intriguing result from Felts' work is that subcutaneous transplantation of 5-day-old rat phalanges forms a secondary center of ossification and growth plate at only the proximal end of the bone (Felts, 1959).

In our culture experiments, neonatal (postnatal day 0 or P0) MTs continued to grow longitudinally and increased by more than 50% in length over 6 days (starting length mean 1.93 mm, P2: 2.65, P4: 2.99, P6: 3.10) (Figure 9.2) (Reno, 2006). This essentially matched the growth of MTs *in vivo*; however, growth failed to progress further after 6 days in culture. Cellular proliferation, as detected by BrdU incorporation, was largely restricted to epiphyseal and columnar cells in the first two days of culture (Figure 9.2). In contrast to normal MT growth, the primary center of ossification did not progress in culture.

One evident difference between the two ends of cultured MTs was the pace of columnar chondrocyte differentiation (Figure 9.2). After 2 days of culture, the columnar zones at each end were still identifiable, but the distal one was better defined. After 6 days, in most cases the proximal columnar zone was completely obliterated, while the distal columnar chondrocytes better retained their flattened phenotype and organization. The differential behavior of the two ends appears to be pre-patterned in the bone prior to entering the culture environment. These results are similar to those of Glickman *et al.* (2000), who surgically swapped growth plates between different anatomical sites in rabbits and found that transplanted growth plates, while slower than untransplanted controls, retained the growth properties of their source location.

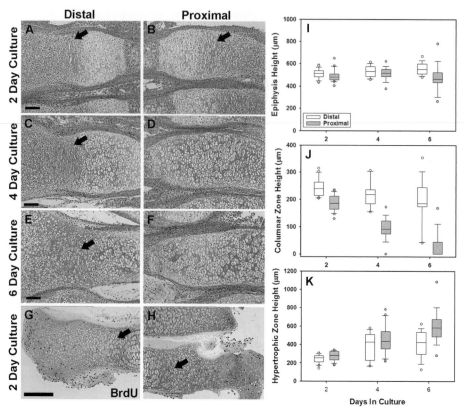

Figure 9.2 Differential preservation of the distal growth plate columnar zone in cultured metatarsals. After 2 days in culture both the distal (A) and proximal (B) ends preserve a columnar zone (arrows) between epiphyseal and hypertrophic chondrocytes. At 4 days, the distal end (C) still preserves a distinct columnar zone (arrow), while proximally (D) it has degraded substantially. After 6 days of culture, (E) a thin layer of flattened chondrocytes remains distally, while (F) the proximal end is composed entirely of hypertrophic cells. Columnar cells show the highest proportion of BrdU incorporation compared to other chondrocyte populations at both the distal (G) and proximal (H) ends. Scale bars are 100 μm. Box and whisker plots illustrate the different behaviors of the columnar zones at each end during organ culture. (I) The epiphyses of each end remained essentially constant. (J) In contrast, while the columnar zone was preserved through 6 days of culture in the distal end, it was much reduced or lost proximally. (K) The hypertrophic zones of each end expanded substantially due to the lack of progression of the primary center of ossification. Data aggregated from nine separate culture experiments.

9.7   Potential Differences in Ihh Signaling in Proximal and Distal MTs

As the IHH/PTHrP feedback loop is crucial for maintaining a functional growth plate, it is reasonable to hypothesize that modification of one of its components may underlie growth plate loss. In many cases, growth plates of knockout and transgenic mice with altered IHH/PTHrP signaling resemble direct ossification with accelerated chondrocyte differentiation and disorganized columnar zones (Reno *et al.*, 2006). To address this hypothesis, we surveyed protein expression using immunohistochemistry just prior to the visual differentiation of the proximal and distal ends in P0 and P2 mouse MTs. At these ages, PTHrP is observed across the entire cartilaginous ends of the proximal and distal MT. Particularly intense staining was found in articular and periarticular chondrocytes where the gene is known to be expressed (Lee *et al.*, 1996; St-Jacques *et al.*, 1999) and in prehypertrophic cells which express *Pthr1*. As expected, PTHR1 was observed in prehypertrophic and hypertrophic chondrocytes, the adjacent perichondrium, and faintly in the epiphyseal chondrocytes of both ends. No differences were observed between each end at this age (data not shown).

IHH is detectable in many of the chondrocytes across both proximal and distal cartilaginous regions fitting its role as a diffusible morphogen regulating multiple steps during endochondral ossification (Figure 9.1C) (Long and Ornitz, 2013). At P2, staining is detected in articular, epiphyseal, and columnar chondrocytes at both ends, but most intensely in prehypertrophic cells where it is known to be expressed (Figure 9.3).

For PTCH1, strong staining occurs in prehypertrophic and epiphyseal chondrocytes (Figure 9.3). Positive staining was also seen in columnar and articular chondrocytes and in the perichondrium. The most intense and consistent staining occurred in chondrocytes across the entire proximal epiphysis and in the portion of the distal epiphysis adjacent to the columnar zone. For the rest of the distal end the staining pattern was variable. Commonly a gradient of PTCH1 expression was observed with weaker staining further from the columnar zone. In some cases, no PTCH1 was detectible in the distal epiphysis and growth plate, while at the other extreme strong staining was nearly uniform across the epiphyseal chondrocytes similar to the proximal end (Figure 9.3).

We used embryonic alligators to further explore the association of PTCH1 with growth plate formation. As anticipated, PTCH1 expression occurred in prehypertrophic cells and continued throughout the remaining hypertrophic chondrocytes (Figure 9.3). More importantly, at both ends PTCH1 was observed in round epiphyseal chondrocytes adjacent to the columnar chondrocytes, while expression was reduced in those cells closer to the articular surface. Thus, alligator PTCH1 expression matched the gradient pattern that was commonly observed in mice.

While the variability in the mouse is problematic, it can be concluded that (1) chondrocytes in the epiphysis nearest to the columnar zone show strong PTCH1 expression in the distal end prior to growth plate formation, and (2) that PTCH1 is strongly and evenly expressed across the proximal epiphysis that does not form a growth plate. Interestingly, the carpals also showed an even pattern of PTCH1 expression to the proximal end at this stage. Despite the variation in staining in the distal epiphyses, there is reason to suspect that the gradient pattern is a real phenomenon. First, it matches previously published results using *in situ* hybridization detection of *Ptch1* mRNA (Long *et al.*, 2001; Koziel *et al.*, 2004; Kuss *et al.*, 2014). Second, it agrees with the pattern observed during growth plate formation in the alligator, and lastly, it corresponds to the regions of cellular proliferation at both the distal and proximal ends of the MT (Reno *et al.*, 2006).

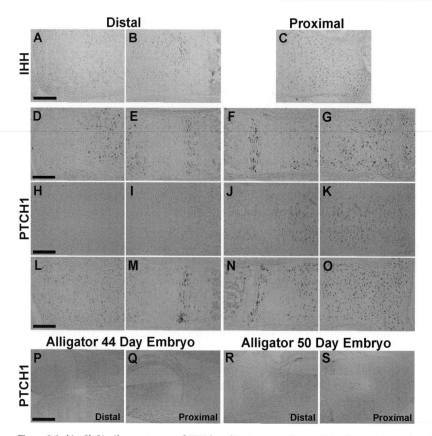

Figure 9.3 (A–C) Similar patterns of IHH localization are detected in the epiphyseal, columnar, and prehypertrophic chondrocytes at each end of P2 MTs. PTCH1 detection is variable in the distal end (D, E, H, I, L, M). Commonly, a gradient of expression is observed in the epiphysis (D), with strong expression detected in prehypertrophic chondrocytes (E, M). However, some specimens show no staining in distal epiphysis (H) or the growth plate (I), and in others staining is uniform across the epiphysis (L). In contrast, proximal staining is highly consistent in prehypertrophic chondroctyes (F, J, N) and uniformly across the epiphysis (G, K, O). (P–S) In the embryonic alligators PTCH1 is detected in epiphyseal chondrocytes adjacent to the columnar zone and prehypertrophic cells at each end, consistent with these bones forming two growth plates in this species. A black and white version of this figure will appear in some formats. For the color version, please refer to the plate section.

For multiple reasons, the differential distribution of PTCH1 between the two ends may reflect the importance of IHH for growth plate function. *Ptch1* is upregulated in response to hedgehog signaling. In its inactivated state, PTCH1 binds to smoothened (SMO), a transmembrane protein that transduces hedgehog signaling. When freed from PTCH1 after binding to a hedgehog protein, SMO stimulates (and/or inhibits) the GLI family of transcription factors (McMahon, 2000). However, PTCH1 itself is a target of GLI, and the increased production of PTCH1 serves to bind the free SMO to attenuate the hedgehog signal (McMahon, 2000). Ectopic or modified expression of IHH leads to altered expression of *Ptch1* in cartilaginous growth plates and epiphyses (Chung *et al.*, 1998). Using mice carrying a hypomorphic allele of exostosin1 (*Ext1*), Koziel and colleagues (2004) demonstrated the sensitivity of *Ptch1* expression to a modulated IHH signal. Mutations in *Ext1* affect heparan sulfate synthesis in the cartilage matrix, which serve to increase the diffusion capacity of IHH proteins. This increased diffusion resulted in a distally expanded expression domain of *Ptch1* in the epiphyses of embryonic radii (Koziel *et al.*, 2004). Thus, the consistently strong staining in proximal MTs may reflect increased Ihh signaling relative to the more variable PTCH1 expression distally.

Three key cellular behaviors were documented during typical growth plate formation in MTs but not in the opposite end during direct ossification: (1) the specific proliferation of reserve chondrocytes, (2) the continued columnar organization of growth plate chondrocytes, and (3) the differentiation of epiphyseal chondrocytes to form a secondary center of ossification. Given that IHH has the functions of increasing chondrocyte proliferation and promoting reserve chondrocyte differentiation, what can be gleaned from the observed patterns of PTCH1 expression? Interestingly, the regions of early PTCH1 expression and proliferation in the distal and proximal epiphyses appear to correspond to the populations of chondrocytes that will be replaced by the primary center of ossification. The distal epiphysis beyond the region of strong PTCH1 expression undergoes replacement by the secondary center of ossification. These chondrocytes will later express PTCH1 as they begin to differentiate into the prehypertrophic stage and express IHH. Alternatively, it is possible that any increased IHH signaling indicated by PTCH1 expression could simply be a by-product of direct ossification itself. At these early stages there are roughly comparable numbers of columnar chondrocytes at each end; however, the proximal population is diminishing through terminal differentiation. This would result in more chondrocytes producing IHH (Kobayashi *et al.*, 2002, 2005). This interpretation may fit with the increased variability observed in PTCH1 staining in the distal epiphysis of mice.

To further explore differences between growth plate formation and direct ossification, we are in the process of conducting a high-throughput mRNA sequencing (RNA-seq) analysis of the proximal and distal chondrocytes in the developing mouse MT (see Chapter 8). This technique will provide a catalogue of genes with expression differences between the two ends (Pareek *et al.*, 2011). While results are preliminary, we have identified some intriguing candidates in P4 MTs when the visual differences in size and organization of the columnar zones first appear. We do not observe strong differences in IHH and PTCH1 expression between the two ends. However, as mRNA is extracted from the entire cartilaginous region on either side of the primary ossification center, this technique will not detect purely spatial differences in gene expression. Intriguingly, given the experiments above regarding differential growth, *Igf1* does appear to have greater expression in the proximal end and may be associated with the rapid differentiation of chondrocytes during direct ossification. We anticipate finding other important genes distinguishing growth plate formation and direct ossification using this technique that will direct us to the specific genes that differentiate growth plates from more generalized endochondral ossification.

9.8   Growth Plate Loss in the Human Pisiform

Another example of evolutionary change through growth plate loss is the human pisiform. In most mammals, including primates and even the early hominid *Australopithecus afarensis*, the pisiform is elongated, while in humans it consists of a small bony pea-shaped nubbin (Figure 9.4). Furthermore, the typical mammalian pisiform forms from two separate centers of ossification while the human only forms one. We recently confirmed that elongated chimp and gorilla pisiforms also form from two separate ossification centers (Kjosness *et al.*, 2014) (Figure 9.4).

Such dramatic differences in morphology and ossification pattern suggest a potential developmental mechanism: the loss of one of the centers of ossification and an associated growth plate. To confirm this, we characterized the nature of the two potential ossification centers in apes. In both chimpanzees and gorillas, the primary center forms during deciduous dental eruption, but the secondary center forms during M2 and M3 eruption. Ossification of the single human center occurs between years seven and twelve (Francis, 1940; Gilsanz and Ratib, 2005), which corresponds more closely with that of the ape secondary center. This suggests that the pisiform is not simply the fusion of two separate cartilage condensations, such as the mammalian hamate or the *os centrale* and scaphoid in African apes (Gillies, 1929; Kivell and Begun, 2007), but instead possesses an active growth plate topped by a secondary center of ossification.

While we cannot confirm the histology of pisiform ossification in developing humans, apes, or other primates due to ethical considerations for acquiring large amounts of embryonic tissue, we instead turned to the mouse. The initial ossification

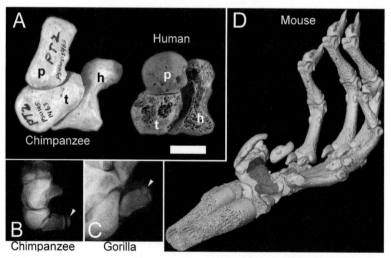

Figure 9.4 (A) Articulated pisiform (p), triquetral (t), and hamate (h) in a chimpanzee and human illustrating the elongated pisiform in the ape (scale bar 1 cm). Radiographs reveal the secondary center in subadult (B) chimpanzee (M2 erupting) and (C) and gorilla (M3 erupting). (D) Micro-CT of a 3-week-old mouse wrist demonstrating the long pisiform (gray) with a separate secondary epiphysis (dark gray).

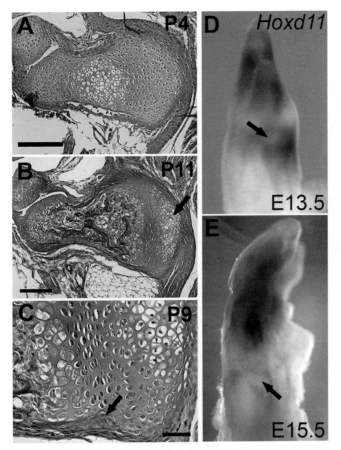

Figure 9.5 (A) Safranin O (red) staining reveals the development of the growth plate in the mouse pisiform. Chondrocyte hypertrophy and calcification is initiating in the central part of the P4 cartilage model. (B) By P11 the pisiform is largely ossified except for the remaining growth plate on the palmar end (right); note the formation of the secondary center (arrow). (C) The pisiform preserves all of the hallmarks of a growth plate with columnar and hypertrophic cells and an encircling bone collar and perichondrial ring (arrow). Scale bars are 100 μm. *In situ* hybridization in (D) E13.5 and (E) E15.5 mouse forelimbs reveal late-stage *Hoxd11* expression surrounding the developing pisiform (arrows). A black and white version of this figure will appear in some formats. For the color version, please refer to the plate section.

center forms relatively early compared to other carpals by P4, and the secondary center initiates at P7 (Figure 9.5A,B). Histological analysis revealed that the intervening cartilage between the two centers maintains all of the hallmarks of a typical growth plate with functional columnar and hypertrophic zones, and an encircling bone collar and perichondrial ring (Figure 9.5C).

The loss of a functioning growth plate and center of ossification in the pisiform constitutes a dramatic developmental and functional shift in the human wrist. Given our results with cultured MTs, such a change is not likely to result simply from an altered biomechanical loading regime brought on by changes in locomotor or manipulative behavior. That is not to say there were not important functional changes placed on the pisiform during human evolution, only that such alterations required changes in early skeletal pattern formation and/or growth plate specification that are largely driven by gene regulatory networks. There are a number of behavioral and morphological transitions involving the hominoid carpus that have impacted pisiform evolution. First, the human and African ape pisiforms appear to be unusual in their opportunity for sliding mobility across the triquetral compared to other primates (Moojen et al., 2001; Jameson et al., 2002). In monkeys and the Miocene hominoid *Proconsul*, the pisiform articulates into a cup-like socket between the triquetral and ulnar styloid (Napier and Davis, 1959; Jouffroy, 1991). Similarly, the gibbon pisiform is buttressed proximally by the novel *os Daubentonii*, despite also having a reduced ulnar styloid. Orangutans have a substantially shortened pisiform that is stabilized by a direct articulation with the hamate hamulus (Lewis, 1972). Interestingly, we have observed that orangutans still form two centers of ossification as other mammals do, despite their short pisiform. Second, the pisiform serves as the insertion for the powerful *flexor carpi ulnaris* (FCU) and the origin of the *abductor digiti minimi*. The FCU is active during both monkey and ape quadrupedal locomotion and is one of two muscles recruited in both hands during percussive tool manufacture (Marzke et al., 1998; Patel et al., 2012). Third, the pisiform is a component of multiple anatomical complexes with important functional and clinical significance. It defines one of the boundaries and potentially the depth of the carpal tunnel, as it is one of the attachment sites for the flexor retinaculum (Marzke, 2010). Tasks that require frequent use of the power squeeze grip such as racquet sports, which are similar to the motions utilized during stone tool production, can result in pain and disability when associated with pisiform instability (Helal, 1978; Marzke, 2010).

It is currently unknown how the length of the ancestral pisiform affected the carpal tunnel, risk of traumatic injury, and stability of the pisotriquetral joint. It is interesting that both humans and highly suspensory orangutans have shortened pisiforms. Therefore, pisiform reduction is not likely to be the result of loss of a locomotor role for the forelimb in humans. Humans and orangutans do differ from African apes by infrequently engaging in quadrupedal locomotion (either knuckle-walking or palmigrade quadrupedalism). Gibbons are also highly suspensory and do not frequently engage in quadrupedal postures, yet still have long pisiforms. However, as described above, hylobatids still have a stable, cup-like socket for their pisiform as opposed to the articulation relocated to the palmar surface of the triquetral in humans and great apes (Lewis, 1972). It is reasonable to hypothesize that human pisiform reduction may reflect improved pisotriquetral joint stability with the advent of repetitive manipulative behaviors brought on by stone tool manufacture and use after 2.6 my (Semaw et al., 2003; Toth and Schick, 2009). This possibility is currently being investigated.

The existence of a pisiform growth plate has particular significance for the patterning of the mammalian wrist. Given the role that *Hox* genes have in the specification and regulation of growth plates (Boulet and Capecchi, 2004), one would expect that *Hox* should have an important role in the development of this bone. This is supported by the phenotypic effects of *Hoxa11* and *Hoxd11* knockout mice. Homozygous deletion of *Hoxa11* or *Hoxd11* results in shortened pisiforms that are commonly fused to the triquetral (Small and Potter, 1993; Davis and Capecchi, 1994; Favier *et al.*, 1995). *Hoxa11;Hoxd11* double heterozygous mice have a slightly shortened pisiform, while inactivation of three alleles results in a grossly malformed pisiform/triquetral mass (Davis *et al.*, 1995; Kjosness *et al.*, 2014). Double homozygous *Hoxa11;Hoxd11* deletion results in complete absence of pisiform and triquetral (Davis *et al.*, 1995).

The biphasic expression pattern of posterior *Hoxa* and *Hoxd* genes in the developing tetrapod limb produces separate expression domains in the zeugopod and autopod (Zakany and Duboule, 2007) (Figure 9.1B). The intermediate "no *Hoxd* land" corresponding to the wrist has been hypothesized to underlie the lack of longitudinal growth in carpals (Woltering and Duboule, 2010). The unique growth plate of the pisiform enables a test of this prediction, with the hypothesis that *Hox* should be found to be expressed in association with the pisiform, but to a lesser degree with other carpals. In accordance with this prediction, *Hoxd11* is detected in developing carpus at E13.5 and is maintained in the medial wrist surrounding the pisiform in E15.5 mice (Figure 9.5D,E). This corroborates previous observations that *Hoxd11* has a stronger expression in the medial compared to lateral wrist at this stage (Koyama *et al.*, 2010) and provides another example of normal variation in ossification providing clues to mechanisms of skeletal development (for further details see Reno *et al.*, 2016).

9.9   Mechanisms of Integration between *Hox* and Growth Plate Patterning

The cases of the mammalian MPs and human pisiform demonstrate that growth plate loss is a viable mechanism for evolutionary change of the skeleton. In addition, they provide important test cases to explore genes and developmental processes specific to growth plate formation: a fundamental aspect of building bones. Comparisons between skeletal sites such as the MTs and carpals have been used to identify the interaction between *Hox* gene patterning and growth plate regulatory pathways. For example, the synpolydactyly homolog (*spdh*) mutant encodes a polyalanine expansion in the HOXD13 protein, which represses the activity of other HOXD proteins in the autopod (Villavicencio-Lorini *et al.*, 2010). Thus, the *spdh* phenotype resembles that of *HoxdDel(11–13)* which has synchronous deletion of *Hoxd11*, *Hoxd12* and *Hoxd13* with severe truncation and fusion of the metacarpals and phalanges (Bruneau *et al.*, 2001). Villavicencio-Lorni and colleagues (2010) recently demonstrated that the MTs of *spdh* mutant mice have a malformed perichondrium with reduced expression of the bone-promoting transcription factor *Runx2*. Similarly, the short radius and ulna in *Hoxa11-/-;d11-/-* mice also fail to express the later phase of *Runx2* and associated short stature homeobox 2 (*Shox2*), indicating inhibition of cartilage differentiation prior to *Ihh* expression and chondrocyte hypertrophy (Figure 9.1D) (Gross *et al.*, 2012).

An association between *Hox* and *Ihh* is intriguing given important roles that the latter gene has in coordinating the multitude of signals influencing chondrocyte behavior in the growth plate and our previous results with PTCH1 in the MT. Gonzalez-Martin and colleagues explored the relationship between *Hox* and *Ihh* in *Hoxdel(11–13)* mouse MPs (Gonzalez-Martin et al., 2014). These shortened bones evinced increased expression of *Gli3*, the negative regulator of *Ihh*. The interaction between GLI3 and IHH has an important role in the differentiation of reserve to columnar chondrocytes (Hilton *et al.*, 2005; Koziel *et al.*, 2005). Crossing *Hox-del(11–13)* and *Gli3-/-* mice rescued MT growth and partially rescued the MC (Gonzalez-Martin et al., 2014). The more complete rescue in the foot likely reflects the expression of *Hoxc* genes in the hind limb (Wellik and Capecchi, 2003). These experiments support a role of *Hox* acting in a dose-dependent manner to initiate chondrocyte differentiation through regulation of *Runx2* and *Ihh* (Figure 9.1D).

Further analysis of *spdh* has revealed additional Hox-mediated pathways that contribute to the assignment of long bone identity. Skeletal elongation is dependent on biomechanical interactions with a fibrous/ossified sheath encasing directionally oriented proliferating and hypertrophying chondrocytes (Kuss *et al.*, 2014). The lack of a well-defined perichondrium and delayed cortical bone formation in *spdh* mice results in the MC undergoing irregular lateral growth and fusion to adjacent bones. This phenotype resembles *Wnt5a-/-* mice, in that the chondrocytes of both genotypes fail to adopt the elongated flattened shape typically observed in perichondrial and columnar cells. Furthermore, both *Hoxd13* and *Wnt5a* are coexpressed in the perichondrium, but in *spdh* mice where HOXD activity is inactive, *Wnt5a* expression is substantially reduced. This suggests that *Hox* also has a role in regulating the chondrocyte cell polarity in both the perichondrium and columnar chondrocytes through Wnt signaling (Yang *et al.*, 2003; Gao *et al.*, 2011; Kuss *et al.*, 2014) (Figure 9.1C). Thus, Hox may act by patterning two of the fundamental progenitor pools and signaling centers of the growth plate: the reserve chondrocyte zone and perichondrium. Interestingly, these are also two sites that distinguish the growth plate forming from the non-forming end of mouse MTs (Reno *et al.*, 2006).

9.10   Anthropological Implications

Skeletal structure and diversity, both within and between species, is one of the primary resources available for biological anthropologists to study the functional evolution of humans and primates. While adaptation through natural selection has shaped our skeleton over the generations, this process cannot be fully understood without knowing how development interprets our genotype into a functional phenotype. Therefore, the process by which skeletons are built and the source of the variation within their construction are fundamental questions for biological anthropology.

Over the past 20 years anthropologists have incorporated the implications of evo–devo research into their studies. Development frequently relies on the reuse of a surprisingly small number of highly conserved "tool kit" genes, regulatory networks, and cellular processes to pattern the embryo. As such, similar genes are re-used not only in the development of different parts of the embryo, but also repeatedly used across the diversity of animals. This means that one of the key mechanisms for generating different outcomes during development is through the regulation of these core sets of developmental control genes. Thus, these genes, as well as the regulatory networks that control their expression and interaction, tend to be highly conserved (Carroll, 2008). The conservation of the "tool kit" and regulatory structure results in the potential for pleiotropic effects across the developing embryo, yet gene regulation has the potential to operate with remarkable specificity (Shapiro *et al.*, 2004; Guenther *et al.*, 2008; Menke *et al.*, 2008). The conservation of key patterning genes combined with the diversity of regulatory potential results in observable patterns of integration and modularity emerging from the developmental process (Wagner, 1989, 2007; Hallgrimsson *et al.*, 2002). This realization has led many to seek out patterns of phenotypic and genotypic modularity in the primate skeleton (Hlusko, 2004). In addition, such a developmental perspective has been used to construct a trait classification system for morphological, functional, and phylogenetic analyses that facilitate the generation of hypotheses concerning the potential pleiotropic relationships of characters in question (Lovejoy *et al.*, 1999).

Anthropologists have been slower to conduct investigations into the developmental basis for primate phenotypic variation and evolution themselves, despite guidelines defined over a decade ago (Chiu and Hamrick, 2002; Carroll, 2003; Hallgrimsson and Lieberman, 2008). Understandably, this delay is due in large part to the practical and ethical difficulties inherent to conducting experimental embryological analyses on humans, apes, and other primates. However, there are a number of ways that these obstacles can be overcome. The first is incorporating the plethora of comparative genomic data available for our species and those of our close relatives. While daunting given the size of these genomes, tools are rapidly being developed to facilitate comparisons between species. Alignments at the USCS Genome Browser (genome.ucsc.edu) are provided that aid in the identification and cataloging of specific genomic differences between ours and other species (Kent *et al.*, 2002). Algorithms have been devised to identify humans specific sites of accelerated mutation, deletion, and duplication in the genome through comparison to other primate and vertebrate genomes that underlie our morphological development (Pollard *et al.*, 2006; Prabhakar *et al.*, 2006, 2008; McLean *et al.*, 2011; Dennis *et al.*, 2012; O'Bleness *et al.*, 2012). In addition, great effort has been expended to identify putative regulatory regions by the Encyclopedia of DNA Elements (ENCODE) Project (Bernstein *et al.*, 2012). Such "genome-first" approaches have found a number of interesting candidate loci with potentially important phenotypic effects involving the brain, limbs, and reproductive anatomy, yet each awaits further functional validation. A limitation of this "genome-first" approach is that candidate loci are sorted by the visibility of the novel genotypes and not the magnitude of their developmental effect or the evolutionary significance of their resulting phenotypes. Therefore, phenotype-driven approaches are also required to better understand human skeletal evo–devo.

Fortunately, the general conservation of genetic and developmental mechanisms means that experimental results from more tractable organisms can be applied to questions of human development (Chiu and Hamrick, 2002; Rolian, 2014). In certain developmental contexts, such as the limb, the mouse is an ideal model to explore primate skeletal development because both mice and primates share generalized pentadactyl limbs and a majority of the mechanisms controlling limb patterning and skeletal growth (Cotney et al., 2013). Molecular phylogenies now show a close relationship between rodents and primates (Kriegs et al., 2006), further supporting the use of mouse models as a resource to understand human and primate skeletal development.

One approach is to combine the analyses discussed above, investigating the developmental variation that occurs within the normal skeleton, with comparative functional genomic data to bridge the gap between genotype and phenotype. For instance, the pisiform provides an exquisite example of the potential site-specific capabilities of genetic cis-regulatory networks. The use of next-generation sequencing technologies to investigate the transcriptome and chromatin structure can be used in comparisons between the mouse pisiform and other carpals to identify the genes and regulatory networks involved in specifying growth plate location (Creyghton et al., 2010; Cotney et al., 2013; Chapter 8). This model has the additional benefit of informing on the developmental basis for the human-specific reduction of the pisiform. The identification of genes and enhancers involved in mammalian pisiform longitudinal growth can be cross-referenced with genomic sites of primate conservation and human uniqueness to pinpoint potential candidate loci underlying the evolution of the human phenotype. New sequence editing techniques like CRISPR/Cas9 are making the possibility of testing the effect of hominoid-specific genotypes within the mouse a practical reality (Menke, 2013). Together, developmental and genetic techniques can provide novel data to inform, and potentially resolve, long-standing debates surrounding the classification of primate morphological traits as homologies or homoplasies by clarifying the underlying mechanisms and processes that ultimately determine morphology (Reno, 2014; see Chapter 8 for discussion of the value of various genetic and developmental biology approaches; see Chapter 4 for detailed discussion of determining homology). Thus, as a field, biological anthropology has the combination of tools (i.e., comparative and functional genomics, the mouse as an appropriate model organism, expertise in phenotypic comparisons) to determine how the unique human skeleton has been built both through evolution and again in each generation through development.

9.11   Experimental Procedures

9.11.1   Immunohistochemistry

Mouse and alligator specimens were prepared and sectioned as previously described (Reno et al., 2006, 2007). For antigen unmasking, sections were incubated with 0.1 units/ml chondroitinase ABC (Sigma, St. Louis, MO) for 10 min at 37°C. Endogenous peroxidase activity was quenched using 1% hydrogen peroxide solution. The following polyclonal antibodies demonstrating cross-reactivity with mouse, rat, and human proteins were used: (1) goat anti-PTHrP raised against peptide at N-terminus of human origin (1:100; sc-9680 Santa Cruz Biotechnology, Santa Cruz, CA); (2) rabbit anti-PPR raised against amino acids 469–593 of human origin (1:100; sc-20749 Santa Cruz Biotechnology); (3) goat anti-IHH raised against the C-terminus of Indian hedgehog of human origin which does not cross-react with other members of the hedgehog family (1:100; sc-1196 Santa Cruz Biotechnology); and (4) goat anti-PTCH1 raised against a peptide mapping to the amino terminus of mouse origin (1:500; sc-6149 Santa Cruz Biotechnology). Depending on the primary antibody, the secondary antibody was either goat anti-rabbit or donkey anti-goat detected with avidin-biotinylated HRP complex (ABC Staining System, Santa Cruz Biotechnology) following the manufacturer's protocol. Slides were counterstained with methyl green.

9.11.2 *In Vitro* Metatarsal Culture

The left and right metatarsal triads containing MT2–4 from newborn mice were dissected from each foot and promptly placed in culture. MT triads were free-floating in 2–3 ml Delbecco's modified Eagles medium (DMEM) plus 10% fetal bovine serum (FBS) and fungicide and antibodies in a 12-well plate. As bone collar growth was one feature distinguishing the two ends of the metatarsal, media containing FBS was chosen because previous analyses have shown that it is necessary to promote bone collar formation (Klement and Spooner, 1992). MTs were incubated at 37°C in a high-humidity atmosphere containing 5% CO_2. Culture media were typically changed on alternate days. MTs were cultured for 2, 4, or 6 days.

For each metatarsal the total length the mineralized region (opaque portion), and the proximal and distal cartilaginous regions (translucent portions) were measured using an eyepiece reticule on a 10× dissecting microscope upon initial dissection and removal from culture. In addition, the lengths of the total metatarsal, the primary center of ossification, and proximal and distal epiphyseal, columnar and hypertrophic zones of MT3 were measured from Safranin O-/Fast Green-stained histological sections.

Specimens were then fixed in 10% neutral-buffered formalin, decalcified in EDTA, embedded in paraffin and sectioned at 6 μm for histological analysis. To assess cellular differentiation, sections were stained using Safranin O/Fast Green.

To assess chondrocyte proliferation the normal culture media was replaced with media containing 1:100 concentration BrdU (BD Biosciences Pharmingen) the evening prior to tissue recovery. BrdU incorporation was detected using BrdU *In-Situ* Detection Kit (BD Biosciences Pharmingen) following the manufacturer's protocol and counterstained with thionin to stain cartilage matrix and identify cell nuclei.

9.11.3 *In Situ* Hybridization

Mouse embryos were dissected from the uterine horn of pregnant FVB/NJ females at embryonic day (E) 13.5 and 15.5 and fixed in 4% paraformaldehyde. Embryos were dehydrated in graded methanol and stored at –20°C. Skin was removed from E15.5 limbs by manual dissection in ice-cold methanol prior to *in situ* analysis. Expression patterns were confirmed in repeated *in situ* analyses containing at least two experimental specimens and one sense control. Whole mount in situ hybridization for a *Hoxd11* riboprobe (a gift from Denis Duboule, University of Geneva) was performed as previously described (Nieto *et al.*, 1996). Proteinase-K treatment prior to hybridization consisted of 10 µg/ml for 30 min (E13.5) or 1 h (E15.5).

9.12   Acknowledgments

We thank Chris Percival and Joan Richtsmeier for the invitation to contribute to the Building Bones symposium and this volume as well as their editorial guidance. We are grateful to Ruth Elsey, Philip Trosclair II, and Dwayne LeJeune of the Louisiana Department of Wildlife and Fisheries at the Rockefeller Wildlife Refuge for providing alligator specimens. We thank Yohannes Haile-Selassie (Department of Physical Anthropology, Cleveland Museum of Natural History) for access to primate skeletons in his care, and Lyman Jellema for curatorial assistance. We thank Tim Ryan (Center for Quantitative Imaging, PSU) and Griffin Jones (Applied Research Laboratory, PSU) for micro-CT scanning and Tim Ryan and Simone Sukhdeo for their assistance during image processing and 3D reconstruction. We also thank Walter Horton for suggesting and advising on the metatarsal *in vitro* culture experiments. Two reviewers provided helpful comments that substantially improved this manuscript. Jasmine Hines and Denise McBurney provided valuable technical assistance. This work was supported by grants from the National Science Foundation (BCS-0311768 and BCS-1540418).

References

Abad, V., Meyers, J. L., Weise, M., *et al.* (2002). The role of the resting zone in growth plate chondrogenesis. *Endocrinology*, 143, 1851–1857.

Akiyama, H., Chaboissier, M. C., Martin, J. F., Schedl, A. and De Crombrugghe, B. (2002). The transcription factor Sox9 has essential roles in successive steps of the chondrocyte differentiation pathway and is required for expression of Sox5 and Sox6. *Genes and Development*, 16, 2813–2828.

Andrey, G., Montavon, T., Mascrez, B., *et al.* (2013). A switch between topological domains underlies *Hoxd* genes collinearity in mouse limbs. *Science*, 340, 1234167.

Ballock, R. T. and O'Keefe, R. J. (2003). The biology of the growth plate. *Journal of Bone and Joint Surgury American Volume*, 85A, 715–726.

Bernstein, B. E., Birney, E., Dunham, I., *et al.* (2012). An integrated encyclopedia of DNA elementsin the human genome. *Nature*, 489, 57–74.

Bisgard, J. D. and Bisgard, M. E. (1935). Longitudinal growth of long bones. *Archives of Surgery*, 31, 569–587.

Boulet, A. M. and Capecchi, M. R. (2002). Duplication of the *Hoxd11* gene causes alterations in the axial and appendicular skeleton of the mouse. *Developmental Biology*, 249, 96–107.

Boulet, A. M. and Capecchi, M. R. (2004). Multiple roles of *Hoxa11* and *Hoxd11* in the formation of the mammalian forelimb zeugopod. *Development*, 131, 299–309.

Bruneau, S., Johnson, K. R., Yamamoto, M., Kuroiwa, A. and Duboule, D. (2001). The mouse *Hoxd13^spdh* mutation, a polyalanine expansion similar to human Type II synpolydactyly (Spd), disrupts the function but not the expression of other *Hoxd* genes. *Developmental Biology*, 237, 345–353.

Capecchi, M. R. (1994). Targeted gene replacement. *Scientific American*, 270, 52–59.

Capecchi, M. R. (1997). Hox genes and mammalian development. *Cold Spring Harbor Symposia on Quantitative Biology*, 62, 273–281.

Carroll, S. B. (2003). Genetics and the making of *Homo sapiens*. *Nature*, 422, 849–857.

Carroll, S. B. (2008). Evo–devo and an expanding evolutionary synthesis, a genetic theory of morphological evolution. *Cell*, 134, 25–36.

Chiu, C. H. and Hamrick, M. W. (2002). Evolution and development of the primate limb skeleton. *Evolutionary Anthropology*, 11, 94–107.

Chung, U. I., Lanske, B., Lee, K., Li, E. and Kronenberg, H. (1998). The parathyroid hormone/parathyroid hormone-related peptide receptor coordinates endochondral bone development by directly controlling chondrocyte differentiation. *Procedings of the National Academy of Sciences USA*, 95, 13030–13035.

Cooper, K. L., Oh, S., Sung, Y., *et al.* (2013). Multiple phases of chondrocyte enlargement underlie differences in skeletal proportions. *Nature*, 495, 375–378.

Cotney, J., Leng, J., Yin, J., *et al.* (2013). The evolution of lineage-specific regulatory activities in the human embryonic limb. *Cell*, 154, 185–196.

Creyghton, M. P., Cheng, A. W., Welstead, G. G., *et al.* (2010). Histone H3K27ac separates active from poised enhancers and predicts developmental state. *Procedings of the National Academy of Sciences USA*, 107, 21931–21936.

Davis, A. P. and Capecchi, M. R. (1994). Axial homeosis and appendicular skeleton defects in mice with a targeted disruption of Hoxd-11. *Development*, 120, 2187–2198.

Davis, A. P. and Capecchi, M. R. (1996). A mutational analysis of the 5' HoxD genes, dissection of genetic interations during limb development in the mouse. *Development*, 122, 1175–1185.

Davis, A. P., Witte, D. P., Hsieh-Li, H. M., Potter, S. S. and Capecchi, M. R. (1995). Absence of radius and ulna in mice lacking hoxa-11 and hoxd-11. *Nature*, 375, 791–795.

De Crombrugghe, B., Lefebvre, V. and Nakashima, K. (2001). Regulatory mechanisms in the pathways of cartilage and bone formation. *Current Opinion in Cell Biology*, 13, 721–727.

Dennis, M. Y., Nuttle, X., Sudmant, P. H., *et al.* (2012). Evolution of human-specific neural *SRGAP2* genes by incomplete segmental duplicaiton. *Cell*, 149, 912–922.

Deschamps, J. (2004). Developmental biology. Hox genes in the limb, a play in two acts. *Science*, 304, 1610–1611.

Dolle, P., Izpisua-Belmonte, J. C., Falkenstein, H., Renucci, A. and Duboule, D. (1989). Coordinate expression of the murine Hox-5 complex homoeobox-containing genes during limb pattern formation. *Nature*, 342, 767–772.

Dolle, P., Dierich, A., Lemeur, M., *et al.* (1993). Disruption of the Hoxd-13 gene induces localized heterochrony leading to mice with neotenic limbs. *Cell*, 75, 431–441.

Duboule, D. (2007). The rise and fall of Hox gene clusters. *Development*, 134, 2549–2560.

Ducy, P. (2000). Cbfa1, a molecular switch in osteoblast biology. *Developmental Dynamics*, 291, 461–471.

Farnum, C. E., Tinsley, M. and Hermanson, J. W. (2008a). Forelimb versus hindlimb skeletal development in the big brown bat, *Eptesicus fuscus*, functional divergence is reflected in chondrocytic performance in autopodial growth plates. *Cells Tissues Organs*, 187, 35–47.

Farnum, C. E., Tinsley, M. and Hermanson, J. W. (2008b). Postnatal bone elongation of the manus versus pes, analysis of the chondrocytic differentiation cascade in *Mus musculus* and *Eptesicus fuscus*. *Cells Tissues Organs*, 187, 48–58.

Favier, B., Le Meur, M., Chambon, P. and Dolle, P. (1995). Axial skeleton homeosis and forelimb malformations in Hoxd-11 mutant mice. *Proceedings of the National Academy of Sciences USA*, 92, 310–314.

Favier, B., Rijli, F. M., Fronmental-Remain, C., Fraulob, V. and Chambon, P. (1996). Functional cooperation between the non-paralogous genes *Hoxa-10* and *Hoxd-11* in the developing forelimb and axial skeleton. *Development*, 122, 449–460.

Felts, W. J. L. (1959). Transplantation studies of factors in skeletal organogenesis I. The subcutaneously implanted immature long-bone of the rat and mouse. *American Journal of Physical Anthropology*, 17, 201–215.

Francis, C. C. (1940). The appearance of centers of ossification from 6 to 15 years. *American Journal of Physical Anthropology*, 27, 127–138.

Fromental-Remain, C., Warot, X., Messadecq, N., Dolle, P. and Chambon, P. (1996). Hoxa-13 and Hoxd-13 play a crucial role in the patterning of the limb autopod. *Development*, 122, 2997–3011.

Gao, B., Song, H., Bishop, K., *et al.* (2011). Wnt signaling gradients establish planar cell polarity by inducing Vangl2 phosphorylation through Ror2. *Developmental Cell*, 20, 163–176.

Gehrke, A. R., Schneider, I., De La Calle-Mustienes, E., *et al.* (2015). Deep conservation of wrist and digit enhancers in fish. *Proceedings of the National Academy of Sciences USA*, 112, 803–808.

Gillies, C. D. (1929). The origin of the os pisiforme. *Journal of Anatomy*, 63, 380–383.

Gilsanz, V. and Ratib, O. (2005). *Hand Bone Age, A Digital Atlas of Skeletal Maturity*. Heidelberg: Springer.

Glickman, A. M., Yang, J. P., Stevens, D. G. and Bowen, C. V. (2000). Epiphyseal plate transplantation between sites of different growth potential. *Journal of Pediatric Orthopedics*, 20, 289–295.

Goff, D. J. and Tabin, C. J. (1997). Analysis of *Hoxd-13* and *Hoxd-11* misexpression in chick limb bud reveals that Hox genes affect both bone condensation and growth. *Development*, 124, 627–636.

Gonzalez-Martin, M. C., Mallo, M. and Ros, M. A. (2014). Long bone development requires a threshold of Hox function. *Developmental Biology*, 392, 454–465.

Gross, S., Krause, Y., Wuelling, M. and Vortkamp, A. (2012). Hoxa11 and Hoxd11 regulate chondrocyte differentiation upstream of Runx2 and Shox2 in mice. *PLoS ONE*, 7, e43553.

Guenther, C., Pantalena-Filho, L. and Kingsley, D. M. (2008). Shaping skeletal growth by modular regulatory elements in the *Bmp5* gene. *PLoS Genetics*, 4, e1000308.

Haines, R. W. (1942). The evolution of epiphyses and of endochondral bone. *Biological Review*, 17, 276–292.

Haines, R. W. (1969). Epiphyses and sesamoids. *In:* Gans, C. (ed.) *Biology of Reptilia*. New York, NY: Academic Press.

Hallgrimsson, B. and Lieberman, D. E. (2008). Mouse models and the evolutionary developmental biology of the skull. *Integrative Comparative Biology*, 48, 373–384.

Hallgrimsson, B., Willmore, K. and Hall, B. K. (2002). Canalization, developmental stability, and morphological integration in primate limbs. *American Journal of Physical Anthropology*, Suppl. 35, 131–158.

Hamrick, M. W. (1999). A chondral modeling theory revisited. *Journal of Theoretical Biology*, 201, 201–298.

Helal, B. (1978). Chronic overuse injuries of the piso-triquetral joint in racquet game players. *British Journal of Sports Medicine*, 12, 195–198.

Hendrikse, J. L., Parsons, T. E. and Hallgrimsson, B. (2007). Evolvability as the proper focus of evolutionary developmental biology. *Evolution and Development*, 9, 393–401.

Hilton, M. J., Tu, X., Cook, J., Hu, H. and Long, F. (2005). Ihh controls cartilage development by antagonizing Gli3, but requires additional effectors to regulate osteoblast and vascular development. *Development*, 132, 4339–4351.

Hlusko, L. J. (2004). Integrating the genotype and phenotype in hominid paleontology. *Proceedings of the National Academy of Sciences USA*, 101, 2653–2657.

Hunziker, E. B. (1994). Mechanism of longitudinal bone growth and its regulation by growth plate chondrocytes. *Microscopy Research and Technique*, 28, 505–519.

Izpisua-Belmonte, J. C., Falkenstein, H., Dolle, P., Renucci, A. and Duboule, D. (1991). Murine genes related to the *Drosophila* AbdB homeotic genes are sequentially expressed during development of the posterior part of the body. *EMBO Journal*, 10, 2279–2289.

Jameson, B. H., Rayan, G. M. and Acker, R. E. (2002). Radiographic analysis of pisotriquetral joint and pisiform motion. *Journal of Hand Surgery American*, 27, 863–869.

Johnson, R. L. and Tabin, C. J. (1997). Molecular models for vertebrate limb development. *Cell*, 90, 979–990.

Jouffroy, F. K. (1991). La "Main Sans Talon" du primate bipéde. *In:* Coppens, Y. (ed.) *Origine(s) De La Bipedie Chez Les Hominides.* Paris: Centre National de la Recherch Scientifique.

Kent, W. J., Sugnet, C. W., Furey, T. S., *et al.* (2002). The human genome browser at UCSC. *Genome Research*, 12, 996–1006.

Kivell, T. L. and Begun, D. R. (2007). Frequency and timing of scaphoid–centrale fusion in hominoids. *Journal of Human Evolution*, 52, 321–340.

Kjosness, K. M., Hines, J. E., Lovejoy, C. O. and Reno, P. L. (2014). The pisiform growth plate is lost in humans and supports a role for Hox in growth plate formation. *Journal of Anatomy*, 225, 527–538.

Klement, B. J. and Spooner, B. S. (1992). Endochondral bone formation in embryonic mouse premetatarsals. *Transactions of the Kansas Academy of Science*, 95, 39–44.

Kobayashi, T., Chung, U. I., Schipani, E., *et al.* (2002). PTHrP and Indian hedgehog control differentiation of growth plate chondrocytes at multiple steps. *Development*, 129, 2977–2986.

Kobayashi, T., Soegiarto, D. W., Yang, Y., *et al.* (2005). Indian hedgehog stimulates periarticular chondrocyte differentiation to regulate growth plate length independently of PTHrP. *Journal of Clinical Investigation*, 115, 1734–1742.

Koyama, E., Yasuda, T., Wellik, D. M. and Pacifici, M. (2010). *Hox11* paralogous genes are required for formation of wrist and ankle joints and articular surface organization. *Annals of the New York Academy of Science*, 1192, 307–316.

Koziel, L., Kunath, M., Kelly, O. G. and Vortkamp, A. (2004). Ext1-dependent heparan sulfate regulates the range of Ihh signaling during endochondral ossification. *Developmental Cell*, 6, 801–813.

Koziel, L., Wuelling, M., Schneider, S. and Vortkamp, A. (2005). Gli3 acts as a repressor downstream of Ihh in regulating two distinct steps of chondrocyte differentiation. *Development*, 132, 5249–5260.

Kriegs, J. O., Churakov, G., Kiefmann, M., *et al.* (2006). Retroposed elements as archives for the evolutionary history of placental mammals s. *PLoS Biology*, 4, e91.

Krumlauf, R. (1992). Evolution of the vertebrate Hox homeobox genes. *Bioessays*, 14, 245–252.

Krumlauf, R. (1994). Hox genes in vertebrate development. *Cell*, 78, 191–201.

Kuss, P., Kraft, K., Stumm, J., *et al.* (2014). Regulation of cell polarity in the cartilage growth plate and perichondrium of metacarpal elements by HOXD13 and WNT5A. *Developmental Biology*, 385, 83–93.

Lacroix, L. (1951). *The Organization of Bones.* Philadelphia, PA: The Blakiston Company.

Lanske, B., Karaplis, A. C., Lee, K., *et al.* (1996). PTH/PTHrP receptor in early development and Indian hedgehog-regulated bone growth. *Science*, 273, 663–666.

Lee, K., Deeds, J. D. and Segre, G. V. (1995). Expression of parathyroid hormone-related peptide and its receptor messenger ribonucleic acids during fetal development of rats. *Endocrinology*, 136, 453–463.

Lee, K., Lanske, B., Karaplis, A. C., *et al.* (1996). Parathyroid hormone-related peptide delays terminal differentiation of chondrocytes during endochondral bone development. *Endocrinology*, 137, 5109–5118.

Lefebvre, V., Behringer, R. R. and De Crombrugghe, B. (2001). L-Sox5, Sox6 and Sox9 control essential steps of the chondrocyte differentiation pathway. *Osteoarthritis and Cartilage*, 9A, S69–S75.

Lewis, O. J. (1972). Evolution of the hominoid wrist. *In:* Tuttle, R. H. (ed.) *The Functional and Evolutionary Biology of Primates.* Chicago, IL: Aldine-Atherdon.

Long, F. and Ornitz, D. M. (2013). Development of the endochondral skeleton. *Cold Spring Harbor Perspectives in Biology*, 5, a008334.

Long, F., Zhang, X. M., Karp, S., Yang, Y. and Mcmahon, A. P. (2001). Genetic manipulation of hedgehog signaling in the endochondral skeleton reveals a direct role in the regulation of chondrocyte proliferation. *Development*, 128, 5099–5108.

Lovejoy, C. O., Cohn, M. J. and White, T. D. (1999). Morphological analysis of the mammalian postcranium: a developmental perspective. *Procedings of the National Academy of Sciences USA*, 96, 13247–13252.

Maes, C. and Kronenberg, H. M. (2012). Postnatal bone growth: growth plate biology, bone formation, and remodeling. *In:* Glorieux, F., Pettifor, J. M. and Juppner, H. (eds.) *Pediatric Bone*, 2nd ed. Oxford: Elsevier.

Mann, R. S., Lelli, K. M. and Joshi, R. (2009). Hox specificity unique roles for cofactors and collaborators. *Current Topics in Developmental Biology*, 88, 63–101.

Marzke, M. W. (2010). Anthropology and comparative anatomy. *In:* Cooney, W. P. I. (ed.) *The Wrist. Diagnosis and Operative Treatment*, 2nd ed. Philadelphia, PA: Wolters Kluwer/Lippincott Williams and Wilkins.

Marzke, M. W., Toth, N., Schick, K., *et al.* (1998). EMG study of hand muscle recruitment during hard hammer percussion manufacture of Oldowan tools. *American Journal of Physical Anthropology*, 105, 315–332.

Mayr, E. (1963). *Animal Species and Evolution.* Cambridge, MA: Harvard University Press.

McLean, C. Y., Reno, P. L., Pollen, A. A., *et al.* (2011). Human-specific loss of regulatory DNA and the evolution of human-specific traits. *Nature*, 471, 216–219.

McMahon, A. P. (2000). More suprises in the Hedgehog signaling pathway. *Cell*, 100, 185–188.

Menke, D. B. (2013). Engineering subtle targeted mutations into the mouse genome. *Genesis*, 51, 605–618.

Menke, D. B., Guenther, C. and Kingsley, D. M. (2008). Dual hindlimb control elements in the *Tbx4* gene and region-specific control of bone size in vertebrate limbs. *Development*, 135, 2543–2553.

Minina, E., Wenzel, H. M., Kreschel, C., *et al.* (2001). BMP and Ihh/PTHrP signaling interact to coordinate chondrocyte proliferation and differentiation. *Development*, 128, 4523–4534.

Minina, E., Kreschel, C., Naski, M. C., Ornitz, D. M. and Vortkamp, A. (2002). Interaction of FGF, Ihh/Pthlh, and BMP signaling integrates chondrocyte proliferation and hypertrophic differentiation. *Developmental Cell*, 3, 439–449.

Moojen, T. M., Snel, J. G., Ritt, M. J., *et al.* (2001). Pisiform kinematics *in vivo*. *Jouranal of Hand Surgury American*, 26, 901–907.

Napier, J. R. and Davis, P. R. (1959). *The Fore-Limb Skeleton and Associated Remains of Proconsul Africanus.* London: British Museum (Natural History).

Nelson, C. E., Morgan, B. A., Burke, A. C., *et al.* (1996). Analysis of Hox gene expression in the chick limb bud. *Development*, 122, 1449–1466.

Nieto, M. A., Patel, K. and Wilkinson, D. G. (1996). *In situ* hybridization analysis of chick embryos in whole-mount and tissue sections. *In:* Bronner-Fraser, M. (ed.) *Methods in Avian Embryology.* San Diego, CA: Academic Press.

O'Bleness, M., Searles, V. B., Varki, A., Gagneux, P. and Sikela, J. M. (2012). Evolution of genetic and genomic features unique to the human lineage. *Nature Reviews in Genetics*, 13, 853–866.

Ogden, J. A., Grogan, D. P., Light, T. R., Albright, J. A. and Brand, R. A. (1987). Postnatal development and growth of the musculoskeletal system. *In: The Scientific Basis of Orthopaedics.* Norwalk, CN: Appleton and Lange.

Pareek, C. S., Smoczynski, R. and Tretyn, A. (2011). Sequencing technologies and genome sequencing. *Journal of Applied Genetics*, 52, 413–435.

Patel, B. A., Larson, S. G. and Stern, J. T., Jr. (2012). Electromyography of wrist and finger flexor muscles in olive baboons (*Papio anubis*). *Journal of Experimental Biology*, 215, 115–123.

Payton, C. G. (1932). The growth in length of the long bones in the madder-fed pig. *Journal of Anatomy*, 66, 414–425.

Pollard, K. S., Salama, S. R., Lambert, N., *et al.* (2006). An RNA gene expressed during cortical development evolved rapidly in humans. *Nature*, 443, 167–172.

Prabhakar, S., Noonan, J. P., Paabo, S. and Rubin, E. M. (2006). Accelerated evolution of conserved noncoding sequences in humans. *Science*, 314, 786.

Prabhakar, S., Visel, A., Akiyama, J. A., *et al.* (2008). Human-specific gain of function in a developmental enhancer. *Science*, 321, 1346–1350.

Reno, P. L. (2006). Ossification of the mammalian metatarsal: proliferation and differentiation in the presence/absence of a defined growth plate. Kent, OH: Kent State University. 155 pp.

Reno, P. L. (2014). Genetic and developmental basis for parallel evolution and its significance for hominoid evolution. *Evolutionary Anthropology*, 23, 188–200.

Reno, P. L. (2016). Evo–devo sheds light on mechanisms of human evolution: limb proportions and spines. *In:* Boughner, J. and Rolian, C. (eds.) *Evolutionary Developmental Anthropology: A Postgenomic Approach to Understanding Primate and Human Evolution.* Hoboken, NJ: Wiley-Blackwell, pp. 77–99.

Reno, P. L., McCollum, M. A., Lovejoy, C. O. and Meindl, R. S. (2000). Adaptationism and the anthropoid postcranium: selection does not govern the length of the radial neck. *Journal of Morphology*, 246, 59–67.

Reno, P. L., Degusta, D., Serrat, M. A., *et al.* (2005). Plio-pleistocene hominid limb proportions – evolutionary reversals or estimation errors? *Current Anthropology*, 46, 575–588.

Reno, P. L., McBurney, D. L., Lovejoy, C. O. and Horton, W. E. (2006). Ossification of the mouse metatarsal: differentiation and proliferation in the presence/absence of a defined growth plate. *Anatomical Record Part A – Discoveries in Molecular Cellular and Evolutionary Biology*, 288A, 104–118.

Reno, P. L., Horton, W. E., Elsey, R. M. and Lovejoy, C. O. (2007). Growth plate formation and development in alligator and mouse metapodials: evolutionary and functional implications. *Journal of Experimental Zoology Part B – Molecular and Developmental Evolution*, 308B, 283–296.

Reno, P. L., Horton, W. E., Jr. and Lovejoy, C. O. (2013). Metapodial or phalanx? An evolutionary and developmental perspective on the homology of the first ray's proximal segment. *Journal of Experimental Zoology Part B – Molecular and Developmental Evolution*, 320, 276–285.

Reno, P. L., Kjosness, K. M. and Hines, J. E. (2016). The role of Hox in pisiform and calcaneus growth plate formation and the nature of the zeugopod/autopod boundary. *Journal of Experimental Zoology Part B - Molecular and Developmental Evolution*, 326, 303–321.

Rolian, C. (2008). Developmental basis of limb length in rodents: evidence for multiple divisions of labor in mechanisms of endochondral bone growth. *Evolution and Development*, 10, 15–28.

Rolian, C. (2014). Genes, development, and evolvability in primate evolution. *Evolutionary Anthropology*, 23, 93–104.

Romereim, S. M. and Dudley, A. T. (2011). Cell polarity: the missing link in skeletal morphogenesis? *Organogenesis*, 7, 217–228.

Sears, K. E., Behringer, R. R., Rasweiler, J. J. T. and Niswander, L. A. (2007). The evolutionary and developmental basis of parallel reduction in mammalian zeugopod elements. *American Naturalist*, 169, 105–117.

Selleri, L., Depew, M. J., Jacobs, Y., *et al.* (2001). Requirement for Pbx1 in skeletal patterning and programming chondrocyte proliferation and differentiation. *Development*, 128, 3543–3557.

Semaw, S., Rogers, M. J., Quade, J., *et al.* (2003). 2.6-Million-year-old stone tools and associated bones from OGS-6 and OGS-7, Gona, Afar, Ethiopia. *Journal of Human Evolution*, 45, 169–177.

Serrat, M. A., Lovejoy, C. O. and King, D. (2007). Age- and site-specific decline in insulin-like growth factor-I receptor expression is correlated with differential growth plate activity in the mouse hindlimb. *Anatomical Record – Advances in Integrative Anatomy and Evolutionary Biology*, 290, 375–381.

Shapiro, M. D., Marks, M. E., Peichel, C. L., *et al.* (2004). Genetic and developmental basis of evolutionary pelvic reduction in threespine sticklebacks. *Nature*, 428, 717–723.

Small, K. M. and Potter, S. S. (1993). Homeotic transformations and limb defects in Hox A11 mutant mice. *Genes and Development*, 7, 2318–2328.

Smits, P., Dy, P., Mitra, S. and Lefebvre, V. (2004). Sox5 and Sox6 are needed to develop and maintain source, columnar, and hypertrophic chondrocytes in the cartilage growth plate. *Journal of Cell Biology*, 164, 747–758.

Spitz, F., Gonzalez, F. and Duboule, D. (2003). A global control region defines a chromosomal regulatory landscape containing the HoxD cluster. *Cell*, 113, 405–417.

Spitz, F., Herkenne, C., Morris, M. A. and Duboule, D. (2005). Inversion-induced disruption of the Hoxd cluster leads to the partition of regulatory landscapes. *Nature Genetics*, 37, 889–893.

St-Jacques, B., Hammerschmidt, M. and McMahon, A. P. (1999). Indian hedgehog signaling regulates proliferation and differentiation of chondrocytes and is essential for bone formation. *Genes and Development*, 13, 2072–2086.

Tarchini, B. and Duboule, D. (2006). Control of Hoxd genes' collinearity during early limb development. *Developmental Cell*, 10, 93–103.

Toth, N. and Schick, K. (2009). The Oldowan: the tool making of early hominins and chimpanzees compared. *Annual Review of Anthropology*, 38, 289–305.

Villavicencio-Lorini, P., Kuss, P., Friedrich, J., *et al.* (2010). Homeobox genes d11–d13 and a13 control mouse autopod cortical bone and joint formation. *Journal of Clinical Investigation*, 120, 1994–2004.

Vortkamp, A., Lee, K., Lanske, B., *et al.* (1996). Regulation of rate of cartilage differentiation by Indian hedgehog and PTH-related protein. *Science*, 273, 613–622.

Wagner, G. P. (1989). The origin of morphological characters and the biological basis of homology. *Evolution*, 43, 1157–1171.

Wagner, G. P. (2007). The developmental genetics of homology. *Nature Reviews in Genetics*, 8, 473–479.

Wellik, D. M. and Capecchi, M. R. (2003). *Hox10* and *Hox11* genes are required to globally pattern the mammalian skeleton. *Science*, 301, 363–367.

Wilsman, N. J., Farnum, C. E., Green, E. M., Lieferman, E. M. and Clayton, M. K. (1996a). Cell cycle analysis of proliferative zone chondrocytes in growth plates elongating at different rates. *Journal of Orthopaedic Research*, 14, 562–572.

Wilsman, N. J., Farnum, C. E., Leiferman, E. M., Fry, M. and Barreto, C. (1996b). Differential growth by growth plates as a function of multiple parameters of chondrocyte kinetics. *Journal of Orthopaedic Research*, 14, 927–936.

Wolpert, L. (1981). Cellular basis of growth during development. *British Medical Bulletin*, 37, 215–219.

Woltering, J. M. and Duboule, D. (2010). The origin of digits: expression patterns versus regulatory mechanisms. *Developmental Cell*, 18, 526–532.

Woltering, J. M., Noordermeer, D., Leleu, M. and Duboule, D. (2014). Conservation and divergence of regulatory strategies at Hox loci and the origin of tetrapod digits. *PLoS Biology*, 12, e1001773.

Yang, Y., Topol, L., Lee, H. and Wu, J. (2003). Wnt5a and Wnt5b exhibit distinct activities in coordinating chondrocyte proliferation and differentiation. *Development*, 130, 1003–1015.

Yokouchi, Y., Nakazato, S., Yamamoto, M., *et al.* (1995). Misexpression of Hoxa-13 induces cartilage homeotic transformation and changes in cell adhesiveness in chick limb buds. *Genes and Development*, 9, 2509–2522.

Yokouchi, Y., Sasaki, H. and Kuroiwa, A. (1991). Homeobox gene expression correlated with the bifurcation process of limb cartilage development. *Nature*, 353, 443–445.

Zakany, J. and Duboule, D. (2007). The role of Hox genes during vertebrate limb development. *Current Opinions in Genetics and Development*, 17, 359–366.

Zakany, J., Kmita, M. and Duboule, D. (2004). A dual role for Hox genes in limb anterior-posterior asymmetry. *Science*, 304, 1669–1672.

Zhao, Y. and Potter, S. S. (2001). Functional specificity of the *Hoxa13* homeobox. *Development*, 128, 3197–3207.

10 Ontogenetic and Genetic Influences on Bone's Responsiveness to Mechanical Signals

Ian J. Wallace, Brigitte Demes and Stefan Judex

10.1   Introduction

The human skeleton is able to alter its structure and strength throughout life in response to the loads it sustains during the physical activities to which we subject our bodies. Typically, skeletal loading shifts the balance in bone turnover toward net formation, which can lead to bigger, stronger bones, whereas decreased loading causes net resorption, which can result in more slender, fragile bones. This phenomenon, commonly referred to as "bone functional adaptation" (Ruff et al., 2006), has fascinated biologists and clinicians for well over a century (Wolff, 1892), for it is an exquisite example of the capacity of organisms to adjust to their environments (West-Eberhard, 2003), and harnessing the sensitivity of our skeletons to mechanical signals provides opportunities for promoting bone health and treating skeletal injuries and degenerative diseases (Ozcivici et al., 2010). The responsiveness of bone to loading is an ancient and widespread evolutionary trait among vertebrates, observable in animals as distantly related to humans as reptiles and birds (e.g., Rubin and Lanyon, 1984).

Biological anthropologists have long been interested in bone's responsiveness to loading, because if our bones are shaped by our physical activity, then it might be possible to infer the lifestyles of ancient human populations by analyzing their skeletal remains (Ruff, 2005). Ancient peoples characterized by thick, strong bones would be interpreted as having been highly active, whereas those with slender, gracile bones would be interpreted as having been more sedentary. Over the last few decades, this model has been the foundation for numerous reconstructions of past human behavior (e.g., Ruff et al., 1984, 1993, 2015; Bridges, 1989; Trinkaus, 1997; Holt, 2003; Marchi et al., 2006; Sládek et al., 2006; Maggiano et al., 2008; Shaw and Stock, 2013). Strong empirical support for this model has been provided by controlled experiments involving animal models such as sheep, pigs, rodents, and fowl that have demonstrated the potential for skeletal loading activities (e.g., running) to promote bone formation, retard bone loss, and, ultimately, enhance structure and strength (e.g., Biewener and Bertram, 1994; Lieberman, 1996; Judex et al., 1997; Lieberman et al., 2001, 2003; Joo et al., 2003; Hamrick et al., 2006; Barak et al., 2011). In addition, compelling evidence for a relationship between skeletal morphology and physical activity patterns in living humans is provided by controlled exercise interventions and studies of athletes documenting enhanced bone structure among individuals who frequently engage in skeletal loading activities (e.g., Daly, 2007; Shaw and Stock, 2009; Behringer *et al.*, 2013; Tan *et al.*, 2014; Warden *et al.*, 2014).

However, a number of anthropologists argue that, although mechanical signals engendered by physical activity affect skeletal structure and strength, this does not necessarily mean that activity patterns can be accurately inferred from human skeletal remains. Several issues have been raised, including the weak correspondence between bone structure and its *in vivo* loading environment (Demes *et al.*, 1998, 2001; Lieberman *et al.*, 2004; Schmitt *et al.*, 2010), the mechanical inefficiency of bone's functional response (i.e., bone formation stimulated by loading does not always occur in areas of the bone surface where mechanical integrity is most challenged) (Bertram and Swartz, 1991; Wallace *et al.*, 2014), and the large influence of genetic background on bone structure independent of functional loading (Lovejoy *et al.*, 2003; Morimoto *et al.*, 2011; Wallace *et al.*, 2012; see also Hrdlička, 1937). In this chapter, we discuss two additional issues that are especially critical, namely, the age-dependency of bone mechanoresponsiveness, and the role of genetics in modulating bone's responsivity to loading.

The chapter begins with a general description of bone's response to mechanical signals, from the organ level to the cellular and molecular levels. In this section, we review research on how bone recognizes its mechanical environment, and how mechanical cues are translated into cellular information affecting bone turnover. Then, we consider research documenting the effects of ontogeny on bone mechanoresponsiveness. Studies of both human and animal models have shown that mechanical signals are most anabolic during the growing years but their potency declines thereafter. Next, we discuss research on genetic regulation of bone mechanoresponsiveness. Currently, the most compelling evidence of genetically determined variation in responsivity comes from experiments with mouse models, particularly inbred strains and outbred stocks. Finally, we end by discussing the implications of this research for anthropological analyses of skeletal remains in which ancient human physical activity patterns are inferred based on bone structure.

10.2   Bone's Response to Loading

Bone's response to mechanical loading is complex, from the organ level, to the tissue level, to the cellular and molecular levels (Figure 10.1). At the organ level, bones are subjected to multiple modes of loading, including axial compression, axial tension, shear, bending, and torsion (Martin *et al.*, 1998). Not surprisingly, the magnitude of stresses endured by a bone during any given functional activity varies greatly according to the structural role of that bone in the activity (Lieberman, 1996) and the intensity of the activity (Rubin and Lanyon, 1982; Burr *et al.*, 1996). Under natural conditions, bones rarely experience a single type of loading, but instead sustain various combinations of loading modes. During striding legged

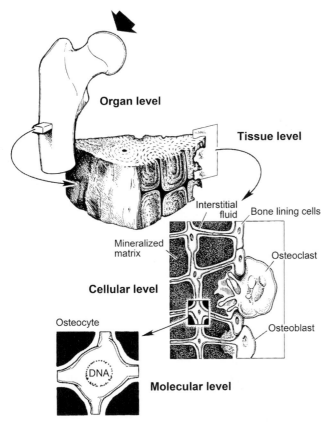

Figure 10.1 Mechanical forces affect bone on progressively smaller scales, from the organ level to the tissue level to the cellular and molecular levels. Figure modified from Rubin *et al.* (1990), and used with permission from Elsevier.

locomotion, for example, limb bones experience a superimposition of bending and axial compression (Rubin and Lanyon, 1982; Demes *et al.*, 1998, 2001; Lieberman *et al.*, 2004), and probably torsion as well (Demes *et al.*, 1998). As a result of this superimposition, dramatically non-uniform gradients of strain develop along limb bone longitudinal axes (Biewener *et al.*, 1986; Biewener and Bertram, 1993) and throughout their transverse cross sections (Rubin *et al.*, 2013).

Whole-bone loading exposes bone tissue to a barrage of biophysical signals including strain, pressure developed in intramedullary canals and within cortices with transient pressure waves, fluid flow through the network of lacunae and canaliculi within the bone matrix, dynamic electric fields, and oscillatory accelerations. Numerous studies have shown that many of these signals are independently able to modulate bone turnover (Thompson *et al.*, 2012). However, they are not mutually exclusive, and they all are generated simultaneously during skeletal loading. This cacophony of mechanical signals is further complicated by the fact that components of individual signals also influence bone turnover. For example, the effects of mechanical strain on bone tissue are known to be threshold-driven, such that certain degrees of strain must be achieved to stimulate a cellular response (Lanyon, 1987); however, a response can be triggered by alterations in several parameters of the strain signal, including the temporal variation of strain (Lanyon and Rubin, 1984), the number of strain cycles (Rubin and Lanyon, 1984), the novelty of strain conditions (Lanyon, 1992), as well as strain magnitude (Rubin and Lanyon, 1985), rate (O'Connor et al., 1982), distribution (Judex et al., 1997), and frequency (Rubin et al., 2001). The cellular response to loading also depends on the timing of sequential loading events, where brief refractory periods between events can enhance the anabolic potential of loading (Srinivasan et al., 2007).

Bone cells are tightly coupled to the extracellular tissue matrix and, therefore, biophysical signals induced at the cellular level depend on tissue-level behavior (Jacobs et al., 2010), as well as the precise location of the cells within the tissue matrix (Rubin et al., 2013). Most tissue-level mechanical signals result in deformation at the cellular level, although it is unclear if deformation per se is what triggers the cellular response (Jacobs et al., 2010). At least four types of cells are involved in bone's response to loading: bone-destroying osteoclasts derived from hematopoietic stem cells, bone-forming osteoblasts derived from mesenchymal stem cells, matrix-embedded osteocytes derived from osteoblasts, and osteoprogenitor cells (i.e., pre-osteoblasts and preosteoclasts). Many researchers envision a clear division of labor among these cells such that osteocytes are the primary sensory cells and osteoblasts and osteoclasts are effector cells (e.g., Burger and Klein-Nulend, 1999; Bonewald, 2006; Jacobs et al., 2010). However, workers have demonstrated that all four cell types are sensitive to mechanical signals, so isolating the critical sensory cell is difficult (Thompson et al., 2012). Nevertheless, osteocytes are particularly well situated to perceive load-generated signals and orchestrate a coordinated response among cells. Osteocytes are distributed throughout the bone matrix in lacunae and network with other osteocytes, osteoblasts, and bone-lining cells by long cytoplasmic processes that occupy canaliculi containing interstitial fluid, enabling intercellular communication through gap junctions between processes, as well as extracellular communication by fluid flow (Riddle and Donahue, 2009). Furthermore, the microarchitecture of both osteocyte processes and lacunae have been suggested to promote the amplification of relatively small tissue-level mechanical signals to ranges that can be sensed by cell bodies (Han et al., 2004; Nicolella et al., 2006).

Several mechanisms by which bone cells may perceive mechanical signals have been proposed, most of which involve force-induced changes in protein configuration (Jacobs et al., 2010; Thompson et al., 2012). Mechanical loads that cause cell deformation will inevitably disrupt the structure of the intracellular cytoskeleton, making cytoskeletal proteins logical candidate mechanosensors (Wang et al., 1993). Membrane-spanning integrins and integrin-associated proteins are also possible mechanosensors, as they link the cytoskeleton to the extracellular matrix and regulate signaling pathways (Wang et al., 2007; Litzenberger et al., 2010). Other trans-membrane proteins are altered by mechanical stimulation, including ion channels and connexin hemichannels, which may also represent incipient molecular mechanotransduction events (Duncan, 1998; Batra and Jiang, 2012). Plasma membrane dynamics provide another possible mechanosensory mechanism through the organization of lipid raft microdomains with the ability to coordinate interactions between regulatory molecules that result in signaling cascades (Simons and Toomre, 2000; Rubin *et al.*, 2007). Much recent work has been devoted to understanding the mechanosensory role of primary cilia, antenna-like structures that extend from cell surfaces (Hoey *et al.*, 2012). Deflections or perturbations of cilia result in increased membrane tension, which may open mechanosensitive membrane channels (Kwon *et al.*, 2011). In all likelihood, the response of bone cells to mechanical signals is defined by multiple mechanoreceptors acting in concert.

Mechanical signals perceived by mechanosensors must be translated into biochemical signals to induce expression of genes that encode proteins involved in bone cell differentiation, proliferation, and survival (RUNX2, COX-2, osteonectin, osteocalcin, osterix, sclerostin, RANK-L, etc.). Numerous mechanically mediated intracellular signaling cascades have been implicated in bone mechanotransduction (Thompson *et al.*, 2012). Some of the better characterized of these include activation of β-catenin (Case and Rubin, 2010), protein kinase signaling (Liu *et al.*, 2008), calcium signaling (Hung *et al.*, 1995), and signaling mediated by G-proteins (Arnsdorf *et al.*, 2009). A coordinated response among cells also requires intercellular signaling. Several cell-to-cell pathways have been proposed that either are activated by, or mediate, mechanical signals (Jacobs *et al.*, 2010). Gap junctions formed between neighboring osteocytes and osteoblasts by alignment of transmembrane connexons provide a critical avenue through which cells can communicate (Yellowley *et al.*, 2000). Two particularly well-studied intermediaries for intercellular communication are nitric oxide and the eicosinoids, prostaglandin and prostacyclin, the release of both of which has been shown to be stimulated by mechanical signals (Rawlinson *et al.*, 1991, 1995; Klein-Nulend *et al.*, 1995) and affect the osteogenic potential of loading (Forwood, 1996; Turner *et al.*, 1996).

10.3   Age-dependency of Bone Responsivity

Human exercise intervention studies have shown that the effects of mechanical loading on the skeleton vary from person to person (e.g., Dalsky *et al.*, 1988; Snow-Harter *et al.*, 1992). The degree of bone loss associated with skeletal unloading (bed rest, spaceflight) has also frequently been observed to vary between individuals (e.g., Laugier *et al.*, 2000; Vico *et al.*, 2000). These studies underscore the fact that the responsiveness of an individual's bone to mechanical signals depends on a number of non-mechanical factors.

Age, in particular, has a strong effect on bone's responsivity to mechanical signals, such that the anabolic potential of loading peaks during the growing years and diminishes thereafter (see Pearson and Lieberman, 2004, for an excellent overview; also see Chapter 7 for a review of mechanical influences on the epiphyseal growth plate). Abundant evidence exists demonstrating that human physical activity during growth promotes bone mass accrual and enhances overall bone strength (Daly, 2007; Behringer *et al.*, 2013; Tan *et al.*, 2014). A recent systematic review of randomized controlled interventions and observational studies demonstrated that exercise augments bone strength in children and adolescents primarily through improvements in periosteal expansion and the geometric components of structural resistance to loading (Tan *et al.*, 2014). For example, in a 16-month prospective study by Macdonald and others (2009), in which young boys (aged 9–11 years) engaged in a school-based exercise program comprised of jumping, skipping, dancing, and playground circuits, positive change during the trial period in tibial shaft second moments of area (a proxy for diaphyseal bending strength) was significantly greater in the exercise group compared with a control group. In contrast, controlled studies of the effects of physical activity on the mature and senescent human skeleton most often fail to reveal skeletal augmentation (Srinivasan *et al.*, 2012). In the rare studies of elderly individuals in which modest positive effects of exercise for bone are detected, they result from a slowing of the rate of normal age-related endocortical bone loss and provide little benefit to overall structural strength (Srinivasan *et al.*, 2012). For example, in a one-year randomized, controlled intervention trial of elderly women (aged 70–78 years) by Karinkanta and colleagues (2007) investigating the skeletal effects of an exercise regimen involving strength, balance, agility, and jumping training, tibial shaft strength decreased over the trial period in both women who trained and those who did not, but the decline was roughly 2% less in the intervention group.

Underlying age-related degradation in bone adaptability to loading are alterations in bone cell numbers (i.e., declining density of osteocytes and osteoblasts), and alterations in cellular function, including attenuated mechanical stimulation of bone cells and changes in load-activated signaling pathways (Srinivasan *et al.*, 2012), as well as changes in extracellular matrix quality (Vashishth, 2007). Aging is associated with a decrease in bone mineral surface-to-volume ratio and an increase in interstitial fluid viscosity, which could reduce the velocity of load-induced fluid flow and likewise the magnitude of biophysical signals directed at bone cells (Rubin *et al.*, 1992). In terms of signaling pathways, age-related alterations have been documented in load-induced activation of second messengers such as calcium (Donahue *et al.*, 2001), activation of kinases downstream of second messengers (Pahlavani and Vargas, 2000), and, even further downstream, activation and DNA binding of transcription factors such as Wnt/β-catenin (Manolagas and Almeida, 2007). In addition, ontogenetic changes in bone's responsiveness to loading may be affected by age-related alterations in levels of circulating hormones (Devlin, 2011). For example, the periosteal osteogenic response to loading during youth is evidently enhanced by the rise in estrogen around the time of puberty (Devlin *et al.*, 2010; see also Devlin and Lieberman, 2007), whereas decreased bone adaptability during adulthood might be exacerbated by the rapid drop in estrogen following female menopause (Lanyon *et al.*, 2004).

Several experiments involving animal models have also demonstrated degradation in bone's responsiveness to loading from growth to adulthood. For example, in an influential study by Rubin and coworkers (1992), exogenous mechanical loads (axial compression) were applied to ulnae of juvenile and adult turkeys for 8 weeks, and the effects of loading were assessed relative to non-loaded contralateral ulnae. In the juvenile group, loading significantly increased periosteal bone formation and led to greater diaphyseal bone quantity. However, in the adult group, loading had little effect on bone turnover or shaft morphology. Another particularly convincing experiment is that of Lieberman and colleagues (2001, 2003), who analyzed the skeletal effects of 3 months of treadmill exercise (30 min/day) in juvenile, subadult, and adult sheep. In the juveniles, animals treated with exercise-loading were found to have significantly enhanced periosteal bone formation in both the femur and tibia and greater diaphyseal polar moments of area (i.e., average shaft bending strength) relative to age-matched controls (Figure 10.2). In the subadults, the skeletal benefits of exercise were less than those observed in the juveniles, and in the adults, no significant improvements in bone formation or diaphyseal strength were detected.

There is currently some controversy in the animal model literature over whether bone mechanoresponsiveness diminishes progressively throughout adulthood into older age or remains stable after its decline following growth. Some animal

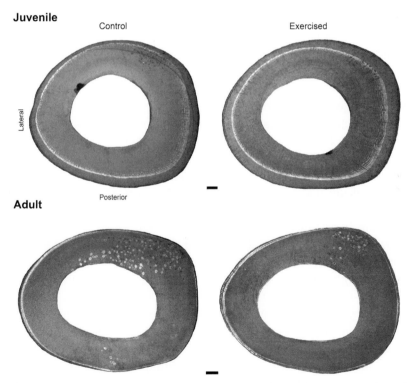

Figure 10.2 Tibial mid-diaphyseal cross sections. Within each age group, the sedentary control sheep and the exercised sheep had similar body masses throughout the experiment. Calcein labels injected after the first week of the 90-day exercise treatment are visible as the light gray rings within the sections and illustrate the periosteal bone added throughout the experiment. Scales = 1 mm. Images courtesy of Daniel Lieberman.

experiments have observed further diminishment in adaptability between early/middle adulthood and senescence (e.g., Turner *et al.*, 1995; Srinivasan *et al.*, 2003), but others have found little change with advanced aging (Brodt and Silva, 2010), and even enhanced sensitivity during old age (Leppänen *et al.*, 2008). Leppänen and colleagues (2008) subjected skeletally mature and senescent rats to treadmill running and found that hind limb bone structure and strength were significantly enhanced by exercise in senescent animals but not mature animals. However, the bones of senescent animals were structurally weaker at the beginning of the exercise treatment, so running presumably engendered greater strains in their bones compared to those of mature animals, which may explain their greater bony response to loading. In other words, the distinct responses observed between the two groups may not have been due to age-related differences in bone tissue mechanosensitivity per se. To circumvent this potentially confounding issue, Brodt and Silva (2010) applied exogenous (supraphysiological) axial compressive loads to tibiae of mature and aged BALB/c inbred mice, which produced similar levels of strain in their diaphyses, and found that loading had a similar positive effect on periosteal bone formation in the two groups. In contrast, Srinivasan *et al.* (2003) observed that diaphyseal cortical bone formation stimulated by exogenous tibial bending was 2.5-fold less in aged C57BL/B6 inbred mice than mature C57BL/B6 mice, despite the fact that loading engendered similar strains in the diaphyses of the two groups. The difference in the results obtained by Srinivasan *et al.* (2003) using C57BL/B6 mice and by Brodt and Silva (2010) using BALB/c mice is intriguing and may indicate that the effects of aging on bone mechanoresponsiveness vary according to an individual's genetic background.

An important issue related to the age-dependency of mechanical influences on the skeleton is the degree to which adult morphology reflects behavior when young. A limited number of early studies suggested that bone gains from youth activity are lost in adulthood (e.g., Karlsson *et al.*, 2000). However, there is now compelling evidence that loading-induced bone enhancement achieved during growth can be preserved into adulthood, although bone gains will erode to some degree if individuals do not remain physically active (Forwood, 2013). This was nicely illustrated in a recent study by Warden and colleagues (2014), who analyzed differences in humeral diaphyseal bone size and strength between the throwing and non-throwing arms of young professional baseball players and former players who had retired from the sport. Throwing activities nearly doubled humeral diaphyseal strength in young active players, but strength gradually diminished into adulthood after throwing activities ceased. However, half of bone size and one-third of bone strength gains were maintained lifelong, decades after the end of the players' active careers. In players that continued throwing during aging, the loss in bone size and strength was less pronounced. Results consistent with these, showing retention of exercise-induced bone structural benefits from youth into adulthood, have also been provided by studies of competitive racquet sports players (e.g., Haapasalo *et al.*, 2000; Kontulainen *et al.*, 2001). Together, these studies demonstrate that a physical activity signal remains evident in skeletal morphology potentially long after cessation of that activity, at least in the case of extreme bone-loading activities such as professional athletics.

10.4 Genetic Regulation of Bone Responsivity

Although human skeletal morphology is clearly influenced by mechanical signals, it is also controlled to a large degree by the genome, a fact underscored by the generally high heritability estimates reported for many bone structural traits. For example, for limb bone shaft size – a trait of interest in many investigations of past human activity – genetic factors have been estimated to account for 25% to over 50% of the morphological diversity within living human populations (e.g., Demissie et al., 2007; Havill et al., 2007). Over the last two decades, linkage studies and human genome-wide association studies have identified numerous genes and genetic loci harboring polymorphisms that affect skeletal structure and strength (Richards et al., 2012), often in a sex- and site-specific manner (Ioannidis et al., 2007). One way in which these alleles exert their influence on the skeleton is by regulating the responsiveness of bone to mechanical signals (Bonjour et al., 2007).

Current knowledge of the precise alleles that affect human bone morphology by modulating mechanotransduction is rather limited, but some candidate alleles have been proposed (e.g., Tajima et al., 2000; Dhamrait et al., 2003; Suuriniemi et al., 2004; Liu et al., 2008; Saxon et al., 2011; Wesselius et al., 2011). Instead, at this time, the most compelling evidence for the influence of genetic variation on bone mechanoresponsiveness comes from research involving mice. Animal models are critical for experimentally defining the genetic regulation of bone mechanotransduction, and mice have become the gold standard for such research because their genetic history and mechanical environments can be strictly controlled. Furthermore, the genes and molecular pathways affecting the skeleton are highly conserved in mice and humans (Karsenty, 2003) and the skeletal response to altered mechanical signals is often observed to be similar in the two species (e.g., Luu et al., 2009).

The vast majority of mouse experiments investigating the influence of the genome on bone functional adaptation have employed inbred strains. Inbred strains are closed populations of genetically identical animals that are bred to maintain homozygosity (Beck et al., 2000). Thus, genetic differences between inbred strains are due to specific allelic differences, similar to the genetic differences between individual humans. Two particular strains have been especially common in bone mechanotransduction research, and, indeed, in biomedical research in general, namely, C3H/HeJ (C3H) and C57BL/6J (B6). In one particularly elegant study, to examine bone mechanoresponsiveness in C3H and B6 mice, Robling and Turner (2002) applied exogenous mechanical loads (axial compression) to ulnae of animals from the two strains. The responsiveness of C3H ulnae was found to be lower in two independent parameters. First, C3H mice required relatively more mechanical strain in their ulnar diaphyses before bone formation was triggered. Second, once the bone-formation threshold was surpassed in C3H ulnae, the increase in bone formation per unit increase of mechanical strain was significantly less than that in B6 mice, and therefore equal changes in suprathreshold strain did not result in equal changes in bone formation between C3H and B6 mice. Findings consistent with these were obtained by Akhter and colleagues (1998), who subjected tibiae of C3H and B6 mice to four-point bending and found that load-induced bone formation was significantly higher in B6 mice than in C3H mice. Similarly, in a study by Kodama *et al.* (2000), C3H and B6 mice were treated with 4 weeks of jumping exercise, which significantly increased cortical area and periosteal bone formation in B6 tibiae (relative to unexercised controls), but no effects of exercise were detected in C3H tibiae. In addition, Judex *et al.* (2002) found that trabecular bone quantity and quality in proximal tibiae of B6 mice, but not C3H mice, were significantly enhanced by low-level mechanical vibration. Together, these studies nicely demonstrate the importance of an individual's particular allelic complement in defining bone mechanoresponsiveness.

Subsequent investigations were aimed at identifying specific regions of the mouse genome harboring polymorphisms responsible for regulating bone mechanotransduction. Kesavan and colleagues (2006) used tibial four-point bending to stimulate bone formation in an F2 population derived from the intercross of C3H and B6 strains. Quantitative trait loci (QTLs) for bone mechanoresponsiveness were then identified by interval mapping on six different chromosomes. Robling and colleagues (2003, 2007) applied exogenous ulnar loads to strains of congenic mice to examine the contribution of four QTLs to regulating bone mechanotransduction. Four congenic strains were created by moving the particular QTLs from C3H onto a B6 background by repeated backcrossing. They found that the responsiveness of each of these strains was significantly different from that of B6 controls, with some strains exhibiting reduced sensitivity and others enhanced sensitivity. Differences in responsiveness were manifest as changes in minimum level of strain required to initiate osteogenesis and/or the ability to form bone per unit of mechanical strain. Together, these results show that bone mechanotransduction is mediated by several gene polymorphisms, which theoretically increases the potential for interindividual variability in bone mechanoresponsiveness.

The interaction between genetics and mechanical signals has also been explored in studies that exposed inbred mice to skeletal unloading. For example, consistent with loading investigations, comparisons of bone's response to unloading have been made between C3H and B6 strains and have shown that both sciatic neurectomy (Kodama *et al.*, 1999) and hind limb unloading through tail suspension (Amblard *et al.*, 2003; Judex *et al.*, 2004) induce greater cortical and trabecular bone loss in B6 mice than C3H mice. Additional studies of inbred mice have identified many QTLs influencing bone's response to unloading and, interestingly, such genomic regions have been found to exhibit little overlap with those known to influence bone's loading response (Judex *et al.*, 2013), further underscoring the complexity of genetic influences on the relationship between bone structure and mechanical signals.

For clinicians, the implications of interindividual variation in bone mechanoresponsivity demonstrated by studies of inbred mice are clear. It partly explains differences among humans in individual rates of bone gain observed in exercise-based interventions and bone loss during spaceflight or bed rest. More generally, it supports the trend towards personalized medicine. From an anthropological perspective, however, the contribution of genetics to shaping interindividual variation in bone's responsivity to loading is arguably less relevant because attempts to reconstruct the physical activity patterns of particular individuals are relatively rare (e.g., Trinkaus *et al.*, 1998), while it is far more common to use samples of skeletal remains to gain insight into behavioral differences between populations (e.g., Ruff *et al.*, 1984; Bridges, 1989; Marchi *et al.*, 2006; Sládek *et al.*, 2006; Maggiano *et al.*, 2008). Therefore, what is perhaps most relevant is the importance of genetics in determining populational variation in bone mechanoresponsiveness.

Because the vast majority of genetic diversity among humans (> 80%) is accounted for by within-population variation (Li *et al.*, 2008), and there is currently limited evidence that alleles affecting bone mechanoresponsiveness are biased toward the small fraction of genetic diversity that is explained by between-population variation (Styrkarsdottir *et al.*, 2010), it is not unreasonable to expect that genetic differences could play a reduced role in affecting skeletal variation between populations than within populations. If so, anthropological analyses that statistically test for populational differences in skeletal morphology relative to within-population variation might be fairly immune to the potentially confounding effects of genetic background on bone mechanoresponsiveness, assuming that sample sizes are sufficiently large.

Nevertheless, a recent study by Meiring and colleagues (2013) suggests that some variation in bone adaptability to loading may indeed exist between certain human populations (e.g., ethnic groups). Previous studies had shown that people of African ancestry tend to have more robust bone structure relative to individuals of European ancestry (Danielson *et al.*, 2013), even during early childhood (Wetzsteon *et al.*, 2011), and that structural differences between these groups relate, at least in part, to genetic differences between Africans and Europeans (Chen *et al.*, 2011). Thus, a reasonable hypothesis is that one way in which gene polymorphisms affect bone structural differences is by enabling the bones of Africans to be more responsive to loading (e.g., Robling and Turner, 2002). Meiring and coworkers (2013) investigated this potential interaction between ethnicity and physical activity on bone structure in a population of pre-/early pubertal black and white South Africans. Individuals were classified according to self-reported physical activity levels over the previous two years as being either highly active or more sedentary. Meiring and colleagues (2013) found that in the low-activity group, black children had significantly larger tibial shafts and greater femoral neck mineral content than did white children. However, no significant differences were detected between ethnic groups in the high-activity group. Among whites, children in the high-activity group had enhanced bone structure relative to their sedentary counterparts, but a similar effect of activity was not observed in black children. Therefore, based on these results, it appears that the bones of white children are in fact more responsive to loading, contrary to expectations. Nevertheless, these findings support the basic idea that bone mechanoresponsiveness can vary at the population level.

Recent research in our laboratory involving outbred mice has provided additional evidence for interpopulation variation in bone mechanoresponsivity (Wallace, 2013; Wallace *et al.*, 2015). By definition, an outbred stock is a closed population of genetically variable animals that is bred to maintain maximum heterozygosity (Chia *et al.*, 2005). Therefore, in outbred mouse stocks, as in human populations, individual animals are genetically heterogeneous, and no two animals are genotypically or phenotypically identical. Commercial mouse breeders maintain large closed populations of outbred mice consisting of several thousand animals per population that have accumulated numerous recombination events. In our recent studies, mice have been employed from two particular commercially available outbred stocks, Hsd:ICR (ICR) and Crl:CD1 (CD1). These stocks were chosen for analysis because their ancestry is especially well documented (Chia *et al.*, 2005; Yalcin *et al.*, 2010) and their genetic architecture displays important similarities to human populations (Aldinger *et al.*, 2009; Yalcin *et al.*, 2010). ICR and CD1 mice have been reproductively isolated for well over 120 generations, which would correspond in humans to at least ~3,400 years of genetic separation (Fenner, 2005). Genetic isolation has led to clear population stratification that is comparable to that of human groups (Aldinger *et al.*, 2009). For example, *Fst*, a measure of genetic diversity between populations, is approximately 0.11 for the ICR and CD1 stocks (Jonathan Flint, personal communication, 2013; from data in Yalcin *et al.*, 2010), whereas closely related human populations typically exhibit values less than 0.05 (Reich *et al.*, 2009), meaning that allele frequency differentiation between ICR and CD1 mice is at least as great as that between many human groups. Average heterozygosity in both stocks is approximately 0.30 (Yalcin *et al.*, 2010), which is well within the range of human populations (Conrad *et al.*, 2006).

To examine the degree to which genetic differences between ICR and CD1 populations influence bone's responsiveness to loading, we conducted an experiment in which growing female mice from each stock were either treated with an exercise regimen for four weeks or served as sedentary controls (n = 20 animals/stock/activity group). A detailed description of the experiment can be found elsewhere (Wallace, 2013). The experiment began shortly after weaning when animals were four weeks of age. The exercise regimen consisted of 30 minutes of treadmill running at a rate of 12 m/min for 5 days/week. Home-cage activity was monitored in all animals during the experimental period using a system equipped with infrared sensor technology; and limb forces were measured with a force plate to verify that they were similar between stocks. After the experiment, animals were euthanized, tibiae were extracted, and cortical and trabecular bone structure was quantified with micro-CT in the mid-diaphysis and proximal metaphysis, respectively. In addition, diaphyseal structural strength was determined by loading tibiae in three-point bending to failure using a mechanical testing machine.

Among the ICR mice, running was found to result in significant improvements in tibial diaphyseal bone quantity, structural geometry, and mechanical properties, as well as enhanced trabecular morphology (Figure 10.3). In contrast, however, among the CD1 mice, the same running regimen had little effect on either tibial cortical

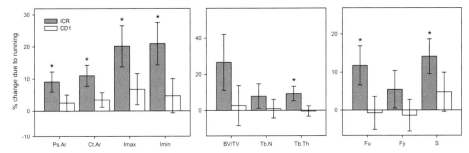

Figure 10.3 Relative difference in tibial bone parameters between controls and runners among ICR and CD1 mice. Left: mid-diaphyseal cortical bone structural parameters. Middle: proximal metaphyseal trabecular bone structural parameters. Right: diaphyseal mechanical properties. Bars equal the percent difference between the runner mean relative to the control mean. Whiskers equal the standard deviation of the sampling distribution of the relative difference. Asterisks indicate statistically significant ($p < 0.05$) differences between activity groups determined by independent-samples t-tests. Ps.Ar, periosteal area; Ct.Ar, cortical area; Imax, maximum second moments of area; Imin, minimum second moments of area; BV/TV, bone volume fraction; Tb.N, trabecular number; Tb.Th, trabecular thickness; Fu, ultimate force; Fy, yield force; S, stiffness.

and trabecular structure or diaphyseal mechanical properties. For example, while exercise treatment led to an average increase of 11% in diaphyseal cortical area among ICR mice, a bone quantity gain of only 3% was detected among CD1 runners relative to controls. In addition, while ICR runners exhibited a 12% increase in the ultimate bending strength of their tibiae, the breaking strength of CD1 runners' tibiae was actually reduced by 1% compared to controls. Importantly, in neither stock was body mass, limb muscle mass, or cage activity level different between runners and controls. Given that most environmental variables were controlled in the experiment, the differential effects of exercise on ICR and CD1 bones can reasonably be assumed to be due to genetic differences between stocks. Therefore, if extrapolation of these data to humans is warranted, then the results suggest that the effects of physical activity on human bone structure and strength cannot be assumed to be the same across different populations (e.g., ethnic groups). Just as the skeletal benefits of mechanical loading can vary from one individual to the next, as demonstrated by inbred mouse experiments, this experiment with outbred mice provides compelling evidence that skeletal adaptability may also vary from population to population.

10.5 Anthropological Implications

The foregoing discussion of bone's response to loading highlights the complexity of the process and its tendency to vary between individuals according to the age at which loading occurs and genetic background. These aspects of bone functional adaptation would seem to greatly undermine the accuracy of anthropological inferences about ancient human physical activity based on skeletal remains. There is clearly a window of opportunity that exists during the growing years when the potential positive influence of loading on bone structure and strength is greatest (see Chapter 12 for evidence that ontogenetic changes in human bone material properties vary between bones under different loading conditions). Adult bones are much less responsive to loading than growing bones, which means that any functional signal present in adult bone morphology is primarily the result of childhood activity (Pearson and Lieberman, 2004). Thus, a researcher's ability to infer anything about adult activity from bone structure is evidently limited. Furthermore, because of genetic influences on bone mechanoresponsiveness, it is possible for the magnitude of the functional signal to vary in the bones of different individuals despite identical physical activity patterns during life (Wallace *et al.*, 2015). Two populations with similar bone structure may have exhibited dramatic differences in activity levels during life; and a population with gracile bones may have actually been more physically active than a population characterized by more robust bone structure. This complexity is inconvenient, but it is unavoidable and should be carefully considered when skeletal remains are used to reconstruct past human physical activity. Alas, skeletal morphology may indeed emit a signal related to functional loading history, but our ability to decipher this functional signal amidst the noise caused by other determinants of bone structure is limited.

Moving forward, a major challenge for anthropologists will be to regard ontogenetic and genetic influences on bone mechanoresponsiveness as more than just variables that confound reconstructions of past human behavior, but as potential sources of novel hypotheses that we should aim to test (Wallace *et al.*, 2010). A nice example of such a hypothesis is Martin and colleagues' (1998) suggestion, made nearly two decades ago, that the skeletal hyper-robusticity characteristic of Neanderthals might not simply reflect extreme high levels of activity, but instead genetic differences from modern humans related to greater bone responsivity to loading. Now, in the age of paleogenetics, we might soon be able to rigorously evaluate this idea. Indeed, it has already been shown that the Neanderthal genome differs from that of modern humans in a region harboring the gene *RUNX2* (Green *et al.*, 2010), which is known to affect skeletal physiology in a variety of ways (Karsenty *et al.*, 2009), including in the regulation of bone's response to mechanical signals (Salingcarnboriboon *et al.*, 2006; Ziros *et al.*, 2008). Multiple *RUNX2* polymorphisms and their influence on human skeletal physiology have been identified (Vaughan *et al.*, 2004; Doecke *et al.*, 2006), and additional allelic variants will likely be discovered. If future studies can determine the precise differences in *RUNX2* between Neanderthals and modern humans, and the effects of *RUNX2* polymorphisms continue to become better understood, then it might not be long before we can make sound statements about how genetically mediated differences in bone mechanoresponsivity may, or may not, have influenced Neanderthal skeletal morphology. Ultimately, in broadening our perspective on bone mechanobiology and our scope of inquiry, anthropologists have great potential to make a significant contribution to enhancing understanding of the complex ways in which human behavior has shaped the evolution of our skeletons.

References

Akhter, M. P., Cullen, D. M., Pedersen, E. A., Kimmel, D. B. and Recker, R. R. (1998). Bone response to *in vivo* mechanical loading in two breeds of mice. *Calcified Tissue International*, 63, 442–449.

Aldinger, K. A., Sokoloff, G., Rosenberg, D. M., Palmer, A. A. and Millen, K. J. (2009). Genetic variation and population substructure in outbred CD-1 mice: implications for genome-wide association studies. *PLoS ONE*, 4, e4729.

Amblard, D., Lafage-Proust, M. H., Laib, A., *et al.* (2003). Tail suspension induces bone loss in skeletally mature mice in the C57BL/6J strain but not in the C3H/HeJ strain. *Journal of Bone and Mineral Research*, 18, 561–569.

Arnsdorf, E. J., Tummala, P., Kwon, R. Y. and Jacobs, C. R. (2009). Mechanically induced osteogenic differentiation – the role of RhoA, ROCKII and cytoskeletal dynamics. *Journal of Cell Science*, 122, 546–553.

Barak, M. M., Lieberman, D. E. and Hublin, J.-J. (2011). A Wolff in sheep's clothing: trabecular bone adaptation in response to changes in joint loading orientation. *Bone*, 49, 1141–1151.

Batra, N. and Jiang, J. X. (2012). "INTEGRINating" the connexin hemichannel function in bone osteocytes through the action of integrin α5. *Communicative and Integrative Biology*, 5, 516–518.

Beck, J. A., Lloyd, S., Hafezparast, M., *et al.* (2000). Genealogies of mouse inbred strains. *Nature Genetics*, 24, 23–25.

Behringer, M., Gruetzner, S., McCourt, M. and Mester, J. (2013). Effects of weight-bearing activities on bone mineral content and density in children and adolescents: a meta-analysis. *Journal of Bone and Mineral Research*, 29, 467–478.

Bertram, J. E. A. and Swartz, S. M. (1991). The "law of bone transformation": a case of crying Wolff? *Biological Reviews*, 66, 245–273.

Biewener, A. A. and Bertram, J. E. A. (1993). Skeletal strain patterns in relation to exercise training during growth. *Journal of Experimental Biology*, 185, 51–69.

Biewener, A. A. and Bertram, J. E. A. (1994). Structural response of growing bone to exercise and disuse. *Journal of Applied Physiology*, 72, 946–955.

Biewener, A. A., Swartz, S. M. and Bertram, J. E. A. (1986). Bone modeling during growth: dynamic strain equilibrium in the chick tibiotarsus. *Calcified Tissue International*, 39, 390–395.

Bonewald, L. F. (2006). Mechanosensation and transduction in osteocytes. *Bonekey Osteovision*, 3, 7–15.

Bonjour, J.-P., Chevalley, T., Rizzoli, R. and Ferrari, S. (2007). Gene–environment interactions in the skeletal response to nutrition and exercise during growth. *Medicine and Sport Science*, 51, 64–80.

Bridges, P. S. (1989). Changes in activities with the shift to agriculture in the southeastern United States. *Current Anthropology*, 30, 385–394.

Brodt, M. D. and Silva, M. J. (2010). Aged mice have enhanced endocortical response and normal periosteal response compared with young-adult mice following 1 week of axial tibial compression. *Journal of Bone and Mineral Research*, 25, 2006–2015.

Burger, E. H. and Klein-Nulend, J. (1999). Mechanotransduction in bone – role of the lacunocanalicular network. *FASEB Journal*, 13, S101–S112.

Burr, D. B., Milgrom, C., Fyhrie, D., *et al.* (1996). *In vivo* measurement of human tibial strains during vigorous activity. *Bone*, 18, 405–410.

Case, N. and Rubin, J. (2010). Beta-catenin – a supporting role in the skeleton. *Journal of Cellular Biochemistry*, 110, 545–553.

Chen, Z., Qi, L., Beck, T. J., *et al.* (2011). Stronger bone correlates with African admixture in African-American women. *Journal of Bone and Mineral Research*, 26, 2307–2316.

Chia, R., Achilli, F., Festing, M. F. W. and Fisher, E. M. C. (2005). The origins and uses of mouse outbred stocks. *Nature Genetics*, 37, 1181–1186.

Conrad, D. F., Jakobsson, M., Coop, G., *et al.* (2006). A worldwide survey of haplotype variation and linkage disequilibrium in the human genome. *Nature Genetics*, 38, 1251–1260.

Dalsky, G. P., Stocke, K. S., Ehsani, A. A., *et al.* (1988). Weight-bearing exercise training and lumbar bone mineral content in postmenopausal women. *Annals of Internal Medicine*, 108, 824–828.

Daly, R. M. (2007). The effect of exercise on bone mass and structural geometry during growth. *Medicine and Sport Science*, 51, 33–49.

Danielson, M. E., Beck, T. J., Lian, Y., *et al.* (2013). Ethnic variability in bone geometry as assessed by hip structure analysis: findings from the hip strength across the menopausal transition study. *Journal of Bone and Mineral Research*, 28, 771–779.

Demes, B., Stern, J. T. Jr., Hausman, M. R., *et al.* (1998). Patterns of strain in the macaque ulna during functional activity. *American Journal of Physical Anthropology*, 106, 87–100.

Demes, B., Qin, Y.-Z., Stern, J. T. Jr., Larson, S. G. and Rubin, C. T. (2001). Patterns of strain in the macaque tibia during functional loading. *American Journal of Physical Anthropology*, 116, 257–265.

Demissie, S., Dupuis, J., Cupples, L. A., *et al.* (2007). Proximal hip geometry is linked to several chromosomal regions: genome-wide linkage results from the Framingham Osteoporosis Study. *Bone*, 40, 743–750.

Devlin, M. J. (2011). Estrogen, exercise, and the skeleton. *Evolutionary Anthropology*, 20, 54–61.

Devlin, M. J. and Lieberman, D. E. (2007). Variation in estradiol level affects cortical bone growth in response to mechanical loading in sheep. *Journal of Experimental Biology*, 210, 602–613.

Devlin, M. J., Stetter, C. M., Lin, H.-M., *et al.* (2010). Peripubertal estrogen levels and physical activity affect femur geometry in young adult women. *Osteoporosis International*, 21, 609–617.

Dhamrait, S. S., James, L., Brull, D. J., *et al.* (2003). Cortical bone resorption during exercise is interleukin-6 genotype-dependent. *European Journal of Applied Physiology*, 89, 21–25.

Doecke, J. D., Day, C. J., Stephens, A. S., *et al.* (2006). Association of functionally different *RUNX2* P2 promoter alleles with BMD. *Journal of Bone and Mineral Research*, 21, 265–273.

Donahue, S. W., Jacobs, C. R. and Donahue, H. J. (2001). Flow-induced calcium oscillations in rat osteoblasts are age, loading frequency, and shear stress dependent. *American Journal of Physiology*, 281, C1635–1641.

Duncan, R. L. (1998). Mechanotransduction and mechanosensitive ion channels in osteoblasts. *In:* Van Duijn, B. and Wiltink, A. (eds.) *Signal Transduction: Single Cell Techniques*. Berlin: Springer, pp. 125–134.

Fenner, J. N. (2005). Cross-cultural estimation of the human generation interval for use in genetics-based population divergence studies. *American Journal of Physical Anthropology*, 128, 415–423.

Forwood, M. R. (1996). Inducible cyclo-oxygenase (COX-2) mediates the induction of bone formation by mechanical loading *in vivo*. *Journal of Bone and Mineral Research*, 11, 1688–1693.

Forwood, M. R. (2013). Growing a healthy skeleton. *In:* Rosen, C. J. (ed.) *Primer on the Metabolic Bone Diseases and Disorders of Mineral Metabolism*. Ames, IA: Wiley-Blackwell, pp. 149–155.

Green, R. E., Krause, J., Briggs, A. W., *et al.* (2010). A draft sequence of the Neandertal genome. *Science*, 328, 710–722.

Haapasalo, H., Kontulainen, S., Sievänen, H., *et al.* (2000). Exercise-induced bone gain is due to enlargement in bone size without a change in volumetric bone density: a peripheral quantitative computed tomography study of the upper arms of male tennis players. *Bone*, 27, 351–357.

Hamrick, M. W., Skedros, J. G., Pennington, C. and McNeil, P. L. (2006). Increased osteogenic response to exercise in metaphyseal *versus* diaphyseal cortical bone. *Journal of Musculoskeletal and Neuronal Interactions*, 6, 258–263.

Han, Y., Cowin, S. C., Schaffler, M. B. and Weinbaum, S. (2004). Mechanotransduction and strain amplification in osteocyte cell processes. *Proceedings of the National Academy of Sciences USA*, 101, 16689–16694.

Havill, L. M., Mahaney, M. C., Binkley T. L. and Specker, B. L. (2007). Effects of genes, sex, age, and activity on BMC, bone size, and areal and volumetric BMD. *Journal of Bone and Mineral Research*, 22, 737–746.

Hoey, D. A., Chen, J. C. and Jacobs, C. R. (2012). The primary cilium as a novel extracellular sensor in bone. *Frontiers in Endocrinology*, 3, 75.

Holt, B. M. (2003). Mobility in Upper Paleolithic and Mesolithic Europe: evidence from the lower limb. *American Journal of Physical Anthropology*, 122, 200–215.

Hrdlička, A. (1937). Human typogeny. *Proceedings of the American Philosophical Society*, 78, 79–95.

Hung, C. T., Pollack, C. R., Reilly, T. M. and Brighton, C. T. (1995). Real-time calcium response of cultured bone cells to fluid flow. *Clinical Orthopaedics and Related Research*, 313, 256–269.

Ioannidis, J. P., Ng, M. Y., Sham, P. C., *et al.* (2007). Meta-analysis of genome-wide scans provides evidence for sex- and site-specific regulation of bone mass. *Journal of Bone and Mineral Research*, 22, 173–183.

Jacobs, C. R., Temiyasathit, S. and Castillo, A. B. (2010). Osteocyte mechanobiology and pericellular mechanics. *Annual Review of Biomedical Engineering*, 12, 369–400.

Joo, Y. I., Sone, T., Fukunaga, M., Lim, S. G. and Onodera, S. (2003). Effects of endurance exercise on three-dimensional trabecular bone microarchitecture in young growing rats. *Bone*, 33, 485–493.

Judex, S., Gross, T. S. and Zernicke, R. F. (1997). Strain gradients correlate with sites of exercise-induced bone-forming surfaces in the adult skeleton. *Journal of Bone and Mineral Research*, 12, 1737–1745.

Judex, S., Donahue, L. R. and Rubin, C. (2002). Genetic predisposition to low bone mass is paralleled by an enhanced sensitivity to signals anabolic to the skeleton. *FASEB Journal*, 16, 1280–1282.

Judex, S., Garman, R., Squire, M., *et al.* (2004). Genetically linked site-specificity of disuse osteoporosis. *Journal of Bone and Mineral Research*, 19, 607–613.

Judex, S., Zhang, W., Donahue, L. R. and Ozcivici, E. (2013). Genetic loci that control the loss and regain of trabecular bone during unloading and reambulation. *Journal of Bone and Mineral Research*, 28, 1537–1549.

Karinkanta, S., Heinonen, A., Sievänen, H., *et al.* (2007). A multi-component exercise regimen to prevent functional decline and bone fragility in home-dwelling elderly women: randomized, controlled trial. *Osteoporosis International*, 18, 453–462.

Karlsson, M. K., Linden, C., Karlsson, C., *et al.* (2000). Exercise during growth and bone mineral density and fractures in old age. *Lancet*, 355, 469–470.

Karsenty, G. (2003). The complexities of skeletal biology. *Nature*, 423, 316–318.

Karsenty, G., Kronenberg, H. M. and Settembre, C. (2009). Genetic control of bone formation. *Annual Review of Cell and Developmental Biology*, 25, 629–648.

Kesavan, C., Mohan, S., Srivastava, A. K., *et al.* (2006). Identification of genetic loci that regulate bone adaptive response to mechanical loading in C57BL/6J and C3H/HeJ mice intercross. *Bone*, 39, 634–643.

Klein-Nulend, J., Semeins, C. M., Ajubi, N. E., Nijweide, P. J. and Burger, E. H. (1995). Pulsating fluid flow increases nitric oxide (NO) synthesis by osteocytes but not periosteal fibroblasts – correlation with prostaglandin upregulation. *Biochemical and Biophysical Research Communications*, 217, 640–648.

Kodama, Y., Dimai, H. P., Wergedal, J., *et al.* (1999). Cortical tibial bone volume in two strains of mice: effects of sciatic neurectomy and genetic regulation of bone response to mechanical loading. *Bone*, 25, 183–190.

Kodama, Y., Umemura, Y., Nagasawa, S., *et al.* (2000). Exercise and mechanical loading increase periosteal bone formation and whole bone strength in C57BL/6J mice but not C3H/Hej mice. *Calcified Tissue International*, 66, 298–306.

Kontulainen, S., Kannus, P., Haapasalo, H., *et al.* (2001). Good maintenance of exercise-induced bone gain with decreased training of female tennis and squash players: a prospective 5-year follow-up study of young and old starters and controls. *Journal of Bone and Mineral Research*, 16, 195–201.

Kwon, R. Y., Hoey, D. A. and Jacobs, C. R. (2011). Mechanobiology of primary cilia. *In:* Gefen, A. (ed.) *Cellular and Biomolecular Mechanics and Mechanobiology*. Heidelberg: SpringerLink, pp. 99–124.

Lanyon, L. E. (1987). Functional strain in bone tissue as an objective, and controlling stimulus for adaptive bone remodeling. *Journal of Biomechanics*, 20, 1083–1093.

Lanyon, L. E. (1992). The success and failure of the adaptive response to functional load-bearing in averting bone fracture. *Bone*, 13, S17–21.

Lanyon, L. E. and Rubin, C. T. (1984). Static *vs* dynamic loads as an influence on bone remodelling. *Journal of Biomechanics*, 17, 897–906.

Lanyon, L. E., Armstrong, V., Ong, D., Zaman, G. and Price, J. (2004). Is estrogen receptor α key to controlling bones' resistance to fracture? *Journal of Endocrinology*, 182, 183–191.

Laugier, P., Novikov, V., Elmann-Larsen, B. and Berger, G. (2000). Quantitative ultrasound imaging of the calcaneus: precision and variation during a 120-day bed rest. *Calcified Tissue International*, 66, 16–21.

Leppänen, O. V., Sievänen, H., Jokihaara, J., *et al.* (2008). Pathogenesis of age-related osteoporosis: impaired mechano-responsiveness of bone is not the culprit. *PLoS ONE*, 3, e2540.

Li, J. Z., Absher, D. M., Tang, H., *et al.* (2008). Worldwide human relationships inferred from genome-wide patterns of variation. *Science*, 319, 1100–1104.

Lieberman, D. E. (1996). How and why humans grow thin skulls: experimental evidence for systemic cortical robusticity. *American Journal of Physical Anthropology*, 101, 217–236.

Lieberman, D. E., Devlin, M. J. and Pearson, O. M. (2001). Articular surface area responses to mechanical loading: effects of exercise, age, and skeletal location. *American Journal of Physical Anthropology*, 116, 266–277.

Lieberman, D. E., Pearson, O. M., Polk, J. D., Demes, B. and Crompton, A. W. (2003). Optimization of bone growth and remodeling in response to loading in tapered mammalian limbs. *Journal of Experimental Biology*, 206, 3125–3138.

Lieberman, D. E., Polk, J. D. and Demes, B. (2004). Predicting long bone loading from cross-sectional geometry. *American Journal of Physical Anthropology*, 123, 156–171.

Litzenberger, J. B., Kim, J. B., Tummala, P. and Jacobs, C. R. (2010). Beta1 integrins mediate mechanosensitive signaling pathways in osteocytes. *Calcified Tissue International*, 86, 325–332.

Liu, D., Genetos, D. C., Shao, Y., *et al.* (2008). Activation of extracellular-signal regulated kinase (ERK1/2) by fluid shear is Ca^{2+}- and ATP-dependent in MC3T3-E1 osteoblasts. *Bone*, 42, 644–652.

Liu, Y.-Z., Wilson, S. G., Wang, L., *et al.* (2008). Identification of *PLCL1* gene for hip bone size variation in females in a genome-wide association study. *PLoS ONE*, 3, e3160.

Lovejoy, C. O., McCollum, M. A., Reno, P. L. and Rosenman, B. A. (2003). Developmental biology and human evolution. *Annual Review of Anthropology*, 32, 85–109.

Luu, Y. K., Capilla, E., Rosen, C. H., *et al.* (2009). Mechanical stimulation of mesenchymal stem cell proliferation and differentiation promotes osteogenesis while preventing dietary-induced obesity. *Journal of Bone and Mineral Research*, 24, 50–61.

Macdonald, H. M., Cooper, D. M. L. and McKay, H. A. (2009) Anterior–posterior bending strength at the tibial shaft increases with physical activity in boys: evidence for non-uniform geometric adaptation. *Osteoporosis International*, 20, 61–70.

Maggiano, I. S., Schultz, M., Kierdorf, H., *et al.* (2008). Cross-sectional analysis of long bones, occupational activities and long-distance trade of the Classic Maya from Xcambó – archaeological and osteological evidence. *American Journal of Physical Anthropology*, 136, 470–477.

Manolagas, S. C. and Almeida, M. (2007). Gone with the Wnts: β-catenin, T-cell factor, forkhead box O, and oxidative stress in age-dependent diseases of bone, lipid, and glucose metabolism. *Molecular Endocrinology*, 21, 2605–2614.

Marchi, D., Sparacello, V. S., Holt, B. M. and Formicola, V. (2006). Biomechanical approach to the reconstruction of activity patterns in Neolithic Western Liguria, Italy. *American Journal of Physical Anthropology*, 131, 447–455.

Martin, R. B., Burr, D. B. and Sharkey, N. A. (1998). *Skeletal Tissue Mechanics*. New York, NY: Springer.

Meiring, R. M., Avidon, I., Norris, S. A. and McVeigh, J. A. (2013). A two-year history of high bone loading physical activity attenuates ethnic differences in bone strength and geometry in pre-/early pubertal children from a low-middle income country. *Bone*, 57, 522–530.

Morimoto, N., Ponce de León, M. S. and Zollikofer, C. P. E. (2011). Exploring femoral diaphyseal shape variation in wild and captive chimpanzees by means of morphometric mapping: a test of Wolff's Law. *Anatomical Record*, 294, 589–609.

Nicolella, D. P., Moravits, D. E., Gale, A. M., Bonewald, L. F. and Lankford, J. (2006). Osteocyte lacunae tissue strain in cortical bone. *Journal of Biomechanics*, 39, 1735–1743.

O'Connor, J. A., Lanyon, L. E. and MacFie, H. (1982). The influence of strain rate on adaptive bone remodelling. *Journal of Biomechanics*, 15, 767–781.

Ozcivici, E., Luu, Y. K., Adler, B., *et al.* (2010). Mechanical signals as anabolic agents in bone. *Nature Reviews Rheumatology*, 6, 50–59.

Pahlavani, M. A. and Vargas, D. M. (2000). Influence of aging and caloric restriction on activation of Ras/MAPK, calcineurin, and CaMK-IV activities in rat T cells. *Proceedings of the Society for Experimental Biology and Medicine*, 223, 163–169.

Pearson, O. M. and Lieberman, D. E. (2004). The aging of Wolff's "Law": ontogeny and responses to mechanical loading in cortical bone. *Yearbook of Physical Anthropology*, 47, 63–99.

Rawlinson, S. C. F., El Haj, A. J., Minter, S. L., *et al.* (1991). Loading-related increases in prostaglandin production in cores of adult canine cancellous bone *in vitro*: a role for prostacyclin in adaptive bone remodeling? *Journal of Bone and Mineral Research*, 6, 1345–1351.

Rawlinson, S. C. F., Mosley, J. R., Suswillo, R. F. L., Pitsillides, A. A. and Lanyon, L. E. (1995). Calvarial and limb bone cells in organ and monolayer culture do not show the same early responses to dynamic mechanical strain. *Journal of Bone and Mineral Research*, 10, 1225–1232.

Reich, D., Thangaraj, K., Patterson, N., Price, A. L. and Singh, L. (2009). Reconstructing Indian population history. *Nature*, 461, 489–494.

Richards, J. B., Zheng, H.-F. and Spector, T. D. (2012). Genetics of osteoporosis from genome-wide association studies: advances and challenges. *Nature Reviews Genetics*, 13, 577–588.

Riddle, R. C. and Donahue, H. J. (2009). From streaming potentials to shear stress: 25 years of bone cell mechanotransduction. *Journal of Orthopaedic Research*, 27, 143–149.

Robling, A. G. and Turner, C. H. (2002). Mechanotransduction in bone: genetic effects on mechanosensitivity in mice. *Bone*, 31, 562–569.

Robling, A. G., Li, J., Shultz, K. L., Beamer, W. G. and Turner, C. H. (2003). Evidence for a skeletal mechanosensitivity gene on mouse chromosome 4. *FASEB Journal*, 17, 324–326.

Robling, A. G., Warden, S. J., Shultz, K. L., Beamer, W. G. and Turner, C. H. (2007). Genetic effects on bone mechanotransduction in congenic mice harboring bone size and strength quantitative trait loci. *Journal of Bone and Mineral Research*, 22, 984–991.

Rubin, C. T. and Lanyon, L. E. (1982). Limb mechanics as a function of speed and gait: a study of functional strains in the radius and tibia of horse and dog. *Journal of Experimental Biology*, 101, 187–211.

Rubin, C. T. and Lanyon, L. E. (1984). Regulation of bone formation by applied dynamic loads. *Journal of Bone and Joint Surgery*, 66A, 397–402.

Rubin, C. T. and Lanyon, L. E. (1985). Regulation of bone mass by mechanical strain magnitude. *Calcified Tissue International*, 37, 411–417.

Rubin, C. T., McLeod, K. J. and Bain, S. D. (1990). Functional strains and cortical bone adaptation: epigenetic assurance of skeletal integrity. *Journal of Biomechanics*, 23, 43–54.

Rubin, C. T., Bain, S. D. and McLeod, K. J. (1992). Suppression of the osteogenic response in the aging skeleton. *Calcified Tissue International*, 50, 306–313.

Rubin, C., Turner, A. S., Bain, S., Mallinckrodt, C. and McLeod, K. (2001). Anabolism: low mechanical signals strengthen long bones. *Nature*, 412, 603–604.

Rubin, C. T., Seeherman, H., Qin, Y.-X. and Gross, T. S. (2013). The mechanical consequences of load bearing in the equine third metacarpal across speed and gait: the nonuniform distributions of normal strain, shear strain, and strain energy density. *FASEB Journal*, 27, 1887–1894.

Rubin, J., Schwartz, Z., Boyan, B. D., *et al.* (2007). Caveolin-1 knockout mice have increased bone size and stiffness. *Journal of Bone and Mineral Research*, 22, 1408–1418.

Ruff, C. B. (2005). Mechanical determinants of bone form: insights from skeletal remains. *Journal of Musculoskeletal and Neuronal Interactions*, 5, 202–212.

Ruff, C. B., Larsen, C. S. and Hayes, W. C. (1984). Structural changes in the femur with the transition to agriculture on the Georgia coast. *American Journal of Physical Anthropology*, 64, 124–136.

Ruff, C. B., Trinkaus, E., Walker, A. and Larsen, C. S. (1993). Postcranial robusticity in *Homo*. I: temporal trends and mechanical interpretation. *American Journal of Physical Anthropology*, 91, 21–53.

Ruff, C. B., Holt, B. and Trinkaus, E. (2006). Who's afraid of the big bad Wolff?: "Wolff's Law" and bone functional adaptation. *American Journal of Physical Anthropology*, 129, 484–498.

Ruff, C. B., Holt, B., Niskanen, M., *et al.* (2015). Gradual decline in mobility with the adoption of food production in Europe. *Proceedings of the National Academy of Sciences USA*, 112, 7147–7152.

Salingcarnboriboon, R., Tsuji, K., Komori, T., *et al.* (2006). Runx2 is a target of mechanical unloading to alter osteoblastic activity and bone formation *in vivo*. *Endocrinology*, 147, 2296–2305.

Saxon, L. K., Jackson, B. F., Sugiyama, T., Lanyon, L. E. and Price, J. S. (2011). Analysis of multiple bone responses to graded strains above functional levels, and to disuse, in mice *in vivo* show that the human Lrp5 G171V High Bone Mass mutation increases the osteogenic response to loading but that lack of Lrp5 activity reduces it. *Bone*, 49, 184–193.

Schmitt, D., Zumwalt, A. C. and Hamrick, M. W. (2010). The relationship between bone mechanical properties and ground reaction forces in normal and hypermuscular mice. *Journal of Experimental Zoology*, 313A, 339–351.

Shaw, C. N. and Stock, J. T. (2009). Intensity, repetitiveness, and directionality of habitual adolescent mobility patterns influence the tibial diaphysis morphology of athletes. *American Journal of Physical Anthropology*, 140, 149–159.

Shaw, C. N. and Stock, J. T. (2013). Extreme mobility in the Late Pleistocene? Comparing limb biomechanics among fossil *Homo*, varsity athletes and Holocene foragers. *Journal of Human Evolution*, 64, 242–249.

Simons, K. and Toomre, D. (2000). Lipid rafts and signal transduction. *Nature Reviews Molecular Cell Biology*, 1, 31–39.

Sládek, V., Berner, M. and Sailer, R. (2006). Mobility in Central European Late Eneolithic and Early Bronze Age: tibial cross-sectional geometry. *Journal of Archaeological Science*, 33, 470–482.

Snow-Harter, C., Bouxsein, M. L., Lewis, B. T., Carter, D. R. and Marcus, R. (1992). Effects of resistance and endurance exercise on bone mineral status of young women: a randomized exercise intervention trial. *Journal of Bone and Mineral Research*, 7, 761–769.

Srinivasan, S., Agans, S. C., King, K. A., *et al.* (2003). Enabling bone formation in the aged skeleton via rest-inserted mechanical loading. *Bone*, 33, 946–955.

Srinivasan, S., Ausk, B. J., Poliachik, S. L., *et al.* (2007). Rest-inserted loading rapidly amplifies the response of bone to small increases in strain and load cycles. *Journal of Applied Physiology*, 102, 1945–1952.

Srinivasan, S., Gross, T. S. and Bain, S. D. (2012). Bone mechanotransduction may require augmentation in order to strengthen the senescent skeleton. *Ageing Research Reviews*, 11, 353–360.

Styrkarsdottir, U., Halldorsson, B. V., Gudbjartsson, D. F., *et al.* (2010). European bone mineral density loci are also associated with BMD in East-Asian populations. *PLoS ONE*, 5, e13217.

Suuriniemi, M., Mahonen, A., Kovanen, V., *et al.* (2004). Association between exercise and pubertal BMD is modulated by estrogen receptor α genotype. *Journal of Bone and Mineral Research*, 19, 1758–1765.

Tajima, O., Ashizawa, N., Ishii, T., *et al.* (2000). Interaction of the effects between vitamin D receptor polymorphism and exercise training on bone metabolism. *Journal of Applied Physiology*, 88, 1271–1276.

Tan, V. P., Macdonald, H. M., Kim, S., *et al.* (2014). Influence of physical activity on bone strength in children and adolescents: a systematic review and narrative synthesis. *Journal of Bone and Mineral Research*, 29, 2161–2181.

Thompson, W. R., Rubin, C. T. and Rubin, J. (2012). Mechanical regulation of signaling pathways in bone. *Gene*, 503, 179–193.

Trinkaus, E. (1997). Appendicular robusticity and the paleobiology of modern human emergence. *Proceedings of the National Academy of Sciences USA*, 94, 13367–13373.

Trinkaus, E., Ruff, C. B., Churchill, S. E. and Vandermeersch, B. (1998). Locomotion and body proportions of the Saint-Césaire 1 Châtelperronian Neandertal. *Proceedings of the National Academy of Sciences USA*, 95, 5836–5840.

Turner, C. H., Takano, Y. and Owan, I. (1995). Aging changes mechanical loading thresholds for bone formation in rats. *Journal of Bone and Mineral Research*, 10, 1544–1549.

Turner, C. H., Takano, Y., Owan, I. and Murrell, G. A. (1996). Nitric oxide inhibitor L-NAME suppresses mechanically induced bone formation in rats. *American Journal of Physiology*, 270, E634–639.

Vashishth, D. (2007). The role of the collagen matrix in skeletal fragility. *Current Osteoporosis Reports*, 5, 62–66.

Vaughan, T., Reid, D. M., Morrison, N. A. and Ralston, S. H. (2004). *RUNX2* alleles associated with BMD in Scottish women; interaction of *RUNX2* alleles with menopausal status and body mass index. *Bone*, 34, 1029–1036.

Vico, L., Collet, P., Guignandon, A., *et al.* (2000). Effects of long-term microgravity exposure on cancellous and cortical weight-bearing bones of cosmonauts. *Lancet*, 355, 1607–1611.

Wallace, I. J. (2013). Physical activity and genetics as determinants of limb bone structure. PhD dissertation, Stony Brook University. Available at: www.paleoanthro.org/dissertations/download/

Wallace, I. J., Middleton, K. M., Lublinsky, S., *et al.* (2010). Functional significance of genetic variation underlying limb bone diaphyseal structure. *American Journal of Physical Anthropology*, 143, 21–30.

Wallace, I. J., Tommasini, S. M., Judex, S., Garland, T. Jr. and Demes, B. (2012). Genetic variations and physical activity as determinants of limb bone morphology: an experimental approach using a mouse model. *American Journal of Physical Anthropology*, 148, 24–35.

Wallace, I. J., Demes, B., Mongle, C., *et al.* (2014). Exercise-induced bone formation is poorly linked to local strain magnitude in the sheep tibia. *PLoS ONE*, 9, e99108.

Wallace, I. J., Judex, S. and Demes B. (2015). Effects of load-bearing exercise on skeletal structure and mechanics differ between outbred populations of mice. *Bone*, 72, 1–8.

Wang, N., Butler, J. P. and Ingber, D. E. (1993). Mechanotransduction across the cell surface and through the cytoskeleton. *Science*, 260, 1124–1127.

Wang, Y. L., McNamara, L. M., Schaffler, M. B. and Weinbaum, S. (2007). A model for the role of integrins in flow induced mechanotransduction in osteocytes. *Proceedings of the National Academy of Sciences USA*, 104, 15941–15946.

Warden, S. J., Mantila Roosa, S. M., Kersh, M. E., *et al.* (2014). Physical activity when young provides lifelong benefits to cortical bone size and strength in men. *Proceedings of the National Academy of Sciences USA*, 111, 5337–5342.

Wesselius, A., Bours, M. J., Agrawal, A., *et al.* (2011). Role of purinergic receptor polymorphisms in human bone. *Frontiers in Bioscience*, 16, 2572–2585.

West-Eberhard, M. J. (2003). *Developmental Plasticity and Evolution*. Oxford: Oxford University Press.

Wetzsteon, R. J., Zemel, B. S., Shults, J., *et al.* (2011). Mechanical loads and cortical bone geometry in healthy children and young adults. *Bone*, 48, 1103–1108.

Wolff, J. (1892). *Das Gesetz der Transformation der Knochen*. Berlin: A. Hirschwald.

Yalcin, B., Nicod, J., Bhomra, A., *et al.* (2010). Commercially available outbred mice for genome-wide association studies. *PLoS Genetics*, 6, e1001085.

Yellowley, C. E., Li, Z., Zhou, Z., Jacobs, C. R. and Donahue, H. J. (2000). Functional gap junctions between osteocytic and osteoblastic cells. *Journal of Bone and Mineral Research*, 15, 209–217.

Ziros, P. G., Basdra, E. K. and Papavassiliou, A. G. (2008). Runx2: of bone and stretch. *International Journal of Biochemistry and Cell Biology*, 40, 1659–1663.

11 The Havers–Halberg Oscillation and Bone Metabolism

Russell T. Hogg, Timothy G. Bromage, Haviva M. Goldman,
Julia A. Katris and John G. Clement

11.1 Introduction

Rather than being a passive responder to other body tissues, bone is a dynamic participant in overall homeostasis, with a major impact on how other tissues behave throughout ontogeny. Bones act as endocrine organs to regulate metabolic rate and cell function in cooperation with adipose tissue, the hypothalamus and pituitary, thyroid, pancreas, and a number of other organs besides (e.g., Confavreaux et al., 2009). In an evolutionary sense, this means that the study of bone histology and physiology should give us fundamental information about evolution of energetics (how individual organisms use available calories) and life history (patterns of growth, reproduction, and lifespan). On the flipside, more information about energetics and metabolic physiology will greatly inform our understanding of skeletal growth processes.

Following this concept, we have recently advanced a hypothesis that the physiological keystone between the bone/energy complex is a biorhythm centered in the hypothalamus of the brain, known as the Havers–Halberg Oscillation (HHO; Bromage et al., 2009). To summarize, this hypothesis argues that a biological clock within the hypothalamus influences metabolism, cell proliferation, and other life history variables through oscillations in output via sympathetic neurons. This biorhythm impacts the growth of bone, such that we can see recorded signatures of it within bone histology (and within teeth).

To date, there has been no synthesis of the major concepts linking the physiology of bone to the physiology of energy homeostasis, with regard to the work of prior researchers that was used to build the HHO model. Likewise, there is no synthesis of the data supporting the HHO model to date, and no evidence published with regard to bone's tissue-specific metabolic rate in order to discuss how the HHO affects bone specifically within the context of the entire organism. This chapter is intended to (1) provide a review of the bone/energy homeostasis literature in light of the HHO; (2) to summarize the HHO research that has been performed thus far and examine how this mechanism impacts the growth of bone such that we can see recorded signatures of it within bone histology (and within teeth); and (3) present new evidence with regard to bone's tissue-specific metabolic rate.

11.2   The Cross-talk between Bone and Energy Homeostasis

Although the information has yet to make it into most physiology or neuroscience textbooks, it is now well-established that the sympathetic nervous system plays a major role in regulating bone mass accrual and bone resorption (e.g., Elefteriou *et al.*, 2014). This effect comes about via direct innervation of bone cells, with multiple humoral factors (e.g., endocrine hormones) playing a role in regulating the sympathetic output (Confavreaux *et al.*, 2009; Elefteriou *et al.*, 2014). These humoral factors, which include hormones such as neuropeptide Y, leptin, adiponectin, and osteocalcin, among others, establish a feedback loop that ties bone growth and remodeling together with overall energy homeostasis (Ducy *et al.*, 1996, 2000a, 2000b; Karsenty, 2001, 2006; Takeda *et al.*, 2002; Hamrick, 2004; Allison *et al.*, 2007; Hamrick and Ferrari, 2008; Lee and Karsenty, 2008; Takeda and Karsenty, 2008; Confavreaux *et al.*, 2009; Driessler and Baldock, 2010; Ducy, 2011; Elefteriou *et al.*, 2014). Ultimately, we argue that this link between bone and energy homeostasis (or metabolism) underlies a fundamental physiological system that is geared to match bone growth, body mass, and metabolic rate to each other in a cohesive life history package among mammals.

The impetus for the discovery of the bone and energy physiology came from the osteoporosis-related studies of Ducy, Karsenty, and colleagues (Ducy *et al.*, 2000a, 2000b; Karsenty, 2001), which were in turn driven by the recognition that there is a low incidence of osteoporosis in obese humans (Ducy *et al.*, 2000a, 2000b). From this observation, these researchers postulated that leptin, a hormone secreted by adipocytes (fat cells) that is known to influence appetite and metabolism, might also have an influential role in bone (Ducy *et al.*, 2000a, 2000b; Karsenty, 2001). They demonstrated that: (1) a high bone mass phenotype in *ob/ob* (leptin-deficient) mice could be corrected with an intracerebroventricular infusion of leptin (Ducy *et al.*, 2000a); (2) osteoblasts from *db/db* (leptin *receptor*-deficient) mice behaved indistinguishably from wild-type osteoblasts in culture; and (3) mice which underwent chemical lesioning of the ventromedial hypothalamic nuclei (where leptin receptors are present to regulate appetite) in the brain exhibited a drastic increase in bone mass, which subsequent leptin treatment could not reverse (Takeda *et al.*, 2002; Takeda, 2008). That is, direct intravenous leptin treatment had no effect on bone because it was the portion of the brain that responds to leptin to regulate bone mass that was damaged. Furthermore, mice which had their leptin receptors deleted from neurons were shown to recapitulate the high bone mass phenotype, in contrast to mice which had leptin receptors removed from their osteoblasts, where no change was observed (Shi *et al.*, 2008). Taken together, these results suggest strongly that leptin has a powerful influence upon bone, but that its mechanism of action upon bone is indirect, relying upon leptin's impact on output from the hypothalamus of the brain.

These authors argued that the brain uses sympathetic nervous system output to regulate bone mass, as influenced by leptin. For the sympathetic nervous system to have such an effect, there must be clear demonstration that it innervates bone tissue directly; there is ample evidence in this regard. Multiple studies have shown that cortical bone, trabecular bone, bone marrow, and periosteum are rich with nerve fibers primarily delivered alongside nutrient arteries. These fibers are predominantly sensory and sympathetic in nature, but parasympathetic fibers have also been identified (Bajayo *et al.*, 2012; Elefteriou *et al.*, 2014). In turn, sympathetic fibers synapse with osteoblasts and osteocytes, influencing these cells directly by releasing the neurotransmitter norepinephrine (also known as noradrenaline) onto β2 (and to a lesser extent β1) adrenergic receptors (Confavreaux *et al.*, 2009; Elefteriou *et al.*, 2014).[1] In addition to adrenergic receptors, osteoblasts also express nicotinic and muscarinic receptors for the parasympathetic neurotransmitter acetylcholine (Shi *et al.*, 2010; Bajayo *et al.*, 2012).[2] Routes of innervation from bone following sensory, sympathetic, and parasympathetic pathways have been found to include diverse connections in the central nervous system (CNS), including the spinal cord, brainstem, paraventricular nucleus of the hypothalamus, prelimbic cortex, and even motor cortex (Denes *et al.*, 2005; Bajayo *et al.*, 2012; Elefteriou *et al.*, 2014). Crucially, chondrocytes in long-bone growth plates also receive direct sympathetic innervation and express β2 adrenergic receptors (Elefteriou *et al.*, 2014). This suggests that the CNS may use the same sympathetic mechanism to coordinate cartilage and bone cell activity together to regulate overall growth of the skeleton and that CNS influence is not just restricted to bone.

A recent study using an experimental mouse model also demonstrates interconnectivity of sensory and autonomic bone innervation pathways. In this study, mice had one forelimb experimentally loaded during a bupivacaine block of their ipsilateral brachial plexus. Bupivacaine is one of the most commonly used local anesthetics, and acts by stopping the conduction of nerve impulses in both sensory and motor nerve fibers. Control mice underwent identical loading without anesthesia (Sample *et al.*, 2008). The anesthetized mice experienced significantly less bone remodeling in the loaded limb, but more importantly experienced no observable remodeling in the unloaded limb. This was contrary to the results in control mice, who demonstrated increased bone deposition in *both* the loaded and unloaded contralateral limb. These results suggest that intact neuronal pathways are necessary for remodeling of bone in response to biomechanical forces, and also

---

[1] Adrenergic receptors are a class of cell membrane proteins that bind specifically to the neurotransmitters norepinephrine and epinephrine. These neurotransmitters are released by postsynaptic sympathetic neurons onto innervated target cells across a synapse to either trigger (typically β1) or inhibit (typically β2) a response in the target cell. The target cells typically are glandular (here including bone cells due to their endocrine role), smooth muscle, or cardiac muscle. In addition to bone, one or both of these receptors can be found on cells in areas such as the brain, cardiac tissue, liver, and bronchi/bronchioles of the lungs.

[2] Nicotinic and muscarinic receptors are similar to adrenergic receptors, except that they are responding to the neurotransmitter acetylcholine, which in this case is released on target tissues primarily by postsynaptic parasympathetic neurons (somatic motor neurons and a few postsynaptic sympathetic neurons also release acetylcholine onto target cells).

that these pathways will respond to changes in loading to affect bone deposition in non-loaded bones. This demonstrates that the CNS is able to act as a central drive to coordinate bone physiology across the body, and likely acts to provide an organism-wide response to changes in loading and also to promote symmetry in the skeleton. These results do not preclude the importance of local bone regulation, but instead add complexity to our understanding of bone growth and remodeling. This system is also likely tied to the leptin physiology, as Rubin and Rubin (2008) point out that the nervous response to loading should physiologically incorporate a host of other tissues and organs, such as the bone marrow cells which will become osteogenic or adipogenic depending on resource availability and loading. This provides yet another physiological link between adipose and osseous tissues.

With this evidence in mind, it should not be surprising that the action of the leptin-sympathetic pathways upon bone is likely much more complex than the original Ducy/Karsenty models proposed. Various experiments have had results that seem to conflict with one another, and authors have interpreted these contradictions to suggest that rather than simply promoting bone resorption or inhibiting bone formation as per the original model, leptin may instead: (1) increase trabecular bone resorption and cortical bone deposition; (2) act differently within bone of the axial and appendicular skeleton; (3) act to increase bone mass across the board; or (4) act simply to increase the rate of bone turnover in general (Hamrick and Ferrari, 2008; Idelevich *et al.*, 2013; Turner *et al.*, 2013). There are many hypotheses, and at this point no clear choice can be made among them. Additionally, there is evidence suggesting that leptin may act peripherally as well as centrally via the hypothalamus, as osteoblasts and osteoclasts do express leptin receptors and peripheral administration of leptin has been shown to increase bone density and bone mineral content in *ob/ob* mice (Steppan *et al.*, 2000). Turner and colleagues (2013) have strongly supported this idea, with the report that wild-type mice whose bone marrow was lethally irradiated and replaced with bone marrow from *db/db*-deficient mice developed a decreased bone mass phenotype. While we do acknowledge the likelihood of peripheral effects of leptin on bone mass, it is important to point out that Turner and colleagues' results for lumbar vertebrae and femora do conflict with one another for certain bone formation measurements. Moreover, results from their ANOVA tests display a lack of statistical significance among their samples as often as they demonstrate significant difference, warranting some skepticism in considering their conclusions. Nevertheless, the picture is more complex than we have recognized, and the direct peripheral effect of leptin needs much more study.

Regardless of the precise action of leptin, the total evidence is strongly in favor of the hypothesis that with or without peripheral action, leptin does act centrally via the hypothalamus to influence bone remodeling, and that this central action is a vital link in the feedback loops of energy metabolism (e.g., Karsenty 2001, 2006; Hamrick *et al.*, 2007; Lee and Karsenty, 2008; Takeda and Karsenty, 2008; Confavreaux *et al.*, 2009; Ducy, 2011). Leptin's action on hypothalamic neurons affects overall sympathetic output, which in turn upregulates the activity of embryonic stem-cell protein tyrosine phosphatase (ESP) in osteoblasts. ESP is a protein that influences the decarboxylation of osteocalcin by osteoclasts. Osteocalcin is a protein secreted by osteoblasts that functions both as a structural protein in bone and as a hormone in the blood serum. Osteocalcin occurs in two forms in the body, a carboxylated and uncarboxylated form, and the uncarboxylated form is the active protein that functions as a hormone (Hinoi *et al.*, 2008; Confavreaux *et al.*, 2009; Ferron and Lacombe, 2014). Therefore, when leptin and the sympathetic nervous system upregulate ESP, there is an increase in the hormone-form of osteocalcin in the blood. Specifically, osteoclasts respond to ESP by freeing an increased amount of osteocalcin from the bone matrix and decarboxylating it (Hinoi *et al.*, 2008; Confavreaux *et al.*, 2009; Ferron and Lacombe, 2014). Released into the serum, the uncarboxylated osteocalcin acts as an endocrine hormone to influence: (1) insulin secretion by the pancreas, (2) proliferation of pancreatic β (insulin-producing) cells, as well as (3) adiponectin secretion by adipocytes. This last function has a consequent effect on insulin sensitivity throughout the body (Lee *et al.*, 2007; Hinoi *et al.*, 2008; Lee and Karsenty, 2008; Confavreaux *et al.*, 2009; Idelevich *et al.*, 2013; Ferron and Lacombe, 2014). Likewise, this serum osteocalcin completes a feedback loop, since the release of osteocalcin influences in turn the release of leptin by adipocytes (Amling *et al.*, 2001; Karsenty, 2001; Elefteriou *et al.*, 2014; osteocalcin: Lee *et al.*, 2007). Importantly, osteoblasts also respond directly to insulin to increase serum uncarboxylated osteocalcin (Ferron and Lacombe, 2014).

The close connection between fat and bone cells in the regulation of overall metabolism makes intuitive sense, for several important reasons. First, as mentioned above, bone marrow contains its own large adipocyte stores, and osteoblasts and adipocytes also share a common lineage from bone marrow pluripotent mesenchymal progenitor cells (essentially, bone marrow stem cells; Berendsen and Olsen, 2014). There is plasticity between these two cell lineages, such that even differentiated osteoblastic or adipogenic cells can re-differentiate between each other (Berendsen and Olsen, 2014). The regulation of mesenchymal cell differentiation and the plasticity of their bone- and fat-cell descendants is known to rely upon a complex array of local, hormonal (including leptin), and mechanical factors, which includes cross-talk between the two different cell lineages. This cross-talk includes the leptin mechanism, as leptin treatment via both peripheral (intravenous) and central (direct hypothalamic injection) administration has been shown to affect the adipocyte–osteoblast system in bone marrow (Hamrick *et al.*, 2005, 2007). These complex relationships between the two cell types suggest that their physiological role within the organism at large should be closely related and that they should help to govern each other's behavior in general. Second, bone growth and remodeling are costly processes, and therefore we expect that bone and metabolic physiology would be integrated so that the body can satisfy the caloric needs of bone growth and remodeling within the overall energy budget of the complete organism. Third, a central axiom of bone biology is that bone mass should scale with body mass to accommodate increasing biomechanical loads at larger sizes, and adipose depots serve as a major component of overall body mass. Last, in addition to controlling bone mass, body mass is the major determinant of metabolic rate among mammals

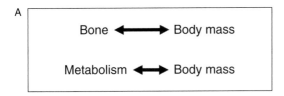

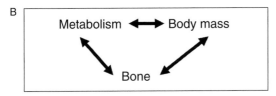

Figure 11.1 Two models regarding the association of body mass, metabolic rate, and bone physiology. (A) Traditional model where body mass is independently associated with metabolism and bone mass, such that any covariation in the latter two variables is a result of both being driven physiologically by body mass. (B) New model, wherein bone has a direct physiological communication with both body mass and metabolism, so that all three variables covary because they are part of a complete physiological loop.

(Sibly and Brown, 2007; Bromage *et al.*, 2009). The correlation between bone size/mass and body mass has been traditionally linked to biomechanical concerns (e.g., Biewener, 1982; Christiansen, 2001), whereas the correlation between metabolism and body mass has typically been observed within the context of efficiency of energetic scaling (e.g., Sibly and Brown, 2007). However, we can now see that the leptin–sympathetic–osteocalcin system serves as a discrete physiological connection between these two correlations to body size, which did not seem so strongly linked before (Figure 11.1). This connection has major implications for our study of the evolution of skeletal growth and life history, which are discussed in the next section.

11.3 Regulation of Bone and Energy Homeostasis by Biological Clocks: the HHO

It is important to understand these connections between bone and energy pathways in order to understand the HHO model, because they form the physiological basis for the hypothesis. We contend that the leptin–sympathetic–osteocalcin system participates with centrally controlled biological rhythms, which act as metronomes to regulate bone growth and coordinate overall life-history physiology. Time is an essential ingredient in nature's pattern generator, and across most organisms we see evidence that growth is dependent on time-linked oscillations in biological activity – in other words, biological rhythms (Roenneberg and Morse, 1993). Fundamentally, organisms must pace their metabolism and growth to match resource availability as well as their overall life-history strategy. This requires the ability to organize physiology through time using internal clocks – mechanisms that allow timekeeping via a regular, predictable oscillation. Just as grandfather clocks keep track of time via regular oscillations of a pendulum, metazoans keep track of time via regular oscillations in protein expression regulated by genes such as *Clock*, *Per*, and *Bmal* (e.g., Fu *et al.*, 2005). The late Franz Halberg, the founding father of the study of these rhythms, coined the term "circadian" to refer to the 24-hour clocks that have recently been the focus of so much attention in physiological research. However, Halberg and colleagues repeatedly demonstrated the existence and importance of longer-term rhythms, that is, those with frequencies greater than one day (e.g., Halberg, 1969).

To bring the story back to bone growth, experimental research has shown that molecular clocks that are entrained centrally by the suprachiasmatic nucleus of the hypothalamus act as major mediators of the leptin/sympathetic pathway (Fu *et al.*, 2005; Hamrick and Ferrari, 2008). In mice, osteoblast activity and proliferation are influenced by 24-hour hypothalamic rhythms under the control of the genes *Clock*, *Per*, and *Bmal* (Fu *et al.*, 2005). These rhythms are transmitted to bone tissue via a corresponding oscillation in the sympathetic output discussed in the previous section; this oscillation also influences heart rate and blood pressure cycles (Ueyama *et al.*, 1999; Fu *et al.*, 2005). Moreover, activation of osteoblast β2 adrenergic receptors (which, as discussed in Section 11.2, are targets of sympathetic innervation) activates transcription of the biorhythm genes *Per1* and *Per2* within these cells (Fu *et al.*, 2005; Elefteriou *et al.*, 2014). Likewise, serum osteocalcin levels have been shown to oscillate over a 24-hour cycle in multiple species, and numerous bone transcription factors undergo daily oscillations within humans, once again showing that bone cell activity cycles under the influence of biological clocks (Zvonic *et al.*, 2007; Allen, 2008).

In these studies of the effect of biorhythms on bone, leptin, and osteocalcin, the focus has been almost entirely in terms of the circadian clock. The longer-period rhythms identified by Halberg and others have not been considered. As we will see, this is likely a side effect of the trend to use mice as model organisms in experimental physiology. However, a growing body of evidence has led us to argue that long-period (i.e., greater than 24-hour) hypothalamic rhythms may be key players in the coordination of skeletal growth, metabolism, and life history, operating through the physiological cross-talk between bone and energy homeostasis described in the previous section.

The first clues leading us to this hypothesis came from an unlikely source: the microstructure of teeth. Dental enamel and dentine display histological signatures of biological rhythms in the form of periodic growth increments, much as tree rings do. There are 24-hour growth lines (cross-striations in enamel, von Ebner's lines in dentine) and longer-period growth lines (striae of Retzius in enamel, Andresen lines in dentine) whose periodicity varies among and within species, but not within individual organisms (Dean, 2000). While the circadian nature of cross-striations and von Ebner's lines has been a long-accepted tenet of tooth biology (e.g., Asper, 1916; Okada, 1943; Boyde, 1979; Lacruz *et al.*, 2012), the biology underlying the longer-period increments remained mysterious for decades. However, beginning in the

1990s, researchers began to notice that the Retzius rhythm was correlated with body mass among anthropoid primates (Dean and Scandrett, 1995; Lacruz et al., 2008; Smith, 2008). Another important clue came in 2005, when Otto Appenzeller and colleagues published a landmark paper suggesting that the human Retzius rhythm is tied physiologically to oscillations in heart rate. They found that both rhythms occur over an approximately circaseptan (near-weekly) interval, and advanced the hypothesis that this is a direct result of circaseptan oscillations in sympathetic nervous output (Appenzeller et al., 2005; see also Wu et al., 1990; Rawson et al., 2000).

Appenzeller's suggestion that hard tissue growth increments may be under the influence of long-period hypothalamic clocks raises the question of how long-term sympathetic rhythms would impact bone, as circadian hypothalamic clocks have such a strong effect on bone as found in the studies cited previously. With osteoblast activity and proliferation occurring in a centrally coordinated, periodic manner (Fu et al., 2005), one would expect to see specific growth increments in bone similar to those in teeth. For example, we know that bone cell proliferation occurs in a coordinated fashion over a 24-hour period in mice according to changes in sympathetic output, as described above. While bone cells are proliferating, they cannot also be secreting osteoid because their chromatid-coiled DNA is unavailable for transcription. Accordingly, when the cells of a bone are proliferating more or less simultaneously under this sympathetic influence, a histological aberration should appear in the bone where the osteoblast epithelium halted its activities for cell division to take place – in other words, a growth increment. The only growth increments in bones comparable to those in teeth are lamellae, but surprisingly, prior to the work of Bromage and colleagues (2009), only two studies attempted to determine whether bone lamellae have periodicity (Okada and Mimura, 1940; Shinoda and Okada, 1988). The evidence is therefore limited, but considering: (1) Appenzeller's hypothesis that Retzius periodicity (RP) and oscillating autonomic output are linked, and (2) the likely correlation between RP and body size, it raises the possibility that lamellae are in fact periodic and that their rhythm is not circadian, but varies among species in a manner similar to the Retzius periodicity.

In the teeth of mice and several small primate species, the RP may be so short that it matches the circadian rhythm (Bromage et al., 2009; Hogg, 2010), such that these animals do not display cross-striations between their striae of Retzius, and in this case we would *expect* to see a periodicity of 24 hours between lamellae, as vital labeling experiments have demonstrated that rats possess (Bromage et al., 2009).[3]

---

[3] With regard to teeth, we can be certain that we are actually seeing striae of Retzius at 24-hour intervals in these animals because striae of Retzius span multiple prisms, allowing us to visibly distinguish them from cross-striations, which are contained only in individual prisms. These daily striae of Retzius could be potentially confused for "laminations," which are not a biological structure but an optical effect resulting from a combination of section thickness and cross-striation alignments in three dimensions (Tafforeau et al., 2007) that can therefore appear similar to striae of Retzius. However, where laminations are visible, striae of Retzius can still be seen spaced periodically among them as clearly identifiable features and this is not the case for these specimens. We are also confident that RP = 1 exists because of vital labeling data we have published on rats (Bromage et al., 2009). Regardless, removal of RP = 1 animals from regressions does not alter the models in a major way (Bromage et al., 2012).

Another alternative is that in the smallest animals the Retzius rhythm does not exist, and that we see only a manifestation of circadian rhythms (see Bromage *et al.*, 2016, for further discussion). In either case, you would see daily-secreted lamellae in the smallest, most active mammals. In larger animals, we would expect that lamellae would be formed over longer intervals than one day. If this pattern is true, it would signify that the intense focus of most chronobiological research on strictly circadian clocks controlling bone formation has resulted from either the coincidence that within mice the Retzius rhythm and the circadian rhythm happen to correspond, or that the Retzius mechanism only exists or else is only influential in larger species (Bromage *et al.* 2012, 2016). In other words, our mouse and rat model organisms have caused us to focus too much on the circadian rhythms that dominate these small species' lives, while overlooking longer-term rhythms that play a larger role in larger-bodied species.

Bromage and colleagues (2009) followed this line of reasoning and performed three tests to help determine how lamellae, Retzius periodicities, and body size are related. First, they tested whether or not lamellae are periodic growth increments, and second they tested whether their periodicity corresponds to that of striae of Retzius. They found that the answer to both questions is "yes": within sheep, macaques, humans, and rats, the Retzius periodicity in teeth matched a lamellar rhythm revealed through vital bone labeling. Third, this study also showed that among anthropoid primates and among a larger mammalian sample, there is a very strong correlation between body mass and Retzius periodicity as previous studies had suggested. Given that daily rhythms in body tissues are shared due to their control by central clocks in the hypothalamus, the most likely explanation for the fact that bones and teeth both display longer-period growth increments with the same periodicity is that both tissues are responding to one common physiological system. Bromage and colleagues (2009) have termed this shared rhythm of bone and teeth the Havers–Halberg oscillation, or HHO, in honor of Clopton Havers and Franz Halberg. Given that the hypothalamus acts as the primary metronome of the body's circadian rhythms as well as the importance of oscillations in sympathetic output with regard to bone (discussed above), we would predict that the hypothalamus would also be the generator of this shared long-term rhythm, and that it is expressed in peripheral tissues via autonomic nervous output.

On a basic level, this correspondence of Retzius and lamellar periodicities gives us a powerful calibration tool for reading histological bone growth records with much more precision than has been possible before. Prior to this discovery, histological assessments of bone growth demanded use of lines of arrested growth (LAGs) – whose resolution is generally limited to seasonal and annual timescales, but whose frequency is not self-evident in the morphology (Woodward *et al.*, 2013) – or else indirect estimates of bone formation rate based on types of bone tissue in a section (woven bone, plexiform, lamellar, etc.; e.g., Lee *et al.*, 2013). If a study required more precision than either technique allowed, then that required use of vitally labeled bones: logistically difficult to create/obtain and not available for fossils. With the HHO connection between teeth and bone, one may create a growth chronology of bone through histological examination of an organism's teeth and gain a direct assessment of its HHO periodicity. Then, with this periodicity, counts and measurements of lamellae in relevant histological sections of bone can provide a direct chronology of that bone's growth down to the resolution of the HHO (1–14 days, depending on species).

This is possible because both bones and teeth are formed by secretory cells that lay down matrix in an appositional manner, which as we now know include growth increments as calibration points for specific periods of time. While it is true that early endosteal primary bone is destroyed in the process of growth of the entire organ as the cortical bone overall expands in diameter, the primary bone that remains still directly encodes a faithful record of its own growth that can be mined for life history information. Likewise, even secondary remodeled osteons contain secreted matrix with lamellae, so they can also be used to garner life-history information, although with more difficulty than primary cortical bone. An example of this technique is available in the studies of Bromage and colleagues (2011, 2015), who were able to detect periods of stress and malnourishment in bones of human individuals from Malawi and place those episodes directly within the chronology of the individuals' lifespans using their HHO as obtained from teeth as a calibration point. Because the individuals in the study had known life-history data available (age, domicile, weight, height, etc.), these studies were able to check the validity of their calculations based on the known events.

On a broader level, the HHO has the potential to provide more than just a powerful tool for creating growth chronologies, it also provides us with a physiological mechanism that may reveal a great deal about why and how bone growth and life histories evolve the way they do. Multiple follow-up studies have demonstrated complex scaling patterns of HHO periodicity with respect to body mass, brain mass, and metabolism (Bromage *et al.*, 2009, 2012; Hogg *et al.*, 2015). There is ample physiological and histological evidence to suggest that this scaling is connected to bone growth, and to overall organismal growth and life history. For example, it is known that mammalian cells *in vivo* have their own specific metabolic rates, which largely vary according to the body mass of the species in question, as a component of Kleiber's law. This law specifically states that metabolic rate scales with body mass, at a ¾ power relationship, such that larger animals have lower metabolic rates per unit body mass (Kleiber, 1947). However, when fibroblasts from different mammal species are extracted from their host organisms and placed in identical conditions *in vitro*, they become metabolically indistinguishable (Brown *et al.*, 2007). This suggests that central control is vital to pace cellular activity according to an organism's life-history profile in order to match metabolic activity appropriate to its overall mass and calorie needs. In other words, it is the neuroendocrine system that tells elephant cells to behave like elephant cells and raccoon cells to behave like raccoon cells, not any inherent genetic program contained entirely within these cells themselves. Moreover, because osteoblasts divide in a coordinated fashion under the direction of rhythmic output from the sympathetic nervous system, we expect osteoblast proliferation to scale with the rhythms that control them. Indeed, this is what we see in interspecific studies, as osteocyte lacunar density (a function of how frequently osteoblasts divide as they become incorporated into bone) scales inversely with body mass (Bromage *et al.*, 2009). In effect, smaller mammal species tend to possess a high-frequency HHO and have high osteocyte density (relatively frequent cell proliferation events), while large mammals tend to exhibit the opposite pattern. Combined with the bone-energy homeostasis discussed in the previous section, it becomes evident that the correlations in body/brain size, metabolism, and the growth rate of bone tissue are likely of significance for study of life-history evolution.

Therefore, we predict that the HHO mechanism should influence energy expenditure via osteocalcin and leptin relays as well as coordinate cell proliferation. If we assume that animals larger than a mouse have osteoblast proliferation that is coordinated by the sympathetic nervous system, as do mice, but that their cells are driven to divide over a multi-day cycle following the HHO rhythm, we have a fairly efficient explanation for scaling of growth and metabolic rate in mammals of different size. To be specific, a mouse (HHO of one day or else following only a circadian pattern) will receive 14 signals for its cells to proliferate in a 2-week period, due to the 24-hour oscillation in sympathetic output that mice have been demonstrated to experience. In the same time interval, an elephant's cells (HHO of 14 days) will receive only one signal to proliferate (Bromage *et al.*, 2009). It follows that the mouse's skeleton would tend to grow at a relatively much greater rate – which we know they do, because mouse lamellae and elephant lamellae are of comparable width even though their HHO periodicity differs by a factor of 14 (Bromage *et al.*, 2009). It also becomes evident that this greater rate of cell proliferation and activity would be correlated with a more frenetic calorie expenditure per unit time for the mouse, and a greater basal metabolic rate relative to body mass. Thus we can see how mammals of small body mass have rapid cell division, rapid growth, and a relatively fast metabolism, whereas larger animals have the opposite pattern – and all of this can be tied together neatly by a single system in the form of the HHO model. Luckily, bone is intrinsically linked to adipocytes and the energy system, so that as it experiences upshifts or downshifts in its own activity under sympathetic influence, the physiological literature has demonstrated that it has the potential to influence other body systems to help maintain a coordinated physiology.

Thus we can see that the HHO could play a major role in our understanding of bone growth and life history by serving as a single, elegant mechanism that can help us tie together overall growth, metabolism, reproductive output, lifespan, and many other life-history variables that need to evolve in a coordinated fashion, maintaining cohesive life histories consistent with their metabolic ecology (Bromage *et al.*, 2012). If the model can be validated it should be possible to assess evolution of life history among different species by tracking the evolution of their HHO mechanisms in concert with key variables such as body mass, brain mass, and basal metabolic rate (e.g., Bromage *et al.*, 2009, 2012).

Since the original model, we have also added significant details to our understanding of how HHO biology might guide the evolution of bone growth and life history. Hogg and colleagues (2015), for example, have shown that lemurs have radically low HHO periodicities compared to anthropoid primates. Among anthropoids the range of mean HHO periodicities across species ranges from 1 to 11 days, whereas for lemurs it is limited to 2–4 days – this despite the fact that both taxa share a similar range of body mass variation. Hogg and colleagues interpreted the restricted range of lemur HHO variation as being tied to a long period of independent evolution in the environment of Madagascar, as that environment became increasingly unpredictable through geologic time. Under this idea, the narrow range of HHO periodicities in lemurs is a metabolic adaptation that is part of a suite of bizarre life-history adaptations in this group (Hogg *et al.*, 2015). Importantly, they also argued that *Daubentonia*, the extant lemur species that has arguably the most stable and predictable resource base, has the HHO periodicity, metabolic rate, and other life-history characteristics that most resemble those of anthropoids. These findings demonstrate that ecology could play major roles in determining exactly how HHO physiology coordinates growth and metabolism, which is an important component needed if the model is to be further corroborated.

Moreover, Bromage and Janal (2014) have demonstrated that tissue- and organ-specific metabolic rates among anthropoids correlate strongly with HHO periodicity. For different organs they found a range of regression slopes between 0.2 and 0.28 when excluding RP = 1 species from analyses (the authors argued that RP = 1 species present a biological anomaly); importantly, they found an arithmetic mean for all organs (except the brain) at an approximately ¼ power scaling relationship (slope of 0.25). However, they found that brain mass scales at a power of 0.31, which demonstrates that the high metabolic demands of brain tissue likely have a major influence on the growth of other tissues. As tissue masses increase with body size, the 0.31 slope demonstrates that brain mass will be increasing at a faster rate. Assuming a finite energetic model (i.e., each animal only has access to a finite resource base that it can marshal to support growth, reproduction, homeostasis, and other necessary activities such as predator avoidance), the authors argue that "payment" for brain tissue must come from other tissues. Tissues which scale with body size at a slope below 0.25 are good candidates, and it is important to point out that the digestive tract falls into this category at 0.23. This presents a situation in line with the expensive tissue hypothesis of Aiello and Wheeler (1995), where evolution of modern humans is characterized by a trade-off between brain size and the size of some other tissues, especially the digestive tract. This may help explain the unusual correlations between brain mass, body mass, and HHO seen previously among lemurs (Hogg *et al.*, 2015). However, we do not currently know how bone tissue metabolism scales with respect to body mass and HHO, as there are not enough direct data available for it to have been assessed in the Bromage and Janal study.

A major prediction of the HHO model is that if the hypothalamus is driving a multidien (i.e., multiple-day) biological clock that is entraining multiple body systems to act according to its rhythm, then we should see oscillations in multiple metabolites (specific chemical compounds that are products of physiology) over a time span matching that of the biological rhythm recorded in the striae of Retzius. In the most recent paper published on the HHO model, Bromage and colleagues (2016) performed a metabolic study of pigs that provides the strongest evidence in support of the HHO model to date. In this study, the authors took daily blood samples of 36 cross-bred pigs and used mass spectrometry to quantify the entire metabolome (all present serum metabolites) of each sample. They found a 5-day oscillation in metabolite levels that matched the 5-day Retzius period in the teeth of the sample pigs. Although the specific neurological pathway controlling these oscillations is still unknown, this provides very solid evidence that a central biological clock is coordinating many body systems in a manner similar to what the HHO model predicts.

11.4   Tissue-specific Metabolic Rate of Bone and the HHO

11.4.1   Framework

Because the HHO model is aimed in large part at helping us understand bone growth processes, it is important to see how the correlation of bone metabolism with HHO fits in with the other tissue metabolisms published in Bromage and Janal (2014). This would provide insight as to the types of metabolic demands that bone growth places on the body, compared to other tissues, and therefore give us further insight into the evolution of skeletal growth.

Unfortunately, there are no published data directly assessing the tissue-specific metabolic rate of bone *in vivo* among different mammal species. Therefore, we sought out proxy variables that would provide insight into bone metabolism across species.

Osteocyte lacuna density (OD, number of osteocyte lacunae per unit area of bone), should be a good indicator of bone metabolism, as larger numbers of cells will necessarily require more energy expenditure. According to this model, a species with higher osteocyte density will have higher bone-specific metabolism than species with lower density. Therefore, we analyzed data on OD from extant lemurs and modern humans to assess scaling patterns of bone-specific metabolism.

However, we also wanted to seek out a more direct physiological marker of relative bone metabolism. Serum levels of the bone-produced hormone osteocalcin are commonly used in the literature as a marker for bone metabolism, as are levels of bone-specific alkaline phosphatase (bALP, a byproduct of osteoclast activity). Because osteocalcin in its uncarboxylated form serves as a "keystone" hormone in the neuroendocrine feedback loops regulating bone and energy metabolism, as described above, it is an especially important indicator of bone metabolism on which to focus. Although uncarboxylated osteocalcin is the form of the hormone that is known to influence metabolism, sufficient published data for this particular version of the hormone are not available. Therefore, we operate under the assumption that increased total osteocalcin will be accompanied by an overall increase in the uncar-boxylated version.

11.4.2 Osteocyte Density Methods and Results

To assess intraspecific variation we gathered OD data from six species of extant lemurs as well as a modern human sample, which includes a population from Australia (n = 11) and one from Malawi (n = 10). Human specimens were acquired from the Victorian Institute for Forensic Medicine (Australia) and the University of Malawi College of Medicine (Malawi), respectively. All specimen collection protocols were approved by local ethics committees. The protocol for gathering OD data from midshaft femoral cross-sections is reported in Bromage and colleagues (2015). For the human sample, we assessed the natural logarithm (ln) of OD against ln age, height, and body mass using bivariate ordinary least-squares regression and multiple regression; for lemurs we assessed only ln OD in bivariate regression against ln of the species mean body mass.

Among lemurs (Figure 11.2), there is a reasonably strong relationship between ln body mass and ln OD, at r^2 = 0.566. This relationship is not statistically significant (p = 0.08). We propose that the non-significance is an artifact of the small

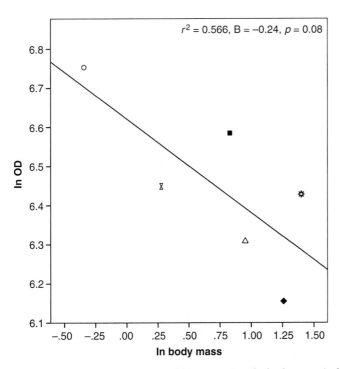

Figure 11.2 Bivariate regression of ln OD against ln body mass in lemurs. Circle, *Hapalemur griseus*; triangle, *Daubentonia madagascariensis*; star, *Propithecus coquereli*; square, *Eulemur fulvus*; hourglass, *Avahi laniger*. All data taken from Hogg *et al.* (2015).

sample size (n = 6), given the moderately strong value of the r^2 statistic. Given this likelihood, plus the fact that selecting α at 0.05 as the boundary for statistical significance is an artificial human designation, we take the conservative approach in not eliminating the possibility of a real biological relationship between ln body mass and ln OD within lemurs. We think a biological link is likely because ln OD is negatively correlated with ln body mass across species as the HHO model predicts, and significant correlations have been found in prior studies (Bromage *et al.*, 2009, 2015). Importantly, the slope of this relationship is –0.24, signifying that species with larger body mass have relatively fewer osteocytes per unit bone, and therefore there is a lower relative metabolic rate for bone tissue in the larger-bodied species (in other words, a lower tissue-specific metabolic rate). With regard to soft tissues, Bromage and Janal (2014: 655) found that in an anthropoid sample, "the slope arithmetic mean for body and tissue masses RI [= RP or HHO periodicity] ≥ 2 is 0.25, equal to the slope with ¼ power that typifies some relationships between life-history characteristics and body size." The relationships found in the prior study also reflect a decrease in specific metabolic rate with increasing body size. Therefore, although the regression slopes are opposite, our results match those of Bromage and Janal by providing evidence that for both bone and soft tissues, specific metabolic rate decreases with increasing body size at a near ¼ power rate. If the slopes shared the same positive or negative value, they would actually be demonstrating *opposite* biological relationships between bone and soft tissue with body mass. These are only suggestions presented by the data we have thus far; our conclusions here are perforce limited by the small sample size. However, we feel that these first-stage results are supportive of the HHO model and warrant further study.

That being said, as discussed above, lemurs are unusual compared to anthropoid primates with regard to their HHO periodicity scaling, for reasons probably stemming from their long-term independent evolution within Madagascar. Unfortunately there are presently insufficient corresponding anthropoid ln OD data to compare against that of the lemurs, so we cannot say if the lemur OD scaling is significantly different from that of the anthropoids as is the case with their HHO periodicity, or whether the OD scaling of both groups follows a similar pattern which their HHO periodicity does not. These factors also suggest that we must be careful not to extrapolate too much meaning from the OD data that we have available at this point.

In multiple regression analysis of our human sample, we found that none of the predictors were significantly related to ln OD; although ln height approaches significance, we think this is likely due to a collinearity bias. In bivariate regression, ln height was a significant predictor for ln OD (see Table 11.1 and Figure 11.3A). We think that height is a better predictor than body mass because in modern industrialized society the variance in body mass per given height is abnormally high due to prevalence of obesity, sedentary lifestyles, etc., in some populations (such as Australia), hence the large confidence interval in regressions of ln body mass against ln height in our modern human sample (Figure 11.3B). In other words, among modern humans height is likely a poor predictor for body mass. In general, therefore, our

Table 11.1 Regression statistics for ln OD against ln age, ln body mass, and ln height among modern humans from Malawi.

Model for ln OD	Variable assessed	Variable r² (if avail.); p	B	Std error	Beta	95% confidence interval for B	
						Lower bound	Upper bound
Multiple regression, all variables r² = 0.316, p = 0.085, n = 21	ln age	0.30	0.11	0.10	0.03	–0.10	0.31
	ln body mass	0.91	0.02	0.17	0.22	–0.35	0.38
	ln height	0.08	0.53	0.28	0.46	–0.06	1.12
Bivariate regression n = 21	ln age	0.10; 0.16	0.15	0.10	0.32	–0.06	0.37
	ln body mass	0.09; 0.19	0.22	0.16	0.30	–0.12	0.55
	ln height	**0.27; 0.02**	**0.60**	**0.23**	**0.52**	**0.13**	**1.07**

Bold font = statistically significant

results agree with the prediction that ln OD, and therefore bone metabolism, scale with body size. Our results are also similar to those of Bromage and colleagues (2015), who had demonstrated that in the Malawi sample alone, the correlation between ln OD and ln body mass among humans is *positive*, rather than negative as determined from interspecific samples (i.e., Bromage et al., 2009; this study). We view this difference from interspecific results as being related to physiological constraints within the human species. That is, humans have a large range of body sizes but our variation in duration of growth does not have an equivalent range. Therefore, individuals who are programmed to reach a larger body size must grow more quickly, and consequently have higher cell-proliferation rates (for further discussion see Bromage et al., 2015).

11.4.3 Osteocalcin and bALP Methods and Results

For osteocalcin and bALP analyses, we gathered data on serum values of these two hormones for seven mammal species from the literature (Table 11.1). All animals were from captive or domesticated populations. We included data only from young adults, to control for changes in osteocalcin and bALP levels through the juvenile period and the documented age-related decline in the levels of these two markers (Allen, 2008; Kilgallon et al., 2008). Ln values of serum osteocalcin and bALP were regressed against ln body mass data drawn from the literature, matched to breed where applicable (Table 11.2).

Serum osteocalcin was strongly and significantly correlated to body mass (Figure 11.4). The relationship is negative, with a slope value (β) of –0.24. As with ln OD results, the decrease in osteocalcin levels with increasing body size signifies relatively lower metabolic rates for bone tissue at a relatively large

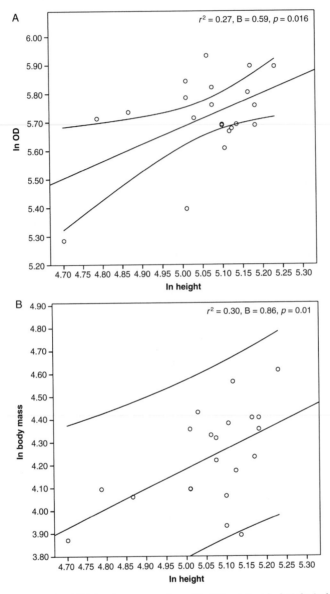

Figure 11.3 (A) Bivariate regression of ln OD against ln height in humans. (B) Bivariate regression of ln body mass against ln height in humans. Although the correlation is significant, the 95% confidence interval is large.

mass, occurring at a slope whose magnitude (irrespective of the positive or negative value of the integer) approaches a ¼ power scale. For bALP, there was no significant correlation and the relationship was negative ($\beta = -0.126$). The slope value for osteocalcin is critical, as it suggests that bone metabolism scales with body mass in a similar manner to most soft tissues as in Bromage and Janal (2014). Again, our negative slope and the positive slopes of the Bromage and

Janal study both signify decreases in relative metabolic rate of tissues with a concomitant increase in body size, so even though the slopes seem superficially opposite one another (in that ours have a negative value), the numbers are in fact in agreement. The fact that the raw magnitude of the slopes are similar between the two studies is likely biologically meaningful; although our species sample is very different from that of the prior study, the close correspondence of the scaling power is unlikely to be coincidental. It is also interesting to note that the slope value for ln bALP vs. ln body mass (Figure 11.4) is very close to one-half that of osteocalcin. Also, raw bALP values (i.e., without logarithmic transformation) do correlate strongly with ln body mass (r^2 = 0.612, B = −10.2, p = 0.02). While ln osteocalcin and ln bALP do not correlate significantly with one another (r^2 = 0.464, p = 0.06), their correlation does approach significance. It may be that the small sample size is influencing this result. However, when ln osteocalcin is regressed against raw bALP values and vice versa, strong and significant relationships do appear (r^2 = 0.671, p = 0.13; r^2 = 0.678, p = 0.12). The sum of this evidence suggests that we should not discount bALP as an indicator of bone tissue metabolism and a predictor of HHO biology, and that larger samples may help clarify its role.

Regardless, osteocalcin data suggest that like the majority of tissues, the relative metabolism of bone scales negatively with body mass, at a scaling relationship that approximates −0.25. As shown above, we know that smaller mammals will tend to have a relatively higher number of osteocalcin-producing cells, because osteocyte density is also known to scale negatively with body mass across species. Relatively more osteocalcin-producing cells seems likely directly linked to the higher osteocalcin levels we demonstrate in these smaller mammals, for obvious reasons. Therefore, following our assumption above, there should be a higher level of the uncarboxylated version of the osteocalcin hormone to help drive the frenetic metabolism of smaller mammals. This increased metabolic rate will provide more relative energy throughput to pay the expensive costs of rapid bone growth (which in turn drives high osteocalcin levels, and so on). The converse situation will tend to occur in larger mammals.

11.4.4 Discussion

Lemur and other mammal osteocyte density data suggest that across species, osteocyte density (and therefore osteoblast proliferation, as matrix production seems to be tied to osteoblast numbers; see Bromage *et al.*, 2009) may be scaling in a manner similar to osteocalcin. However, data from additional species are needed to verify this because lemurs are known to be unusual in their HHO expression (Hogg *et al.*, 2015). This supports our hypothesis; however, we would argue that the serum markers we tested are a more reliable direct indicator of bone physiology, because assessment of osteocyte density cannot take into account differences in the relative metabolic rates of individual cells compared across taxa (only the overall contribution of the *number* of cells to bone tissue). Because osteocalcin levels should rise

Table 11.2 Raw data for analyses of osteocalcin and bALP.

Species (breed)	Osteocalcin total ng/ml [ln] (ref)	bALP U/l [ln] (ref)	body mass, kg [ln] (ref)
Mus musculus	220 [5.394] (Richman et al., 1999)	155 [5.3043] (Richman et al., 1999)	0.026 [-3.650] (Poggi et al., 2007)
Rattus norvegicus	66 [4.19] (Lian et al., 1989; Srivastava et al. 2000)	–	0.353 [-1.043] (Martinez et al. 2010)
Canis familiaris (beagle)	19.4 [2.965] (Allen, 2008)	15.3 [2.728] (Allen, 2008)	8.9 [2.186] (Crippa et al., 1992)
Papio hamadryas F	24.59 [3.202] (Havill et al., 2006)	41.52 [3.726] (Havill et al., 2006)	18.84 [2.936] (Havill et al., 2006)
Papio hamadryas M	32.8 [3.490] (Havill et al., 2006)	52.2 [3.955] (Havill et al., 2006)	29.97 [3.400] (Havill et al., 2006)
Homo sapiens F (modern)	25.3 [3.230] (Binkley et al., 2000)	22.5 [3.114] (Binkley et al., 2000)	53.6 [3.982] (Binkley et al., 2000)
Homo sapiens M (modern)	31.1 [3.437] (Binkley et al., 2000)	24.5 [3.199] (Binkley et al., 2000)	60.2 [4.098] (Binkley et al., 2000)
Equus caballus (standardbred)	6.7 [1.902] (Lepage et al., 1990)	41 [3.714] (Trumble et al., 2008)	455 [6.120] (Malinowski et al., 1996)
Elephas maximus	15 [2.708] (Kilgallon et al., 2008)	30 [3.40] (Kilgallon et al., 2008)	3903 [8.269] (Kilgallon et al., 2008)

and fall according to both total cell number and the activity level of osteoblasts, as well as being linked to overall metabolic systems as described above, it is the most telling factor in our assessment here. Still, we acknowledge that future studies with larger sample sizes are needed to corroborate this further.

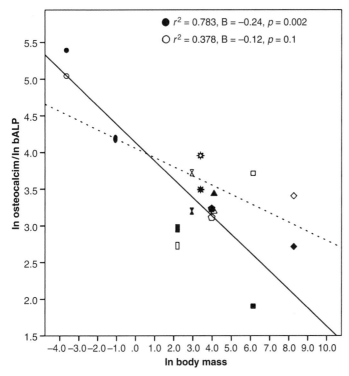

Figure 11.4 Bivariate regression of ln osteocalcin/ln bALP serum levels in young adult mammals. Black-filled shapes/solid line, osteocalcin; hollow shapes/dotted line, bALP. Circle, *Mus musculus*; oval, *Rattus norwegicus*; rectangle, *Canis familiaris* (beagle); hourglass, female *Papio hamadryas*; star, male *Papio hamadryas*; pentagon, female *Homo sapiens*; triangle, male *Homo sapiens*; square, *Equus caballus* (standard-bred); diamond, *Elephas maximus*.

Ultimately, as osteocalcin release and osteoblast proliferation are both known to operate under the control of hypothalamic clocks (Fu *et al.*, 2005; Allen, 2008), we predict that the HHO acts as the central clock, which manifests the genetically programmed scaling laws of metabolism and size. The fact that osteocalcin levels and possibly osteocyte density appear to scale with body mass in a manner that closely resembles soft-tissue-specific scaling is strong circumstantial evidence that this is the case. The similar scaling pattern of tissue-specific metabolism between bone and soft tissues also suggests that the HHO is exclusively linked to hard tissues, but has correlations with organismal physiology and life history in general. This further corroborates interpretations of the pig metabolome data presented by Bromage and colleagues (2016).

11.5   Anthropological Implications

All in all, bone tissue clearly has a major role to play in the regulation of the body's metabolic systems. Moreover, experimental studies have demonstrated that the neuroendocrine system, centered in the hypothalamus, exerts direct control over bone growth and remodeling through a combination of sympathetic postsynaptic potentials and humoral factors including leptin. We have amassed substantial indirect evidence that this control operates according to a biological rhythm known as the HHO, also generated in the hypothalamus, which varies among taxa and which is expressed histologically in bones and teeth as periodic growth increments. The periodicity of these increments demonstrates that variations in the HHO rhythm are correlated with differences in size and overall life history. Therefore, we postulate that a major purpose of the HHO is to operate as a physiological mechanism that maintains the pace and pattern of bone growth within the context of species' overall life histories. With regard to bone metabolism, our results also suggest that bone metabolism seems to scale at a 0.24 rate, close to the 0.25 mean for non-nervous tissues. Although we admit that taken separately the small sample sizes for our ln OD and osteocalcin studies provide only weak to moderate support for this contention, the fact that both analyses agree despite small sample sizes and different sample species adds a great deal of strength to the argument. Being close to the 0.25 mean suggests that bone is not one of the tissues that is sacrificed to fuel brain size following the expensive tissue hypothesis, unlike stomach or spleen mass which scale at 0.2 and 0.19, respectively (Bromage and Janal, 2014). A likely explanation for this is that the mechanical function of bone at increasing body sizes is so important that bone is typically not sacrificed to pay for the calorie expenditures associated with increased brain size. This is of importance for understanding bone growth and evolution of skeletal form in general.

Admittedly, much of the evidence to support the HHO model at this point is indirect, being drawn from histology and inferred from the current state of knowledge in the areas of bone and neuroendocrine physiology; the pig metabolome data of Bromage and colleagues (2016) is the most direct evidence we have. Thus far we have tracked the hard-tissue manifestation of a multidien biological rhythm that is shared between bones and teeth, we have a large amount of data regarding the relationships between those rhythms and predictor variables related to life history, and we have direct evidence that multiple body systems oscillate according to the same rhythm thanks the pig metabolome data. We have examined Retzius periodicities, osteocyte density, and metabolic scaling within the framework of the predictions of the HHO model. In all of these areas, the predictions of the model (which, again, is built upon our current understanding of neuroendocrine interactions with the skeleton and energy homeostasis) have been supported. However, to gain the most solid corroboration of the HHO model, we need to isolate the "smoking gun," as it were, using physiological studies that can directly identify the specific neuroendocrine mechanisms in the hypothalamus and experimentally manipulate the system. This requires several key components. First, we need direct measurements of sympathetic nervous activity oscillating according to a timescale that matches an organism's HHO. Second, we need follow-up studies to identify the nucleus – again, most likely within the hypothalamus – that generates this rhythm. Once this nucleus is identified, we can use experimental models to examine the effects that a knockout of this nucleus would have on teeth, bone, and indeed cell proliferation and metabolism in general. Lastly, genetic studies would be needed to identify the sources of variation in the HHO, through which we could better understand its evolution. Likewise, more samples are also needed with regard to HHO rhythms in various mammal taxa, such that we can understand the influence that ecology has on bone growth and life history via evolution of the HHO. These are all research areas currently under development, and without these data presently being available we freely acknowledge that the HHO model is a provisional tool for exploring life-history evolution, albeit a potentially powerful one. Using the data available we have created the model and begun the monumental task of gathering evidence to support or refute it, and this chapter is intended as a review of the progress to date.

That being said, we have seen that a better understanding of the HHO has potential for giving us a tool to assess changes in skeletal growth among primates as well as for assessing overall life-history evolution. This tool has direct relevance for understanding hominin evolution and the evolution of variation within the modern human species. As noted above, the ability to determine individual organisms' HHO rhythms using histological analysis of teeth gives us a means to calibrate growth and remodeling schedules within bone tissue, so that we can directly assess evolutionary changes in skeletal growth patterns within extant organisms, saving ourselves the cost and time investment of longitudinal studies of living animals. Moreover, this calibration tool allows us to directly assess skeletal growth processes in fossil organisms within a precise chronological framework. Consequently, this provides the ability to directly measure the response of bone tissue to nutrition, pathology, seasonality, and miscellaneous sources of stress within the fossil record. For example, we can assess how skeletal growth responds to changing rainfall patterns within individual lifetimes and also make comparisons across individuals, as has already been done among modern humans (Bromage *et al.*, 2011, 2015).

Ideas developed here relating to overall HHO periodicity patterns can be used to assess how ecology and phylogeny drive life-history evolution among different primate species and groups. This has the capacity to inform our understanding not only of the evolutionary history of specific groups such as the lemurs or the homi-nins, but also to increase our knowledge of larger-scale evolutionary processes. As discussed above, assessment of HHO periodicity has already given us a tremendous insight into the differences in the evolution of ontogeny between lemurs and anthropoids that likely result from factors associated with lemurs' long evolutionary history in Madagascar. The observation that lemurs are highly restricted in their HHO patterns compared to anthropoids and seem to have decoupled their maturation rate from their body mass in a unique way (Hogg *et al.*, 2015) suggest additional meaningful avenues of research.

Also, with regard to bone-tissue-specific scaling, it is important to reiterate that bone metabolism likely scales similarly to that of other tissues, excepting the brain (although sample size limitations must be dealt with before this can be stated with certainty). The fact that brain mass scales differently with respect to HHO has major implications for hominin evolution inasmuch as encephalization is a major feature in the evolutionary history of this group. For example, our data provide further support for the expensive tissue hypothesis, and raise the idea that if we consider the brain as an "expensive tissue" following Aiello and Wheeler (1995), then bone does not seem to be one of the tissues where the body goes through "cost-cutting" in order to pay for that large brain within the overall limited resource budget. The tissue-specific data likewise suggest that encephalization patterns in hominins may be part of (and may have driven) an overall growth and life-history trend that diverges from those of their anthropoid relatives, much as the unusual lemur ecology drives its own pattern. This is an especially important question, because modern human life history is so different from that of the other hominoids; we have a relatively higher energy budget and a higher reproductive output, coupled with a paradoxically long juvenile period and lifespan (Schultz, 1960; Harvey and Clutton-Brock, 1985; Leigh, 2004, 2012; Reiches *et al.*, 2009; Isler and van Schaik, 2012; Pontzer, 2012; Schwartz, 2012). Therefore, much research into hominin life history has been devoted to (1) ascertaining when in our evolutionary past this separation from the apes occurred, and (2) discerning what drove our unique life-history adaptations. To this end, more detailed HHO variation data for the hominins and non-hominin apes may help us finally pinpoint detailed answers to such questions.

Acknowledgments

This research was funded by the 2010 Max Planck Research Award which is endowed by the German Federal Ministry of Education and Research to the Max Planck Society and the Alexander von Humboldt Foundation in respect of the Hard Tissue Research Program in Human Paleobiomics.

References

Aiello, L. C. and Wheeler, P. (1995). The expensive-tissue hypothesis: the brain and the digestive system in human and primate evolution. *Current Anthropology*, 36(2), 199–221.
Allen, M. J. (2008). Biochemical markers of bone metabolism in animals: uses and limitations. *Veterinary Clinical Pathology*, 32(3), 101–113.
Allison, S. J., Baldock, P. A. and Herzog, H. (2007). The control of bone remodeling by neuropeptide Y receptors. *Peptides*, 28, 320–325.
Amling, M., Pogoda, P., Beil, F. T., *et al.* (2001). Central control of bone mass: brainstorming of the skeleton. *Advances in Experimental Medicine & Biology*, 496, 85–94.
Appenzeller, O., Gunga, H. C., Qualls, C., *et al.* (2005). A hypothesis: autonomic rhythms are reflected in growth lines of teeth in humans and extinct archosaurs. *Autonomic Neuroscience*, 117, 115–119.
Asper, H. (1916). Uber die "Braune Retzius" sche Parallelstreifung im Schmelz der Menschlichen Zahne, Schweiz. *Vierteljahrschrift Zahnheilk*, 26, 277–314.
Bajayo, A., Bar, A., Denes, A., *et al.* (2012). Skeletal parasympathetic innervation communicates central IL-1 signals regulating bone mass accrual. *Proceedings of the National Academy of Sciences*, 109, 15455–15460.
Berendsen, A. D. and Olsen, B. R. (2014). Osteoblast–adipocyte lineage plasticity in tissue development, maintenance and pathology. *Cellular and Molecular Life Sciences*, 71, 493–497.

Biewener, A. A. (1982). Bone strength in small mammals and bipedal birds: do safety factors change with body size? *Journal of Experimental Biology*, 98, 289–301.

Binkley, N. C., Krueger, D. C., Engelke, J. A., Foley, A. L., and Suttie, J. W. (2000). Vitamin K supplementation reduces serum concentrations of under-γ-carboxylated osteocalcin in healthy young and elderly adults. *American Journal of Clinical Nutrition*, 72(6) , 1523–1528.

Boyde, A. (1979). Carbonate concentration, crystal centers, core dissolution, caries, cross striations, circadian rhythms, and compositional contrasts in the SEM. *Journal of Dental Research*, 58(B), 981–983.

Bromage, T. G. and Janal, M. N. (2014). The Havers–Halberg Oscillation regulates primate tissue and organ masses across the life history continuum. *Biological Journal of the Linnean Society*, 112(4), 649–656.

Bromage, T. G., Lacruz, R., Hogg, R. T., *et al.* (2009). Lamellar bone reconciles enamel rhythms, body size, and organismal life history. *Calcified Tissue International*, 84, 388–404.

Bromage, T. G., Juwayeyi, Y. M., Smolyar, I., *et al.* (2011). Enamel-calibrated lamellar bone reveals long period growth rate variability in humans. *Cells Tissues Organs*, 194(2–4), 124–130.

Bromage, T. G., Hogg, R. T., Lacruz, R. S. and Hou, C. (2012). Primate enamel evinces long period biological timing and regulation of life history. *Journal of Theoretical Biology*, 305, 131–144.

Bromage, T. G., Juwayeyi, Y. M., Katris, J.A., *et al.* (2015). The scaling of human osteocyte lacuna density with body size and metabolism. *Comptes Rendus Palevol*, 15(1), 32–39.

Bromage, T. G., Idaghdour, Y., Lacruz, R. S., *et al.* (2016). The swine plasma metabolome chronicles "many days" biological timing and functions linked to growth. *PLOS ONE*, 11, e0145919.

Brown, M. F., Gratton, T. P. and Stuart, J. A. (2007). Metabolic rate does not scale with body mass in cultured mammalian cells. *American Journal of Physiology – Regulatory, Integrative, and Comparative Physiology*, 292, R2115–R2121.

Christiansen, P. (2001). Mass allometry of the appendicular skeleton in terrestrial mammals. *Journal of Morphology*, 251(2), 195–209.

Confavreaux, C. B., Levine, R. L. and Karsenty, G. (2009). A paradigm of integrative physiology, the crosstalk between bone and energy metabolisms. *Molecular and Cellular Endocrinology*, 310, 21–29.

Crippa, L., Ferro, E., Melloni, I., *et al.* (1992). Echocardiographic parameters and indices in the normal Beagle dog. *Laboratory Animals*, 26, 190–195.

Dean, M. C. (2000). Incremental markings in enamel and dentine: what they can tell us about the way teeth grow. *In:* Teaford, M. F., Smith, M. M. and Ferguson, M. W. J. (eds.) *Development, Function, and Evolution of Teeth.* Cambridge: Cambridge University Press, pp. 119–130.

Dean, M. C. and Scandrett, A. E. (1995). Rates of dentine mineralization in permanent human teeth. *International Journal of Osteoarchaeology*, 5, 349–358.

Denes, A., Boldogkoi, Z., Uhereczky, G., *et al.* (2005). Central autonomic control of the bone marrow: multisynaptic tract tracing by recombinant pseudorabies virus. *Neuroscience*, 134, 947–963.

Driessler, F. and Baldock, P. A. (2010). Hypothalamic regulation of bone. *Journal of Molecular Endocrinology*, 45, 175–181.

Ducy, P. (2011). The role of osteocalcin in the endocrine cross-talk between bone remodelling and energy metabolism. *Diabetologia*, 54(6), 1291–1297.

Ducy, P., Desbois, C., Boyce, B., *et al.* (1996). Increased bone formation in osteocalcin-deficient mice. *Nature*, 382(6590), 448–452.

Ducy, P., Amling, M., Takeda, S., *et al.* (2000a). Leptin inhibits bone formation through a hypothalamic relay: a central control of bone mass. *Cell*, 100(2), 197–207.

Ducy, P., Schinke, T. and Karsenty, G. (2000b). The osteoblast: a sophisticated fibroblast under central surveillance. *Science*, 289(5484), 1501–1504.

Elefteriou, F., Campbell, P. and Ma, Y. (2014). Control of bone remodeling by the peripheral sympathetic nervous system. *Calcified Tissue International*, 94, 140–151.

Ferron, M. and Lacombe, J. (2014). Regulation of energy metabolism by the skeleton: osteocalcin and beyond. *Archives of Biochemistry and Biophysics*, 56(1), 137–146.

Fu, L., Patel, M. S., Bradley, A., Wagner, E. F. and Karsenty, G. (2005). The molecular clock mediates leptin-regulated bone formation. *Cell*, 122(5), 803–815.

Halberg, F. (1969). Chronobiology. *Annual Review of Physiology*, 31, 675–726.

Hamrick, M. W. (2004). Leptin, bone mass, and the thrifty phenotype. *Journal of Bone and Mineral Research*, 19(10), 1607–1611.

Hamrick, M. W. and Ferrari, S. L. (2008). Leptin and the sympathetic connection of fat to bone. *Osteoporosis International*, 19, 905–912.

Hamrick, M. W., Della Fera, M. A., Choi, Y., et al. (2005). Leptin treatment induces loss of bone marrow adipocytes and increases bone formation in leptin-deficient *ob/ob* mice. *Journal of Bone and Mineral Research*, 20(6), 994–1001.

Hamrick, M. W., Della Fera, M. A., Choi, Y., et al. (2007). Injections of leptin into rat ventromedial hypothalamus increase adipose apoptosis in peripheral fat and in bone marrow. *Cell and Tissue Research*, 327, 113–141.

Harvey, P. H. and Clutton-Brock, T. H. (1985). Life history variation in primates. *Evolution*, 39, 559–581.

Havill, L. M., Rogers, J., Cox, L. A. and Mahaney, M. C. (2006). QTL with pleiotropic effects on serum levels of bone-specific alkaline phosphatase and osteocalcin maps to the baboon ortholog of human chromosome 6p23–21.3. *Journal of Bone and Mineral Research*, 21(12), 1888–1896.

Hinoi, E., Gao, N., Jung, D. Y., et al. (2008). The sympathetic tone mediates leptin's inhibition of insulin secretion by modulating osteocalcin bioactivity. *Journal of Cell Biology*, 183, 1235–1242.

Hogg, R. T. (2010). Dental microstructure and growth in the cebid primates. PhD Dissertation, City University of New York.

Hogg, R. T., Godfrey, L. R., Schwartz, G. T., et al. (2015). Lemur biorhythms and life history evolution. *PLOS ONE*, 10, e0134210.

Idelevich, A., Sato, K. and Baron, R. (2013). What are the effects of leptin on bone and where are they exerted? *Journal of Bone and Mineral Research*, 28(1), 18–21.

Isler, K. and Van Schaik, C. P. (2012). Allomaternal care, life history and brain size evolution in mammals. *Journal of Human Evolution*, 63, 52–63.

Karsenty, G. (2001). Central control of bone formation. *Advances in Nephrology*, 31, 119–133.

Karsenty, G. (2006). Convergence between bone and energy homeostasis: leptin regulation of bone mass. *Cell Metabolism*, 4, 341–348.

Kilgallon, C., Flach, E., Boardman, W., et al. (2008). Analysis of biochemical markers of bone metabolism in Asian elephants (*Elephas maximus*). *Journal of Zoo and Wildlife Medicine*, 39(4), 527–536.

Kleiber, M. (1947). Body size and metabolic rate. *Physiological Reviews*, 27(4), 511–541.

Lacruz, R. S., Dean, M. C., Ramirez-Rozzi, F. and Bromage, T. G. (2008). Megadontia, striae periodicity and patterns of enamel secretion in Plio–Pleistocene fossil hominins. *Journal of Anatomy*, 213, 148–158.

Lacruz, R. S., Hacia, J. G., Bromage, T. G., et al. (2012). The circadian clock modulates enamel development. *Journal of Biological Rhythms*, 27(3), 237–245.

Lee, A. H., Huttenlocker, A. K., Padian, K. and Woodward, H. N. (2013). Analysis of growth rates. *In:* Padian, K. and Lamm, E. T. (eds.) *Bone Histology of Fossil Tetrapods.* Berkeley, CA: University of California Press, pp. 217–252.

Lee, N. K. and Karsenty, G. (2008). Reciprocal regulation of bone and energy metabolism. *Trends in Endocrinology and Metabolism*, 19(5), 161–166.

Lee, N. K., Sowa, H., Hinoi, E., et al. (2007). Endocrine regulation of energy metabolism by the skeleton. *Cell*, 130, 456–469.

Leigh, S. R. (2004). Brain growth, life history, and cognition in primate and human evolution. *American Journal of Primatology*, 62, 139–164.

Leigh, S. R. (2012). Brain size growth and life history in human evolution. *Evolutionary Biology*, 39, 587–599.

Lepage, O. M., Marcoux, M. and Tremblay, A. (1990). Serum osteocalcin or bone Gla-protein, a biochemical marker for bone metabolism in horses: differences in serum levels with age. *Canadian Journal of Veterinary Research*, 54, 223–226.

Lian, J., Stewart, C., Puchacz, E., *et al.* (1989). Structure of the rat osteocalcin gene and regulation of vitamin D-dependent expression. *Biochemistry*, 86, 1143–1147.

Malinowski, K., Christensen, R. A., Hafs, H. D. and Scanes, C. G. (1996). Age and breed differences in thyroid hormones, insulin-like growth factor (IGF)-I and IGF binding proteins in female horses. *Journal of Animal Science*, 74, 1936–1942.

Martinez, C., Gonzalez, E., Garcia, R. S., *et al.* (2010). Effects on body mass of laboratory rats after ingestion of drinking water with sucrose, fructose, aspartame, and sucralose additives. *The Open Obesity Journal*, 2010(2), 116–124.

Okada, M. (1943). Hard tissues of animal body – highly interesting details of Nippon studies in periodic patterns of hard tissue are described. *Shanghai Evening Post, Medical Edition*, 43, 15–31.

Okada, M. and Mimura, T. (1940). Zur Physiologie und Pharmakologie der Hartgewebe. IV. Mitteilung: Tagesrhythmus in der Knochenlamellen- bildung. *Proceedings of the Japan Pharmacological Society*, 95–97.

Poggi, M., Bastelica, D., Gual, P., *et al.* (2007). *C3H/HeJ* mice carrying a toll-like receptor 4 mutation are protected against the development of insulin resistance in white adipose tissue in response to a high-fat diet. *Diabetologia*, 50, 1267–1276.

Pontzer, H. (2012). Ecological energetics in early *Homo*. *Current Anthropology*, 53, S346–358.

Rawson, M. J., Cornelissen, G., Holte, J., *et al.* (2000). Circadian and circaseptan components of blood pressure and heart rate during depression. *Scripta Medica*, 73, 117–124.

Reiches, M. W., Ellison, P. T., Lipson, S. F., *et al.* (2009). Pooled energy budget and human life history. *American Journal of Human Biology*, 21, 421–429.

Richman, C., Baylink, D. J., Lang, K., Dony, C. and Mohan, S. (1999). Recombinant human insulin-like growth factor-binding protein-5 stimulates bone formation parameters *in vitro* and *in vivo*. *Endocrinology*, 140(10), 4699–4705.

Roenneberg, T. and Morse, D. (1993). Two circadian oscillators in one cell. *Nature*, 362, 362–364.

Rubin, J. and Rubin, C. (2008). Review: Functional adaptation to loading of a single bone is neuronally regulated and involves multiple bones. *Journal of Bone and Mineral Research*, 23(9), 1369–1371.

Sample, S. J., Behan, M., Smith, L., *et al.* (2008). Functional adaptation to loading of a single bone is neuronally regulated and involves multiple bones. *Journal of Bone and Mineral Research*, 23(9), 1372–1381.

Schultz, A. H. (1960). Age changes in primates and their modification in man. *In:* Tanner, J. M. (ed.) *Human Growth*. New York, NY: Pergamon, pp. 1–20.

Schwartz, G. T. (2012). Growth, development, and life history throughout the evolution of *Homo*. *Current Anthropology*, 53(S6), S395–S408.

Shi, Y., Yadav, V. K., Suda, N., *et al.* (2008). Dissociation of the neuronal regulation of bone mass and energy metabolism by leptin *in vivo*. *Proceedings of the National Academy of Sciences*, 105(51), 20529–20533.

Shi, Y., Oury, F., Yadav, V. K., *et al.* (2010). Signaling through M3 muscarinic receptor favors bone mass accrual by decreasing sympathetic activity. *Cell Metabolism*, 11, 231–238.

Shinoda, H. and Okada, M. (1988). Diurnal rhythms in the formation of lamellar bone in young growing animals. *Proceedings of the Japan Academy*, 64(Series B), 307–310.

Sibly, R. M. and Brown, J. H. (2007). Effects of body size and lifestyle on evolution of mammal life histories. *Proceedings of the National Academy of Sciences*, 104(45), 17707–17712.

Smith, T. M. (2008). Incremental dental development: methods and applications in hominoid evolutionary studies. *Journal of Human Evolution*, 54, 205–224.

Srivastava, A. K., Bhattacharyya, S., Castillo, G., *et al.* (2000). Development and application of a serum C-telopeptide and osteocalcin assay to measure bone turnover in an ovariectomized rat model. *Calcified Tissue International*, 66, 435–442.

Steppan, C. M., Crawford, D. T., Chidsey-Frink, K. L., Ke, H. and Swick, A. G. (2000). Leptin is a potent stimulator of bone growth in *ob/ob* mice. *Peptides*, 92(1–3), 73–78.

Tafforeau, P., Bentaleb, I., Jaeger, J. J. and Martin, C. (2007). Nature of laminations and mineralization in rhinoceros enamel using histology and X-ray synchrotron microtomography: potential implications for palaeoenvironmental isotopic studies. *Palaeogeography, Palaeoclimatology, Palaeoecology*, 246, 206–227.

Takeda, S. (2008). Central control of bone remodeling. *Journal of Neuroendocrinology*, 20(6), 802–807.

Takeda, S. and Karsenty, G. (2008). Molecular bases of the sympathetic regulation of bone mass. *Bone*, 42, 837–840.

Takeda, S., Elefteriou, F., Levasseur, R., *et al.* (2002). Leptin regulates bone formation via the sympathetic nervous system. *Cell*, 111(3), 305–317.

Trumble, T. N., Brown, M. P., Merritt, K. A., *et al.* (2008). Joint dependent concentrations of bone alkaline phosphatase in serum and synovial fluids of horses with osteochondral injury: an analytical and clinical validation. *Osteoarthritis and Cartilage*, 16(7), 779–786.

Turner, R. T., Kalra, S. P., Wong, C. P., *et al.* (2013). Peripheral leptin regulates bone formation. *Journal of Bone and Mineral Research*, 28(1), 22–34.

Ueyama, T., Krout, K., Nguyen, X. and Karpitskiy, A. (1999). Suprachiasmatic nucleus: a central autonomic clock. *Nature Neuroscience*, 2, 1051–1053.

Woodward, H. N., Padian, K. and Lee, A. H. (2013). Skeletochronology. *In:* Padian, K. and Lamm, E. T. (eds.) *Bone Histology of Fossil Tetrapods*. Berkeley, CA: University of California Press, pp. 195–216.

Wu, J. Y., Cornelissen, G., Tarquini, B., *et al.* (1990). Circaseptan and circannual modulation of circadian rhythms in neonatal blood pressure and heart rate. *Progress in Clinical and Biological Research*, 341A, 643–652.

Zvonic, S., Ptitsyn, A. A., Kilroy, G., *et al.* (2007). Circadian oscillation of gene expression in murine calvarial bone. *Journal of Bone and Mineral Research*, 22(3), 357–365.

12 Structural and Mechanical Changes in Trabecular Bone during Early Development in the Human Femur and Humerus

Timothy M. Ryan, David A. Raichlen and James H. Gosman

12.1 Introduction

Many evolutionary functional morphology studies within biological anthropology assume a direct relationship between skeletal form and biomechanical function. Such studies often rely heavily upon the fundamental concept of "bone functional adaptation," or the idea that bone tissue is responsive to and reflective of skeletal loading throughout an organism's life. As a result, cortical and trabecular bone structure are treated as more or less faithful records of activity during an individual's lifetime and are therefore generally considered robust indicators of behavior and behavioral variation in past and present populations and species. Many studies on human and non-human primates and other mammals have suggested a link between cortical bone cross-sectional geometric properties (Larsen, 1995, 2015; Lieberman, 1997; Bridges *et al.*, 2000; Ruff, 2005b, 2009; Carlson and Judex, 2007; Shaw and Stock, 2009a, 2009b; Wallace *et al.*, 2013) or three-dimensional trabecular bone structure (MacLatchy and Müller, 2002; Ryan and Ketcham, 2002b, 2005; Lazenby *et al.*, 2008b, 2011; Barak *et al.*, 2011; Wallace *et al.*, 2013; Ryan and Shaw, 2012, 2015; Matarazzo, 2015) and the loads engendered during different physical activities. Other studies, however, have called into question the functional significance of cortical and trabecular bone structural variation in primates and other mammals (Fajardo *et al.*, 2007; Carlson *et al.*, 2008; Ryan and Walker, 2010; Shaw and Ryan, 2012; Wallace *et al.*, 2014, 2015; Chapter 10). In order to gain a better understanding of the functional significance of cortical and trabecular bone structural variation in adult organisms, it is critical to develop a more robust understanding of the factors that contribute to bone development during ontogeny and that ultimately contribute to building adult bone morphology.

Many morphological features of the vertebrate postcranial skeleton develop in response to specific behaviors and the resultant mechanical stimuli. Within humans, various important functional characters of the postcranial skeleton, including the femoral bicondylar angle (Tardieu and Trinkaus, 1994), the lumbosacral angle (Abitbol, 1987), epiphyseal morphology (Carter *et al.*, 1989), cortical bone structure of long bones (Ruff, 2003a, 2003b; Shaw and Stock, 2009b), and three-dimensional trabecular bone architecture (Ryan and Krovitz, 2006; Gosman and Ketcham, 2009; Zeininger, 2013; Raichlen *et al.*, 2015), have been demonstrated to be the products of an ontogenetic response to the loads induced during bipedal walking or running.

The ontogenetic changes in trabecular bone architecture in humans have received increasing attention over the last decade. While many studies have documented the processes of endochondral ossification and early trabecular bone development and growth in a range of organisms (Nafei *et al.*, 2000a, 2000b; Tanck *et al.*, 2001; Wolschrijn and Weijs, 2004; see Chapter 7 for a review of endochondral ossification), and several studies have documented early patterns of ossification in fetal, neonatal, and juvenile humans (Byers *et al.*, 2000; Salle *et al.*, 2002; Cunningham and Black, 2009a, 2009b, 2010; Reissis and Abel, 2012), there has been comparatively little work on trabecular bone development in humans within the context of postnatal locomotor ontogeny (Ryan and Krovitz, 2006; Gosman and Ketcham, 2009; Abel and Macho, 2011; Maclean *et al.*, 2014; Raichlen *et al.*, 2015).

Analyses of the developing human ilium suggest early construction of a genetically patterned trabecular bone scaffold through the processes of endochondral ossification, with later structural modifications possibly in response to locomotor and postural loading changes (Cunningham and Black, 2009a, 2009b; Abel and Macho, 2011). Work on femoral and tibial metaphyseal ossification indicates broadly similar patterns of trabecular bone development in these elements (Ryan and Krovitz, 2006; Gosman and Ketcham, 2009). The modeling of trabecular bone architecture in both femur and tibia during the juvenile period is characterized by an increase in the bone volume fraction through increasing trabecular thickness with a concurrent decrease in the number of trabeculae (Ryan and Krovitz, 2006; Gosman and Ketcham, 2009). These analyses also demonstrate the differentiation of age- and gait-related structural zones within the femoral head and neck and the proximal tibia, suggesting that the trabecular bone is adapting to the normal loads occurring during walking. In more recent work, Raichlen and colleagues (2015) linked trabecular bone structural changes in the distal tibia to locomotor kinematic changes in the ankle joint during ontogeny. Taken together, these three studies indicate that a link can be made between three-dimensional trabecular bone microstructure and specific events during gait maturation, including changes in the orientation and bone volume fraction at the proximal femur, alterations in the relative bone volume fraction between the tibial condyles, and shifts in the fabric anisotropy and orientation of trabecular bone at the ankle joint in association with changes in step-to-step variation during gait maturation.

The objective of this study is to compare the structural and mechanical changes in the trabecular bone of the proximal femoral and humeral metaphyses in a sample of juvenile humans ranging in age from 6 months to approximately 10 years of age. The comparison of structural features and calculated elastic properties of these skeletal elements will provide novel data that will illuminate how developmental and mechanical factors interact and ultimately contribute to adult morphology and intraskeletal variability. We predict that trabecular bone structure in the femur and humerus will have similar structural and mechanical characteristics early in development as a result of similarities in the patterned process of endochondral ossification. We expect that mechanically relevant trabecular bone features, and consequently elastic properties, will increase at a more rapid rate during growth in the proximal femoral metaphysis than in the humerus in response to the heightened locomotor demands on the lower limb. This research tests the hypothesis that ontogenetic patterns of trabecular bone structure reflect general developmental processes influenced by site-specific joint and regional kinematics and kinetics in the postcranial skeleton. We propose that the onset and maturation of bipedal gait is a key component in the ontogenetic development of trabecular bone in the lower limb skeleton. Although there is significant individual (Sutherland *et al.*, 1988; Raichlen *et al.*, 2015) and possibly cultural variation (Tracer, 2002), the changes in load magnitude due to increasing body mass as well as alterations in load orientation due to locomotor maturation during the juvenile period represent a unique natural experiment with which to test the functional significance of developmental changes in bone structure.

12.2   Materials and Methods

For this study, one femur and humerus from 33 individuals were selected from the Norris Farms #36 archaeological skeletal collection. The individuals ranged in age from 6 months to approximately 10.5 years as determined by tooth crown and root formation and eruption (Milner *et al.*, 1990). The Norris Farms #36 site is a late prehistoric cemetery site from the central Illinois River valley dating to about AD 1300 with graves containing between one and several individuals associated with the Oneota cultural tradition of village agriculturalists (Santure *et al.*, 1990). Juvenile and adult individuals from this collection have been used in previous studies of trabecular and cortical bone development and structural variation (Ryan and Krovitz, 2006; Shaw and Ryan, 2012; Ryan and Shaw, 2012, 2015; Gosman *et al.*, 2013). Specimens used in the current analysis were selected based on the state of preservation of both the proximal femur and proximal humerus. Only bones judged to be in good condition, with minimal or no breakage or weathering of the cortical bone and no apparent signs of pathologies affecting limb bone size, shape, or structure, were used. The sex of each individual was unknown.

All bone specimens were scanned at the Center for Quantitative Imaging (CQI) at the Pennsylvania State University using either an HD-100 benchtop microcomputed tomography (μCT) system or the OMNI-X HD-600 industrial μCT system. Each bone was mounted in a florist foam base and transverse cross-sectional scans were collected for the entire proximal metaphysis beginning at the proximal-most edge and proceeding distally through approximately one-third of the shaft. The epiphyses were not scanned for either bone used in this study. The μCT scans were collected with slice thicknesses and spacing ranging from 0.0218 to 0.0460 mm depending on the size of the specimen. Specimens were scanned with source energies of between

90 and 130 kV and between 40 and 150 μA depending on specimen size. The μCT scan data were collected with 2,400 projections with a running average of three samples per projection, and 41 slices per rotation. Images were reconstructed with a 1024 × 1024 pixel grid and a field of view ranging in size from 17.40 to 40.96 mm, resulting in reconstructed pixel sizes of between 0.017 and 0.040 mm. In all cases scans were collected at the maximum resolution obtainable based on specimen size. The original 1024 × 1024 16-bit TIFF images were cropped to the maximum extents of the bone and were converted to 8-bit data using ImageJ (Schneider *et al.*, 2012). This processing step resulted in a reduction of the number of grayscale values in the histogram (to 256 gray values), but no loss of voxel (3D pixel) resolution. Six humeri and one femur were excluded from the analysis due either to internal damage to the trabeculae or excessive mud or debris filling the intertrabecular spaces. The following analyses, therefore, were conducted on a total of 27 humeri and 32 femora from 33 separate individuals.

To facilitate both morphometric and finite element analyses of the three-dimensional structure of trabecular bone in the growing metaphysis, a single cubic volume of interest (VOI) with an edge length of 5 mm was defined within each femoral and humeral metaphysis. Because the VOIs were not scaled to joint or body size, the VOIs represent a larger portion of the metaphysis in the younger individuals in the sample. Due to the significant shape differences between the femoral and humeral metaphyses as well as the significant shape changes during ontogeny in both bones, it is not possible to define anatomically or developmentally homologous VOIs between the two bones and across all ages. The VOIs were positioned similarly across all individuals in the study with the center 5 mm below the proximal margin of the bone and centered in the transverse plane between medial, lateral, anterior, and posterior extents of the bone. In the older individuals, at least, the VOIs were positioned in locations that represent approximately similar biomechanical regions, tracking the leading edge of ossification. The goal was to ensure that the VOIs lay within the zone of initial bone response to external loads.

The three-dimensional trabecular bone structure was quantified using the BoneJ plugin for ImageJ (Doube *et al.*, 2010). Each VOI was segmented using the iterative isodata segmentation algorithm (Ridler and Calvard, 1978; Trussell, 1979). In all cases the data were visually inspected to ensure that a reasonable threshold value was calculated and used for subsequent quantification of the bone architecture. Several common trabecular bone structural variables were quantified in BoneJ using model-independent methods: bone volume fraction (BV/TV), trabecular thickness (Tb.Th), trabecular separation (Tb.Sp), connectivity density (Conn.D), and degree of anisotropy (DA). Detailed explanations for the variables used are provided in Shaw and Ryan (2012) and Doube *et al.* (2010). In brief, bone volume fraction (BV/TV) was calculated as the number of bone voxels divided by the total number of voxels in the VOI. Trabecular thickness (Tb.Th) and trabecular separation (Tb.Sp) were calculated using model-independent distance transform methods (Hildebrand and Rüegsegger, 1997). Connectivity density (Conn.D) was calculated using the topological approach of Odgaard and Gundersen (1993). Degree of anisotropy (DA) was determined based on the mean intercept length (MIL) method with DA calculated as 1 – (tertiary eigenvalue/primary eigenvalue), where the eigenvalues represent the axes of the best fit ellipsoid of the distribution of vector orientations and the intercept lengths.

The elastic stiffness constants of the trabecular bone structure within each cubic VOI were determined using micromechanical finite element analyses (μFE). Models were constructed by converting each voxel into an 8-noded brick element, resulting in highly accurate geometric representations of the trabecular bone structure (van Rietbergen, 2001; van Rietbergen *et al.*, 1995, 1996, 1998). Bone tissue was modeled as linear elastic and isotropic with stiffness constants of 1 GPa and Poisson ratio of 0.3 following Ulrich and colleagues (1999). The exact input of Young's modulus value is of little consequence for the current analysis as the goal of the study is only to assess the relationship between structure and elastic stiffness constants, not to accurately predict strain in the bone structure. The resultant primary Young's modulus values can be scaled easily because of the linear elastic analyses. In this study, we use this normalized tissue modulus as defined by Ulrich and colleagues (1999) to represent a unit Young's modulus value for comparison across two skeletal sites and between individuals. The number of elements in the models used in this study ranged from 162,000 to 2.1 million with an average of approximately 617,000 elements. A total of six μFE analyses were run for each VOI, simulating three compressive tests in orthogonal directions and three shear tests. The complete stiffness matrix of the structure, containing the nine independent elastic constants for each cube, was calculated based on the results of the six μFE analyses (van Rietbergen *et al.*, 1995). The primary Young's modulus was calculated for each VOI. All finite element analyses were performed with the Scanco Image Processing Language Finite Element v1.13 code.

Locally weighted polynomial regressions (LOESS) with a smoothing parameter of 0.8 were used to characterize the relationships between trabecular bone structural variables, calculated primary Young's modulus, and age. Spearman's rank order correlation coefficients (r_s) were calculated to assess correlations between each quantified variable (trabecular bone measures and μFE model-calculated primary Young's modulus) and age, as well as between the calculated primary Young's modulus and each measured trabecular bone variable. Ordinary least-squares linear regressions were used to assess the relationships between predicted elastic properties and each of the trabecular bone structural variables in the femur and humerus separately. All variables except BV/TV were $\log_{10}$-transformed for regression analyses. In all analyses, null hypotheses were rejected if $p < 0.05$. Statistical analyses were performed using IBM SPSS 22 and R (R Development Core Team, 2013).

12.3   Results

Visual inspection of the three-dimensional data suggests broadly similar trabecular bone structure between the proximal femur and humerus in young human infants (Figure 12.1). By at least three years of age, however, the trabecular bone architecture near these two joints has diverged significantly, with the proximal femoral trabecular bone displaying a more robust structure with apparently more bone volume and thicker trabeculae (Figure 12.1). The quantitative analysis of bone structural characteristics bears out this observed pattern (Table 12.1). Values for all measured morphometric variables are very similar in both elements at young ages (approximately 0.5 years of age). After one year of age, BV/TV and Tb.Th increase in both elements, but the rate at which these variables increase appears to be different in the femur and humerus. Femoral BV/TV and Tb.Th increase more rapidly and reach higher values by approximately 3 or 4 years of age. Other trabecular structural variables near these joints show broad similarity during ontogeny with only apparently minor differences between the two bones in features such as Tb.Sp, Conn.D, and anisotropy (Figure 12.2). The μFE calculated Young's modulus

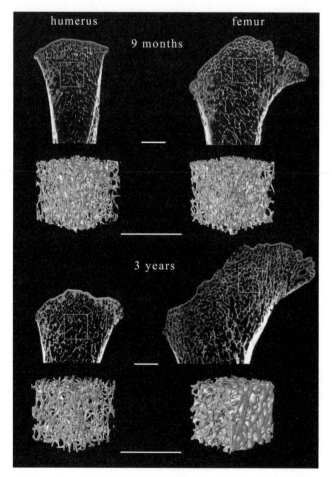

Figure 12.1 Coronal sections and three-dimensional reconstructions of the proximal humeral (left) and femoral (right) metaphyses of a 9-month-old (top) and 3-year-old (bottom) used in this study. White boxes show location for each volume of interest. Scale bars are 5 mm.

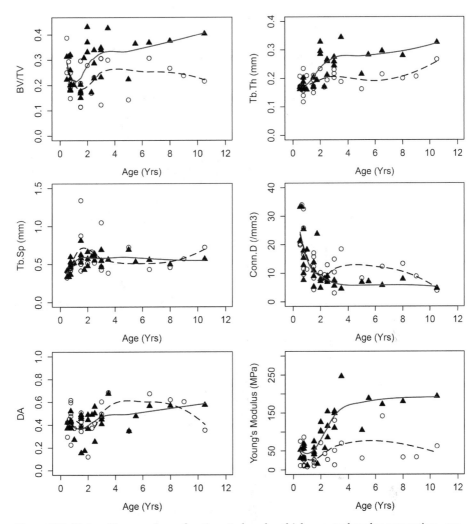

Figure 12.2 Plots of bone volume fraction, trabecular thickness, trabecular separation, connectivity density, degree of anisotropy, and estimated primary Young's modulus against age. Young's modulus values are reported as a normalized relative unit bone tissue modulus based on μFE model input modulus value of 1 GPa. Symbols: white circles, humerus; black triangles, femur. Locally weighted polynomial regressions (LOESS) with a smoothing parameter of 0.8 are plotted for the humerus and femur for each variable.

values follow patterns similar to those of the BV/TV and Tb.Th with a distinct divergence after about two years of age. The femoral trabecular bone increases in stiffness rapidly between 2 and 4 years of age before leveling off. By contrast, estimated Young's modulus, values in the metaphyseal trabecular bone of the humerus remain mostly lower than those of the femur and only increase slightly during ontogeny.

Spearman's rank-order correlation coefficients indicate that all of the proximal femoral trabecular bone variables are significantly correlated with age except

Table 12.1 Results of quantitative analyses of trabecular bone structure and estimated Young's Modulus for each individual in the sample.

Burial number	Age (years)	Humerus						Femur					
		BV/TV	Tb.Th (mm)	Tb.Sp (mm)	Conn.D (/mm³)	DA	Young's Modulus (MPa)	BV/TV	Tb.Th (mm)	Tb.Sp (mm)	Conn.D (/mm³)	DA	Young's Modulus (MPa)
172	0.5	0.387	0.208	0.325	20.26	0.296	76.16	0.313	0.170	0.337	33.26	0.371	52.66
202	0.5	0.251	0.172	0.406	19.89	0.423	11.26	0.223	0.162	0.418	21.43	0.423	31.01
85	0.63	0.294	0.161	0.350	34.05	0.450	60.72	0.313	0.170	0.337	33.26	0.371	54.50
57	0.75	0.191	0.157	0.456	16.53	0.504	26.13	0.227	0.168	0.464	17.97	0.424	31.60
140	0.75	0.206	0.140	0.426	25.91	0.477	33.73	0.184	0.202	0.597	7.62	0.375	28.36
142	0.75	0.249	0.171	0.421	17.46	0.597	86.58	0.260	0.188	0.462	15.35	0.432	69.27
167	0.75	0.195	0.166	0.477	9.61	0.617	32.48	0.320	0.188	0.366	25.45	0.522	55.68
173	0.75	0.318	0.235	0.449	11.55	0.410	12.17	0.201	0.171	0.529	12.82	0.405	63.24
247	0.75	0.149	0.118	0.500	32.59	0.226	10.34	0.180	0.165	0.488	10.01	0.439	63.66
58	1	0.213	0.210	0.513	11.41	0.373	8.38	0.202	0.161	0.517	18.25	0.271	11.68
117	1.5	0.297	0.211	0.416	17.12	0.509	40.99	0.151	0.172	0.624	5.27	0.382	47.53
131	1.5	0.209	0.173	0.503	15.79	0.427	26.13	0.203	0.172	0.525	13.80	0.473	58.52
135	1.5	0.176	0.166	0.550	12.34	0.471	27.17	0.176	0.169	0.584	10.98	0.489	40.50
162	1.5	0.115	0.150	0.877	8.28	0.345	11.09	0.169	0.204	0.813	5.21	0.456	41.98
221	1.5	0.114	0.195	1.340	4.26	0.393	19.31	0.203	0.202	0.586	9.00	0.153	75.23
79	1.75	–	–	–	–	–	–	0.308	0.194	0.430	23.85	0.173	15.70
88	2	0.279	0.234	0.517	10.26	0.121	71.75	0.431	0.295	0.479	7.91	0.367	126.00
124	2	–	–	–	–	–	–	0.331	0.328	0.664	4.85	0.445	100.86
171	2	–	–	–	–	–	–	0.370	0.285	0.573	7.25	0.490	102.60
65	2.3	0.170	0.170	0.666	9.50	0.375	42.77	0.173	0.171	0.603	8.12	0.491	57.09
153	2.5	0.232	0.195	0.519	12.95	0.415	27.37	0.287	0.260	0.640	6.91	0.561	115.47
160	2.5	–	–	–	–	–	–	0.228	0.212	0.610	9.00	0.254	85.69
177	2.5	–	–	–	–	–	–	0.339	0.266	0.552	7.53	0.503	153.72

25	3	0.307	0.231	0.470	10.40	0.604	13.11	0.348	0.275	0.546	7.28	0.473	149.16
76	3	0.306	0.203	0.427	14.94	0.498	130.79	0.339	0.259	0.468	7.48	0.408	154.44
161	3	0.123	0.217	1.050	3.09	0.461	51.30	0.232	0.245	0.690	5.59	0.449	110.83
183	3.5	0.300	0.189	0.386	18.49	0.685	70.74	0.426	0.344	0.562	4.56	0.674	246.37
115	5	0.143	0.163	0.725	8.31	0.347	30.78	0.224	0.215	0.691	6.86	0.347	104.51
30	5.5	–	–	–	–	–	–	0.364	0.283	0.531	7.11	0.477	188.42
29	6.5	0.307	0.215	0.433	12.35	0.674	141.66	0.368	0.296	0.557	5.75	0.566	172.53
260	8	0.267	0.201	0.458	13.36	0.620	33.16	0.375	0.280	0.498	7.97	0.568	179.77
113	9	0.238	0.207	0.571	8.96	0.603	33.50	–	–	–	–	–	–
89	10.5	0.216	0.267	0.722	3.91	0.353	62.61	0.403	0.326	0.567	4.69	0.574	193.49

Table 12.2 Spearman's rank-order correlation coefficients between age and each measured trabecular bone variable as well as estimated Young's modulus.

Bone	BV/TV	Tb.Th	Tb.Sp	Conn.D	DA	Young's Modulus
Humerus	0.160	0.510	0.091	−0.469	0.181	0.352
	ns	< 0.01	ns	< 0.05	ns	ns
Femur	0.580	0.772	0.348	−0.673	0.460	0.818
	< 0.01	< 0.001	ns	< 0.001	< 0.05	< 0.001

Table 12.3 Spearman's rank order correlation coefficients between estimated Young's modulus and each measured trabecular bone variable.

Bone	BV/TV	Tb.Th	Tb.Sp	Conn.D	DA
Humerus	0.403	0.254	−0.346	0.128	0.358
	< 0.05	ns	ns	ns	ns
Femur	0.760	0.824	0.102	−0.600	0.527
	< 0.001	<0.001	ns	< 0.001	< 0.01

Tb.Sp (Table 12.1). By contrast, only Tb.Th and Conn.D are significantly correlated with age in the humerus. Additionally, the correlation coefficients for these two variables are lower than those for the corresponding variables in the femur, suggesting a stronger correlation between these variables and age in the proximal femur.

Assessing the relationships between primary Young's Modulus and each of the quantified trabecular bone structural variables can provide insight into the relative significance of each structural feature in determining trabecular bone stiffness. Estimated primary Young's modulus values are strongly correlated with BV/TV in both the femur and humerus, although the correlation is much stronger in the femur (Table 12.2). In addition, estimated Young's modulus is significantly correlated with Tb.Th, Conn.D, and DA in the femur, but not the humerus. With the exception of some of the youngest individuals in the sample, BV/TV, Tb.Th, and Young's modulus are always higher in the femur than in the humerus. Ordinary least-squares linear regression results further reveal the relationships between estimated Young's modulus and trabecular bone structural features. Primary Young's modulus is significantly correlated with BV/TV in the humerus (slope = 1.96, $p < 0.05$, $r^2 = 0.14$). No other regression analyses for the humeral trabecular bone variables approach significance. By contrast, Young's modulus shows a significant relationship with all femoral trabecular bone variables except Tb.Sp (Figure 12.3). These include BV/TV (slope = 2.50, $p < 0.001$, $r^2 = 0.41$), Tb.Th (slope = 2.40, $p < 0.001$, $r^2 = 0.64$), Conn.D (slope = −0.793, $p < 0.001$, $r^2 = 0.37$), and DA (slope = 1.21, $p < 0.01$, $r^2 = 0.25$).

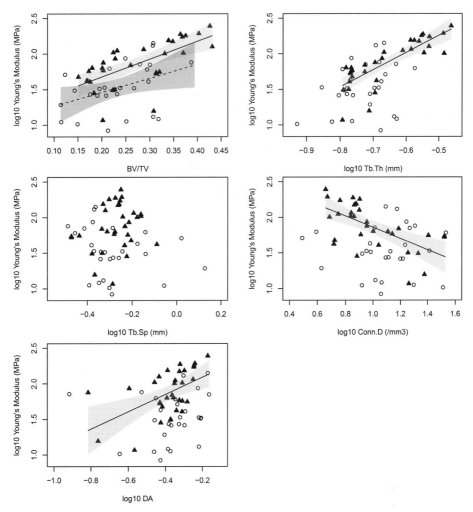

Figure 12.3 Bivariate plots of $\log_{10}$ Young's modulus vs. each trabecular bone variable. Ordinary least-squares regression lines and 95% confidence intervals (in gray) are plotted for each significant result. Symbols: white circles, humerus; black triangles, femur.

12.4   Discussion

12.4.1   Ontogenetic Alterations in Trabecular Bone Structure and Mechanics

This study provides novel insights into the role of mechanical loading on the functional adaptation of trabecular bone in the human postcranial skeleton. Previous data on trabecular bone ontogeny suggest that femoral and tibial trabecular bone develops in response to changes in loading associated with the initiation and maturation of bipedal walking as well as changes in body mass (Ryan and Krovitz, 2006; Gosman and Ketcham, 2009). The results of this study support and extend that work, demonstrating distinct differences in femoral and humeral metaphyseal trabecular bone characteristics after approximately one year of age. The increase in bone volume fraction, accomplished primarily through the thickening of the trabeculae, combined with the decrease in number of trabecular struts, as indicated by changes in connectivity density, results in significant alterations in the mechanical properties of metaphyseal trabecular bone during ontogeny. The structural and mechanical differences in humeral and femoral trabecular bone appear to be driven by the early divergence in loading and usage patterns between the upper and lower limbs in human juveniles, a pattern matched quite nicely in the development of cortical bone strength characteristics (Ruff, 2003b). Although debate continues over the functional significance of trabecular bone structural variation in humans and other primates (Fajardo *et al.*, 2007; Carlson *et al.*, 2008; Ryan and Walker, 2010; Shaw and Ryan, 2012; Ryan and Shaw, 2012, 2015; Wallace *et al.*, 2013; Chapter 10), the results of the current analysis, together with those from other analyses of ontogenetic changes in trabecular bone (Ryan and Krovitz, 2006; Gosman and Ketcham, 2009; Raichlen *et al.*, 2015), suggest that the divergent and distinct morphologies of the proximal femur and humerus in humans develop only after the divergence of limb use following the onset of unassisted bipedal walking at approximately one year of age (Sutherland *et al.*, 1988; Sutherland, 1997).

The relationships between trabecular bone structural characteristics and primary Young's modulus provide insights into the mechanical significance of the various structural features. While primary Young's modulus, a measure of bone stiffness, was significantly correlated with most bone variables in the femur (all except trabecular separation), Young's modulus was only correlated with bone volume fraction in the humerus. This similarity between humeral and femoral metaphyseal trabecular bone matches a wealth of data from other studies indicating a relationship between bone volume fraction and various mechanical properties (e.g. Hodgskinson and Currey, 1990; Ulrich *et al.*, 1999; Mittra *et al.*, 2005) and underscores the mechanical importance of bone volume fraction in the growing skeleton. The femur, however, has more robust trabecular bone than the humerus, a feature that develops only after the onset of bipedal walking.

These results extend previous work on bone development in humans that show a strong mechanically mediated growth response during locomotor maturation (Ruff, 2003a, 2003b; Ryan and Krovitz, 2006; Gosman and Ketcham, 2009; Cowgill *et al.*, 2010; Gosman *et al.*, 2013). The divergent structural and mechanical patterns in humeral and femoral trabecular bone match those found in other analyses of cortical (Ruff, 2003a, 2003b, 2005a) and trabecular bone morphology (Ryan and Krovitz, 2006; Gosman and Ketcham, 2009; Reissis and Abel, 2012; Raichlen *et al.*, 2015), but contrast with work on the trabecular structure in the developing ilium (Cunningham and Black, 2009a, 2009b; Abel and Macho, 2011). Ruff (2003a, 2003b, 2005a) demonstrated that femoral and humeral strength characteristics of cortical bone in the femur and humerus of *Homo* develop only after the adoption of bipedal walking at about one year. Between the ages of 1 and 3 years, there is a rapid increase in strength characteristics, followed by slow change until adolescence at which time adult proportions are reached. The results for BV/TV from the oldest individuals in the current sample (i.e., those older than 8 years) are already within the range of variation seen in adult humans from the same population. Shaw and Ryan (2012) report mean BV/TV values of 0.265 and 0.401 for the humerus and femur, respectively, from a mixed sample of young adult males and females. The mean BV/TV values for the three oldest individuals in the sample used in this study fall just below the corresponding values from adults with a value of 0.240 for the humerus and 0.389 for the femur. The other comparable variables reported by Shaw and Ryan (2012) show greater divergence from the adult pattern. Trabecular thickness and separation are both lower and connectivity density higher in 8–10.5-year-olds in the current sample compared to the adults, suggesting a continued pattern of growth with increasing thickness and decreasing number of trabeculae into adolescence and early adulthood.

The accelerated growth between 1 and 3 years corresponds well to the onset of bipedalism at about 1 year of age and the stabilization of gait at approximately 3.5–4 years (Sutherland et al., 1988; Sutherland, 1997; Stanitski et al., 2000). Reissis and Abel (2012) quantified characteristics of fetal bone development in humans, demonstrating that both humeral and femoral metaphyseal bone develop similarly, with no significant structural differences in bone volume fraction, trabecular number, or trabecular thickness at fetal ages between four and nine months. Reissis and Abel's (2012) data match the results from the current analysis in showing no difference in trabecular structure between the femur and humerus in young, preambulatory infants.

Work on bone development in pigs and dogs provides further evidence for a generalized developmental process in bone development, mediated by mechanical loading and perhaps other biological factors during ontogeny. Analyzing bone microarchitecture and mechanical properties in pig tibiae and vertebrae, Tanck and colleagues (2001) found that trabecular bone increases in volume and anisotropy with age and body mass. Interestingly they found a time lag between the increase in bone volume and degree of anisotropy, suggesting that the initial response to increased loads is to add bone mass and then refine that mass later into a more mechanically efficient, anisotropic structure. Wolschrijn and Weijs (2004) found that the bone volume fraction and trabecular thickness of the canine ulnar coronoid process increase with age while trabecular number displays the opposite trend, decreasing in older individuals. They suggest that dogs may retain primary bone from the fetal growth stage until several weeks after birth as a result of the delayed maturation of motor control and gait development (Wolschrijn and Weijs, 2004).

In contrast to these data suggesting a strongly mechanically mediated developmental mechanism in cortical and trabecular bone growth, work on the juvenile human ilium suggests distinct regional organization of trabeculae that appears to parallel the structural organization observed in adults (Cunningham and Black, 2009a, 2009b; Abel and Macho, 2011). This adult-like pattern is typically associated with the bone growth response to forces generated during locomotor and postural loading. The presence of this iliac trabecular structure in very young, preambulatory individuals, therefore, strongly suggests a distinct genetic patterning of trabecular bone architecture in the ilium (Cunningham and Black, 2009a, 2009b; Abel and Macho, 2011; see Chapter 6 for evidence of regional variation in the development of cortical bone material properties in the mandible), although the unique endochondral ossification patterns of this bone (Cunningham and Black, 2010) may play a role as well. Although the general process of development is likely similar, trabecular bone structure in the appendicular skeleton appears to develop somewhat differently than that of the ilium, with no evidence for a pre-locomotor scaffold or distinct patterning of metaphyseal bone (Ryan and Krovitz, 2006; Gosman and Ketcham, 2009; Raichlen *et al.*, 2015). It seems likely that a combination of genetic and mechanical factors work together to produce intraskeletal variability within anatomically specific developmental shape and size constraints and that the relative influence of these factors varies across the skeleton (Willmore *et al.*, 2007; Lazenby *et al.*, 2008a). Variation in adult trabecular bone structure across the skeleton suggests significant complexity in the role of genetic, mechanical, and other factors in driving local bone morphology (Ulrich *et al.*, 1999; Morgan *et al.*, 2003; Ryan and Shaw, 2012; Shaw and Ryan, 2012; Chirchir, 2015).

12.4.2 General Model for Trabecular Bone Development

The interactions among mechanical loading, the general processes of growth and development, and variability in skeletal responsiveness account for skeletal adaptation during ontogeny and into early adulthood (Turner and Robling, 2003; Pearson and Lieberman, 2004). Following this period, the skeletal response is greatly reduced (Forwood and Burr, 1993), but it does continue over a longer time frame with the possibility of cumulative long-term effect (Pearson and Lieberman, 2004; Valdimarsson *et al.*, 2005; Ruff, 2006). Therefore, adult bone morphology represents a composite of structural features established initially during early development and throughout ontogeny and modified by various biological mechanisms and functional adaptation during maturity. Data from this study, as well as previous work on ontogenetic alterations in bone at a variety of skeletal sites, provide a framework for understanding bone growth within a functional and locomotor developmental context in humans and other mammals.

The initial architecture of metaphyseal trabecular bone is dictated by the patterned organization of cartilage cells and the process of endochondral ossification forming the primary spongiosa (Carter and Wong, 1988; Carter *et al.*, 1989, 1991). The initial primary spongy bone, deposited during endochondral ossification, is rapidly replaced by secondary trabecular bone early in life. In humans, this occurs within the first year. The resulting bone has fewer thicker trabecular struts than seen in younger individuals. The internal bone architecture in the very young neonatal individuals, those less than about 3–5 months of age in humans, is clearly still arranged in columnar structures generated during calcification of the cartilage model during early bone growth (Martin *et al.*, 1998; Carter and Beaupre, 2001; Currey, 2002). These columns of bone progressively develop into trabecular structures that are more similar to what is recognizable as adult bone architecture. In

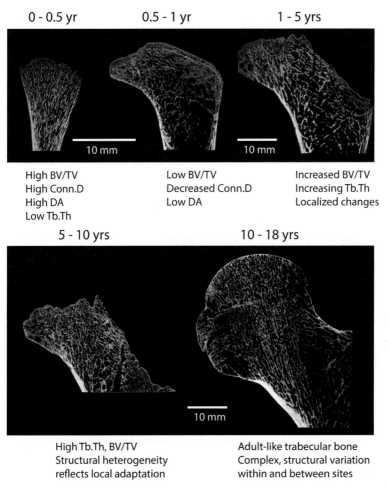

Figure 12.4 Description of generalized trabecular bone development in the human postcranial skeleton. Displayed are coronal sections through the proximal femur of five individuals representing each developmental period outlined in the text – neonatal, infancy, early childhood, middle childhood, puberty/adolescence. Characteristics of trabecular development are listed below each image and are discussed in more detail in the text.

humans, the differences in bone structure between fetal age and older, bipedal toddlers are evident from μCT scan data of the proximal femoral metaphysis (Figures 12.1 and 12.4). In older individuals after about 1 year of age, there is also evidence of biomechanical differentiation within the proximal femur. The primary trabecular arcades, with distinct orientation and anisotropy characteristics, develop in conjunction with the thickening of the cortex of the inferior femoral neck, suggesting a link to the loads generated during bipedal walking.

Several age-specific predictions can be made regarding the general development of trabecular architecture throughout human ontogeny based on this basic model of trabecular bone growth and development (Figure 12.4). These predictions are derived from the existing data from the literature on trabecular bone growth (Byers *et al.*, 2000; Nafei *et al.*, 2000a, 2000b; Parfitt *et al.*, 2000; Tanck *et al.*, 2001; Salle *et al.*, 2002; Wolschrijn and Weijs, 2004; Ryan and Krovitz, 2006; Cunningham and Black, 2009a, 2009b, 2010; Gosman and Ketcham, 2009; Abel and Macho, 2011; Reissis and Abel, 2012; Maclean *et al.*, 2014; Raichlen *et al.*, 2015):

1. **Neonatal (0–0.5 years).** This pre-locomotor stage in humans is characterized by relatively dense, homogeneous, and numerous primary and early secondary trabeculae. Bone volume fraction and trabecular number (as measured by connectivity density) are high, while trabecular thickness is relatively low. This structure is also characterized by high anisotropy (high DA) reflecting the initial ossification of the cartilage model.

2. **Infancy (0.5–1 years).** Trabecular structure is reorganized during this period through rapid bone loss reflected in lower bone volume fraction, a decreased number of trabeculae, and a loss of defined spatial organization (lower DA).

3. **Early childhood (1–5 years).** This period is characterized by the initial differentiation of skeletal sites as a result of increasing body mass and the onset of unassisted bipedal walking. In the lower limb elements, this leads to increasing bone volume fraction through increased trabecular thickness. Bone mass increases are accomplished primarily by increasing thickness rather than number of trabeculae. Some elements display increasingly localized structure including changes in fabric anisotropy and spatial arrangement depending on local biomechanical and growth characteristics. Changes in trabecular architecture, especially anisotropy, match changes in locomotor biomechanics from more variable loading patterns to more predictable loading patterns (Raichlen *et al.*, 2015).

4. **Middle childhood (5–10 years).** This period sees stabilization of an adult-like gait pattern and the onset of more independent activities. Trabecular bone is characterized by heterogeneity of structure within and between sites (variable bone volume fraction, stabilization of trabecular thickness), an increase in anisotropy (higher DA) in localized and stereotypically loaded regions, and an increase in plate-like trabecular structures in high strain regions.

5. **Puberty/adolescence (10–18 years).** Body mass increases as a result of the pubertal growth spurt and individuals realize a more fully active adult lifestyle. This time period is characterized by attainment of adult-like trabecular structure with heterogeneous bone volume fraction, stabilization of trabecular thickness, and a spatially defined fabric change in the degree of anisotropy and principal orientation reflecting functional differentiation and a generally greater complexity of structural organization.

More inter- and intraspecific data are needed to more fully elucidate these patterns of bone development in humans and to understand the functional significance of trabecular bone structural variation. The data presented here provide unique insights into these processes but also have several limitations. The sample size used here, while relatively large for a μCT study of trabecular bone development, is somewhat small, especially at older ages. A larger sample, especially at older ages and one that extends into adulthood, would augment and strengthen the patterns documented here. In addition, the use of an archaeological sample introduces a significant amount of uncertainty into the study because we ultimately do not know important details about the behavior, diet, health status, and culture of the individuals used in the study. These issues are common within anthropological analyses. The similarities across many of the studies of trabecular bone development in different human populations (Ryan and Krovitz, 2006; Gosman and Ketcham, 2009) and other species (Tanck et al., 2001; Wolschrijn and Weijs, 2004) strongly suggests we are documenting generalized developmental processes common at least to mammalian species.

12.4.3 Anthropological Implications

Understanding ontogenetic developmental trajectories of bone macro- and microstructure in various regions of the skeleton is important for a wide array of important questions within evolutionary functional morphology, skeletal biology, paleoanthropology, and biological anthropology as a whole. Included among the potentially important issues that can be addressed with ontogenetic trabecular bone data are fundamental questions related to bone functional adaptation, the reconstruction of behavioral patterns in fossil organisms and past human populations, the evolution of human life history, the analysis of factors affecting skeletal growth (e.g., nutritional stress) within the bioarchaeological record, and the development of models to better understand factors driving bone loss later in life. Specifically, analysis of ontogenetic changes in trabecular bone architecture can provide a foundational framework within which questions of the functional and biological significance of bone structural variation can be addressed (also see Chapter 6 for study of ontogenetic changes in mandibular cortical bone properties).

Within biological anthropology, there has been growing interest in the three-dimensional structure of trabecular bone and its potential utility for understanding the evolutionary morphology of extinct humans and other primates, and in particular for reconstructing the behavioral patterns of extinct taxa (Ryan and Ketcham, 2002a; Desilva and Devlin, 2012; Barak et al., 2013; Su et al., 2013; Chirchir et al., 2015; Skinner et al., 2015). Such behavioral reconstructions in fossil taxa and archaeological samples depend on establishing a strong link between variation in skeletal structures and biomechanical function within extant humans and other primates. Robust ontogenetic data can provide profound insights into the complexity of mechanical and non-mechanical influences on adult bone morphology (Ruff, 2005b), but this area remains somewhat untapped within biological anthropology and functional evolutionary morphology.

The results of the current analysis, together with previous work on bone development in the postcranial skeleton (Ryan and Krovitz, 2006; Gosman and Ketcham, 2009; Raichlen et al., 2015), suggest that changes in locomotor loading are reflected in distinct, mechanically mediated skeletal markers. These skeletal markers of development and locomotor loading can, in turn, be useful not only for reconstructing locomotor behavior and locomotor evolution in hominins, but also for understanding evolutionary changes in life history patterns of hominins and other species (Raichlen *et al.*, 2015). Importantly, further refinement of our understanding of ontogenetic changes in cortical and trabecular bone structure across the post-cranial skeleton in humans and other primates could also allow for more effective reconstructions of locomotor transitions in the fossil record.

In addition to functional and paleoanthropological analyses, data on ontogenetic changes in trabecular and cortical bone also have the potential to inform on questions of significant interest to bioarchaeologists and skeletal biologists. An anthropological perspective on bone development that potentially incorporates temporal, spatial, and even cultural variation in the populations analyzed has the potential to produce important new insights into past and present human skeletal health and variation in the dynamics of bone growth across human populations. Of particular importance may be the potential to use ontogenetic data on bone growth in the postcranial skeleton to address important contemporary health issues such as the role of mechanical loading, diet, culture, and genetics in age-related bone loss.

12.5   Acknowledgments

We thank Chris Percival and Joan Richtsmeier for inviting us to participate in this volume. We also thank Terrance Martin of the Illinois State Museum for access to the Norris Farm #36 skeletal material. George Milner assisted with access and relevant data related to the Norris Farms #36 collection. This research was supported by grants from the Leakey Foundation (TMR) and National Science Foundation BCS-1028904 (TMR), BCS-1028793 (JHG), and BCS-1028799 (DAR).

References

Abel, R. and Macho, G. A. (2011). Ontogenetic changes in the internal and external morphology of the ilium in modern humans. *Journal of Anatomy*, 218, 324–335.

Abitbol, M. M. (1987). Evolution of the lumbosacral angle. *American Journal of Physical Anthropology*, 72, 361–372.

Barak, M. M., Lieberman, D. E. and Hublin, J. J. (2011). A Wolff in sheep's clothing: trabecular bone adaptation in response to changes in joint loading orientation. *Bone*, 49, 1141–1151.

Barak, M. M., Lieberman, D. E., Raichlen, D., *et al.* (2013). Trabecular evidence for a human-like gait in *Australopithecus africanus*. *PLoS ONE*, 8, e77687.

Bridges, P. S., Blitz, J. H. and Solano, M. C. (2000). Changes in long bone diaphyseal strength with horticultural intensification in West-Central Illinois. *American Journal of Physical Anthropology*, 112, 217–238.

Byers, S., Moore, A. J., Byard, R. W. and Fazzalari, N. L. (2000). Quantitative histomorphometric analysis of the human growth plate from birth to adolescence. *Bone*, 27, 495–501.

Carlson, K. J. and Judex, S. (2007). Increased non-linear locomotion alters diaphyseal bone shape. *Journal of Experimental Biology*, 210, 3117–3125.

Carlson, K. J., Lublinsky, S. and Judex, S. (2008). Do different locomotor modes during growth modulate trabecular architecture in the murine hind limb? *Integrative and Comparative Biology*, 48, 385–393.

Carter, D. R. and Beaupre, G. S. (2001). *Skeletal Function and Form*. Cambridge: Cambridge University Press.

Carter, D. R. and Wong, M. (1988). The role of mechanical loading histories in the development of diarthrodial joints. *Journal of Orthopaedic Research*, 6, 804–816.

Carter, D. R., Orr, T. E. and Fyrhie, D. P. (1989). Relationships between loading history and femoral cancellous bone architecture. *Journal of Biomechanics*, 22, 231–244.

Carter, D. R., Wong, M. and Orr, T. E. (1991). Musculoskeletal ontogeny, phylogeny, and functional adaptation. *Journal of Biomechanics*, 24, 3–16.

Chirchir, H. (2015). A comparative study of trabecular bone mass distribution in cursorial and non-cursorial limb joints. *Anatomical Record*, 298, 797–809.

Chirchir, H., Kivell, T. L., Ruff, C. B., *et al.* (2015). Recent origin of low trabecular bone density in modern humans. *Proceedings of the National Academy of Sciences of the USA*, 112, 366–371.

Cowgill, L. W., Warrener, A., Pontzer, H. and Ocobock, C. (2010). Waddling and toddling: the biomechanical effects of an immature gait. *American Journal of Physical Anthropology*, 143, 52–61.

Cunningham, C. A. and Black, S. M. (2009a). Anticipating bipedalism: trabecular organization in the newborn ilium. *Journal of Anatomy*, 214, 817–829.

Cunningham, C. A. and Black, S. M. (2009b). Development of the fetal ilium: challenging concepts of bipedality. *Journal of Anatomy*, 214, 91–99.

Cunningham, C. A. and Black, S. M. (2010). The neonatal ilium-metaphyseal drivers and vascular passengers. *Anatomical Record*, 293, 1297–1309.

Currey, J. D. (2002). *Bones: Structure and Mechanics*. Princeton, NJ: Princeton University Press.

Desilva, J. M. and Devlin, M. J. (2012). A comparative study of the trabecular bony architecture of the talus in humans, non-human primates, and *Australopithecus*. *Journal of Human Evolution*, 63, 536–51.

Doube, M., Kłosowski, M. M., Arganda-Carreras, I., *et al.* (2010). BoneJ: free and extensible bone image analysis in ImageJ. *Bone*, 47, 1076–1079.

Fajardo, R. J., Muller, R., Ketcham, R. A. and Colbert, M. (2007). Nonhuman anthropoid primate femoral neck trabecular architecture and its relationship to locomotor mode. *Anatomical Record*, 290, 422–436.

Forwood, M. R. and Burr, D. B. (1993). Physical activity and bone mass – exercises in futility. *Bone and Mineral*, 21, 89–112.

Gosman, J. H. and Ketcham, R. A. (2009). Patterns in ontogeny of human trabecular bone from SunWatch Village in the Prehistoric Ohio Valley: general features of microarchitectural change. *American Journal of Physical Anthropology*, 138, 318–332.

Gosman, J. H., Hubbell, Z. R., Shaw, C. N. and Ryan, T. M. (2013). Development of cortical bone geometry in the human femoral and tibial diaphysis. *Anatomical Record*, 296, 774–787.

Hildebrand, T. and Rüegsegger, P. (1997). A new method for the model-independent assessment of thickness in three-dimensional images. *Journal of Microscopy*, 185, 67–75.

Hodgskinson, R. and Currey, J. D. (1990). Effects of structural variation on Young's modulus of non-human cancellous bone. *Proceedings of the Institution of Mechanical Engineers. Part H, Journal of Engineering in Medicine*, 204, 43–52.

Larsen, C. S. (1995). Biological changes in human populations with agriculture. *Annual Review of Anthropology*, 24, 185–213.

Larsen, C. S. (2015). *Bioarchaeology: Interpreting Behavior from the Human Skeleton*. Cambridge: Cambridge University Press.

Lazenby, R. A., Angus, S., Cooper, D. M. L. and Hallgrimsson, B. (2008a). A three-dimensional microcomputed tomographic study of site-specific variation in trabecular microarchitecture in the human second metacarpal. *Journal of Anatomy*, 213, 698–705.

Lazenby, R. A., Cooper, D. M., Angus, S. and Hallgrimsson, B. (2008b). Articular constraint, handedness, and directional asymmetry in the human second metacarpal. *Journal of Human Evolution*, 54, 875–885.

Lazenby, R. A., Skinner, M. M., Hublin, J. J. and Boesch, C. (2011). Metacarpal trabecular architecture variation in the chimpanzee (*Pan troglodytes*): evidence for locomotion and tool-use? *American Journal of Physical Anthropology*, 144, 215–225.

Lieberman, D. E. (1997). Making behavioral and phylogenetic inferences from hominid fossils: considering the developmental influence of mechanical forces. *Annual Reviews in Anthropology*, 26, 185–210.

MacLatchy, L. and Müller, R. (2002). A comparison of the femoral head and neck trabecular architecture of *Galago* and *Perodicticus* using micro-computed tomography (µCT). *Journal of Human Evolution*, 43, 89–105.

Maclean, S. J., Black, S. M. and Cunningham, C. A. (2014). The developing juvenile ischium: macro-radiographic insights. *Clinical Anatomy*, 27, 906–914.

Martin, R. B., Burr, D. B. and Sharkey, N. A. (1998). *Skeletal Tissue Mechanics*. New York, NY: Springer-Verlag.

Matarazzo, S. A. (2015). Trabecular architecture of the manual elements reflects locomotor patterns in primates. *PLoS ONE*, 10.3, e0120436.

Milner, G. R., Smith, V. G., Santure, S. K., Harn, A. D. and Esarey, D. (1990). Oneota human skeletal remains. *In: Archaeological Investigations at the Morton Village and Norris Farms 36 Cemetery*. Springfield, IL: Illinois State Museum.

Mittra, E., Rubin, C. and Qin, Y.-X. (2005). Interrelationships of trabecular mechanical and microstructural properties in sheep trabecular bone. *Journal of Biomechanics*, 38, 1229–1237.

Morgan, E. F., Bayraktar, H. H. and Keaveny, T. M. (2003). Trabecular bone modulus–density relationships depend on anatomic site. *Journal of Biomechanics*, 36, 897–904.

Nafei, A., Danielsen, C. C., Linde, F. and Hvid, I. (2000a). Properties of growing trabecular ovine bone – Part I: Mechanical and physical properties. *Journal of Bone and Joint Surgery. British Volume*, 82B, 910–920.

Nafei, A., Kabel, J., Odgaard, A., Linde, F. and Hvid, I. (2000b). Properties of growing trabecular ovine bone – Part II: Architectural and mechanical properties. *Journal of Bone and Joint Surgery. British Volume*, 82B, 921–927.

Odgaard, A. and Gundersen, H. J. G. (1993). Quantification of connectivity in cancellous bone, with special emphasis on 3-D reconstruction. *Bone*, 14, 173–182.

Parfitt, A. M., Travers, R., Rauch, F. and Glorieux, F. H. (2000). Structural and cellular changes during bone growth in healthy children. *Bone*, 27, 487–494.

Pearson, O. M. and Lieberman, D. E. (2004). The aging of Wolff's "law": ontogeny and responses to mechanical loading in cortical bone. *Yearbook of Physical Anthropology*, 47, 63–99.

R Development Core Team. (2013). *R: A Language and Environment for Statistical Computing*. Vienna: R Foundation for statistical Computing.

Raichlen, D., Gordon, A., Foster, A., *et al.* (2015). An ontogenetic framework linking locomotion and trabecular bone architecture with applications for reconstructing hominin life history. *Journal of Human Evolution*, 81, 1–12.

Reissis, D. and Abel, R. L. (2012). Development of fetal trabecular micro-architecture in the humerus and femur. *Journal of Anatomy*, 220, 496–503.

Ridler, T. W. and Calvard, S. (1978). Picture thresholding using an iterative selection method. *IEEE Transactions on Systems, Man and Cybernetics*, SMC-8, 630–632.

Ruff, C. B. (2003a). Growth in bone strength, body size, and muscle size in a juvenile longitudinal sample. *Bone*, 33, 317–329.

Ruff, C. B. (2003b). Ontogenetic adaptation to bipedalism: age changes in femoral to humeral length and strength proportions in humans, with a comparison to baboons. *Journal of Human Evolution*, 45, 317–349.

Ruff, C. B. (2005a). Growth tracking of femoral and humeral strength from infancy through late adolescence. *Acta Paediatrica*, 94, 1030–1037.

Ruff, C. B. (2005b). Mechanical determinants of bone form: insights from skeletal remains. *Journal of Musculoskeletal & Neuronal Interactions*, 5, 202–212.

Ruff, C. B. (2006). Gracilization of the modern human skeleton – the latent strength in our slender bones teaches lessons about human lives, current and past. *American Scientist*, 94, 508–514.

Ruff, C. B. (2009). Relative limb strength and locomotion in *Homo habilis*. *American Journal of Physical Anthropology*, 138, 90–100.

Ryan, T. M. and Ketcham, R. A. (2002a). Femoral head trabecular bone structure in two omomyid primates. *Journal of Human Evolution*, 43, 241–263.

Ryan, T. M. and Ketcham, R. A. (2002b). The three-dimensional structure of trabecular bone in the femoral head of strepsirrhine primates. *Journal of Human Evolution*, 43, 1–26.

Ryan, T. M. and Ketcham, R. A. (2005). The angular orientation of trabecular bone in the femoral head and its relationship to hip joint loads in leaping primates. *Journal of Morphology*, 265, 249–263.

Ryan, T. M. and Krovitz, G. E. (2006). Trabecular bone ontogeny in the human proximal femur. *Journal of Human Evolution*, 51, 591–602.

Ryan, T. M. and Shaw, C. N. (2012). Unique suites of trabecular bone features characterize locomotor behavior in human and non-human anthropoid primates. *PLoS ONE*, 7, e41037.

Ryan, T. M. and Shaw, C. N. (2015). Gracility of the modern *Homo sapiens* skeleton is the result of decreased biomechanical loading. *Proceedings of the National Academy of Sciences of the USA*, 112, 372–377.

Ryan, T. M. and Walker, A. (2010). Trabecular bone structure in the humeral and femoral heads of anthropoid primates. *Anatomical Record*, 293, 719–729.

Salle, B. L., Rauch, F., Travers, R., Bouvier, R. and Glorieux, F. H. (2002). Human fetal bone development: histomorphometric evaluation of the proximal femoral metaphysis. *Bone*, 30, 823–828.

Santure, S. K., Harn, A. D. and Esarey, D. (1990). *Archaeological Investigations at the Morton Village and Norris Farms 36 Cemetery*. Springfield, IL: Illinois State Museum.

Schneider, C. A., Rasband, W. S. and Eliceiri, K. W. (2012). NIH Image to ImageJ: 25 years of image analysis. *Nature Methods*, 9, 671–675.

Shaw, C. N. and Ryan, T. M. (2012). Does skeletal anatomy reflect adaptation to locomotor patterns? Cortical and trabecular architecture in human and nonhuman anthropoids. *American Journal of Physical Anthropology*, 147, 187–200.

Shaw, C. N. and Stock, J. T. (2009a). Habitual throwing and swimming correspond with upper limb diaphyseal strength and shape in modern human athletes. *American Journal of Physical Anthropology*, 140, 160–172.

Shaw, C. N. and Stock, J. T. (2009b). Intensity, repetitiveness, and directionality of habitual adolescent mobility patterns influence the tibial diaphysis morphology of athletes. *American Journal of Physical Anthropology*, 140, 149–159.

Skinner, M. M., Stephens, N. B., Tsegai, Z. J., *et al.* (2015). Human evolution. Human-like hand use in *Australopithecus africanus. Science*, 347, 395–399.

Stanitski, D. F., Nietert, P. J., Stanitski, C. L., Nadjarian, R. K. and Barfield, W. (2000). Relationship of factors affecting age of onset of independent ambulation. *Journal of Pediatric Orthopedics*, 20, 686–688.

Su, A., Wallace, I. J. and Nakatsukasa, M. (2013). Trabecular bone anisotropy and orientation in an Early Pleistocene hominin talus from East Turkana, Kenya. *Journal of Human Evolution*, 64, 667–677.

Sutherland, D. (1997). The development of mature gait. *Gait and Posture*, 6, 163–170.

Sutherland, D. H., Olshen, R. A., Biden, E. N. and Wyatt, M. P. (1988). *The Development of Mature Walking*. London: MacKeith Press.

Tanck, E., Homminga, J., Van Lenthe, G. H. and Huiskes, R. (2001). Increase in bone volume fraction precedes architectural adaptation in growing bone. *Bone*, 28, 650–654.

Tardieu, C. and Trinkaus, E. (1994). Early ontogeny of the human femoral bicondylar angle. *American Journal of Physical Anthropology*, 95, 183–195.

Tracer, D. P. (2002). Did the australopithecines crawl? *American Journal of Physical Anthropology*, 34, 156–157.

Trussell, H. J. (1979). Comments on "Picture thresholding using an iterative selection method". *IEEE Transactions on Systems, Man and Cybernetics*, SMC-9, 311.

Turner, C. H. and Robling, A. G. (2003). Designing exercise regimens to increase bone strength. *Exercise and Sport Sciences Reviews*, 31, 45–50.

Ulrich, D., van Rietbergen, B., Laib, A. and Rüegsegger, P. (1999). The ability of three-dimensional structural indices to reflect mechanical aspects of trabecular bone. *Bone*, 25, 55–60.

Valdimarsson, O., Sigurdsson, G., Steingrimsdottir, L. and Karlsson, M. K. (2005). Physical activity in the post-pubertal period is associated with maintenance of pre-pubertal high bone density – a 5-year follow-up. *Scandinavian Journal of Medicine & Science in Sports*, 15, 280–286.

van Rietbergen, B. (2001). Micro-FE analyses of bone: state of the art. *Advances in Experimental Medicine and Biology*, 496, 21–30.

van Rietbergen, B., Weinans, H., Huiskes, R. and Odgaard, A. (1995). A new method to determine trabecular bone elastic properties and loading using micromechanical finite-element models. *Journal of Biomechanics*, 28, 69–81.

van Rietbergen, B., Weinans, H., Huiskes, R. and Polman, B. J. W. (1996). Computational strategies for iterative solutions of large FEM applications employing voxel data. *International Journal for Numerical Methods in Engineering*, 39, 2743–2767.

van Rietbergen, B., Odgaard, A., Kabel, J. and Huiskes, R. (1998). Relationships between bone morphology and bone elastic properties can be accurately quantified using high-resolution computer reconstructions. *Journal of Orthopaedic Research*, 16, 23–28.

Wallace, I. J., Kwaczala, A. T., Judex, S., Demes, B. and Carlson, K. J. (2013). Physical activity engendering loads from diverse directions augments the growing skeleton. *Journal of Musculoskeletal and Neuronal Interactions*, 13, 283–288.

Wallace, I. J., Demes, B., Mongle, C., Pearson, O. M., Polk, J. D. and Lieberman, D. E. (2014). Exercise-induced bone formation is poorly linked to local strain magnitude in the sheep tibia. *PLoS ONE*, 9, e99108.

Wallace, I. J., Gupta, S., Sankaran, J., Demes, B. and Judex, S. (2015). Bone shaft bending strength index is unaffected by exercise and unloading in mice. *Journal of Anatomy*, 226, 224–228.

Willmore, K. E., Young, N. M. and Richtsmeier, J. T. (2007). Phenotypic variability: Its components, measurement and underlying developmental processes. *Evolutionary Biology*, 34, 99–120.

Wolschrijn, C. F. and Weijs, W. A. (2004). Development of the trabecular structure within the ulnar medial coronoid process of young dogs. *Anatomical Record*, 278A, 514–519.

Zeininger, A. (2013). Ontogeny of Bipedalism: Pedal Mechanics and Trabecular Bone Morphology. PhD, University of Texas.

Appendix to Chapter 3: Detailed Anatomical Description of Developing Chondrocranium and Dermatocranium in the Mouse

Kazuhiko Kawasaki and Joan T. Richtsmeier

A.1 Introduction

In Chapter 3, we presented an abbreviated anatomical description of the developing chondrocranium and dermatocranium. Here, we provide further details for interested readers. Following the protocol outlined in Chapter 3, we combine our own laboratory observations of C57BL/6J mouse development with historical works to provide a detailed description of the development and ossification of the chondrocranium and the spatiotemporal associations between the chondrocranium and its topologically associated dermatocranial elements. The developmental descriptions are based on timed matings and expressed in terms of embryonic days postconception (e.g., 17 days postconception is E17) and postnatal days (e.g., P2 = second postnatal day). Because many structures are transient, they are described according to their appearance during developmental time that is approximate because of variation in developmental timing among samples (Flaherty et al., 2015). All figures mentioned in this Appendix and the list of Abbreviations and their definitions appear in Chapter 3. References that are not listed in the References section of Chapter 3 are shown at the end of the Appendix text.

A.2 Chondrocranium – Overall Structure and the Relationship with the Cranial Base

The chondrocranium is that part of the endoskeleton that protects the brain and three principal sense organs but does not include the pharyngeal endoskeleton (comprised of Meckel's cartilage, Reichert's cartilage, malleus, incus, stapes, ala temporalis, and other components). The separation of the chondrocranium and the pharyngeal skeleton, as well as the exclusion of the pharyngeal skeleton from our definition of the chondrocranium, is primarily due to the incorporation of the endoskeletal upper jaw into the braincase over evolutionary time. Notably, the ascending lamina of the ala temporalis (Figures 3.1 and 3.2A,B) is derived evolutionarily from the ascending process of the palatoquadrate (Maier, 1987; Hopson and Rougier, 1993; Kielan-Jaworowska *et al.*, 2004) that arose as the dorsal component (i.e., the upper jaw cartilage) of the mandibular arch.

Portions of the chondrocranium are named for soft tissue organs that they protect: *braincase*, *nasal capsule*, and *otic capsule*. The *braincase* consists of the floor, roof, and lateral wall, which protect the brain and partly contributes to protection of the eyes. The *nasal capsule* protects the olfactory organs and olfactory bulbs, whereas the *otic capsule*, composed of the pars cochlearis (PCO) and pars canalicularis (PCA), accommodates the organs of hearing and balancing (pars cochlearis protecting the saccule and cochlear duct, and pars canalicularis protecting the semicircular canals and utricle). These and all other anatomical abbreviations in this chapter are defined in a list found within section 3.5.3.

The cranial base has played an important role in anthropological research but a definitive definition of the term is hard to come by. The cranial base as envisioned by many anthropologists is usually an amalgam of four bones (ethmoid, sphenoid, temporal, occipital) that combine to form the endocranial surface of the floor of the skull, located largely underneath the brain. In the strict sense, however, parts of the frontal and parietal also contribute to the cranial base in humans. The cranial base consists of the anterior, middle, and posterior cranial fossae (only an anterior part of the posterior cranial fossa in some definitions) and all midline structures, extending from the crista galli anteriorly to the foramen magnum posteriorly (Enlow, 1990; Lieberman et al., 2000). The term "chondrocranium" is often used as a synonym for the embryonic cartilaginous cranial base by anthropologists. However, the cartilages that compose the embryonic skull include far more than the cartilages that serve as the model for the bony cranial base. A notable example is the lateral wall of the cartilaginous braincase, part of which forms as the chondrocranium but is eventually resorbed and substituted by dermal bones. To resolve this confusion, we provide a detailed description of the development of the chondrocranium below.

A.2.1   Braincase Floor

Although the composition of the cranial base varies among species, the midline floor of the braincase contributes to the cranial base consistently in vertebrates. In the mouse, the braincase floor arises as the trabecular (T), hypophyseal (H), acrochordal (AR), and parachordal (P) cartilages arranged along the anterior–posterior axis (see the scales in Figure 3.3). These cartilages subsequently fuse and develop into the bony braincase floor, consisting of the mesethmoid (see Section A.2.4), presphenoid (PS), basisphenoid (BS), and basioccipital bones (BO in Figure 3.2E).

The braincase floor forms by E12.5 with the appearance of the parachordal cartilage (Figure 3.3). The parachordal cartilage forms as a broad posterior half and a narrow anterior half that splits anteriorly forming a "Y." The posterior half joins laterally with the occipital arch (OA), leaving the foramen hypoglossum (fhg) midway along this joint (Figure 3.3A). The trabecular cartilage forms also at E12.5 and serves as the septum nasi (SN), an anterior extension of the braincase floor. The hypophyseal cartilage is the next to form by E13.5, anterior to the parachordal cartilage, with the hypophyseal fenestra (fhy) forming at the center of this cartilage (Figure 3.3B). Between the hypophyseal and parachordal cartilages, the acrochordal cartilage forms and fuses posteriorly with the parachordal cartilage, leaving the basicranial fenestra (fb) in the medial region of the Y. Anteriorly, the acrochordal cartilage connects with the hypophyseal cartilage via a thin (or fenestrated) cartilage plate (Figure 3.3B). The notochord runs along the dorsal surface of the parachordal cartilage, and the anterior end of the notochord rests on the acrochordal cartilage at E13.5 (de Beer, 1937). At this stage, the hypophyseal cartilage laterally extends the processus alaris (PAL) and joins with the ala temporalis (AT) (de Beer and Woodger, 1930). Connections between the braincase floor and the otic capsules are described in the section on the otic region (Section A.2.5). As the trabecular cartilage extends posteriorly and connects with the hypophyseal cartilage, a continuous braincase floor is formed by E14.5 (Figure 3.2A).

Perichondral/endochondral ossification of the braincase floor begins with the basioccipital between E14.5 and E15.5. The basioccipital grows anteriorly from the central aspect of the posterior end (bounding the foramen magnum (fmg)) by replacing the parachordal cartilage and reaches the level of the basicranial fenestra by E16.5 (the basicranial fenestra closes at E17.5 in Figure 3.2E). Subsequently, the basisphenoid arises by ossification of the hypophyseal cartilage initially on both sides of the hypophyseal fenestra (Figure 3.2E; the hypophyseal fenestra closes around E16.5). The presphenoid appears by ossification of that part of the trabecular cartilage lying medial to the pila metoptica (PMO; Figure 3.2A,E) at E17.5 and extends anteriorly to the level of the base of the pila preoptica (PPO) at P0. As ossification progresses in the braincase floor, these bones become connected by cartilaginous joints, referred to as synchondroses. The spheno-occipital synchondrosis forms between the basisphenoid and basioccipital medial to the sphenocochlear commissure (CSC; Figures 3.2F and 3.3B) by P0 (McBratney-Owen et al., 2008). The intersphenoid synchondrosis forms subsequently at P7, as the presphenoid grows posteriorly towards the anterior end of the basisphenoid.

Dermatocranium Associations – Vomer, Palatine, and Pterygoid. Between E14.5 and E15.5, cartilages of the braincase floor associate with three bilateral pairs of forming dermatocranial bones that are members of the palatal series defined in early vertebrates (Goodrich, 1930; Romer and Parsons, 1977): the vomers (VM), palatines (PL), and pterygoids (PTG-VT and PTG-DS in Figure 3.2C,D). The palatine bones arise first by E15.5 ventral to the pila metoptica (Figure 3.2C and Table 3.1) and grow anteromedially and posterolaterally with the lateral edge inclined ventrally. By E16.5, the medial edge bends dorsally forming a vertical plate (vppl), and a horizontal plate (hppl) buds off medially from the vertical plate along the midline (Figure 3.4) (Fawcett, 1917). At E17.5, the vertical plate of the palatine anteriorly approaches the posterior end of the nasal capsule (cupula nasi posterior, CNP; Table 3.1) and posteriorly overlies the anterior end of the ventral element of the pterygoid. At this stage, the horizontal plate of the palatine spreads anteriorly below the presphenoid (Table 3.1) and forms a suture posteriorly with the anterior end of the ventral element of the pterygoid (Figure 3.4B). The intersphenoid synchondrosis forms dorsal to this suture at P7. At E17.5, the laterally spreading vertical plate extends posteriorly toward the anterior edge of the processus alaris and the ala temporalis (Fawcett, 1917; Eloff, 1948), leaving a narrow gap that remains at least partially patent at P14 after the ala temporalis and the processus alaris ossify.

Around E15.5, the vomers arise as a pair of nearly vertical plates medial to the posterior end of the paraseptal cartilages (PC in Figure 3.2A) and lateral to the ventral edge of the septum nasi (Figure 3.2C; Table 3.1). As each vomer extends anteriorly at E16.5, the plates grow dorsolaterally and medioventrally, and the two plates ventrally contact each other or open slightly (Figure 3.4), separating the ventral edge of the septum nasi from the medial border of the paraseptal cartilage on each side. Posterior to the paraseptal cartilage, the ventral edges of the vomers separate widely and underlie the septum nasi. At E17.5, the ventral edge of each vomer anteriorly form a suture with the dorsal edge of the posterior end of the palatine process of the premaxilla (pppm). By P0, the posterior end of the vomer becomes a narrow process extending toward the septo-paraseptal fissure (fsp in Figure 3.2A) formed between the septum nasi and the lamina transversalis posterior (LTP). More anteriorly, the ventral edge of the vomer widens and curls laterally, and the curled posterior edge apparently contacts the anterior edge of the lamina transversalis posterior (Table 3.1).

Each of the paired pterygoid bones appears around E15.5 from two separate ossification centers, which form the ventral (PTG-VT) and dorsal elements (PTG-DS) (Figure 3.2C,D). The ventral elements are the first to develop ventral to the hypophyseal cartilage (Table 3.1) and medial to the ventral ridge (pterygoid process) that formed at the bottom of the ala temporalis. The dorsal elements form next near the posterior end of the ventral element and extend posterolaterally along the ventral surface of the alicochlear commissure (CAC; Table 3.1) that connects the hypophyseal cartilage with the pars cochlearis (PCO in Figure 3.2A,F) (de Beer and Woodger, 1930). Soon after their formation, the posterior end of the ventral element connects with the medial end of the dorsal element (Figure 3.4). At E16.5, the ventral element extends posteriorly beneath the medial end of the dorsal element, while the dorsal surface of the dorsal element connects with the base of the alisphenoid (perichondrally ossified ala temporalis; Figure 3.1). At E17.5, the anterior end of the ventral element forms a suture with the posterior edge of the palatine. The dorsal elements are homologous with the reptilian pterygoid, whereas the ventral elements are derived from the ectopterygoid (Parrington and Westoll, 1940; Presley and Steel, 1978; Moore, 1981). Both elements thus originate as members of the palatal series of dermatocranial elements, but a medioventral portion of the ventral element is composed of cartilage. This pterygoid cartilage (CPTG in Figure 3.4B) is considered as secondary cartilage (de Beer, 1937; Presley and Steel, 1978; Moore, 1981), as it arises after deposition of the bone matrix in the rat (Presley and Steel, 1978). However, the pterygoid cartilage and the bony ventral element arise nearly simultaneously around E15.0. This observation is consistent with a different hypothesis that the pterygoid cartilage is derived from the palatoquadrate (Zeller, 1987). The pterygoid cartilage gradually undergoes endochondral ossification and persists postnatally at least to P14.

A.2.2   Lateral Wall and Roof of the Occipital Region

The part of the chondrocranium composing the lateral wall and roof of the occipital region arises as the paired occipital arches (OA in Figure 3.3B) and the tectum posterius (TP). As early as E12.5, the occipital arches grow and join with the posterolateral edges of the parachordal cartilage (P in the scale of Figure 3.3). At E13.5, each occipital arch grows dorsally as a relatively thick plate along the posterior edge of the pars canalicularis (PCA in Figure 3.2B). The morphological similarity of the occipital arch and the neural arch of the first cervical vertebra suggests that these arches are serial homologs (de Beer, 1937). The occipital arch dorsally continues to the tectum posterius that appears as a thin cartilage with a meshwork-like texture. The occipital arches, tectum posterius, and parachordal cartilage bound the foramen magnum (fmg in Figure 3.3B). The tectum posterius blends with the parietal plate (PP) anteriorly, dorsal to the posterior edge of the pars canalicularis.

By E15.5, perichondral/endochondral ossification begins at a middle region of the occipital arch, spreading from the posterior edge to the anterior edge, to form the exoccipital bone (EO in Figure 3.2E). The exoccipital grows dorsoventrally and ventrally reaches the foramen hypoglossum (fhg) that originated at the boundary between the occipital arch and parachordal cartilage by E16.5. As the exoccipital extends medially beyond this foramen by P0, the anterior intraoccipital synchondrosis, connecting the exoccipital and basioccipital bones (BO), forms within the parachordal cartilage.

During this process, the paracondylar processes (PPC), which are homologous with the transverse processes of the vertebrae (de Beer, 1937), grow anterolaterally from the anterior edge of the occipital arches at E15.5 (Figure 3.2A). By E16.5, the base of the paracondylar process gradually undergoes ossification but its apex remains cartilaginous even at P14. The posterior edge of the exoccipital bounding the foramen magnum is partly covered with cartilage at E16.5, forming the occipital condyle (OC), while the remainder of the occipital arch largely ossifies.

The supraoccipital bone (SO) appears bilaterally at E17.5 by perichondral/endochondral ossification of the tectum posterius on both sides of the posterior edge near the midline. These two bony plates spread superiorly and join along the midline (Figure 3.2E), while the inferomedial edge remains cartilaginous until around P2. As the supraoccipital spreads laterally, the posterior intraoccipital synchondrosis forms between the supraoccipital and exoccipital bones at P7.

Dermatocranium Association – Interparietal. At E15.5, progressive chondrification of the tectum posterius obscures its border with the occipital arch (dotted line in Figure 3.2B) and the parietal plate. At this stage, the interparietal (IP) bone arises as a pair of thin dermatocranial plates, which soon join at the midline to form a crescent-shaped bone (Figure 3.2D). The lateral extremities of the interparietal overlie the parietal plate (Table 3.1), while a thin medial extension of the parietal plate extends anterior to these lateral extremities. The relatively broad medial region of the interparietal coincides with the anterior edge of the tectum posterius (Table 3.1), which appears as a meshwork because of poor chondrification. At E17.5, the interparietal anteriorly overlies the posterodorsal edge of the parietal plates (Figure 3.2E). The portions of the parietal plate and the tectum posterius that are overlain by the interparietal bone are poorly chondrified, appearing as a coarse meshwork from this stage onward.

As the interparietal and supraoccipital bones grow, the tectum posterius is reduced to a narrow channel between these two bones and narrow marginal regions, superimposed by the interparietal, by P7. In the region deeply covered by the interparietal, the tectum appears poorly chondrified, looking like a fragmented meshwork. By P14, the tectum between the interparietal and supraoccipital is completely resorbed, and only a small poorly chondrified cartilage remains within the supraoccipital bone near the boundary with the parietal bone (PR in Figure 3.2E; lateral to the interparietal). In our observations, although bone and cartilage continue to grow, chondrification is relatively poor in all regions of the chondrocranium that are covered by a dermal bone. We propose this as evidence of a growth mechanism, by which localized expansion of dermal bone and resorption of cartilage are coordinated and coupled. Similar patterns are observed also in the preoccipital region, as we describe below.

A.2.3   Lateral Wall and Roof of the Preoccipital Region

The lateral wall of the preoccipital region bridges the nasal capsule and the occipital cartilages and is composed, from anterior to posterior, of the sphenethmoid commissure (CSE), ala orbitalis (AO), orbitoparietal commissure (COP), and parietal plate (PP) (Figure 3.2B). The pila preoptica (PPO) and pila metoptica (PMO), which connect with the braincase floor, also contribute to the lateral wall (Goodrich, 1930; Moore, 1981). While dermatocranial bones (frontal, parietal, and squamosal) develop superficial and dorsal to these cartilages (Figure 3.2C,D), some cartilages are progressively resorbed and eventually completely substituted by these bones.

In Lacertilia (Gaupp, 1900) and other reptiles (de Beer, 1937), the dorsal region of the lateral wall comprises the teania marginalis, a simple ribbon-like structure, but this region is more complicated in the mouse (summarized above). In most primates, including humans, the orbitoparietal commissure is absent (i.e., there is a large gap in the sidewall.), presumably in association with the increased brain volume (Starck, 1975).

In mice, the ala orbitalis arises medial to the eye and joins anteriorly with the dorsal ridge of the nasal capsule via the sphenethmoid commissure (Figure 3.3B), while the orbitoparietal commissure appears posterior to the eye and grows anteriorly from the parietal plate between E12.5 and E13.5. The ala orbitalis connects with the orbitoparietal commissure in most samples, but in some samples they are still separated in a region posterior to a large apically expanding plate (Figure 3.3B), the tectum transversum (TTR in Figure 3.2B) (de Beer, 1937). On each side, medial to the ala orbitalis, the orbital cartilage (O; lateral) and the hypochiasmatic cartilage (Y; medial) arise between E12.5 and E13.5 (Figure 3.3) (McBratney-Owen et al., 2008). These two cartilages join with a narrow process extending medially from the orbital cartilage by E13.5. At E14.5, the orbital cartilage also extends a U-shaped rod laterally, anteriorly, and then medially with the medial (distal) end reaching the trabecular cartilage (T in Figure 3.3B). As the lateral edge of the U-shaped rod merges with the ventral edge of the ala orbitalis, the orbital and hypochiasmatic cartilages are integrated into the ala orbitalis (Figure 3.2B) (Eloff, 1948). The hypochiasmatic cartilage medially fuses with the trabecular cartilage at E15.5. Once fused, the trabecular cartilage connects with the lateral wall (ala orbitalis) by the two roots, pila preoptica and pila metoptica that bound the foramen opticum (fop) (Goodrich, 1930). The pila preoptica initiates perichondral/endochondral ossification at E17.5, and the area surrounding the foramen opticum ossifies into the orbitosphenoid by P7.

Dermatocranium Associations– Frontal, Parietal, and Squamosal. The frontal bones (FR) appear by E14.5 as a pair of dermatocranial bones (Figure 3.2C,D). Before mineralization, the matrix of the frontal bone is discernible as a lattice-like matrix immediately dorsal to the ala orbitalis (Table 3.1), spreading from the sphenethmoid commissure to the anterior edge of the tectum transversum. Mineralization initiates within this matrix, but the exact location varies among samples. From E15.5 to E16.5, the frontal extends anteriorly to the sphenethmoid commissure (Table 3.1). The posterior edge of the frontal only slightly overlaps with the ala orbitalis but not with the tectum transversum (Figure 3.2D and Table 3.1). As the frontal expands apically and posteriorly at E17.5, the underlying cartilages are resorbed rapidly, thereby limiting the superimposition of frontal ossification with surrounding cartilages spatially and temporally.

Appearing later than the frontal bones, the parietal bones (PR) are discernible before mineralization at E14.5 as a lattice-like matrix that slightly overlies the dorsal edge of the tectum transversum and spreads dorsally (Table 3.1). Anteriorly, the matrix extends towards the dorsal extension of the anterior edge of the tectum. Mineralization initiates between E14.5 and E15.5 along (or slightly above) the dorsal edge of the tectum transversum (Figure 3.2D). Between E15.5 and E16.5, the parietal bone overlies the tectum transversum considerably and extends anteriorly up to the dorsal extension of the anterior edge of the tectum. The portion of the tectum transversum that is superimposed by the parietal bone is weakly chondrified and appears meshwork-like. Posteroventrally, the parietal grows toward the dorsal edge of the orbitoparietal commissure (Table 3.1). Any region of the tectum and orbitoparietal commissure that is superimposed by the expanding parietal undergoes a rapid resorption beginning at E16.5. By 17.5, the posterior aspect of the parietal bone slightly overlies the anterior edge of the parietal plate that appears poorly chondrified at the site of this overlap (Table 3.1). At this stage, the majority of the tectum transversum is considerably resorbed, but its anterior edge marginally remains and is aligned with the anterior edge of the parietal bone. Thus, as the

frontal bone extends posteriorly, its approaching edge contributes to a suture forming with the parietal along a line initially defined and maintained by the anterior
edge of the tectum transversum (Figure 3.2B,D). This growth pattern suggests that
the location of the future frontal–parietal (coronal) suture is predetermined by the
anterior edge of the tectum transversum, which arose by E13.5, long before mineralization of these bones.

The squamosal (SQ) appears between E14.5 and E15.5 as a bilateral pair of dermatocranial bones (Figure 3.2C,D). Each squamosal initially forms as a squamous
basal plate (sbp) and an outer ridge (Figure 3.4), appearing immediately lateral to
the ventral edge of the orbitoparietal commissure (Table 3.1) (de Beer and Woodger,
1930). The ridge develops into the zygomatic process (zps) anteriorly and the retrotympanic process (rtps) posteriorly (Figure 3.4). At E16.5, the condylar process
of the mandible articulates with the squamosal at the hollow where the zygomatic
process branches off from the squamous basal plate. Between E15.5 and E17.5,
the squamous basal plate slightly overlies the ventral edge of the orbitoparietal
commissure, while it grows medioventrally toward the posterodorsal edge of the
alisphenoid (part of the membrane bone outgrowth from the ala temporalis, shown
in Figure 3.1). The caudal process (cps in Figure 3.4), extending caudodorsally from
the base of the retrotympanic process, completely superimposes the lateral wall
where the underlying cartilage is rapidly resorbed.

After E16.5, as the frontal, parietal, and squamosal bones gradually expand to
overlie the ala orbitalis, orbitoparietal commissure, and/or the tectum transversum, the cartilages beneath these dermal bones are progressively resorbed. As a
result, between E17.5 and P0, the tectum transversum and its ventral connection
with the ala orbitalis and the orbitoparietal commissure degenerate into a narrow
tract along the gap formed by the frontal, parietal, and squamosal bones with little
overlap between the tract and these bones. The remnant of the cartilage is completely resorbed at P0. These observations concur with our finding in the occipital
region: thick bone does not form or grow to overlie thick cartilage.

Fragmentary secondary cartilages arise along the posterior edge of the parietal
bone and within the forming interparietal (sagittal) suture at E16.5. The secondary
cartilages remain in the unossified region at P4, and a small cartilaginous nodule
persists within the posterior fontanelle, surrounded by the parietal and the interparietal (IP) bones, at P7.

A.2.4   Olfactory Region

Among the components of the nasal capsule, the lateral walls (parietes nasi, PN)
arise first at E12.5, followed by the roof (tectum nasi, TN) at E13.5 (Figure 3.3). The
anterior region is not well chondrified at early stages (Zeller, 1987). The tectum
nasi forms a furrow called the sulcus dorsalis nasi (SDN) along the dorsal midline,
and the sulcus connects inferiorly with the septum nasi (SN in Figure 3.3B) that
separates the left and right nasal passages (Figure 3.2A). The tectum nasi laterally
joins with the paries nasi, also establishing a furrow, within which the foramen

epiphinale (fep) forms near the posterior end (Figure 3.2E). At E13.5 and later, the paries nasi is separated into the anterior (pars anterior, PAT), intermediate (pars intermedia, PIT), and posterior (pars posterior, PPT) regions by the sulcus anterior lateralis (SAL) and sulcus posterior lateralis (SPL; the scale of Figure 3.2A,B). The dorsal ridge of the pars intermedia continues to the sphenethmoid commissure (CSE in Figure 3.2B). Around E14.5, the posterior end of the paries nasi connects with the trabecular cartilage (T in Figure 3.3) immediately anterior to the pila preoptica through the lamina orbitonasalis (LON, consisting of the pars posterior and the posterior end of the pars intermedia) (Fawcett, 1917). The orbitonasal fissure (fon) forms between the posterior edge of the pars posterior and the anterior edge of the ala orbitalis (AO).

At E14.5, the fenestra nasi (fn) becomes bounded anteriorly by the cupula nasi anterior (CNA) and posteroventrally by the laminae transversalis anterior (LTA). The laminae transversalis anterior arise as a pair of triangular plates, separated from each other along the midline (Figure 3.2A) (Zeller, 1987). Posteroinferior to the fenestra nasi, the processus alaris superior (PAS) extends anterolaterally. By E15.5, the lamina transversalis anterior connects with the septum nasi medially and the paries nasi dorsally so that this region is surrounded by a ring of cartilage: the zona annularis (ZA; the scale of Figure 3.2A) (Fawcett, 1917).

At E14.5, a pair of paraseptal cartilages (PC) arise along the septum nasi inferolateral to its inferior edge (Figure 3.2,B). The paraseptal cartilage accommodates the vomeronasal organ and separates it from the septum nasi. Between E15.5 and E16.5, the inferior edge of the pars posterior medially forms the lamina transversalis posterior (LTP), which is separated from the septum nasi by the septo-paraseptal fissure (fsp; Figure 3.2A) (Fawcett, 1917; Eloff, 1948). The posterior end of the capsule is referred to as the cupula nasi posterior (CNP). At this stage, the floor of the nasal capsule (solum nasi) consists of the lamina transversalis anterior, paraseptal cartilage, and lamina transversalis posterior. The fenestra basalis (fbs) forms as the elongated gap between the inferior edge of the paries nasi and the paraseptal cartilage or septum nasi (Figure 3.2A).

Various paired nasal turbinals grow inside the nasal capsule (Fawcett, 1917; Starck, 1979; Maier and Ruf, 2014). The ethmoturbinal I (ETB1) extends inward from the sulcus posterior lateralis at E13.5 and splits into two branches near the bottom at E15.5. The ethmoturbinals II (ETB2) and III (ETB3) grow posteroventral to the ethmoturbinal I at E14.5 and E16.5, respectively. These ethmoturbinals posteriorly connect with the lamina cribrosa (LCB in Figure 3.2E) (Maier and Ruf, 2014). The nasoturbinal develops antero-posteriorly inside the pars anterior at E14.5, while the maxilloturbinal forms along the ventral edge of pars anterior at E15.5. Generally in mammals, the ethmoturbinals are covered with the olfactory epithelium, whereas both the nasoturbinal and maxilloturbinal are covered with the respiratory epithelium (Moore, 1981; Harkema et al., 2006). In addition to the nasal turbinals, the crista semicircularis (CS) extends inward from the sulcus anterior lateralis at E14.5 (Starck, 1979). The paired laminae cribrosa form at E15.5 as the posterior roof of the nasal capsule. The two laminae are separated medially by the septum nasi, the dorsal corner of which forms the crista galli (CG in Figure 3.2E). The laminae cribrosa support the olfactory bulbs, which receive olfactory nerve filaments from the nasal capsule through the foramina cribrosa.

Perichondral/endochondral ossification of the olfactory region initiates relatively late at a mediodorsal region of the laminae cribrosa, ethmoturbinals, nasoturbinals, and maxilloturbinals around P4, while the tectum nasi, paries nasi, and paraseptal cartilage are progressively resorbed. A central portion of the posterior edge of the septum nasi begins to ossify into the mesethmoid at P4, but anteriorly and dorsally it remains cartilaginous at P14. In addition, the anterior-most cartilages of the nasal capsule, which are not associated with any bone (Figure 3.2E), also persist at P14.

Dermatocranium Associations – Premaxilla, Maxilla, Lacrimal, and Nasal. The paired dermatocranial premaxillae (PMX) begin ossification between E14.5 and E15.5 in the alveolar process (avppm) along the inferior border of the pars anterior (Figures 3.2C,D, 3.4, and Table 3.1). The alveolar process subsequently grows superolaterally to form the ascending portion of the premaxilla. At E16.5, the growing ascending portion forms the posterodorsal process (pdppm) along the surface of the pars anterior. Within the alveolar process, a large pit forms anterolaterally to accommodate the developing incisor. The alveolar process also grows medially and continues to the palatine process (pppm in Figure 3.4) that elongates posteriorly along the ventral surface of the paraseptal cartilage (Table 3.1). The posteriorly growing palatine process extends superiorly along the medial surface of the paraseptal cartilage (medial ascending process) at E17.5 and along the lateral surface of the paraseptal cartilage (lateral ascending process) at P0 (Eloff, 1948). By P7, the palatine, medial ascending, and lateral ascending processes unite at the posterior end of the paraseptal cartilage. The paraseptal cartilage begins to be resorbed by P1 and almost completely disappears by P7, leaving the premaxillae to provide postnatal protection for the vomeronasal organ (Eloff, 1948).

The paired dermatocranial maxillae (MX) arise slightly later than the premaxillae between E14.5 and E15.5 (Eloff, 1948), the medial aspect of the alveolar process (avpm) appearing beneath the pars intermedia (Figure 3.2C,D, and Table 3.1). From the lateral portion of this process, the zygomatic process (zpm) extends posterolaterally, while the lateral ascending portion of the frontal process (fplap) elongates superomedially (Figure 3.4) (Eloff, 1948). The lateral ascending portion terminates slightly anterior to the lateral apex of the pars intermedia and abruptly turns 90 degrees anteriorly to form the lateral bar. The medial ascending portion of the frontal process (fpmap) grows along the sulcus anterior lateralis and joins the anterior end of the alveolar process inferiorly (Figure 3.4) (Eloff, 1948). At E16.5, as the posterior edge of the premaxilla approaches the anterior edge of the medial ascending portion of the maxilla (Figure 3.4), the premaxilla–maxillary suture forms in line with the sulcus anterior lateralis (Figure 3.2B). At this stage, the lateral bar connects with the two ascending portions of the frontal process to form the infraorbital foramen (iof). The lateral bar also grows dorsally and forms a dorsal ascending lamina of the frontal process (fpdal) alongside the pars intermedia. At E16.5, the alveolar process extends medially and continues to the palatine process (ppm), which elongates anteriorly inferolateral to the septum nasi (inferior to the vomer; Figure 3.4 and Table 3.1). At P2, the anterior end of the palatine process of the maxilla underlies the posterior end of the palatine process of the premaxilla, forming a suture inferior to the posterior end of the paraseptal cartilage (Table 3.1). Furthermore, the posterior end of the palatine process of the maxilla forms a suture with the anterior end of the palatine bone (PL) at the level of the posterior end of the nasal capsule.

The paired dermatocranial lacrimal (LA) bones appear between E15.5 and E16.5 as tiny nodules and grow into thin plates on each side lateral to the pars intermedia (Table 3.1), posteromedial to the dorsal end of the lateral ascending portion of the maxilla (Figure 3.2D). At E16.5, the orbital crest (cola) forms apparently parallel to the ridge of the pars intermedia and splits the plate into the facial (fpla) and orbital (opla) processes (Figure 3.4) (Wible, 2011). The facial process is inserted between the pars intermedia and the lateral ascending portion of the maxilla. The orbital crest articulates with the posterior edge of the lateral ascending portion anteriorly around P2 and with the anterior end of the supraorbital crest of the frontal (FR) postero-dorsally at P4 (Wible, 2011). The orbital process reaches the paranasal process (PPN in Figure 3.2E; Table 3.1), a cartilaginous hamulus holding the nasolacrimal duct, inferiorly at P2 (Macklin, 1921).

The nasal (NA) bones form as a pair of dermal bony plates that cover the tectum nasi and a dorsal portion of the pars anterior (Figure 3.2D and Table 3.1). Each nasal plate begins ossification at E16.5 from two sites: one on the anterolateral corner of the plate slightly dorsoposterior to the fenestra superior (de Beer and Woodger, 1930) and the other on the medioposterior corner slightly anterior to the crista galli (Figure 3.2D,E). The ossification progresses along the edge of each plate, and the medial region ossifies subsequently by E17.5. Anteriorly, the nasal bones reach the level of the posterior edge of the lamina transversalis anterior, coincident with the anterior edge of the premaxilla on the lateral and ventral sides (Figure 3.4). The lateral edge of the nasal forms a suture with the dorsal edge of the premaxilla at E17.5 (Wible, 2011), and the posterior edge of the nasal aligns with the posterior edge of the posterodorsal process of the premaxilla along the sulcus anterior lateralis (Figures 3.2E and 3.4). The posterior edge of the nasal reaches the dorsal edge of the lamina cribrosa (Table 3.1) and the anterior edge of the frontal at P0.

A.2.5 Otic Rregion

Each auditory capsule consists of two parts, the dorsolateral pars canalicularis (PCA) and the ventromedial pars cochlearis (PCO, Figure 3.2F). The auditory capsule begins chondrification by E12.5 from the lateral side of the pars canalicularis (Figure 3.3A) (de Beer and Woodger, 1930), and by E13.5, the semicircular canals and the endolymphatic duct form internal to the pars canalicularis (Kaufman and Bard, 1999). By contrast, chondrification of the pars cochlearis appears to be only superficial, the dorsal half appearing poorly chondrified even at E14.5, especially around the stapes (ST) cartilage (Figure 3.2B). The crista parotica (CPR in Figure 3.2B) is a shallow ridge, formed by the lateral surface of the pars canalicularis that overhangs the pars cochlearis (de Beer and Woodger, 1930). On the medial surface of the pars canalicularis, the foramen endolymphaticum (fed) opens as a long tract beside the posterior edge, and the subarcuate fossa (fsa) becomes evident in the upper half between E14.5 and E15.5 (Figure 3.2F) (Fawcett, 1917). At E15.5, as chondrification progresses on the ventral side of the pars cochlearis, the fenestra ovalis (fov) becomes discernible medial to the stapes (Figure 3.2B), and the foramen perilymphaticum (fpl) opens on the posterior wall (de Beer and Woodger, 1930). A forming cochlear duct is first detected as an internal ridge. The suprafacial commissure (CSF) bridges the pars cochlearis and the pars canalicularis on their anterior surfaces (Figure 3.2F), and the internal acoustic meatus (mai) forms on the dorsal surface of the pars cochlearis, bounded in part by the pars canalicularis. At E15.5, Reichert's cartilage (RC, an element of the pharyngeal skeleton) attaches laterally to the crista parotica (Figure 3.2B), anterior to which the tegmen tympani (TGT) dorsally roofs a hollow called the epitympanic recess (Fawcett, 1917). The epitympanic recess and its posterior extension, fossa incudis, accommodate the incus and part of the malleus cartilages at E16.5.

The auditory capsule is linked with surrounding cartilages by seven commissures: the alicochlear (CAC), sphenocochlear (CSC), chordo-cochlear (CCC), parietocapsular (CPC), orbitocapsular (COC), supraoccipitocapsular (CSOC), and exoccipitocapsular commissures (CEOC in Figure 3.2F) (Starck, 1979). As early as E13.5, the pars cochlearis connects with the hypophyseal cartilage (H) via the alicochlear commissure (i, CAC) and with the acrochordal cartilage (AR) via the sphenocochlear commissure (ii, CSC in Figure 3.3B) (McBratney-Owen et al., 2008). These cartilages bound the foramen caroticum (fct in Figure 3.2F). At E15.5, the pars cochlearis connects with the parachordal (P) via the chordo-cochlear commissure (iii, CCC), whereas the pars canalicularis joins with the parietal plate (PP) via the parietocapsular commissure (iv, CPC). At E16.5, the pars canalicularis connects with the orbitoparietal commissure (COP) via the orbitocapsular commissure (iv, COC) (Fawcett, 1917; Zeller, 1987), and the pars canalicularis connects with the tectum posterius (TP) via the supraoccipitocapsular commissure (vi, CSOC). When the posterior intraoccipital synchondrosis is formed between the supraoccipital (SO) and exoccipital (EO) bones at P7, the anterior end of this synchondrosis continues to the supraoccipitocapsular commissure anteroinferiorly. The pars canalicularis connects with the exoccipital bone at the base of the cartilaginous paracondylar process (PPC) through the exoccipitocapsular commissure by E17.5 (vii, CEOC). The exoccipitocapsular fissure (feoc), bounded by the supraoccipitocapsular and exoccipitocapsular commissures, is soon filled by a thin cartilaginous plate. The chordo-cochlear commissure, which posteriorly continues to the anterior intraoccipital synchondrosis, borders the foramen jugulare (fj) anteromedially and the basicapsular fissure (fbc) posterolaterally, while the supraoccipitocapsular commissure borders the supraoccipitocapsular fissure (fsoc) posteriorly.

Perichondral/endochondral ossification of the auditory capsule initiates at three different locations to form the petromastoid part of the temporal bone at P1 (Thomas, 1926). Two of the three ossification centers are located around the boundary between the pars cochlearis and the pars canalicularis: one in the anterior region around the tegmen tympani (TGT in Figure 3.2B) and the other in the posterior region around the foramen perilymphaticum (fpl). An additional ossified region is found on the dorsal surface of the pars cochlearis medial to the internal acoustic meatus at P1. However, this region connects with the posterior ossification center via a narrow tract and appears to be an anterior extension of the posterior bone. The presence of the third ossification center described by Thomas (1926) was not confirmed in our observation, possibly due to different samples used in the two studies (Thomas investigated "yellow mice"). Ossification progresses in the pars cochlearis at P2 and subsequently extends to an inferior region of the pars canalicularis. At P7, the lateral surface of the pars canalicularis is still largely cartilaginous but mostly ossified by P14.

Dermatocranium Association– Squamosal. The tegmen tympani anteriorly continues to the orbitocapsular commissure, and both structures are located medial to the retrotympanic process (rtps) of the squamosal (SQ) at E16.5. At P2, secondary cartilage develops at the posterior end of the retrotympanic process (Table 3.1), which articulates with the pars canalicularis by P7.

References (not included in citations for Chapter 3)

Enlow, D. H. (1990). *Facial Growth*. Philadelphia, PA: Saunders.

Gaupp, E. (1900). Das chondrocranium von *Lacerta agilis*. *Anatomische Hefte*, 14, 434–594.

Harkema, J. R., Carey, S. A. and Wagner, J. G. (2006). The nose revisited: a brief review of the comparative structure, function, and toxicologic pathology of the nasal epithelium. *Toxicologic Pathology*, 34, 252–269.

Kielan-Jaworowska, Z., Cifelli, R. L. and Luo, Z.-X. (2004). *Mammals from the Age of Dinosaurs: Origins, Evolution, and Structure*. New York, NY: Columbia University Press.

Maier, W. (1987). The ontogenetic development of the orbitotemporal region in the skull of *Monodelphis domestica* (Didelphidae, Marsupialia), and the problem of the mammalian alisphenoid. *In:* Kuhn, H.-J. and Zeller, U. (eds.) *Morphogenesis of the Mammalian Skull*. Hamburg: Paul Parey.

Parrington, F. R. and Westoll, T. S. (1940). On the evolution of the mammalian palate. *Philosophical Transaction of the Royal Society B*, 230, 305–355.

Starck, D. (1975). The development of the chondrocranium in primates. In: Luckett, W. P. and Szaley, F. S. (eds.) Phylogeny of the Primates. New York: Plenum Press.

Thomas, L. J. (1926). Ossification centers in the petrosal bone of the mouse. *Anatomical Record*, 33, 59–68.

Index